Klemens Joos
Convincing Political Stakeholders

Klemens Joos

Convincing Political Stakeholders

Successful lobbying through process competence in the complex decision-making system of the European Union

WILEY-VCH Verlag GmbH & Co. KGaA

1. Auflage 2016

All books published by Wiley-VCH are carefully produced. Nevertheless, authors, editors, and publisher do not warrant the information contained in these books, including this book, to be free of errors. Readers are advised to keep in mind that statements, data, illustrations, procedural details or other items may inadvertently be inaccurate.

Library of Congress Card No.:
applied for
A catalogue record for this book is available from the British Library.

Bibliographic information published by the Deutsche Nationalbibliothek
The Deutsche Nationalbibliothek lists this publication in the Deutsche Nationalbibliografie; detailed bibliographic data are available on the Internet at
<http://dnb.d-nb.de> abrufbar.

Printed in the Federal Republic of Germany
Printed on acid-free paper
Translation: Deman Übersetzungen / Ian Rhodes
Layout: pp030 – Produktionsbüro Heike Praetor, Berlin, Germany
Cover design: Schindler Parent GmbH, Meersburg, Germany
Cover photo: © KEFFECT DESIGN GBR, Constance/Wilm Ihlenfeld@fotolia
Satz: inmedialo UG, Plankstadt
Druck & Bindung: CPI books GmbH, Leck

Print ISBN: 978-3-527-50865-5

For my wife and children

Contents

Preface

Back in 1990, political Europe was still called the European Community, the European Union had not yet been "born" and the common currency, the euro, did not yet exist. This was when, as a student at Ludwig-Maximilians-University (LMU) in Munich, I founded EUTOP International GmbH as a service provider for structural support of the work of lobbyists at European and member state level.

Since then, the exciting topic of lobbying at the European institutions has held me in its thrall professionally and scientifically, and as an author and publisher. In 1997, I obtained my doctorate on the topic *Representing the Interests of German Companies vis-à-vis the Institutions of the European Union* from the Faculty of Business Administration at Munich's LMU (Munich School of Management) – a pioneering work at the time, since there were practically no scientific publications to draw on. Based on an organisational science approach, my doctorate dealt with the necessity of structural, process-oriented lobbying at a point in time when the complex multi-level system of the European Union, based on a variety of different formal and informal processes and procedures, was just beginning to emerge. However, it was already clear to keen observers at that time that content-related work alone – i.e. disregarding the procedural aspects of political decisions – would no longer lead to success in lobbying. What was already hinted at in my book, *Lobbying in the new Europe*, published in 2011, will now be extensively analysed and explained in this publication – the paradigm shift triggered in political lobbying due to the enormous increase in the importance of procedural issues.

The initial idea for this book came to me during the "Convincing Political Stakeholders" master seminar which I have been organising for a number of years as a visiting lecturer at the Munich School of Management at LMU whilst searching for a quick and in-depth introduction to the topic. This has led to a book which readers can use in various ways: it offers students and interested members of the public a quick introduction to process-oriented lobbying at the institutions of the European Union.[1] At the same time, it is intended to provide lobbyists, decision-makers in companies, associations and organisations as well as legislators and executives with a navigation tool in their daily work.

Enthusiasm and a wealth of ideas are always the nucleus for a new work. However, theories only crystallise and concepts only mature in dialogue with others, as was the case with this book. My thanks here are directed first and foremost to Professor Anton Meyer, Professor of Business Administration and Chair of the Institute for Marketing at LMU Munich, and Professor Armin Nassehi of the Institute of Sociology at the LMU Faculty of Social Sciences. The personal discus-

---

1 For the sake of completeness, I would like to add that certain of the book's passages have already been published in some of my earlier works. They have been adapted for this book.

sions conducted during the development of this book helped me extensively to clarify my ideas. I would particularly like to thank both of the above for declaring their willingness to write ground-breaking contributions to my book. At this point, thanks are also due to the team surrounding Professor Meyer for its involvement (in alphabetical order): Michael Dürr, Ana Jakić, Anja Meindl, Carola Neumann, Lena-Marie Rehnen and Maximilian Wagner. Finally, the contributions and discussions provided and conducted by my students during the seminars also gave rise to valuable notes and stimuli which have been integrated into this illustration.

However, my thanks also extend to the many helping hands who provided assistance in terms of research and sifting through the extensive material. These are as follows (in alphabetical order): Thomas Bobinger, Clara Freißmuth, Christiane Hofferbert, Bettina Hornbach, Malte Kilian, Julia Klohs, István Kornis, Arne Leimenstoll, Carolin Maug, Matthias Pfeil, Michael Schaaff, Walter Tombrock, Clarissa Warsberg and Jan Weisensee.

Special thanks go to Dr Alois Maderspacher, Dr Stefan Herold and Dr Christian Fackelmann – they supported the development of this book in various ways and provided me with valuable tips in revising the draft texts and editing the manuscript.

Finally, I would like to thank Julia Klohs, Stefanie Valdés-Scott and Christian Schaufler for their outstanding organisational support. Particular thanks go to Markus Wester for the support provided by my publisher, Wiley.

Suggestions from readers are always welcome. Please feel free to contact me at cps@dr-joos.eu.

Munich, August 2016   *Klemens Joos*

List of abbreviations

ACE	Alliance for Beverage Cartons and the Environment
ACEA	European Automobile Manufacturers' Association
ALDE	Alliance of Liberals and Democrats for Europe (political group in the EP)
AMA	American Marketing Association
Approx.	Approximately
BDA	Confederation of German Employers' Associations
BDI	Federal Association of German Industry
BDU	Bundesverband Deutscher Unternehmensberater e. V. (Association of German Management Consultants)
BGL	Bundesverband Güterkraftverkehr und Logistik (Federal Association Road Transport and Logistics)
Bn	Billion(s)
BSE	Bovine Spongiform Encephalopathy
BVerfGE	(Rulings of the) Federal Constitutional Court
CBI	Confederation of British Industry
CC	Content Competence
CEEP	European Centre of Employers and Enterprises providing Public Services
CEFIC	European Chemical Industry Council
CEO	Corporate Europe Observatory/ Chief Executive Officer
CEPS	Centre for European Policy Studies
CFSP	Common Foreign and Security Policy
CoR	Committee of the Regions
Coreper	Permanent Representatives Committee
CSDP	Common Security and Defence Policy
CSR	Corporate Social Responsibility
DG	Directorate General
DGB	German Trade Union Federation
DIHK	German Chambers of Industry and Commerce
EAEC	European Atomic Energy Community
EC	European Community
ECB	European Central Bank
ECJ	European Court of Justice
ECR	European Conservatives and Reformists (political group in the EP)
ECSC	European Coal and Steel Community
EEAS	European External Action Service
EEC	European Economic Community
EEG	German Renewable Energy Act

EESC	European Economic and Social Committee
EFDD	Europe of Freedom and Direct Democracy (political group in the EP)
EFSA	European Food Safety Authority
EFSF	European Financial Stability Facility
EFSM	European Financial Stabilisation Mechanism
EFTA	European Fair Trade Association
EMA	European Medicines Agency
EMU	European Economic and Monetary Union
ENF	Europe of Nations and Freedom (political group in the EP)
EP	European Parliament
EPACA	European Public Affairs Consultancies Association
EPC	European Policy Centre
EPC	European Political Cooperation
EPP	European People's Party
ESC	Economic and Social Committee
ESCB	European System of Central Banks
ESDP	European Security and Defence Policy
ESM	European Stabilisation Mechanism
Etc.	Et cetera
ETI	European Transparency Initiative
ETUC	European Trade Union Confederation
EU	European Union
e.V.	Registered association
ff.	Following
G7	Group of 7
G20	Group of the twenty most important industrialised and emerging markets
GG	Grundgesetz (Basic Constitutional Law of Germany)
Greens/EFA	The Greens/European Free Alliance (political group in the EP)
GUE/NGL	European United Left/Nordic Green Left (political group in the EP)
IGO	Intergovernmental Organisation
IHK	Chamber of commerce and industry
IPCC	Intergovernmental Panel on Climate Change
ISO	International Standard Organisation
ISV	Industry Structure View
IT	Information Technology
LMU	Ludwig-Maximilians-University
LP	Limited Partnership
LSE	London School of Economics
Ltd.	Limited liability company

M	Million(s)
MBA	Master of Business Administration
MBV	Market-based View
MEP	Member of the European Parliament
MLG	Multi-Level Governance
MSA	Multiple Stream Approach
MSc	Master of Science
NA	Non-Attached Members (MEPs not being part of a political group)
NGO	Non-Governmental Organisation
No.	Number
NPE	New Political Economy
NSA	National Security Agency
N.U.	Name unknown
OECD	Organisation for Economic Co-operation and Development
OEEC	Organisation for European Economic Co-operation
OJ	Official Journal
OLAF	Office Européen de Lutte Anti-Fraude (European Anti-Fraud Office)
§	Paragraph
PA	Public Affairs
PCC	Perspective Change Competence
PJC	Police and Judicial Co-operation in criminal matters
PLC	Public Limited Company
PR	Public Relations
PR	Permanent Representation
PStC	Process Structure Competence
PSuC	Process Support Competence
QM	Quality Management
RBV	Resource-Based View
Reg.	Regulation
Retd.	Retired
RoPEP	Rules of Procedure of the European Parliament
S&D	Progressive Alliance of Socialists and Democrats (political group in the EP)
SEA	Single European Act
SEAP	Society of European Affairs Professionals
SHV	Stakeholder View
SL	Successful lobbying
SME	Small and Medium-sized Enterprises
SRI	Stanford Research Institute
SRM	Single Resolution Mechanism
SSM	Single Supervisory Mechanism

StGB	Strafgesetzbuch (German Penal Code)
s.v.	sub voce
TCE	Treaty establishing a Constitution for Europe
TEU	Treaty on the European Union
TFEU	Treaty on the Functioning of the European Union
TL	Treaty of Lisbon
TRC	Transaction Costs
TTIP	Transatlantic Trade and Investment Partnership
TÜV	Technical Inspection Association
UNICE	Union of Industrial and Employers' Confederations of Europe
UNO	United Nations Organisation
US	United States
USA	United States of America
USD	US dollar
VDA	Verband der Automobilindustrie (German Association of the Automotive Industry)
VdC	Verband der Cigarettenindustrie (German Cigarette Industry Association)
VKU	Verband kommunaler Unternehmen e.V. (German Association of Municipal Companies)
Vol.	Volume
WHO	World Health Organisation
WSA	World Steel Association
WTO	World Trade Organisation

Introduction

The world has changed …

The first few years of the new millennium have led to far-reaching upheavals of a political and social nature, and the world has become vastly more complex across all areas of social experience: a few keywords such as globalisation, digitisation and internet, climate change and financial crisis are sufficient to make the extent of these changes clear.

All of this has consequences for the political arena, since these problems are transnational and can no longer be resolved at individual state level. This simultaneously reveals the nation state's increasingly restricted ability to act. The result is a change in the relationships between nation states which goes hand-in-hand with increasing interdependence and thus a decrease in nation state sovereignty.

Nowhere is this more apparent than in the development of political Europe, from the alliance of the six Western European states back in the 1950s to the complex, multi-level system of the European Union, which is attempting to integrate the interests of (still) 28 member states, their regions and half a billion citizens. This gives rise to a variety of decision-making levels, barely transparent formal and informal procedure paths and a gradual decrease in the importance of the individual member states. This complex multi-level political system intensified even further when the Treaty of Lisbon came into effect on 1st December 2009, raising it to a new level of complexity. New, complex rules of procedure, increases in competence for the European Parliament and much more besides have led to a sharp rise in the number of decision-makers involved in a political process. Consequently, the outcome of European decision-making processes has become even more unpredictable than before. These processes appear intransparent and inaccessible.

These are the framework conditions and challenges with which lobbying is faced today. In view of the complex political and legal circumstances of the EU and the multitude of actors and decision-making levels, lobbying work can no longer restrict itself to just the executive and legislative levels of an individual member state. Instead, the focus is increasingly shifting from Europe's capitals to the "European capital city" of Brussels. The affected parties – companies, associations and organisations, but also the EU member states and EU regions themselves – have recognised this. They are all setting up representative offices. More offices, more lobbyists – but is it a case of "the more the better"?

The increase in the number of lobbyists in Brussels is also going hand-in-hand with an increase in content competence. As it is often assumed that the primary objective of lobbying in a decision-making process is to achieve a specific result using content, i.e. factual arguments, in practice, the focus has been less on process competence than on content competence. The core focus of the activity of associations and organisations, but also of economic lobbyists such as corporate representative offices and external service providers (e.g. public affairs agencies and law firms) is on content-related work: participation in public consultations, drawing up exhaustive argumentation papers and expert opinions, execution of media campaigns. However, this practice appears to be extensively divorced from the EU's significant developmental trends, as these are much more concerned with procedural questions ("processes") of European policy: which levels of the EU are involved in political decisions? At which level (EU or member state) are decisions ultimately made? Which institutions decide on which topics with which voting modalities?

Added to this is the EU's continuous increase in competence: ever more areas of policy are falling under the complex decision-making procedures of this dynamic multi-level system, involving supranational (European), national and regional levels. The actors at the relevant levels do not act in isolation from each other in this. Instead, co-operation and a willingness to compromise are required if an actor wishes to achieve his objectives, each of which is determined through constitutional and political competencies, potential influences and interests. To be able to act successfully against this backdrop of decision-making processes in the EU, a lobbyist must possess extensive process competence. In addition to knowledge of the material – formal and informal – decision-making processes, he must also have corresponding access options (networks across institutions, parliamentary groups and member states) at all decision-making levels throughout the EU. With the "EU construction site" now stretching from Portugal to Finland and from Ireland to Cyprus, there are only a very small number of actors who can manage this.

Convincing political stakeholders intends to deal with these questions and challenges. In addition to analysing the multi-level system of the EU and the changes to the political and legal framework of lobbying related to reforms, particularly to the Treaty of Lisbon, the book aims to offer a practical guide to lobbying at the EU institutions. The book is structured as follows:

- The beginning is marked by fundamental thoughts on the topic of lobbying and stakeholders from Professor Armin Nassehi and Professor Anton Meyer with his co-authors (in alphabetical order) Ana Jakić, Anja Meindl, Carola Neumann and Maximilian Wagner. These precede the actual exposition. This involves matters of diverging interests in a modern society in which the different perspectives and interests of stakeholders exist simultaneously and encounter one another on an equal footing. Perspectives beyond the classic shareholder value approach are shown from the point of view of corporate management in view of complex framework conditions, and the importance of political stakeholders is additionally emphasised. Finally, the importance of the intermediary in lobbying is analysed, derived from theories on market exchange relationships.

- Chapter 2 defines the necessary terms and deals with questions concerning the function and legitimation of lobbying in political systems, particularly the exchange of interests and information at EU level.
- Chapters 3, 4 and 5 show the complexity of the framework conditions for lobbying in the EU. They demonstrate the vital importance of processes in politics and show the complexity of the interactions of EU institutions with the actors of civil society in the decision-making process. To achieve this, all relevant actors and institutions as well as the sometimes complicated formal and informal (decision-making) procedures and legislative processes are introduced.
- Chapters 6 and 9 are designed as "practical chapters". They are dedicated to the specific practice of lobbying and introduce the instruments required for modern stakeholder management (Chapter 6), whose application is then explained on the basis of case studies (Chapter 9). Chapter 6 should ideally be read in conjunction with Chapter 10, which shows approaches to the continued development of the present concepts of lobbying instruments. Section 8.2 by Professor Anton Meyer and the co-authors Michael Dürr and Lena-Marie Rehnen can also be read in this context. It describes the challenges involved in undertaking successful lobbying and maintaining competitive opportunities from the point of view of small and medium-sized enterprises (SMEs). Use of the lobbying instruments has to be learnt. Chapter 7 therefore describes the challenges currently faced by lobbyist training and shows an approach to the future structure of this and the development path to becoming a professional "governmental relations manager". Section 8.1 by Professor Armin Nassehi can also be read in this context.
- Finally, Chapter 10 is a resumé of the significant information contained in this book and a plea for the necessity of supplementing and updating the instruments for successful lobbying in the EU in the light of the Treaty of Lisbon. The content competence of the lobbying clients must be intermeshed with the process competence of an intermediary (external lobbying service provider) to achieve a successful conclusion under the new framework conditions of the Treaty of Lisbon.

The overview subsequently inserted here is intended to provide the reader with a quick navigational aid to reading this book and to enable the specific selection of those sections of relevance to him. The thesis-like summaries of Chapters 2 to 7 should be pointed out to readers who have very little time. At least an overview of the central content of the book can therefore be obtained by reading just a few pages.

Overview: the individual sections of the book

Chapter 1 – Fundamental thoughts on the topic of lobbying and stakeholders

Chapter 1 offers a general introduction to the topic of lobbying and stakeholders. In their guest contributions, Armin Nassehi and Anton Meyer (with his co-authors) reveal fundamental thoughts and ideas:

1.1 Differences of interest, stakeholders and translation conflicts *(Armin Nassehi)*

Armin Nassehi initially explains the divergence of interests in a modern society in which the different perspectives and interests of stakeholders not only exist simultaneously but also encounter one another on an equal footing – there is no longer any hierarchical structure of stakeholder interests. What is true or false is always dependent on the situation. For lobbying, this means that a concern also has to be translated into the perspective of the other party to enable it to be formulated in such a way that a decision is possible in the first place.

1.2 Stakeholder orientation: perspectives of corporate management beyond the classic shareholder value approach in the face of more complex framework conditions *(Anton Meyer, Maximilian Wagner, Ana Jakić and Carola Neumann)*

Anton Meyer, Maximilian Wagner, Ana Jakić and Carola Neumann describe the commercial importance of stakeholder orientation and the stakeholder approach, which will be more important for modern corporate management in the future than the present, classic shareholder approach. They make clear the relevance of politics as a stakeholder for companies and thus the importance of functioning communication between companies and stakeholders. This communication is vitally necessary for companies to obtain their "licence to operate" and also maintain it in the long term.

1.3 Importance of the intermediary in lobbying derived from mutual market relationship theories *(Anton Meyer and Anja Meindl)*

Anton Meyer and Anja Meindl integrate lobbying into economic theory and explain the existence and importance of intermediaries within mutual market relationships, segueing into the requirement of an independent intermediary in lobbying.

Chapter 2 – Lobbying – an approach: fundamentals and introduction

The second chapter delimits the various areas of communication and lobbying – public relations, public affairs, general lobbying and governmental relations – from each other in terms of their different addressees, objectives, instruments and time frames. Chapter 2 also deals with questions of legitimation and the status of lobbying in political systems.

Chapter 3 – Politics as a process: from content to process competence

Chapter 3 deals with the importance of processes in politics and the reshaping and reformulation of political contents through processes. Against this backdrop, the procedural dimension of politics must be given increased consideration in lobbying than was previously the case. This part of the book is therefore also a plea for the necessity of a paradigm shift in lobbying, away from purely content-oriented arguments (content competence) towards increasingly process-oriented work (process competence), and thus ultimately the intermeshing of content and process competence.

Chapter 4 – The European Union as the target of lobbying: political system and peculiarities in comparison with national (member state) systems

The fourth chapter presents the institutional framework in the multi-level system of the EU. It shows how this multi-level system with its numerous actors and decision-making levels has developed historically and is to be classified in terms of political theory. Chapter 4 also offers an overview of the way in which the individual EU institutions function and the legal framework of their actions.

Chapter 5 – Legislative procedures and other legal regulations as the framework of lobbying in the EU

Chapter 5 offers an overview of the legal framework of lobbying in the EU. In addition to the formal legislative procedures, supplemented by informal procedures such as the informal trialogue between the Commission, Parliament and Council, the options available to lobbyists to access the EU institutions, as regulated by EU legislation, are also described. Alongside the information on institutions provided in Chapter 4, Chapter 5 is therefore also an important basic prerequisite for understanding the "complexity trap of the EU".

Chapter 6 – Governmental relations: process management in practice

Chapter 6 explains the structural instruments (who takes action) and the process-oriented instruments (which lobbying tools are used) of lobbying. The reader is provided with a detailed insight into the governmental relations "toolbox".

Chapter 7 – Training: ways to becoming a governmental relations manager

The paradigm shift in lobbying, from content to process competence, demands new training methods for lobbyists. Specific governmental relations manager training would push forward the professionalisation and definition of the vocation of lobbyist and simultaneously meet the requirements of politicians and lobby groups (such as companies, associations, organisations, etc.). Such specialised training could also make a significant contribution to increased transparency while improving the image of lobbying. Chapter 7 shows how this training could be structured in the future.

Chapter 8 – Discourse: future challenges

8.1 Professionalism means translation competence *(Armin Nassehi)*

Armin Nassehi's contribution deals with the competencies which new elites have to develop in a complex society. Today and in the future, professionalism above all means the competence of a change of perspective and being able to mediate and "translate" between various functional and professionalisation areas.

8.2 Convincing political stakeholders: specifics and challenges for SMEs using the example of Bavaria *(Anton Meyer, Michael Dürr and Lena-Marie Rehnen)*

The increased importance of politics as a stakeholder for companies has already been dealt with in the first chapter. In Section 8.2, Anton Meyer, Michael Dürr and Lena-Marie-Rehnen analyse the topic from the perspective of small and medium-sized enterprises (SMEs) using the example of Bavaria. To maintain their competitive opportunities, they will be compelled to interconnect more intensively for the purpose of lobbying.

Chapter 9 – Case studies

The ninth chapter deals with the practical implementation of the book's contents and shows, on the basis of two fictitious example cases, how lobbying projects can be successfully structured through the complementary implementation of the relevant client's content-oriented lobbying structures and the external process competence of an intermediary.

Chapter 10 – Summary and outlook: necessity of supplementing and updating the instruments for successful lobbying in the EU in the light of the Treaty of Lisbon

Based on the knowledge of process competence, Chapter 10 shows approaches to a further differentiated, organisational science-oriented approach to lobbying. Under the generic term of process competence, a distinction is made in this case between (1) the provision of procedural structures (including networks as well as organisational and personnel structures); (2) perspective change competence and (3) subsequent process support. When intermeshed with the client's content competence, this understanding of process competence offers a significantly greater likelihood of success as part of specific lobbying projects. This complementary procedure of client and intermediary is finally made tangible on the basis of a "formula for successful lobbying".

Chapter 1   Fundamental thoughts on the topic of lobbying and stakeholders

1.1 Differences of interest, stakeholders and translation conflicts

By Armin Nassehi

Interests always occur in the plural. An interest can only be held by someone who encounters other interests. This indicates that interests always refer to specific viewpoints – or to express it more precisely: interests only exist wherever the same object, the same problem, the same circumstances, the same resource, etc. is presented from very different perspectives. At the same time, this divergence also unites the different interests, since they refer directly to each other. This therefore usually involves something like the unity of differences of interest. Only when these are determined will it also be possible to understand the interests of different viewpoints or stakeholders.

Classic conflicts of interest are those such as the differences of interest between unions and management. One side has an interest in higher wages, the other side has an interest in lowering labour costs – the unity of the difference of these divergent interests lies in the fact that they are related to each other in a complementary manner. Another classic case would be a company's negotiations with the responsible state bodies regarding permissible emissions in industrial production. One side is interested in asserting specific environmental standards whereas the other side is interested in improving or maintaining its own market position. Again, the divergent interests are related in a complementary, almost dichotomous, manner in this case. Such divergences of interests produce conflict systems in which each utterance by the actors involved is drawn into the vortex of this divergence. Even if the representative of a company proposes a solution, in the second case for instance, this is ascribed to his interest, just as a trade unionist's concession in collective bargaining is always regarded as driven by interest.

Interests do not simply exist – they are attributed by observers. To genuinely be able to understand the divergent interests of different stakeholders within a conflict and develop tools to enable different stakeholders to productively relate to one another, it is not at all necessary to decode the "real" interest at first, i.e. to fathom out what an actor really "means". What is of particular interest is rather the fact that modern societies are characterised by their constant understanding of actor positions as a specific expression of different viewpoints.

The form of functional differentiation inherent to a modern, complex society (see Section 1.1.1), which then leads to a precise understanding of stakeholders (see Section 1.1.2), should therefore initially be pointed out in the following. Following on from this, I will use the term "translation" to attempt to indicate the form which an appropriate strategy for dealing with complexity must take (see Section 1.1.3).

1.1.1 Complexity and differentiation

Calling modern society complex is almost a platitude. However, what complexity means is rarely specified more precisely on use of this diagnosis. The fact that things are complex means considerably more than the implicitness that things are difficult rather than simple. So what does complexity mean?

Even pointing out the divergent interests of different stakeholders indicates complexity. The fact that there can be different, mutually exclusive perspectives of the same object indicates that what we see depends on our relevant viewpoint. Stakeholders differ particularly due to the fact that they are stakeholders in terms of a topos, but that they have different perspectives, interests and success criteria within this. This may appear trivial at first glance, since it has always been thus. However, the particular feature of a modern society lies in the circumstance that these different perspectives not only occur simultaneously but that they also encounter one another on an equal footing.[1] A modern society suspends the logical figures of the *principle of non-contradiction* and *excluded middle*.

According to the principle of non-contradiction, a sentence cannot be true or false at the same time. Evidently this no longer applies empirically, because a situation is basically different for different stakeholders, with the result that different sentences about an object can apply as well as the fact that a specific sentence can apply to one but not the other.

According to the principle of excluded middle, a statement is either true or false. This principle is also empirically suspended when different perspectives of the object encounter each other on an equal footing.

Both figures of classical logic get by without the observer. One simply has to imagine that things are ultimately as they are independent of the observer. If this were the principle according to which the world was constructed, it would be possible to distinguish different stakeholders according to whether they have the right or wrong perspective of something specific. However, what we are dealing with here is situations in which effectively contradictory perspectives of the same object are both different and also each indisputably legitimate. The relationship between stakeholders is not therefore characterised by the question of which of the perspectives should continue to apply and which must be discarded. What is instead involved is how a society deals with the fact that it is not all cast from the same mould, that its different perspectives cannot simply be mapped onto each other

---

1   See Nassehi (2015), p. 97 ff.

without leaving a remainder and that we have ultimately come to terms with the fact that this is precisely what a modern society has to deal with.[2]

Such a situation is complex because it is aware of several links to a situation and because there are simultaneously several possibilities for considering an object. To express this in a very simplified form: in the old world, something was either true or false, either legitimate or not; one was either a believer or a heretic, either a legitimate spokesperson or not. Ultimately, everything was pigeon-holed in these distinctions, at least in clear, hierarchically structured classifications. Conversely, things can no longer be placed into such simple contexts in the modern world. The fact that something is valid or not is effectively dependent on different perspectives, and social modernisation is always characterised by the fact that one becomes more or less accustomed to how dependent on viewpoints the worlds in which we live are. Such worlds are complex insofar as they cannot be regarded one-dimensionally – and they develop forms for handling this multi-dimensionality. The historic development of the market economy, for example, was a reaction to increased complexity since it established different interests and viewpoints; the establishment of democracy in politics virtually anticipates the multi-dimensionality of interests and perspectives for solutions; modern science is only possible because it permits competing forms of knowledge.

The simultaneity of differences therefore indicates differentiation, in this case the functional differentiation of society. System differentiation is misunderstood when it is confused with the division of labour, since the division of labour ultimately necessitates an operational unit beyond the differentiated systems that divides something which already exists in such a way that things are meaningfully related to one another. Whoever divides labour must already presuppose an idea of the unity of labour in order to be able to divide it so that different operations can be undertaken on the same workpiece.

With reference to social theory questions, the division of labour as a social differentiation principle would necessitate pre-differentiation unity. The paradigmatic case of such a social theory originates from Émile Durkheim, who does not see the "division of social labour" as being held together at random by a social moral. Such a differentiation theory is not really consistent, because it regards differentiation as a subordinate principle and understands social diversity in terms of unity and not, conversely, social unity in terms of the differentiation. The unity of a functionally differentiated society consists of its differentiation – and, as the sole principle of unity, the operational substrate of "communication" is assumed as the common operational basis of everything societal in this system theory perspective which originates from Niklas Luhmann.[3]

---

2 See Nassehi (2011); Luhmann (1997).
3 See Luhmann (1997).

Functional systems begin and end with positive and negative code values – in the case of the economic system – this is the distinction between payments or non-payments, mediated through money. Money is perhaps the simplest medium, since it leaves little scope for interpretation. It is able to simulate hard factualities and can be translated into all possible goods, services, experiences, etc. if only one is able to pay. Again, however, it only follows its own logic in this. This is why this particularly potent medium has never been able to solve social problems – and has thus been the crucial culmination point for criticism. The market alone is unable to establish any order, it cannot sustain populations, it cannot ensure justice and it is not interested in how goods and opportunities are distributed. All of this is of no interest to the market because it cannot ultimately be mapped economically in the narrower sense of the word. In this regard, the economic market is effectively an operationally closed system of payments which in turn have consequences – for payments.

Such a description of the economic system is based above all on the closed way in which it operates but disregards the system's openness. Because whilst the ultimately blind mechanism of the system-based cycle of payment processes in chains of payments and their consequences for solvency generate radical immanence in terms of their cumulative impact, the operations themselves are ultimately unable to perceive their systematic nature. "The openness of the economy is thus expressed in the fact that payments are bound to reasons for payments, which ultimately refer to the system's environment."[4] What one then sees are other market participants with their purposes and intentions, narratives about price developments, supply and demand on product and service markets, availability of capital and, by no means least, assessments of how others will act on the market and how this will develop. The market then appears as a network. It was Harrison C. White[5] who most clearly pointed out that it is above all mutual observations and battles for position on the part of market participants in markets which render consumption or investment decisions plausible. Information, observations, assessments, customs, prejudices, expectations and, by no means least, appropriate descriptions of the market arise in networks. The market is characterised primarily by the fact that nobody has complete information, as it would otherwise collapse, because if everybody did (supposedly!) the right thing on a market, i.e. invest in the same stocks or purchase the same products, if they were actually so well informed that they could no longer take a risk, profit and loss opportunities would disappear and everything would ultimately meet in the middle, in which only monopolists would then remain.

The remarkable thing about the economic system it that it operates inexorably according to its own logic but that one constantly has to make sense of it and find

---

4 Luhmann (1988), p. 59.
5 See White (1981; 2002).

categories in order to achieve the bases for decision-making. Not for no reason has the differentiation of a modern, market-oriented economic system always been related to the moralisation of the economy and the politicisation of markets. And not for no reason do forms of self-interpretations and reflection theories, which serve no purpose other than to make sense of what is inexorably taking place, arise around this ultimately purely economically-based interface logic: the fact that the conditions for the success of payments and non-payments are to be sought exclusively in further payments and non-payments.[6]

Society's operational order problem is resolved through the differentiation of code-based interface logics and the systemic cycle of functional systems – conversely, the practical order problem of dealing with the consequences of this differentiation in society is resolved through two mechanisms: on one hand by the formation of organisations, which provides patterns for handling the different interface logics in the long term and consequentially, on the other hand, the establishment of specific organisation-based action types in the form of audience and service roles, profession types, expectation styles and mentalities. It is ultimately these two mechanisms which manifest themselves as the economic system (and all other functional systems) to a normal observer, i.e. observers such as those in the networks described by Harrison White which ensure that order patterns, which then use the code accordingly, arise above the brutal logic (in the sense of a factum brutum) of economic interface conditions.

I describe this duality of the economy firstly as a very simple, systemically self-contained autopoiesis of payments, and secondly as an area of an economic practice which above all has to demonstrate its plausibility within social expectations, consequences and forms in order to point out that the same mechanism also applies to other functional systems. It is simply most clearly demonstrable using the obstinacy of the economy. However, it is also true of the political, the scientific, the legal, the religious or the educational functional system that its systemic closure lies exclusively in very simple coding and symbolically generalised interface forms. The political system is able to observe everything, but the conditions for success are exclusively dependent on whether political communication leads to the maintenance of power or pushing through decisions using the resource of power. What Harrison White says about the network conditions of markets then also applies here: it is mutual observations, assessments, expectations of political actors which lead to corresponding self-interpretations, i.e. to the maintenance of political programs and differences, to the remarkable interaction of factual assessments of the "situation" with the actual "political" sense of such assessments in terms of the code-based conditions for success. Similar effects can also be demonstrated for other functional systems.[7]

---

6 See Händler (2012).
7 See Nassehi (2012).

It is the different conditions for success which fundamentally distinguish economic and political operations. The connectivity of economic operations is generated solely in terms of expected effects as regards the ability to pay and the balancing of scarcity; in the political system, however, it is dependent on the extent to which political operations serve to maintain power or lead to collectively binding decisions in terms of an assignable collective. What sounds very formal here is ultimately determined through the simplicity of the coding – and accordingly leads to complex forms. In particular, the negotiable interaction between the different operation forms is complex in this case. As the conditions for success of economic and political operations are fundamentally different, the theory of functional differentiation suggests that anything approaching the co-ordination of both modes of operation is ultimately out of the question – and must nevertheless take place time and again at certain points. This makes it clear why the relationship between these two functional systems has become the central problem of social disputes in functionally differentiated societies and actually influences the self-interpretation of society. All of the keywords of such debates – political economy of capitalism, social market economy, neoliberalism, socialism, new deal, etc. – are aimed at the relationship between the two modes of operation, which is ultimately irreconcilable in operational terms. Formally, as in the discussion surrounding the minimum wage which extensively marked 2013's German parliamentary election campaign, this means that, from an economic perspective, the concept is focussed on the economic consequences of such an instrument, whereas the question concerning voter loyalty or the electability of the concept is registered from a political perspective. It is interesting that neither of the two perspectives is more appropriate, simply because the conditions for appropriateness are different.

Incidentally, this argument cannot be used to argue either in favour of or against a universal minimum wage. It is more important to point out that even such a simple example is able to show that the different logics of both functional systems apply irreducibly – and that specific solutions are still found for each of them. It should at any rate have become clear that the operational relationship between the economy and politics (and science, law, religion, etc., although this is not the issue here) is genuinely difficult, irreducibly difficult. This is perhaps why we imagine successful socialisation to be such that the different parts are interrelated in such a way that they do not mutually interfere with their conditions for success too extensively. The classic image of an integrated, western post-war industrial society with its stable institutional arrangement may well come close to this ideal – but it is increasingly coming under pressure. A great deal can be said about this in social theory terms, but the following is crucial here: this differentiation theory design can now be used to determine the reference problem, in which the reference problem of a convincing political stakeholder is to be systematically sought. The issue of lobbying or the negotiation of interests of different provenance and above all different fundamental logics, namely a primarily economic and a primarily political logic, is directly concerned with the differentiation principle of a modern society. It does not involve simply divergent interests, nor does it involve pitting the economic interests of industries, associations or companies, for instance, against the political interests of regional, national or European political levels. These are not simply power struggles between various interests, in which the stronger opponent wins or in which consensuses can be reached. Instead, it involves the fact that governmental relations have to work with the circumstance that different forms of success and knowledge encounter each other here, and have to find forms for co-ordinating these different conditions for success.

Ultimately, such processes are translation processes. Modern societies can simply no longer be regarded as communities cast from the same mould; their complexity is also underestimated if is it assumed that only a balance of interests is involved. Today, the primary issue is whether the different perspectives, logics and conditions for success can be translated into each other. Contemporary conflicts concerning solutions and divergent interests therefore arise primarily in the form of translation conflicts.

Political and economic actors, for example, are aware of each other, have an image of their opposite party and are ultimately reliant on dealing with mutual expectations. These expectations – this is the crucial aspect – are not controlled centrally, they are not integrated in the sense that an instance for co-ordinating the two logics with each other could be designated. Instead, this co-ordination takes place in the present, in practical form, in real time and in the form of temporary adaptation processes in each case. This is carried out through fiscal policy measures as well as through legal specifications for work safety, environmental protection, credit protection, minimum wages, collective bargaining autonomy or product control; it is carried out through investment decisions with the option of switching to geopolitical areas; it is carried out through the creative layout of legal specifications as well as through attempts to reach a compromise between companies and administrations; it is reflected in concepts such as emissions trading or agreements between industry associations and the public sector; it is carried out through the exertion of influence by trade associations, trade unions or stakeholders on parties, parliaments and public opinion, etc.

With this both unsystematic and incomplete list, it should be pointed out that the loosely coupled, different logics of a political and economic nature have diverse points of intersection and contact, but no one-to-one interface which could genuinely co-ordinate both logics. This is precisely the point in the system at which lobbying, persuading, convincing and negotiating processes take place. The non- or semi-public form of lobbying which is often the subject of public criticism, the negotiation of specific issues and individual cases, and by no means least the clear formulation of own objectives and interests are inseparable parts of modern society. Whoever wishes to conduct the mental experiment of how these forms of lobbying could be forgone can only possibly encounter two models: either a dictatorial form of politics which, without looking at specific cases, specifies structures to which adherence is simply mandatory, or a completely deregulated economy. Neither can be desirable. This is because in the former case, this would not only lead to a loss of legitimation in political terms, but it would also rule out opportunities for learning, because only a normative expectation style could be used as the possible basis. In the second case, this would mean that the adaptation of economic dynamics to social requirements would lead to considerable problems, thus significantly overloading the political system's possibilities for action.

These short comments should already have made it clear that such forms of lobbying and negotiation between stakeholders of different provenance must never be treated as an anomaly or special interest in order to adequately understand the problem. In modern society, forms of organisation in which the different logics of society have to be re-referenced to each other occur at different points and in different areas. The case in question here falls into this context and can only be understood appropriately from there.

The above considerations are rather general in nature and do not argue using specific cases but instead provide an insight into the social framework in which lobbying takes place. Their specific form will be dealt with in the following chapters. Two aspects should be pointed out very briefly here; the concept of the stakeholder and the rather more competence theory-based aspect of translation.

1.1.2 One theory of the "stakeholder"

The concept of the stakeholder is largely undisputed in the commercial and management-oriented literature.[8] Interestingly, it is often used in connection with business ethics issues, which is only logical since the consideration of stakeholders firstly also takes into account the different interests of an economic process and secondly is also able to portray non-economic interests in the narrower sense, e. g. the interests of affected parties, the public, customers, etc. If one therefore wishes to model divergent interests, the stakeholder model can be used not only to give consideration to different actors but also the type of their interests or their perspectives in order to enable a better understanding of the process. In this regard, political actors, bureaucracies and administrations as well as media and scientists are also stakeholders in processes involving the specific mediation of interests but also participation in the formulation of policies.

The above described structure of functional differentiation makes it clear that diverse perspectives, each of which stake their own claim to the outcome of processes without the occurrence of a central form of final decisions through level hierarchies, encounter each other at the interfaces of different societal functional sys-

---

8   See e. g. Freeman (1984).

tems and logics. Not even society's political system is able to stake such a claim, leading to the representation of the structure of modern society when such processes are modelled in a stakeholder model.

1.1.3 Translation conflicts

Finally, brief reference should be made to the structure of the implied differences in perspective. It has already been indicated in the above that conflicts in modern societies do not so much involve mere conflicts concerning finite resources in the sense that things simply have to be distributed better to find something approaching a balance. Resource conflicts naturally play a significant role, but regarded in terms of the system, translation conflicts come to the fore. What is involved in the issue of lobbying? It also involves preparing the concern of, for example, an industry association or a company such that one's own concern is not simply pushed through. Whoever wishes to assert a concern must anticipate the other party's logic, so must ask himself what is politically and legally possible; must see, for instance, that, from a political perspective, the challenges are entirely different to those that emerge when the same problem is viewed from one's own economic or corporate perspective. This literally involves translation: I have to translate my concern into the other party's perspective to enable it to be formulated such that a decision is possible in the first place. In turn, I must be able to understand the other party's translation to determine what is possible and what is not.

The representation and assertion of interests are not simply a power struggle between communicating tubes in the sense that what one party receives the other has to give, and vice versa. This would be a simplistic perspective. What is instead involved is determining how actors arrive at common solutions from different perspectives – and if not that, then different solutions which are acceptable to both.

This can be formulated as translation rather than integration.[9] Modern social forms are simply not always already integrated, not organised collaboratively and certainly not co-ordinated through common interests. Instead, these different logics have to be translated into each other, whereby a translation process is by no means simply a transfer process.

The insight that the translation of contents cannot amount to transfer from one context to another is not new. The modern translation approach breaks with Humboldt's or Herder's romantic concepts of translation as an act of "faith" which helps to transport what is "foreign" into what is "familiar" in order to further the "development" of one's own nation. Since the 1920s at the latest, however, the clear distinction between the original and the translation has been elimi-

---

9 See Nassehi (2015), pp. 270 ff.

nated. Walter Benjamin[10] developed a lovely image for this: he compares translation with the image of a tangent touching a circle; they come into contact at one point and then each go their own way.

This way was subsequently pursued further by theoreticians such as Jacques Derrida,[11] who is interested in the fact that the translation is in no way dictated by the original. The possibility of the pure translation from one language into another was not therefore discussed any further but rather the question of how the relevant translation context determines how a text to be translated is culturally shaped. The translation is not therefore carried out according to the image of the output material but ultimately according to one's own image, the translator's image. The relationship between what is translated and the translation thus ultimately disappears in the indeterminacy of the relevant character systems. It is precisely this indeterminacy which defines the location of negotiation or translation processes and which constitutes the social significance of lobbying.

1.2 Stakeholder orientation: perspectives of corporate management beyond the classic shareholder value approach in the face of more complex framework conditions

By Anton Meyer,[*] Maximilian Wagner, Ana Jakić and Carola Neumann

1.2.1 "Be ahead of change"[12]: challenge of stakeholder orientation

"New Group strategy: E.ON is to concentrate on renewable energies, power networks and customer solutions, and will be hiving off its majority stake in a new, listed company for conventional power generation, global energy trading and exploration & production."[13]

On the same date, Spiegel Online reported:

"Strategy change: E.ON plans to dispose of its nuclear, gas and coal business. Utility company E.ON is undertaking a radical strategy change. It plans to dispose of its conventional power supply business. The Group will instead be concentrating on renewable energies and service products."[14]

---

10 See Benjamin (1992).
11 See Derridaand Venutti (2001).
*   In addition to my three co-authors, I would also like to thank the former employees of the Institute of Marketing at Ludwig-Maximilians-University in Munich; Professor Andreas Munzel, Dr Jan Engel and Dr Anna Girard, and also particularly Professor Manfred Schwaiger and Professor Anja Tuschke, for their contributions and commitment in establishing the "Convincing Stakeholders" seminar in the M.Sc. study program within the Munich School of Management at Ludwig-Maximilians-University.
12 Peter Drucker.
13 E.ON (2014).
14 Diekmann (2014).

Admittedly, such an offensive and equally courageous, radical strategy change is an "extreme" example to make it clear that it is not (no longer) sufficient to include customers and commerce plus market influencers, competitors, debt capital providers or internal target groups such as employees and equity providers in the calculation of a company's target groups.[15] Other stakeholder groups in a company often have to be taken into account from a strategic point of view because they are of great importance to the future success of the company. With the above strategy change, E.ON is also attempting to integrate stakeholder groups previously neglected by the company into its strategic calculation as a utility company and also satisfy their interests. This realisation is not limited solely to E.ON. In many industries (e.g. power supply, telecommunications and financial services sectors), the issue of a licence to operate is no longer any guarantee that a company will find political and social acceptance, support and tolerance to enable it to successfully further develop and defend its competitive advantages in its core business in the future. Framework conditions – irrespective of whether they are determined by the environment, company or politics – can change and lead to the fact that companies are unable, or not permitted, to continue their previous core business as they no longer have the social legitimation. In short, the licence to operate for a company's future constantly has to be earned anew. Boundary conditions are transformed into target groups, important stakeholders whose goals, interests and plans the company's management must interact and deal with. The objective is to convince diverse social and political stakeholders of the benefit, nature and content of the company's activity and its effects (or at least achieve their continued toleration).

The reasons for reorientation and strategy changes by companies are not only due to technological changes. In recent years, a variety of social, political, ecological and economic developments such as globalisation, European integration, German reunification, the dissolution of the Eastern Block, the Internet and economic crises, environmental catastrophes, etc. have led to an increase in social criticism regarding the behaviour of companies and their shouldering of responsibility for negative developments as well as the need for transparency – and thus also requirements on successful communication on the part of such companies. One consequence of these developments (see following summary) is that the intensifying involvement of the company's environment in all corporate planning, decisions and actions plus the communication of these are attaining ever increasing strategic and operational importance. This noticeable development can be described with the keywords "stakeholder orientation", "stakeholder approach", "stakeholder view" or "stakeholder theory", and is the subject of this article.

To be able to understand the far-reaching consequences of these developments, it is initially necessary to take a closer look at the drivers of this increasing stake-

---

15 See also the example case of the "Enron débâcle" in Culpan and Trussel (2005).

holder orientation. Central issues which are promoting these changes include: what are the social, political and economic development trends enabling or necessitating increased stakeholder orientation that companies will have to deal with in the 21st century? What are the challenges that they will pose to the companies' own actions?

1.2.2 Drivers of stakeholder orientation

1.2.2.1 Internet and digitisation

Buzzwords such as the Internet, Web 1.0, Web 2.0, the "Internet of Things", digitisation but also data protection, data espionage and copyright protection are major talking points. The Internet and its precursors (such as Arpanet) – the bright idea of a few highly intelligent military minds and scientists – have revolutionised the way in which contemporary societies interact. Communication, as well as many other digitisable value creating processes between individuals and/or organisations,increasingly takes place in the online environment. All stakeholder groups, not only customers or employees, are constantly accessible 24/7, in real time, personalised – but also anonymous – (in)visible to each other and to other stakeholders. The spread of "smart devices" and interconnectedness via social media are leading to the fact that information, opinions, experiences and comments can be exchanged at rapid speed around the globe. However, it is always uncertain as to whether these statements are true or perhaps falsified.

Knowledge of, about and amongst all stakeholders substantially increases the transparency of many processes and promotes what is often a viral spread of all kinds of information on the Internet. All stakeholders have the same tools and means at their disposal for representing their interests in society, politics and business and for making themselves heard. Together with their members and other stakeholders, they can exchange ideas, form bonds and interconnect to contribute to value creation.[16] The consequences can be both positive and negative in nature. Fans of certain brands, celebrities, stars, companies or not-for-profit organisations can push them extensively – but can drop them again equally quickly if displeased, and destroy brand values(s), which have taken decades to build up, in a matter of days. The above mentioned developments and the resulting influence exerted by stakeholders on the economy and society must always be evaluated ambivalently: for instance, hackers can disable entire industrial plants, as was recently the case with the TV station TV5MONDE, but can also improve security systems and software products – or even revolutionise them. Without the Internet, political movements and developments such as the Arab Spring would not have spread at such a dynamic pace, but neither would the Islamic State organisation have seen the swell in ranks which it is currently experiencing.

---

16 See Kornum and Mühbacher (2013), p. 1461; Driessen, Kok and Hillebrand (2013), p. 1465; Korschun/Du (2013), p. 1495.

"Where there is much light, the shadow is deep" – this aphorism from Johann Wolfgang von Goethe once again proves true.

In summary, it must be assumed that the Internet and digitisation speed up development processes in society and the economy like a catalyst and enable all stakeholder groups to actively influence and participate in corporate processes and decisions. Conversely, of course, this also applies to the influence which companies have over their stakeholders.

1.2.2.2 Climate change and demographic trend

Ecological changes can be observed across the globe. Climate change is manifesting itself, for instance, in the melting of the polar ice caps combined with the threat to animal species, which touches people on an emotional level, such as the polar bear or the whale. The precise causes and effects remain the subject of dispute, but man's influence has now been scientifically proven. In our view, one factor which fosters this negative development is an excessive desire to achieve short-term profits and sales growth coupled with short-term, aggressive marketing practices. One further aspect is the explosion in global population growth in developing countries. The people there often do not have the knowledge or the opportunities required to make sparing use of resources. At the same time, it is not possible to demand that they make use of the same tools available to saturated national economies with ageing and declining populations such as many of the economically dominant industrialised nations in the west. In addition, emerging markets such as China and India, but also Brazil or Russia, still have a vast amount of catching up to do in terms of environmental protection. Whilst some are insisting on their right to economic growth and consumption, the others are admonishing them to use and consume goods and resources more consciously and sparingly. At first glance, economic growth and a simultaneous increase in environmental awareness appear irreconcilable. Multinational companies which act globally on markets are operating in precisely this area of conflict. They have to meet the widely divergent needs and expectations of their customers and stakeholders – the simplest method, resolving this task in a standardised way as possible for all parties, is often the wrong approach. What constitutes waste for some is part of the standard of living and the expected quality of life for others. Society's implicit demand on companies to take a more social approach can already be seen extensively across Europe: today, it is no longer sufficient to evaluate quality of life on the basis of economic and material prosperity indicators. Instead, criteria such as adherence to specific values by companies and their suppliers (even across entire value creation networks), conserving resources, the respectful treatment of employees and authentic behaviour towards customers, etc. are playing an increasingly important role.[17]

---

17 See Meyer and Niedermeier (2011).

1.2.2.3 More social responsibility on the part of citizens and companies: increased complexity of political decision-making processes in the European Union

What is known by the generic term "Hartz IV" (German unemployment benefit) simultaneously equates to more personal responsibility for each citizen and the related restructuring of public expenditure for politicians. At present, it is the "break even" austerity policy publicised by Finance Minister Wolfgang Schäuble which, for many citizens, is associated with hardship and increased personal responsibility for their own security in the event of disease, accident or old-age poverty.

What the Federal Republic of Germany has achieved in a radical reform process, namely ensuring the competitiveness of German companies in a globalised economy, still remains to be confronted by some other European countries. The dispute regarding the continued development of European society is therefore a fundamental problem which also extensively concerns companies. In the future, they may well be required to take on increased responsibility in terms of child care or old-age provisions for their employees.

1.2.2.4 Globalisation and critical trends in a globally interconnected economic and financial world

Like many technological developments, globalisation, too, offers opportunities and risks. As a stakeholder group, customers benefit from lower prices – and opine: "Tight is right". On the other side of the fence, companies see themselves facing increased competitive pressure which not only compels them to lower production costs but also, logically, to subject their employees – the company's internal stakeholders – to rationalisation measures in terms of payment (minimum wages), social benefits or precarious working conditions. Suppliers, also stakeholders, additionally have to optimise their production and supply conditions to ensure their existence. This process runs through all partnerships within the value creation network of each company. Locations (countries, regions, communities) which offer liberal tax regimes and other regulations favourable to companies are also relevant stakeholders and compete against each other. Their concern is to secure jobs and ensure that their citizens prosper. In this environment, regional coalitions of states assume an existential importance for states, citizens and companies. One of the fundamental objectives within the EU (European Union) is to harmonise living conditions for all citizens in the member states. This can lead to the increasing communitisation of the different policy areas (with regard to the process of European integration and the European treaties, see Chapter 4). Whilst competing fiscal and tax policies in the member states may be advantageous for individual states, regions and companies, they may possibly have significantly destabilising consequences for the EU states and the European economy as a whole. The complexity, lack of transparency and interactions of political decision-making processes in the EU are on the increase, as are the interactions between the political decisions of the various member states and the decision-making levels of the member states.

The issue of the communitisation of the policy areas has the potential for considerable conflict within the EU. The situation becomes even more difficult when the negotiations surrounding further treaties with external EU partners are added, as currently seen in the efforts involving the transatlantic free trade agreement with the USA – Transatlantic Trade and Investment Partnership (TTIP). Back in the 1990s, this Transatlantic Trade and Investment Partnership treaty's predecessor failed due to France's veto following fierce resistance from NGOs (non-governmental organisations), amongst others. Individual negotiation items such as the issue of fracking licenses or the authorisation of genetically modified foods call into question fundamental principles such as the precautionary principle of the state for its population as prevalent in Europe. This easily eclipses opportunities such as the equality of a construction company in a Baltic state with a bidder in California in a public invitation to tender within the future scope of TTIP. The topic of international arbitrage actually affects state sovereignty rights, and the negotiations, which have thus far been conducted mainly in secrecy, strongly suggest that this involves a fierce dispute between powerful stakeholder groups in the USA and EU as well as major, globally operating companies. Citizens are merely being informed about the results which are achieved.

1.2.2.5 New organisational structures for the representation of civil interests

In view of the above described political and economic changes, certain of the current social developments are understandable. When official institutions and their representatives lose credibility and operate in realms which the "normal citizen" no longer understands, and the ability of trade unions to exert an influence is on the wane, non-governmental forms of organisation increase in importance. In this case, civil interest groups, which also increasingly represent local interests, form alongside the classic development, human rights or environmental policy NGOs such as Greenpeace, Human Rights Watch and the World Wide Fund For Nature, etc. These are aimed primarily at the moderate representation of their own interests, but radical groups, which come together at specific times, in specific locations or for specific issues, are also often formed at "their fringes". Examples of this include radical groups at the inauguration of the European Central Bank building in Frankfurt's banking district following the sub-prime crisis or during the "Stuttgart 21" railway construction protest. All of these actions document citizens' growing need to increasingly make themselves heard as the "actual sovereign" through their own commitment and to play an active role in political and social decision-making processes. The fear of no longer being able to independently structure one's own life but instead being controlled by economic, state or social crises whose origin is far removed from one's own environment is driving people to become active and take to the streets. The virtual counterpart of this is the previously addressed social, digital media, which extensively facilitate the possibility of exchange for these interest groups and also extensively promote it.[18]

1.2.2.6 Interim result

Faced with the conflicting priorities of intensifying competitive pressure and increasing demands for responsible activities, companies in the 21st century are being compelled to operate increasingly pro-actively and less reactively. They, and above all corporate management, play a key role in the structuring of future framework conditions for the coexistence of societies in a globalised world. The many legitimate interests of diverse parties have to be reconciled with one another. In this, companies can act as valuable advisors to government representatives, e.g. when structuring new international treaties: they are able to bring their entire economic expertise to bear. They can also become champions of the citizens, since the latter's interests also determine the companies' own interests. After all, their customers, employees and suppliers also number amongst their ranks. The common understanding of many textbooks and practitioners concerning the framework within which a company acts is that these are predetermined and cannot, or can barely, be influenced or shaped by companies. Within this understanding, framework conditions merely offer static business opportunities and threats to which the companies can react. Since this is only partially correct and companies most certainly can actively help to structure framework conditions, both monitoring and early warning systems are important for companies that want to have a strategic "edge". Above all, however, the attempt to change framework conditions through lobbying and the political representation of interests, etc. is not only legitimate but also necessary, irrespective of whether the objective is to facilitate future strategies or prevent the deterioration of their current business. In the final analysis, active political lobbying can therefore be regarded as an offensive attempt to actively structure the framework in order to represent and implement one's own and stakeholders' interests better, and ultimately to create common value creation for the stakeholder network in collaboration with the stakeholder network in question.

1.2.3 Ideal of the honourable merchant: a stakeholder-oriented concept?

The ideal of the honourable merchant takes on new topicality as part of the above described changes. The honourable merchant is the ideal for responsible economic operators. It stands for a pronounced sense of responsibility for one's own company, for society and for the environment or for "conscious" stakeholder orientation. An honourable merchant's behaviour is based on virtues aimed at ensuring

---

18 With regard to the growing importance of NGOs, see also the German Federal Agency for Civic Education (2010).

long-term economic success without opposing the interests of society:[19] he conducts business in a sustainable manner.

There is no single definition for "honourable", since the term has to be reexamined every time according to the historic context. Today, for instance, the merchant is often represented by companies and their salaried managers, whose scope of responsibility is significantly wider than that of their historic predecessors. What remains unchanged, however, is an ethical basis which emerges from social responsibility. One key term in this context is that of reciprocity, the principle of mutuality in social interaction, i.e. giving and taking as a characteristic of the honourable merchant. As reciprocity is part of a behavioural norm in every society[20] and, at the same time, the honourable merchant is not subject to any separate code, he, like every member of society, is obligated to society in general.[21] It can accordingly be concluded that this central norm of behaviour also applies to the honourable merchant. Concepts such as corporate social responsibility and corporate ethics are becoming increasingly important in economic and business affairs for precisely the same reasons.[22]

One aspect is becoming clear in this: the more extensively companies succeed in integrating their interests into the common good, i.e. integrating all stakeholder interests into their corporate policy – as far as possible – the more successful these companies will be. Even if their objective is to credibly help structure favourable framework conditions for their future activities.

Conclusion

Stakeholder-oriented corporate management aligns its interests with the common values and feels obligated to and responsible for not only the interests of the owners but, like an honourable merchant, also the common good. This also serves as a superordinate, integrative objective in the alignment and reconciliation of interests with all other stakeholders. In a global world, this logically leads to the question: "What is meant by the global common good, the 'common good' of 'global society'?".[23]

1.2.4 Complex and dynamic perspectives of stakeholder orientation

When taking various stakeholder interests into consideration in the corporate policy and analysing the stakeholders' interconnectedness at global, regional and local level as well as the dynamics of this, useful contributions can be made by the stakeholder theory, which is based on its numerous precursor theories. Accordingly, sustainable corporate success can only be ensured if companies regard

---

19 See Klink (2008), p. 72.
20 See Phillips (2014), p. 26.
21 See Klink (2008), p. 72.
22 See Ulrich (2014), pp. 19 ff.
23 See Wahlers (2009), p. 3.

themselves as part of an ecosystem or a holistic stakeholder network. This value creation network not only includes equity providers, customers, employees, entrepreneurs and managers but all suppliers, competitors, alliance partners, trade unions, regulatory authorities, social and political organisations (NGOs), citizens' initiatives, governments, authorities, associations and other participants as legitimate stakeholders (stakeholder groups) interconnected with and between each other as well as with the focal company. On this basis, all actors in this stakeholder network are able to interact with one another and jointly structure value creation contributions and relationships, co-creation is the characteristic, central design element in this. As both a prerequisite and consequence, the actors should be familiar with, understand and respect these mutual interests and take them into account in their decisions and their behaviour. The normative bases of the stakeholder theory and its instrumental conclusions and methods can support stakeholder management in the resulting, complex tasks.

The following quotations are intended to serve as a simple introduction to the abstract deliberations on the stakeholder theory:

"The behavioural norm of reciprocity exists in every human society."[24]

"One crucial difference between the stakeholder theory and many predecessor theories on strategic management is the fact that the stakeholder theory explicitly recognises the role of ethics and values and takes it seriously. Perhaps the most important task as part of the management of stakeholder relationships is the development of a common vision – a co-ordinating ethic – which aligns the interests of value-oriented people with one another."[25]

"There are as many authentic values which can form the umbrella of stakeholder relationships as there are companies. However, what is common to all of them is that they are ultimately always ethical values. No vision and no value system could fulfil this commonality-giving function if it is not also based on benefits for the community […] All companies act in a network of relationships with their stakeholders."[26]

The economy is not an end in itself but has the task of supplying society with goods. *"As a sub-area of society, the economy performs a service function, is so to speak subordinate to society and is subject to changes in the social state of consciousness, which it in turn influences."*[27]

"The permanent link between the economy and society is a fact which cannot be disputed. At the same time, this applies a polarity, a tension which is not resolvable, between society and the sub-area of the economy."[28]

---

24 Philipps (2014), p. 26.
25 Philipps (2014), p. 29.
26 Philipps (2014), p. 30.
27 Meyer (1973), p. 21.
28 Meyer (1996), p. 13.

For a long while, the shareholder value approach was the dominant corporate management practice approach. Public enterprises, the majority of family-owned companies and small and medium-sized enterprises (SMEs) are explicitly excluded from this. The objective was to increase the market value of the equity capital, the fundamental interest of each shareholder, since this was the basis for evaluating the company's success. Back in the 1970s, with the oil embargo, car-free Sundays as a result of the Yom Kippur War, the collapse of the international monetary system (Bretton-Woods) and discussion surrounding the boundaries of belief in growth and progress, the corporate environment became less predictable and "more risky" from a strategic point of view. This growing risk led to increased consideration in strategic management.

At the latest since the dot-com crisis (2000), the financial crisis (2007), and the changing framework conditions and profound processes of transformation in society, politics and the economy in recent decades (see Section 1.2.2), a reorientation is being seen in corporate management and business administration, leading to a paradigm shift from shareholder value to stakeholder orientation. In their book entitled *Stakeholders Matter – A New Paradigm for Strategy in Society*, published in 2011, Sybille Sachs and Edwin Rühli explain this reorientation as follows:

"The dominant shareholder-value model has led to mismanagement, market failure and a boost to regulation, as spectacularly demonstrated by the events surrounding the recent financial crisis. 'Stakeholders Matter' challenges the basic assumptions of this model, in particular traditional economic views on the theory of the firm and dominant theories of strategic management, and develops a new understanding of value creation away from pure self-interest toward mutuality. This new stakeholder paradigm is based on a network view, whereby mutuality enhances benefits and reduces risks for the firm and its stakeholders. The understanding of mutual value creation is operationalized according to the licence to operate, to innovate and to compete."[29]

R. Edward Freeman, the scientific pioneer of the stakeholder approach, comments on this in his preface to the publication by Sachs and Rühli:

"When the authors claim that a new paradigm emerged for strategic management, they are being too modest. Their proposals do no less than rewrite the contract between business and society. First of all, they broaden the notion of business as the engine of economic activity by focusing on value for shareholders rather than economic value for shareholders. Business in the twenty-first century must be seen as an institution which creates value for customers, suppliers, employees, communities, financiers and society."[30]

---

29 Sachs and Rühli (2011), p.I.
30 Sachs and Rühli (2011), p. XV.

If the new credo of corporate management is now stakeholder management and no longer shareholder value maximisation, it involves an incomparably more complex approach and process for formulating and communicating, implementing and checking corporate goals and corporate strategies and measuring their success. After all, this necessitates involving all companies and all stakeholder groups, which are influenced by the focal company and which in turn influence the company, in decisions and activities, and meeting their requirements. In this reorientation process, a one-dimensional maximisation approach is increasingly transformed into a complex, interaction-oriented reconciliation of interests process equating to a difficult balancing act. Added to this is the fact that the stakeholder management approach goes hand-in-hand with a loss of control due to the qualitative nature of the stakeholder relationship construct. Awareness of this is a central element of successful stakeholder-oriented thinking.

Since, as lecturers within the Munich School of Management at Ludwig-Maximilians-University, we want to prepare our students for the challenges accompanying this paradigm shift that they will encounter in corporate practice, we have been offering the "Convincing Stakeholders" (customers, employees, managers, investors, etc.) seminar since the introduction of the Master of Science study programme in business administration (winter semester 2008/2009) as part of the subject-related basics and an additional seminar on the topic of "Convincing Political Stakeholders" since the winter semester of 2013. Using the example of political lobbying by companies and associations, the latter demonstrates the form taken by professional lobbying for specific stakeholder groups in corporate practice.

To be able to understand the basis and the precursors of stakeholder management, we would like to answer the following questions in the next section:

How did stakeholder approaches and theories develop? What were their important predecessors? Who are the most important representatives? Which publications and findings are central to this development? And finally, what are the benefits of these findings to the practice of stakeholder management?

1.2.5 Stakeholder theory: central contributions, development stages and selected key findings

The paradigm shift towards a stakeholder orientation was based on a variety of theoretical preliminary works in the field of corporate ethics and on the relationship between the economy and society in various scientific disciplines such as philosophy, sociology, psychology, economics and business administration. The stakeholder orientation also benefited from best-sellers by certain management gurus, first and foremost Peter Drucker, and the study of the behaviour of many family-owned companies and SMEs which have been successful and engaged in sustainable management for a number of decades or centuries (see the left column of Figure 1.2).

1.2.5.1 Central contributions to the stakeholder theory

Important contributions to the development of the stakeholder theory arose from the inadequacies of the prevailing shareholder value approach: above all, these can also be found in strategic management[31] and occurred – as is so often the case – at the fringes of the domain rather than in the mainstream. With the growing "impact of crises and shortfalls", they attracted attention in the fields of organisational theory[32] and corporate ethics.[33] Due to its references to the area of corporate social responsibility (CSR), it was also dealt with and implemented there[34] and subsequently also in the "sustainability debate".[35], [36]

This is hardly surprising, since it is ultimately the common concern of stakeholder management, CSR, corporate citizenship and corporate ethics to relativise, push back, overcome or replace the shareholder value approach with the objective that the corporate environment and particularly society as a whole (also indirectly nature) or individual social groups have more influence on or in corporate decisions.

It is also understandable that these new perspectives of stakeholder orientation were not bid an immediate and uncritical welcome, and are still not, by salaried managers and their principals. At first glance, the classic shareholder value approach (in comparison with the stakeholder theory) has the advantage of simplicity and also puts forth logical arguments. A company should be run by the management such that, above all, the interests of the owners are represented by the managers and, thinking in the short term, this means maximum possible residual profits. The simple reason for this is that the managers are their principals' actors and their fiduciary task as their trusted representatives is to increase the principals' wealth and profits. This task is a simpler maximisation task (at least at first glance) than weighing up diverse stakeholder interests against each other. This short-term view is also more prevalent amongst companies represented on the capital market due to high-frequency trading and the specific strategies induced by this as well as speculative transactions with stocks, options and short selling. At second glance – if one thinks in terms of cause and effect relationships and manages accordingly, particularly in the longer term and from the perspective of sustainability instead of just short-term profit maximisation – the various perspectives converge. This may be one reason why this paradigm shift, as we observe it, progressed rather slowly in the past and only picked up pace with the increasing real and digital, global interconnectedness of the economy and society.

---

31 See e.g. Freeman (1984).
32 See e.g. Donaldson and Preston (1995); Jones (1995).
33 See e.g. Phillips (1997).
34 See e.g. Wood (1991).
35 See Steurer, Langer, Konrad and Martinuzzi (2005).
36 In this regard as a whole, see Laplume, Sonpar and Litz (2008), pp. 1156 ff.

1.2.5.2 Three stakeholder theory development stages

The development of the stakeholder theory can be roughly subdivided into three stages: the *(preliminary) development stage*, the *growth stage* and the *maturity stage.*

In the initial stage, the (preliminary) development stage, the first stakeholder theory approaches were developed as a response to the shareholder value approach prevailing within management. In the mid-1980s, this phase reached its conclusion with the central publication by *R. Edward Freeman (1984): Strategic Management – A Stakeholder Approach,* one of the best known representatives of the stakeholder theory and stakeholder management, because his work can be regarded as the prototype of a comprehensive treatise on stakeholder management. Freeman understands stakeholders to be specific groups, or individual persons, which exert an influence on an organisation or are affected in some way by these organisations' activities.[38] He portrayed the stakeholder view of a company in a so-called simplified hub and spoke model (see Figure 1.1).

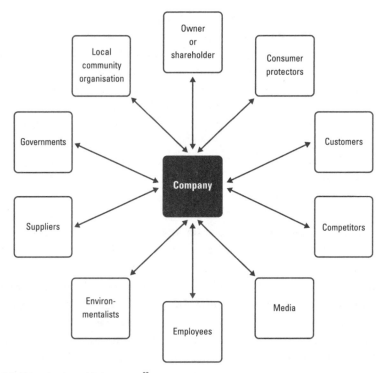

Figure 1.1: Hub and spoke model of a company[37]

---

38 See Freeman (1984), p. 25.
37 Own illustration, based on Freeman (1984), p. 25.

On this basis, he developed an extensive framework for the management process for stakeholder management and pleads for a voluntaristic philosophy in this. Finally, he discusses the structural consequences for the co-ordination functions on the management level, on the functional management disciplines and the new roles of the CEO. The stakeholder approach and the view that the management should not only primarily represent the interests of the owners, but that further external and internal target and stakeholder groups as well as the quality of the relationships with these are important to the company's success, were dealt with long before this by management gurus such as Peter Drucker and a number of theoreticians in the social and management sciences, etc. (see the left column of Figure 1.2). Accordingly, the theory developments in this initial stage are based on this preliminary theoretical work.

Freeman (1984) points out that the term stakeholder probably occurred first in 1963 in an internal memorandum at the Stanford Research Institute (SRI), where it was originally defined as *"those groups without whose support the organization would cease to exist"*.[39] As explained above, Freeman extends this term to include all individual persons and groups which can influence the achievement of an organisation's goals, or which are affected by the achievement of an organisation's goals. The latter also refers to stakeholders who may be affected in the future. The strategic and integrative orientation of his approach is revealed in the following quotation:

"Groups which 20 years ago had no effect on the actions of the firm, can affect it today, largely because of the actions of the firm which ignored the effects on the groups. Thus, by calling those affected groups 'stakeholders', the ensuing strategic management model will be sensitive to future change, and able to turn new 'external changes' into internal changes. One way to understand the definition is to think of the stakeholder concept as an umbrella for the problems in business strategy and corporate social responsiveness. To be an effective strategist you must deal with those groups that can affect you, while to be responsive (and effective in the long run) you must deal with those groups that you can affect."[40]

With his comprehensive and integrative approach (from both a theoretical point of view and a management perspective), Freeman is responding to the social, political and environmental challenges of the 1970s, the emergence of consumer protection and environmental protection as well as further challenges.[41] His approach shows how important the establishment and maintenance of relationships are, particularly with all types of external stakeholder, whilst simultaneously demonstrating that this approach can be used for all types of organisation.

---

39 Quoted from Freeman (1984), p. 31.
40 Freeman (1984), p. 46.
41 As described, for instance, in the 1973 Davos Manifesto and in "Die Grenzen des Wachstums"; see
   e.g. Steinmann (1973) or Meadows, Meadows, Randers and Behrens (1972).

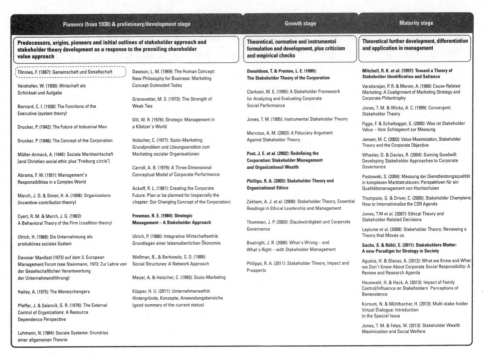

Figure 1.2: Selected contributions on the development of stakeholder theory & stakeholder management[42]

For strategic management, he also developed a comprehensive range of planning, analysis and control instruments up to and including a strategic early warning system based on existing instruments, and integrated this range of instruments into his stakeholder management framework and the existing strategic management processes. Further on in the development stage, important theoretical distinctions, further developments and substantiation of the stakeholder approach, which provide new perspectives, now take place on the basis of Freeman's framework concept. These are joined in the growth and maturity stage of the stakeholder theory by works on specific theoretical questions or works which particularly concern the management applications specified by Freeman.

Based on this pioneering work, the second stage, the *growth stage*, of the stakeholder theory and stakeholder management in the 1990s, is marked by further theoretical substantiation, the development of certain topic areas, critique of the overall approach and empirical checks (See Figure 1.2).

The article by *Donaldsonand Preston (1995): The Stakeholder Theory of the Corporation: Concepts, Evidence and Implications,* is central to this period since it summarises the findings concerning the stakeholder approach and their substantiation thus far.

---

42 Own illustration: extensive own further development of a portrayal by Munzel and Ullmer (2009, unpublished, Institute for Marketing) and Zakhem, Palmer and Stoll (2008) as well as a review by Laplume, Sonpar and Litz (2008).

The authors distinguish between three dimensions[43] of the stakeholder theory:[44]

- A *descriptive/empirical perspective* (i. e. a perspective which describes the theory and explains relationships which can be observed in the real world).
- An *instrumental/predictive perspective* (i.e. a perspective which postulates the theory, explains positive cause and effect connections between stakeholder management and the achievement of corporate goals and thus has a predictive value).
- A *normative perspective* (i.e. that decisions made on a normative basis choose the right alternatives).

These differ according to the statements they make and therefore also have different implications. At the same time, however, it must also be remembered that the three dimensions are related, and mutually support and influence each other.

Under certain circumstances, the *descriptive perspective* is useful in order to describe and understand which stakeholders a company has, which interactions also take place between the company and these stakeholders, i.e. what type of interactions these are, what strategic importance various stakeholder groups have for the company and what specific contributions they make.

On the basis of "if-then" relationships, the *instrumental perspective* of the theory enables predictions regarding the advantageousness of various uses of resources for a specific objective (profitability, growth, return on investment) to be made in the search for solutions or competitive advantages. In this phase of stakeholder development, this is methodically implemented with the aid of statistical methods or empirical methods such as monitoring, surveys, case studies and experiments. Margolis and Walsh (2003), for instance, analysed more than 120 studies in terms of the relationships between the financial results of companies and the implementation or omission of stakeholder-related corporate policies/practices, discovering positive relationships in over 70 studies, negative relationships in 30 studies and mixed relationships in the remainder.[45] In another study, Banks and Vera (2007) determined that stakeholder management has a positive impact on both the financial and social performance of a company.[46]

The *normative perspective* refers to the ethical and social value basis and responsibility of a company, i.e. the fact that stakeholder management which is based on norms behaves according to its ethical, moral and social standards (e.g. principles of justice/fairness) in its relationships/interactions with stakeholders.[47]

---

43 See Donaldson and Preston (1995), p. 65. Called "descriptive accuracy", "instrumental power" and "normative validity" in the original. The authors also mention that more then 12 books and 100 scientific articles on the stakeholder concept have appeared in the ten years following Freeman's publication (1984).
44 See Pastowski (2004), pp. 10 ff.
45 See Margolis and Walsh (2003), pp. 273 ff.
46 Quoted from Sachs and Rühli (2011), p. 43.
47 See also Donaldson and Preston (1995).

Criterion	Approach
Descriptive or empirical	• What is the nature of the company? • What do managers think about management? • What do management boards think about the interests of stakeholders? • How are specific companies managed?
Instrumental/ predicative	• Conventional statistical methods for generating implications for stakeholder management
Normative	• Interpretation of the corporate culture on the basis of philosophical, ethical and social responsibility

Figure 1.3: Characteristics of the stakeholder approach[48]

As Donaldson and Preston (1995) add, this is joined by the fact that, in addition to these three theory dimensions, the stakeholder theory is also "managerial" when it does not merely describe, explain and predict cause and effect relationships but also

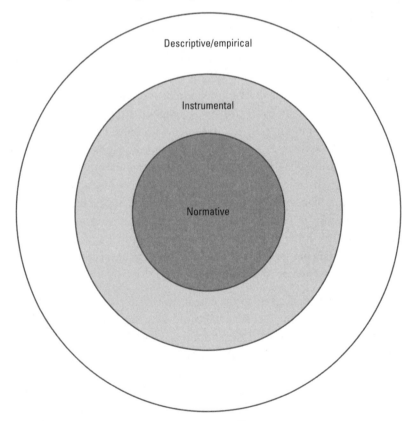

Figure 1.4: Three aspects of the stakeholder theory and their relationship[49]

---

48 Own illustration, based on Pastowski (2004), p. 10.
49 Own illustration, based on Donaldson and Preston (1995), p. 74.

develops "management recipes", i.e. it advises. – "[...] it also recommends attitudes, structures, and practices that, taken together, constitute stakeholder management. Stakeholder management requires, as its key attribute simultaneous attention to the legitimate interests of all appropriate stakeholders, both in the establishment of organizational structures and general politics and in case-by-case decision making [...]. The theory does not imply that all stakeholders (however they may be identified) should be equally involved in all processes and decisions."[50]

In response to the question of how the three dimensions build on one another, the authors state that the core of the stakeholder theory is normative and supplies the reasoning and justification, the moral reference points and responsibility (inner motives = normative basis of the theory) for the other dimensions (see Figure 1.4).

This is also confirmed by the following quotation:

"Thus, the normative principles that underlie the contemporary pluralistic theory of property rights also provide the foundation for the stakeholder theory as well."[51]

Another crucial development step in the stakeholder theory during this phase was that not only relationships between the focal companies and their stakeholders were studied or, as in the "classic" input-output model, only in one direction and for a few central value creation partners, but relationships in both directions to and from the focal company with all of its stakeholders and between all of these stakeholders (see Figure 1.5). Accordingly, the network perspective was introduced into stakeholder management at this point.

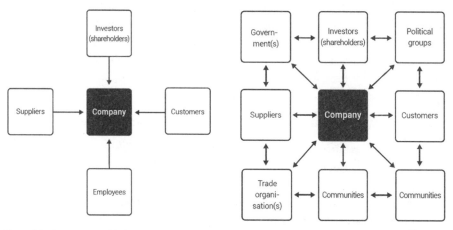

Figure 1.5: Input-output model of the company versus the stakeholder model as a comprehensive relationship network[52]

---

50 Donaldson and Preston (1995), p. 67. With regard to the three dimensions of the stakeholder theory according to Donaldson and Preston (1995) and their relevant approaches, see the overview in Figure 1.3.
51 Donaldson and Preston (1995), p. 85.
52 Own illustration. The illustration on the left is based on Donaldson and Preston (1995), p. 68. The illustration on the right is also based on Donaldson and Preston (1995), p. 69 and Pastowski (2004), p. 10.

1.2.5.3 Maturity phase as part of stakeholder management

In the third phase, the maturity phase, a high number of contributions were made to further develop specific theoretical topics and practical applications of the stakeholder theory and stakeholder management. We will briefly outline and acknowledge a small selection of these contributions as examples. Prior to this, however, we will present two comprehensive and fundamental contributions which attempt to pick up on Freeman's (1984) extensive overall analysis and continue it in theoretical and content terms. These are the book publications by *Post, Preston and Sachs (2002): Redefining the Corporation, Stakeholder Management and Organizational Wealth,* and *Sachs and Rühli (2011): Stakeholders Matter – A New Paradigm for Strategy in Society.* Common to both contributions is that they further develop the network perspective, the ideas of stakeholder commitment, collaboration and co-creation in the stakeholder theory and stakeholder management and furnish them with new perspectives.

Driven in part by the inadequacies (e. g. market failure, crises, mismanagement) of the shareholder value approach and also particularly against the background of the downsides of globalisation, Post, Preston and Sachs (2002) come to the conclusion in their aforementioned book, as previously stated in this contribution, that the essence of companies should be redefined.

"The conventional concept is descriptively inaccurate and ethically unacceptable [...]. The corporation cannot – and should not – survive if it does not take responsibility for the welfare of all its constituents, and for the well-being of the larger society within which it operates. The contractual agreements and government regulation it must follow are not always enough."[53] Accordingly, the authors define their "stakeholder view (SHV) of the corporation" as follows: *"The corporation is an organization engaged in mobilizing resources for productive uses in order to create wealth and other benefits (and not to intentionally destroy wealth, increase risk, or cause harm) for its multiple constituents, or stakeholders."*[54]

In their view, this definition is more suitable/contemporary because it:[55]

- Is extremely realistic, since it describes this more precisely.
- Provides management with better guidelines concerning its areas of responsibility.
- Gives consideration to the fact that corporate success has multiple facets and has to be regarded from various perspectives, i. e. including that the owners' interests do not always take top priority and are never the only interests which count.

---

53 Post, Preston and Sachs (2002), pp. 16 – 17.
54 Post, Preston and Sachs (2002), p. 17.
55 See Post, Preston and Sachs (2002), p. 17.

- Continues to determine which stakeholders should be identified and which are the legitimated and important stakeholders. Particularly those that are not bound to the company by contracts and not voluntarily, and which are thus often easily overlooked. The concerns and interests of these stakeholders should also be registered and addressed.

Post, Preston and Sachs (2002) modify Freeman's understanding of stakeholders, as this has since been criticised due to its excessively wide perspective (amongst others, Freeman also included competitors and their interests, which are contrary to those of the focal company and therefore do not usually have a stake in the focal company). Post, Preston and Sachs (2002) regard stakeholders as "*individuals and constituencies that contribute, either voluntarily or involuntarily, to its wealth-creating capacity and activities, and that are therefore its potential beneficiaries and/or risk bearers*".[56] Accordingly, stakeholders have three essential characteristics:

1. Stakeholders provide tangible (monetary) and intangible (e.g. social acceptance) *resources* which are crucial to the success of the company.
2. Stakeholders are directly or indirectly affected by the company's *activities* in a *positive* or *negative* manner. They thus bear a risk ("value at risk") and their prosperity is dependent on the company's fate.
3. Stakeholders have sufficient *power* to influence the company's performance. This also means that they can mobilise political instances, for example, for the benefit (or to the disadvantage) of the company in order to support or prevent corporate activities.

In addition to the classic resources (capital, labour, land), *resources* in this case also include the "licence to operate". *Risks* can be financial in nature, career opportunities, the quality of products or service, or effects on the environment and local residents. The *power* of stakeholders is not only of a financial nature but can also refer to the possibility of mobilising political power or the power of social movements (e.g. through social media including the withdrawal of resources).

In the portrayal of their stakeholder model focussed on bilateral stakeholder relationships (see Figure 1.6), Post, Preston and Sachs (2002) point out that the arrows always point in both directions because this is intended to designate mutual exchange or interactions ("benefits" or "harms" or combinations of these).[57]

At the same time, there are not only bilateral relationships between stakeholders and the company, but also indirect relationships and thus often multiple linkages to other stakeholders via the relationships between stakeholders, e.g. via the same communities. In addition, individual stakeholders can simultaneously have sever-

---

56 Post, Preston and Sachs (2002), p. 19.
57 See Post, Preston and Sachs (2002), p. 22.

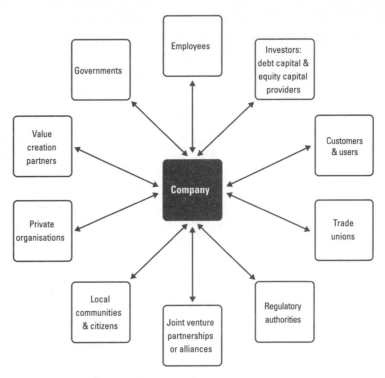

Figure 1.6: The company and its stakeholders[58]

al roles (e.g. employee, stockholder, customer, neighbour, trade union member, etc.). And naturally, the relationships between the company and specific stakeholders also change depending on the relevant concerns and circumstances – they are extensively characterised by dynamics.

Before we now ask which value contributions the various stakeholders can make to the common "organisational wealth" according to the SHV described by Post, Preston and Sachs (2002), the meaning of organisational wealth as a target variable and the benefit which can arise from this for all concerned must first be clarified. The three authors explain:

"Organizational wealth is the cumulative result of corporate performance over time, including all of the assets, competencies, and revenue-generating capacities developed by the firm. Compared to less successful companies, wealthier firms can pay higher wages and offer better career opportunities, take greater risks, provide greater customer benefits".[59] And based on Sveiby (1997), they go on to explain: *"Organizational Wealth is the summary measure of the capacity of an organization to create benefits"*.[60]

---

58 Own illustration, based on Post, Preston and Sachs (2002), p. 22.
59 Post, Preston and Sachs (2002), p. 36.
60 Post, Preston and Sachs (2002), p. 45.

The central source of organisational wealth is the relationships with the most important stakeholder groups. The specific value contributions made by these stakeholder groups are shown in Figure 1.7:

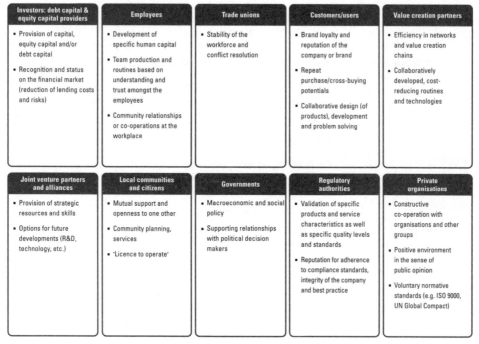

Figure 1.7: Value contributions of different stakeholders to organisational wealth[61]

The authors then place the SHV into relation with the two other prominent approaches, the resource-based view (RBV) and the industry structure view (ISV) or the similar market-based view (MBV), on the basis of three dimensions (Figure 1.8).

They arrive at the result that *a company's SHV is the more comprehensive basis* for strategic management since it integrates the perspectives of the ISV and the RBV, extending and completing them with the relationship between the company and society and between the company and politics. This is not least important from a management perspective because the involvement of and relationship with these two stakeholders (society and politics) are critical to success.[62]

The authors underscore this with the following explanation: *"The corporation's most important asset – and the only one it cannot create or replace on its own – is its acceptance within society as a legitimate institution."*[63]

---

61 Own illustration, based on Post, Preston and Sachs (2002), p. 47.
62 See Post, Preston and Sachs (2002), pp. 231, 291.
63 Post, Preston and Sachs (2002), p. 256. The authors also practised and harmonised their findings on three companies which have implemented the stakeholder approach over a long period of time spanning several decades in order to check the consistency of their concept on these examples (see Post, Preston and Sachs (2002), p. 2).

Dimensions	Resource-based view (RBV)	Industry structure view (ISV)	Stakeholder view (SHV)
Unit of analysis	Company	Industry	Network of a company's stakeholders
Main sources of organisational wealth	▪ Tangible assets ▪ Human resources ▪ Knowledge ▪ Technology ▪ Financial resources ▪ Intangible resources	▪ Negotiating power via-à-vis suppliers and customers ▪ Market power via-à-vis competitors	▪ Relationships leading to higher earnings and/or lower costs and risks ▪ Relationship benefits which enable growth in wealth
Means for maintaining organisational wealth	▪ Imitation barriers at corporate level	▪ Market entry barriers at industry level ▪ Production savings/sunk costs ▪ Regulation by governments	▪ Company-specific connections between stakeholders and implicit agreements leading to higher earnings and/or reduced costs and risks

Figure 1.8: The sources of organisational wealth from the perspective of three different theoretical approaches[64]

Stakeholders Matter – A new Paradigm for Strategy in Society by Sachs and Rühli (2011)

Sachs and Rühli (2011) base their work on the SHV formulated by Post, Preston and Sachs (2002). The latter applied the SHV to a network in which the interactions primarily took place between the focal company and its stakeholders.[65] Sachs and Rühli (2011) adopt a multilaterally more complex network perspective for the SHV which goes beyond bilateral interactions between a company and its network. The addition of this perspective is used to analyse relationships between all partners within a network, with the result that focus is not placed on a specific company which has stakeholders but in which "the company" itself is a stakeholder. This "evolutionary" network perspective, which goes beyond bilateral dialogues, is a central element of their new stakeholder paradigm. They explain "*we understand value creation between firm and stakeholders in the context of relation-*

---

64 Own illustration, based on Post, Preston and Sachs (2002), p. 54.
65 See Post, Preston and Sachs (2002), p. 41.

al embeddedness based on mutual multilateral processes [...] We assume that if corporations want to tap their stakeholders potentials as a source of continuous value creation, they need more than bilateral dialogues. Rather they need collaborative procedures to build common ground with their multiple stakeholders in a network view". [66] They develop their understanding of the stakeholder paradigm and its assumptions on the basis of this network perspective, which is founded on the "mutuality" and not the "self-interest" of all parties concerned. At its core, they operationalise this using a concept of three licenses (see Figure 1.9):[67]

- *"Licence to operate"* with the central stakeholders of society and politics (*cast of stakeholders* in the original).
- *"Licence to innovate"* with the resource owners as central stakeholders.
- *"Licence to compete"* with all direct and indirect stakeholders in the network.

This concept with the three licences is then exhaustively explained and the important challenges of this paradigm shift are then briefly outlined. On the whole, this is an interesting, very wide-ranging – perhaps even too wide-ranging – concept and is not yet complete, as the authors themselves state with the following remark during their explanations on the three licences: the work *"is not complete, considerable work has to be done".* [68]

---

66 Sachs and Rühli (2011), p. 41.
67 See Sachs and Rühli (2011), p. 93.
68 Sachs and Rühli (2011), p. 94.

```
┌─────────────────────────────────────────────────────────────┐
│                     Stakeholder paradigm                      │
│        Value creation with and for stakeholders through a     │
│            network-based perspective of mutuality             │
└─────────────────────────────────────────────────────────────┘
```

Operationalisation based on RBV, ISV and
the socio-political perspective

```
┌─────────────────────────────────────────────────────────────┐
│                 Framework of the three licences               │
│        (comprehensive application for mutual value creation)  │
└─────────────────────────────────────────────────────────────┘
```

Aspects	Licences		
	To operate	To innovate	To compete
Stakeholder make-up	▪ Social and political stakeholders	▪ Owners of the resources	▪ Direct and indirect stakeholders in the network
(Value) contribution	▪ By (in)voluntary stakeholders	▪ By (un)limited resources	▪ Through co-operation, co-opetition, competition
Distribution	▪ According to the (in)voluntary contributions	▪ According to resource distribution	▪ According to the direct and indirect contributions in networks
Strategies	▪ Improvement of common solutions; exploration of common objectives with social and political stakeholders	▪ Innovative resource pooling and development; capacity for interacting with stakeholder	▪ Positioning / benchmarking
Evaluation of the process and the result	▪ Value creation stimulated through (dis)similarities	▪ Value creation through innovative solutions	▪ Value creation through motivation within and between networks

Figure 1.9: Core elements of the three licences for operationalising the stakeholder paradigm[69]

---

69 Own illustration and translation, based on Sachs and Rühli (2011), p. 93.

1.2.6 Stakeholder management and strategies

Tried and tested strategic management and marketing concepts and methods can essentially be applied for stakeholder management but require certain modifications in terms of the special considerations of the various stakeholder relationships. As part of stakeholder analyses, these are above all concepts such as *segmenting – targeting – positioning*[70] and findings and methods pertaining to relationship marketing in general, business relationships and relationship quality[71] as well as interactive communication theories, particularly social media.[72]

To clarify the central, basic question[73] of who the important stakeholders of a specific company or network are, the overview of stakeholder groups relevant to the company can be classified according to bilateral stakeholder relationship characteristics[74] or can be subdivided into three categories according to proximity to the company's activities (see Figure 1.10).[75]

According to Mitchell, Agle and Wood (1997), the status of *stakeholder groups* in society can be assessed based on the dimensions of power, legitimacy and urgen-

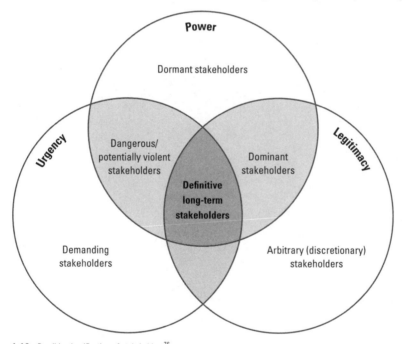

Figure 1.10: Possible classification of stakeholders[76]

---

70 See Kotler and Armstrong, pp. 237 ff.
71 See Morgan and Hunt (1994); Diller, Haas and Ivens (2005).
72 See Hennig-Thurau, Malthouse, Friege, Gensler, Lobschat, Rangaswamy and Skiera (2010); Malthouse, Haenlein, Skiera, Wege and Zhang (2013).
73 With regard to this and other basic questions, see the overview by Laplume, Sonpar and Litz (2008), Tables 3–6, pp. 1162–1167.
74 See Mitchell, Agle and Wood (1997), p. 874.
75 See Post, Preston and Sachs (2002), p. 55.
76 Own illustration, based on Mitchell, Agle and Wood (1997), p. 874.

cy. The *power* of stakeholders results from financial resources and the possibility of influencing media, etc. *Legitimacy* represents the stakeholder group's degree of recognition in society. *Urgency* represents the stakeholder's requirement on the company to meet its demands as quickly as possible.[77]

In the *first category* of the model by Post, Preston and Sachs (2002), and thus closest to the company, the authors describe stakeholder groups which invest tangible and/or intangible resources. These include employees (investment in the form of labour, for instance), customers (investment in the form of purchasing products and services) and shareholders (financial investment). The *second category* encompasses stakeholder groups which influence the entire industry, e.g. trade unions, alliances, joint ventures and regulatory authorities. Finally, the *third category* includes stakeholder groups which have a social and political influence.[78] Examples of these include the European Commission and the Council of Ministers,

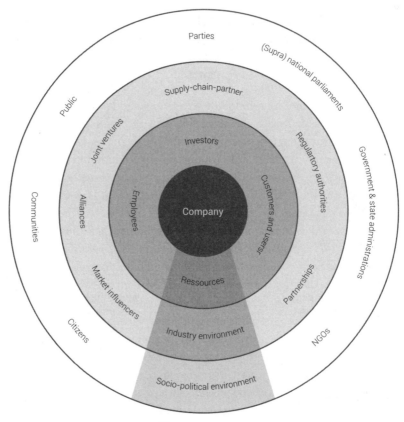

Figure 1.11: The stakeholder view of the company[79]

Comment: The relationship and complement between RBV, ISV and SHV are again clearly indicated in this figure. It shows the various "stakeholder layers" according to the three perspectives and proximity to the core of acompany, but not necessarily their relative importance.

77 See Mitchell, Agle and Wood (1997), p. 874.
78 See Post, Preston and Sachs (2002), p. 55.
79 Own illustration and further development based on Post, Preston and Sachs (2002), pp. 55ff.

governments and state administrations. However, the proximity of a stakeholder group to the company in the graphic has no bearing on its actual significance (see Figure 1.11).

The model which is shown is referred to as central-instrumentalistic and places a company at the centre of the action (see Figure 1.12). Accordingly, only relationships between the company and the stakeholder groups are analysed. To enable to eliminate this simplification, as already explained in this contribution, companies can be viewed as part of a network with their stakeholders. This enables both the interdependencies between the individual stakeholder groups to be mapped[80] and the multilateral stakeholder dialogue to be registered.[81] As part of the network system, the company is an actor through which other stakeholders belonging to the network system communicate and interact.

In everyday management, many other stakeholder group and relationship categorisations are possible and useful depending on the specific objectives. Categorisation of the various "target groups" by type or the strategic importance of this target group's resources, the type of benefit/damage, the type of interests/topics, de-

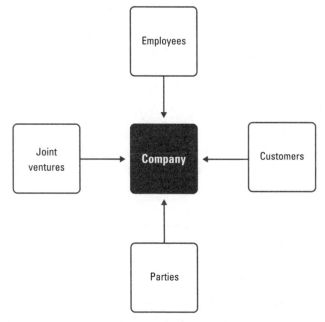

Figure 1.12: Central-instrumentalistic stakeholder approach: The company at the centre of the action – a simplified example[82]

---

80 See Rowley (1997); Vanderkerckhove and Detchev (2005).
81 See Calton and Kurland (1996).
82 Own illustration, based on Rowley (1997), p. 89; comment: the arrows symbolise direct relationships between the listed stakeholder groups.

mands, attitudes, quality and strength of the relationships with the focal company, etc. is conceivable.[83]

The various stakeholder groups should be categorised and prioritised for the entire company, into individual locations/regions, individual divisions and strategic business units, since both fundamental strategic behaviour and specific behaviour towards different stakeholder groups can be defined and co-ordinated on this comprehensive basis.

The central question of which strategies companies can implement in stakeholder management, with reference to specific stakeholder groups, arises at this point. Meffert, Burmann and Kirchgeorg (2012) suggest four options[84]:

1. Strategy of innovation (proactive strategy):
   Characteristics: above average, proactive activity; active structuring of the relationship with various stakeholder groups; anticipation of the expectations and requirements of the stakeholder groups.
   Company example: Apple, pioneer in the field of technology and technology services.

2. Strategy of avoidance/adaptation through retreat:
   Characteristics: defensive/reactive activity; comprehensive analysis of competitor activities and market events; addressing the stakeholder groups' most essential expectations.
   Company example: Blackberry, "conventional" smartphones not introduced until 2013.

3. Strategy of resistance:
   Characteristics: proactive and reactive activity; fighting against certain stakeholder group demands (proactive) or refusal to meet specific expectations/requirements of the stakeholder groups (reactive).
   Company examples:
   (Active): Abercrombie & Fitch consciously decides not to offer clothing in larger sizes, leading to discontent amongst various stakeholder groups.
   (Reactive): Shell: the intended sinking of the Brent Spar oil storage platform in the North Atlantic.

4. Strategy of avoidance through problem shifting:
   Characteristics: reactive activity; passive structuring of the relationship with various stakeholder groups; shifting of problems in order not to have to meet requirements.

---

83 Payne, Ballantyne and Christopher (2005) distinguish here between various "markets" which are of significance to the company: customer markets, referral markets, influencer markets, employee markets, supplier markets and internal markets; for an alternative classification of stakeholders, see e.g. Payne, Ballantyne and Christopher (2005), p. 860.
84 See Meffert, Burmann and Kirchgeorg (2012), pp. 330–331.

Company example: travel company TUI withdrew from a holiday destination in the Caribbean because the very demanding internal environmental protection guidelines could not be guaranteed in that specific destination.

Figure 1.13: Stakeholder group-oriented strategies in the situational context[85]

These types of strategy reveal different approaches to integrating stakeholders into the planning and implementation of corporate activities. This raises the question of how companies should determine the preferred strategy. As can be seen in Figure 1.13, the strategy must always be selected in terms of the company's own strength and the influence of the stakeholder groups concerned.

The company's strength is determined through its competitive position and the available internal resources. Conversely, the strength of the stakeholder groups' influence is mainly dependent on their status in society and the importance of the concern in public debate. Over time, each company has developed appropriate instruments to meet the requirements of evaluating its own strength. Once both the company's strength and the strength of the stakeholders' influence have been evaluated, the appropriate strategy can then be selected (for examples of specific companies, see strategy types 1– 4 in the preceding section).

1.2.7 Example applications of the stakeholder view in marketing

The understanding of marketing and of corporate management in general changes during the course of increasing stakeholder orientation. *Marketing* can accordingly be defined as follows: *"[...] creating superior benefits for an organisation's different stakeholder groups/stakeholders with the active involvement of all value creation partners in order to sustainably achieve above average increases in value".*[86] In practice, marketing can be undertaken defensively or offensively. Of-

---

85 Own illustration, based on Meffert, Burmann and Kirchgeorg (2012), p. 331.
86 Meyer and Davidson (2016).

fensive marketing then means *"[...] accessing and exploiting the entire potential of marketing [...] leading markets, delivering* superior customer benefits, *taking* risks *and forcing* competitors *to become* imitators".[87] Offensive marketing is designed not to regard the behaviour of customers/stakeholders as given but also as changeable, and also to be able to offensively change customer structures and further develop internal resources.[88] This also applies accordingly to offensive stakeholder management. With its definition published in 2013, *"Marketing is the activity, set of institutions, and processes for creating, communicating, delivering, and exchanging offerings that have value for customers, clients, and society at large"*[89], the American Marketing Association endorses this wide understanding of marketing.

One further indication that stakeholder orientation is increasing in importance is shown, for example, by the fact that the *Journal of Business Research* dedicated an entire issue to this topic in 2013. In the introductory article by Kornum and Mühlbacher (2013), the two authors push the topic of "multi-stakeholder virtual dialogue" and deal with the contents of this special issue. The crucial element is interaction with and between stakeholders, particularly in the online area. A variety of partially uncontrollable interactions and the resulting, complex relationships means that modern stakeholder management offers new opportunities, and particularly that it also faces new challenges. In this context, the objective must be to integrate the relevant stakeholders into the corporate processes and to understand and be able to analyse a concept of the connections as part of one's own, and optimally also the connections between different, stakeholder networks. This resulting complexity leads to the fact that companies are having to rethink or rather "think ahead" in terms of marketing and strategy and develop or continue to develop new skills. Hillebrand, Driessen and Koll (2015) provide an initial approach to potential stakeholder-related marketing capabilities.

The application of the stakeholder view to established tools in the marketing and strategy fields demands their adaptation to this holistic way of thinking. For example, the integration of social and political stakeholder concerns into Porter's classic value creation chain (see Figure 1.14) can be used to show the consequences of continuously integrating stakeholder-relevant topics into companies' value creating processes.[90] It becomes clear here that all value creating processes are ultimately co-creation activities or the results of co-creation processes by diverse stakeholders (stakeholder groups). However, it must be noted that the above mentioned representation as a value creation chain as part of input-output relationships is basically correct. If the stakeholder view is applied rigidly, however, the value creation chain should be transformed into a value creation network

---

87 Meyer and Davidson (2001), p. 65.
88 Meyer and Davidson (2001).
89 American Marketing Association (2013).
90 See Porter and Kramer (2006), p. 8.

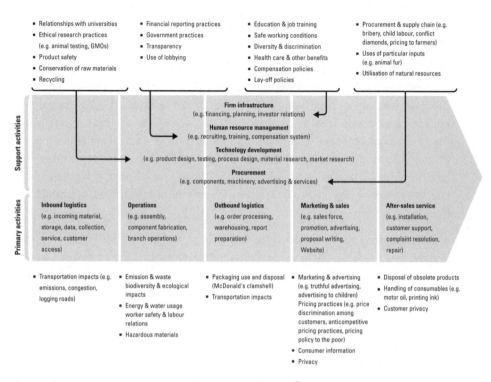

- Relationships with universities
- Ethical research practices (e.g. animal testing, GMOs)
- Product safety
- Conservation of raw materials
- Recycling

- Financial reporting practices
- Government practices
- Transparency
- Use of lobbying

- Education & job training
- Safe working conditions
- Diversity & discrimination
- Health care & other benefits
- Compensation policies
- Lay-off policies

- Procurement & supply chain (e.g. bribery, child labour, conflict diamonds, pricing to farmers)
- Uses of particular inputs (e.g. animal fur)
- Utilisation of natural resources

Support activities

Firm infrastructure
(e.g. financing, planning, investor relations)

Human resource management
(e.g. recruiting, training, compensation system)

Technology development
(e.g. product design, testing, process design, material research, market research)

Procurement
(e.g. components, machinery, advertising & services)

Primary activities

Inbound logistics
(e.g. incoming material, storage, data, collection, service, customer access)

Operations
(e.g. assembly, component fabrication, branch operations)

Outbound logistics
(e.g. order processing, warehousing, report preparation)

Marketing & sales
(e.g. sales force, promotion, advertising, proposal writing, Website)

After-sales service
(e.g. installation, customer support, complaint resolution, repair)

- Transportation impacts (e.g. emissions, congestion, logging roads)

- Emission & waste biodiversity & ecological impacts
- Energy & water usage worker safety & labour relations
- Hazardous materials

- Packaging use and disposal (McDonald's clamshell)
- Transportation impacts

- Marketing & advertising (e.g. truthful advertising, advertising to children) Pricing practices (e.g. price discrimination among customers, anticompetitive pricing practices, pricing policy to the poor)
- Consumer information
- Privacy

- Disposal of obsolete products
- Handling of consumables (e.g. motor oil, printing ink)
- Customer privacy

Figure 1.14: Porter's value creation chain extended by social and political issues[91]

which takes up stakeholder concerns at all potential interaction points between the company and stakeholders as relevant.

From a theoretical, scientific perspective, it is interesting that, entirely irrespective of the theoretical concepts of the stakeholder view referred to here and without mutual references, the theoretical developments towards a new marketing logic over the past ten years reveal a number of similarities in terms of their content. Starting with the publication by Vargo and Lusch entitled *"Evolving to the New Dominant Logic for Marketing"* in the *Journal of Marketing* in 2004, many theoretical findings and implications have been published, particularly in terms of the co-creation construct.[92] Certain of the fundamental premises of the service-dominant logic postulated by Vargo and Lusch therefore bear great similarity to the assumptions of the modern stakeholder theory, such as *"all social and economic actors are resource integrators"*,[93] which can also be found in some instances in earlier explanations in scientific service marketing literature.[94] These theoretical

91 Own illustration, based on Porter and Kramer (2006), p. 8.
92 See also Prahalad and Ramaswamy (2004).
93 Vargo and Lusch (2008), p. 7.
94 See Lusch and Vargo (2006).

convergences in the various management disciplines could indicate an extensive paradigm shift.

This is also being revealed in a rethinking process for both the brand and brand management in the areas of brand understanding and brand strategy. Branding processes are increasingly being regarded as dynamic, interactive and social processes, subsequently leading to a, partially extensive, loss of control over brand images by brand owners. This resulting loss of control is severely hampering traditional brand management. Examples which immediately come to mind are the contributions by fans or critics of brands in various social media channels or the effects caused by the image-damaging conduct of some drivers of certain car brands.

This new logic is also revealed in the importance and understanding of corporate brands, which are viewed as central, intangible assets by many companies and as an increasingly important co-ordination instrument by global companies. The importance of various stakeholder groups to the image and value of corporate brands was recognised around ten years ago.[95] This development is referred to as "brand democratisation". This means that the importance of brands and their personality is being publicly discussed – made easier by Web 2.0 – and developed jointly in dialogue with various stakeholder groups in the co-creation process. The range of this dialogue is vast due to the diverse stakeholders' interconnectedness. Accordingly, brand management is now no longer regarded primarily as an autonomous management process by a company but as a dynamic process of exchange and interaction between stakeholder groups and the company. This leads to a change in the importance and role of the brand managers within the company, since they should systematically involve all internal and external stakeholders in the brand management process if possible but must nevertheless ensure that the brand core is maintained.[96] If the interdependencies of the different stakeholder groups between each other without the involvement of brand management are added, this "co-ordination process" is made difficult.[97]

On the basis of the service-dominant logic, Merz, He and Vargo (2009) show how the understanding of a brand and the related shift in the importance of various brand resources have continued to develop from a "product branding logic" (identification logic) to the "stakeholder-focussed branding logic", a dynamic, interactive and social process (see Figure 1.15).

---

95 See Balmer and Gray (2003); Chun and Davies (2006).
96 See Kornum and Mühlbacher (2013); Gyrd-Jones and Kornum (2013).
97 See Vallester and Wallpach (2013).

The new logic: from branding "to" ...   ... to branding "with"

Product focus, brand era 1900 - 1930	Benefit focus, brand era 1930 - 1990	Relationship focus, brand era 1990 - 2000	Stakeholder focus, brand era 2000 and in future
• The brand for recognition • The brand as a legal system • The brand for orientation • The brand as a symbol for constant quality	• The brand as a vehicle for enriching product benefit through personal and symbolic images • The brand for differentiation • The brand for symbolic image	• The brand as a dyadic relationship partner • The customer as a value creation partner • The employees as value creation partners	• Brand as a dynamic, interactive and social process • Brands have network-like relationships with all stakeholders

Figure 1.15: Transformation of branding logic induced through service-dominant logic[98]

1.2.8 Summary and outlook

To put it in a nutshell: in both corporate practice and science, strategic focus is increasingly shifting away from the shareholder approach to the stakeholder approach with the objective of maximising *organisational wealth*. In this, companies should be regarded as part of a network of interdependent relationships. This means that companies should not only integrate their relationships with their stakeholders but also the relationships between their stakeholders into their corporate decisions.[99] Accordingly, the topic of "*stakeholder multiplicity*" will also continue to increase in importance in science and practice in the future.[100] What must a company consequently internalise? Based on Freeman's (2004) explanations and the increasing importance of stakeholder network systems, the following is suggested:

- Society and politics, etc. are not boundary conditions but important stakeholders.
- The influences of one's own corporate activities on other stakeholders should be taken into consideration.
- The stakeholders' modes of behaviour, values and requirements should be understood and analysed in this regard.
- Companies should understand how stakeholder groups are interconnected with each other.
- Companies should analyse interdependencies and interactions between the stakeholder groups and also take these into account in their strategic and operational decisions.

---

98 Own illustration, based on Merz, He and Vargo (2009), p. 331.
99 See Matzler, Pechlaner and Renzl (2003); Holtbrügge and Puck (2009).
100 See Neville and Menguc (2006).

Legal status	Origin	
	National	International
Public	• State institutions (e.g. government, local administration)	• Supranational organisations (e.g. EU, IMF, WTO)
Private	• Non-governmental organisations (NGOs) (e.g. trade unions, associations, media)	• International non-governmental organisations (e.g. Greenpeace, Amnesty International)

Figure 1.16: Origin and legal status of socio-political stakeholder groups[101]

- Stakeholder orientation should start with corporate processes and structures.
- The stakeholders' interests should be balanced over time.

The complexity of corporate management increases as a result. The former socio-political "framework conditions" are an integral part of a company's stakeholder network, and in many cases, relationships with socio-political stakeholder groups (see Figure 1.16) such as NGOs and politics are equally as important as those with equity providers, customers, employees and suppliers.

In the sense of pro-active management, it is therefore most certainly better to also engage in dialogue with these (socio-political) stakeholders in good time to find out, understand and, if possible, also give consideration to their interests and not only to start this process when the "licence to operate" or own competitive advantages are at risk. What applies to a company – that it is simultaneously a stakeholder in a network and has stakeholders – is also true of politics and NGOs – they are stakeholders and they also have stakeholders themselves. They too can lose their competitive advantages and their "licence to operate". The principle of reciprocity and fairness should apply to us all.

1.2.9 Closing remarks

The stakeholder approach will replace the shareholder approach! Or: the shareholder approach will become an aspect of the more extensive stakeholder approach and will consequently be integrated into it. Ultimately because the shareholder approach has led too frequently to excessively one-sided, short-term and exaggerated profit seeking due to the manner in which it has been applied in practical management. Occasionally, the shareholder value approach is (partly) responsible for a number of crises and poor decisions in society, nature and the economy in general. The conceptions of man at the root of the shareholder value approach, such as that of the rational "Homo oeconomicus", the models and management philosophies derived from these and resulting management misconduct are no longer compatible with the complex and dynamic reality, and are cer-

---

101 Own illustration, based on Holtbrügge, Berg and Puck (2007), p. 50.

tainly no longer desirable in their excessive form. A company's or a national economy's financial performance indicators are important; taken on their own, however, they are too one-sided and are only a tool, a prerequisite, part of a complex benefit construct for man and society or the sum of all stakeholders. Social acceptance is a significantly more important aspect for all companies. This is already a crucial asset of each company today and will increasingly become so in the future. Not least because this is the only asset which cannot be manufactured or procured autonomously but is developed jointly via interactions in complex network structures and always remains dynamic. The assumption that a licence to operate, once acquired, is final is erroneous – a nostalgic anecdote from a time long gone – in short: simply false. Instead, the "licence to operate" constantly has to be "earned" anew.[102]

1.3 Importance of the intermediary in lobbying derived from mutual market relationship theories

By Anton Meyer and Anja Meindl

General information on the terms stakeholder and stakeholder management has been provided in the above. The following contribution now applies this to the specific case of lobbying. See Chapter 4 for an overview of stakeholders in the EU. In addition to the EU institutions (Commission, Parliament and Council), social stakeholders (e. g. companies, NGOs, churches, social organisations, trade unions, etc.) are also presented there and their characteristics and features are dealt with. See Chapter 2 for a definition of the term lobbying and the delimitation of various types of lobbying. This section integrates lobbying into economic theory (Section 1.3.1). In terms of political lobbying or governmental relations managers (see Chapter 7) which assume the role of intermediaries within the EU's political stakeholders, theories which explain the existence and importance of intermediaries within mutual market relationships can be called on to legitimise the existence of governmental relations managers and understand their special role and importance.

1.3.1 Intermediaries

1.3.1.1 Definitions

The starting point for the scientific assessment of intermediaries is the early trade theories of the 18th century.[103] The term comes from *inter* (Latin) = between/among/during and *medius* (Latin) = the middle, lying in between. The diverse forms of intermediaries, concerning trade, innovation, marketing, financial or

---

102 See Post, Preston and Sachs (2002), p. 248.
103 See Steuart (1767).

digital intermediaries, are reflected in the variety of multiple and different definitions, making a uniform definition of the term difficult. Figure 1.17 shows a small selection of typical definitions. To generate a uniform understanding of the term for this publication, we will use the following definition as the basis: an intermediary is *"[...] an independent, profit-maximizing economic agent mediating between two market sides in presence of market imperfections"*.[104] Markets and their imperfection are therefore central to the concept of intermediation.

A *market* is to be regarded as a complex network of economic and social relationships[105] and describes the point at which the supply of and demand for materials, services or opportunities (in the sense of rights) meet.[106] Markets should enable exchange. However, an exchange is only potentially possible if, in addition to the correspondingly necessary need for both parties to engage in exchange, the exchange intentions of the seller and buyer also coincide in time, and the transaction is not limited by physical location. This means that it must be specifiable in terms of both material (what is to be exchanged), personnel (which agents are involved) as well as space (where can an exchange take place) and time (when can an exchange take place) and must be understood as a sub-system of the total quantity of economic interdependencies to be regarded in isolation. Accordingly, a market is generally defined as "the (depending on the purpose of the investigation) material, personal, temporal and spatial delimitation of a quantity (> 1) of goods, buyers and sellers which together form a network of economic and social relationships".[107]

What is common to all definitions is the assumption that intermediaries assume a potential central position within the value creation chain between the "manufacturing" seller and the consuming buyer, whereby intermediation is also characterised by its conditionality on and relativity to supply and demand, and intermediaries are viewed as crucial mediators in the value creation chain in all concepts.[108] We understand intermediaries to be independent economic market participants which strive to achieve individual profit maximisation.[109] What is crucial is that the involvement of intermediaries as so-called "market makers"[110] or "matchmakers" makes this exchange possible in the first place, particularly in geographical and temporal terms, or at least facilitates access to the markets.[111]

---

104 Rose (1999), p. 51.
105 See Piekenbrock and Hennig (2013), p. 164.
106 See Homburg and Krohmer (2006), p. 2; Meyer (1973), pp. 40 ff.
107 Piekenbrock and Hennig (2013), p. 165.
108 See Chircu and Kauffman (1999), p. 109; von Walter and Hess (2005), p. 19; Rose (1999), p. 51.
109 See Rose (1999), p. 51. We are therefore delimiting our understanding of intermediaries to cases which receive a form payment for their commitment. This is called commission and excludes friendly turns or favours (see von Walter and Hess (2005), p. 40; Picot, Reichwald and Wigand (2003), p. 377).
110 Cummins and Doherty (2006), p. 360.
111 See Hess and von Walter (2006), p. 3. Intermediaries can accordingly be regarded as special system or market influencers, and can primarily and above all be assigned to the group of market advisors; see Meyer (1973), p. 88.

Steuart (1767), p. 177	"This operation is trade: it relieves both parties of the whole trouble of transportation, and adjusting wants to wants, or wants to money. The merchant represents by turns both the consumer, the manufacturer, and the money. To the consumer he appears as the whole body of manufacturers; to the manufacturers, as the whole body of consumers; and to the one and the other class his credit supplies the use of money."
Oxford Advanced Learner's Dictionary, (2005), p. 812	"A person or an organization that helps other people or organizations to make an agreement by being a means of communication between them."
Picot et al. (2003), p. 377	"The term intermediary is generally used to denote any actor on a market who is neither a supplier nor a buyer, but either facilitates the overall functioning of the market or first enables the market to function, receiving a commission or similar compensation for this."
Yavas (1995), p. 18	"One of the main explanations of intermediaries in search markets ... is that they **resolve ... inefficiencies in return for a profit.**"
Zeithaml/Bitner (2003), p. 367	"Service intermediaries perform **many important functions for the service principal** – **coproducing** the service, making services **locally available**, and functioning as the **bond between the principal and the customer.**"
Rose, F., 1999, The Economics, Concept, and Design of Information Intermediaries, p. 51	"An intermediary is an **independent, profit-maximizing economic agent mediating between two market sides** in presence of market imperfections. Intermediation is the **bridging the incompatibilities** between the two (market) sides involved in a transaction by transformation of output attributes of the supply market side to appropriate input attributes of the demand market side."
Lee, J., Son J.-Y., Suh, K.-S., 2010, International Journal of Electronic Commerce, p. 70	"Online marketplaces are often established and run by a third-party intermediary that **matches buyers and sellers, and facilitates transactions between them.** This is because intermediaries hold a proprietary position as the sole owners of trans- action information. By **amassing and analyzing** a vast amount of transaction information, intermediaries are able to play a crucial role as the **provider of a knowledge platform** through which participating sellers can obtain valuable market knowledge about customers and competitors."
Donnelly, J. H., 1976, Journal of Marketing, p. 56 f.	"Channels of distribution have evolved in many service industries, which use **separate organizational entities** as intermediaries **between the producer and user of the service.** These intermediaries play a **variety of roles in making the services available** to prospective users." „**Any extra-corporate entity between** the **producer of a service** and **prospective users** that is utilized to **make the service available** and/or more convenient is a marketing intermediary for that service."

Figure 1.17: Example definitions of intermediaries

The assumptions on which this advantageousness is based or how it occurs can be explained using various economic and behavioural science theories.

1.3.1.2 Intermediaries explained using economic theories

Intermediaries play no role in neoclassical theories, as their fundamental assumption of perfect markets[112] leaves no scope for middlemen.[113] These are unable to either make use of asymmetrically distributed information[114] or skim off margins since perfect markets guarantee uniform and transparent prices.[115] Neo-institutional assumptions of imperfect markets are therefore a necessary prerequisite for the scientific analysis and legitimation of intermediaries.[116] In this sense, the existence of intermediaries in markets from a (welfare) economic perspective is then conversely based above all on the fact that intermediaries typically reduce market inefficiencies (subject to corresponding remuneration), as the following explanations will show.[117] At the end of this section, we will list a selection of literature which explains the role of intermediaries using political and sociological theories. However, the core of this section is an explanation of the economic theory.

1.3.1.2.1 Transaction cost theory

The transaction cost theory[118] deals with costs which occur when property rights are transferred.[119] Due to the underlying behavioural assumptions (limited rationality, asymmetrical information distribution and opportunism) and the influence of uncertainty, the frequency of exchange and resource-specific equipment of the transaction partners, these are confronted by a range of problems which can reduce the value of the transaction or prevent it in its entirety.[120] The formal statement of the theory is that minimising the costs related to the transaction has the effect of maximising the efficiency of the transaction.[121] Transaction costs arise both prior to the completion of a contract (caused by the search for information, as part of negotiations and contract design) and after the completion of a contract due to monitoring the implementation of, and possible adjustments to, the contract.[122] Intermediated transactions are advantageous when they help the market participants to reduce the transaction costs involved by more than the costs caused by the intermediary's remuneration.[123] However, these costs must not be simply transferred to the other contracting party, as a result of which one

---

112 The assumptions of a perfect market include complete market transparency, immediate responses, the absence of preferences plus strictly rational decision-making behaviour on the part of sellers and buyers, the absence of transportation costs plus the occurrence of supply and demand at the same time; see Mecke, Piekenbrock and Sauerland (2014); Hess and von Walter (2006), p. 3; Scholes, Benston and Smith (1976), p. 217; Allen and Santomero (1998), p. 1462.
113 See Hess and von Walter (2006), p. 3; Scholes, Benston and Smith (1976), p. 217.
114 See Leland and Pyle (1977), p. 383.
115 See Hess and von Walter (2006), p. 3; Jevons (1871), pp. 91–92.
116 See Scholes, Benston and Smith (1976), p. 217.
117 See Yavaş (1995), p. 18.
118 See Coase (1937); Williamson (1975; 1985).
119 See Picot, Dietl and Franck (2008); Wareham, Zheng and Straub (2005).
120 See Meffert and Bruhn (2003), p. 41; Meffert,Burmann and Kirchgeorg (2008), p. 39; Cummins and Doherty (2006), pp. 359, 394; Anderson and Anderson (2002), p. 53.
121 See Williamson (1985), p. 22.
122 See Picot, Dietl and Franck (2008), p. 42; Ebers and Gotsch (2006), p. 278.
123 See von Walter and Hess (2005), pp. 33–34; Yavaş (1995), p. 18.

party would be worse off than without the integration of an intermediary;[124] instead, TA2 > TA1 and TN2 > TN1 must apply in addition to T2 + T3 > T1 to achieve a Pareto optimum situation as shown in Figure 1.18.

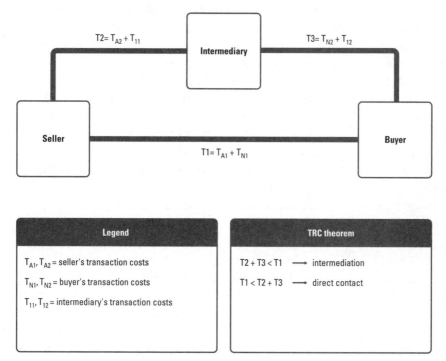

Figure 1.18: Intermediation for the reduction of transaction costs[125]

Intermediaries are in a position to minimise transaction costs since they are able to reduce the contract partners' uncertainties, internalise transaction-specific investments and use them to their advantage.[126] In particular, transaction-specific investments (e.g. to establish an extensive sales network or build up industry-specific knowledge) are responsible for high transaction costs.[127] An intermediary can not only repeatedly use these specific assets in similar transactions with other customers[128] but can also exploit his experience, his capital and his lower opportunity costs to obtain or improve resources and thus increase the frequency of a transaction, thereby achieving effects of scale[129] and obtaining a better result.[130] It should, however, be noted that the relationship with the intermediary also gives rise to uncertainties for his customer, as the customer is unable to assess either the quality of the service received or the intermediary's opportunism, with the result

---

124 See Wiese (2010), p. 271.
125 Source: Own illustration, based on Walter and Hess (2005), p. 34.
126 See Ebers and Gotsch (2006), p. 283.
127 See Williamson (1985), p. 52.
128 See Scholes, Benston and Smith (1976), p. 222.
129 See Ebers and Gotsch (2006), p. 283.
130 See Zeithaml and Bitner (2000), p. 351.

that the involvement of an intermediary may be disadvantageous in comparison with direct contact with the seller.[131] Under the general assumption of the risk neutrality of all agents,[132] the transaction costs rise with increasing uncertainty. The more important the transaction is for the agent and the more damage a possible mistake on the part of the intermediary can cause to his customer's reputation, the greater the influence of the uncertainty becomes.[133] Intermediation may nevertheless lead to efficiency advantages, as value creation by the customer himself also gives rise to uncertainties in terms of the quality of performance.[134] As service providers, intermediaries are accordingly extensively dependent on the trust of their clients.[135] By indicating his (greater) professionalism (competence, experience, etc.), his higher service standards and a fundamentally trusting relationship, the intermediary can reduce transaction-related uncertainty in comparison with direct contact between the transaction partners.[136] In conformance with this, the prospect theory[137] shows that a certain result is preferable to an uncertain one, even if the uncertain alternative were to promise a better result in monetary terms.

1.3.1.2.2 Search theory

The chance of finding the best possible transaction partner[138] involves search costs, as these costs increase as the number of contacts made rises and the time required for the search increases.[139] The search cost theory[140] focuses on the trade-off between the costs related to the ex-ante evaluation of a further potential partner – especially on the part of the buyer. Intermediaries offer advantages in search cost theory terms because they reduce the contact points of a search and enable potential transaction partners to be identified more efficiently and effectively (e.g. through specialisation in a specific niche market segment),[141] leading to a reduction in search costs[142] for both market participant sides and optimisation of the transaction process. The Baligh-Richartz effect (see Figure 1.19) shows the savings potentially possible due to the existence of an intermediary, which represents the central mediating "node" between the two sides of the market. [143]

---

131 See Ebers and Gotsch (2006), pp. 279, 282–283.
132 See Geyskens, Steenkamp and Kumar (2006), p. 520; Ebers and Gotsch (2006), p. 281.
133 See Zeithaml and Bitner (2000), p. 351.
134 See Lusch, Brown and Brunswick (1992), p. 129.
135 See Meffert and Bruhn (2012), p. 91.
136 See Smith, Carroll and Ashford (1995), pp. 10-11.
137 See Kahnemann and Tversky (1979).
138 The offer tabled by the seller (in terms of price and quality) and buyer (in terms of its reservation price) may differ significantly. Due to non-transparent markets, no transaction partner can ever be in possession of all information concerning the other party (see Spulber (1996a), pp. 560–561; Stigler (1961), pp. 213–214; Diamond (1987), p. 429; Pratt, Wise and Zeckhauser (1979), p. 204).
139 See Stigler (1961), pp. 215–216; Burdett and Judd (1983), p. 955; Albrecht (2011), p. 238.
140 See Stigler (1961).
141 See Spulber (1996a), pp. 560–561; Stigler (1961), pp. 216, 220; Cosimano (1996), p. 134.
142 The search costs now consist of the reduced time for searching for information and the commission which has to be paid to the intermediary.
143 See Baligh and Richartz (1964), pp. 670–671; Toporowski (1999), p. 81.

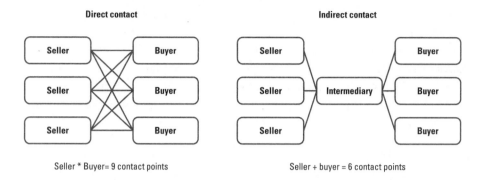

Figure 1.19: Simplification effect due to the integration of intermediaries[144]

The *Baligh-Richartz effect* states that the costs of finding (potential) partners increase with an increasing number of possible contact partners and points. Based on a minimum of two agents on both sides of the market, an intermediary, as a central point of contact, disproportionately reduces the costs if the number of market participants rises.[145] If the number of intermediaries on one value creation level increases excessively, however, this effect disappears[146] until a further intermediate stage which reduces the number of contact points again is integrated.[147] Ideally, all market participants would contact the intermediary and abandon their own search completely, thus finding their most suitable transaction partner through this intermediary.[148]

The search cost theory also assumes that the delay in each transaction (arising from the search for an additional alternative or due to the establishment of irrelevant contacts) increases its costs. The theory analyses the optimal strategy of an individual when a choice has to be made from a range of uncertain possibilities. In mathematical terms, the search cost theory calculates the ideal end point of a search. Individuals with low search costs will prefer direct contact, whereas individuals with high search costs will decide in favour of the integration of an intermediary.[149]

1.3.1.2.3 Intermediation theory of the firm

The intermediation theory of the firm essentially regards all companies on the market as intermediaries.[150] Companies only enter a market if they are able to reduce the transaction costs in comparison with a direct exchange relationship be-

---

144 Source: Own illustration, based on Walter/Hess (2005), p. 23.
145 See Baligh and Richartz (1964), pp. 670–671.
146 See Toporowski (1999), p. 81.
147 See Baligh and Richartz (1964), pp. 670–671.
148 See Stigler (1961), p. 216; Scholes et al. (1976), p. 223; Bhargava and Choudhary (2004), p. 23; Baye and Morgan (2001), p. 454.
149 See Stigler (1961), p. 187; Butters (1977), pp. 257–258; Burdett and Judd (1983), p. 457; Posey and Yavaş (1995), p. 536–538; Posey and Tennyson (1998), p. 257.
150 See Spulber (1996).

tween suppliers and customers.[151] Companies must therefore generate profits which are advantageous to both transaction partners across all costs and value creation points in comparison with direct exchange.[152] Intermediaries (firms) can achieve economies of scale for themselves,[153] reduce the transaction partners' risks[154] and establish a reputation[155] for their mediation services[156] which not only reduce the transaction costs but also the involved agency costs (see the following).

1.3.1.2.4 Principal agent theory

The principal agent theory[157] deals with situations in which a principal (the person or party issuing an order) uses the services or competencies of an agent (the recipient of the order) in order to fulfil his interests and issues a payment for this.[158] However, the agency theory is concerned less with determining the comparative cost advantages arising due to an agent than his potential for ensuring the practical implementation and execution of the service as efficiently as possible, i.e. with minimal agency costs.[159] Agency costs are caused by divergent interests and asymmetrical information between the principal and agent, whereby it is assumed that the agent is better informed than the principal in terms of his capabilities, true intentions, competencies, level of knowledge and behaviour.[160] Added to these are the agent's different risk affinity[161] and potential opportunistic behaviour at the expense of the principal.[162] The principal's calculation weighs up these costs against the advantages arising due to the agent through his ability to make use of the latter's specific competencies, e.g. his tacit knowledge, access to a valu-

---

151 See Spulber, Pandian and Robertson (2003), p. 256.
152 See Spulber (1996a), p. 560; Spulber, Pandian and Robertson (2003), p. 256; Backhaus and Voeth (2010), pp. 13 – 14; in addition to the market opportunities for companies, transaction options particularly arise from the specific resources which a company possesses and its corresponding competencies (see Spulber, Pandian and Robertson (2003), p. 256). In conformity with the resource-based view (see Peteraf (1993); Prahalad and Hamel (1990); Wernerfelt (1984)), intermediaries should concentrate on their core competencies to enable this comparative advantage to be maintained in the long term (see Spulber, Pandian and Robertson (2003), p. 264; Peng and York (2001), p. 328; Bhattacharya and Thakor (1993), p. 8).
153 See Spulber, Pandian and Robertson (2003), p. 257; Chan (1983), p. 1545; Scholes, Benston and Smith (1976), p. 222; Diamond (1984), p. 393; Bhattacharya and Thakor (1993), p. 8.
154 See Spulber, Pandian and Robertson (2003), p. 257; Allen and Santomero (1998), p. 1462; Burani (2008), p. 77; Santomero (1984), p. 577.
155 For an appropriate definition of reputation, we concur with Simon (1985), p. 37, who views reputation as the result of satisfactory experiences which customers have had with a company and its services, and Spence (1974), p. 107, who defines "reputation as [the] outcome of a process in which firms signal their key characteristics to constituents to maximize their social status" (Schwaiger (2004), p. 48).
156 See Spulber, Pandian and Robertson (2003), p. 257; Scholes, Benston and Smith (1976), p. 223; Hagel III and Rayport (1997), p. 54.
157 See Berle and Means (1932); Coase (1937); Jensen and Meckling (1976).
158 See Ebers and Gotsch (2006), pp. 258, 263; Jensen and Meckling (1976), p. 308; Eisenhardt (1989), p. 58.
159 See Jensen and Meckling (1976), pp. 308 – 309; Ebers and Gotsch (2006), p. 259.
160 See Ebers and Gotsch (2006), p. 261.
161 Risk neutrality is assumed for the principal, whereas the agent is characterised by risk aversion; see Anderson and Oliver (1897), p. 79; Basu, Lal and Srinivasan (1985), p. 272.
162 See Picot, Dietl and Franck (2008), p. 74; Eisenhardt (1989), p. 58; Picot (1991), p. 150.

able network, specific experience, time, etc. or also basic enablement of a transaction which the principal would be unable to conduct without the agent since, for example, he does not have the necessary competencies.[163] Intermediaries can essentially be regarded as their customers' agents.[164] Involving an intermediary can be beneficial in terms of costs, space, time, flexibility, quantitatively and qualitatively better arrangements, leading to reduced search times and lower transaction costs or, in extreme cases, even initiating and enabling transactions in the first place.[165] As the integration of an intermediary initially causes additional costs,[166] this party must consequently be able to achieve disproportionately high savings, leading to a Pareto optimum situation for all parties concerned.[167] This is made possible by the intermediary's problem solving inherent in the principal-agent relationship arising from "hidden characteristics", "hidden intention", "hidden knowledge" and "hidden action".

If the principal makes incorrect assumptions regarding the agent's competencies and potentials in the case of "*hidden characteristics*", the better informed intermediary can point this out to him or support him *a priori* in selecting more suitable transaction partners[168] and thus reduce the agency costs in the superordinate agent relationship.[169] Ross extends the idea of the "hidden characteristics" to an advisory opportunity for intermediaries.[170] Accordingly, intermediaries can offer the transaction partners additional benefits by indicating characteristics and skills to the partners which the other partner seeks, desires or requires.

Following the completion of the contract, the agent's "*hidden intentions*" can harm the principal, e.g. due to the opportunistic exploitation of loopholes in the contract or the principal's dependency due to specific investments.[171] An intermediary who is better informed – in comparison with the principal – can point out these risks, make the agent's actual objectives clear to the principal, help him to avoid contractual loopholes and install incentive and control mechanisms, or himself take over the agent's specific investments and objectives and thus reduce the principal's dependency on the agent.[172]

---

163 See Ebers and Gotsch (2006), p. 258.
164 See Ross (1973), p. 134; Jensen and Meckling (1976), pp. 309–310; Pratt and Zeckhauser (1985), p. 2.
165 See Rosen (2013), p. 628; Spulber, Pandian and Robertson (2003), pp. 260-261.
166 As costs are also incurred for searching for, monitoring and checking the intermediary in addition to his commission (see Yavaş (1995), p. 18; Ebers and Gotsch (2006), p. 262; Diamond (1984), p. 393).
167 See Diamond (1984), p. 399; Wiese (2010), p. 12.
168 See Anderson and Oliver (1987), p. 79; Basu, Lal and Srinivasan (1985), p. 272; Akerlof (1970), pp. 489, 495.
169 See Kennes and Schiff (2008), p. 1192; Bhargava and Choudhary (2004), pp. 24, 27; Ross (1989), p. 551.
170 See Ross (1989), p. 550.
171 See Ebers and Gotsch (2006), p. 264.
172 See Mass (2010), pp. 5–6; Diamond (1984), p. 394.

In the case of *"hidden knowledge"*, the principal can neither understand nor assess the result of the agent's work, or in the case of *"hidden action"*, the principal cannot comprehend or judge the agent's value creation contribution with certainty.[173] The better informed intermediary can help the principal to evaluate the results and additionally influence the installation of control and information mechanisms.[174]

In each case, the intermediary increases the transparency of the agent's area of responsibility for the principal by making the transmission of knowledge and information and the agent's behaviour obsolete.[175] From an agency theory perspective, the justification for the existence of intermediaries is based on the superiority of his information,[176] his specialisation, his economies of scale and scope and his reputation as a superior information service provider,[177] as a result of which he gains trust for the neutral, discrete handling of important (e.g. financial or strategic) information and consequently obtains this more easily, quickly or at all.[178] In order to guarantee efficiency, it must be ensured that the intermediary himself does not reveal opportunistic behaviour, thus making the principal-intermediary relationship more predictable and calculable than the superordinate principal-agent relationship.[179] The reputation of an intermediary as a faithful service provider is consequently crucial to success and is underscored e.g. by signing a code of ethics, through adherence to specific service standards, by the provision of certificates and the long-term establishment of authentic and serious business relationships.[180]

1.3.1.3 Behavioural theories

In contrast to the theories dealt with so far, all of which assume an economic perspective of intermediaries, the structural hole theory[181] and the social exchange theory[182] offer a behavioural science perspective.

---

173 See Ebers and Gotsch (2006), p. 264.
174 See Mass (2010), pp. 5-6; Ebers and Gotsch (2006), pp. 265–266.
175 See Draper and Hoag (1978), p. 597; Campbell and Kracaw (1980), p. 864; Brealey, Leland and Pyle (1977), p. 383; Chemmanur and Fulghieri (1994), p. 58; Santomero (1984), pp. 577–578; Bhattacharya and Thakor (1993), p. 14; Spulber, Pandian and Robertson (2003), p. 261.
176 See Chan (1983), p. 1545; Luo and Donthu (2007), p. 454; Gopalan, Nanda and Yerramilli (2011), p. 2083; Eisenhardt (1989), pp. 61, 64.
177 See Scholes, Benston and Smith (1976), p. 223.
178 See Hagel III and Rayport (1997), p. 54.
179 See Gopalan, Nanda and Yerramilli (2011), pp. 2084–2085; Campbell and Kracaw (1980), p. 876; Chemmanur and Fulghieri (1994), p. 58; Peng and York (2001), p. 330; Spulber (1996b), p. 149; Diamond (1984), p. 393; Draper and Hoag (1978), p. 596; Brealey, Leland and Pyle (1977), p. 383.
180 See Bailey and Bakos (1997), p. 3; Ebers and Gotsch (2006), pp. 265–266; Diamond (1984), p. 394; Chan (1983), p. 1560; Gopalan, Nanda and Yerramilli (2011), pp. 2083, 2085; Bhattacharya and Thakor (1993), pp. 18–19; Spulber (1996b), p. 148.
181 See Burt (1992).
182 See Homans (1958); Thibaut and Kelley (1959); Blau (1964).

1.3.1.3.1 Structural hole theory

Like the search theory, the structural hole theory[183] deals with the structure of social networks and their influence on the "searchability" of potential transaction partners.[184] It is assumed that, as of a certain size, clusters form in social networks; these are characterised by the fact that intensive connections exist between the agents within the cluster but only very weak connections between the clusters.[185] Consequently, information within a network cluster reveals greater redundancy than outside. Markets are susceptible to so-called structural holes such as limited access to information or contacts. Individuals can generate competitive advantages if they are able to bridge these structural holes by positioning themselves at as many interfaces as possible.[186]

Figure 1.20 clearly shows the advantageous role of intermediaries: it shows an intermediary I at the interface between three clusters (C1, C2 and C3) and an agent A who is searching for possible transaction partners. According to the structural hole theory, A can very easily establish contacts within his cluster C2, exchange information and find out the prices of all market participants in this cluster.[188] However, direct access to the agents in clusters C1 and C3 is not possible for A due to his lack of connections. A is therefore reliant on the assistance of the intermediary I, who can provide him with access to the clusters. Accordingly, the justification and advantageousness of intermediaries are found in markets in which

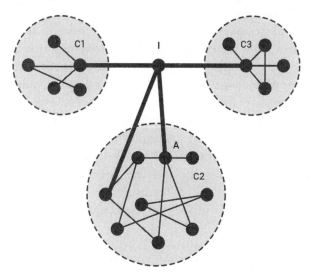

Figure 1.20: Clusters within a social network[187]

---

183 See Burt (1992).
184 See Burt (1997), p. 340; Zaheer and Soda (2009), p. 2.
185 See Markovsky (1993), p. 153.
186 See Zinkhan (1994), p. 152; Burt (1997), p. 340; Han (2011), p. 5; Piekenbrock and Hennig (2013), p. 164.
188 See Burt (1997), p. 341; Stigler (1961).
187 Source: Own illustration, based on Burt (1997), p. 341.

they are able to bridge structural holes through diversified contacts and enable their customers to access new markets, market segments, information and additional transactions.[189] Intermediaries can also be integrated into one's own network, thus reducing the costs of managing this network; however, this transforms one's own, previously "strong" connections into "weak" ones,[190] leading to second order structural holes. Radical development towards exclusive relationship management by an intermediary is not therefore very advisable because of loss of control, the reliability and quality of the transferred information and the risk of opportunistic behaviour on the part of the intermediary.[191] Due to such a mediating position, intermediaries would increasingly extend their influence over the entire network.[192]

1.3.1.3.2 Social exchange theory

The central assumption of the social exchange theory is that the behaviour of individuals is not only influenced by the behaviour of the agents involved directly in the transaction but also by so-called "peers".[193] "Peers" are all agents within an individual's social network which extensively influence the individual through their opinions and behaviour, e. g. colleagues, family members, relatives or friends.[194] Contrary to the transaction cost theory, the social exchange theory assumes that the advantages arising from repeated behaviour in the form of learning effects and trusted, stable relationships,[195] which can reduce uncertainties and thus costs, do not only extend to the agents immediately involved but can also be achieved by observing other market players or the experiences of peers.[196] Accordingly, participants who enter a new market and have no personal experience, often rely on the existing and consequently more easily assessable transaction forms,[197] leading to the occurrence of a dominant "exchange rule" – a direct or indirect form of exchange which is typical of a specific market. The social exchange theory can therefore explain empirical transaction forms from behavioural science perspectives. However – and this limitation should be explicitly mentioned – it offers no assessment of whether the selected form of exchange is efficient, when it becomes inefficient or which factors should necessitate a change because the effectiveness of the system is declining significantly.[198] Whereas transaction cost-related approaches, with their precise calculation of all relevant costs, are not very practical for deriv-

---

189 See Zinkhan (1994), p. 153; Markovsky (1993), p. 154; Granovetter (1973), p. 1378; Baye and Morgan (2001), p. 457; Mass (2010), p. 8; Peng and York (2001), p. 328.
190 See Zinkhan (1994), p. 152; Granovetter (1973), pp. 1365–1366.
191 See Zinkhan (1994), pp. 152, 154; Fleming and Waguespack (2007), p. 168; Granovetter (1983), p. 202.
192 See Zaheer and Soda (2009), pp. 9, 23, 26.
193 See Emerson (1976), p. 336; Meeker (1971), p. 485; Homans (1958), pp. 597–598.
194 See Homans (1958), p. 600; Nord (1969), p. 177; Emerson (1954), pp. 688, 693.
195 See Luo and Donthu (2007), pp. 454–455.
196 See Blau (1964), p. 194; Campbell (1961), p. 106.
197 See Emerson (1976), p. 341; Zaheer and Soda (2009), pp. 9–10; Bhattacharya and Thakor (1993), p. 38.
198 See Emerson (1976), p. 339; Pillkahn (2012), p. 170.

ing direct action implications since the complete registration of all costs appears unrealistic, the social exchange theory's contribution to an explanation is also limited. This is particularly due to the fact that the basis of the decision in favour of intermediated or direct relationships in a given market is not transparent or comprehensible but that this relationship pattern is merely explained through the assumption of the trusting imitation of dominant market structures.[199]

1.3.2 Summary

As the attentive reader has almost certainly noticed, all of the outlined theories which explain the role of intermediaries in markets necessarily require the existence of a market. But when does a "market" for political lobbying occur? As long as a citizen or a company attempts to represent his or its political interests himself or itself before the political institutions, there is not yet a market. A market only occurs when a company determines a need and consequently seeks and finds a professional service provider for representing or supporting the representation of its political interests. The market is therefore first manifested in the relationship between the company and governmental relations manager; all further stakeholders materialise around this basic relationship. Whether this exchange relationship exists for a short period of time on an event-, project- or "issue"-related basis or leads to a longer commercial relationship with permanent representation and an intensive, long-term information flow, changing concerns and further services is dependent on further need and the quality of the service relationship.

To conclude, the role of governmental relations managers as central intermediaries within the framework of the EU should be dealt with based on the presented economic and behavioural science theories, which explain the existence of intermediaries in markets, make them understandable, legitimise them and also demonstrate their advantages. To be able to exert an influence as a stakeholder as part of the EU's political activity, it is not only first necessary to understand a complex system of institutions and decision-making processes but also to have relationships with the key institutions and individuals which enable access to information, topics or "an audience". The transaction costs and also the search costs which would be incurred in order to find a suitable contact for a corporate concern or issue at all and then formally position and communicate it correctly would be insurmountably high for an individual stakeholder. It would also be difficult to position oneself at each relevant decision-making interface and keep abreast of all information flowing in the diverse committees and institutions. In addition to a great deal of time, this task also necessitates long-term experience and above all reputation, familiarity, an excellent network and constant, active interconnectedness. In this regard, the existing structures within the framework of European politics are entirely justified, since they contribute to the effective and efficient ex-

---

199 See Homans (1958), p. 598.

change of information and political interests. However, it is worth considering whether the increased professionalisation of political lobbying and governmental relations managers would not be advisable for the benefit of society as a whole in view of their importance and the extent of their influence. This would particularly be linked to a defined vocational profile on the basis of specific training and extensive quality assurance measures (see Chapter 7).

Chapter 2   Lobbying: an approach. Fundamentals and introduction

2.1 Introduction

Most people have at least a vague concept of what is meant by the representation of interests or lobbying. The topic is regularly the subject of generally unflattering media reports on current affairs and debates (e.g. the accusation that individual draft laws are "whispered into the ear" of the responsible ministry by the industry concerned). Conversely, NGOs generally enjoy greater credibility amongst politicians and the public in terms of the phenomenon of lobbying. They are often regarded *per se* as the counterbalance to economic interests and the representatives of public interest objectives. Whether correctly or incorrectly, what information on environmental protection is likely to be taken more seriously? Information issued by Greenpeace and the WWF or by Shell and BP, which are planning to extract oil?[1]

Only rarely is lobbying the subject of a general debate dealing with such questions. Consequently, only selected aspects are ever portrayed and commented on. As is so often the case, however, aspects of lobbying are less obvious than they appear: if we depart from the level of (not infrequently prejudiced) everyday knowledge, there emerges, on closer scrutiny, a multi-layered phenomenon with various forms and characteristics, approaches and objectives. The following is therefore concerned with approaching the topic of lobbying from various perspectives in order to determine its complexity and place it into a bigger context. Only then can a sustainable and informed understanding of lobbying emerge from these rather vague impressions.

Section 2.2 therefore deals with the terminological and functional delimitation of various sub-areas of lobbying. The following questions are addressed:

- What are the various concepts that need to be distinguished in the area of lobbying? How are the individual sub-areas defined in terminological terms and what is their historic background? How are the individual terms and concepts delimited from each other and what are their strengths and weaknesses?
- What tasks does lobbying (in the broadest sense) undertake for the represented party, i.e. what are its essential objectives and functions for companies and other economic and societal actors?

Section 2.3 then examines lobbying in relation to politics, dealing with issues surrounding the legitimation of lobbying in general and specifically within the system of the EU:

---

1   Geiger (2006), p. 24.

- What is the importance of interests and the representation of these interests in the political system?
- How is lobbying evaluated in terms of political science?
- What are the European legal bases and regulations for lobbying amongst the EU institutions?

2.2 Lobbying as a structured communication process

2.2.1 Introduction and question

The word "lobbying" often evokes negative associations in the public sphere/ media – whether it be the suspected one-sided representation of economic interests to the detriment of third parties, the accusation that power is being secretly exercised behind the scenes or even the accusation of corruption and nepotism.[2] This is particularly true of the practice of "lobbyism". But does this really do political, economic and social reality justice? Or is professional lobbying a legitimate aspect of democratic politics, does the "mediation of interests (…) belong to a democracy like the piston to the cylinder"?[3]

Regarded historically, lobbying or the representation of interests has been around since the birth of politics. Because politics involves the exchange of ideas, arguments and, of course, interests. Different groups within a society have different ideas of how the community, the *res publica*, should be structured, and attempt to make their arguments and ideas heard by decision-makers. This was already the case in antique times, in the Attic Democracy or in the Roman Republic. In the Middle Ages and the early modern age, audiences with influential persons, for example, were used as a method for bringing arguments to their attention. These most certainly also involved individual interests, such as those of Augsburg merchant Jakob Fugger, who used his middleman Johannes Zink to establish relationships with the Holy See, the royal Hungarian court and the Republic of San Marino.[4] However, there were also groups such as guilds and trade associations which wanted to articulate and assert their interests and preserve their prerogatives. The targeted representation of interests increased in the industrialised world of the 19th century, and the association structure which is still partially in place today slowly developed – particularly the emergence of trade unions on one side and economic and agricultural associations on the other side of the political spectrum. Today, of course, the field of lobbying is significantly more differentiated, and an increasing trend towards professionalisation has been developing since the 1980s. This has led to the emergence of the "lobbying" that we are familiar with

---

2 See the recent book by Hans-Martin Tillack (2015).
3 Kleinfeld, Willems and Zimmer (2007), p. 7.
4 Heitz (2011), pp. 60–61.

today. As will be shown below, companies, agencies and law firms, but also churches and think tanks or NGOs such as Greenpeace, engage in lobbying in addition to associations.

The modern term "lobbying" originates from the 19th century. The Oxford English Dictionary (OED) lists 1837 as the year in which the term *to lobby* was first used in its present sense. The word *lobbyist* then emerged in 1863. In etymological terms, *lobbying* is derived from *lobby*, which in turn originates from the Medieval Latin word *lobia* for covered walk or colonnade.[5] The meaning of *lobby = lobbying* is probably derived from the fact that "lobbyists" asked members of parliament to support their petitions during parliamentary debates and votes in the lobby of the British parliament.[6] A different tale is recounted in the USA: here, the term is traced back to a custom of US President Ulysses Grant (who held office from 1869 to 1877). He could often be found relaxing in the lobby of the Willard hotel in Washington D.C., where he was always surrounded by a growing number of "lobbyists" attempting to engage in informal discussions in which to present their concerns to him.[7]

Although the word lobbying may only be a good 170 years old, the activity it describes has been around since the emergence of state systems.[8] However, the lobbying with which we are familiar today has only developed since the end of the 19th century. Nevertheless, the term now appears to have become a fashionable word. The basic word, *lobby* "can apparently be outstandingly combined with almost any modifier":[9] car lobby, pharmaceuticals lobby, agricultural lobby, civil service lobby and bank lobby are just a few examples of this. Nonetheless, there is still no simple, concise and universally recognised definition of lobbying or – synonymously – the representation of interests, despite the term's frequent use.[10] As can be seen from the list above, this can lead to a certain confusion of terms. For instance, the terms lobbying, governmental relations or public affairs are occasionally used synonymously even amongst scientists and practitioners;[11] in the media, even (comparatively simple) delimitation from public relations often appears not to be entirely familiar. The logical consequence of this (too) is that the democratic legitimation, the purpose and the function of lobbying – from the perspective of both an individual company and that of politics and society – often remain hidden to the public (with regard to the democratic legitimation of lobbying, see Section 2.3).

---

5 See van Schendelen (2013⁴), p. 57.
6 See Lösche (2007), p. 20.
7 See Köppl (2008), p. 191.
8 See van Schendelen (2006), p. 132.
9 König (2007), p. 10.
10 In English, the word "advocacy" is also increasingly being used for "lobbying".
11 See McGrath (2005), p. 15.

Against this backdrop, the first part of this portrayal deals with two issues:

- To attain a working definition which is suitable for this portrayal, it is first necessary to distinguish between and delimit various concepts. What, therefore, is meant by the terms lobbying, representation of interests and governmental relations? How is their content delimited from that of public relations and public affairs (see Section 2.2.2)?
- The perspective of the commercial enterprise will then be examined: what are the essential objectives and functions of lobbying from a corporate perspective (see Section 2.2.3)?

2.2.2 Definitions and delimitations

2.2.2.1 From investor relations to governmental relations: lobbying as an indispensable element of corporate communication

Terms such as public relations, public affairs, lobbying and governmental relations essentially belong to the field of corporate communication (see Figure 2.2). Since lobbying mostly involves the representation of companies' interests, the term "corporate communication" is used below. However, the statements apply not only to private companies but also to associations, organisations and even the EU member states and their regions (which also undertake lobbying at European level, as evidenced by the variety of regional representations in Brussels, for instance).

Corporate communication is the management of communication processes between the company and the outside world.[12] Corporate communication contributes to a company's added value by – to express it in simplified terms – creating images of the company and projecting them to the outside world.[13] This enables the company's internal visions (mission statement) and external effects (image) to be harmonised with one another, which in turn boosts the company's reputation and thus contributes to added value.[14]

External corporate communication primarily involves public relations (PR). PR is initially aimed generally at the company's outside world, i.e. consumers, peers and other companies, predominantly through the use of (mass) media. The content is usually designed to achieve a certain scatter effect and is often based on classic advertising. One example of PR is extensive multi-channel campaigns undertaken by companies by means of advertisements in printed media, the Internet and own information publications as well as press conferences and public appearances by company representatives. Information concerning new brands or product ranges, strategy changes, restructuring or changes to the company's image is often issued in this way.

---

12 See Mast (2008³), p. 26; the internal dimension of corporate communication (e.g. with employees, the employees' committee, etc.) will not be dealt with in any greater detail in this book.

13 See Schmid and Lyczek (2008), p. 133.

14 See Schmid and Lyczek (2008), pp. 131 ff.

One special case of external communication is the company's contact with its equity capital providers, called investor relations. By tradition, maintaining investor relations, in the sense of sound capital market communication, is indispensable for a company. Particularly in difficult times – such as the global financial and economic crisis from 2007 onwards – it is vital to actively seek dialogue with investors and implement confidence-building measures: as a result of general uncertainty and fear of the future, the stock markets react increasingly nervously to any situation in which there is no clear information. Professional capital market communication performs a valuable orientation function here and shores up the company's valuation. In contrast to other branches of corporate communication, investor relations is subject to stringent legal regulations – particularly if a company is listed on the stock exchange, for instance (disclosure requirements, etc.).[15]

Conversely, public affairs (PA) can be regarded as a sub-area of PR which is targeted towards politics and a limited public. PA's group of addressees is therefore smaller than that of PR: here, the communication addressees are no longer the broader public but above all administrations and politicians as well as non-governmental organisations (e.g. consumer protection organisations, environmental protection or patient organisations). PA focuses on strategic information management between politics and companies on one hand and society on the other.[16] PA work is therefore primarily content-oriented. The main purpose of PA is to establish and maintain constructive relationships with politicians in order to obtain an insight into, and exert an influence on, the political realm. The tools used to do this are often similar to those of PR. Examples of PA include organising events with representatives from the fields of politics and economics with reference to a topic of relevance to the company or the creation of information material for specific political and societal groups. What are called grass roots campaigning and grass roots lobbying also deserve a mention in this context. These terms involve the mobilisation of large groups of "normal" citizens to inform political representatives of their opinions in various ways. The use of media is one of the most effective tools in grass roots lobbying, because the more media attention an issue receives, the more likely it is that decision-makers will deal with it. Grass roots lobbying frequently makes use of digital communication tools such as blogs, tweets or Facebook campaigns. All of these activities have the objective of ensuring greater public understanding of and increased attention for the relevant issue. More or less the reverse variant is grass top lobbying, which is aimed at mobilising leading personalities within various groups, professional and specialist associations and well-known personalities that are able to influence public opinion.[17]

By contrast, lobbying or the representation of interests is aimed solely at politicians and administrations. The target group therefore becomes increasingly

---

15 See Mast (2008), p. 336.
16 See Althaus, Geffken and Rawe (2005), p. 7.
17 With regard to this topic, see Althaus (2013).

smaller, with blurred boundaries to the area of PA. The representation of interests primarily involves a certain quasi measurable level of involvement in specific political decisions. The communication content in this case is more sensitive than that of PA. The requisite conditions are confidentiality and discretion – crucial characteristics of lobbying. Successful implementation necessitates precise planning in advance and extensive knowledge of the political arena. The tools and instruments of PR and PA are usually unsuitable for this, since scatter effects have to be avoided. However, PR and PA tools most certainly can provide useful support for the lobbying process.

So-called governmental relations is a special form of lobbying and the representation of interests. This differs from the general concept of lobbying in terms of its time horizon, target group, content and objective: whilst lobbying is also aimed at short-term decisions on individual cases – whether as part of subsidy decisions (budget lobbying) or the issue of an individual permit, governmental relations is aimed at involvement in the legislative activity of state institutions as a long-term, structural approach. It is often commenced long before the actual legislative decision and can accompany the entire decision-making process under certain circumstances. The part of governmental relations aimed at the legislative procedure can therefore also be referred to as "legislative lobbying"[18]. Governmental relations communication is also specific and targeted exclusively at decision-makers and opinion leaders in politics (especially members of government) and the executive level – addressees are therefore political representatives in parties and legislators as well as members of the executive level. Governmental relations are particularly process-oriented.

In contrast above all to classic PR, the improvement of public reputation plays practically no role whatsoever in terms of the objective of governmental relations. The content of governmental relations differs from the more general concept of lobbying due to its specific focus on the legislative and executive activities of state institutions: examples of this include the targeted, discrete establishment of contact with, and direct dissemination of information to, previously identified decision-makers or the legislative and executive working levels involved in the initiative, often as part of personal, confidential meetings.

The discussion on the various corporate communication concepts clearly reveals specialisation according to the type of work and tasks as well as quantitative adaptation of the target group (see the graphic in Figure 2.1).

Whilst PR is aimed at reaching the largest possible group of recipients, the objective of governmental relations is the provision of information to a specific group, i.e. limited to just a few individuals, identified through process-oriented work

---

18 Bouwen (2002), p. 366 with further references ("legislative lobbying").

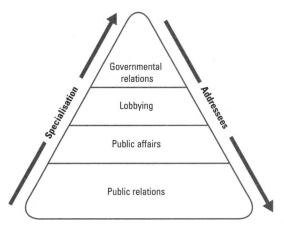

Figure 2.1: Term delimitations

(process competence). The character of the information also differs to the extent that PR is usually used to convey more general information, whereas the content in the field of governmental relations is aimed at specialists, i.e. the depth of the information can therefore be significantly greater. The content is also increasingly sensitive, occasionally involving corporate secrets or other data and content not intended for public consumption. Against this background, it goes without saying that any communication must be confidential and discrete. On the whole, it is therefore clear that there are considerable differences between the individual concepts of corporate communication. So that a company can develop an effective and efficient communication strategy, it must be aware of these differences – as regards both the terminology and the possible uses and limitations of the individual methods of communication that are used.

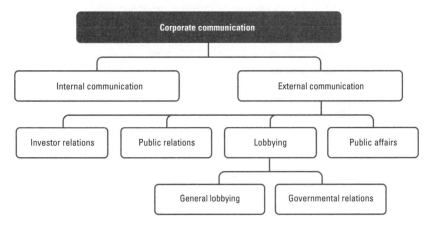

Figure 2.2: Lobbying as an element of corporate communication

2.2.2.2 Lobbying as the communication of individual interests in the political system

To date, there is no clear definition of lobbying. There is neither a uniform term nor a uniform definition. Many terms are used in parallel or as synonyms: e.g. lobbying, public affairs, political communication or governmental relations. Nor has science thus far developed a clear definition: Peter Lösche, for example, describes the term as follows: lobbying is "influencing primarily state representatives, from the community to the national and European level, (...) in order to help structure legislation or the execution and implementation of legislation in one's own individual interest".[19] Conversely, Van Schendelen understands lobbying as "the build-up of unorthodox efforts to obtain information and support regarding a game of interest in order to get a desired outcome from a power holder".[20] In turn, the European Commission defines the term as "[involving] all activities (...) intended to exert an influence on the European institutions' and bodies' policy-making and decision-making process".[21] An older but frequently quoted definition originates from Thomas Milbrath, one of the pioneers of scientific work on lobbying in the USA: "[L]obbying is stimulation and transmission of a communication, by someone other than a citizen acting on his own behalf, directed to a governmental decision-maker with the hope of influencing his decision".[22] The aspects of communication, interest and politics are common to all of these definitions. At the same time, this trio of terms also represents the essence of lobbying: ultimately, social actors are concerned with the procurement, selection and evaluation of information from the political arena and, in the opposite direction, the exertion of a direct or indirect, actor-oriented influence in the executive and legislative decision-making processes. This interest-led reciprocal relationship reveals the "intermediary" character of the mediation of interests, which thus brings together the concepts of communication, interest and politics (see Figure 2.3).[23]

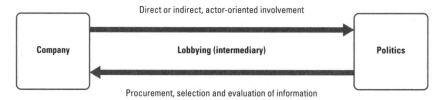

Figure 2.3: Lobbying as an intermediary system

---

19 Lösche (2007), p. 20.
20 van Schendelen (2013⁴), p. 58.
21 European Commission (2006), p. 5.
22 Quoted from McGrath (2005), p. 17.
23 Lösche (2007), p. 13.

Interest in this case is a constituent characteristic of politics: in addition to their property as the fundamental motivations behind the actions of social actors, interests are so to speak the "raw material of politics".[24] By articulating and asserting their interests, the actors hope to achieve political advantages in the battle of interests. Politics is therefore always driven by interests, and competition between interests is a natural foundation of democratic politics. The European Commission also refers to this aspect in its Green Paper on the European Transparency Initiative: "Lobbying is entirely legitimate in a democratic system. It is irrelevant who undertakes this lobbying: individual citizens or companies, civil society organisations, other stakeholders or companies which represent third parties (public affairs advisors, think tanks and lawyers)".[25]

The negative connotations of the concept of lobbying are therefore hardly justifiable in factual terms: "Modern societies and democratic systems of government are unimaginable without the bundling, representation and assertion of interests".[26] The above outlined origin of the concept of lobbying in the venerable democracies of Great Britain and the United States also proves this historically.[27]

By nature, the represented interests are always individual interests – they are not based on "general" interests, a point which is frequently raised as grounds for criticising lobbying. On closer examination, however, there is no tenable foundation to this criticism: nobody will seriously be able to claim to speak with omnipotence for the generality. Apart from very general objectives (such as the preservation of jobs or protection of the environment), no interest is "generally applicable" in this sense – which measures are right or wrong is always dependent on the individual perspective. Even the categories listed above cannot be used without further qualification in the majority of cases: which interest is to be given priority in the closure of an environmentally harmful factory – that of the 5,000 employees threatened with unemployment or that of the environment, i.e. ultimately that of the thousands of people living in the surrounding area? Regarded in this way, lobbying can only logically be the (justified) representation of individual interests, and politics can only ultimately be a compromise in the comparison and consideration of these interests (see Sections 2.3.1, 2.3.2 and 2.3.3).

In turn, the often criticised lack of transparency in lobbying is an expression of the sensitivity of the communicated content and has nothing to do with secretiveness but is instead concerned with safeguarding internal corporate information on the one hand and with the strategic avoidance of premature public exposure on the other. The latter is plausible to anyone who has ever been involved in poli-

---

24 Meyer (2010[3]), p. 105.
25 European Commission (2006), p. 5
26 Kleinfeld, Willems and Zimmer (2007), p. 7.
27 It must be noted here that, whilst lobbying is also the subject of controversial discussion in both countries, it by no means has such a poor reputation as e.g. in continental Europe; for greater detail, see Joos (2011), pp. 223–245.

tics: if initiatives are disclosed prematurely, there is a risk of their being "talked to death" and ultimately of failure or – at best – a return to minimal positions. However, the lowest common denominator is neither the ideal of democracy nor a particularly efficient procedural outcome. The next chapter will return to the democratic legitimation of lobbying in greater detail (see Section 2.3).

This illustration focuses on an analysis of the mediation of corporate interests, but also applies to all actors involved in lobbying, and thus also to associations, organisations and even the EU member states and regions. Lobbying is therefore defined as follows in the sense of a working definition:

Lobbying is:

- Firstly the procurement, selection and evaluation of information which can lead to a competitive advantage or prevent a competitive disadvantage for the represented company (or the association, the organisation, the EU member state/region).
- Secondly the direct or indirect involvement of a company (or an association, an organisation, an EU member state/region) in legislative and/or executive (EU) decision-making processes by means of information, with the objective of achieving competitive advantages or averting competitive disadvantages.[28]

In this case, lobbying is to be regarded as a dynamic, ongoing process which gives consideration to discontinuities in the political and administrative sectors.[29] Figure 2.3 shows the model of lobbying as an intermediary system (with regard to the "intermediary system", see also Section 2.3.3).

2.2.3 Lobbying as an element of corporate communication

In Section 2.2.2, the definitions and delimitations of political lobbying were explained and lobbying determined as an element of corporate communication. The following section will now reveal the practical methods through which corporate interests can be integrated into the political arena. Two questions require answering in this:

- Which type of lobbying can benefit a company in which situations?
- Which communication strategy considerations have to be made and which practical deliberations have to be involved in implementing different communication strategies?

This will clearly show that there are essentially three dimensions to lobbying for companies. Firstly, lobbying can be used as an early warning system to identify relevant political issues and trends. Secondly, lobbying, in its classic form, encompasses the support of decision-making processes in the political arena. Thirdly,

---

28 Joos (1998), p. 27.
29 See Joos (1998), p. 27.

political crisis management can be undertaken by means of lobbying. It must be noted at this point that the three dimensions do not stand in isolation from each other. Their nature and orientation overlap to a certain extent, and they should ideally be undertaken as complementary elements of a corporate lobbying strategy.

2.2.3.1 Lobbying as an early warning system: identification of issues and trends

In the political arena, both major and minor political events are often foreshadowed. In reality, however, the political processes reported on by mass media are only a very small part of all political initiatives. Nor are the political issues restricted solely to the genuinely political arena but often emerge from the area of civil society. These can lead to both risks and opportunities for companies. The latter necessitates dealing actively and extensively with political issues. However, "companies generally tend not to deal with the environmental risks of the political-societal and the legal arenas",[30] but these risks have to be identified and assessed as precisely as possible in order to make them manageable.[31] On the other hand, the volume of political news is now vast. Expertise and political sensitivity are needed to filter out information that is genuinely important for orientation from the flood of announcements – and especially to establish sensible correlations. This is all the more true for political issues which are not reported on in the media. On analysis, it is also important to give consideration to the fundamental links between the micro and macro levels and observe possible interconnections and interactions with other issues. Against this backdrop, lobbying can be viewed as preventive action for identifying issues and trends in the political arena.[32]

Lobbying, also in the sense of political risk management, accordingly begins long before actual dialogue with political decision makers.[33] It tends to take place at the end of the lobbying process; a significant part of the overall work must already have been completed by then. Only the extensive preparation of dialogue determines whether an issue will succeed in the lobbying process. The foundation of effective lobbying is therefore the broad-based identification and analysis of relevant issues, often without a specific lobbying assignment. It is also necessary to keep an eye on the political arena from a personal point of view in order to remain constantly up to date. Only in this manner can the legislative and executive decision-makers be identified as quickly as possible if a crisis should arise. This prior knowledge cannot be underestimated, since it enables effective lobbying virtually from a standing start if necessary. In view of this, lobbying is ideally designed as a structural and continuous process.

---

30 Hofmann and Frevel (2007), p. 80.
31 See Hofmann and Frevel (2007), p. 80.
32 See Bender and Reulecke (2003), pp. 117 ff.
33 See Bender and Reulecke (2003), p. 35.

Successful lobbying is based on profound and extensive preparation. This "managing the fieldwork"[34] includes sounding out the political terrain. In this, information is initially obtained by means of comprehensive press and media evaluation, followed by continuous contact and dialogue with insiders, i.e. politicians, civil servants and other decision-makers. It is fundamentally the case that "a lobbyist who wishes to undertake preventive lobbying must necessarily be involved where the ideological and programmatic groundwork on the relevant topic area is being done."[35] It is vital to act as discretely as possible, i.e. to attract as little public attention as possible, as undesired political issues may otherwise "surface". In short, the objective is to let sleeping dogs lie.[36] At the same time, however, it must be noted that communication cannot be designed as a one-way street. During a lobbying process, it is important to ensure extensive information transparency, i.e. "all information relevant to decision-making must be as complete as possible".[37] True to the intermediary character of lobbying, this information transparency must be reciprocal; this also testifies to integrity and fairness towards the contact persons.[38]

Issue management is crucially important to successful lobbying.[39] As Henry Kissinger put it: "An issue ignored is a crisis invented".[40] The function of issue management is to "identify and deal with issues which have (…) the potential for crisis at an early stage"[41] and to precisely determine and classify the issue. In this, the issue and opinion landscape is initially "scanned" to achieve a broad-based information perception. Actual monitoring then involves specifically tracking a selected issue. Actively searching for an issue by the lobbyist himself is also important: firstly because a basic knowledge of the backgrounds is often important from the beginning, and secondly because he is ideally closer to the political action than the company which he is representing.

The "supreme discipline" of preventive lobbying, namely the possibility of structuring the debate surrounding potentially problematic issues from the word go, also requires mentioning in this context. This enables, for instance, the prevention of "certain opinions, trends and undercurrents from being placed on the political agenda".[42] Achieving this would undoubtedly be the ideal case for the company, but it rarely occurs in practice and is only possible with an excellent political network. Anticipating issues also necessitates outstanding work in terms of the "early warning system" (keywords: information management, monitoring), which will be introduced in the next section.

---

34 van Schendelen (2013[4]) p. 245.
35 Bender and Reulecke (2003), p. 118.
36 Bender and Reulecke (2003), p. 119.
37 Joos (1998), pp. 89–90.
38 See Joos (1998), p. 90.
39 See Ingenhoff and Röttger (2008).
40 Quoted from Bender and Reulecke (2003), p. 35.
41 Kretschmer and Elbe (2007), p. 89.
42 Bender and Reulecke (2003), p. 117.

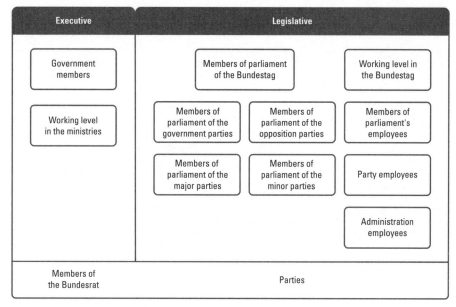

Figure 2.4: Addressees in the political environment – Federal Republic of Germany[43]

A thorough key player analysis is required to identify possible contacts. The key question for this is: who are the relevant persons involved in the executive and legislative political decision (see also Chapters 3 and 6)? It must also be determined who represents which opinions regarding the issue, and who is the opinion leader. Based on purely politico-legal structures, this is not always immediately apparent. Instead, the actual power context has to be observed,[44] which in turn necessitates an in-depth knowledge of political decision-making processes: in addition to the formal criteria, particular consideration must also be given to the topical and personal links between the actors. This leads to a relatively large group of potential addressees for the company's interest, as Figure 2.4 shows using the example of the Federal Republic of Germany.

The bases of the fundamental scheme in Figure 2.4 also apply to other political systems in the EU member states.[45] As outlined at the start, however, solely taking national circumstances into account is not sufficient. Without considering European circumstances, lobbying would occasionally amount to nothing. The political and institutional multi-level interdependence within the EU accordingly necessitates expansion to the EU level.[46] Figure 2.5 therefore shows the addressee

---

43 Source: Bender and Reulecke (2003), p. 47.
44 Bender and Reulecke (2003), p. 45.
45 The institutional characteristics of individual elements and also political decision-making processes therefore differ significantly in some cases, but the fundamental arrangements of the separation of powers – particularly the dualism of the executive and legislature – exist in all EU member states, see Ismayr (2008[4]), pp. 9–64.
46 See Section 4.5 on the political system of the EU.

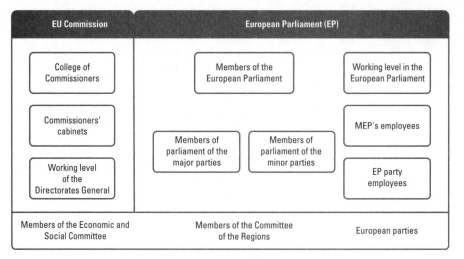

Figure 2.5: Addressees in the political environment – European Union[47]

structure within the EU and gives consideration to the special characteristics of the political, institutional circumstances of the EU's political system.[48]

In all of this, it must be remembered that a lobbyist's working network should not merely be limited directly to the political arena. The pre-political sphere should also be entered, primarily to pick up news and "background noise" but also for specific information research. Contact with PR and PA agencies, journalists, (specialist) lawyers and colleagues from the lobbying industry should therefore be sought and maintained. An excessively strategic approach to establishing one's own network is not to be advised in any case: firstly, pure efficiency evaluation is not particularly compatible with the social phenomenon of networking, and secondly, when one first gets to know a person, it is impossible to foresee what importance they may subsequently assume for one's own interests.

2.2.3.2 Lobbying as a long-term project: structural support of decision-making processes

2.2.3.2.1 General

Lobbying processes – particularly in the area of governmental relations – should be long-term and structural in nature. Structural governmental relations means: not only acting for the client with regard to a specific project and from time to time but, continuously and with foresight, supporting the client's interest in the political arena. In this form, lobbying is to be regarded as an active undertaking

---

47 Source: according to Bender and Reulecke (2003), p. 47.
48 As shown in Section 4.5 using the political system of the EU, subdivision and designation according to conventional categories such as executive, legislative, but also government or opposition, are only possible with concessions in the political system of the EU. For the sake of simplicity, however, the basic scheme of Figure 2.4 has been retained in Figure 2.5.

which is dedicated with foresight to targeted communication with executive and legislative decision-makers.

A sufficient number of trustworthy contacts are the central resource of lobbying. Contact management is therefore of paramount importance to the lobbying process (with regard to the establishment and management of communication networks, see Section 3.7).

Fundamental premises for dialogue with politicians and administrative decision-makers are knowledge, honesty and professionalism. This basically involves sounding out the interests of all concerned and adopting their perspective. In the dialogue, it must be explained, why from the point of view of a political decision-maker, a certain decision makes sense but another does not. It must also be ascertained whether there is any information that is as yet unfamiliar to the decision-maker, but which may be important for his decision.

Three basic rules of lobbying can be listed:

1. First obtain precise information, then act.

2. Communicate your own concerns clearly, openly and honestly.

3. Adopt the dialogue partner's perspective and learn to understand him.

Particularly the latter – the dialogue partner must always have his political counterpart's perspective in mind as well – is extremely important. The questions to be asked are therefore firstly how important the issue is or could be to the decision-maker, and secondly whether and to what extent his own interests match those of the relevant company.[49]

In addition to establishing contacts, however, extending and maintaining them also necessitate particular commitment. Above all, the maintenance of contacts should be undertaken thoroughly. This firstly encompasses apparently banal activities such as sending birthday cards, letters of congratulation on promotions or election to specific committees or positions. In order to leave a lasting (positive) impression on your opposite number, contact should also be maintained at regular intervals, even without any specific occasion. The most favourable case is a personal meeting, e.g. a joint meal with the relevant persons. Attending events such as specialist conferences or party events is also appropriate, as the relevant experts or politicians can usually be encountered there. If a personal discussion is not possible due to time and/or geographical constraints, contact should at least be maintained by telephone. Irrespective of the specific, practical form, a constant and continuous presence is required without being obtrusive.

However, the long-term orientation of the lobbying process not only offers advantages at the contact level. Changes in the political landscape can also offer good

---

49 See N.U. (2009b), pp. 16–17.

opportunities for lobbying. Interests can be conveyed very well to the political arena, particularly after elections and during the subsequent coalition negotiations.[50] Trustworthy contacts which have been established long before such an election are then accordingly valuable. The period of time between elections – and especially the time just prior to the elections – can be outstandingly used for corresponding content preparation.[51]

2.2.3.2.2 Information management

The flow of information from the political institutions now resembles a genuine flood in the form of personal messages, statements, resolutions and other memoranda. Several hundreds of official statements are issued by the EU institutions alone each day. Some 11,000 legislative acts, i.e. regulations, directives and decisions, were dealt with during the Barroso Commission's term from 2010 to 2014.[52] If the national policy data are added, this figure quickly rises to tens of thousands.[53] Although it was designed to increase the transparency of the political process and provide the public with comprehensive information, the policy of open information is having virtually the opposite effect: the glut threatens to overwhelm outsiders and often leads to confusion rather than information transparency. The great diversity also makes the search for specific content laborious. On the other hand, the official news aimed at the broad public only remains superficial and contains few details. Detailed monitoring of the relevant legislative activity of the EU's institutions and member states, in particular, is therefore of prime importance. From the perspective of lobbying, searching in and analysing the areas planned by the client form the basis of successful lobbying. Regularly and extensively scrutinising political information output is crucial, as it can be used to determine a variety of useful information and details. This activity therefore takes up a large part of the lobbyist's human and time resources. Specific know-how, specialist knowledge and human resources are also required here to systematically and analytically penetrate the maze of information, forward the significant content to the client in condensed form and ultimately provide company-specific interpretations. In addition, the lobbyist's ability to obtain and classify corresponding marginal notes and background information for the client alongside the officially published notifications is especially important. This is the source of genuine added value for the companies, which can thus obtain important facts in structured form. The topic of information management is picked up on at several points throughout the book (see particularly Chapter 1 and Section 6.3).

---

50 See N.U. (2009c), pp. 26–29; Altmeyer (2009); Amann, Becker, Dohmen and Traufetter (2013), p. 30. However, it must be remembered that politicians are addressed from all sides in such a phase – the lobbyist's professional manner is all the more important at this point.
51 See Waldermann (2009).
52 Own calculation according to EUR-LEX statistics, http://eur-lex.europa.eu/statistics/legislative-acts-statistics.html (last accessed on 8.5.2015).
53 The German Bundestag alone published over 14,800 printed documents during the 17th legislative period; see https://www.bundestag.de/drs (last accessed on 7.5.2015).

2.2.3.2.3 Strategy consulting

The development and implementation of objective, specific problem solutions are necessary to transport the client's interest into the political sphere. In the case of a commercial enterprise, the economic framework conditions are constantly under precise scrutiny, whereas the social and political environment is paid less attention under certain circumstances. This stands in sharp contrast to potential opportunities, but also threats, which may arise for the company as a result of decisions made by public institutions, particularly the European institutions. Legal and regulatory decisions directly or indirectly determine the company's economic framework. Companies should not therefore only monitor their market or industry environment but also social, cultural or scientific currents and trends, as these may in turn result in determining regulations in the future (see Section 6.3). This becomes particularly clear in the case of extensively regulated industries such as the energy or telecommunications industries: in some cases, deficits in recognising and handling legal developments can negate entire business models (consider e.g. the splitting of energy group E.ON which was completed in April 2015 as part of the turnaround in German energy policy[54] or the scheduled abolition of cellular telephony roaming charges[55]). Against this backdrop, companies must position themselves strategically in the long term within the political sphere in order to be able to react appropriately and effectively to external stimuli or to anticipate them.

A lobbyist brings his knowledge and his experience to bear as an external consultant in order to support the company in both establishing such fundamental structures and strategically implementing specific lobbying projects. Chapter 6 explains exhaustively how this can be accomplished (see Section 6.5).

2.2.3.2.4 Events

The organisation and hosting of events in the political arena is another important element of holistic lobbying. Such events serve firstly to establish contacts; secondly, they offer the opportunity to exchange information in an informal atmosphere: corporate representatives and politicians can become personally acquainted with each other and discuss current issues. These events also offer the company the opportunity to visibly represent and portray itself to politicians ("image building"). A successful event can therefore enhance the company's reputation amongst executive and legislative decision-makers.

Such events can assume various forms; workshops, dialogue forums or specialist presentations are common examples. The pinnacle of such events is almost certainly the parliamentary evening, typically with fifty to a hundred participants in a corresponding setting. Representatives of the European Parliament, particularly

---

54 See N.U. (2015d).
55 See European Commission (2015a).

the members of relevant and important committees, the political group function-aries and their employees, further relevant politicians and decision-makers from the EU institutions are invited, for example. In addition to the formal part of the evening, such as a presentation by a political specialist of relevance to the compa-ny, the informal setting leads to numerous opportunities for topical and personal exchange between decision-makers.

Planning and organising such events necessitates a high level of professionalism and commitment. Perfect organisational preparation and hosting of the event are the basic prerequisites for success.

2.2.3.2.5 Integration of corporate interests

Ultimately, the objective of lobbying is always the transfer of a company's inter-ests into the political sphere. One of the most important instruments for achieving this, personal dialogue with legislative and executive decision-makers, has already been introduced above. Another indispensable element is written comments such as statements and position papers.[56] Written documents guarantee a certain sus-tainability and obligation. Due to the written form, the addressee literally has something "tangible in his hand", which may stimulate recapitulation and reflec-tion. The addressee can also refer back to details such as facts and figures at a later point in time. Own stances on issues which are to be transferred to the political arena can be formulated precisely in the position papers. So-called statements are usually requested by politicians prior to hearings in committees; they are the for-mulation of the opinions to be put forth. However, statements on current issues can also always be submitted without solicitation. The point in time of submission must be noted. Even the best paper is futile if it is submitted too late. The earlier the text is received by the addressees, the greater the likelihood of its being noted and possibly taken into consideration. Ideally, such a paper is available to the ad-dressees at the start of their opinion-forming process.

As in the case of personal communication, various "tradecraft" aspects have to be observed with written comments. These will be introduced in the section on the instruments of lobbying (see Section 6.4). At this point, however, it should be pointed out that the documents should be written in clear language and as suc-cinct a form as possible. Of course, the basic rules of professional lobbying also apply here: objectivity, honesty and integrity are equally as important in written statements as in personal dialogue.[57]

2.2.3.3 Lobbying as political crisis management: lobbying as "fire-fighting"

Despite the best contact and issue management preparations and constant pres-ence in the political arena, it is still possible that developments or events requiring

---

56 See Bender and Reulecke (2003), pp. 71–72.
57 See N.U. (2009b), p. 17.

rapid response may occur virtually out of the blue. Such an "exogenous shock" is not unusual in itself, as issues which have been dormant for a long while and were hardly virulent in the first place but then attract attention due to current occurrences often come into the focus of decision-makers in the political sphere. Entirely new developments, which necessitate legislation from the point of view of politicians, can also arise. Past examples of this include the introduction of a tax on alcopops in 2003,[58] legislation surrounding the issue of fine particulate emissions[59] or also the (renewed) phasing-out of nuclear energy in the wake of the reactor disaster in Fukushima.[60] There are also cases of "botched"[61] legislation, which can have significant impacts on a company. In comparison with the above outlined "normal" procedure of a lobbying process, it is significantly more difficult to achieve success under these circumstances, particularly if an initiative had already been decided on politically or is already in the formal legislative procedure. Although it is actually too late for the integration of corporate interests, particularly in the latter case, action options are still available even then – albeit under the prerequisite that the lobbyist essentially has access to actors in the political sector concerned.[62] The following can be used as a rule of thumb: the better the lobbyist is also networked outside of specific issues in the political arena, the greater the likelihood of his being able to convey the company's interest to the addressees in an emergency: "Whoever first considers how to contact politicians in a crisis will have a tough job."[63] In such situations – in contrast to the above outlined pro-active working method – lobbying is compelled to react to certain exogenous influences. What is initially required here is to remain calm and attempt to help structure the relevant agenda in order to (re)gain "interest sovereignty". Conversely, hectic activism can unnecessarily "cause a stir" and accordingly have a disadvantageous effect.

If such an emergency arises, the regular steps of lobbying must be shortened and compressed to a greater or lesser extent – depending on the specific situation. The status quo must first be analysed precisely. Various scenarios – from best case to worst case – should then be immediately developed and assessed. This is helpful to assess the corresponding situation. A continuous, fact-oriented policy of information to the political actors is also important. Consideration must also be given

---

58 See Rickens (2004).
59 Since 1980, for example, various limit value guidelines have been issued by the EC or EU, but these were only implemented to a certain extent in Germany. In response to the public debate raging since 2004/2005, the issue of fine particulates was increasingly picked up on by politicians, i.e. in terms of the introduction of particulate filters for diesel-powered vehicles, extended emission protection, etc.; see N.U. (2005), pp. 78–94.
60 See Fischer (2011), p. 2.
61 See Wiegand (2009), p. 5; see also Karpen/Nünke/Breutz (2008).
62 This demonstrates the irreplaceability of good networking in the political arena: a complete cold start in an urgent political issue usually has little likelihood of success. If no trustworthy contacts whatsoever are therefore available, only the sub-optimal option of indirect address through a mail shot or possibly the media still remains.
63 Bender and Reulecke (2003), p. 144.

to whether a more offensive communication policy may be useful. Conventional company-specific crisis communication can be used as the basis for this.[64]

Naturally, the operational measures implemented in a crisis must take effect as soon as possible. Setting clear priorities is first required for this in order to enable the targeted implementation of all available personnel and resources. In organisational terms, it is necessary to open up direct decision-making and co-ordination channels between companies and lobbyists, to which the establishment of a task force consisting of just a few persons can contribute. Goal-oriented lobbying instruments must also be selected, firstly in terms of the time constraint and secondly in terms of their effectiveness. Under the given circumstances, the instruments may have to be implemented independently of each other, possibly even at the same point in time. Occasionally, more unconventional methods can also be used: a mail shot from the company to all members of parliament, in which the corporate management points out the consequences of a political initiative, would be possible for instance. Support through the implementation of classic campaigning (and thus public relations or public affairs) instruments such as e.g. an opinion piece by a high-ranking company representative, the placement of advertisements in a newspaper or the distribution of information material to political decision-makers is also conceivable.

Despite these options, the short-term approach naturally gives rise to not inconsiderable risks: the time pressure leads to the risk of not being able to fully ascertain and think through facts and connotations. The information situation may also be inadequate on the whole. It is also possible that not all relevant contact persons may be available *ad hoc*. In the worst case, it may ultimately prove impossible to halt a political decision or influence it in the company's interests.[65] Such "fire-fighting" should therefore be avoided in lobbying wherever possible, since a lobbying process always has the best likelihood of success when it is structural and thus long-term in nature. Precautions should be taken for the event that critical situations nevertheless occur: for example, corresponding occurrences can be theoretically played through during calm phases in order to be better prepared in an emergency. If necessary, a prophylactic crisis infrastructure can be set up as a result of such simulations.[66]

On the whole, it is clear that the individual dimensions of lobbying cannot be regarded in isolation from each other. The successful effect of lobbying is best able

---

64 Unlike conventional crisis communication, such an offensive communication policy is of course not aimed primarily at the broad public; the implementation of such PR instruments is intended here as the exception or an addition to the outlined instruments; for general information on corporate crisis communication, see Töpfer (2008[2]) and Mast (2008), pp. 371–387.

65 If an issue really is already so advanced, it may occasionally be better not to undertake any actions in order not to appear unprofessional to politicians or the public (in the sense of acting too late or inadequately). In this case, an honest lobbyist, as an external consultant, has the professional duty to point out the hopelessness of the situation to his client.

66 See Bender and Reulecke (2003), p. 143.

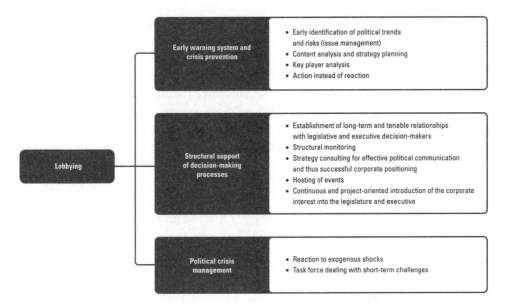

Figure 2.6: Possible uses of lobbying for companies

to develop if the three dimensions are used to complement each other, since the circumstances accompanying the lobbying process can change. Regarded over a longer period of time, experience has shown that the lobbyist finds himself "caught between action and reaction": during phases of the early warning system and when giving support for decision-making processes, he may not be in sole control of the process, but is nevertheless pro-actively engaged, whereas he is required to respond at short notice in an emergency.[67] It is therefore vital to always act with a view to the possible need for "fire-fighting" even in the (relatively) calm phases in order to lay the foundations for successfully dealing with emergencies.

The above addressed operation steps and instruments are exhaustively portrayed and explained in the following in terms of their practical aspects and implementation options.

2.3 Legitimation of lobbying

Section 2.2 made clear what exactly is meant by lobbying. Section 2.3 will now deal more extensively with its legitimation in the political and social arena. How can the lobbyist best respond to the frequently asked question of the political or democratic legitimation of lobbying?

---

67 Bender and Reulecke (2003), p. 120.

Firstly, lobbying is usually criticised by the European public. "Lobbyist" is regarded by many as a derogatory term, and lobbying is often considered to be something dishonest or improper.[68] Media reports usually have a negative connotation: "Powerful whispering voices",[69] "In lobby-land"[70] or "The lobby republic"[71] are the headlines concerning the topic of lobbying. The titles of relevant books also speak a clear language: back in 1955, questions were raised in Germany about the "rule by associations".[72] Further examples of titles and headlines include "The bought state. How corporate representatives in German ministries write their own laws",[73] "The lobbyists: who really rules us?",[74] "The puppet masters. Managers, ministers, media – how Germany is governed".[75] The corresponding titles for the EU are: "Europe's puppet masters. Who really rules in Brussels?",[76] "Europe's supermarket. Selling out our democracy",[77] "Brussels injections. Corruption, lobbyism and EU finances".[78] This list could be continued *ad nauseam*.

The topic of lobbying is therefore subject to extensive public attention. Each year, for example, the "Worst EU Lobbying Award" is presented to civil servants, politicians and companies in Brussels; this is done to publicly pillory what the presenters consider to be particularly controversial lobbying activities in order to contain their effects. This "scandalisation" of the topic contributes to the "myth of lobbying", which is constantly reinforced through suggestive media reporting and is occasionally reduced to a simple scheme of good and evil.[79] The topic of lobbying is also outstandingly suitable for nourishing and ostensibly confirming existing prejudices and resentments such as "Big business determines politics, not the voters". It must be noted here that this assumption is false – if the situation were so simple, there would be no need for lobbying.

What are the objections raised against lobbying? One of the strongest, and at the same time most incorrect, accusations is the assumption of a connection between lobbying and corruption. This focuses on the insinuation that lobbyists buy political advantages. The affair and subsequent trial surrounding the so-called "armaments lobbyist" Karl-Heinz Schreiber[80] in Germany and the scandal concerning

---

68 See Lösche (2005), p. 53; McGrath (2005), p. 3.
69 Speth (2009), p. 8.
70 Hardinghaus (2006), p. 48.
71 N. U. (2003b).
72 Eschenburg (1955).
73 Adamek and Otto (2008).
74 König (2007).
75 Gammelin and Hamann (2005).
76 Gammelin and Löw (2014).
77 Misik and Reimon (2014).
78 Rubner (2009).
79 See Kleinfeld, Willems and Zimmer (2007), p. 10.
80 Schreiber's activities had nothing whatsoever to do with lobbying as defined above – Schreiber was involved in the mediation of business contracts and apparently had (excessively) close business relationships with one or more politicians. Insofar as the criminal allegation, which was not the object of the proceedings before Augsburg district court, is concerned – this involves corruption and not lobbying in the legal sense.

former EU Commissioner Edith Cresson are two prominent examples similar to the "Abramoff affair" in the USA or the *Bangemann* scandal at the Spanish company Telefónica at the end of the 1990s. Particularly in terms of the accusations of corruption, lobbying is regarded as an "attack on common decency"[81] and also as "shadow politics".[82] However, a clear distinction must be made between legal and legitimate lobbying and illegal, criminal corruption. The former has nothing to do with the latter. The crossing of legal boundaries is the exception, as confirmed by the rule of professional and legally sound lobbying.

Another category of accusations is politically theoretical nature and primarily insinuates that lobbying undermines democracy. Some believe that lobbying erodes the primacy of politics.[83] Elsewhere, it is actually claimed that lobbyists are the "fifth power"[84] in the state – alongside the legislature, the executive, the judiciary and the media as the fourth power. It is stated precisely that "Lobbyism is a power without legitimation".[85] In the eyes of critics, the apparently undemocratic character of lobbying is due to the fact that the iron democratic principle of "one man, one vote" is undermined by (asymmetrical) lobbying. The underlying fear is that politics could ultimately be transformed into political patronage in the sense that a small minority obtains advantages over the vast majority. The lack of transparency of lobbying is criticised with equal frequency in this context: political decisions are made in a manner which is incomprehensible to the public since only the politicians, not the lobbyists, appear in public.

These objections are by no means new; for example, Jean-Jacques Rousseau wrote in his classic work "The social contract": "Nothing is more dangerous than the influence of private interests in public affairs, and the abuse of the laws by the government is a less evil than the corruption of the legislator, which is the inevitable sequel to a particular standpoint."[86] Subsequent criticism has persisted to the present day. Sociologist Max Weber also warned of the "nepotism" and "alliance[s] of all kinds" in his writings.[87] In his famous essay entitled "Politics as a vocation", Weber also foresees the possible danger of an increase in the power of "stakeholders" in the party democracy.[88] Economist Mancur Olson in turn pointed out the negative influence of stakeholders in terms of states' capability for institutional change.[89] In an interview, the former president of the German Federal Constitutional Court, Hans-Jürgen Papier, stated: "In general, lobbyism can pose a latent risk to the democratic constitutional state."[90] Even more prominently, however, at

---

81 Rubner (2009), p. 10.
82 von Alemann and Eckert (2006), p. 3.
83 Leif (2010), p. 8.
84 Leif and Speth (2006).
85 Leif and Speth (2006) p. 352.
86 Rousseau (2005; original 1762), p. 124.
87 Weber (1988), p. 499.
88 Weber (1988), p. 544.
89 See Olson (1985).
90 N.U. (2010b), p. 6.

a different place in the same interview,[91] he significantly qualified this criticism: "The assertion of individual interests, which may well include economic interests, the bundling of such interests in powerful associations and the conveyance of these interests to the governmental administration and the members of the German Bundestag – in other words, the organised representation of interests – naturally [form part of] our parliamentary democracy. (...) There is therefore most certainly no cause to generally demonise the activity of lobbyists, irrespective of whether they are acting for trade associations, trade unions, individual major companies, non-governmental organisations, churches or other social groups."[92] Ultimately, there are also good reasons which speak in favour of the transparent and legitimate representation of (organised) interests. First and foremost, the complexity of modern societies, can no longer be comprehended by one single individual (see Section 1.1). Decision-makers need, and therefore seek, to exchange information with the parties concerned and lobbyists in modern democracies. "Without external know-how and without the input of stakeholders at all stages of decision-making, decision-makers are barely able to obtain an overview of the consequences of their decisions or (...) failure to make decisions."[93] Professional and transparent lobbying can help to reduce the complexity of decision-making to a manageable level and therefore also significantly increase the quality of political decisions.

The following will now deal with rebutting the accusation that lobbyism is "a power without legitimation".[94] The relationship between interests and lobbying, and the state and politics, must first be analysed in detail. This concerns fundamental questions such as the role of interests in a democratic political system and the resulting legitimation of lobbying.

2.3.1 Politics as the contest between various interests with the objective of consensual solutions

Whoever wishes to recognise the necessity and the democratic legitimation of lobbying must first demonstrate a certain understanding not only for the interests behind the individual actors but also and above all for the functionality and the actors of practical politics. In turn, the ability to understand and anticipate politics and its developments requires an intimate, comprehensive and direct knowledge of the real political circumstances beyond official statements and medial reporting. To express it differently, one has to engage with the "logic of politics". In view of the complexity of political reality, a knowledge of the formal circumstances and an awareness of the information released officially or through the media alone are not sufficient – all too frequently, these only reveal a small, some-

---

91 Papier (2007).
92 Papier (2007).
93 Griesser (2014), p. 63.
94 Leif and Speth (2006), p. 352.

times distorted, glimpse of politics. The "why" of lobbying only becomes clear against this background.

"Politics is the art of the possible" – goes a widespread saying ascribed to Otto von Bismarck. Politics is omnipresent each and every day: political issues are found on the front page of newspapers, they consume news programmes on the television and provide talk shows with discussion topics. Almost every "responsible citizen" has an idea of politics. But what is actually meant by the term "politics": "what is politics?"[95]

The word politics originates from the ancient Greek: *Tà politikà* "designates public matters referring to the polis which concern and obligate all citizens (=polítes). *Politiké téchne*, the art of leadership and administration of public tasks in the interest of the community of citizens/the common good of the polis".[96] To a certain extent, each human society needs rules to which each of its members must adhere to co-exist as a community. The scope and structure of these rules are basically undefined and variable – the regulations are determined through policy making.[97] This is what politics involves: "Policy making (…) generates those regulations of co-existence which should apply bindingly to the whole of society."[98] The medium of policy making is power. According to the classic definition by sociologist Max Weber, power is "the probability that one actor within a social relationship will be in a position to carry out his own will despite resistance regardless of the basis on which this probability rests".[99] To enable this initially formless power to be applied, a constant method of asserting it is required: authority.

In turn, Max Weber defines the term authority as "the probability that a command with a given specific content will be obeyed by a given group of persons".[100] However, authority is not given, and nor does it exist, *per se*; it is established and structured in a specific manner by people through actions. Authority can therefore have diverse forms and characteristics. So that authoritative commands have a likelihood of being obeyed, the authority must be supported through its legitimation. Legitimation can in turn have various bases: "tradition",

---

95 Meyer (2003).
96 Nohlen (1998), p. 488; "Polis" is the name given to the ancient Greek city state; at that time, politics was "a policy of citizenship", i.e. politics was the common property of the citizens of the polis; during the early modern age, the term politics underwent a semantic transformation with the formation of modern states.
97 The framework assumed here is the modern age state consisting of a uniform state territory, a state populace (sovereign) and the state authority (in the sense of sovereignty), see Reinhard (2007), pp. 11 ff.; as an organisation in its specific form, which essentially persists to the present date, this (national) state has arisen since the 17th century in Europe; during the course of its development, politics has increasingly become a matter for representatives; in the modern age context, "politics" therefore differs from the ancient "policy of citizenship", see Reinhard (2007), pp. 37 ff.; the following explanations refer to the modern age, national form of statehood, because supranational power and authority structures only began to form in the middle of the last century; with regard to the political system of the EU, see Chapter 4.
98 Meyer (2003), p. 48.
99 Weber (1984), p. 89.
100 Weber (1984), p. 89.

"affectual" or "value-rational beliefs" or a "positive statute whose legality is be-
lieved".[101] For the latter case, "this legality (…) can be regarded as legitimate" if it
is based on an "agreement of the parties interested in this" or on "imposition […]
and obedience".[102] In modern, democratically constituted political systems, the
legitimation of authority on the part of the elected government is given through
various arrangements on a contractual basis and is more or less accepted as such
– at least by the vast majority of citizens. First and foremost, the constitution is to
be stated here as a central body of law which internally regulates the relationship
of the rulers and ruled and thus constitutes the state's authority.[103] In a democracy, the state populace lends itself the constitution; this thus represents the supreme norm which limits the power of the state authority versus those subjected
to the norm.[104] The state populace, as the sovereign authority, chooses its government, which exercises state authority for a specific period of time, in elections.
The so-called separation of powers exists in all other regards, i.e. jurisprudence
(judiciary), the legislature (legislative) and the government (executive) are separate in principle.[105] The institution of the constitutional state, through which the
state authority and its institutions are permanently bound to an objective legal
system, is also characteristic. The modern state therefore not only has the monopoly on power – both internally and externally – but also the legal monopoly.[106]

With regard to the political system, two dimensions of the legitimation of political
authority arise through the temporary delegation of the exercise of state authority
to the government: input legitimation and output legitimation.[107] Input legitimation refers to the "derivation of authoritative requirements as authentically as possible from the preferences of the members of the community".[108] Output legitimation focuses on the fact "that the exercise of authority should effectively promote the interests of the members".[109] To put it another way: "input legitimacy is
based on the recognisability and effective recognition of the quality of the political
policy and decision-making process. Conversely, the recognisability and effective
recognition of the products and results of the political policy and decision-making
process are relevant in the case of output legitimacy."[110] In science, it is above all
input legitimation in the sense of the "consent of the governed" which is regarded
as the crucial normative criterion for legitimation, as these decisions do not necessarily have to be made by democratically elected "governors" in the case of output
legitimation, which is based solely on the benefit of decisions for the ruled.[111] Fig-

---

101 Weber (1984), p. 62.
102 Weber (1984), p. 62.
103 See Vorländer (1999), pp. 9 ff.
104 See Kriele (2003), p. 239.
105 See Kriele (2003), p. 101.
106 Frevel (2004), pp. 66–67, Reinhard (2007), p. 22.
107 See Scharpf (2004).
108 Scharpf (2004).
109 Scharpf (2004).
110 Schmidt (2008), pp. 282–283.
111 See Scharpf (2004).

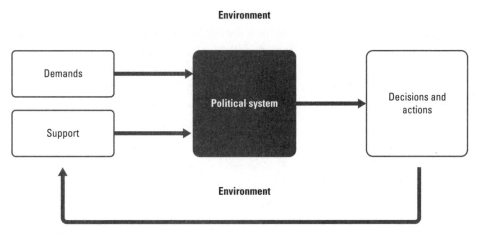

Figure 2.7: The political system in its environment

ure 2.7 shows the connection between input and output and the political system in its environment in schematic form.

However, Weber's categories of power and authority are not sufficiently far-reaching for a contemporary definition of the conceptual content of politics. In view of the historic events and developments in the 20th century, the "definition of politics"[112] has been modified in scientific discussion.[113] In order to characterise politics appropriately, further identifying characteristics have been determined in the wake of Weber's definitions, namely conflict, interest and consensus[114] – which are also essential aspects for an understanding of the interface between politics and lobbying. In modern, democratically constituted communities, a wide variety of (often contrary) opinions and ideas about public affairs usually exists in parallel – in theory, as many as there are members of the community. This pluralism of interests existing in parallel often leads to conflicts, which should ideally be resolved in a consensus in the sense of the common good. Accordingly, politics is the "public conflict of interests under the conditions of power and the need for consensus".[115]

Conflict is thus a central characteristic of politics. If there were no conflicts, there would probably be no need for politics either. At the same time, there would be hardly any social, and certainly no political, development without conflicts; conflicts are therefore equally as important for the political system as their amicable (if possible) resolution by means of consensus, through which interest-driven, latent tensions are optimally reduced. In turn, interests are not only the fundamental motivations for the actions of social actors and thus the "raw material of poli-

---

112 See Schmitt (1932).
113 See von Beyme (1996), p. 24.
114 See Meyer (2003), p. 110 ff. and pp. 124–125.
115 Nohlen (1998), p. 489.

tics".[116] By asserting their interests, the actors hope to achieve political advantages. As has already been mentioned, the trio of interests, conflicts and consensus is constitutive for politics. Although only consensus usually has positive connotations today, its prerequisites of "interest" and "conflict" must also be accepted as something normal and simply necessary; conversely, party political dispute, above all, is often regarded as unproductive and even unseemly in public. However, it is simply impossible to achieve consensus without conflict.[117]

Particularly under the framework conditions of democracy, politics is always characterised by confrontation, negotiation, co-ordination and compromise. In contrast to other societal action areas, particularly in comparison with the economy, this naturally leads to frictional losses and inefficiencies which occasionally cause democratic politics to appear ineffective.[118] However, this is precisely what constitutes the specific character of democratic politics: the battle between various opinions with the objective of a consensus-oriented political solution. Winston Churchill's famous statement is also to be understood in this sense: "Many forms of Government have been tried, and will be tried in this world of sin and woe. No one pretends that democracy is perfect or all-wise. Indeed, it has been said that democracy is the worst form of government except all those other forms that have been tried from time to time."[119]

2.3.2 Lobbying as the aggregation of interests

The question "why lobbying?" can now be answered more easily against the above outlined political backdrop. It must be noted that lobbying has increasingly become the focus of scientific interest, particularly over the last few years.[120] Democracy theory approaches and considerations are at the forefront: lobbying ensures opinion forming and diversity, and therefore realises the pluralism of opinions and views in political discourse.[121] It is in any case a platitude that a democracy needs opinion diversity if it does not wish to be deprived of its procedural bases. The articulation of interests on the part of society is the crucial contribution for this (see Section 2.3.4.1)

In particular, many experts regard the quality of opinion forming and public discussion at EU level to be inadequate. The Europeanisation of politics in the EU member states is closely linked to this. The connection between communal, regional, national and European political levels characterised by science as multi-level interdependence also poses a challenge to democratic institutions. If the sci-

---

116 Meyer (2003), p. 110.
117 See Mouffe (2007), pp. 7–14.
118 See Frevel (2004), pp. 114 ff.
119 Quoted from House of Commons (1947).
120 See McGrath (2005), p. 6. The scientific judgement is significantly better than that of public opinion. It is regrettable that these research results are barely taken note of in the broad public.
121 Historical foundation of this, Article 10 of the Federalist Papers, in: Hamilton, Madison and Jay (2007), pp. 93–100.

entific findings concerning this topic are followed, lobbying above all includes the following necessary and positive aspects:

- Interest aggregation and mediation.
- Realisation of political participation.
- Provision of political consulting for economic actors.
- Meeting the corporate needs of companies in the process of communication with politicians.

There would be no politics without interests. Interest aggregation and mediation are therefore essential for democratic conditions: important information, which would almost certainly not be generated there without external input, is transferred into the political system, through the articulation of interests from the social sphere. The aspect of political participation is closely related to this: ultimately, politics should be oriented towards the interests of those affected by policies and should also include them.[122] In the sense of "government for the people by the people", it is necessary for politicians to recognise the interests of social actors on one hand; on the other hand, the population in a democracy must also be able to become involved in politics outside of the elections which are only held periodically. Examples of this include citizens' initiatives and referendums, but also efforts towards active participation in the form of lobbying. As individual political decisions can often have completely different, complex consequences, the advantages and disadvantages of political actions must be assessed as well as possible. In view of this, lobbying also represents a form of political consulting.[123] As no political entity ever has knowledge of all that is necessary in principle, the required external expertise benefits politicians in this way. Politicians therefore require – also without solicitation – feedback from those affected by political decisions in order to enable the avoidance, and undesired side-effects, of these decisions.[124] Added to this is the fact that many political initiatives are now extremely complex in terms of both the functional object and their interactions and consequential effects, and would be extremely difficult to implement without the necessary external expert knowledge, as is shown by the issue of genetic engineering, for instance. One example of political consulting is the institution of the parliamentary hearing during a legislative proposal, in which the representatives of social and economic concerns are questioned by the members of parliament and can have their expert opinion placed on record. A similar direction is taken by the consultation of interested representatives of civil society by the Commission on specific issues such as e.g. the White Paper on "Democratic European Governance".[125] To a certain extent, this also prevents a minority from dictating to the majority, which may otherwise lead to possible conflicts. A member of the German Bundestag therefore

---

122 See Langguth (2007), p. 184.
123 See Lösche (2006), p. 334.
124 This particularly applies to EU politics.
125 See European Commission (2001).

sums this up as follows: "For me, lobbying is an important element of parliament-arianism. It serves to provide information and is used for decision-making in the parliamentary legislative process."[126] In turn, society itself has a requirement to obtain information from politics.

2.3.3 Lobbying as a tool for forming communication interfaces between politics and the affected parties: necessity of an intermediary

Mutual dependencies between politics and the affected parties (citizens, organisa-tions, small and large companies and, under certain circumstances, also member states or their – in many cases federal – subdivisions such as the German federal states in the multi-level system of the European Union) are typical of modern, open social systems. For example, the economy is not an entity outside of society – this is the impression that sometimes arises when economic development such as e.g. fierce price competition and the resulting pressure on wages are regarded as an external factor without looking for the trigger amongst the people (i.e. the buyers) themselves. The economy is a part of society; "politics for the people" is inconceivable without "politics with the economy". In turn, the economy is reliant on economically attractive framework conditions and interested in the discontin-uation of unnecessary regulation; "economy without politics" cannot therefore exist either.

Against this background, the regular, complementary exchange of standpoints and perspectives is necessary. However, company representatives and economists are constantly criticising the lack of competence demonstrated by politics and politicians in economic affairs.[127] The general message is that economically sub-optimal political results are achieved due to a lack of expertise on the part of poli-ticians, and that political desires and concepts are not based on any realistic as-sumptions.

These findings are both correct and incorrect. What is correct is firstly that "talk-ing at cross purposes" is indeed often observed in communication between econ-omists and politicians; because politicians, too, often demonstrate a lack of under-standing towards demands from economic circles. Secondly, it is true that politi-cal processes and decisions hardly ever follow pure cost/benefit calculations but are instead products of compromises which can only be understood from the po-litical process (see above). From an economic point of view, many political results are therefore "second-best solutions", often characterised by the principle of the minimal consensus – the ideal of economic efficiency criteria looks somewhat dif-ferent. However, it is particularly these characteristics which are the key constitu-ent features of politics. As stated in the section on the nature and logic of political

---

processes, democratic politics consists of precisely these categories. Regarded from this standpoint, the finding that politics and politicians are lacking in economic competence is therefore incorrect: when evaluating political performance, economic representatives simply use an unsuitable catalogue of concepts with which political work cannot be registered or can only be registered to an inadequate extent.

The reason why politicians and economists often demonstrate a mutual lack of understanding is due primarily to the different perceptions and basic assumptions of both groups of actors. The economy, for example, is regularly focussed on profit maximisation and (cost) efficiency. Conversely, these categories are of scant importance in politics; as described above, power and authority are the central concepts here. These divergent basic concepts are an expression of the functionally differentiated character of modern society. Modern, collaborative society is thus characterised by sustained differentiation into subsystems such as e. g. the political system, the economic system, the legal system, etc. The theoretical rationale for these relationships originates from the sociologist Niklas Luhmann, who undertook extensive research into the emergence and structure of these functional systems as part of the system theory which he developed.[128] Expressed in very condensed and simplified form, the subsystems according to Luhmann each lead separate lives which are focussed upon themselves. According to their structure, they are self-referential and autopoietic, i. e. their communication refers only to themselves and they always create or stabilise themselves from within themselves.[129]

Whilst communication with other subsystems, the "environment", is not entirely impossible, external information is only received partially and selectively according to the functional area of the subsystem. Expressed in simplified terms, this means that the subsystems cannot communicate with one another in a complementary manner; speechlessness and incomprehension prevail between them so to speak.

This is the perspective of the macro-sociological theory – in the light of Luhmann's system theory; however, common experience causes this theoretical finding to appear empirically saturated. However, this observation is apparently problematic under the real conditions of a pluralistic, democratic system of government, as a lack of communication would constantly lead to sensational, undesirable developments with negative consequences for society. The formation of communication interfaces between politics and the economy is therefore all the more important.

Professional, structured and goal-oriented lobbying can make an integrative and necessary contribution to this by creating options for overcoming the system

---

128 See Luhmann (1984); as an introduction to the system theory by Niklas Luhmann: Horster (2005).
129 Baecker (2009), pp. 100 ff.

boundaries through mutually understandable communication between politics and the economy, and both structuring and supporting these. Figure 2.8 shows this in the sense of lobbying as a system of discourse and negotiation: in such a system, lobbying should guarantee through intermediary structures what cannot succeed through direct communication due to a lack of common socialisation on the part of political and economic elites. In the best case, this thereby ensures that politicians and economists make the best possible, sustainable decisions, whose results ultimately benefit all concerned, in mutual collaboration. Politicians and economists state their needs and expectations, exchange information and consequently make the necessary decisions. Exchange which is desirable from a political and societal perspective can also take place in the pre-political sphere, irrespective of specific lobbying processes. In turn, such a voluntary value system would be a way to reduce actual or supposed differences (of interests) between the affected parties and politics.

In this dialogue, both the affected parties and politicians make requirements on good and professional lobbying (for details on these requirements, see Sections 7.3.1.2 and 7.3.1.3). The reliable, objective and transparent mediation of information on backgrounds and the possible consequences and problems which may arise from legislation is particularly important to politicians. Politicians also demand that lobbyists have an understanding of the formal and informal political processes and procedures (Chapter 3) and the political culture – which differ from those familiar to the affected parties from their institutions (e. g. an organisation, an association or a company). And, of course, politicians also expect lobbyists to reveal a high level of integrity and adhere to all compliance regulations. In turn, the affected parties expect information about the political system, political procedures, issues and networks. In particular, companies also expect their lobbyists to have a business mindset and implement their objectives vis-à-vis politicians.

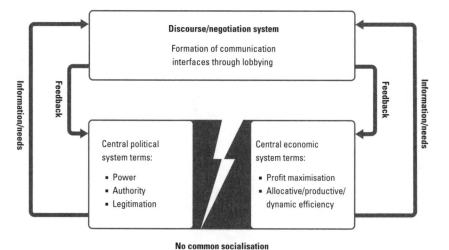

Figure 2.8: Lobbying as a system of negotiation for forming communication interfaces

Consequentially, the affected parties want their interests to be represented professionally and with integrity.

Ideally, an intermediary who is familiar with, and can give consideration to, both sides' requirements exists for dialogue between politicians and the affected parties. This intermediary must mediate and translate between the different cultures. He must be able to switch perspectives and place himself in the other party's position. Such an intermediary additionally offers the advantage that, as an independent third party, he is more credible to politicians than lobbyists who are employed by an association or company. On the other hand, he is also able to be more objective towards his clients and clearly point out which objectives are possible and which are not, unlike an employed lobbyist who is integrated in hierarchical and disciplinary terms (with regard to onepager and perspective change, see Chapters 6 and 10).

Lobbying serves as an intermediary system in the broadest sense of the economic-political mediation of interests. In the following, this will be briefly explained using the example of the private sector, since this is the most familiar case of lobbying. However, as has been emphasised several times, the intermediary system of lobbying also applies to case examples involving other affected parties such as associations, organisations and even EU member states and regions vis-à-vis the Union and its institutions.

As an intermediary system, lobbying links the two external systems of politics and the economy by overcoming existing barriers to communication through its mediation activity. It acts as a type of translation mechanism between the two systems; by transforming the information from both external systems, it enables one party to receive the interests articulated by the other party. Communication can be stimulated by both parties. However, the relevant interests of politics and the economy do not simply exist alongside each other. By interposing lobbying, they communicate with each other and frequently only take on their specific structure in their reciprocal relationship (for an illustration, see Figure 2.3 in Section 2.2.2.2).[130]

Lobbying as such is therefore positioned between the two systems of politics and the private sector. It helps both sides to give their interests an organisational structure, formulate them appropriate to the addressees and convey them to the other arena. In such a system, the communication process is conceivable in both directions. The private sector can introduce legitimate interests into the political and administrative sphere. Politicians and civil servants can therefore access important factual information and structure their legislation more effectively. Equally, however, politics and administration (i.e. the EU institutions) can also make contact with the private sector via the intermediary (lobbyist) and thus point out

---

130 Joos (1998), p. 85.

or pave the way for the orientation of corporate policy, e.g. by holding out the prospect of subsidies or tax breaks for specific behaviour on the part of companies. In the intermediary system of lobbying, this therefore enables politicians and administrators to convey their desires, such as the creation of jobs or more ecologically sound production as well as allowing them to co-influence business location decisions.[131]

2.3.4 Political science concepts for analysing and evaluating lobbying: overview

The necessity of interests and lobbying in politics ultimately exists due to purely practical considerations: politicians obtain necessary information, the complexity of the decision-making situation is reduced, communication between politicians and the affected parties is facilitated and improved through professional lobbying, and the effectiveness and quality of political decisions are increased in the final analysis. An overview of some political science concepts should also help to position and evaluate this finding in terms of political theory. It must be remembered in this case that the analytical concepts of neo-pluralism, neo-corporatism, the exchange theory and the governance approach each have different starting points. They all interpret politics, state and government differently. Neo-pluralism and neo-corporatism describe mutual relationships between the state and stakeholders: they therefore deal primarily with the input side of political decision-making. This perspective differs significantly from action-oriented concepts such as exchange theory and the governance approach. In view of this, the following explanations are not limited to one single analysis concept – an assessment or evaluation can only be undertaken once the phenomenon of lobbying has been analysed from the various perspectives.

2.3.4.1 Neo-pluralism

Closely associated with Ernst Fraenkel, neo-pluralism is regarded as the successor to the classic pluralistic considerations of David Truman or Harold Laski. The fundamental concept here is the free and unhindered competition of interests, a crucial element of a democratic society. If a specific concern is organised, it is faced by another interest in a heterogeneous society. In an initially passive state, self-regulation of the interests always takes place, enabling a solution for the common good. "Just as in a market, numerous stakeholders compete for political influence in pluralistic systems. Political decision-makers in government, administration, parliament and parties act so to speak as arbitrators between these interests, but also pursue their own interests at the same time."[132]

---

131 See Joos (1998), p. 86.
132 Nohlen and Schultze (2010⁴), s.v. pluralism.

However, neo-pluralism acknowledges that this self-regulation only functions in the ideal case. Within debate, for instance, representatives of public and usually non-specific concerns are only inadequately able to make themselves heard.[133] Conversely, organised stakeholders, often from the private sector, are able to assert their interests more easily.[134] Fraenkel, too, acknowledges this initially negative characteristic, but nevertheless considers this orientation to be advantageous, as the common good can only be determined in this manner.[135] Precisely this cannot be defined prior to a debate; instead, it arises from compromises by the different stakeholders during the course of a long-term process. Because the "common good is not a social reality but a regulatory ideal".[136] The coexistence of competing interests, in particular, is a quintessential aspect of democracy. Common good is not defined in advance or determined by the state; it arises from political competition. Interests can most certainly be organised autonomously and integrated professionally in order to ensure that they are recognised. Only this enables a balance of powers. However, all sides must adhere to the generally accepted and legally established rules in this process.[137] In contrast to his peers, Fraenkel assigns a more active role to the state.[138] It is therefore in the state's interest to integrate its own concerns.[139] The legislator is also obliged, with the aid of the constitution or by law, to establish framework conditions which ensure balanced competition between interests and are supported by a recognised code of values.[140]

In addition to the parties, the organised interests and the representation of interests are the crucial intermediaries in linking the political preferences of society (citizens, economy, stakeholders) and the processes in the "central political decision-making system".[141] For democratic states, it is therefore clear that "the common good can be established and asserted not *despite* the activity, but precisely *thanks to* the involvement, of interest groups [emphases in the original]".[142] Organised interests provide information through direct and indirect channels (lobbying, elections or via the parties themselves) and support political decision-making.[143] Some practitioners of lobbying also view their work in a neo-pluralistic sense: "Democracy can only function if the opinion of all social actors is integrated – and then weighed up by politicians. The societal relevance and media salience of the issues play a very crucial role in this. Ultimately, it involves lobbying as part of the democratic process."[144]

---

133 See Fraenkel (1964), p. 44; Michalowitz (2007), p. 29 ff.; Böhret, Jann and Kronewett (1979), p. 173.
134 See Heitz (2011), pp. 88–89.
135 See Straßner (2006), pp. 78–79.
136 Fraenkel (1964), p. 42.
137 Kohler-Koch, Conzelmann and Knodt (2004), p. 228.
138 See Böhret, Jann and Kronewett (1979), pp. 169, 173–174; Erdmann (1988), p. 375.
139 See Straßner (2006), pp. 81-82.
140 See Fraenkel (1964), pp. 42, 147–150; Straßner (2006), pp. 80-81; Lösche (2007), p. 104.
141 Straßner (2006), p. 79.
142 Fraenkel (1964), p. 46.
143 See Fraenkel (1964), p. 42; Michalowitz (2007), p. 30.
144 Tietmeyer (2013), p. 170.

However, the organisation and representation of interests are also subject to criticism: firstly, there is the so-called free-rider problem, which may distort the interests. If there are no incentives to take part in lobbying, individuals attempt to profit from the efforts of the group without themselves taking action. This often results in predicaments, particularly for public lobbying. In companies, for example, all employees benefit from a collective agreement negotiated by the trade union, not only paying union members. In addition, interests see themselves faced with resources which are apparently still unevenly distributed. Here, critics tend to see the dominance or even preference of economic interests in the political process.[145]

Nevertheless, current societal responses to preliminary decisions in the area of major state and private sector projects confirm that this trend is developing in the opposite direction. The potential of citizens' initiatives in the public arena therefore appears to be strong, despite all of the criticism that has been levelled.[146] One example is the resistance of citizens' initiatives to major projects such as the construction of the new railway station in Stuttgart (Stuttgart 21) or to power lines and wind parks stemming from the turnaround in German energy policy.

2.3.4.2 Neo-corporatism

In the concept of neo-corporatism, lobbying is not regarded as the influence of particular interests on the common good but as a necessity for efficient governance. Lobbying therefore contributes to the governability of modern democracies. The incorporation of organised interests into the political process facilitates the political controllability of society and improves the quality of political problem solving.[147] In other words: if the affected parties, e.g. employers and employees, are included in labour and social legislation negotiations via associations and trade unions, the laws will have increased bearing on the reality of the lives of those affected and will therefore be more efficient than if politicians decide on them without the input of the affected parties.

Whilst neo-pluralism regards stakeholders and lobbying as intermediaries in the political decision-making process, other theories recognise and demand the increased interconnection of state institutions and stakeholders. The latter are increasingly involved in political decisions and can even act on behalf of the state. Neo-pluralism is therefore not sufficiently far-reaching for many authors.[148] The theory of neo-corporatism picks up on these concepts.

For neo-corporatism, organised interests and lobbying are more than intermediaries; they are assigned a role which integrates them more extensively into the po-

---

145 See Straßner (2006), p. 85; Reutter and Rütters (2007), pp. 123–124; Crouch (2008), p. 5.
146 See Brettschneider (2011), pp. 40–41; Bebnowski (2013), p. 146; Thaa (2013), pp. 7–8.
147 Kohler-Koch, Conzelmann and Knodt (2004), pp. 229–230.
148 See Köppel and Nerb (2006), p. 292; Schmitter (1979), p. 16; Schmitter (1974), p. 96.

litical process.[149] State instrumentalisation of associations is dealt with, which is why neo-corporatism is also referred to as a directed form of identifying interests.[150] "Corporatism can be defined as a system of interest representation in which the constituent units are organized into a limited number of singular, compulsory, non-competitive, hierarchically ordered and functionally differentiated categories, recognized or licensed (if not created) by the state and granted a deliberate representational monopoly within their respective categories in exchange for observing certain controls on their selection of leaders and articulation of demands and supports."[151]

With the objective of achieving a homogeneous common good in an efficient manner, the state accordingly selects specific interests which it integrates into the political process in the long term. The stakeholders must make concessions to the state to attain influence over the decision-making process.[152] At the same time, the state attempts to minimise the number of co-operation partners by subdividing them into hierarchical umbrella organisations in order to avoid a possible free-rider problem.[153] As the normative level of neo-corporatism is still fed by interests of unequal power, the establishment of institutional exchange not only promotes the stakeholders' cooperation in this way but also the implementation of the state's own interests. It is fundamentally possible for such institutionalised exchange to be initiated both by the state and through society.[154] A look at the European level reveals numerous points of reference, e.g. the Commission's structural exchange with organised interests, which represent a corporatistic structure and could lead to a further increase in the Commission's power.[155] However, neo-corporatism cannot be used as the sole concept to explain the European level, which is why the processes at European level can be more appropriately described as "quasi-corporatistic or as pluralistic with corporatistic" elements.[156]

In the sense of neo-corporatism, the manner in which stakeholders are integrated is therefore regarded as the "response to the problems of state control of complex industrialised societies".[157] Organised interests incorporate the heterogeneous interests of society, are involved in the political decision-making system and can even take over state tasks. In this mutual relationship, the state can use the resources of the incorporated stakeholders in order to compensate for information deficits, increase legitimacy or reduce administration costs. In turn, the organised interests can assert their own interests, since they are frequently involved in the

---

149 See Schmitter (1979), p. 16; Köppl (2006), p. 281.
150 See Böhret, Jann and Kronewett (1988), p. 185.
151 Schmitter (1979), p. 13.
152 See Michalowitz (2007), p. 32, Heitz (2011), p. 87.
153 See Janning (2009), p. 136.; Köppel and Nerb (2006), p. 294; von Aleman and Heinze (1981), p. 55.
154 See Schmitter (1974), pp. 102–103; Köppel and Nerb (2006), p. 293; Michalowitz (2007), p. 34.
155 See Michalowitz (2007), pp. 32-33; Heitz (2011), pp. 90–91.
156 Michalowitz (2007), p. 33.
157 Böhret, Jann and Kronewett (1988), p. 183.

decision-making process.[158] According to Philippe Schmitter, this institutionalised participation therefore leads to more stable political structures.[159] Lobbying is thus upgraded to a "symbiotic" exchange relationship.[160]

One criticism levelled at the neo-corporatistic concept is the possible trade-off between process efficiency and declining legitimacy, which is triggered through the selective participation procedure. Authors also pick up on the fact that neo-corporatism has brought forth a state sponsored elite cartel, which arises from asymmetrical resource distribution but also from its sole focus on umbrella organisations.[161] Although not all interests can be organised in umbrella organisations and their hierarchical structures cannot prevent occasional dissenters, it is conceded that both social control and the stability of western democracies can be better recorded in neo-corporatism, thus enabling diverging interests to be balanced more effectively.[162]

2.3.4.3 Exchange theory

Both neo-corporatism and neo-pluralism have proved unsuitable for portraying and explaining the individual characteristics of political decision-making within the EU in theory. Whilst neo-pluralism cannot explain how or why interests or their representatives organise themselves, neo-corporatism is unable to adequately reflect the number and diversity of lobbyists and interest groups acting within the framework of the EU. Nor is it able to portray the manner in which organised interests, which are more individually controlled than consistently institutionalised, participate in the EU.[163] Against this background and also due to the shift in research interest towards action-oriented questions, the analysis and theoretical modelling of the actions of systems are decreasing and are shifting more towards those of individual actors. Focus in this case is being placed on economic models which base individual behaviour on cost/benefit calculations.[164] In political science, this concept is above all used in the rational choice theories, according to which the actors follow their preferences in accordance with benefit-maximising procedures. Action options are analysed under the given prerequisites, opportunity and transaction costs are compared and the best option is selected (with regard to the problem of applying economic models on political processes and decision-making, see Chapter 3).

Here, the political system and lobbying are subjected to a process-oriented approach.[165] As in the case of economic models, political approaches can also use

---

158 See Böhret, Jann and Kronewett (1988), p. 179; Gründinger (2012), p. 23.
159 See Köppel (2006), pp. 82, 181–182.
160 Köppel (2006), p. 283.
161 See Köppel (2006), p. 282; Lösche (2007), p. 110.
162 See Böhret, Jann and Kronewett (1988), pp. 180, 183, 186; Janning (2009), p. 152.
163 See Michalowitz (2007), pp. 31–32.
164 See Heitz (2011), p. 96.
165 Michalowitz (2014), p. 18.

products and goods as the basis. This concept makes use of exchange theory.[166] As its basis, it assumes that the interaction of actors, following the – economic – law of supply and demand, is based on the exchange of goods in the sense of e.g. services, knowledge or information. The fact that both actors benefit from the exchange, albeit not necessarily to the same extent, is of significant importance in this.[167] On this basis, interdependence between the actors can actually arise if one actor's goods are vital for the other to achieve its objectives.[168] Following this approach, political lobbying is conceived as an exchange relationship between private (companies, stakeholders and organisations) and political actors, whose most important goods are information on the one hand and involvement in political decision-making or advantageous decisions on the other hand. This is based on the fact that not only lobbyists attempt to obtain access to political decision-making, but that political actors are also reliant on close exchange with the private sector to ensure that their political strategies are effective or to recognise problems and needs in good time.[169]

These assumptions are based on rationalistic neo-institutionalism, which assumes that actors "[adapt] to the standards and rules of the political system to the extent necessary for their success" and that "the conditions of the political system" determine the actors' behaviour.[170] Consequently, the actors develop strategies with which they can best maximise their benefit or achieve their objective as effectively as possible under the given institutional framework.[171] Political lobbying is therefore portrayed as a plausible and legitimate exchange relationship.

What is problematic about the assumption of an ideal type of exchange, however, is that many aspects have to be included in political decision-making and the information provided by a private actor is often not sufficient on its own to make sustainable decisions. Nor is there any actual transfer of ownership of a good from one actor to another – because, ultimately, both the private and the political actor possess the information. An exchange can therefore also take place unilaterally, i.e. without any consideration, if the private actor supplies the information but the political decision which is taken is not in its favour.

Pieter Bouwen dealt with this problem in his "theory of access". Whilst he substantiates the exchange theory by also using the resource of "information" as the basis, he does not regard the consideration as "influence on political decision-making" but instead, as part of his research on lobbying in the EU, as "access" to political institutions. Whilst this access does not necessarily equate to influence, it

---

166 Heitz (2011), p. 98.
167 Heitz (2011), p. 99, Michalowitz (2007), p. 39, Bouwen (2001), p. 5.
168 Bouwen (2001), p. 8.
169 See Bouwen (2001), p. 5.
170 Michalowitz (2007), p. 38.
171 Heitz (2011), pp. 96–97.

is a necessary condition for, and thus an indicator of, it.[172] According to Bouwen, there are three types of the "access good" information:[173]

1. "Expert knowledge" is the private sector's expertise and know-how which is vital to be able to understand markets. This knowledge is necessary to be able to develop and evaluate laws for a specific sector.

2. "Information on the common European interests" includes private sector information which is necessary to filter out or define the interest and the needs of an economic, political or social sector in Europe.

3. "Information on the comprehensive member state interest" includes private sector information which is necessary to filter out or define the interest and the needs of economic, political or social sectors of individual member states.

The exchange of goods is therefore shifted away from the political decision as such and further external factors; the exchange takes place bilaterally insofar as both actors agree on a fictitious, underlying exchange contract. According to the theory, this is to be assumed.

The exchange theory or the theory of access can be summed up as follows: it regards lobbying as a rational exchange transaction between private and political actors, at least major parts of which are based on mutual dependency. Lobbying is therefore not only a means required by private actors to harmonise their activities with political trends but is also vital for political actors in order to adapt their measures to the actual socio-economic circumstances.

2.3.4.4 Governance approach

Since the mid-1990s, a further theoretical concept focussed on the importance of individual actors has emerged: the "governance approach".[174] It is understood to be a "continuous political process of setting explicit goals for society and intervening in it in order to achieve these goals".[175] In accordance with the narrow, and thus analytically applicable, definitions, however, "governance" means that political decision-making is not monopolised by national governments but is instead undertaken through a variety of public, semi-public and private actors across various levels (sub-state, national and supranational).[176] The implementation and co-ordination of political strategies through a variety of actors can also be regarded as the adoption of this approach.[177] In this regard, governance can also be defined as a shift in competence or power for political decision-making: following this approach, a horizontal shift to semi-public institutions and private actors, for exam-

---

172 Bouwen (2001), p. 2.
173 Bouwen (2001), p. 7.
174 Michalowitz (2007), p. 27.
175 Jachtenfuchs and Kohler-Koch (2004), p. 99.
176 See Hooghe and Marks (2001), pp. 2–3, Krahmann (2003), pp. 10 ff., Heitz (2011), p. 93.
177 Krahmann (2003), p. 11.

ple, is also taking place in addition to the vertical shift towards supranational and sub-national levels.[178]

The background is a co-operative conception of statehood. A state's sovereignty is reduced in a complex and globalised world. This means that the state is no longer superior to society and is also no longer able to control it hierarchically. The state is therefore merely a subsystem alongside other functional systems. With the differentiation of society (see Section 1.1), the state also has to enter into negotiations with all other subsystems. Due to this form of governance, lobbying is transformed into the mediation of interests, and organised interests themselves become involved in political-societal control process. Lobbying therefore takes on an intermediary role. It represents interests vis-à-vis politics and must simultaneously mediate the politics to its clients and explain negotiated compromises.[179]

This joint political decision-making between actors from different sectors is also described by some authors as governance through networks. Rod Rhodes, for example, describes governance through the attributes of "interdependence between organizations" and "continuing interactions between network members", through the existence of "game-like interactions" and through "a significant degree of autonomy from the states".[180] Like the representatives of the exchange theory or the "theory of access" (see Section 2.3.4.3), Rhodes ascribes mutual dependency to the members of the networks due to their respective resources. According to Rhodes, the exchange partners therefore form themselves into profitable networks.[181] This is closely linked to policy network analysis, which investigates the interaction of states and stakeholders "within issue-specific processes"[182] (see also Chapter 3). In turn, other authors regard policy networks as the structure of the political system and governance as governance in and with them.[183] In each case, the governance approach postulates that political decision-making without government ("governance without government", i.e. a kind of self-administration) and "governance with governments" (joint political decision-making by different public, semi-public and private actors) exist in addition to "governance by government".[184]

One special case of the governance approach is multi-level governance, which places particular focus on the many different levels on which the actors are found and on the diversity of political decision-making arenas. This variant particularly applies to the European Union.[185] The core concept of this type of governance is as follows: "Political actors consider problem-solving the essence of politics and

---

178 van Waarden and van Kersbergen (2004), p. 153.
179 Kohler-Koch, Conzelmann and Knodt (2004), pp. 228–229.
180 Rhodes (2007), p. 1246.
181 Rhodes (2007), p. 1245.
182 Michalowitz (2007), p. 35.
183 See Krahmann (2010), p. 22.
184 See Daase and Friesendorf (2010), p. 3.
185 See van Waarden and van Kersbergen (2004), p. 153, Jachtenfuchs and Kohler-Koch (2004), p. 103.

that the setting of policy-making is defined by the existence of highly organised social subsystems […]. The 'state' is […] segmented and its role has changed from authoritative allocation 'from above' to the role of 'activator'. Governing the [European Community] involves bringing together the relevant state and societal actors and building issue-specific constituencies. Thus, in these patterns of interaction, state actors and a multitude of interest organisations are involved in multilateral negotiations about the allocation of functionally specific 'values'".[186]

The integration of non-state actors therefore plays a central role in the governance approach, particularly against the background of its development. The approach was developed following the end of the East-West conflict and the bipolar, international system when state structures and both international and supranational institutions were undergoing extensive diversification and duplication. The trend at that time towards economically inspired strategies for increasing the efficiency of political initiatives through the division of labour and the outsourcing of tasks also extensively influenced the conception of this approach. The involvement of private actors, organised interests and lobbying in the political process is therefore understood as a logically consistent and legitimate historical development which is attributable e. g. to efforts to achieve greater efficiency and effectiveness in political decision-making.

This involvement is also explicitly desired by the EU's political decision-makers: to gain public acceptance, the European Commission is making efforts to involve non-state organisations in political decision-making and called for greater participation and openness in its White Paper on "European Governance".[187] The quality of consultation can be improved through the involvement of experts and stakeholder organisations in decision-making, and the EU's legitimacy can also be increased by opening the political process up to private actors.[188]

2.3.5 Fundamentals of European law

In addition to the political theory considerations regarding the legitimation of lobbying, the question of its legal basis must also be raised. This is also due to the fact that the criticism levelled at lobbying, particularly at European level, is not limited merely to moral arguments (coupled with the accusation that individual interests are placed before the general good in some kind of "reprehensible" manner), but also calls the legality of lobbying into question.

Time and again, spectacular cases of the exercising of an illegal influence on the EU legislative process serve to fan the flames of such criticism: in March 2011, for example, journalists from the *Sunday Times* exposed four Members of the Euro-

---

186 Eising and Kohler-Koch (1999), p. 5.
187 European Commission (2000), p. 5; European Commission (2001), pp. 2, 5; see Jachtenfuchs and Kohler-Koch (2004), p. 105.
188 See European Commission (2001), p. 5, Jachtenfuchs and Kohler-Koch (2004), pp. 105–106.

pean Parliament as corrupt by offering them, in the guise of lobbyists, 100,000 euros for previously agreed, proposed changes to legislation. Three of them accepted the money.[189] This ended the political career of two of them and/or had significant consequences under criminal law. The following question is all the more important in view of this: how and to what extent is political lobbying legally legitimate and which procedures must be adhered to in the context of the EU?

To get straight to the point, legitimate lobbying has nothing to do with the bribery and corruption outlined above. The objective must be to achieve a clearly defined distinction between the lawful and unlawful activity of the lobbyist on the one hand and the public authority on the other hand.

Each action which is in compliance with, or does not violate, applicable laws can be regarded as a lawful activity. Or, as lobbying researcher Alexander Classen accurately formulated it: "If behaviour complies with the legal regulations or does not violate them, it is legal."[190] One example of this could be a telephone call made by a lobbyist to a public authority, in which the former sets forth his arguments on a specific issue to the latter. However, not everything that is legally permissible is also morally correct. This is the reason why there are voluntary self-obligations on the part of lobbyists which supplement and surpass the legal regulations (see Section 2.3.5.2).

2.3.5.1 Primary legal fundamentals

Lobbying is covered by European primary law. Article 11 (1) TEU makes it clear that the EU institutions "[shall,] by appropriate means, [give] citizens and representative associations the opportunity to make known and publicly exchange their views in all areas of Union action." This very first paragraph makes it clear whom this exchange of views should benefit, i.e. (a) the citizens and (b) the representative associations in equal measure. The subsequent paragraphs do not ultimately specify in detail which instruments are available to the EU institutions in this exchange of views. The following are stated:

- Regular dialogue (Article (2) TEU).
- Broad consultations (Article 11 (3) TEU).
- The European citizens' initiative (Article 11 (4) TEU).

The obligation to exchange views with the population is therefore by no means limited solely to dialogue with organised associations and lobbyists, but also explicitly includes citizens and organised civil society. The EU institutions' open dialogue with all types of lobbyist is therefore set down in EU primary law.

---

189 N. U. (2011b).
190 Classen (2014), p. 290.

2.3.5.2 Regulations for lobbyists (code of conduct) and European Union officials

The fact that the EU institutions are obligated qua European treaties (e.g. preamble and Article 11 TEU) to public accessibility and transparency in their decision-making processes and that the institutions are *de facto* reliant on information from an organised civil society and the specialist knowledge of companies, NGOs and associations in this necessitate contact between EU officials and lobbyists. This exchange of views requires rules, which are also established by the EU. Lobbying in Brussels does not therefore only have to submit to the rules of the political process in general (see also Chapter 3) but also very specific rules, which are established by politicians (or the legislative and executive levels) and which represent framework conditions which have to be taken into consideration for lobbying. In addition to the primary law requirements, however, these official rules of contact are also an expression of the legitimacy of lobbying amongst the EU institutions. With regard to the establishment of the European Transparency Register, for instance, it is stated that "European policy-makers do not operate in isolation from civil society, but maintain an open, transparent and regular dialogue with representative associations and civil society".[191] This can again be seen as a clear commitment by the European institutions to fundamentally open and legally legitimated dialogue with lobbyists.

The regulations subdivide lobbying into two spheres: "recipients" and "senders". Consequently, specific regulations regulate the behaviour of the employees of EU institutions or EU parliamentarians (recipients) and others the procedure of lobbyists (senders).[192] The regulations are so to speak the link which enables communication between both spheres and, at the same time, guarantees transparent and regulated information exchange. The presence of such rules *de facto* testifies to the acceptance or legitimation of lobbying in the political system of the EU (for details on the legal framework of access to the individual institutions, see Section 5.3).

2.3.5.2.1 Regulations for lobbyists

The code of conduct of the European Transparency Initiative (ETI) is aimed directly at lobbyists. Initiatives for a code of conduct emerged at the start of the 1990s in the European Parliament, long before the Parliament was practically made equal to the Council in its importance to the legislative process with the Treaty of Lisbon. In 1996, these initiatives led to an initial code of conduct and a register for lobbyists at the European Parliament. The European Commission followed in 2008. It had launched the European Transparency Initiative back in 2005; in 2011, the Commission and Parliament defined a joint register, a code of conduct (see Figure 2.9 in the following) and a complaints mechanism in an inter-

---

191 European Parliament (2015b), Annex IX, Point B, Recital 2.
192 Greenwood (2011³), p. 53.

Code of Conduct

"The parties hereto consider that all interest representatives interacting with them, whether on a single occasion or more frequently, registered or not, should behave in conformity with this code of conduct.

In their relations with EU institutions and their Members, officials and other staff, interest representatives shall:

a) always identify themselves by name and, by registration number, if applicable, and by the entity or entities they work for or represent; declare the interests, objectives or aims they promote and, where applicable, specify the clients or members whom they represent;

b) not obtain or try to obtain information or decisions dishonestly or by use of undue pressure or inappropriate behaviour;

c) not claim any formal relationship with the European Union or any of its institutions in their dealings with third parties, or misrepresent the effect of registration in such a way as to mislead third parties or officials or other staff of the European Union, or use the logos of EU institutions without express authorisation;

d) ensure that, to the best of their knowledge, information, which they provide upon registration, and subsequently in the framework of their activities covered by the register, is complete, up-to-date and not misleading; accept that all information provided is subject to review and agree to cooperate with administrative requests for complementary information and updates;

e) not sell to third parties copies of documents obtained from EU institutions;

f) in general, respect, and avoid any obstruction to the implementation and application of, all rules, codes and good governance practices established by EU institutions;

g) not induce Members of the institutions of the European Union, officials or other staff of the European Union, or assistants or trainees of those Members, to contravene the rules and standards of behaviour applicable to them;

h) if employing former officials or other staff of the European Union, or assistants or trainees of Members of EU institutions, respect the obligation of such employees to abide by the rules and confidentiality requirements which apply to them;

i) obtain the prior consent of the Member or Members of the European Parliament concerned as regards any contractual relationship with, or employment of, any individual within a Member's designated entourage;

j) observe any rules laid down on the rights and responsibilities of former Members of the European Parliament and the European Commission;

k) inform whomever they represent of their obligations towards the EU institutions. Individuals who have registered with the European Parliament with a view to being issued with a personal, non-transferable pass affording access to the European Parliament's premises shall:

l) ensure that they wear the access pass visibly at all times in European Parliament premises;

m) comply strictly with the relevant European Parliament Rules of Procedure;

n) accept that any decision on a request for access to the European Parliament's premises is the sole prerogative of the Parliament and that registration shall not confer an automatic entitlement to an access pass."

Source: European Commission (2014) "Transparency Register/Code of Conduct",
http://ec.europa.eu/transparencyregister/public/staticPage/displayStaticPage.do;TRPUBLICID=vGQnVm1YYJHVkJPpgsYGn8JCZQ4b6 TG76Tg9GnD6jZlKvJXMpk41!1756804907?locale=de&reference=CODE_OF_CONDUCT (last accessed on 29.05.2015).

Figure 2.9: "Code of Conduct" (in Annex 3 of the interinstitutional agreement from 2014 on the Transparency Register)

institutional agreement.[193] The Council, which supported this initiative,[194] does not maintain a register itself.

The European Transparency Register is used for the "registration and monitoring of organisations and self-employed individuals engaged in EU policy-making and policy implementation".[195] The central concern is adherence to laws and ethical principles. "... [A]voiding undue pressure, illegitimate or privileged access to information or to decision makers."[196]

Critics find fault with the fact that entry in the Transparency Register is voluntary and not mandatory, as is the case in the USA, for instance.[197] Another shortcoming, which is also constantly criticised by lobbyists, is that by no means all interest groups in Brussels are subject to the regulations of the European Transparency Initiative.[198] Whilst law firms, for example, are explicitly listed in the Transparency Register, the activities of lawyers are not included in the register's scope when these involve e. g. "advisory work and contacts with public bodies in order to better inform clients about a general legal situation or about their specific legal position, or to advise them whether or not a particular legal or administrative step is appropriate or admissible under the law as it stands".[199] The activities of social partners as participants in social dialogue are also excluded. Another group of lobbyists which is not subject to the regulations consists of the representatives of local, regional and communal authorities, such as e. g. the representations of the German federal states or state parliaments. Nor are the representatives of parties or churches and religious communities ever affected. It is merely "expected" of these groups that they register themselves,[200] despite their similarities to private company lobbying.[201]

2.3.5.2.2 Regulations for European Union officials

In addition to the regulations aimed directly at lobbyists, there are also regulations for the officials of the EU, e. g. the Members of the Commission, the EU parliamentarians or the EU civil servants. The prudent and lawful conduct of a lobbyist, called compliance, demands adherence to those regulations affecting him personally and also gives consideration to the rules applicable to his contact persons.

The primary law actually states that Members of the Commission must refrain from any action "incompatible with their duties"; during their term of office, they are prohibited from engaging in "any other occupation, whether gainful or not"

193   van Schendelen (2013[4]), p. 311.
194   European Commission (2015g).
195   *Official Journal of the EU*, L 191/29 from 22.7.2011, Article I.1.
196   European Commission (2015g).
197   Rubner (2009), pp. 206 – 207.
198   Rubner (2009), pp. 119 – 120; van Schendelen (2013[4]), p. 386.
199   *Official Journal of the EU*, L 191/30 from 22.7.2011.
200   *Official Journal of the EU*, L 191/30 from 22nd July 2011.
201   van Schendelen (2013[4]), p. 311.

(Article 245 TFEU). There is also a *Code of Conduct for Commissioners*; this is particularly aimed at avoiding conflicts of interest in the performance of their duties. For example, other professional activities, whether gainful or not, are prohibited (Article 1.1) and Members of the Commission must also "declare any financial interest or asset which might create a conflict of interests in the performance of their duties" (Article 1.3). No gift with a value of more than 150 euros may be accepted (Article 1.11).

The present Commission President, Jean-Claude Juncker, wants to see these standards raised. In his "Political Guidelines for the next European Commission" published on 15th July 2014, he dedicated an entire chapter to the topic of lobbying, in which he pleads for increased transparency in contact with stakeholders and lobbyists: "Our citizens have the right to know with whom Commissioners and Commission staff, Members of the European Parliament or representatives of the Council meet in the context of the legislative process."[202] Since the new Commission came to power in 2014, for instance, commissioners are obliged to make personal meetings with lobbyists public on their respective website.[203]

In accordance with the *Rules of Procedure of the European Parliament*, the principles of "disinterest, integrity, openness, diligence, honesty, accountability and respect for Parliament's reputation" (Annex 1, Article 1) apply to members of the parliament in the exercise of their mandate. They must additionally resolve possible conflicts of interest and notify the parliamentary President of these if necessary (Annex 1, Article 3), and must also submit a declaration concerning their financial interests (Annex 1, Article 4). Gifts may only be accepted if they are "given in accordance with courtesy usage" and do not exceed a value of 150 euros (Annex 1, Article 5).

The regulations for EU civil servants particularly include the *Staff Regulations of Officials of the European Economic Community*,[204] which e.g. specify that civil servants must not accept any instructions from persons or organisations outside of their institution; they must carry out the duties assigned to them "objectively, impartially and in keeping with [their] duty of loyalty to the Union" (Article 11). Nor must civil servants "accept ... any honour, decoration, favour, gift or payment of any kind whatever" (Article 11). Information that has not been published must not be disclosed by civil servants (Article 17). Article 12 of the Staff Regulations additionally states: "An official shall refrain from any action or behaviour which might reflect adversely upon his position." However, there are also further regulations. In addition to the Staff Regulations, for example, the Commission has also issued a *Code of Good Administrative Behaviour for Staff of the European Commis-*

---

202 Juncker (2014), p. 13.
203 European Commission (2014a).
204 Council of the European Economic Community, Council of the European Atomic Energy Community (2015).

sion in Their Relations with the Public. This provides e.g. for the protection of personal data and secret information as well as a principle of non-discrimination and the proportionality and consistency of the administration. In the case of lobbying, this means that all stakeholders concerned should be treated equally.

Whilst these regulations are aimed primarily at EU officials by regulating their contact with the external world, they also indirectly influence the behaviour of lobbyists. This is because a professional lobbyist will be familiar with these regulations governing his contact persons and will tailor his own behaviour to them in order not to embarrass his counterpart by compelling him to draw attention to these regulations. Any contrary activity could endanger a valuable lobbying contact.

2.3.5.3 Further legal regulations and voluntary commitment of lobbyists

In addition to the above cited European standards, member state regulations may also be relevant to lobbying in Brussels depending on where the lobbying takes place or the nationality of the persons involved. For example, § 334 (bribery) or § 108e StGB (bribery of members of parliament) would also be relevant to German nationals.[205] However, this is only mentioned for the sake of completeness, because these criminal offences naturally have nothing whatsoever to do with professional lobbying.

In practice, the legal standards are supplemented by voluntary commitments by lobbyists. Both the European Public Affairs Consultancies Association (EPACA) and the Society of European Affairs Professionals (SEAP) recommend that their members are listed in the voluntary Transparency Register and abide by the code of conduct. They have additionally developed their own codes.[206]

Individual lobbying companies are going beyond this and are thus setting benchmarks for others. Exemplary lobbying companies – more precisely, the lobbying agencies – are e.g. voluntarily undergoing various transparency, data protection, quality management, legal and financial compliance audits.[207] Companies' in-house lobbying departments must additionally give consideration to the internal compliance regulations. The compliance standards are therefore being driven beyond the legislation by the industry itself. This trend towards voluntary controls ultimately leads to the situation that other lobbying companies will also have to comply with these standards if they wish to remain present on the market (with regard to lobbyists' integrity and compliance, see also Section 7.3.1.3).

The professionalism of a lobbying company can generally be recognised by how strictly it adheres to codes of conduct and which voluntary commitment and control mechanisms it has imposed on itself. An unprofessional lobbying company

---

205 Classen (2014), pp. 108–109.
206 EPACA (2015); SEAP (2015).
207 EUTOP International GmbH, for example (2015).

interprets the rules more loosely, according to the maxim "What is not expressly prohibited is permissible", whereas a professional lobbying company interprets the rules strictly. Only in this way can a relationship of trust be established between politicians, stakeholders and lobbyists in the long term.[208] In addition, the lobbying agencies also have a competitive interest in strictly interpreting and rigidly adhering to the codes of conduct. Prudent conduct can also make a difference in terms of the desired result, and can therefore increase the effectiveness of lobbying.[209] Adherence to all regulations is crucially important to a lobbyist's reputation. If even the slightest doubt is cast on his integrity due to (even unconscious!) misconduct, his reputation and credibility are tarnished, if not actually ruined. In some cases, this can make it impossible to remain in this profession.

2.4 Summary

Chapter 2 deals with two major issues. The first issue focuses primarily on conceptual questions concerning lobbying:

- What are the various concepts that need to be distinguished in the area of lobbying? How are the individual sub-areas defined terminologically and what is their historic background? How are the individual terms and concepts delimited from each other and what are their strengths and weaknesses?
- What tasks does lobbying (in the broadest sense) undertake for the represented party, i.e. what are its essential objectives and functions for companies and other economic and societal actors?

The second issue deals with the relationship between lobbying and politics. The analysis focuses on the following questions:

- What is the importance of interests and the representation of these interests in the political system?
- How is lobbying evaluated in terms of political science?
- What are the European legal bases and regulations for lobbying amongst the EU institutions?

The key results for the first issue can be summed up as follows:
(1) The term lobbying can be defined as:
   – firstly the procurement, selection and evaluation of information which can lead to a competitive advantage or prevent a competitive disadvantage for the represented company (or the association, the organisation, the EU member state/region);

---

208 van Schendelen (2013[4]), p. 313.
209 van Schendelen (2013[4]), p. 313.

    – secondly the direct or indirect involvement of a company (or an association, an organisation, an EU member state/region) in legislative and/or executive (EU) decision-making processes by means of information, with the objective of achieving competitive advantages or averting competitive disadvantages.

(2) Conceptual delimitation from public relations and public affairs is essential for a correct understanding of lobbying. Whilst public relations is concerned with the external portrayal of a company to a broad (media) public and therefore, by no means least, with image management; public affairs targets a smaller group of addressees: it deals with strategic information management between politics, companies and society, a "limited public" so to speak. The focus in this is clearly on content (preparation of analyses, planning and hosting of events, etc.), and less on process support. The latter is the domain of lobbying, which is concerned above all with measurable involvement in specific legislative and executive decisions.

(3) Governmental relations has become established as a special form of lobbying (representation of interests). In content terms, governmental relations is delimited through its specific orientation towards the legislative and executive activity of state institutions (occasionally referred to more narrowly as "legislative lobbying"), and in temporal terms through its structural (i.e. long-term) approach: whilst general lobbying is also aimed at short-term individual decisions, governmental relations usually commences at a far earlier point in time and accompanies the entire decision-making process or the relevant environment, sometimes over several years under certain circumstances. Governmental relations are primarily process-oriented; the content bearer is the company (or the association or organisation).

(4) In addition to investor relations and public relations, lobbying, and particularly governmental relations, is generally part of strategically focussed corporate communication. In contrast to investor relations (as capital market communication which is actually legally required in certain cases) and public relations (as an external portrayal and image management tool), the importance of governmental relations as a lever for specific participation in decision-making processes is only gradually becoming recognised by many companies.

(5) Lobbying is an important part of corporate environmental management: continuous, precise analysis of a company's political environment is an essential basis for long-term corporate strategy decisions; the implementation of these decisions can be extensively promoted through specific communication with legislative and executive decision-makers. Lobbying can help not only extensively regulated industries, but ultimately any company dependent on legislative or administrative decisions, to achieve competitive advantages or avoid the occurrence of competitive disadvantages.

(6) There are essentially three dimensions to lobbying for companies:
   - Firstly, lobbying can be used as an early warning system to identify relevant political issues and trends. Effective lobbying starts long before the actual decision-making process: precise issue management, i.e. the continuous monitoring and content-related support of an issue, continuous dialogue with potential decision-makers (which necessitates correct key player analysis) and the establishment of reciprocal information transparency are essential criteria without which subsequent participation in decision-making processes is unlikely to succeed.
   - Secondly, lobbying, in its classic form, encompasses the support of decision-making processes in the political arena. In addition to information management, which is also essential in this case, the strategic component increases in importance in structural co-operation. Governmental relations means not only acting for a company with regard to a specific project and from time to time but continuously supporting it in the political arena. However, this necessitates long-term, trusting legislative and executive contacts. Contact management is therefore of prime importance to the lobbying process. The extension and maintenance of the network necessitate particular commitment.
   - Thirdly, political crisis management can be undertaken by means of lobbying in order to avoid possible worst case scenarios for the company through strategic responses to unforeseen (usually exogenous) events. However, sound networking in the political arena is particularly required for this; actions "from a standing start" are usually unsuccessful.
(7) These three dimensions of lobbying do not stand in isolation from each other; instead, their nature and orientation overlap to a certain extent, and they should ideally be undertaken as complementary elements of a corporate lobbying strategy.

The results for the second issue can be summed up as follows:
(8) There would be no politics without interests. The importance of interests and lobbying in a democratic system can be described in precisely this way. Particularly under the framework conditions of democracy, politics is always characterised by confrontation, negotiation, co-ordination and compromise. However, this is precisely what constitutes the specific character of democratic politics: the battle between various opinions with the objective of a consensus-oriented political solution.
(9) Against this background, lobbying ensures opinion forming and diversity, and therefore realises the pluralism of opinions and views in political discourse. Interest aggregation and mediation are therefore essential for democratic conditions: important information, which would almost certainly not be generated there without external input, is transferred into the political system through the articulation of interests from the social sphere. An im-

portant task, because many experts particularly regard the quality of opinion forming and public discussion at EU level to be inadequate.

(10) In this dialogue, both the affected parties and politicians require good and professional lobbying. The reliable, objective and transparent mediation of information on backgrounds and the possible consequences and problems which may arise from legislation is particularly important to politicians.

(11) Ideally, an intermediary who is familiar with, and can give consideration to, both sides' requirements exists for dialogue between politicians and the affected parties. This intermediary must be able to switch perspectives and place himself in the position of the different parties involved in an issue in order to understand their interest situation and decision tendency, and to be able to tailor his actions and arguments to these.

(12) The political science concepts explained in this book show that lobbying is also an essential part of the political system from a political science perspective:

- The fundamental concept of neo-pluralism here is the free and unhindered competition of interests, a crucial element of a democratic society. If a specific concern is organised, it is faced by another interest in a heterogeneous society.
- In the concept of neo-corporatism, lobbying is not regarded as the influence of particular interests on the common good but as a necessity for efficient governance. Lobbying therefore contributes to the governability of modern democracies. The incorporation of organised interests into the political process facilitates the political controllability of society and improves the quality of political problem solving.
- As its basis, exchange theory assumes that the interaction of actors, following the – economic – law of supply and demand, is based on the exchange of goods in the sense of e.g. services, knowledge or information. The fact that both actors benefit from the exchange, albeit not necessarily to the same extent, is of significant importance in this.
- The following applies in the governance approach: with the differentiation of society, the state also has to enter into negotiations with other subsystems. Due to this form of governance, lobbying is transformed into the mediation of interests, and organised interests themselves become involved in the political-societal control process. Lobbying therefore takes on an intermediary role. It represents interests vis-à-vis politics and must simultaneously mediate the politics to its clients and explain negotiated compromises.

(13) Political lobbying is not an undesired foreign body in the EU system; instead, the European treaties actually obligate the EU institutions to engage in exchange with civil society (citizens, organisations and companies): according to Article 11 (1) TEU, the EU institutions "[shall,] by appropriate means, [give] citizens and representative associations the opportunity to make known and publicly exchange their views in all areas of Union action". Reg-

ulations for the information mediators (e. g. Transparency Register and Code of Conduct) and for the information recipients (e. g. Code of Conduct for Commissioners or *Rules of Procedure of the European Parliament*) define in detail how this information exchange should take place.

Politicians are not passive vis-à-vis lobbying. The primacy of politics still applies. First of all, apparently abstract elements such as the political process, the formal and informal procedures, regulations and the institutions themselves have a significant influence on the structure of practical lobbying. The reason for this is that lobbyists are first and foremost passive vis-à-vis these circumstances – these are the framework conditions to which they have to adapt. To a certain extent, they have to abide by the ground rules which others have established. Politicians also have the option of choosing from the variety of arguments and interests which are presented to them. Naturally, decision-makers also pursue their own political agenda and interests, e. g. they not only take the lobbyists' arguments into account in their decision-making horizon but also their national origin, their party membership, their constituency or their region of origin, etc. The political decision as a whole is therefore far more complex and cannot simply be reduced to the exchange of arguments and information with lobbyists. Professional lobbying will also always factor a political decision-maker's extended decision-making horizon into its process support. Lobbying in the EU has to undergo a paradigm shift in this regard, as Chapter 3 will show.

Chapter 3 Politics as a process: paradigm shift from content competence to process competence in lobbying

3.1 Introduction and question

Politicians often talk of pursuing "content-relate politics".[1] Ideas, programmes, policy drafts and visions – in short: political content – are also available for the electorate to select in political debates and especially in election campaigns. When this content is implemented in politics, i.e. when it becomes laws, it naturally affects citizens' lives and influences the work and success of citizens' initiatives, associations, NGOs or companies. Content therefore appears to be the central element of politics. And so it is hardly surprising that the activity of classic lobbying instruments (corporate representative offices, associations, public affairs agencies, law firms) is focussed on content-related work: participation in public consultations, drawing up exhaustive discussion papers and expert opinions, letters and E-mails to decision-makers, hosting of issue-related events and conducting media campaigns.

In a democracy, however, politics is not simply a procedure at the end of which the best content and arguments, e.g. under welfare economic aspects, gain the upper hand. This is often misunderstood by the general public. Politics not only consists of content; it also has a procedural dimension which is at least equally as important. Political decisions are the culmination of an occasionally complex process which is characterised on the one hand by formal conditions such as legislative procedures, rules of procedure or instruction relationships and on the other hand by informal rules. And political processes have their own specific character, which differs significantly from the processes in other societal action areas such as the economy, for example. Political processes follow their own logic, which does not always meet external, rationalistic expectations at first glance. There are nevertheless analysis methods which help to structure the political process into various phases and stages, thus also making it comprehensible and understandable to outsiders who are not involved directly in the process (see Sections 3.3 and 3.4). This opens up time slots in which it is possible for lobbyists to support the political process and introduce legitimate interests.

The actors involved have to make decisions in each phase and at each stage of the political process. Models which are actually intended to help explain decision-making processes often presuppose opportunistic-rational and schematic-general modes of behaviour, such as that of homo economicus, who is ostensibly always concerned with benefit maximisation and his advantage. This may cause stake-

---

1 See Lindner (2015).

holders to gain the impression that politics is a constant which cannot be changed from the outside but which also appears to be easily predictable and foreseeable. In particular, economic decision-makers often perceive politics as an unchangeable constant for a company which can be disregarded in decision-making processes with the ceteris paribus assumption. However, politics is an entirely variable parameter, and its content is changing continually.[2] The political decision-making process is too dynamic and volatile, and has too many variables, for such rationale-based models to appear helpful. Because the result of political decisions is not defined *a priori*, as is assumed e.g. according to the homo economicus concept. According to the "homo politicus" concept, which corresponds much more to the realities of politics, a decision-maker gives consideration to a variety of parameters in his decision making and weighs these up precisely before making a decision. His decisions are usually open (see Section 3.8).

The central questions of this chapter are therefore:

- What importance is attached to content, procedures and processes, in politics?
- How are political processes structured, and how can lobbying adapt to them?
- How can time slots and decision-making windows, which arise in the political process, be used for lobbying?
- How does a political actor make decisions, and how can the decision-making process of such a "homo politicus" be decrypted for outsiders?

One essential core competence, on which lobbying must concentrate, is already becoming clear: process competence. Since the early days of European unification, knowledge of the relevant European decision-making procedures and mastery of the formal and informal decision-making mechanisms of European politics (process competence) have been a crucial factor in successful lobbying. Since the Treaty of Lisbon came into force on December 1st 2009, at the latest, process competence has been equally as important as content competence in the highly complex, multi-level system of the EU: process competence is a vital prerequisite of long-term, successful lobbying in Europe. No matter how "good" an argument is, it will not be heard if it is not introduced to the right decision-makers in the right form and at the right point in time according to the specified rules. It must therefore be concluded that it is almost more important for a lobbyist to be perfectly familiar with the rules of the relevant political decision-making process than to have the better arguments.[3]

The political science theories, concepts and approaches introduced in the following are not documented exhaustively and to the full depth of their scientific discussion, but are instead only used insofar as they are of relevance to lobbying.

---

2 Joos (2015), p. 408.
3 Joos (2011), p. 31; Joos (2014), pp. 40–43.

3.2 Content as the key element of politics?

In the media industry, "content is king!". This is particularly used to describe the importance of content in online media. Content is especially important in search engine optimisation (SEO) for websites or blogs, since the site concerned will not be listed in a prominent position ("at the very top") in search engines without relevant content, or will perhaps not be listed at all and cannot therefore be found and consulted.[4] Irrespective of this, it is precisely this content which interests readers, listeners and viewers in a medium. The dictum "content is king!", which may appear to possess universal validity at first glance, is automatically transferred to many areas of life. After all, focus on content is trained: even schoolchildren learn to concentrate on content, whether it be during lessons or in class tests. In discussions, children are taught to concentrate on content and the "better" arguments, since these will ultimately prevail in disputes. Later on, positions are often awarded according to the applicants' qualifications and content-related knowledge; when in the job, work is usually evaluated according to content-related criteria. And the majority of lobbying companies also give priority to recruiting personnel with content competencies.[5] It is therefore hardly surprising that this trained, basic assumption is projected onto many other areas of life – including politics.

One of the central focuses of politics is indeed on content, interests, ideas, visions, content-related discussion and competition between ("better") arguments. Content and ideas extensively influence politics. The philosopher Georg Wilhelm Friedrich Hegel attributed tremendous power to ideas in the world of political activities. For example, the French Revolution would not have been possible without the ideas and content of the Enlightenment. It was not the result of the bourgeoisie's interests and the decline of the aristocracy but instead created a reality according to the concepts of the Enlightenment. In this sense, Karl Marx saw the "transformation of philosophy into practice" in revolution and political change.[6] The modern politics familiar in the western world since the end of the 18th century is therefore inscribed with a strong content-related element, an idealistic concept, which is still manifested today in programme parties (such as communist parties) and topical parties (e.g. from the ecology camp and the environmental movement). However, so-called people's parties (above all major social democratic and conservative parties), which attempt to address wide areas of the population and as many social milieus as possible, offer political agendas which are based on issues and content. Politics is also distinguished and categorised according to

---

4 Definition e.g. at: seo-united.de.
5 See Godwin, Ainsworth and Godwin (2013), pp. 216–217.
6 Münkler (2013), pp. 32–33; an introduction to and summary on Hegel can also be found in: Hartmann, Meyer and Oldopp (2002), pp. 16––176.

content-related topics, e.g. in foreign, domestic, environmental, economic or social policy areas.

The understanding of a modern, pluralistic democracy is based on a variety of ideas, political content and interests, which represented by social groups and parties, are in (controlled) competition with each other.[7] In the battle for popularity amongst the electorate, political parties therefore position themselves using programmes and programmatic statements, i.e. content, in order to delimit themselves from one another. Political agendas and election manifestos provide information on a party's basic political orientation and serve their politicians as a guideline for their political actions. In the election campaign conducted in Germany in 2013, for example, issues such as the demand for a "veggie day" by Bündnis90 and the Greens,[8] the demand for a passenger car toll for foreign-registered vehicles by the CSU[9] or the demand for a statutory minimum wage by the SPD[10] went head-to-head. If such content-related positioning does not take place or only takes place to a certain extent, "more content" is often demanded by citizens and the media in public debate. Or the accusation is levelled that the parties no longer differ from one another due to a lack of content-related positioning.[11] A pragmatic political style based on processes and factual issues is also frequently criticised.[12] Conversely, a (moral) quality characteristic is recognised in politics oriented towards content;[13] because politicians who concentrate on content are apparently not concerned with striving to attain personal power and personal advantages.

At first glance, content also appears to be especially important in EU politics. Opinions and interests from all member states collide with each other, and with 28 member states, 28 different opinions are also theoretically possible in the Council of the EU. When dealing with issues such as limiting $CO2$ emissions from passenger cars, for example, different ideas such as how the content of the regulation's text is to be structured can then most certainly clash. Countries in which small passenger cars with lower CO_2 outputs per km are produced are much more easily satisfied with tighter limits than countries such as Germany, in which passenger cars with higher CO_2 emissions per km are primarily manufactured.[14] A content-related compromise then has to be found here. Content therefore also appears to be the central element of European politics.

It therefore comes as little surprise that focus is also frequently placed on content-related work in lobbying amongst the EU institutions. It is the political content

---

7 Kevenhörtster (2008[3]), pp. 217–228.
8 Bündnis90 and the Greens (2013).
9 CSU (2013).
10 SPD (2013).
11 See N.U. (2014c); N.U. (2009a); Maxwill (2015).
12 Langguth (2009); Braun, Blechschmidt, Brössler and Fried (2010).
13 See interview with FDP chairman Christian Lindner (2015).
14 Sinn (2013).

However, fundamental questions arise in view of such a focus on contents: how do we define what the "better" content and therefore the "better" argument is? Is the evaluation of content and arguments not dependent on the relevant boundary conditions in which they are put forward? In other words: does the validity of content change when it is placed in a different context? Is it then still valid at all? In other words, is the evaluation of the content not also incumbent upon a process?

The question of who has the better argument or what is right and wrong cannot even be answered clearly in science. In 1962, scientific philosopher Thomas S. Kuhn wrote in his epochal work The Structure of Scientific Revolutions how even scientific facts are subject to evaluation and classification through the scientific environment, i.e. the leading scientists of their age.

He is talking here about powerful paradigms (doctrines/ideologies) which assert or deny the validity of various scientific results. Because scientific knowledge is not merely the result of the positivistic accumulation of facts over time: the more one deals with an issue, the more certain one becomes that previous views of the world, which are readily labelled as "errors" or "superstition" today, were not "less scientific nor more the product of human idiosyncrasy than those of today".[1] Such concepts were further developed at the end of the 20th century. Accordingly, the "perspective" on the facts and the scientific explanatory models are the crucial factor that categorises them as "better" or "poorer", "right" or "wrong". It was therefore required that subjectivity and relativism should be seriously in science, as a result of which, however, scientific knowledge also lost its absolute objectivity and status as "privileged knowledge".[2]

If it is therefore never absolutely clear, even in "objective" science, which content is "right" or "true", but this is instead always the result of an evaluation by the environment, how should it then be possible to objectively find the "better" argument in a political community with a variety of actors and interests? Here, once again, content-based evaluation is always dependent on the relevant societal environment (e.g. trade unions or employers), which always lays claim to, and redefines, the criteria of "good for the common interest". Politics therefore often faces the difficult decision of correctly evaluating and classifying political content: are economic policy interests and the preservation of jobs or environmental policy objectives and the preservation of nature for coming generations the "better" argument? The result will always be a content-based compromise which bundles a number of (also competing and contradictory) interests and arguments.

[1] Kuhn (2012[4]), pp. 2-3. [2] Nye (2003), p. 1.

Figure 3.1: Discourse: the relative value of content

that lobbyists want to help structure because, ultimately, policy-making directly affects the lives of people and companies. Law firms, for example, help their clients to analyse the content of legal texts or to draw up expert opinions and exhaustive position papers. Public relations and public affairs agencies conduct media campaigns to inform the public. In-house lobbyists and external service providers collect the necessary information and content for lobbying projects, and analyse and process them. Associations, NGOs and corporate representative offices prepare content for communication with politicians, particularly for public consultations. Ultimately, focus here is placed on the content competence of lobbying.

In summary, it must therefore be stated that this firstly shows how important the content-related dimension of politics is. The content helps to distinguish between parties and politicians. Political content which is implemented influences the lives of citizens, and the work and success of companies and organisations. Discussion surrounding political contents is part of our political culture. It is therefore content which sets the political process in motion in the first place.

On the other hand, however, it also raises the question of whether, if only the content of politics is analysed, an important aspect is not overlooked, namely the political process, i.e. the decision-making processes and, in relation to this, the exchange of information and issues, and the formation of coalitions and majorities. One aspect which is crucial to an understanding of political pluralism is that, in addition to the diversity of opinions and interests, a pluralistic system is also concerned with the creation of participation options and access to political decision-makers. Otherwise, the exchange of opinions and competition between arguments would not at all be possible on a political level.[15] However, these participation options only arise if actors are familiar with the formal and informal political procedures and processes. Does the complexity of a multi-level system such as the EU, with its variety of decision-making processes and decision-makers, not demand particular consideration of the formal and informal decision-making processes? Joschka Fischer, Germany's former foreign minister, recently concisely summed up the importance of procedural issues in the political "mechanism" in general: "Initially, I had no idea how important issues of responsibility are in politics. Take coalition agreements, for example: responsibilities are the central issue there. Essentially, a coalition without any content-related agreements can be formed with a partner with whom one gets on well. You simply have to clarify the matter of responsibility in the individual policy areas yourself."[16] So isn't "Process is king" actually more appropriate?

3.3 Classic dimensions of politics: polity, policy, politics

Before political processes can be precisely analysed, all of the different meanings of the term "politics" must first be defined accurately. Its use in the vernacular shows how "vague" the term "politics" is: it can mean the totality of political decision-makers, the politicians. However, it can also be used to mean "political activity", the issues and news which reach the public realm and are further discussed there. It can be used to designate the political objectives and programmes of parties or also the synthetic summarisation of all political content within the country. In short, there is no one single "politics". Political science distinguishes between three dimensions of politics; derived from practice, these are polity, policy and politics.

---

15 Badie, Berg-Schlosser and Morlino (2011), s.v. pluralism.
16 Dankquart (2011).

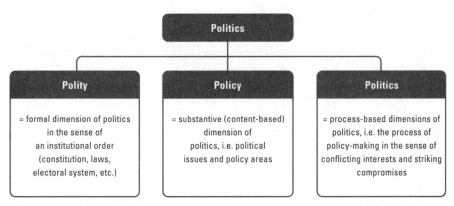

Figure 3.2: The three dimensions of politics

- *Polity* is the *formal dimension* of politics. This involves its normative, structural and constitutional elements, i.e. the (historically established) institutional order which makes politics and policy possible in the first place. Examples of the central institutions of a political system are the parliament, the government and the judiciary, but the form of government (republic, monarchy), the political validity of a country, e.g. as a democracy, and the unwritten standards of the political culture also form part of the scope of polity.[17] With reference to the European Union, polity means a complex, dynamic, multi-level system – consisting of the EU member states, EU regions, the European public (or preferably in the plural, the European publics) and the EU institutions – with various decision-making and legislative procedures (one of which is the ordinary legislative procedure in combination with the so-called informal trialogue, see Chapter 5) which specify the legal framework for EU politics (see Section 4.5).
- The term *policy* describes the *content-related dimension* of politics (also called the substantive dimension). This can refer to specific political programmes and specific political objectives and tasks, but also entire political areas such as social, domestic, economic or environmental policy.[18] In the EU, the European Commission, which has the right of legislative initiative, uses White Papers as the basis with which to announce its political objectives e.g. the more effective control of corporate fusions in the EU in 2014.[19]
- Conversely, *politics* designates the *procedural dimension* of politics. This involves "the active, more or less conflict-based process of political structuring which is above all undertaken in political negotiations and exchange processes, and in which consideration is given to the different, partly similar or conflicting, partly neutral, partly unifying interests of the parties and political intentions, their demands and objectives, etc.".[20] Specifically, these are processes of

---

17 Bernauer, Jahn, Kuhn and Walter (2013[2]), p. 36.
18 Bernauer, Jahn, Kuhn and Walter (2013[2]), p. 36; Nohlen and Schultze (2010[4]), s.v. policy.
19 European Commission (2014b).
20 Nohlen and Schultze (2010[4]), s.v. politics.

opinion forming (e. g. demonstrations and public discussions), decisions (e. g. as part of legislative procedures) and processes of implementation (e. g. enactments of administrative regulations, monitoring adherence to laws and sanctions in the case of misconduct).[21]

From the point of view of lobbying and stakeholders, polity is a given variable which does not change or only changes over a very long period of time. The treaties on the European Union (TEU) and the functioning of the European Union (TFEU), for example, can only be amended through ratification (ordinary amendment procedure according to Article 48 TEU) by all member states or with the approval of all member state parliaments (simplified amendment procedure according to Article 48 TEU). In contrast, national constitutions are usually easier to restructure. The German constitution (GG), for example, can be amended with a two-thirds majority in the Bundestag and Bundesrat (Article 79 GG). Polity is therefore a fixed framework which lobbyists must use for orientation and which they must "always bear in mind" for their work. The content-related dimension (policy) is more important for lobbying. As shown in Section 3.2, however, content alone is not the crucial factor in politics. In addition, content and arguments are usually formulated by political actors at the executive and legislative level, i. e. in the governments, the parliamentary groups and parties as well as by the stakeholders (companies, associations, organisations; at EU level, this can also be the EU regions and EU member states). They are therefore also predetermined for the lobbyist and can only be changed to a minor extent. Lobbying work particularly remains focussed on the procedural dimension of politics through monitoring and long-term and structural process support. This dimension of politics is more or less the lobbyist's access level to politicians. As part of what is called policy-making – the procedural procedure leading to the formulation of political ideas and objectives, and ultimately to a policy – he is able to support the political process and integrate his clients' legitimate interests during the time slots which open up in this process. Consequently, it must be stated here that the procedural dimension of politics is of supreme importance for lobbying, and that it is almost more important for lobbyists to be familiar with the processes and both formal and informal rules of the relevant political decision-making process than "merely" to have their sights on political content (policy) and hold the better arguments. Because in a democracy, it is particularly the political process that undertakes qualitative classification regarding which are actually the better arguments and which interests are ultimately asserted.

---

21 Bernauer, Jahn, Kuhn and Walter (2013[2]), p. 36.

3.4 Procedural dimension of politics

3.4.1 "Complexity trap" of polity: process competence for the political system in the European Union

Even the first political dimension, the polity of the EU, poses a particular challenge to the process competence of lobbying. It must be stated that it is not only since the Treaty of Lisbon came into force on December 1st, 2009, but chiefly since then that the EU's polity has become a complex, dynamic, multi-level system with a seemingly vast number of political decision-makers and many different decision-making levels. Only the capability of decoding this veritable "complexity trap" in its processes enables success to be achieved in structuring the EU's polity and reducing its complexity so that efficient and effective lobbying is possible at all. The problem will only be outlined cursorily at this point. Chapter 4 will deal in depth with the institutions and their interaction in the complex structure of the EU due to their importance to lobbying, because the polity sets out the framework for the political processes, within which policy and politics can develop.

The implementation of the treaties on European integration, particularly from the Single European Act (SEA, 1987) up to and including the Treaty of Lisbon (2009), has seen a constant power shift from the member states to the EU and increasing communitisation of more and more areas of policy, which are subject to the complex formal and informal decision-making procedures of the EU.

The dynamic, multi-level system of the European Union reveals actors and decision-makers at the *regional* level (e.g. the German federal states, or provinces and regions in other member states, which are represented in the Committee of the Regions), at the *national* level (the member states, which are represented in the Council of the EU) and the *supranational* level (e.g. the European Parliament and the Commission). At the EU level alone, several institutions (usually the Commission, Parliament and Council) engage in close exchange before and during the legislative procedure (see Chapter 5). In their daily work, this system of negotiation goes far deeper than the inter-institutional relationships reveal at first glance. Decisions are pre-negotiated in a variety of bodies and committees.[22] The situation is similar at member state and regional level. This requires successful lobbying to be able to analyse and evaluate the relevant constitutional and political competencies, options for exerting an influence and interest positions. The search for the right contact persons amongst the relevant actors therefore regularly becomes a challenge, even for the lobbying agencies engaged by international companies and large associations, with their more extensive resources and larger staffs. Numerous questions are thrown up: which levels of the EU are involved in

---

22 Kohler-Koch, Conzelmann and Knodt (2004), p. 172.

political decisions? Which institutions decide with which voting arrangements on which topics? At which level (EU or member state) are decisions ultimately made?

The EU treaties, the Treaty on the European Union (TEU) and the Treaty on the Functioning of the European Union (TFEU), which deal with the voting arrangements and the various legislative procedures, as well as the various institutions' rules of procedure, provide an initial, formal answer. However, questions concerning the informal decision-making processes such as the so-called informal trialogue (see Chapter 5), and as regards political majorities and networks, still remain unanswered.

On the executive side, the EU is lacking in a "government" in the sense of member state constitutions; executive tasks are undertaken by both the Commission and the Council. Governance in the multi-level system additionally makes things difficult. European lobbying must be aimed at the European executive, the European Commission and European Council (the heads of state and government of all member states) and at the member state level (the member state governments). Depending on the legislative procedure, the Committee of the Regions and the Economic and Social Committee may also have to be included in lobbying. Lobbying should therefore be established across member states and institutions under all circumstances. However, it is also vital not to neglect the legislature (consisting of the European Parliament and the Council of the EU, i.e. the EU Council of Ministers). A cross-member state approach, which again includes the Council members (i.e. *de facto* the member state governments), is also required here. Above all, however, this must also be a cross-party approach and must give consideration to the parties represented in the European Parliament, in which case the national origin of the members of parliament can again play an important role.[23]

Complexity therefore arises from the formal structures, circumstances and regulations (polity) as well as from the constitutional reality of the EU and the manner in which governance is undertaken and with which actors. This already shows how important an understanding of formal and informal responsibilities, procedures and processes is in lobbying; process competence is required to continue to structure these and make them understandable, manageable and plannable for lobbying clients. The European integration development trends of EU politics are initially more likely to raise procedural questions (process questions) before content can be introduced into the European political system in the first place. In other words: the reduction of EU polity complexity through process competence comes first.

---

23 Joos (2014), p. 42.

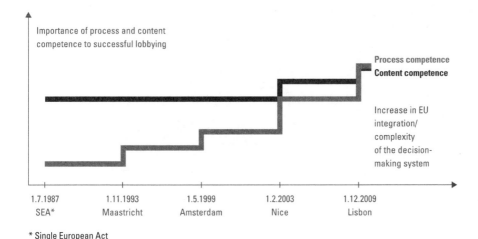

Figure 3.3: Change in the importance of process and content competence for successful lobbying during the development of the EC or EU

3.4.2 Policy cycle

In a work on lobbying amongst the EU institutions, it is therefore worthwhile to precisely analyse the procedural dimension of politics. The political content is also ultimately subject to this dimension. The political process, i.e. its structure and procedure in the specific case, is crucially important in terms of which content is implemented in policies and which is not. In political science, so-called policy analysis (also called policy research) deals with precisely this problem. It shows how the content-related dimension of policy is defined and moulded by the procedural dimension (politics). The content-related results of politics arise from a process, so to speak. This process is the above mentioned policy-making. It begins with the articulation and definition of issues and problems, and ends with the binding specification of programmes and measures.[24] In short, it involves "what governments do, why they do it, and what difference it makes".[25] Back in 1956, Harold Laswell proposed subdividing the processes of policy-making into phases (sometimes also referred to as *stages*),[26] the sequence of which is now known as the *policy cycle*. Since then, this model has undergone constant further development, and a distinction is now made between six different phases: (1) problem definition; (2) agenda setting; (3) policy formulation; (4) policy implementation; (5) policy evaluation and (6) policy termination.[27]

---

[24] Jann and Wegrich (2014³), p. 97; Blum and Schubert (2009), p. 8.
[25] Dye (1976).
[26] Lasswell (1956).
[27] The six phases are cited according to Jann and Wegrich (2014), pp. 105–122. The number and designation of the individual phases can vary depending on the author. Lasswell (1956), for example, spoke of seven stages. However, the central analysis units of problem definition, agenda setting, policy-making, implementation and evaluation are found virtually everywhere. See: Badie, Berg-Schlosser and Morlino (2011), s.v. policy cycle.

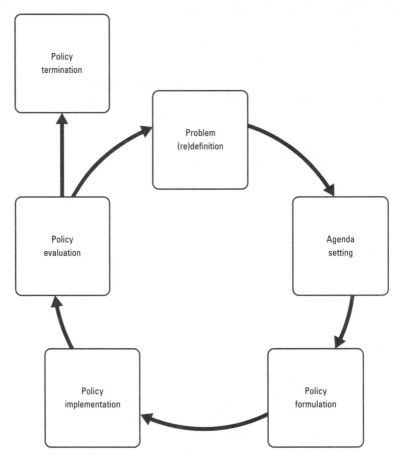

Figure 3.4: The ideally typical phases of the policy cycle[28]

The policy cycle traces the emergence and implementation of political content (policy) and reveals the close interconnection between policy and politics. Polity specifies the framework for this process. The phases of the policy cycle plausibly make it clear how processes play an essential role, even in the substantive (content-related) dimension of politics (policy): "The emphasis of the policy cycle perspective is on the *process* [emphasis in the original] of policy actions and interactions involving many different political and bureaucratic players."[29] Here, policy-making is nothing other than a solution-oriented sequence of steps applied to eliminate social problems.[30] The individual phases of the policy cycle will be briefly outlined in the following six sections.

---

28 Taken from: Jann and Wegrich (2014³), p. 106.
29 Badie, Berg-Schlosser and Morlino (2011), s. v. policy cycle.
30 Jann and Wegrich (2014³), p. 97.

3.4.2.1 Problem definition

The first phase, problem definition, involves collective needs, deficits and dissatisfactions, which are conveyed to the political, administrative system from the outside and for which a solution is sought. However, societal construction of the problem, e.g. via scientific findings, information dissemination, (proactive) lobbying, is required so that a problem gains political attention.[31] This means that, firstly, the problem must be defined and secondly, the necessity of control intervention by politicians must be articulated.[32] This phase is characterised by a low level of institutionalisation.[33] A variety of stakeholders and actors take up the issues and problems, e.g. parties, citizens' initiatives, churches, intellectuals, private individuals, companies, associations or organisations (see also Section 2.3.1).

3.4.2.2 Agenda setting

Agenda setting is a transitional phase between problem definition and policy formulation. The issues have been brought to *attention* in phase 1; in the agenda-setting phase, they are now taken into *consideration* by the political, administrative decision-makers.[34] This therefore involves the reduction of issues and problems to be decided on by political players. Political resources are required to help structure the agenda. Formulated differently, the issues and problems have the greatest likelihood of success if they come e.g. from key ministerial officials and members of parliament or important representatives of public opinion (such as journalists).[35] The following additionally applies: "Framing an issue is most likely to be successful, if it can be linked with existing widely held norms or concerns."[36] This framing and the perspective change often related to it will be dealt with in greater detail in Chapter 6 (see also Chapter 10).

Due to its vertical (e.g. EU regions, EU member states) and horizontal structure (e.g. supranational institutions such as the European Parliament or European Commission), the European Union offers lobbyists a variety of options for effective agenda setting.[37] Here, lobbyists must determine who extensively determines, or perhaps even controls, the agenda. This can be an individual (e.g. a rapporteur in the European Parliament or a commissioner) or an institution (e.g. the European Commission).[38] An understanding of agenda control therefore also forms part of an understanding of agenda setting. Within the EU, control over the political agenda is primarily held by the European Commission due to its key role as the initiator of legislative processes (see Chapter 5).[39] As it often seeks advice and

---

31 Knoepfel,Larrue, Varone and Veit (2011), p. 55.
32 Jann and Wegrich (2014³), p. 107.
33 Kevenhörster (2008³), p. 341.
34 Knoepfel, Larrue,Varone and Veit (2011), p. 55.
35 Kevenhörster (2008³), p. 343.
36 Young (2010⁶), p. 52.
37 Young (2010⁶), p. 53.
38 Majone (2006), p. 229; see Hartlapp, Metz and Rauh (2014), p. 7 ff.
39 Majone (2006), p. 231.

support from external experts in this, however, this gives rise to the possibility of agenda setting here in order to promote a policy proposal via access to the Commission's administrative and working levels. Nor must it be forgotten that both the Parliament and the Council can request the Commission to take the initiative, thereby also resulting in options for agenda setting in these institutions.[40] With the European citizens' initiative according to Article 11 TEU in conjunction with Article 24 TFEU, citizens can not only trigger legislative initiatives (in the sense of the enactment of entirely new regulations) but can also request that existing regulations be amended. However, the Commission's right of initiative persists – it merely has to deal with the citizens' initiative, in the same manner as with a petition. It is therefore extremely important for lobbyists to be present during this early stage and to support the process so that legitimate interests can be introduced. This can only be accomplished if lobbying is long-term and structural in nature, and constantly "remains on the ball" in the European and member state political system.

3.4.2.3 Policy formulation and decision

In the third phase, a political, administrative programme is developed, i. e. the objectives of problem solving as well as the necessary instruments and procedures are selected.[41] The programme proposals are then condensed to form decisions.[42] Policy formulation and decisions are interdependent. A specific content-related formulation can make a decision/approval possible or necessary in the first place, because the content may require other ministerial departments or another ministry in the member states or another Directorate General in the European Commission to deal with it, or may necessitate the involvement of another expert committee in the European Parliament. In extreme cases, reciprocal offsetting and the exchange of issues and policy (so-called log rolling) occur. This may particularly be the case if unanimity is demanded in the Council of the EU. One example of this was the Savings Taxation Directive in the year 2000. Hans Eichel, German's minister of finance at that time, reports that Italy had announced a "veto" during the negotiations if the Council did not simultaneously increase Italy's milk quotas when it voted to approve the Savings Taxation Directive. It should incidentally be noted that this policy was not formally the responsibility of the Council of Finance Ministers. However, Italy's tactic was successful: by telephone, the finance ministers persuaded their relevant member states' ministers of agriculture to give the required assurances. Only this encouraged Italy to approve the Savings Taxation Directive.[43]

---

40 Young (2010[6]), p. 53.
41 Knoepfel, Larrue, Varone and Veit (2011), p. 55; Jann and Wegrich (2014[3]), p. 110.
42 Kevenhörster (2008[3]), p. 346.
43 Joos (2014), p. 36.

The political arena therefore changes over time. Whilst many different issues are still on the table and numerous actors and stakeholders are involved in issue definition and agenda setting at the start of a policy cycle in the EU, and also generally, experience has shown that these numbers decline as the process continues. The issues are bundled to form packages, and the actors and stakeholders have joined together in groups and formed coalitions. At the end, only proponents and opponents are left facing each other, and only detailed aspects such as funding, possible exceptions and the time of implementation remain to be clarified.[44] However, these detailed aspects also give rise to a variety of points of reference for successful lobbying.

Decisions are not therefore made solely based on the specifications of democratic institutions such as parliament or government, but also on the basis of intensive relationships with stakeholders, professional groups and clients of all kinds.[45] This is particularly the case in the EU, where the institutions are required to engage in intensive dialogue with civil society (Article 11 TEU). With regard to the decision-making process, see, above all, Section 3.8.

At EU level, the policy formulation process is similar to that of agenda setting: the legislative proposals are primarily formulated in the Commission. The administration plays a material role in this – and later on in policy implementation. However, it is also interesting how decisions and policy formulations come about in the institutions, since they could at least *de facto* delegate parts of this process. The two regulatory agencies, the European Medicines Agency (EMA) and the European Food Safety Authority (EFSA), for example, are the Commission's most important advisors in their respective specialist field. At EU institution level, "external" advice is obtained with regard to questions and decisions in these areas.[46]

In summary, it remains to be stated that lobbying must give consideration to both the most important actors as well as the potential and actual parameters of policy formulation and decision-making (e.g. the party membership of a Member of the European Parliament), i.e. also the potential "veto players". This means that focus must also be placed on those actors which show the least enthusiasm towards a policy and "could block everything". The Commission, for example, could refuse to table a legislative proposal for a decision. Each individual member of the Council could be a veto player. If unanimity is required, a veto by an individual member state is sufficient; in the case of decisions requiring a qualified majority, a blocking minority of at least four EU members, which must in turn represent a sufficiently large section of the EU's population, suffices (see Chapter 5 for detail). However, the European Parliament can also withhold its approval in the ordinary legislative procedure.

44 Schendelen (2013), p. 175.
45 Kevenhörster (2008[3]), p. 21.
46 Pollack (2010[6]), p. 33.

3.4.2.4 Policy implementation

The implementation phase involves the practical handling, the implementation and the execution of a policy. The special consideration of the implementation phase is that political and administrative actions cannot be ultimately controlled through objective specifications, action programmes or laws, and that the intentions of political programmes can be delayed, modified and, in the worst case, even thwarted in this phase, e.g. due to the lack of implementation, selective implementation or reformulation of a policy by the administration (bureaucratic drift).[47]

The key elements of this phase are: programme clarification (how and by whom should the programme be implemented? How is a law to be interpreted?), resource provision (distribution of financial resources, selection of organisational units and personnel for executing the programme) and decision (how is a decision made in an individual case?).[48]

Within the EU, it is not always the institutions in Brussels that are responsible for implementing policies. Some policies, such as those concerning cartel or competition issues, are aimed at the Commission; others, such as the Stability and Growth Pact, are aimed at the member state governments. Above all, the EU policies which directly impact individuals and companies are regulations and directives. Whilst the former have a direct impact, the latter first have to be implemented by the member states.[49] Process support opportunities particularly arise for lobbyists on implementation by the member states, since directives can most certainly still allow the member states scope for interpretation.

3.4.2.5 Policy evaluation

In the fifth phase, the results of implementation are evaluated: have the state activities and policies helped to solve the problem? Has a policy also had unforeseen and unintended results? Administrative evaluation is undertaken by the administration, and political evaluation by the actors of the political system, whether through the government (e.g. by means of government reports), by the political opposition or through public debate.[50]

In EU politics, the evaluation process is difficult, as definition and structuring take place at supranational, European level (in this regard, particularly the Commission and Parliament), as does decision-making (even though the Council is an inter-governmental committee). However, implementation (see Section 3.4.2.4) is usually carried out at national, member state level. Directives are implemented by the member states. Of course, regulations which apply directly throughout the EU

---

47 See Jann and Wegrich (2014[3]), pp. 114–117; Knoepfel, Larrue, Varone and Veit (2011), p. 55.
48 Jann and Wegrich (2014[3]), p. 114.
49 Young (2010[6]), p. 62.
50 Jann and Wegrich (2014[3]), pp. 117–122.

also develop their effects in the member states. The European Union nevertheless subjects its policies to constant evaluation. The Commission actually refers to this as one of its main tools for measuring the success of its policies: "Evaluation is the main tool used by the European Commission to assess the extent to which EU action is achieving the set policy objectives, and how performance can be improved in future. The Commission requires that all activities addressed to external parties must be regularly evaluated in proportion with the resources allocated and the expected impact."[51]

Added to this are reactions to EU policies directly from the member states; these can also be termed "evaluation in the wider sense". The public, stakeholders or also member state governments critically assess EU politics and EU legislation. The German federal government, for instance, has brought proceedings before the European Court of Justice (ECJ) against the classification of what is called EEG apportionment as a subsidy in the sense of European law (in Germany, the expansion of renewable energy is being funded e.g. through surcharges on electricity bills as part of the German Renewable Energy Act (EEG)).[52] The ECJ's rulings can therefore also amount to the evaluation of policies; ultimately, the ECJ checks policies as regards their legality. In colloquial terms, a variety of feedback loops are in place in the EU.

3.4.2.6 Policy termination

Evaluation may also result in the termination of a political programme. Often, however, this does not mean that a policy is completely ended; instead, a policy change takes place and the policy cycle starts again from the beginning.[53]

The amendment of the regulation on maximum CO2 emissions for passenger cars is an example of a policy termination which led to a policy modification by imposing new CO_2 emission limits on new passenger cars in order to achieve the set climate protection targets. Once the EU Commission had ascertained that the desired climate targets could not be achieved with the existing regulation, the regulation was revised and a proposal for a new regulation submitted. This procedure presented all actors and the lobbyists with a further opportunity to support the policy process. The policy cycle started again.

The criticism levelled at this model is that the policy cycle takes a rather hazy approach to analysing the major political processes. A rational, linear, systematic and problem-oriented procedure is suggested.[54] It is claimed that policy-making does not necessarily take place in the sequence proposed by the policy cycle: sometimes, a policy is formulated even before it has been publicly recognised as a

---

51 European Commission (2005–2015).
52 Schultz (2015).
53 Jann and Wegrich (2014³), p. 120.
54 Badie, Berg-Schlosser and Morlino (2011), s.v. policy cycle; Blum and Schubert (2009), pp. 130–134.

problem.[55] The impression can also arise that there is only one policy cycle, whereas there are a number of cycles, including asynchronous ones, at the various levels of a governmental system.[56] This is particularly important in the multi-level governance system of the EU. Ultimately, it is bemoaned that this merely involves a heuristic description, but that this does not explain why it behaves in such a manner.[57]

What is firstly relevant to lobbying is that it is bound to the circumstances and framework specified by the multi-level system of the European Union. Here, policy cycle analysis reveals a variety of access options, which can and should be exploited, for process support. It helps to structure the complex procedures of the political process and thus reduce their complexity. However, it must always be remembered that this is a model, and that it perhaps does proceed somewhat too hazily. Politics can sometimes be a very amorphous process, with a variety of institutional (e.g. Commission, Parliament) or individual actors (e.g. Commissioners, members of parliament), with member states and regions, all of which are attempting to introduce their respective content and interests into the process. It is all the more important for lobbying to also constantly keep sight of the informal processes of policy-making as well as the formal procedures and, by maintaining corresponding structures (representations and personnel on site), to be able to monitor the variety of processes running asynchronously and in parallel (monitoring).

3.5 Temporal dimension of politics

It has become clear that the above mentioned political dimensions, particularly the policy-making process with the policy cycle, run against the backdrop of a further political dimension, time. Polity (EU treaties, institutions and their tasks, etc.) is "created", changed over time and adapted to new conditions (e.g. the EU's eastward enlargement). It is therefore subject to temporal determinisms, but moves slowest when regarded in terms of time.[58] Policies also "have their time" and are subject to societal flows and interests which change over time. At the time of political Europe's establishment in the 1950s, environmental policy was far less important than it is in the EU today. The importance of time and correct timings is most clearly revealed in the case of politics, with many parallel procedures and decision-making processes of daily political activity. Although not all of the phases run precisely in the above listed policy cycle sequence in practice, it becomes clear that policy-making is a process and, consequently, that a time compo-

---

55 Young (2010[6]); Blum and Schubert (2009), p. 130.
56 Young (2010[6]), p. 47.
57 Jann and Wegrich (2014[3]), pp. 122–123.
58 With regard to time determinism, to which polity is subject, see Plato's *state*, with an introduction to constitutional change, in: Nohlen and Schultze (2010[4]), s.v. time and politics.

nent is immanent in the political system as a whole.[59] The temporal dimension does not involve the content-related logic underlying a political decision, but is instead concerned with the political management of time.[60]

The relevance of political time slots to policy research is shown e.g. in the so-called "multiple stream approach" (MSA). According to this, political decisions arise from the interaction of problems, political action options and conflicted decision-making processes which develop independently of one another. Political decisions only become possible if the actors concerned succeed in linking these three "streams".[61] However, this linking cannot take place at any time or under all conditions. The key question in the MSA is: "(…) what makes an idea's time come?".[62] Time therefore becomes an important variable.

The opening of time slots, in which the establishment of contact between lobbyists and politicians appears to be most promising, in each phase of the policy cycle is of particular importance to lobbying. Formulated in common parlance: it is important to wait for the right moment. This is regardless of whether formal deadlines for inputs and proposals have to be observed or consideration simply has to be given to political decision-makers' schedules. It would certainly not be helpful to want to contact Members of the European Parliament and their employees in Brussels if the Parliament is currently meeting in Strasbourg. This would be time management at the micro level. At the macro level, it is necessary to regard the policy cycle as a whole and monitor it sensitively. Because, as has been shown, time is a political resource: "Even when time is scarce and the margins for its use as a background factor of action small, the differences in the competence of using time may gain significance, and playing with the margins of temporality can be trusted into a decisive instance in a political struggle."[63] The tactical use of time is revealed in the fact that actors who imagine themselves to be "certain of victory" because e.g. they believe that they have public opinion and political majorities behind them, want to drive forwards and speed up the policy cycle, whereas those who feel disadvantaged by a policy and see themselves on the "losing side" will be more likely to attempt to delay and slow things down.[64] This therefore results in various policy-making time slots in the political process; these can be subdivided into endogenous, exogenous and structural time slots.[65]

3.5.1 Endogenous time slots

Endogenous time slots arise due to the nature of the political process and the policy cycle. This means that the actors seek opportunities to open up a time slot from

---

59 With regard to the temporal dimension of politics, see Palonen (2003).
60 Rüb (2006), p. 24.
61 See Brückner (2013), p. 50.
62 Kingdon (2003), p. 1.
63 Palonen (2003), p. 174.
64 Schendelen (2013), p. 175.
65 de Figueiredo (2004), pp. 5 ff.

the "problem stream" – which is not easy, because political processes are usually characterised by significant time pressure and unclear preferences.[66] The circumstance that politicians are often on the lookout for issues with which they can be identified is helpful in this case. Potential problems and possible solution approaches compete for attention and recognition here. However, only a limited number of issues can be taken up.[67] As time is a scant resource in the political process, the responsible decision-makers' preferences are usually formed according to the particular situation ("Strike whilst the iron is hot."/"Make hay whilst the sun shines."). It can be seen here that the solution option and problem are not inevitably directly related. Focus is on the "solution". It seeks out a suitable problem onto which it can dock. It is not the content of the solution and its importance to the elimination of the problem which are crucial, but the solution itself as an act of decision.[68] This may, for example, be the case during election campaigns or if a government's standing in the opinion polls is low and it wants to improve its reputation amongst the electorate through (inverted) "actionism". It is therefore in the nature of the democratic political system that its actors pick up on socially "popular" sentiments and orient their decisions towards these. Endogenous time slots can also arise from policy evaluation and policy termination (see Sections 3.4.2.5 and 3.4.2.6) if the evaluation of a policy leads to the conclusion that it must be amended or abolished. This results in opportunities for lobbyists to make contact at the right point in time, as the "cards are reshuffled" in such a time slot and it is therefore possible to introduce interests into a policy which is to be amended or its successor.

3.5.2 Exogenous time slots

Time slots can also arise as a result of exogenous events which are initially outside of the ongoing political processes and the policy cycle. These are usually crises, which politicians quickly embrace and to which they have to find answers. Issues and policies which have thus far been disregarded by politicians or which have only been dealt with on the margins therefore shift to the centre of political attention.[69]

A particularly striking exogenous time slot, which opened up in energy policy, was seen in 2011 in the EU member state of Germany. Whilst 2010 was marked by energy and economic policy considerations related to the extension of the remaining operating times of nuclear power plants, the situation changed abruptly following the damage suffered by a Japanese nuclear power station in Fukushima in 2011. The Fukushima catastrophe triggered a major public debate surrounding the future energy policy in Germany, during the course of which German Federal

---

66 See Brückner (2013), p. 65.
67 See Brückner (2013), p. 54.
68 Rogge (2010), p. 211.
69 Young (2010[6]), pp. 52–53.

Chancellor Angela Merkel, who had "accepted" the residual risk of nuclear power up to that point, reassessed the situation. [70] Environmental policy arguments (reactor safety, the problem of final radioactive waste storage) and – according to some – political opportunities (Landtag elections) now gained the upper hand over supply security arguments. This led to a turnaround in Germany's energy policy and the acceleration of its phasing-out of nuclear energy.[71] At European level, the BSE crisis is one example which made the headlines. Whilst food safety regulations were handled rather sloppily in the 1980s, this changed with the emergence of what was termed "mad cow disease" (bovine spongiform encephalopathy, BSE) and the extensive media coverage which ensued. The result was more cautious food safety regulation.[72] Such exogenous events therefore gave rise to new political facts, which opened up decision-making windows and led to policy reappraisal and amendments. Because the dictum "if the facts change, I change my mind" is not infrequently true in politics, too.

3.5.3 Structural time slots

When time slots are opened up due to constantly recurring events rather than one-off incidents, they are referred to as structural time slots. For instance, structural time slots open up during the course of a change in the political power and legitimacy structure (reassignment of political positions in the executive and legislature) and are therefore also based on institutionalised time rhythms. For Germany, these include elections at European, federal, state and communal level as well as the reassignment of official positions.[73] Other recurring events which open up structural time slots for a policy include annual reports on political issues such as the German Government's poverty report. This offers lobbying aimed at social policy a good opportunity to make contact and actively support the policy cycle. Statistics as well as new scientific and economic findings can help to make a potential problem "quantifiable" in order to steer political attention to a specific issue. The actors involved then have the opportunity to intervene into the decision-making process and speed up decision-making. On the other hand, the objective may be to delay a decision, in the hope that future findings and insights will strengthen one's own bargaining position.[74]

Structural time slots are simpler to assess and easier to calculate in strategic terms due to the recurring events on which they are based.[75] All events produced due to the political system fall into this category: parliamentary dissolutions, coalition changes, no-confidence votes, procedural deadlines, decision deadlines, etc. In the

---

70 N.U. (2011a).
71 With regard to the turnaround in German energy policy in general: Baden-Württemberg State Centre for Political Education.
72 Young (2010[6]), p. 53.
73 Rüb (2006), p. 24; de Figueiredo (2004), p. 7.
74 Rüb (2006), p. 4.
75 Kaiser (2010).

political decision-making process, lobbyists are only able to make use of spontaneous, pragmatic and intuitive actions as an instrument of lobbying to a limited extent. In addition to the question of when time slots open and close, the matter of the right "timing" and an understanding of the underlying processes (process competence) is therefore also relevant. The institutional framework enables the temporal structuring of decision-making processes and political decision-making.[76]

The recognition of time slots is one of the most difficult aspects of a lobbyist's work. Major exogenous crises and events are also easily identifiable to laymen, but the "minor events" which sometimes open up endogenous and structural time slots can only be detected through structural monitoring of the political system. The lobbyist must be so close to the political action that he can virtually "hear the [political] grass growing". In other words, he must be very familiar with the political processes and political discussions and content in order to know which stage a policy is currently in and whether it will make it from the problem definition phase to the agenda setting phase. In part, this is also dependent on the assertiveness of the political actors who take up such an issue. If the topic is appropriate, it is even possible for an actor to make the legitimate interests of the interest group concerned his own and therefore (along with the lobbyists and interest group) "take responsibility for the issue" and personally drive the political process (policy cycle) forwards (so-called endogenous approach, see Section 7.3.1). If lobbyists succeed in identifying the relevant actors and decision-makers at such an early stage of the policy cycle, they have the opportunity of making contact with the relevant contact persons and supporting the process early on. Effective time and process management are therefore at least as important for political lobbying as performing tasks at the content-related, factual level. Temporal prioritisation, called "temporal sorting", plays a central role in this context.[77] This results in a clear advantage to lobbyists which work on a process basis (such as governmental relations agencies) vis-à-vis those which tend to focus on content, and which have less of an affinity towards political processes and may therefore possibly miss the endogenous, exogenous and structural time slots which occur.

3.6 Political actors

As has been shown, politics has an extensive procedural dimension. However, this process necessitates the activity of actors. "Today, it is no longer sufficient to simply base politics on societal problems and political pressure due to problems, and to attempt to transform objective pressure stemming from problems directly into collective actions. Ultimately, the fact that societal problems make it onto the po-

---

76 See Brückner (2013), pp. 65 and 71.
77 See Zahariadis (2003), pp. 4–5.

litical agenda and are transformed into political programmes is dependent on whether the relevant actors notice these problems, recognise their concern [or the need for action] and mobilise resources for political problem solving."[78] Actors are those who act politically (Lat. *actor*, the one who does something, who acts) and are involved in decisions.[79] They pursue specific interests and action objectives, have the resources to act as well as normative orientations and possess the capability to act strategically. Some take part in the entire political process, whilst others are only involved in certain phases.[80] The political process is inconceivable without actors; they articulate the political content and interests: "Just as interests cannot materialise in the political process without actors, the actors that play a role in the political process always defend interests, even if they do not appear to do so at first glance."[81] From an action theory perspective, they consciously or unconsciously introduce their interests, values, objectives and preferences according to what is possible in the situation.[82]

At first glance, the actors in politics appear to be clearly identifiable: politicians. They are at the centre of media attention, particularly if they hold high offices. Commissioners, party whips, rapporteurs in the Parliament, high-ranking party officials, member state ministers or opposition leaders make policy. However, this is done in co-operation with civil servants and/or political employees from the institutions in which they work. They are all so-called individual actors.[83] As already indicated, however, the individual actors only occur very rarely as lone wolves in political activities. They are usually organised collectively, e. g. in political parties or political groups in parliament. Stakeholders such as trade unions, associations, churches, organisations and think tanks are also so-called collective actors. However, individual actors can also be found in the polity institutions, e. g. in the EU Commission or the Council. These so-called institutional actors make up the third group.[84]

Although the following will deal primarily with the individual, collective and institutional actors, it must nevertheless be emphasised that the member states and regions play a significant role as political actors in the multi-level system of the European Union; they can occur as both institutional and collective actors, e. g. the government of a member state. However, they are also – usually indirectly – represented by individuals. The member states are institutionally represented in the European Council and in the Council of the EU (also commonly referred to as the Council of Ministers); in turn, the regions are represented in the Commit-

---

78 Schneider (2014³), p. 282.
79 Nohlen and Schultze (2010⁴), s. v. actor.
80 Jarren and Donges (2011³), p. 129.
81 Meyer (2003), p. 114.
82 See Nohlen and Schultze (2010⁴), s. v. actor.
83 Blum and Schubert (2009), p. 52.
84 Political actor could also be categorised differently from the perspective of political communication: interest articulation actors, interest aggregation actors and policy assertion actors (see Jarren and Donges (2011³), p. 130).

tee of the Regions. However, both member states and regions are represented by individual persons in all EU institutions: each EU state has a Commissioner; Commission officials originate from the 28 member states and are employed on the basis of proportionality; in addition to the parties/groups, the parliamentarians also and above all represent their nations and constituencies/regions, where they are ultimately elected. Although it should not actually play a role at European level, the respective national and regional origin of political actors cannot be entirely overlooked. The reason for this is that, in the complex, multi-level political system of the EU, member states and regions face precisely the same challenges as other political actors, and have to proceed in precisely the same manner as these in implementing their interests. This could also include the instrumentalisation of the actors' national or regional origin (see Sections 4.5.2 and 4.5.3).

It must also be remembered that the political process in itself can become an actor and decision-maker, if legislative procedure and rules of procedure deadlines compel actors to act, for instance. Even if the actors do not consciously intervene into, or halt, a political process, the process can bring about a decision by itself: if, for example, the European Parliament does not issue a statement during certain phases in the ordinary legislative procedure, it virtually approves a submission through its lack of action[85] (see Chapter 5). The actors should have acted consciously and intervened into the process in order to be able to help structure it in this case. The process itself therefore indirectly becomes the "actor" and "decision-maker".

3.6.1 Individual actors[86]

"Politicians", as "the makers" of policy, are at the centre of media attention. As explained in Section 3.5.1, politicians are often on the lookout for issues with which they can make a name for themselves, whether this be through projects in their constituency (e. g. infrastructure) or innovative (and headline-grabbing) policies at national level. As individual, political actors, it is the task of politicians to pick up on "popular" societal sentiments and participate in political agenda setting. Ultimately, they are the representatives of their voters and often hold offices with a legal or even constitutional status, through which they exercise the power delegated to them. They are therefore the most familiar individual actors in politics.

In political reality, however, not only officials and political representatives are involved in politics, i. e. in policy-making. Many more individual actors are engaged in political activities in the background than actually appear in the spotlight. In political reality, power is not exercised solely by politicians. This does not arise

---

85 See Article 294 TFEU, the second reading in the ordinary legislative procedure: "If, within three months of such communication, the European Parliament approves the Council's position at first reading or has not taken a decision, the act concerned shall be deemed to have been adopted in the wording which corresponds to the position of the Council."

86 This section is a revised version from Joos (2011), pp. 32–35.

from a more restrictive definition of legitimacy but from everyday political practice. The reasons for this are that, due to the wealth of appointments and information, and ultimately because of the above average complexity of the content, politicians require support. No politician can take note of everything that is presented to him, not even what interests him directly. Politicians are reliant on their employees to cope with their workload. It is therefore clear that these employees have a certain degree of influence over political processes. This is a product of their jobs; they write speeches and press releases, manage appointments and process incoming and outgoing mail. Whilst the actors behind the scenes are bound by instructions, they have a significant influence on the politicians. It is therefore worthwhile for lobbying (on the basis of two examples: one at European and one at member state level) to analyse this group of individual political actors.

Example of the office manager

The position of office manager is a common one on the political scene.[87] The office manager is a loyal and close confidante of his superior. The office manager typically co-ordinates the staff of a Commissioner, high-ranking EU official, minister, state secretary or members of parliament, and is therefore a prime example of an individual acting behind the scenes. His duties often include processing mail, managing the appointment schedule and co-ordinating work within the office. Above all, however, he pre-selects information and presents the main points to his superior.[88] He also prepares the bases for decision-making and, indeed, also voices his own opinions and priorities. This clearly shows the power that the office manager wields: by no means least, he decides what information is submitted to the actual political decision-maker or whether or not someone is granted an appointment for a meeting. The office manager occasionally steers his superior's entire working day. Often, he also advises the latter on important political matters. Without any doubt, an office manager has a certain level of influence on the politician and thus on political activity as a whole – he therefore has more power than his position would suggest in purely hierarchical terms.[89]

Example of the Chief Whip or parliamentary manager

The example of the parliamentary manager can be cited from a member state perspective: all parliamentary groups in Germany's Bundestag have parliamentary managers who perform this function alongside their elective office.[90] They are nevertheless often unknown in public. Without them, however, almost nothing would happen in parliament: "Parliamentary managers are the machine operators, technicians, the stokers of power. They decide on opportunities within the parliamentary group, on speaking times, resources, offices, agendas, motions, etc.

---

87 See Kuhn (2007).
88 See Schneider (2007).
89 See Neukirch (2009).
90 For exhaustive information see Petersen (2000).

(...) They are the silent string-pullers in the background."[91] They ensure the party takes a co-ordinated stand and endeavour to ensure unanimity in parliamentary votes. The parliamentary managers are therefore amongst the most influential politicians. This is particularly due to the fact that they act as close confidantes and advisors to the parliamentary group leader by defining issues and approaches together with him and keeping him abreast of opinions and processes within the political group. The position of parliamentary manager therefore involves the greatest possible influence within the group. However, it has no legal basis in the rules of procedure of the German Bundestag – let alone in the German constitution or the *Abgeordnetengesetz* (Act on the Legal Status of Members of the German Bundestag). It merely originates from the rules of procedure of the relevant political groups.

Such a function can also be found in other parliaments: in British parliamentarianism, the influential organisers behind the scenes are referred to as "whips".[92] Their primary task is to co-ordinate voting behaviour; they also organise their parties' interests in terms of parliamentary work. There is no directly comparable position in the European Parliament; the closest equivalent here would be the Quaestors in the Bureau of Parliament, who are responsible for MEP administration and budget issues. In addition to the two outlined positions, there are, of course, also other powerful functions in the political system which are not necessarily recognised as such, e.g. the group specialists.[93] The Commissioners' cabinets or the rapporteurs in the European Parliament are examples of this at EU level (see Chapter 4).

As a rough summary, it can be stated that politicians and their employees embody the individual level of polity.

For lobbying, this results in the necessity of identifying the key players amongst the individual actors for a specific initiative and providing them with targeted information. The key persons in the European Parliament, for example, include the rapporteurs and shadow rapporteurs in the committees; these are charged by the committee majority (rapporteur) or by the parliamentary groups (shadow rapporteur) with looking after a specific dossier. Further opinion leaders include the so-called co-ordinators (the groups' specialist policy speakers) and the chairpersons and deputy chairpersons of the committees themselves. If the dossier concerned is very complicated and technical, cross-committee and cross-faction work groups are often set up (as, for example, in the case of the European Services Directive in the European Parliament[94]). Since these work groups are tasked with finding a compromise, maintaining close contact with the group members may also be appropriate under certain circumstances.

---

91 Walter (2007).
92 Parliament of the United Kingdom.
93 See Püschner (2009), pp. 33–40.
94 See Arnold (2008), p. 25 ff.

3.6.2 Collective and corporate actors

Politics does not consist solely of individuals operating independently/in isolation from each other. The political actors are usually organised in groups, i.e. in citizens' initiatives, a political movement or in parties which, insofar as they are represented in parliament, in turn form parliamentary groups. Strictly speaking, a government or the totality of EU Commissioners is also such a collective of political actors. These are examples of collective actors within polity institutions. However, there are also collective actors which are not employed within one of the state institutions. These include the corporate actors, e.g. corporate associations and trade unions. Collective and corporate actors cannot be clearly distinguished from one another and are interwoven "phenomena". However, corporate actors reveal a higher level of organisation with hierarchies than a group of individual actors in a collective (e.g. a citizens' initiative), and the representatives of the corporate actors are not reliant on their basis for each decision within their activities.[95] Collective and corporate actors play a particular role in policy-making in the EU, which is afforded them according to Article 11 TEU. Paragraph 2 states: "The institutions shall maintain an open, transparent and regular dialogue with representative associations and civil society."

In particular, consolidation of the internal market in recent decades has led to the intensification of efforts by corporate actors at EU level.[96] With its intermesh of European, member state and regional political processes, the EU multi-level system offers numerous opportunities for participating in political decision-making.[97] However, a high level of organisation on the part of European associations is not necessarily equivalent to extensive "capability to act". Due to the heterogeneous interests of their members, European associations are often faced with the difficulty of bundling different positions at several levels and transforming them into clear and meaningful standpoints. The association does not always succeed in making the transition from a communication forum to a crucial collective, political actor. According to political scientists Rainer Eising and Beate Kohler-Koch, it is not therefore surprising that "European association federations" are "declining in value as dialogue partners for the European institutions"[98] (with regard to the heterogeneity problem of associations, see also Section 6.4.1.1).

As the institutional framework of the EU fosters the level of organisation of European interest groups, the corporatist and collective actors – like lobbying in general – have now become extensively differentiated in Brussels. Transnationally organised corporate associations (e.g. European Automobile Manufacturers' Association, ACEA), trade unions (e.g. European Trade Union Confederation, ETUC)

---

95 Blum and Schubert (2009), p. 53.
96 Eising and Kohler-Koch (2005), p. 15.
97 See Eising and Kohler-Koch (2005), p. 25.
98 Eising and Kohler-Koch (2005), p. 15.

and other organisations (NGOs, environmental associations, charity and human rights groups, churches, etc.) are now extensively present with their own representative offices in Brussels. In science, they are usually described as the representatives of idealistic issues or specific social groups. The European Commission and the European Parliament also support the co-operation and mergers of such collective actors financially, in order to enable non-economic groups and those with low participation to become involved in European decision-making.[99]

The media, which are often referred to as the fourth power alongside the legislature, the executive and the judiciary, are not to be underestimated as political actors. The mediation of political information through mass media has now assumed tremendous importance. This – incomplete – list shows that political actors are often so-called collective actors which are characterised by a certain degree of organisation, interest aggregation and, above all, a certain goal orientation.

3.6.3 Institutional actors

The so-called institutional actors are a third important group of political actors. The political system of the EU is characterised by the fact that the various legislative and executive competencies are not held by any one of the EU institutions alone, but by the Commission, the Council and the European Parliament, sometimes individually, sometimes in complex interaction.[100] The institutional actors therefore have extensive political influence – not only at EU level.

The Commission not only has a legislative monopoly which enables it to submit proposals on any issue and at any time in the area of European legislation; it is also responsible for drawing up a range of other legally non-binding documents (Green and White Papers, road maps, memoranda and recommendations). It accordingly assumes a privileged role within European legislation which enables it to pre-structure the political decision-making processes. As a result of this, the Commission is also regarded as a central contact for organised interests.[101] The European Commission's consultation offers include meetings with experts, NGOs and organised civil society, the work of advisory committees and expert groups as well as workshops, seminars, conferences and online consultations.[102] This formal process of information exchange is directly sought and maintained by the European Commission. In addition, interest groups make efforts to engage in exchange with the Commission via informal channels. These include bilateral meetings with the employees of the departments in the Directorates General and in the President's, the Vice Presidents' and the Commissioners' cabinets.

---

99 See Eising and Kohler-Koch (2005), p. 24.
100 Schmedes (2010), p. 23.
101 Kaiser (2010).
102 See Kohler-Koch and Quittkat (2011), pp. 74–75.

Although it does not have the direct right of initiative, the European Parliament has increasingly gained in importance as an institutional political actor for lobbyists through the successive expansion of the scope of the co-decision procedure (also referred to as the "ordinary legislative procedure" since the Treaty of Lisbon) to almost all important areas of policy. The Members of the European Parliament maintain correspondingly open dealings with the different interest groups. Through this contact, the elected representatives hope to achieve "not only access to special knowledge but also recourse to the Union citizens and their concerns".[103] As the offices of the members of parliament have relatively few employees (one to two local assistants); the specialist advice of stakeholders is readily accepted and co-operation is also undertaken across parliamentary groups. In this context, it must be mentioned that there is no stringent whip line in the European Parliament.[104] The voting behaviour of the individual members of parliament is therefore significantly more individual than in the member state parliaments. The Federal Association of German Industry (BDI) comes to the conclusion that the voting behaviour is more difficult to assess than, for example, in the German Bundestag.[105] In the European Parliament, a distinction can be made between formal (public consultations, issue-related events, parliamentary evenings, etc.) and informal lobbying (one-to-one meetings with the members of parliament). Intensive and trusting, long-term maintenance of contacts is usually the basic prerequisite for successfully introducing interests using the informal route, and should not therefore first start with the submission of specific concerns. Reaching out to important members of parliament and their assistants as well as group and committee employees at an early stage is therefore appropriate for lobbying.

As an institutional actor, the Council of the EU also plays an essential role. It decides, i.e. together with the Parliament, on laws which are enacted in the ordinary legislative procedure. The primary contact for lobbying in this case is always the EU Council Presidency, as it is responsible for finding compromises within the Council, and regularly draws up compromise texts which are forwarded to the national delegations for examination. At the start of the procedure, the chairperson of the Council work group responsible for the legislation is therefore firstly an important point of contact. During the procedure, the focus shifts to the individual member states. At this point in time, the Council is no longer addressed as an "institutional actor". Interaction between interest groups and the Council then usually takes place indirectly via the permanent representations of the 28 member states (from the responsible attaché to the ambassador) or at national level via the relevant governments (from the responsible ministry official to the minister).[106]

---

103 Schemdes (2010), p. 23.
104 European Parliament (2015).
105 Federal Association of German Industry BDI (2009).
106 See Schemdes (2010), p. 23.

It is to be assumed that the relevant actors do not proceed unilaterally but are bound to one another through legislative procedures, rules of procedure, etc., and co-operate collectively or in sub-groups. Individual actors are integrated into a collective or an institution, for example. Through the new Commission structure created in 2014 and special instructions respectively, Commissioners and Commission officials, for instance, are bound more extensively than before to the way in which their institution functions.[107] On the other hand, the previously mentioned bureaucratic drift also exists. This means, for example, that Commission officials at the working level, whether as a result of delegation or on their own initiative, make decisions or modify policy proposals without these being known at the "higher levels".[108] "In any political system, countless important policy decisions are made by the bureaucracy rather than the legislature. By delegating decisions, the legislature takes advantage of the bureaucracy's expertise in the policy area under consideration."[109]

The individual actors' scope of action and the policy-shaping power of the (institutional) system into which they are integrated must be regarded as complementary (so-called actor-centred institutionalism).[110] It must also be stated that "state programmes are not normally produced by one unitary actor which has all of the required resources at its disposal (…), that they are [instead] the product of strategic interactions between several or a variety of political actors, each of which has its own understanding of the nature of the problem and the feasibility of specific solutions, and each of which additionally has separate individual and institutional [and collective] self-interests plus normative preferences and own resources."[111] The central objective of successful lobbying work must be to give consideration to all actors (individual, collective and institutional) which are directly and indirectly involved in the political process.

3.7 Political networks

As individual political actors, politicians are basically only subject to their conscience and general laws. However, politicians are very rarely able to make decisions independently and alone – with the exception of special power assigned through the constitution, such as that enjoyed by heads of government and presidents, for instance. However, these are usually also limited in their freedom to act and make decisions. As a rule, individual politicians, and in some cases even large institutions such as ministries, do not have the resources (employees, specialist

---

107 N.U. (2015a).
108 N.U. (2015a).
109 This also makes the administration an interesting contact for lobbying (Bennedsen and Feldman (2006), p. 643).
110 Mayntz and Scharpf (1995); Scharpf (2000); a good summary of the approach can be found in: Waschkuhn (2002), pp. 116–121.
111 Scharpf (2000), p. 34.

knowledge, majorities, etc.) which would be required for autonomous policy-making.[112] As was clearly shown in the agenda setting phase of the policy cycle (Section 3.4.2.2), it is not sufficient to generate impartial "pressure due to a problem" in order to place an issue on the political agenda, because in the modern, complex world of politics, there are now only a very few "impartialities" according to which a judgement could be made (see Section 3.2). Whether something is placed on the political agenda is much more dependent on the fact that relevant actors become aware of a problem and want to adopt it.[113] Networks form in politics as a result of this circumstance; politics becomes the "complex bargaining of multiple and heterogeneous actors".[114] Networks are a necessity in political practice, because an individual actor, even if this involves an institutional actor (such as the Commission) or a collective actor (such as a political group in the European Parliament), does not have the resources necessary for an autonomous policy by itself. The various policy sectors are so complex that all actors also require specialist information from other sectors and thus form connections, the number of which increases exponentially. This is evaluated positively in political science, because the bigger a network, the more opinions are represented in it; the more actors compete with one another within it, the better the policy output. Networks are also important in policy implementation[115] – a recognition that has only emerged since the 1970s. Up to that point, a rather more mechanistic understanding prevailed: the state plans, regulates and controls individual areas of policy as a dominant and extensively autonomous actor.[116] Interestingly, this image is still sometimes predominant in public opinion today. Not least because of this, the media and the public have a rather reserved view of political networks, and occasionally refer to them as "old boy networks" or "nepotism".[117] Science bemoans the fact that the networks are self-contained and that outsiders are therefore unable to obtain access. Networks can also materialise or exist purely due to reasons of personal loyalty between their members.[118]

Regarded rationally, a network is at first nothing other than a "mesh of (social, economic and/or political) relationships, designed more or less for continuity and based on voluntariness and reciprocity".[119] Not only are such networks voluntary (formally, there is not even any whip line[120]), the members of a network do not even have to agree on all points of a policy. However, they all have the same language (political and content-related technical terms) and points of reference, which enable them to discuss and establish a platform for debate.[121]

---

112 Schneider (2014[3]), p. 198.
113 Schneider (2014[3]), p. 212.
114 Schneider (2014[3]), p. 212.
115 Badie, Berg-Schlosser and Morlino (2011), s.v. policy network.
116 Blum and Schubert (2009), p. 59.
117 See Blum and Schubert (2009), p. 60; Jansen (2003[2]), p. 11.
118 Kevenhörster (2008[3]), p. 334.
119 Nohlen and Schultze (2010[4]), s.v. network.
120 European Parliament (2015).
121 Badie, Berg-Schlosser and Morlino (2011), s.v. policy network.

Policy networks can be found at all levels of politics (local, regional, national, European and international level), as well as in institutions such as parliaments, ministries, in the administration and also in the interest groups. The individual actors form networks which then become visible in the shape of collective actors such as parties or political groups. However, they can also remain informal and invisible to the public. One example of an informal, non-public network was the so-called Andean Pact, an amalgamation of young politicians from the German conservatives (CDU), particularly in the 1980s and 1990s. Conversely, a publicly known network is found in the European Parliament. The conservatives and social democrats there have been co-ordinating with one another more extensively than ever before since the 2014 elections. The major coalition in the European Parliament continues to persist. Whilst there is no formal coalition agreement, agreements should no longer take place solely on an *ad hoc* basis.[122]

There is also a variety of acquaintances and networks which often form at the so-called working level between peers and across departments and entire institutions. Of course, similar personal connections exist amongst politicians within parties and parliamentary groups, as well as across group boundaries, when parliamentarians are familiar with and hold one another in high regard, e.g. through their work in a committee, or if they hold the same concern. Nationality as an informal bond between individual actors in the EU has already been mentioned. Like informal processes, networks are not specified in constitutions or EU treaties and are not therefore part of the formal polity; as they also correspond to the constitutional reality and the political culture in the member states and the EU, however, they are indeed a part of politics and have a significant influence on the structure of policies and decisions.[123] The influence of networks is particularly recognised and investigated by the political science governance approach.[124]

This now results in two challenges for lobbying: it must identify networks and their members, and must seek contact with them; secondly, lobbying must speak the networks' language, i.e. it must be conversant with the specialist terms, the points of reference and the status of the discussion. A network analysis helps to reveal the actual balance of power and actor relationships. Focus is placed on the backgrounds – how contacts are established and a network is formed. This can be based on personal friendships or also on exchange relationships, i.e. one Member of Parliament has supported another in a previous issue (contact establishment, securing a majority, etc.) and support is now requested in turn.[125]

Of course, there are more than one or just a few networks existing in parallel. One has to move away from the idea that there is only *one* political platform and *one*

---

122 Gutschker (2014).
123 Blum and Schubert (2009), pp. 59–60.
124 Lang and Leifeld (2008), p. 227; Michalowitz (2007), pp. 35–36.
125 See Michalowitz (2007), pp. 35–36.

political process. There are effectively a variety of different main and secondary arenas in the various policy areas.[126] Accordingly, there are a large number of networks, which differ in terms of their number of members, content-related issues, opinions and lifetime. They can also overlap due to the actors' being members of several networks at the same time. Members of the European Parliament, for example, can be members of several networks – in a national, a party and/or group network and possibly an issue network pertaining e.g. to social, economic or environmental policy or concerning specific legislative proposals. Whilst the former networks are easier for outsiders to recognise and comprehend, lobbyists require special process competence to discern issue networks: to do this, lobbyists must have precise knowledge of the individual actors, and the issues and interests in which they are involved. Without doubt, this necessitates long-term and precise knowledge of the political landscape, which calls for structural, sustainable and long-term lobbying, because such networks, which have grown over a number of years and decades under certain circumstances, can only be discovered *ad hoc* by chance, and *ad hoc* access to such circles is difficult to impossible.

Nonetheless, the networks amongst the EU institutions show great openness. The Commission is generally described as very open to the concerns of stakeholders. A representative of the European Chemical Industry Council (CEFIC), for instance, states: "Picking up on the point of openness (…) [it] is amazingly simple to get into the Commission. You are phoning and then there is a certain guy. They can't help you, they put you on to someone who can. It is open and transparent. You are trying to do that in Whitehall or Paris or Bonn and at close shop and secrecy and so on".[127] This openness implies that, in practice, there are hardly any self-contained in-group networks which are difficult to access by outsiders. Queries can be easily submitted by E-mail, and personal meetings are also possible. However, the Commission's openness also means increased competition between the interest groups for the civil servants' attention. As the Commission's civil servants are lacking in an extensive consultancy staff with in-depth, special knowledge, they are particularly interested in practically oriented information and data, which should certainly be taken to heart in the sense of effective lobbying: "Although the Commission is considered open and accessible, an interest's effectiveness in influencing policy directly continues to be determined by its ability to establish a positive reputation in the European political process. That is to say, by the extent to which it can establish its reputation as a provider of reliable, issue-specific and pan-European information."[128]

Due to this great importance of networks in the political process, it is essential to lobbying work for lobbyists to establish their own networks in the long term. It is an undisputed fact that the likelihood of a lobbyist's success increases when he

---

126 Kevenhörster (2008³), p. 333.
127 Quoted from Lahusen and Jauß (2001), p. 44.
128 Coen (2007), p. 339

can call on an extensive network of political contacts.[129] This primarily involves the establishment and the management of communication networks.[130] In this, the lobbyist's task is to mediate and support contact with decision-makers from the institutions of the EU and its member states. This task is sometimes very difficult. The persons employed in the political sector are usually confronted with a heavy workload and many enquiries each day. Finesse and diplomacy are therefore required. Added to these are occasionally a certain degree of class consciousness and genuine "esprit de corps". Executive-level politicians and employees are entirely aware of their elevated positions and their special working environment. EU institution employees, who have usually undergone a demanding, multi-stage selection procedure, are particularly aware of their status. This similarly applies to ministerial officials and politicians at the national level. It must not be overlooked that these are highly professional individuals who are fully aware of the influence that they wield and should accordingly be treated with the due respect. On the one hand, the establishment and maintenance of these contacts are the lobbyist's elementary skills; on the other hand, they are the high art of lobbying; they require a great deal of finesse as well as a high level of diplomatic and political instinct. In practice, this process is equivalent to tightrope walking: on the one hand, the interests should be communicated with a certain commitment and tenacity to underscore the necessity of political action.[131] On the other hand, one should never overburden or even annoy one's counterpart. The latter is a deadly sin in lobbying, and executive employees, in particular, justifiably deplore such faux pas.[132]

The essential advantage of this approach lies in the ability to establish long-term and trusting relationships with (political) decision-makers. Without such relationships, lobbying would hardly be successful, particularly in situations in which quick, direct access to decision-makers is necessary. In this context, it must again be noted that the political contact network should be structured as broadly as possible. This is especially important in the party political framework, since election results can result in power shifts – in the worst case, the lobbyist then loses his greatest capital, namely contact to high-ranking government representatives. To prevent this from happening, the lobbyist should be prepared and also maintain contact with a sufficient number of (current) opposition politicians.[133]

Finally, it should be mentioned that a lobbyist's working network should not merely be limited directly to the political arena. The pre-political sphere should also be entered, above all to pick up news and "background noise", but also for specific information research. Contact with PR and PA agencies, journalists, (specialist) lawyers and colleagues from the lobbying industry should therefore be

---

129 Brückner (2013), p. 61.
130 Kevenhörster (2008³), p. 335.
131 See Bender and Reulecke (2003), p. 120.
132 See Kreimeier (2009).
133 N. U. (2009d).

sought and maintained. An excessively strategic approach to establishing one's own network is not to be advised in any case: firstly, pure efficiency evaluation is not particularly compatible with the social phenomenon of networking, and secondly, the importance which a person may subsequently attain for one's own initiatives cannot usually be foreseen at the point in time of mutual acquaintance.

3.8 Laws of (political) decisions

So far, this chapter has underscored the importance of procedure and analysed the political actors and their interaction in the political process; the final section will now deal with how political decisions are made. This is particularly important because political processes are not completely foreseeable; depending on the actors involved in them, they may take a different course and lead to different results: "And particularly because these actors reveal different objectives and interests, have different levels of resources and can each interpret situations differently, the results of political processes are sometimes not predictable in terms of a specific result. The political process is contingent [random], i.e. it can take different courses and lead to different results depending on the actors involved."[134]

At the end, decisions are made in each phase of the political process by individual actors, irrespective of whether these act collectively or in an institution. There are, of course, exceptions. These may be, for example,majority decisions in parliaments, in government cabinets or at party conferences. However, this too always involves a collective of individuals, all of whom first have to arrive at a decision. "Public opinion" can also be perceived as collective pressure (e.g. poll values), which then compels the political actors to make decisions. As has already been indicated, a decision can also be made on a purely procedural basis (e.g. after the expiry of a deadline or approval through a lack of action). Usually, however, an individual has to make the decision. In election campaigns, party strategists consider: which issues are politically relevant? Which of them should be placed on the political agenda? Officials in the EU Commission and rapporteurs in the European Parliament ask themselves questions such as: How should the content of a draft law be structured? At member state executive level, ministers and their civil servants ask: what implementation options are available and which are actually used? Ultimately, therefore, a few individuals make decisions. The considerations underlying their decision-making have to be known in order to then enable competent support through lobbying.

Political decision-making processes have their own specific character, which differs significantly from those in other societal action areas such as the economy. These processes follow their own logic, which does not always meet external, ra-

---

134 Jarren and Donges (2011³), pp. 129–130.

tionalistically characterised expectations at first glance. There are nevertheless analysis methods which help to make the political process, with its various phases and stages, comprehensible and understandable to outsiders.

3.8.1 Homo economicus or homo politicus?

Rationalism is predominantly expected of decision-makers. It is simply assumed that they weigh up their decisions and then decide rationally. Economy, for example, can be such a rational decision-making criterion. It is therefore hardly surprising that the image of man as homo economicus, who always strives to achieve his own economic, rational advantage with maximum benefit, is extensively known and ascribed with universal validity.

The idealistic nature of homo economicus is an economic theory construct of an "ideal human being who thinks and acts exclusively according to economic motives"[135]. He is interested in economic objectives and strives to attain maximum benefit, which he wishes to achieve with efficient use of resources. He accomplishes this through his rational behaviour, which is characterised by an – apparent – knowledge of all the information. The theoretical concept of homo economicus was developed primarily to be able to describe and explain economic decision-making processes.[136] However, it is also an extremely popular, durable and successful analysis concept which has been transferred to all areas of life – including the political sphere (New Political Economy/public choice).[137] It is therefore presumed that politicians decide according to what is best for asserting their interests, and that voters decide in favour of the party and the programme that best benefit them personally rather than the country. It is claimed that such decisions are also made rationally, not emotionally.[138] Political rationality is described from the economic standpoint.[139] Parties work towards vote maximisation and voters behave rationally in politics.[140] The concept of rational, benefit maximising homo economicus also pressed forwards into other areas of life. The concept was noticeably universalised. It was applied, for example, to explain the stability of marital relationships or the influence of sentences on the crime rate. [141]

Since the emergence of the financial crisis in 2008, however, general criticism of the explanatory concept and guideline model of homo economicus has become louder, and its usefulness and laws have been subjected to increasingly critical scrutiny even for explaining economic decisions. From a philosophical perspective, such a concept "casts a shadow over the economy and society", and ultimate-

---

135 Pollert, Kirchner and Polzin (2013), p. 23.
136 See Pollert, Kirchner and Polzin (2013), p. 23.
137 A concise summary of the economic theory of democracy can be found in: Kirchgässner (2013[4]), pp. 113–134.
138 Kerscher (2013), pp. 48–49.
139 Downs (1968), p. 14.
140 Downs (1968), p. 14.
141 Kerscher (2013), p. 49.

ly leads to a "societal dead end".[142] Leading politicians such as German Federal Chancellor Angela Merkel are calling it into question and pleading for more realistic further development which meets the complex and dynamic requirements of reality. "This also means we are confident that homo economicus is far more than simply a being with economic data, and that the influences of behavioural economics and much more besides are also integrated into a viable theory for society."[143] From the field of macroeconomics, it is stated: "As economists, we will not be able to reveal ways to achieve sustainable prosperity with the ideal of homo economicus alone. We need additional concepts that use other driving forces rooted in man, such as social integration, trust and empathy."[144]

The author of this book clearly pointed out the weaknesses of this concept as a basic assumption for lobbying work in his dissertation in 1997.[145] The central idea of this is that the topic of lobbying involves an *interdependent area* between politics and the economy. Traditionally, however, the economic sciences have thus far often assumed that *the economy is independent of politics*. Trends within the economic sciences, such as the New Political Economy (NPE) and institutional economics, developed approaches which drew attention to the interdependencies of economic and political behaviour.[146] In common parlance: politics affects economic success (e.g. competition regulations, tax policy) and the economy affects politics (e.g. employment situation, tax revenue). Based on the criticism of the homo economicus concept, a further step in the debate concerning the theory is leading to the acceptance of human behaviour (i.e. behaviour which is controlled by internalised norms such as culture, morals, etc.) as an economic variable in order to better model the boundary conditions to which decision-makers are actually subject.[147] The human image of homo economicus additionally assumes that decision-makers are not exposed to any uncertainties, have complete and infinite information transparency and can therefore ultimately assess the effect of their decision.[148] In reality, however, actors only have limited cognitive options for recording and processing information.[149] Added to this is the fact that complete information transparency is not available. Politicians are often reliant on specialist information "from external sources", and in a complex world, the desired and undesired effects of political decisions cannot be conclusively foreseen. The concept of homo economicus – and the related hypothesis of rational action – is consequently being increasingly superseded by sociological theories of human action (homo socialis, homo institutionalis, homo behavioralis).[150]

---

142 Kerscher (2013), p. 13.
143 Merkel (2014).
144 Snower (2014).
145 For more information, see: Joos (1998), pp. 33 – 37. The date difference arises from the fact that the dissertation was submitted in 1997 and printed in 1998.
146 See Joos (1998), pp. 33 – 34.
147 See Schmidtchen (1993), p. 2.
148 Joos (1998), p. 34.
149 Schmidtchen (1993), p. 2.
150 See Joos (1998), pp. 33 ff.; with regard to the debate: Manzeschke (2010).

The fact that the training undergone by economists, and thus a vast number of representatives in large and important interest groups (companies, trade associations and trade unions), still remains oriented towards the homo economicus concept is problematic, however. Economics students then internalise this conception of man more extensively than students of other subjects.[151] This leads to an impact which lessens the influence of other concepts and human images.[152] Whilst future corporate managers will be prevented from an excessively idealistic approach to problems and a "naive moral concept" in this manner,[153] this conception of man will not necessarily give them conceptual access to politics, and only conveys a limited understanding of political decision-making processes. This can lead to incorrect basic assumptions, e.g. that politics, from the perspective of a company, is an external, constant and unchangeable variable whose decisions can be anticipated. In the case of corporate decisions involving the political sphere, these incorrect basic assumptions can then lead to mistakes, sometimes resulting in severe commercial consequences. Ultimately, the concept of homo economicus was developed to enable the successful analysis of economic issues/models, not to analyse political decision-making processes.[154]

What will be the consequences for stakeholders as regards the representation of their interests vis-à-vis politics when the universality of the homo economicus concept is abandoned, and it is conceded that it is not suitable for explaining decision-making processes in all spheres of life? If the concept of homo economicus cannot therefore be applied to politics, this leads to three major challenges for lobbying. Firstly, it must be stated that the results of political decisions are not, or are only conditionally, foreseeable or "predictable", because they are not aimed at a rationality oriented towards maximum benefit. This is not intended to imply that political decisions are "irrational"; instead, their rationality arises from various exogenous and endogenous/internalised variables which cannot be explained solely with the classic homo economicus concept. Accordingly, lobbying must remain very close to the political activity to be able to analyse decision-making processes. Secondly: if complete information transparency is not given for political decision-makers, lobbying must ensure, by supplying (specialist) information, that political decision-makers have all of the information they require for their decisions. This must take place at the right point in time in the political process and vis-à-vis the right addressees. And thirdly: if processing the wealth of information encounters resource limits, a successful lobbying company must prepare the often complex and highly detailed (specialist) information for political decision-makers so that it is sufficiently brief and understandable (see the explanations on the one-pager instrument in Section 6.4.2.1.7).

---

151 Siebenhühner (2001), p. 347.
152 See Kerscher (2013), p. 17.
153 Kerscher (2013), p. 16.
154 Kerscher (2013), p. 17.

Use of the homo politicus concept originating from political philosophy is suggested for further analysis, since this enables a better explanation of the criteria of political processes and decisions.[155] However, to qualify this, it must be stated in advance that all of the concepts which attempt to explain human behaviour involve idealistic types, and that none of these concepts can claim to be able to fully interpret human behaviour. Mixes of the various concepts are much more frequently found in empirical research.[156] This means that not every political decision-maker is 100% a homo politicus; he can also occasionally behave in a benefit maximising manner in the sense of homo economicus. Due to their socialisation in the political system, it nevertheless appears plausible that political decision-makers are more likely to bear similarity to homo politicus than homo economicus.

The concept of homo politicus dates back to Aristotle, who spoke of man as a *zoon politikon*, a being that seeks a fellowship and lives in community (a *polis*). Modern conceptual ideas assume that homo politicus is interested in the community, in contrast to homo economicus, whose behaviour as a benefit maximiser is oriented towards purely economic objectives.[157] "As such, homo politicus is a community being; for him, the community is not a means for achieving private purposes or objectives, but a necessary condition of his existence."[158] He attempts to discern what is best for the community and is in the public interest, and strives to achieve political justice. "Political justice denotes the ordering of a political community, which meets with general approval; i.e. all individuals have good reason to agree with it and, thus, approval of such an ordering may be expected ex ante."[159] The realisation of this ideal also encompasses the maintenance of a liberal constitution and fair participation opportunities for all, "e.g. the equitable access of all citizens to political decisions, and the same basic and political rights for all".[160] These orientation criteria differ fundamentally from those of homo economicus and explain why a change in perspectives must take place in lobbying (i.e. communication between stakeholders which occasionally regard their individual interests in absolute/superficial terms) and politics (with regard to the onepager, see Section 6.4.2.1.7).

Homo politicus is also characterised "by his capability to make free decisions and thus also spontaneous and flexible actions, with the result that his actions are not clearly predictable and social change on the basis of behaviour which does not conform to standards is possible".[161] His public interest orientation through reasonable thought is what primarily distinguishes him from other constructs used to

---

155 Vowe (2005), p. 93.
156 Vowe (2005), p. 93.
157 Vowe (2005), p. 93.
158 Faber, Manstetten and Petersen (1996), p. 17.
159 Faber, Petersen and Schiller (2002), p. 328.
160 Siebenhüner (2001), p. 350.
161 Siebenhüner (2001), p. 350.

explain human behaviour. To do this, homo politicus integrates a variety of parameters into his decision-making and weighs up precisely before he decides.[162] In this regard, German Federal Chancellor Angela Merkel explains that political decision-making in democracies is subject to a multi-layered process and "that calculations must not be based solely on economically rational considerations (…). Instead, social developments and cultural backgrounds are the object of investigations".[163] This decision-making process will be analysed in greater detail in the following section.

3.8.2 Decision-making by homo politicus

Homo politicus' decision-making process is preceded by a premise: the imperative compulsion to have to reach a decision or, to express it differently by again citing Federal Chancellor Merkel: "Politicians must always reach decisions, even if analyses or theories are entirely contradictory. They additionally bear responsibility for implementing their decisions."[164] Even for the decision-maker, it is not always clear how one or another decision is reached. "The essence of ultimate decision remains impenetrable to the observer – often indeed to the decider himself. (…) There will always be the dark and tangled stretches in the decision making process – mysterious even to those who may be most intimately involved."[165] This evaluation by John F. Kennedy, 35th President of the United States of America, shows how difficult it is to portray political decisions and explain them to outsiders such as lobbyists – or even insiders. Too many individual, content-related, procedural and political criteria play a role, and at the end, it is often no longer understandable which criterion was the crucial factor, with the result that Kennedy saw no option other than to speak of "dark and tangled stretches" in the decision-making process. However, there are helpful ways and means for shedding light in this darkness. The following will only briefly refer back to some of the findings from decision theory insofar as they can be used to explain the results of political decision-makers' decisions and for lobbying.[166]

Like any other human being, homo politicus' decisions are oriented towards various categories which help him to evaluate the available information and in decision-making as a whole. Such categories can include benefit maximisation and economy, as has already been shown using the example of homo economicus; whether this rationalistic approach to decisions matches reality has already been called into question. What is more important is to also give consideration to social influence, cultural background and – particularly important in politics – political preferences as decision-making categories. This results in the above mentioned,

---

162 Vowe (2005), p. 93.
163 Merkel (2014).
164 Merkel (2014).
165 Allison (1971), p. i.
166 A more detailed explanation of decision theory approaches must be forgone at this point. For an overview of decision theory approaches, see Rogge (2010), pp. 206–209.

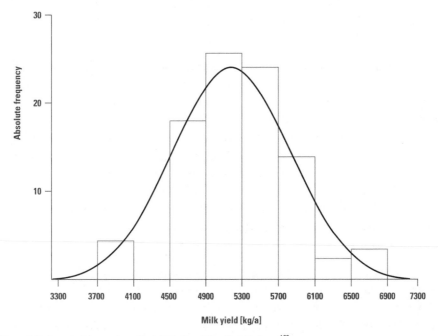

$$f(x)=a*e^{-b*x^2} \text{ with } a,b > 0$$

Constant a determines the size of the curve in the y direction; constant b determines whether the bell curve is flatter or steeper (a small constant b causes the bell curve to be flatter). The function values are always greater than 0, and the curve conforms asymptotically to the x axis for $x \rightarrow \pm \infty$.

Figure 3.5: Mathematical equation of a symmetrical bell curve[167]

Figure 3.6: Approximately normal, empirical distribution of the milk yield of cows[169]

internalised categories and norms which play a role in homo politicus' decision-making (and also that of other people), irrespective of exogenous, rational norms (economy, benefit maximisation, etc.). As these internalised categories and norms are not immediately recognisable to outsiders, the result of homo politicus' decisions is not *a priori* "predictable", and not always ultimately understandable ("The essence of ultimate decision remains impenetrable to the observer."). It should also be noted that this is true for each individual political decision-maker, and that the problem is "infinitely" potentiated due to the number of political decision-makers in the sometimes lengthy political process in a complex multi-level system such as the EU. Political decisions are therefore characterised by their

---

167 Source: Precht, Kraft and Bachmaier (2005[7]), p. 127.
169 Source: Precht, Kraft and Bachmaier (2005[7]), p. 127.

open outcome (in contrast to the predictability of the results of classic homo economicus' decisions).

To explain this decision result openness, the decision-making of actors from the economic, political and also the private sphere should first be dealt with in general terms. This (not empirical) everyday observance is used to develop a model which helps to explain the decision-making process of political decision-makers. Apparently unrelated to decision-making processes at first glance, graphical representation of the Gaussian normal distribution in combination with the law of large numbers can provide a rough description and also a visual idea of how decisions by individual decision-makers (not only in politics) can be explained. The results of decision-making thus become more understandable and clearer to outsiders.

The bell curve of the Gaussian normal distribution is widely known. In addition to describing the distribution of measurement errors in experiments, it is also generally used as a model to describe the distribution of the occurrence of natural phenomena. In statistics, the normal distribution is the most important continuous distribution, because many random variables which occur in practice are approximately normally distributed. With such normally distributed random variables, the density function assumes the shape of a bell: if a continuous characteristic is observed very frequently, this frequency's distribution can be plotted. Practice shows that, in the majority of cases, such an empirical frequency distribution can be approximated through a virtually symmetrical bell curve as a distribution density.[168]

The bell curve therefore portrays the following scenario: if the milk yield of cows is analysed, for example, it is shown that only a very few cows produce a particularly high or particularly low volume of milk, and that the majority lie somewhere in the "middle". The distribution of body sizes amongst schoolboys in a class is similar. Only a very few are particularly tall or particularly short. The majority are of medium height. The impression is confirmed if a high number of persons, i.e. several hundreds of thousands, are included in this example. The more schoolboys are included, the more "perfect" the curve becomes.[170] This is attributable to the law of large numbers: when tossing a coin, for example, "heads" or "tails" should appear with equal frequency as long as the coin is tossed enough times in succession. However, this does not necessarily have to be the case if it is tossed 100, 1,000 or 10,000 times. Nor does the law state that "tails" will necessarily occur the next time after "heads" has appeared a high number of times. Each toss of the coin must be evaluated independently of the previous and the following toss. The law of large numbers demands evening out "in the long term".[171] Formulated verbally, the law states:

---

168   Precht, Kraft and Bachmaier (2005[7]), p. 127.
170   Due to reasons of unambiguousness and clarity, Herrnstein and Murray consciously chose a pure boys' class; Herrnstein and Murray (1994), pp. 553–556.
171   Precht, Kraft and Bachmaier (2005[7]), p. 96.

"If a random experiment is repeated with sufficient frequency under the same conditions, the relative frequency of a specific event arbitrarily approximates the theoretical probability of this event."[172]

As already indicated, the bell curve therefore describes a deviation from the mean. If we look at the interval of the deviations from -3 to 3 (Figure 3.7), 99.7% of all cases are covered. Only a very few extreme cases are located outside of this interval. However, the following is remarkable: in any distribution, regardless of whether it involves the milk production of cows, the size of schoolboys or the distribution of intelligence in the population, approx. 68.27% of cases are found in the interval between the deviations -1 and 1. This shows that there is a certain degree of natural uniformity in the world which is manifested in many aspects of life.[173]

In model form, this natural uniformity can also be transferred to the results of decision-making processes. Amongst the variety of decisions made in daily life, it can be stated from experience – not empirically – that perhaps 5–15% of cases which are submitted to someone for a decision are rejected on principle. Approximately a further 5–15% of cases are supported out of conviction. This low number of cases is comparable with the low incidence of very tall and very short schoolboys. As has already been mentioned, however, the majority of schoolboys are of medium height. This means that, in most cases, decision-making processes are volatile. In the majority of cases submitted for a decision, the decision-maker (in politics, in companies, associations, organisations or in a private household) is not *a priori* fixed in his decision. Formulated differently, this means that in ap-

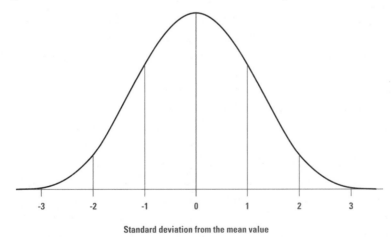

Standard deviation from the mean value

Figure 3.7: Bell curve with standard deviations from the mean[174]

---

172 Precht, Kraft and Bachmaier (2005[7]), p. 96.
173 Herrnstein and Murray (1994), p. 557.
174 Source: Herrnstein and Murray (1994), p. 557.

prox. 70–90 % of the cases submitted each day for a decision: "I can decide this way or that." In this broad spectrum, decision-makers are amenable to arguments, and the result of the decision is initially open.

If decision results are schematically depicted in a bell curve, and this is subdivided into sections, the following picture emerges:

1. Rejection due to basic and general misgivings.

2. Rejection due to serious misgivings.

3. Rejection due to slight misgivings or approval despite slight misgivings.

4. Approval because the environment (e.g. friends or family) agrees/approves.

5. Approval due to a basically positive attitude towards the issue, even if this has not completely sunk in/been understood.

As politics is ultimately structured by human beings, this model can also be applied to explain decision-making amongst political decision-makers. This particularly refers to individual actors, e.g. an office manager (who decides whether a message is important enough to be forwarded to his superior) or a responsible civil servant in a Directorate General within the Commission (who has a certain room to manoeuvre in structuring e.g. a draft directive and can decide how a specific formulation turns out). Politicians, usually parliamentarians and Council members, then in turn decide whether to accept these text formulations in this form. In addition to purely factual and content-related arguments, however, political decision-makers in particular include further – political – criteria in their decision.

Lobbying experience again shows here that decisions are made in a 5–15, 70–90, 5–15 pattern.[175] Of course, the decision-maker's political conviction plays a major role in this. Approx. 5–15 % of the cases submitted for a decision are approved on principle because the decision-maker supports the issue due to extensive political conviction. In these cases, he is even prepared to "sacrifice" other issues to which he is committed, merely to enable such a primary issue or a "pet area of concern" to be implemented. The decision-maker will also assume a "leading role" in such an issue; in such a primary issue, he will essentially take a positive approach to everything that may contribute to its realisation and exploit all procedural "angles" to drive his issue forwards. A European Parliament committee member will regularly attempt to become the rapporteur for a primary issue and thus exert particular influence on the debate. The forerunner will actively engage in the discussion and not miss a single vote. If the forerunner is a Commissioner, he will pay particular attention to the work in his Directorate General, always be kept abreast of the status of the procedure and take corrective action through intervention if necessary.

---

175 See Joos (2015), pp. 414 ff.

Gaussian (or normal) distribution in combination with the law of large numbers

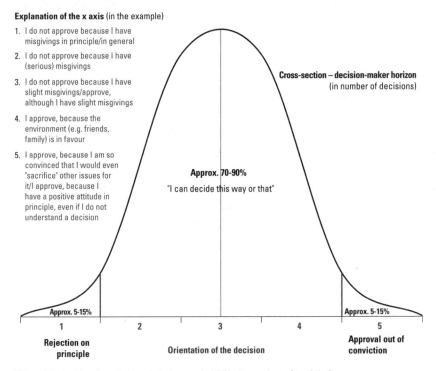

Explanation of the x axis (in the example)

1. I do not approve because I have misgivings in principle/in general

2. I do not approve because I have (serious) misgivings

3. I do not approve because I have slight misgivings/approve, although I have slight misgivings

4. I approve, because the environment (e.g. friends, family) is in favour

5. I approve, because I am so convinced that I would even "sacrifice" other issues for it/I approve, because I have a positive attitude in principle, even if I do not understand a decision

Cross-section – decision-maker horizon
(in number of decisions)

Approx. 70-90%
"I can decide this way or that"

Approx. 5-15%

Approx. 5-15%

| 1 | 2 | 3 | 4 | 5 |

Rejection on principle

Orientation of the decision

Approval out of conviction

Figure 3.8: Decisions by sector, from "rejection on principle" to "approval out of conviction"

The process is similar in the estimated 5 – 15 % of cases which a decision-maker rejects out of principle and deep political conviction. Such a principled and un-compromising attitude can often be observed in the case of ethical issues (e.g. as-sisted suicide, asylum) or also in politically, ideologically charged issues. Often, an uncompromising camp that is difficult to move towards a more flexible attitude is also found in environmental topics such as climate change or energy issues such as attitudes towards nuclear power. With both forerunners and "those unwilling to compromise", arguments often fail to fall on fertile ground. Procedural and cross-issue approaches (log rolling) are then often the only way to reach a com-promise.[176]

It is also true in the case of political decision-makers that their decision is not *a priori* fixed in around 70 – 90 % of cases. In a manner similar to private individuals or decision-makers in companies, political decision-makers are guided by certain criteria which offer orientation in their decisions and which shed light on and un-tangle the "dark and tangled stretches". The decision-maker's environment also plays a major role in the development of his decision-making categories here.

---

176 Joos (2015), pp. 414 ff.

The allocation of his attention poses a particular challenge to a political decision-maker. He receives too many signals from different directions and different sources (flood of information); he has too many tasks to deal with, strategies and plans to consider and too many contacts to maintain to devote the same amount of attention to everything that he encounters. Whilst purely rationalistic decision theories (rational choice) only assign a subordinate role to the factor of time, and decisions are accordingly made in a timeless vacuum,[177] time is a very important dimension in politics in practice (see Section 3.5). Attention and time become important factors in the decision-making process, because both are limited.

In view of this, political decision-makers (but also decision-makers in companies, associations, organisations and in the private sphere) develop categories which provide them with orientation in the decision-making process, help them to use resources economically and manage this limited attention and time.[178] These categories have to be researched in order to make the results of political decision-making more understandable. Cognitive psychology points out that people have a preference for simplicity. People therefore also prefer consistency to chaos and unpredictability. Emotions (in combination with cognition) also play an important role in the decision-making process.[179] The importance of emotion in the decision-making process also explains the strict attitudes of decision-makers in the case of basic rejection (refusal) and absolute endorsement (assumption of the leading role). The formulation of categories for orientation in decision-making is ultimately a process of simplification which reduces the complexity of the decision to a manageable level. Against this "psychological background", it is therefore hardly surprising that some of the categories which political decision-makers apply on a daily basis may appear entirely banal. They are nevertheless very effective, but are not always known to outsiders.

In practice, for example, a Member of Parliament's political group membership can play a role, but his nationality and region of origin may also be relevant to his decisions. A member of the Commission, for example, may have the following criteria which positively influence decision-making: the concern comes from a Directorate with which co-operation has so far been positive; the concern comes – albeit actually irrelevant at European level – from the Commissioner's home country; the concern comes from a colleague who has previously supported the Commissioner. Loyalty is a valuable commodity in politics. The following factors have more of a negative influence on the decision: the concern comes from a Directorate with which co-operation in the past has been negative; the concern comes from a colleague who has never supported the Commissioner before or who has previously refused to co-operate with him; serious or slight misgivings in general may also act as negative arguments against the concern.

---

177 Rogge (2010), p. 207.
178 Badie, Berg-Schlosser and Morlino (2011), s.v. rationality, bounded.
179 With regard to the importance of cognitive psychology in political decisions, see e.g. Badie, Berg-Schlosser and Morlino (2011), s.v. Psychological Explanations of International Politics.

Figure 3.9: Decisions of a political decision-maker: example of an EU Commissioner

Of course, restrictions and regulations also arise through the political process it-self. Decisions must not be unlawful, they must be appropriate to the framework of polity and the institution in which the decision-makers are employed (actor-centred institutionalism has already been mentioned). It is therefore not yet suffi-cient "to know which decision-making rule has effectively been applied in a politi-cal decision-making process [hierarchical, majority, consensual decision-making procedure]. To precisely understand its effect, the institutional context in which this procedure was used and the manner in which it was linked with other decision-making rules must also be determined".[180] Stakeholders will also attempt to support the decision-making process and in turn introduce information and proposals.[181]

If this approach is applied to the variety of decisions in the EU's political process, it is revealed for the practical purposes of lobbying that the majority of decision-makers do not have any preconceived opinion on an issue and that their decisions are open. They aim to "familiarise themselves with the issue" before making a de-cision. Here, lobbying has the opportunity to provide the decision-making pro-cess with relevant support through reliable, objective and transparent informa-

---

180 Eberlein and Grande (2014³), p. 174.
181 See Nohlen and Schultze (2010⁴), s.v. decision theory.

tion, and to convince the decision-maker of the correctness of a decision. Content-related work is highly important at this point and should by no means be underestimated. However, content can only be conveyed if it slots into the rules of the relevant decision-making or legislative procedure. Even if an individual contact person wishes to promote certain issues as a "forerunner" or reject them as a "non-compromiser" in the political process, each individual offers the opportunity of identifying those issues for which he can be successfully brought on board for the interest of the affected party; because he will only reject approx. 5 – 15 % of issues on principle. And a new opportunity arises with each individual contact person in the political process. The likelihood of successfully promoting a lobbying concern is therefore good.

When examining certain laws of (political) decisions, it is better to focus more extensively on "theories of attention and search" than "theories of choice among readily available goals, preferences and consequences".[182] Other political scientists affirm this, stating: "Knowledge of political decision-making procedures is important, as these apparently do not represent arbitrarily applicable and exchangeable, simply and clearly effective mechanisms."[183] When analysing the political process, concentration must consequently be focussed primarily on the decision-making process and not prematurely only on the content-related result of the decision.

3.9 Summary

The maxim "politics is the art of the possible" is attributed to Otto von Bismarck. Ultimately, this saying states that politics is a process whose end result is not maximum output, but only a compromise within the bounds of the given possibilities. This process of compromise is sometimes a protracted and complex process whose result cannot be foreseen.

Chapter 3 deals with the following key questions:

- What importance is attached to content, and what to procedures and processes, in politics?
- How are political processes structured, and how can lobbying adapt to them?
- How can time slots and decision-making windows which arise in the political process be used for lobbying?
- How does a political actor make decisions, and how can the decision-making process of such a "homo politicus" be decrypted for outsiders?

---

182 Badie, Berg-Schlosser and Morlino (2011), s. v. rationality, bounded.
183 Eberlein and Grande (2014³), p. 174.

(1) Politics is subdivided into three dimensions: polity, policy and politics.
  - *polity* is the *formal dimension* of politics. This involves its normative, structural and constitutional elements, i.e. the (historically established) institutional order;
  - the term *policy* describes the *content-related dimension* of politics (also called the substantive dimension). This can refer to specific political programmes and specific political objectives and tasks, but also entire political areas such as social, domestic, economic or environmental policy;
  - *politics* designates the *procedural dimension* of politics. Specifically, these are processes of opinion forming (e.g. demonstrations and public discussions), decisions (e.g. as part of legislative procedures) and processes of implementation (e.g. enactments of administrative regulations, monitoring adherence to laws and sanctions in the case of misconduct).

(2) From the point of view of lobbying, polity is a given variable which does not change or only changes over a very long period of time, and to which lobbying must be oriented. The development of European integration from the "Europe of 6 member states" in the 1950s to the "Europe of 28 member states" is associated with an increase in the complexity of political processes, particularly with the amendments to the Treaty of Lisbon (dealt with exhaustively in Chapter 4).

(3) The content-related dimension of politics is of central importance to lobbying. The contents help to distinguish between parties and politicians. Political content which is implemented influences the lives of citizens, and the work and success of companies, associations and organisations. Discussion surrounding political content is part of our political culture. It is therefore content which sets the political process in motion in the first place.

(4) In complex political systems such as the EU, the procedural dimension of politics noticeably increases in importance. In practice, it is at least as important for lobbyists to be familiar with the processes and both formal and informal rules of the relevant political decision-making process as to "merely" have their sights on political content (policy) and hold the better arguments: in a democracy, it is particularly the political process in which arguments are qualitatively evaluated and which is crucial as to which interests are ultimately asserted in a decision-making process. Lobbying requires significant process competence.

(5) Process competence remains necessary in lobbying to be able to manage and reduce the complexity arising from the formal structures, circumstances and regulations (polity) as well as the constitutional reality of the EU and how governance is undertaken and with which actors. This particularly involves an understanding of formal and informal responsibilities, procedures and processes, as well as their structuring, in order to make them understandable, manageable and plannable for lobbying clients (against this background, see also Chapter 10 on process structure and process support competence in particular).

(6) By no means least, process competence is required in lobbying in order to be able to support the procedural dimension (politics) of politics (see the process support competence needed after a successful change of perspectives, Chapter 10). The political process, i. e. its structure and procedure in the specific case, is crucially important in terms of which content is implemented in policies and which is not. The content-related results of politics arise from a process, so to speak. Policy-making is a process which is represented in the policy cycle: this begins with the articulation and definition of issues and problems and ends with the binding specification of programmes and measures. A distinction is sometimes made between six different phases: (1) problem definition; (2) agenda setting; (3) policy formulation; (4) policy implementation; (5) policy evaluation and (6) policy termination.

(7) The temporal dimension of politics must not be forgotten. Time is a political resource. The opening of time slots, during which the establishment of contact between lobbyists and politicians appears to be most promising, in each phase of the policy cycle, is of particular importance to lobbying. Formulated in common parlance: it is important to wait for the right moment.

(8) The political process requires the activity of actors. They articulate political content and interests, pursue specific interests and action objectives, have the resources to act as well as normative orientations and possess the capability to act strategically. Some take part in the entire political process, whilst others are only involved in certain phases. Lobbyists must establish contact with them.

(9) Networks are a necessity in political practice: an individual actor, even if this involves an institutional actor (such as e. g. the Commission) or a collective actor (such as e. g. a political group in the European Parliament), does not have the resources necessary for an autonomous policy by itself. The high complexity of the various policy sectors means that all actors are reliant on specialist information from other sectors. At the same time, this increased complexity and the EU's multi-level system lead to the fact that the required number of contacts increases exponentially.

(10) This results in two challenges for lobbying: (i) identification of networks and their members plus the establishment of contacts and (ii) ability to communicate with the various networks, i. e. mastery and knowledge of specialist terms, points of reference and the status of the discussion in individual issues. A network analysis helps to reveal the actual balance of power and actor relationships.

(11) Political decision-making processes have their own specific character, which differs significantly from those in other societal action areas such as the economy. They follow their own logic, which does not always meet external, rationalistically characterised expectations at first glance. The political actors have to make decisions in each phase of the political process. "Decisions are not only made around the cabinet table and in parliaments, but in many

locations throughout all phases of the political process: in ministries, at party headquarters, in association offices, etc. (…) When regarded from this perspective, modern political processes are nothing other than a long chain of decisions, whose beginning is difficult if not impossible to discern and whose end is often nothing more than a new decision."[184]

(12) Particular attention must be focussed on the decision-making processes of individual political actors' (e.g. parliamentarians and their employees, Commission officials, office managers, speakers, Commissioners, heads of Directorates, etc.) and their networks (e.g. party membership, nationality, etc.). Each and every day, they make decisions which influence the political process, drive it forwards, change it or perhaps even stop it. Political decision-makers do not use the universally accepted model of the rationalistic, benefit maximising homo economicus for orientation. Homo politicus, oriented towards the common good and the principle of political justice, is instead used as the role model here. This also explains why successful lobbying must guarantee translation from the sphere of economics to the political sphere (perspective change) (see Chapters 6 and 10).

(13) The result of the individual decisions is only *a priori* fixed to a minor extent. A decision-maker rejects approximately 5 – 15 % of the cases submitted for a decision out of basic conviction. A positive decision is made in roughly the same number of cases due to basic conviction. It follows from this that the result of the decision-making process is open in approx. 70 – 90 % of cases. This is also the spectrum in which decision-makers are open to arguments; provided that the corresponding process competence is available to contact the right decision-makers at the right point in time in the "Brussels thicket".

As the result of Chapter 3, the following general rule can be formulated in terms of the importance of content in decision-making processes: *the simpler* the structure of a decision-making process – low number of decision-making levels, simple procedural rules, few decision-makers – *the greater the relevance of individual content and arguments* for a specific decision. In such a system, a decision is accordingly based primarily on content-related aspects. The structure of the decision-making process is transparent; it has no or only little influence on its outcome. Such conditions are usually found in extensively hierarchical decision-making structures (i.e. also in autocratic systems).[185]

The more complex the structure of a decision-making process is – numerous decision-making levels, complex procedural rules, numerous decision-makers and usually diverging interests – *the greater the relevance of the decision-making structures and processes for a specific decision.* The European Union is a prime example of a complex system. Content and arguments remain relevant; however,

---

[184] Eberlein and Grande (2014[3]), p. 151.
[185] With regard to hierarchical decision-making structures, see Eberlein and Grande (2014[3]), pp. 154 – 157.

their individual relevance to the result of a decision-making process tends to increase as the complexity increases. In such a system, a decision is accordingly based extensively on procedural aspects; there is a risk of content-related arguments being disregarded in the decision-making procedure due to procedural reasons. Depending on the stage of the political process, the weight of the content in the argumentation set changes, because the different actors also have different content-related preferences, and weaken or give up their positions by way of reaching a compromise in order to achieve other objectives.

All of this demonstrates the necessity of a paradigm shift in lobbying amongst the EU institutions (but also in the member states). The strong leaning of the classic lobbying instruments' (corporate representative offices, associations, public affairs agencies, law firms) towards content-related work is not on its own sufficient for successful lobbying, since the political content is constantly reformed and reformulated in the decision-making and compromise-striking process. Consequently, the procedural dimension of politics must be given greater consideration than before. It is more important to keep an eye on this dimension and constructively support the political process than to rely solely on the "power" of "better" arguments. Only then is there a likelihood that legitimate interests will be heard and taken into consideration.

In concrete terms, this means that an understanding of the political processes (process competence) is at least as important for lobbying as knowledge of, and work on, the political contents (content competence). Without process competence, it is no longer possible to convey the content, in an understandable form, to the relevant decision-makers within the dynamic multi-level system of the EU, with its vast number of individual political actors (the Commission alone has over 30,000 employees[186]). It stands to reason that the complex decision-making processes can no longer be adequately supported with content-related work alone. The decision-making processes and the criteria according to which decisions are made must also be known and used.

---

186 European Commission (2014b).

Chapter 4   European Union as the target of lobbying: political system and peculiarities in comparison with national (member state) systems

4.1 Introduction and question

In addition to Chapters 2 and 3, this chapter, too, deals with the framework for lobbying. Whereas Chapter 3 was concerned with the importance of processes in politics in general and underscored the importance of process competence in lobbying, Chapter 4 is dedicated to the framework of the EU in particular, and deals with the following questions:

- Which consequences for political lobbying arise from the historical course of European integration? How far has European integration already progressed?
- What are the significant changes arising from the Treaty of Lisbon?
- Who are the political stakeholders (from the point of view of lobbyists) in the EU? How is the political system of the EU characterised? How does it differ from the member states as a result of this?

Today's European Union has its roots in the period following the Second World War. Many of the complex structures and partially overlapping competencies have originated historically. Over time, a complex multi-level system has arisen, with actors and decision-makers at regional (sub-national), member state (national) and European (supranational) level (see Sections 4.2 and 4.3). This historic overview is followed by a portrayal of European integration, which explains the steps taken towards integration with the aid of so-called integration theories, and which shows the extent to which European integration has already progressed from a political science perspective (see Section 4.4). The last major move towards greater integration occurred with the Treaty of Lisbon, which led to crucial changes and strengthened the Union both externally and internally. In its practical, i.e. specific, effects (effectualness), it is virtually equal to the Treaty establishing a Constitution for Europe (TCE), as crucial elements of the latter were taken over.

An overview-like portrayal of the political stakeholders in the EU rounds off this section of the book (see Section 4.5). It starts with a list of important EU institutions. Firstly, the function of the relevant institution is outlined in the sense of institutional theory. Secondly, however, the institutions should also be analysed as veritable political actors (stakeholders) which, under certain circumstances, follow their own agenda and pursue their own interests in the political process of the EU. This change in perspective towards stakeholders draws attention to further, central actors which are often overlooked as part of pure institutional theory –

particularly the EU member states with their sub-national units, the regions, but also (organised) civil society, which plays an important role in the EU. In the analysis, all of the levels, the supranational level of the EU institutions, the national level of the member states with their sub-national units and the level of civil society, are categorised as political stakeholders, since they are all ultimately part of the complex multi-level system of the EU and are involved in the decision-making process and the implementation of European decisions. Consequently, a fundamental understanding of these relationships is vital for successful and efficient lobbying in order to be able to understand legislative procedures, decision-making processes and thus the characteristic procedures of lobbying in Brussels.

4.2 Short history of European integration

"History is past politics and politics is present history."[1] Political Europe, the European Union, is the result of decades of development. Many institutions and their interactions can only be understood in the light of the history of European integration. A brief outline of the ideas concerning political unification of the continent and an overview of the history of the European institutions should help to understand and classify the complexity of the present day Europe of the EU. Nor should it be overlooked that Europe also has a geographical and a cultural dimension, both of which are interwoven with the political dimension, since this plays a particular role in discussion surrounding future EU expansion.

The ancient Greeks explained the name given to the European continent with the well known myth of the Phoenician princess Europa, whom Zeus, in the form of a bull, kidnapped and brought to Crete from the area which is now Lebanon. The continent on which she landed, although it was only an island thereof, was named after her to console the abducted woman.[2] However, the ancient world was not only familiar with the myth. Europe was also recognised as a cultural society, which was subsequently described as the Christian Occident in the Middle Ages.[3] And by no means least, Europe was also a geographical term encompassing the northern area of the known world at that time. The question of where the eastern border of the continent was to be drawn was the subject of dispute then, as it is today. The Urals have only been generally accepted in this role since the 18th century.[4] And although both are members of the Council of Europe, the ex-

---

1 Remark by Oxford historian Edward A. Freeman; with regard to the discussion surrounding the authorship of the quotation: Hesketh (2014), pp. 105–108.
2 With regard to the historical, linguistic derivation of the term Europe from the Semitic *ereb* ("dark" or "evening"), which refers to the sunset, i. e. the west (see the origin of the word Asia from *assu*, which refers to the rising sun, i. e. the east), see Mittag (2008), pp. 21–22.
3 Mittag (2008), pp. 25–30.
4 Mittag (2008), pp. 21–25.

tent to which Russia and Turkey belong to Europe is still discussed today.[5] The concept of a political Europe had also been around since the Middle Ages.[6] Since then, there have been many different ideas on how to unify the continent politically. These usually involved a complex system which, according to modern terminology, would lie somewhere between a confederation or a federation under international law; even today, the EU is difficult to categorise using classic constitutional terms. The predominant situation of rivalry and constant military conflicts based on territorial, economic and dynastic, then subsequently national, interests was to be halted.[7] The concepts of the *Grand Dessin* put forth by the Duke of Sully (1638), who envisaged a power-political equilibrium of 15 states of roughly the same size for Europe, and Immanuel Kant's globally oriented essay *Perpetual Peace* (1795), which proposed a type of federal "League of Nations", for instance, remained important. Reference was still being made to both of these progressive thinkers after 1945, when today's political Europe was being established.[8]

During the course of globalisation at the end of the 19th century, the networking of European states increased prior to the First World War. International congresses, which were characterised above all by the European powers, e. g. the Berlin Congress of 1878, the Berlin Africa Conference of 1884–85 and the Hague Peace Conferences of 1899 and 1907, are examples which show how the European states were able to exchange and co-ordinate their interests at intergovernmental level. Europe's "primal catastrophe", regarded by many contemporaries as the "last days of humanity" (Karl Kraus), nevertheless occurred in 1914–1918. The First World War cost the lives of over 20 million people.[9] The Paris Peace Conference was intended to restore lasting peace to Europe and the world. However, it was already foreseeable for contemporaries such as the economist John Maynard Keynes, who took part in the peace conference, that the peace treaties which were concluded would not have positive consequences – particularly in terms of Europe's economic recovery and peacekeeping.[10] The Treaty of Versailles concluded with Germany was aimed more at reparations than compensation.

Despite this difficult situation, intensive discussion concerning Europe and the desire for European unification arose amongst the continent's elites during the inter-war period. Many hundreds of documents on this matter were published, and there were around a dozen associations with the objective of European integration.[11] The most well known of these is the Paneuropa Union founded in 1922 by Austrian Count Richard Coudenhove-Kalergi, which advocated the United

---

5 Whilst both countries are members of the Council of Europe, misgivings particularly exist as regards discussion concerning Turkey's accession to the EU (see Loth (2014), p. 367).
6 Schmale (2000), pp. 83–90.
7 Simms (2013); Ferguson (2011), pp. 19–43.
8 Brunn (2009³), p. 20.
9 Clark (2012), p. xxiii.
10 Keynes (1920).
11 Schmale (2000), pp. 109–112.

States of Europe.[12] The business world also revealed its readiness to engage in European groupings such as the World Steel Association (WSA), a cartel for regulating market share in the European steel industry formed in 1926. Post 1945, the European unification movement was concerned with both political considerations and economic structures.[13] At first, however, increasing nationalism, fascism and National Socialism in the 1920s and 1930s scuppered any such plans.[14] The global economic crisis also dampened hopes of possible unification. Instead of cross-border free trade, it led to protectionism, customs barriers and partitioning.[15] The Second World War and the Holocaust, triggered by the German Empire's desire for hegemony in Europe, left a trail of devastation, crimes and death in their wake. Over 50 million people lost their lives in Europe.

An entire continent faced a new beginning, and this time, it was also prepared to find a common route out of this catastrophe. In 1946, Winston Churchill – Britain's Prime Minister from 1940 to 1945 and 1951 to 1955 – marked the first milestone on the road to European unification with his famous speech at Zurich University: "Our constant aim must be to build and fortify the strength of the United Nations Organisation. Under and within that world concept, we must re-create the European family in a regional structure called, it may be, the United States of Europe. The first step is to form a Council of Europe."[16]

However, the framework conditions had changed since the inter-war period; the Cold War was already casting its shadows at the end of the 1940s, splitting Europe into east and west, as shown by the Berlin Blockade of 1948 or the foundation of two German states in 1949. An "Iron Curtain"[17] divided the continent. This was the backdrop against which European unification was to take place, although it first began in Western Europe, and Central and Eastern Europe were only included following the collapse of the communist Eastern Block.

Historians (political science integration theories will be dealt with in Section 4.4) highlighted various factors as motivation for the European integration process: firstly, the idealism of the persons and politicians concerned, and secondly, the national (security) interests of the involved states and the maintenance of peace in Europe. Added to these were economic interests in overcoming the constraints of national markets, and ultimately exogenic drivers such as the aforementioned Cold War, the oil crises during the 1970s, the collapse of Bretton Woods' interna-

---

12 Coudenhove-Kalergi (1923), p. 153.
13 Brunn (2009³), p. 24.
14 Schmale (2000), p. 108; "Whilst National Socialism developed concepts for Europe, these were anti-European when measured against the tradition of the idea of Europe." (Schmale (2000), p. 116).
15 Pressler (2013), p. 112; Brunn (2009³), p. 25.
16 Winston Churchill on 19th September 1946, in his speech to the young academics at Zurich University, in: Lipgens and Loth (1988), p. 665.
17 The term "Iron Curtain" in connection with the division of Europe was first coined in 1945 by German Propaganda Minister Joseph Goebbels (See Mazower (2008), p. 554).

tional monetary system or the implosion of the Eastern Block in 1989/90, as well as Europe's attempt to assert itself in a globalised world.[18]

Despite considerations during the inter-war period, the emergence of the EU in post-war Europe was "not a concept developed on the drawing board that was implemented one-to-one in political practice. Instead, integration has constantly continued to develop since the 1950s."[19] The European institutions have therefore grown organically, which has sometimes led to redundancies and overlapping competencies, some of which are still present today and do not always simplify the political process.

In 1948, the Organisation for European Economic Co-operation (OEEC) was founded as part of the Marshall Plan.[20] Also in 1948, France, the UK and the Benelux countries established the intergovernmental Brussels Treaty for co-operation in the field of security policy. When Germany and Italy acceded in 1954, the Brussels Treaty was renamed the Western European Union. It subsequently became redundant alongside the EU's Common Foreign and Security Policy, and was dissolved again in 1997. The Council of Europe – as demanded by Churchill in his Zurich speech – followed in 1949, but this is now of lesser political importance alongside the EU. It is, however, important as an intergovernmental institution for fostering a culture of human and civil rights in Europe.[21]

The precursors of today's EU institutions arose with the European Coal and Steel Community (ECSC). It was founded with the so-called Treaty of Paris in 1951, and was based on a plan developed by French Foreign Minister Robert Schuman (Schuman Plan). The treaty came into force in 1952. Its intention was to integrate Germany into a West European alliance of states and guarantee France's military and also economic security against its neighbour, Germany, which was once more gaining in strength. The European Coal and Steel Community placed Germany's, France's, Italy's and the Benelux countries' coal and steel industry under the supervision of a High Authority with supranational competencies. The European Commission subsequently emerged from this. A special Council of Ministers, a parliamentary assembly and a European Court of Justice were introduced. These were also the forerunners of today's institutions.[22] The European Coal and Steel Community was the first step towards a supranational institution to which the member states gave up parts of their sovereignty over their national coal and steel industry.

The next milestone occurred in 1957 with the signing of the Treaties establishing the European Economic Community (EEC) and a European Atomic Energy

18 Brunn (2009[3]), pp. 12 – 15; Loth (2014), pp. 9 ff.
19 Weidenfeld (2013[3]), p. 69.
20 With the accession of the USA and Canada in 1960, it was raised to a global level, and was renamed the Organisation for Economic Co-operation and Development (OECD) in 1961.
21 Weidenfeld (2013[3]), p. 70; Schmale (2000), pp. 226 – 234.
22 Brunn (2009[3]), pp. 70 – 87; Wessels (2008), pp. 61 – 66.

Council of Europe

The Council of Europe is an intergovernmental state organisation. It is not to be confused with the Council of the European Union or the European Council. The Council of Europe is not an EU institution; it is independent of the EU. It was founded in 1949, has its headquarters in Strasbourg and now has 47 members, including all EU member states as well as non-EU states such as Switzerland, Turkey, Ukraine, Georgia, Azerbaijan or Russia.

The Council of Europe is particularly involved in maintaining and fostering basic rights such as the freedom of expression, and in the protection of human rights. Signed in 1950, its best known convention is probably the European Convention on Human Rights (ECHR), which came into effect in 1953 and can also be enforced before the European Court of Human Rights in Strasbourg (ECHR).

Further information in the Internet at: www.coe.int

Figure 4.1: Council of Europe

Community (EAEC or Euratom) in Rome – the so-called Treaties of Rome. Together with the ECSC Treaty, there were now three European Treaties. The EEC became "the sustainable foundation on which (...) integration could be established".[23] The objective was a common market without customs duties and other trade barriers between the member states. The EEC also formed the cornerstone for the common agricultural policy. Through the Merger Treaty which came into effect in 1967, the three individual treaties were ultimately merged to become the European Communities (EC). During the course of this, the High Authority of the ECSC and the EEC and Euratom Commissions were amalgamated to form the European Commission. In parallel, as a counterbalance to a certain extent, 1959/60 saw the establishment of the EFTA, a free trade zone between Denmark, the UK, Norway, Austria, Portugal, Sweden and Switzerland. Due to its free trade-based agenda, the EFTA did not develop the same integration efforts as the ECSC and EEC.[24] Following the accession of many EFTA members to the EC or EU, the EFTA now only has four geographically remote members: Iceland, Liechtenstein, Norway and Switzerland.

The following decades revealed alternating phases of consolidation and expansion, while the road towards European unification became rockier: "This resulted in a process of European integration consolidation lasting over 30 years, which was constantly beset by setbacks, and partly fostered and partly hampered by several rounds of expansion."[25] The doubling of the number of EC members by the mid-1980s made decision-making through the *de facto* principle of unanimity practised for decisions in the European Council increasingly complicated and

---

23 Brunn (2009³), p. 118.
24 Schmale (2000), pp. 240–241.
25 Herz and Jetzlsperger (2008²), p. 41.

laborious. Reorientation of the community procedures, particularly the voting rules, for increased efficiency, became increasingly unavoidable. The Single European Act (SEA) signed in 1986 thus heralded in the most extensive reform of the EC to date. It came into effect in July 1987. Implementation of the single internal market, encompassing the free movement of goods, services and capital, by the end of 1992, was resolved with the SEA. Integration efforts were given new impetus thanks to the SEA. The Maastricht Treaty, which was signed in 1992 and came into effect on 1st November 1993, was the high point of European unification thus far and led to a new depth of integration. Through this treaty, the European Union (EU) was created as a common framework for the treaties which had so far existed in parallel. The EU was therefore based on three pillars: firstly the European Communities, secondly the newly incorporated Common Foreign and Security Policy (CFSP), and thirdly Police and Judicial Co-operation in criminal matters (PJC), which was also new. A core competence of the participating nation states, namely monetary policy, was surrendered in its entirety to the European level for the first time with the foundation of the European Economic and Monetary Union (EMU), which led to the common currency of the euro. Due to the introduction of the legislative co-decision procedure, the European Parliament, thus far extensively powerless, now became a co-shaper of European policy.

The fall of the Iron Curtain in 1989/90 brought forth a multitude of new accession candidates. The Eastern and South Eastern European states and the Baltic states, in particular, sought to join the EU. To cope with EU expansion, the existing institutional and contractual arrangements had to be modified, as the EU otherwise threatened to become "practically ungovernable". The "complicated architecture of the Union, the impenetrability of the convoluted treaties and the lack of democratic legitimacy of Union activities" also made revision of the Maastricht Treaty necessary.[26] The attempt to ensure the Union's ability to enlarge with the Treaty of Amsterdam in 1997 failed. Nor did the Treaty of Nice, which came into effect in 2003 and was intended to make Europe capable of expansion, lead to the desired results: "Instead of simplifying structures, increasing the transparency of the system and strengthening the Union institutions' decision-making capability, the mechanisms became even more complicated."[27]

In light of the reform attempts' poor results, it became increasingly clear that European integration had reached a crossroads. Both questions regarding the purpose, i.e. the objective of the EU, and questions concerning which competencies were to be surrendered to the Union and which were to remain with the nation states arose.[28] The previously pragmatic approach to unification had come to an end. However, the planned eastern enlargement was still pushed forwards and

---

26 Brunn (2002), pp. 281–282.
27 Herz and Jetzlsperger (2008[2]), p. 67.
28 Herz and Jetzlsperger (2008[2]), p. 71.

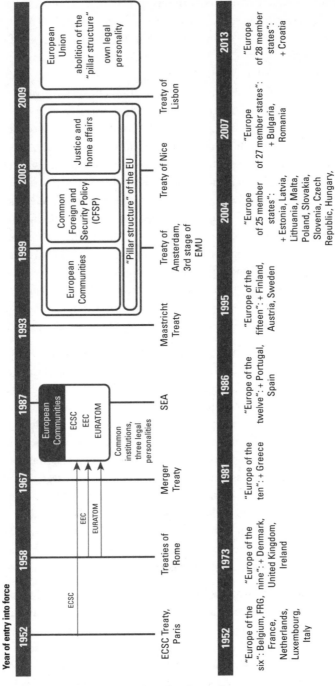

Figure 4.2: From ECSC to Europe of 28 states – the history of the European Union

was completed in 2004 and 2007. In parallel, however, further consideration was given to the purpose of the EU as part of the "post-Nice process". The two main objectives were firstly to make the EU "more efficient, more democratic, more publicly accessible and more transparent", and secondly to clearly separate and delimit the responsibilities of the member states and the EU.[29] Meanwhile, discussion on European policy was centred on the issue of a European constitution, through which the various parallel treaties were to be systematised and unified. A draft constitution, the most important point of which was the amalgamation of the European Treaties and thus the annulment of the EU's three-pillar structure, was presented in 2003.[30] Legislation and the procedures were also systematised, and state attributes such as a common European anthem and flag were introduced. Although the Constitutional Treaty which had been developed was the "most transparent, inclusive and probably also the most democratic draft constitution negotiated in the history of European integration",[31] it foundered in mid-2005 against referenda in France and the Netherlands – although the Constitutional Treaty was either accepted in almost all of the other states or was on the point of being ratified. Once it was subsequently determined that the European Constitution was unobtainable, the European Council decided to consistently sound out the possibilities of further integration.

Agreement regarding the form and content of the reform was reached during the first half of 2007. At the subsequent Intergovernmental Conference in Portugal, the "Treaty of Lisbon amending the Treaty on European Union and the Treaty establishing the European Community" was signed on 13th December 2007. The substance of the European Constitution was essentially maintained in the Treaty of Lisbon in terms of institutional and political projects; changes were particularly implemented with regard to the Charter of Fundamental Rights, issues of responsibility and symbols such as a common European anthem or flag.[32] Whilst the Treaty of Lisbon still failed to fundamentally eliminate the Treaties' confusing entanglement, the restructuring of the EU, which had been necessary for some time, did succeed as a result of it. The Treaty of Lisbon eliminated the distinction between the Union and Community (the previous pillars) and merged them both to form a single organisation with the uniform name "European Union".[33]

Despite the extensive, forward-looking revision of the EU through the Treaty of Lisbon, the question of "Which Europe?"[34] still remains unanswered.[35] Compared to political and economic integration, social and cultural integration are still lag-

---

29 Clemens, Reinfeldt and Wille (2008), p. 235.
30 Herz and Jetzlsperger (2008[2]), p. 75.
31 Herz and Jetzlsperger (2008[2]), p. 82.
32 See Clemens, Reinfeldt and Wille (2008), p. 237.
33 See Clemens, Reinfeldt and Wille (2008), p. 239; the legal personality of the EC was transferred to the Union as a whole.
34 Herz and Jetzlsperger (2008[2]), p. 115.
35 See Article 1 TEU.

ging far behind. As the historic outline shows, the European unification process underwent highs and lows of varying intensity; phases of dynamic progress were interspersed with periods of standstill.[36] The primary objective at the beginning of European unification, to prevent war between the European states for all time, increasingly fell behind the objective of economic modernisation and prosperity during the course of increasing integration. In terms of these objectives, European unification over the past six decades has been a resounding success – not least because the story of unified Europe's success did not follow a master plan at any time. Ultimately, a destroyed, politically divided Europe has developed into the largest economic arena in the world, unifying 28 states with over 500 million inhabitants[37] in peace and economic prosperity. Taken as a whole, the positive aspects of European unification far outweigh the negative sides of the integration process.

Whether the Treaty of Lisbon will now give the EU the hoped-for, permanent institutional stability or even purpose in the long term remains to be seen[38] – further discussion surrounding the design and structure of the EU are not out of the question in the future. New facts triggering such debate have arisen through the European sovereign debt crisis alone. The EFSM, EFSF and ESM "safety nets" may result in the transfer of further competencies to the supranational institutions of the EU. One example of this is the so-called Banking Union and the related transfer of banking supervision (Single Supervisory Mechanism, SSM) to the ECB. German politicians can certainly envisage using the crisis as an opportunity for further integration. In January 2014, Germany's Federal Minister of Finance, Wolfgang Schäuble, demanded a parliament for the Eurogroup, a further step towards deeper integration.[39] In August 2011, the Federal Minister of Labour at the time, Ursula von der Leyen, again picked up on Winston Churchill's idea of the United States of Europe.[40]

4.3 Fundamental changes due to the Treaty of Lisbon

The overview of the history of European integration has shown that the EU has long since shed its status of an international organisation (comparable e.g. with the United Nations). Instead, it is undergoing "a constant development process of communitarisation, characterised by qualitative changes in the direction of a thus far unknown form of organisation based on federal models."[41] The last major in-

---

36 See Judt (2006), pp. 598 ff.
37 See EUROSTAT (2014).
38 See Clemens, Reinfeldt and Wille (2008), p. 248.
39 See N. U. (2014b).
40 N. U. (2011c).
41 Calliess (2010), p. 45.

tegration step was the Treaty of Lisbon, which came into effect on 1st December 2009. Since then, 28 states, from Portugal to Finland and from Ireland to Cyprus, have been bound more closely together than ever before in history. This is manifested, for example, in the so-called Union citizenship which each national of an EU member state has.[42] The EU member states' passports are all Bordeaux red, and the European flag with its 12 stars now also flutters in front of official buildings alongside the member states' national flags – to quote just a few examples. Section 4.3.1 will again deal intensively with the issue of the similarities and differences between the failed Constitutional Treaty and the Treaty of Lisbon.

The Treaty of Lisbon is of central, ground-breaking importance for lobbying amongst the EU institutions, because lobbying at the executive and legislative levels can only take place in the framework specified by politicians.[43] This refers less to the legal determinants such as the registration or compliance requirements made on the lobbyists,[44] but rather to the conditions and relationships within politics itself. Which institutions does a political system provide for, particularly at the legislative and executive level, how is its personnel – the decision-makers – recruited, how are the individual decision-making processes formally and informally structured, etc.? Through its organisational chart and its conditional contexts, each political system simultaneously defines the possibilities and approach points for political lobbying. So how did the Treaty of Lisbon ("Reform Treaty") change the EU's organisational chart, and what are the consequences of this for the practice of lobbying at both European and member state level?

One of the Treaty's main objectives was a fundamental reform of the EU's political system.[45] Three aspects are of particular interest in this:

- Firstly, strengthening the EU externally by raising its foreign policy profile.
- Secondly, strengthening it internally by maintaining the EU's ability to act in an environment which is changing rapidly in view of global crises and challenges by reducing the individual member states' ability to block decisions.
- Thirdly, increasing the EU's democratic legitimation by enhancing the role of the European Parliament in the legislative procedure.

A few examples will be used to briefly show how the EU is strengthened externally. Internally – i.e. in the EU's relationship with its member states – the transition from the principle of unanimity to the majority principle in the votes taken in the Council of the EU in the majority of important policy areas is of particular importance, since this makes it difficult or impossible for individual member states to block legislative initiatives. Added to this is the strengthening of the European Parliament as part of the so-called ordinary legislative procedure (see also Chapter 5).

---

42 With the Maastricht Treaty, which came into effect on 1st November 1993.
43 See Joos (1998), p. 29.
44 See e.g. Joos and Waldenberger (2004), pp. 45–73.
45 Woods and Watson (2012), p. 17; Seeger (2008), p. 63.

4.3.1 "Lisbon": Treaty or Constitution?

Ireland's former Prime Minister, Bertie Ahern, who was in office when the Treaty of Lisbon was ratified, stated in a newspaper interview in 2007: "90 per cent of it [the Constitution] is still there. (...) These changes [the Lisbon Treaty] haven't made any dramatic change to the substance of what was agreed back in 2004."[46]

So is the Treaty of Lisbon a Constitution in all but name and the EU *de facto* a type of "state" or state structure? To deal with these questions, the genesis of the Treaty of Lisbon will first be placed into its historical context (Section 4.3.1.1). The process implemented by the German Council presidency to prepare for the negotiations leading to the Treaty of Lisbon will then be analysed (Section 4.3.1.2). It will become clear that the chosen negotiation method constituted a novelty in the negotiation of European Treaties. It will be shown that the Constitutional Treaty served as the basis for these negotiations and that the member states did not swerve extensively from the base text during the Intergovernmental Conference in 2007. Finally (Section 4.3.1.3), the differences between and common features of the Constitutional Treaty and the Treaty of Lisbon which came into effect in 2009 will be pointed out and evaluated qualitatively.

Treaty of Lisbon

The Treaty of Lisbon was formulated following the failure of the Constitutional Treaty in 2005. It strengthened the EU externally and internally:

Externally – i.e. in the EU's relationship vis-à-vis non-member states and international organisations – the EU became a separate legal personality and was given its own diplomatic service (European External Action Service, EEAS), headed by the High Representative of the European Union for Foreign Affairs and Security Policy.

Internally – i.e. in the EU's relationship with its member states – the EU's organisation was strengthened through the abolition of the three pillar model. The European Council, which has existed since 1974, became an EU institution and is headed by a President.

On elevation of the codecision procedure to the ordinary legislative procedure, the European Parliament was placed on an equal footing with the Council in practical terms. In addition, more policy areas than ever before are decided on according to the majority principle in the Council.

A qualified majority is now reached in the Council when 55% of the member states, which must represent 65% of the EU population, issue their approval. A blocking minority is also achieved when at least four states, which represent 35% of the population, do not issue their approval.
The Treaty was signed in Lisbon in 2007 and came into force on 1st December 2009.

Figure 4.3: Treaty of Lisbon

---

46 Bertie Ahern in an interview (Irish Independent on 24th June 2007), quoted in: Miller (2009).

4.3.1.1 Genesis of the Treaty of Lisbon

The negotiation process for the Treaty of Lisbon (TL) differs significantly from the development process of previous European Treaties. A detailed portrayal of the negotiation process far exceeds the framework of this book. However, at least the most important facts must be dealt with in the following, since they show the essential role played by individual decision-makers – particularly through their process competence. Without chronological placement into the historical context, it would also not be possible to explain how the relevant actors succeeded in preserving the substance of the failed Constitutional Treaty ("TCE").

Context: genesis of the Constitutional Treaty and constitutional crisis

What later became the Treaty of Lisbon was based on the draft of a Constitutional Treaty for Europe, which was formulated for the first time in the history of European unification as part of a Convention (2002–2003), then further negotiated by the heads of state and government as part of an Intergovernmental Conference and ultimately signed by the heads of state and government on 29th October 2004.[47] The Convention, and particularly the President of the Convention, former French President Valéry Giscard d'Estaing, interpreted the mandate given by the heads of state and government in the Laeken Declaration in 2001 on the development of a new fundamental treaty very loosely.[48]

A number of disputed issues concerning individual chapters of the Constitutional Treaty were decided on at the end of the Convention in the small Convention Praesidium group, and were submitted as an overall package to the subsequent Intergovernmental Conference. Under the prevailing time pressure, this "all or nothing" tactic led to an unforeseeable effect, since the accession of ten new EU members from Eastern and Southern Europe in May 2004 was on the agenda. Although the member states criticised the Convention's draft as overstepping the Laeken mandate due to the new developments it contained, it would simply have taken too much time to restart the entire Convention process again and have a more limited submission for an Intergovernmental Conference drawn up. It was also a matter of consensus that the EU required a new Treaty basis, prior to the implementation of eastward enlargement, in order to maintain the EU's ability to act and to absorb the new voices which would soon be heard in the EU institutions. The EU members at that time feared that amendments to the Treaty after eastward enlargement could not be undertaken with the same ambitions as was possible with the EU of 15 member states.

In view of this time pressure, the Intergovernmental Conference adopted the Convention's draft, with a few changes to the details, in 2004 and submitted the Constitutional Treaty to the member states for ratification. Barely a year later, the

---

47 Craig (2011²), pp. 73 ff.
48 Kaunert (2009), p. 468.

EU was thrown into what was thus far its most serious internal crisis, named the "constitutional crisis". In referenda held in France (54.7%) and the Netherlands (61.5%) – two of the EEC's founding members – the Constitutional Treaty was rejected with resounding majorities in 2005. The constitutional crisis, which dragged on until the Treaty of Lisbon came into effect on 1st December 2009 and made itself felt in all of the EU's political debates and legislative proposals during this period, shook the EU to the very depths of its identity. The implicit, permissive consensus which had been presumed up to that point was gone. Instead, it was established that the population's attitude towards constantly progressing European integration had changed. The EU was facing a fully fledged crisis of confidence, acceptance and legitimation which went far beyond the rejection of individual, unpopular areas of policy.[49] The political motto during this period was therefore to demonstrate the ability to act based on the Treaty of Nice but not to conduct any destructive debates which would prove harmful to Europe due to excessively ambitious proposals.[50] Controversial and emotionally charged, major projects undertaken in 2010 – 2014, such as the Banking Union, the debate on Eurobonds, common unemployment insurance or common taxes such as the financial transaction tax, which shook the very foundations of state sovereignty, would have been inconceivable in the 2005 – 2009 period.

Way out of the constitutional crisis

Resubmission of the Constitutional Treaty without amendments was politically out of the question – also in view of the likelihood of further defeats at the polls (e.g. in the United Kingdom).

In a period of reflection spanning several years from June 2005 – 2007, which Sweden's Communication Commissioner and current Foreign Minister, Margot Wallström, dubbed "Plan D" (democracy, dialogue and debate), the EU heads of state and government decided to shelve the Constitutional Treaty in political terms but not to declare it a failure.[51] The Constitutional Treaty was still ratified by a total of 18 states,[52] also through a referendum in Luxembourg. A group of member states joined forces under the name Friends of the Constitutional Treaty and, from 2007 onwards, campaigned not to ignore the successful ratifications but instead to recognise them as a desire for a new basis for the EU Treaty.

However, an historic time slot enabling a new attempt at reforming the Treaty did not arise until 2007. A role was played in this by political changes in the member states, as was the long period without elections in the major member states, which is something of a rarity in the European electoral calendar. France elected a new

---

49 Laumen and Maurer (2006).
50 Phinnemore (2013), p. 21.
51 Phinnemore (2013), p. 20.
52 Ratification completed or the parliamentary procedure run through to such an extent that ratification was practically completed.

President, Sarkozy, who was not tainted by the failed referendum on the Constitutional Treaty. The European Council meeting in June 2007, at which the negotiating mandate for the Treaty of Lisbon was resolved, was also Blair's final appearance as a head of government on the European stage. In the UK, Prime Minister Blair was preparing to hand over office to his party colleague Gordon Brown – Blair was not therefore compelled to take account of the political price of Treaty ratification by Britain's eurosceptical parliament during the Treaty negotiations. Following Germany's parliamentary elections in 2005, Federal Chancellor Merkel was governing in a stable, grand coalition, and took over the EU Council Presidency in rotation in January 2007.

In 2007, political Europe was looking expectantly towards Germany, the second-largest EU member state, which had held the Council Presidency since the failed referenda and was expected to breathe new life into the reform process.[53] Politically, the EU was facing a further major challenge at this point in time: a surge in public attention towards the dangers of climate change. This was triggered, amongst other things, by a report by the British economist and government advisor, Nicholas Stern, concerning the economic consequences of future climate change and the fourth IPCC[54] climate assessment report. Political debate within Europe was subsequently intensified by Chancellor Merkel's and Minister of the Environment Gabriel's trip to Greenland and the high-profile images of this trip. In recognition of the fact that no one member state alone is able to halt climate change, a reformed EU, in which climate-related efforts could be better bundled and asserted vis-à-vis major powers such as China and India in international climate negotiations, was seen as the preferred instrument in the fight against climate change.

Amidst the constitutional crisis and climate debate, the German Council Presidency chose the 50th anniversary of the Treaties of Rome on 25th March 2007 to gather the heads of state and government in Berlin and, as part of the "Berlin Declaration", obligate them to formulate a new basis for the EU by the European elections in May 2009.[55] On 19th June, the German Council Presidency circulated the draft mandate for the planned Intergovernmental Conference; it was accepted four days later by the European Council.[56]

With unanimous acceptance of the negotiating mandate for the Intergovernmental Conference, the German Council Presidency had pulled off a master-stroke. It was now left to the Portuguese Council Presidency to transform the mandate into a final Treaty text in an Intergovernmental Conference. After a very short Inter-

---

53 The United Kingdom took over the Council Presidency on 1st July 2005, but refused to engage in any discussion concerning the future of the Constitutional Treaty in the European Council (see Phinnemore (2013), p. 21).
54 Intergovernmental Panel on Climate Change (IPCC).
55 European Parliament/Council of the EU/Commission of European Communities (2007).
56 European Council (2007).

governmental Conference lasting only three months, the heads of state and government approved the Constitutional Treaty in October 2007, signed it on 13th December 2007 and commenced ratification according to the constitutional rules of their respective national states. Hungary became the first member state to ratify the Treaty of Lisbon on 17th December 2007, four days after it was officially signed by the heads of state and government.[57]

Ireland was the only member state to hold a referendum; on 12th June 2008, this plunged Europe into a state of shock through its rejection of the Treaty of Lisbon (53.4%). The French Council Presidency for the first half of 2008 thereupon issued a statement to the effect that the ratification process would be continued unchanged. Irish doubts, which had become apparent through the referendum, were to be dispelled through additional guarantees and, based on experiences with Nice and Maastricht, the country was to cast a second vote on 2nd October 2009. Once again, European introspection and the EU's constant dealings with the basis of its own Treaty were overtaken by external developments, which significantly increased the pressure on all actors at all levels of government – the collapse of Lehman Brothers and the subsequent banking crisis, which hit Europe with full force.

Initial indications of the subprime crisis first occurred in 2006/2007 in the USA – unsecured mortgages led to widespread evictions and major losses on the balance sheets of American banks.[58] In September 2008, Lehman Brothers filed for insolvency without the US government coming to its rescue. Whilst some European politicians were casting gloating glances to the west, the United Kingdom had already experienced a run on its fifth largest mortgage bank, Northern Rock, back in September 2007.[59] By the time of the second Irish referendum, the financial and banking crisis was in full swing in Europe, and was threatening to turn into a sovereign debt crisis due to the extensive state guarantees given to ailing banks. Irish banks which had close ties to the English-speaking markets were hit particularly hard by the crisis. As EU-wide austerity debates, rescue programmes for states and Troika reports were still inconceivable at that point in time, the majority of Irish viewed their EU membership in 2009 as an economic shield which was intended to protect them against the unchecked force of the financial markets. The second referendum therefore endorsed the Treaty of Lisbon with 67.1% of the votes. The Irish guarantees, which the European Council accepted on 19th June 2009, also contributed to this change in sentiment amongst the Irish population.[60] This was a political commitment, not an amendment to the Treaty of Lisbon, which had already been ratified by the majority of member states at that time. Amongst other aspects, these guarantees ensured that each member state would also be able to provide its "own" Commissioner in the future.

---

57 Langhorst and Ullrich (2008).
58 Bianco (2008).
59 N.U. (2008).
60 European Council (2009).

The final obstacles to the ratification of the Treaty of Lisbon involved constitutional law misgivings in some member states, including Germany and the Czech Republic. Whilst the German Federal President signed the Treaty following the Federal Constitutional Court's Lisbon ruling on 30th June 2009, the eurosceptic Czech President, Vaclav Klaus, refused to sign although the Czech parliament had accepted the Treaty. The Treaty was not able to come into force until 1st December 2009, after the resistance offered by President Vaclav Klaus has been overcome by extensive pressure on the part of the Czech parliament and due to the Czech constitutional court's rubber-stamping of the Treaty. Beforehand, however, the European Council had to adopt an additional protocol providing exceptions from the EU Charter of Fundamental Rights for the Czech Republic. [61]

4.3.1.2 How the chosen process determined the substance of the Treaty of Lisbon

In the preceding explanations, it has been shown that the realisation of the Treaty of Lisbon can only be explained in connection with the Constitutional Treaty. One further important point in analysing and explaining its content substance is the procedural component of its genesis. In the long history of the Treaty of Lisbon's evolution (Laeken Declaration 2001 – entry into force of the Treaty of Lisbon at the end of 2009), it is worthwhile taking a closer look at the negotiations surrounding the Treaty of Lisbon during the 2007–2008 period from a procedural perspective. The following section deals in detail with the German Council Presidency's preparation of the Intergovernmental Conference in 2007.

Three procedural factors explain how it was possible to rescue the substance of the Constitutional Treaty for the Treaty of Lisbon:

1. The establishment of a "base camp" consisting of an alliance of institutional and state actors dedicated to rescuing the TCE or at least its content.

2. The informal process which the German Council Presidency pursued to prepare the negotiating mandate for the Intergovernmental Conference in 2007.

3. The special form of the negotiating mandate, which played a major role as an agenda-setter.

Base camp and game of chess

There is no question that a project as significant and extensive as a Constitutional Treaty, which had failed so resoundingly in two referenda held in two founding states could not have been continued without a pro-active and well organised alliance. At the time of the German Council Presidency, such an alliance had already been established, and crucially influenced the narrative with which the necessity

---

61 Gehring, Delinic and Paul (2009).

of a Reform Treaty was explained.[62] In something resembling a military campaign, the key players, who considered a new Treaty basis for the EU indispensable and wanted to hang onto the substance of the Constitutional Treaty, had organised themselves into a "base camp", inspired each other over a period of months and kept the debate concerning the Constitutional Treaty going.

In January 2006, the European Parliament kicked things off by approving the Duff-Voggenhuber report, which called for the rescue of the TCE. In its *Rome Manifesto* in March 2006, the European People's Party (EPP) demanded that the European Council should give the process new impetus during the first half of 2007 (German Council Presidency). What was important about this manifesto was that the signatories also included nine heads of government or state, including Federal Chancellor Merkel and the future President of France, Sarkozy. This meant that two persons, who were to play key roles in negotiating and ratifying the Treaty of Lisbon over the coming years, were already campaigning to maintain the Constitution's substance back in 2006.[63] These demands were supported by a number of other member states, whose governments primarily voiced their opinions through newspaper interviews. These included Spain, the largest EU country, and Austria, which held the Council Presidency in 2006, but also Estonia and Finland. An informal meeting of the member states' Foreign Ministers in Klosterneuburg from 27th to 28th May 2006 confirmed the growing consensus that the German Council Presidency should attempt to guide the EU out of its blockade.[64] In her speech on 9th May 2006, the German Federal Chancellor stated that Europe must give itself a "constitutionality".[65] The German Council Presidency subsequently found further support in the Friends of the Constitutional Treaty, the informal group of member states which had already ratified the TCE, plus Ireland and Portugal.[66]

Following the constant efforts of individual key figures and the formation of alliances arguing against the more sceptical member states, the European Council's conclusions in June 2006 gave Chancellor Merkel the mandate to conduct consultations with the member states and, during the German Council Presidency, to develop proposals for possible solutions to the constitutional crisis.[67] It was vitally important that these efforts were flanked by various key players, consisting of institutional or state actors, because a Council Presidency is supposed to represent the consensus of the member states without itself extensively pushing in a specific direction. Large member states, in particular, often generate tension with smaller member states when pursuing their interests. Such confrontation would have been counterproductive amidst the political sentiment at that time and following

62 Phinnemore (2013), pp. 40 ff.
63 Phinnemore (2013), p. 26.
64 Phinnemore (2013), p. 26.
65 Phinnemore (2013), p. 29.
66 Phinnemore (2013), p. 60.
67 European Council (2006).

the carefully established political compromise to search for a solution to the constitutional crisis. The tactical interaction of diverse actors, who took turns in their roles as process drivers with specific demands, enabled the German Council Presidency to act as a compromise-finder and bridge-builder, and to keep the negotiation process moving. At the same time, the alliance of Constitution proponents ensured that the substance of the Constitutional Treaty was not disfigured beyond recognition in the process.

Berlin Declaration and Sherpa consultations: informal processes as the way to success

Once Germany had taken over the Council Presidency on 1st January 2007, the Berlin Declaration soon emerged as the formal start of a new Basic Treaty process for the EU – which soon came to be known as the Reform Treaty. This was to be signed by the heads of state and government in Berlin on the 50th anniversary of the Treaties of Rome. This very first opportunity revealed the German Council Presidency's process competence: as not all heads of state and government wanted to sign the Declaration calling for a fresh start to the reform process, the Presidents of the European Parliament, the European Commission and the Council were unceremoniously asked to sign it.[68]

The Berlin Declaration, which is often mentioned only as a footnote in the history of European unification, did not develop its effect as a result of this diplomatic crutch, however, but due to the process in which it was formulated.

The necessity of co-ordinating the text of the Berlin Declaration between the member states offered the Cabinet Offices a helpful pretext for exchanging views concerning the fate of the Constitutional Treaty.[69] As the intention was to avoid public debate and nevertheless quickly arrive at a result which offered a way out of the constitutional crisis, the German Council Presidency asked for the nomination of so-called "Sherpas" on 2nd January (one day following the start of the Council Presidency).[70] In international negotiations, Sherpas are high-ranking government representatives who have the trust of their heads of government. These were to represent their governments during the exploratory talks concerning the Berlin Declaration. It quickly became clear that the German Council Presidency was not using these exploratory talks solely for the Berlin Declaration, but was already sounding out options and negotiating positions for the Reform Treaty.[71]

With two exceptions, the Sherpa meetings took place as part of bilateral talks with German government officials, very rarely at multilateral gatherings. These Sherpa activities were accompanied by bilateral meetings between Federal Chancellor Merkel and her government colleagues. In public, the Federal Chancellor's meet-

---

68 Phinnemore (2013), p. 68.
69 Phinnemore (2013), p. 68.
70 Phinnemore (2013), p. 53.
71 See Phinnemore (2013), p. 68.

ings also became known as the "confessional meetings". Merkel's express wish was that the appointed Sherpas should also be authorised to speak for the respective government. In this manner, the Sherpas were to act as focal points in the exploratory talks. This was a top-down approach – the German Chancellor had declared the way out of the constitutional crisis to be a top priority: this was to be the responsibility of the state chancelleries, not the foreign ministries. The German Federal Foreign Office was only to be involved due to Germany's special Council Presidency role. Merkel's own focal point was Uwe Corsepius, who was employed as Merkel's European policy advisor at the Federal Chancellery at that time.[72]

In contrast to previous Treaty negotiation processes, this consciously avoided the route via the permanent representations in Brussels, which represented their governments' positions bottom-up in drawn-out statements. In addition, confidentiality was of great importance to the German Council Presidency, since public utterances could have led to the national governments becoming entrenched in their demands if they had been supported by the public. In view of the short span of the German Council Presidency, there was no time for face-saving, detailed solutions. The permanent representations in Brussels, which were known to be "information-leaking sieves", were not an option for the Federal Chancellor.[73]

Instead, all of the Sherpa consultations were conducted in Berlin with the participation of representatives of the President of the European Parliament, the European Commission and the General Secretariat of the Council as well as the member states. The Council Secretariat was a special interface in Merkel's efforts to determine a way out of the crisis, and initial, confidential consultations had already taken place prior to the German Council Presidency.[74]

The Constitutional Treaty was chosen as the starting point of the Sherpa exploratory talks, not the Treaty of Nice. The German Council Presidency, in particular, insisted that as much of the Constitutional Treaty's political substance as possible should be saved. The same line was taken by the Friends of the Constitutional Treaty. As has already been described, the backing of this group, which the present President of the Commission and former Prime Minister of Luxembourg, Jean-Claude Juncker, played a part in initiating, was extremely important to the German Council Presidency's efforts due to process reasons.[75]

A negotiating mandate without freedom to negotiate

Whilst the German Council Presidency had defined a process which was intended to show a way out of the constitutional crisis at the start of the Presidency (confidential, bilateral Sherpa exploratory talks in Berlin), the solution to the constitutional crisis

---

72 See Phinnemore (2013), pp. 53 ff.
73 Phinnemore (2013), p. 55.
74 Phinnemore (2013), p. 55.
75 Phinnemore (2013), pp. 60 ff.

remained unclear. Chancellor Merkel gave an insight into Germany's concepts for a solution in her speech to the European Parliament on 17th January: the Constitutional Treaty should be used as a springboard for a Reform Treaty. To achieve this, the individual member states' objections to the Constitutional Treaty would have to be determined and focus placed on a small number of very specific issues.[76]

It fell to Jean Claude Piris, head of the Council's legal department and legal expert in all Treaty amendments since 1990, to propose a solution to the German Council Presidency.[77] Between 2005 and 2006, Piris and his staff had already run through options and formulated a Treaty text containing parts of the TCE as proposed amendments to the existing Treaties.[78] Piris responded to the question concerning the process intended to lead to the member states' agreeing to a text by proposing that a very short Intergovernmental Conference be held and equipped with a detailed negotiating mandate. Previous negotiating mandates for Intergovernmental Conferences contained barely more than a few lines of specifications, whereas Piris estimated that this would stretch to 50 pages. The Intergovernmental Conference was to be depoliticised and reduced to a "technocratic exercise" which was merely to implement the detailed political mandate.[79]

In mid-January, the German Council Presidency was convinced of this proposal, and the corresponding government authorities began drafting a mandate which had never existed before in this form in the history of the EU. It was based on the concept of "reverse engineering". Instead of beginning with a blank sheet of paper, the Constitutional Treaty was used as the basis, and those passages which had to be amended to achieve unanimous approval of the new text were determined. This was based on a top-down approach, which the Council Presidency pursued with great political commitment.[80] The theory that the substance of the TCE has survived in the form of the TL can be underpinned on the basis of the negotiating mandate. A more detailed look at this curiosity of European unification history is therefore worthwhile.

In the Sherpa consultations, the Council Presidency had attempted to determine which amendments to the Constitutional text were necessary so that the member states could accept a new Treaty. It was strictly ensured that no other member state was fully apprised of the compromises which were discussed bilaterally:[81] this method guaranteed that process management remained firmly in the hands of the Council Presidency.

The draft mandate, which the German Council Presidency circulated on 19th June 2007 – two days prior to the crucial European Council summit meeting –

76 Phinnemore (2013), p. 64.
77 Phinnemore (2013), p. 65.
78 Phinnemore (2013), p. 65.
79 Phinnemore (2013), p. 66.
80 Phinnemore (2013), p. 110.
81 Phinnemore (2013), p. 134.

contained what the Chancellor had promised in her public speeches and bilateral consultations: a specific and clear mandate for an Intergovernmental Conference, consisting of 11 pages and Annexes running to more than 5700 words.[82] The draft mandate was accompanied by specific instructions:

1. The mandate was to be the sole basis for negotiations.

2. No issues outside of the mandate were to be dealt with.

3. The innovations introduced by the Treaty of Lisbon were to be retained.

Possible compromise texts in Treaty language, which were intended to allay the concerns raised by some member states during the bilateral consultations, were already enclosed with the draft mandate.[83]

Following receipt of the draft mandate, the Sherpas had 48 hours in which to familiarise themselves with and evaluate the proposals. The message of this undiplomatic process trick was clear: either this mandate is accepted or the process fails.

When the European Council summit meeting came to an end on 23rd June 2007, the German Council Presidency had achieved the impossible: all 27 heads of state and government had agreed to a mandate for an Intergovernmental Conference under the Portuguese Council Presidency. During the course of the heated negotiations, the draft mandate had grown to 16 pages and over 8500 words, corresponding roughly to the version of the consolidated EU Treaty at that time.[84] The content which the future Treaty of Lisbon would have was exhaustively reflected in the mandate. It defined the form of the future Treaty as an amendment agreement to the existing Treaties, specified what should happen with the content of the Constitutional Treaty, introduced new articles, protocols and declarations, and, in Annexes, even set forth the precise language version of the necessary Treaty amendments.[85]

In particular, the draft specified that the Intergovernmental Conference should implement the mandate during the formulation of the final Treaty text rather than engaging in negotiations. The specified objective was to integrate the innovations introduced by the Intergovernmental Conference in 2004 into the existing European Treaties. This refers to nothing other than the innovations in the Constitutional Treaty which were adopted during the Intergovernmental Conference in 2004.[86] This specification was clearly formulated in the final mandate. Changes to these innovations, which had been formulated in the light of the past six months' consultations, were listed separately and individually.

The German Council Presidency's plan proved successful during the Intergovernmental Conference in 2007. Whilst the Intergovernmental Conferences for the

---

82 Phinnemore (2013), p. 134.
83 European Council (2007).
84 Phinnemore (2013), p. 134.
85 European Council (2007).
86 Köppl (2008), pp. 230 ff.

Constitutional Treaty or the Treaty of Amsterdam were to last a further one and a half years, the 2007 Intergovernmental Conference was over after just three months, and dealt above all with transforming the unanimously adopted mandate into a formal Treaty text.

Conclusion

The genesis of the Treaty of Lisbon clearly and comprehensibly shows that the vast majority of the innovations introduced in the Constitutional Treaty for Europe continue to live on in the Treaty of Lisbon. Attempts have been made to quantify how much of the Constitutional Treaty's substance is found in the Treaty of Lisbon. Experts' assessments on this issue vary between 80 – 96 %[87] – something of which the majority of citizens, companies, associations and organisations, as well as a high number of executive and legislative level representatives of the EU member states and regions, are likely to be unaware.

The course of the German Council Presidency additionally offers two messages:

1. In an EU which now comprises 28 member states, a fundamental knowledge of the legal, political and informal processes is the key to a successful Council Presidency and the successful conclusion of a technical or political dossier.

2. The political "game of chess", including the relevant decision-makers at the executive and legislative level, must be mastered to ensure the desired result through alliances.

4.3.1.3 Evaluation of the differences between the Constitutional Treaty and the Treaty of Lisbon

In the following, the common features and differences between the Constitutional Treaty and the Treaty of Lisbon will be analysed and qualitatively assessed. As described in the preceding chapter, "reverse engineering" was employed in the negotiations concerning the Treaty of Lisbon: the government representatives did not commence the negotiations with a blank sheet of paper, but instead used the Constitutional Treaty as the basis for their work. They merely amended the provisions identified as critical during the consultation process which took place under the German Council Presidency. The mandate for the 2007 Intergovernmental Conference lists these identified provisions in detail in an Annex. Three years following the 2004 Intergovernmental Conference during which the Constitutional Treaty had been negotiated, the European Union saw itself faced by a range of new challenges. The 2007 Intergovernmental Conference reacted to these new challenges by giving the EU the necessary competencies or implicitly confirming existing competencies through specific Treaty articles.

The crucial differences between the Constitutional Treaty and the Treaty of Lisbon lie in the "elimination" of elements of statehood from the Constitutional

---

[87] Phinnemore (2013), p. 143; see Open Europe (2007).

Treaty, as demanded by certain member states at that time. For instance, the term "constitution" was removed from the Treaty of Lisbon, and the constitutional symbolism forgone in light of the rejection of the Constitutional Treaty in the two EU founder states, France and the Netherlands.[88] Use of the term constitution and the occasional use of constitutional and statehood symbolism had been regarded critically from the very beginning. Firstly, these characteristics were deemed by part of the population to have negative connotations. Secondly, the Constitutional Treaty's ambitions were limited, and fell far short of the formal legal requirements of a constitution. For instance, the name "Constitutional Treaty for Europe" indicated that this did not involve a nation state constitution, but that the Treaty, like all previous European Treaties, had ultimately arisen on the basis of intergovernmental treaty agreements.[89]

Forgoing the constitutional symbolism affected the structure of the Treaties: whilst the Constitutional Treaty still provided for a uniform constitutional document into which all previous EU Treaties were to be integrated, the Treaty of Lisbon was subdivided into two Treaties under primary law, the "Treaty on the European Union" (TEU) and the "Treaty on the Functioning of the European Union" (TFEU), which replaced the "Treaty establishing the European Community".[90] Both Treaties are assigned equal status and are the Treaties on which the EU is based. A uniform treaty structure containing all protocols, declarations and Treaties would almost certainly have contributed to making it legible to and ensuring its transmission to citizens; however, this splitting into two Treaties had no bearing on the substance, since it is irrelevant which of the two Treaties contains a provision due to their equal status under primary law.

Following the criticism levelled at the TCE's constitutional symbolism, the European flag and the anthem were omitted during the TL negotiations. However, they continue to be used on a voluntary basis and have not disappeared from public life.[91]

During the negotiations, the member states decided to delete the planned preamble of the Constitutional Treaty and instead include a reference to "the cultural, religious and humanist inheritance of Europe" in the TEU's preamble. As a preamble has no direct legal effects on the EU's competencies (but can instead serve merely as an aid for structuring individual regulations), this, too, cannot be regarded as a substantial change to the Constitutional Treaty.[92]

The designation "Foreign Minister" of the EU was also eliminated, and is now called the "High Representative of the Union for Foreign Affairs and Security Pol-

---

88 Köppl (2008), pp. 232 ff.
89 Köppl (2008), pp. 230 ff.
90 Köppl (2008), pp. 232 ff.
91 Köppl (2008), pp. 233 ff.
92 Köppl (2008), pp. 232 ff.

icy", without any substantial changes being made to the position's competencies, tasks or "toolbox".[93]

Changing the names of the legal instruments of law, framework law and resolution, as planned in the Constitutional Treaty, back to regulation, directive and decision was a purely symbolic measure.[94] As this amounts to a difference purely in the nomenclature, but not the effect, of these legal instruments, this dispensation with nation state symbolism has no specific effects on the functioning of the EU either.

As constitutions in democratically constituted states usually include a catalogue of basic rights at the beginning of the document, the "Charter of Fundamental Rights" was not incorporated completely into the text of the Treaty of Lisbon, as was planned in the Constitutional Treaty, in the process of renouncing the constitutional symbolism. This had no bearing on the Charter of Fundamental Rights' effectiveness, since it became legally binding through a reference in Article 6 of the TEU, although Poland and the UK succeeded in ensuring in the negotiations that the Charter is not applicable to them in specific cases.[95]

At the instigation of France which, under President Sarkozy, assumed the position during the negotiations that the Constitutional Treaty had been rejected by the French due to its neoliberal orientation in the 2005 referendum, the reference to "free and undistorted competition" was deleted as a Union objective in the Treaty of Lisbon.[96] Legal scholars view this change as purely cosmetic, since similar formulations are still found in the Treaty of Lisbon.

During the Lisbon negotiations, the Netherlands advocated strengthening the national parliaments.[97] The subsidiarity principle was reinforced and the national parliaments involved more extensively in its verification and compliance. However, this innovation had little bearing on the inter-institutional power structure of the decision-making process of the EU institutions, as the European Commission is able, with the exception of a very few cases, to ignore the national parliaments' subsidiarity concerns.

Poland opened up a political Pandora's Box during the negotiations on the Treaty of Lisbon: the voting rules in the Council. However, the final result also falls into the "cosmetic change" category, because ultimately, the heads of state and government did not agree to a change in the voting rules but merely to a postponement of these rules' coming into effect. The double majority in the Council therefore came into effect in November 2014 rather than in November 2009. A transitional period, in which the old (Nice) procedure applies at the request of a member state, is additionally in place until 2017.

---

93 Köppl (2008), pp. 233 ff.
94 Craig (2011²), pp. 73 ff.
95 Miller (2007).
96 Nowag (2012), p. 398.
97 Phinnemore (2013). p. 117.

Constitutional Treaty	Treaty of Lisbon[1] (Reform Treaty)
The Constitutional Treaty was structured according to the constitutional concept, which involved revoking all existing treaties and replacing them with a uniform text with the designation "Constitution".	The constitutional concept was abandoned in the Treaty of Lisbon. The term "constitution" is not used. The Treaty on the European Union (TEU) retains its designation, and the Treaty establishing the European Community (EC Treaty) is named the Treaty on the Functioning of the European Union (TFEU).
The Constitutional Treaty used the title "Union Minister for Foreign Affairs".	The title "High Representative of the Union for Foreign Affairs and Security Policy" was set down in the Treaty of Lisbon.
The Constitutional Treaty used the designations "law" and "framework law".	In the Treaty of Lisbon, the existing designations "regulation", "directive" and "decision" (or "resolution") are retained.
Article I-3 of the Constitutional Treaty contained the reference to "free and undistorted competition" as a Union objective.	The reference to "free and undistorted competition" as a Union objective from Article 3 TEU was deleted in the Treaty of Lisbon.
In the Constitutional Treaty, Article I-8 mentions the symbols of the EU, such as the flag, anthem and motto.	Article I-8 was deleted in the Treaty of Lisbon.
In the Constitutional Treaty, Article I-6 defined the priority of EU legislation.	The Treaty of Lisbon contains a declaration referring to the existing case law of the European Court of Justice.
The complete text of the Charter of Fundamental Rights was contained in the Constitutional Treaty.	Cross-reference in the Treaty of Lisbon (Article 6 TEU) to the agreed version of the Charter of Fundamental Rights.
The Constitutional Treaty contained no article regulating the role of the national parliaments in the subsidiarity check.	In the Treaty of Lisbon (Article 5 TEU), a general article regulates the role of the national parliaments in the subsidiarity check.
In the Constitutional Treaty (Article I-25), the procedure of decision-making with a double majority is applied directly when the Treaty comes into effect.	The agreed procedure for decision-making with a double majority only came into effect on 1st November 2014 (Article 16 TEU).
In the Constitutional Treaty, Article III-180 contained a provision permitting the European Council to implement measures in the event of supply difficulties. This provision was worded generally.	The provision from the Constitutional Treaty was adopted in the Treaty of Lisbon (Article 122 TFEU), and a reference to the spirit of solidarity between the member states and to the special case of energy in the event of difficulties in the supply of specific products was included.

A provision according to which competencies can be expressly returned to the national level in the course of a future Treaty amendment was finally included. This is an unnecessary clarification because, as the "Masters of the Treaties", the member states are, and always have been, able to shift competencies in either direction

Constitutional Treaty	Treaty of Lisbon[1] (Reform Treaty)
In the Constitutional Treaty, Article III-254 permitted the European Commission to develop a common European space policy. No restriction regarding the depth of integration of this policy area.	In the Treaty of Lisbon, a clause prohibiting harmonisation of the member states' legal regulations (Article 189 TFEU) was added to the provision of Article III-254 concerning the European space policy.
The Constitutional Treaty (Article III-233) did not include combating climate change as part of measures implemented at international level as a political objective.	The requirement for combating climate change as part of measures implemented at international level is specified in the Treaty of Lisbon (Article 191 TFEU).
In the Constitutional Treaty, the promotion of energy network interconnection was not listed explicitly in an extensive article concerning energy (Article III-256). Nor was there any reference to the spirit of solidarity between the member states in energy policy.	A reference to the spirit of solidarity between the member states and a new sub-item regarding the promotion of energy network interconnection were added to the article concerning energy in the Treaty of Lisbon (Article 194 TFEU).

[1] European Council (June 2007), http://www.consilium.europa.eu/uedocs/cms_data/docs/pressdata/de/ec/94935.pdf (last accessed on 27.01.2015).

Figure 4.4: Differences between the Constitutional Treaty and the Treaty of Lisbon

at any time in the course of Treaty amendments. The fact that this has not yet occurred in European history is not due to a lack of legal basis for authorisation but to a lack of national interest on the part of the member states, which have time and again come to the conclusion that joint, co-ordinated actions are more advantageous than separate, national approaches.

There have been very few "retrograde" changes to the EU's competencies. These primarily concern legal areas which affect the core area of state sovereignty, whereby only individual member states are affected in part. For example, Ireland and the United Kingdom were given permanent exemption from the previous pillar of EU domestic policy, besides clarifications on how to deal with increasing co-operation in Common Foreign and Security Policy, including clarifications on tax harmonisation.

In part, the shifts in competence and changed legal bases planned by the Constitutional Treaty for the EU were extended in very limited areas. As the debate on a common EU climate policy flared up from 2007 onwards, and the first Ukraine-Russia gas conflict added fuel to the energy security debate in 2006, both of these issues were given specific regulations in the Treaty of Lisbon. Due to other provisions in the EU Treaties, however, it was already *de facto* possible to implement measures in these areas.

Figure 4.4 shows a tabular overview of the differences between the Constitutional Treaty and the Treaty of Lisbon.

4.3.2 Strengthening the EU externally: the EU as a global player

The Treaty of Lisbon significantly strengthened the EU externally. The European Union is a global player and a trade policy heavyweight. It bundles more material and institutional resources than the majority of states in the world. It is militarily active, particularly in the Balkans and Africa. With a population of over 500 million, it has more inhabitants than the USA and Russia together. EU citizens are educated to top standards. European research is world-class. However, complaints are still being voiced that the political infrastructure of the EU is failing to keep pace with this potential, and that "thinking in global political categories" is lacking in Brussels.[98]

However, it was a particular concern of the Treaty of Lisbon to give the EU a foreign policy "face" and create options for its political activities in keeping with its role as a political "global player".[99] The objective was to lend the EU – which was previously regarded as a chorus of many voices rather than as a common voice of the member states in foreign policy terms – a coherent and visible external image.[100] The community of states is engaged in fierce economic competition with old and new economic centres around the globe, such as the USA, China, Japan, Brazil, India and Russia; by no means least as a result of their economic strength, these also make extensive political demands. Europe will only be able to play an equal-status role in this global context, whether this be in the International Monetary Fund, the United Nations Security Council or other international control and co-ordination bodies, if it, as the EU, is able to speak with one voice.[101]

At its core, the Treaty of Lisbon tackles this problem using three measures:

- For example, the EU now has a separate legal personality (Article 47 TEU); as an entity in international law, it is able to conclude international treaties or join international organisations, and therefore become more tangible as a partner for non-Community countries and international organisations.[102]
- As a foreign policy "face" and contact person for international partners, the Reform Treaty also introduced the office of the High Representative of the Union for Foreign Affairs and Security Policy – ultimately a kind of EU Foreign Minister – (Article 27 (2) and (3) TEU). The previous positions of EU External Affairs Commissioner and the EU Head of Foreign Policy have been merged in this office. At the same time, the High Representative is Vice President of the

---

98 Weidenfeld (2013b), p. 186.
99 See Pollak and Slominski (2012²), p. 214; with regard to the previous ranking in the field of foreign relations, see Sabathil, Joos and Keßler (2008), pp. 184–191.
100 Maurer (2008), p. 13.
101 Giegerich and Wallace (2010), pp. 451 ff.
102 European Patent Office (2013); see also Bieber, Epiney and Haag (2013¹⁰), § 3 Ri. 49 ff.; Murswiek (2008), p. 66.

European Commission and Chairman of the Committee on Foreign Affairs (one of the formations of the Council of the EU) (Article 18 (4) TEU).[103]

- Based on the Treaty of Lisbon, the newly established European External Action Service is subordinate to the High Representative (Article 27 (3) TEU); it is made up of officials of the Commission, the Council Secretariat and the diplomatic services of all member states.

Although the success of the EU's uniform public image has been rather poor so far – examples include foreign policy controversy concerning e. g. Libya in 2011 and Syria in 2013 or the tug-of-war, which some international partners found barely comprehensible, concerning EU measures during the euro crisis – the EU's partial foreign policy emancipation from its member states has set a crucial course. This is also true in the area of security policy: the previous European Security and Defence Policy (ESDP) was renamed the Common Security and Defence Policy (CSDP) (see Article 42 (1) TEU). It facilitates military co-operation between the member states. Within the bounds of their capabilities, all member states are obliged to provide mutual assistance: "If a Member State is the victim of armed aggression on its territory, the other Member States shall have towards it an obligation of aid and assistance by all the means in their power (...)" (Article 42 (7) TEU). During the course of this, for example, the European Defence Agency was incorporated in European primary law (Article 43 (3) TEU). It is intended to strengthen Europe's research and development in the defence industry. It offers a platform for permanent co-operation between the member states and the political will for this.[104]

In the field of foreign and security policy, the EU is gathering competencies and creating the option of its own foreign policy strategy, which is at least partly divorced from the member states.[105] Ultimately, this is an important step towards increased "statehood" for the EU[106] and – at least in the long term – towards a reduction of the member states' foreign policy importance.[107]

4.3.3 Strengthening the EU internally: transition from the principle of unanimity to the majority principle in the Council of the EU is becoming the usual case

In addition to raising its external profile, the EU was also strengthened internally. For example, the European Council, consisting of the heads of state and government of the member states, was strengthened. It was given a permanent President and was elevated to the rank of an EU institution. The European Council meet-

---

103 Weidenfeld (2013b), p. 193.
104 Devuyst (2012), p. 170.
105 Mix (2013), p. 2.
106 Murswiek (2008), pp. 66–67.
107 Sceptical, Giegerich and Wallace (2010), p. 454.

ings now take place more regularly and frequently. With the euro crisis, regular meetings of the heads of state and government of those countries which have the euro as their currency were also introduced.[108]

The reform measures in the area of political decision-making procedures have a far greater impact on the practice of lobbying. The focus of one of these measures is the transition from the principle of unanimity to the majority principle in the Council of the EU ("Council of Ministers" or "Council") in over 40 further cases.[109] The majority decision is thus becoming the usual case (Article 16 (3) TEU) and now covers practically all areas of policy which are crucial to citizens and companies – unanimity is now only required in exceptional cases within the Council (with regard to the so-called ordinary legislative procedure, see Chapter 5). In all, essential areas of policy such as the single market, internal affairs, agriculture, energy, intellectual property, public services, the judiciary, migration and much more besides fall under the majority decision rule in the Council.

The result is a considerable loss of influence for the individual member states: whereas the "veto" of a single member state was sufficient to block a decision in the Council or steer it in a desired direction whilst the principle of unanimity was valid, a blocking minority[110] of (at least) four member states, which together constitute more than 35 % of the EU's population, is required to achieve this under the majority principle.[111] Conversely, for example, Germany, France and the UK alone are no longer able to block a majority Council decision. However, the "no" votes of just four states would also only be sufficient if this were to involve the four largest member states, Germany, France, the UK and Italy. Arithmetically, a blocking minority consisting of smaller member states can require up to 13 members.

The extent to which the "communitarisation" of policy areas according to the Treaty of Lisbon has already progressed is revealed by taking a look at those areas which are still subject to the principle of unanimity. In this, a distinction can be made between outwardly directed policy areas (concerning the relationship between the EU and non-EU countries or international organisations) and inwardly directed policy areas (concerning the relationship between the EU and its member states).

Whilst the principle of unanimity still primarily applies in the former area ("outwards"), particularly in terms of accession agreements, certain trade agreements[112] and in defence policy plus (essentially) the Common Foreign and Secu-

---

108 Devuyst (2012), p. 169.
109 See tabular list in German Bundestag (2007), Table 1: Transition to the qualified majority, pp. 142 – 145; Devuyst (2012), p. 169.
110 Since 1.11.2014, see Article 16 (4) TEU; the majority rules according to the Treaty of Nice can still be applied until 31.3.2017.
111 Since 1.11.2014, see Article 238 (3) TFEU.
112 Trade agreements for cultural and audiovisual services plus social, educational and health services.

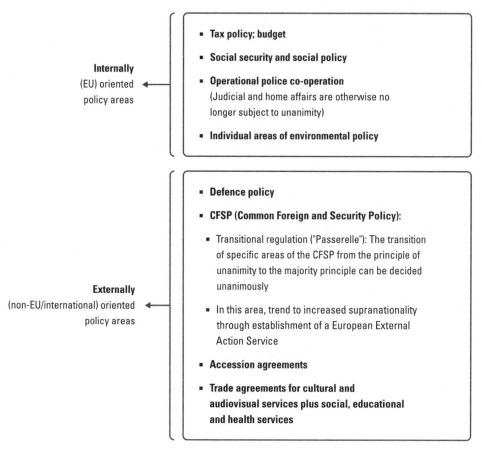

Figure 4.5: After the Treaty of Lisbon – only a very few EU policy areas which still require unanimity in Council decisions

rity Policy (CFSP), the Treaty of Lisbon has also introduced some cases of a qualified majority here (see particularly Article 31 TEU). The Passerelle clause of Article 48 (7) TEU can additionally be used to switch from the principle of unanimity to the majority principle. There is in any case a trend towards increased supranationalism in this area, as shown e.g. by the creation of the previously described External Action Service.

As regards the *inwardly* directed policy areas, only the areas of social security and social policy plus operational police co-operation are still subject to the principle of unanimity, in addition to tax harmonisation and EU budgetary policy. These are joined by individual areas of environmental policy. The instrument of increased co-operation can also be used to transform areas which, in themselves, are still subject to the principle of unanimity, *de facto* into majority principle use cases.

The consequences for the practice of European lobbying are clear: under the principle of unanimity, it is regularly sufficient to convince the crucial decision-makers of an individual member state of one's own concern.[113] The example of the negotiations concerning the Savings Taxation Directive in 2000 shows where this can lead to: Germany's Finance Minister at that time, Hans Eichel, reports[114] of a "veto" threatened during the course of the negotiations by Italy if Italy's milk quotas were not increased – an issue which does not even fall into the finance ministers' area of responsibility. The Italian agricultural lobby's tactic was nevertheless successful: in immediately scheduled telephone calls, the finance ministers persuaded their relevant member states' ministers of agriculture to give the required assurances. Only this caused Italy to agree to the "compromise approach" in the Savings Taxation Directive.

The validity of the majority principle has led to a significant increase in the requirements and the complexity of the lobbying process: even if a lobbyist is sufficiently well interconnected in his "home member state", he often has only a solitary position in EU Europe. It is therefore no longer sufficient to establish contact with individual – crucial – decision-makers in the home member state or to conduct campaigns using public affairs tools in important media within an individual member state. Even if a member state's votes are won for one's concern in this way, the political interests in the other 27 member states may deviate fundamentally from this – from extensive indifference to active opposition. At least a blocking minority of member states is required to support decision-making processes under the majority principle. This means that successful lobbying essentially requires a European approach: what is required are EU-wide cross-institution, -parliamentary group and -member state networks and equivalent (issue-related) coalitions, the establishment of which requires enormous practical effort – if they can be established at all.

This goes hand in hand with the vast increase in the number of action areas. Ultimately, the transfer of a competence does not mean that a policy area is now regulated exclusively at European level. Some are solely the responsibility of the EU, whilst others are regulated in mutual co-ordination with the member states. The conclusion drawn in political science is as follows: "the tasks of co-ordination and the number of possible and also necessary interaction relationships increase exponentially. Only efficiently organised actors with extensive resources can pursue their interests here."[115] It is noticeable that extensive resources alone do not yet lead to success in the representation of interests. Efficient organisation is required or, formulated differently: process competence in lobbying is required (see Chapters 3 and 10).

---

113 See Joos (2011), p. 110.
114 ARD (19.8.2013).
115 Kohler-Koch, Conzelmann and Knodt (2004), p. 171.

4.3.4 Strengthening of the European Parliament

The changes arising from the extension of the European Parliament's legislative responsibilities are equally as drastic for the practice of lobbying as the change in majority requirements in the Council.[116] The Treaty of Lisbon placed the Parliament on an equal footing with the Council in practically all important areas of policy, thus making it a fully-fledged partner in the legislative procedure.[117] As the "ordinary legislative procedure" (Articles 289, 294 TFEU), the co-decision procedure, in which both the European Parliament and the Council must give their approval to adopt a legislative measure, has now become the usual case.[118] Whilst there were 45 areas in which decisions could not be made without the involvement of the Parliament according to the Treaty of Nice, this number has almost doubled to 85 areas according to the Treaty of Lisbon.[119] In addition to the single market – as before – almost all individual provisions in judicial and home affairs policy, the framework decisions concerning agriculture and fisheries policies, trade policy, elements of economic policy co-ordination and the new policy areas of civil protection and administrative co-operation now also lie within the Parliament's area of authority.[120] The Parliament's budgetary powers have also been significantly increased through extension to the agricultural sector – so far at least approx. 45 % of the EU's budget.[121] The EP's rights of control vis-à-vis the Commission have also been extended; for instance, the EP selects the Commission President (Article 17 (7) TEU).[122]

The primary objective of this extension of the Parliament's responsibilities, as the only directly elected EU institution, was to increase the democratic legitimation of European legislation.[123] Naturally, the extension of the Parliament's co-decision powers also significantly affects the representation of political interests: in the policy areas which now fall into the Parliament's area of responsibility, lobbyists now also have to convince the majority of members of parliament (Members of the European Parliament, shortened to MEP) of their concerns – which, in view of the Parliament's composition and its special decision-making structures, not infrequently poses a major challenge. To understand this, one has to be aware of the differences between the European Parliament and the member states' elected assemblies (see Section 4.5.1.1):

---

116 With regard to the gradual strengthening of the European Parliament in the institutional structure, see Joos (1998), p. 159.
117 See Selck and Veen (2008), p. 18.
118 Bieber, Epiney and Haag (2013[10]), § 7 recital 18 ff.; Joos (2011), pp. 100–106.
119 Maurer (2008), p. 10; see German Bundestag (2007), Table 2: Transition to the ordinary legislative procedure, p. 146 ff.
120 Only the Common Foreign and Security Policy has remained as the Council's sole responsibility; with regard to the whole, see: Mangiameli (2012), p. 107.
121 European Commission (2013); see also Hauser (2011), pp. 6687–6688.
122 See Bieber, Epiney and Haag (2013[10]), § 4 Ri. 27.
123 See Maurer (2008), p. 8 ff.; Pollak and Slominski (2012), p. 185.

- For example, the European Parliament has neither government nor opposition groups. The executive level of the EU – with reference to the Commission and (in sub-areas) also the Council – does not arise from the legislative level.
- In addition to voting behaviour according to parliamentary group membership, cross-party voting behaviour characterised by the MEPs' nationality also frequently occurs.[124]

All of this affects issues of "European coalition building" in lobbying,[125] i.e. the formation of alliances amongst the actors at the legislative and executive level: such coalitions usually refer only to individual projects and issues, with the result that new coalitions have to be formed for each concern. Unexpected co-operation options often arise in this process: in the debate concerning the limitation of passenger car CO_2 output, for example, a joint partnership arose between the German automotive industry and trade unions. Industry and organised labour formed a partnership of convenience against Brussels' legislative plans, which they perceived as the threat, one party due to location and competition considerations, and the other party due to concerns about jobs.[126] Accordingly, allies were sought and found across all parliamentary groups, stakeholders and member states in the European Parliament. The previously addressed issue of the lack of government formation from legislative level ranks is expressed here: under certain circumstances, party or parliamentary group membership has little bearing on the direction taken by an MEP's decision. An EU-wide, cross-member state and -party network as well as trusting access to parliamentarians, at least those of the larger member states, have therefore become vital prerequisites of successful lobbying in Brussels.[127]

4.4 Integration theories and the multi-level system of the European Union

Since the EU's high level of integration has already been outlined on the basis of its historic development and a detailed analysis of the last major integration step, the Treaty of Lisbon, the member state integration process (or integration progress) and the EU governance system required for this will now be examined in greater detail on the basis of political science integration theories. The latter is of central importance to process-oriented lobbying, as the co-ordination of its process flows necessitates an extensive knowledge and understanding of the political system of the EU.

---

124 See Wessels (2008), p. 141.
125 Joos (2011), p. 91.
126 See the statements by Erich Klemm, chairman of what was then DaimlerChrysler AG's Central Works Council, and Jürgen Peters, chairman of German metalworkers trade union IG Metall in N.U. (2007).
127 See Joos (2011), p. 93.

Political science has developed various theoretical approaches for categorising and explaining the historic development of the EU. These so-called integration theories can help to identify historic events above and beyond individual cases and to reveal recurring patterns and trends in European integration. They additionally analyse the degree to which European integration has already taken place. Integration therefore refers to both the process and the state of peaceful and voluntary convergence and merger of societies, states and national economies across existing borders.[128]

For lobbying, such interpretations are very helpful for understanding the structure and complexity of the EU. They refer to the relationships between the member states and institutions, and show the influence which these actors have on EU politics. Some theories tend to give the central institutions more influence, whereas others tend to place increased emphasis on the importance of the member states. Such an analysis from a "bird's eye perspective" enables basic categorisation of the roles of institutions, member states and related decision-makers, decision-making structures and processes plus decision-making levels and hierarchies for lobbying.[129] The integration theories have the following tasks:

- They *select* the relevant factors and actors from the irrelevant ones and thus reduce the complexity of the integration process.
- They *order* and structure the integration process so that a distinction can be made between different analysis levels and actor groups.
- They *explain* the integration process. The hypothetically ascertained connections and factors of the integration process are compared against reality and can thus be accordingly interpreted.
- They attempt to *forecast* possible phases, scenarios and thresholds for further integration development.[130]

As a representative selection of integration theories, an overview of federalism, neo-functionalism, liberal intergovernmentalism, supranationalism and multi-level governance (MLG) will be presented (extensively) according to their chronological development.

Whilst the older theories primarily analyse the process of European integration in order to explain how and why this took place, the multi-level governance approach, in particular, goes beyond this. Rather than such an integration analysis, it is instead dedicated to the question of how governance is undertaken in the EU, who the political actors are, what policies are pursued and which decision-making processes exist.[131]

---

128 Weidenfled and Wessels (2006[9]), p. 285.
129 Irina Michalowitz (2007), p. 37, views the benefit of such global theories for lobbying more critically and refers to neo-pluralism, neo-corporatism and political network analysis. These have already been dealt with in greater detail in Chapters 2 and 3.
130 The four functions of integration theories are described in: Weidenfeld (2013[3]), p. 48.
131 See Pollak (2010[6]), p. 16.

4.4.1 Federalism

Federalism is both a political goal and a political science explanatory theory. For some political actors, it is an organisational structure to be achieved for unified Europe. For political scientists, it is a method for explaining the developments and the degree of integration in this unified Europe.[132] In particular, federalism was of great importance in both of its functions (political objective and scientific explanatory theory) at the start of the European unification process.

Federalism as a political objective

The European Movement of the inter-war period was federalist and wanted to establish a unified Europe as a federal state according to the American model. In 1923, Count Coudenhove-Kalergi imagined pan-Europe as a United States of Europe "according to the model of the United States of America". "Pan-Europe would act as a unit in the other parts of the world and vis-à-vis world powers, whilst each state within the federation would enjoy maximum freedom."[133] In his Ventotene Manifesto (1941), the Italian Altiero Spinelli, a progressive thinker and proponent of a federal Europe, subsequently a member of the European Commission and MEP for Italy's communist party, also advocated a European federation and the overcoming of nation state thinking dating from the 19th century: "The question which must be first resolved (…) is that of the abolition of the division of Europe into sovereign states."[134] Winston Churchill's demand for a United States of Europe in 1946 has already been mentioned (see Section 4.2). The following year, he spoke in the Royal Albert Hall of his hope "for the federation of the European States and for the creation of a Federal Constitution for Europe".[135] When the Council of Europe was established, it briefly appeared that the federalistic dream could indeed become reality.

Despite initial hopes, however, the subsequent European Union did not develop in the course or framework of a Constitutional Act. No federal state was created. Nevertheless, the idea of federalism remains an important political ideal today.[136] Particularly in the discussion concerning the purpose of European integration, the idea of a "European Federation" is constantly being brought into play – at the academic level by political scientists[137] and at the political level by politicians, e.g. in 2000 by Germany's Foreign Minister Joschka Fischer,[138] in 2013 by German Minister

---

132 Some political scientists only regard federalism as a political objective, and dispute the fact that it provides any theoretical knowledge; see: Große Hüttmann and Fischer (2005), pp. 54 ff.
133 Coudenhove-Kalergi (1923), p. 153.
134 Lipgens (1985), p. 478. Spinelli remained an advocate of the European federal state throughout his life. In 1958, he published the European Federalist's manifesto. In 1984, just two years prior to his death, he drafted a Constitution for Europe, which was also accepted by the European Parliament but not ratified by the member states.
135 Lipgens and Loth (1988), p. 768.
136 See Große Hüttmann and Fischer (2005), p. 59.
137 Simms (2012), pp. 60 ff.
138 Große Hüttmann and Fischer (2005), p. 42.

for Family Affairs Ursula von der Leyen[139] and in 2014 by the Vice President of the European Commission, Justice Commissioner Viviane Reding.[140]

Federalism as a political science integration theory

As a political science integration theory, the approach developed in the 1960s by Carl Joachim Friedrich is of particular importance.[141] He distanced himself from the idea that federalism is a static concept which could be established in one fell swoop by means of a constitution: "Federalism should not be understood as the designation of a static concept used to identify a special and precisely defined division between various levels of government."[142] Instead, federalism is much more a process "through which specific, independent, politically organised units, whether they be states or other associations, conclude an agreement in order to find political solutions to formulate a common policy and common decisions concerning common problems".[143]

Friedrich nevertheless argues in favour of strong federalistic institutions in this process. A federal union is based on a treaty, and requires:

1. An "assembly of the representatives of the founding communities".

2. An "executive body for the assembly's statements".

3. An "arbitration or judicial body which is responsible for interpreting the Treaty (...)".[144]

In today's EU, these roles are played by the European Council, the Council of Ministers, the European Commission and the European Court of Justice. However, their tasks occasionally overlap. For example, the Commission has both an executive and a legislative role.[145]

Further federalistic elements which reinforce the "central power" in the EU can be recognised e.g. in the extension of the majority principle for voting in the Council and the strengthening of the Parliament through the co-decision procedure, which became the ordinary legislative procedure with the Treaty of Lisbon.[146] Also, Union law takes priority over member state legislation.[147] The subsidiarity principle defined in the Maastricht Treaty is also a federalistic element. It serves as a guideline as to which issues are dealt with at "central" EU level and which at "peripheral" member state level.[148]

---

139 N.U. (2011c).
140 Watt (2014).
141 Friedrich (1964), pp. 154–187; Friedrich (1968).
142 Friedrich (1964), p. 166.
143 Friedrich (1964), p, 166.
144 Friedrich (1964), p. 179.
145 See Grimmel and Jakobeit (2009), p. 37.
146 Weidenfeld (2013³), p. 53.
147 Haratsch, Koenig and Pechstein (2010⁷), p. 85.
148 Große Hüttmann and Fischer (2005), p. 53.

As EU integration progressed as a result of the Treaties from the 1990s, federalism also gained in importance again as an integration theory.[149] As the traditional terms of federalism – e. g. that of the federal state – are not applicable for describing the European Union, modern political scientists are looking, as did Friedrich in the past, for new ways to explain the federal characteristics of the EU: the terms used include "supranational federalism" or also a "fusioned federal state".[150]

4.4.2 Neo-functionalism

In the European political reality of the 1950s, what took place was not the foundation of a federal state but the establishment of a functionally oriented organisation, the European Coal and Steel Community. This was the backdrop against which the political scientist Ernst B. Haas formulated the integration theory of neo-functionalism based on David Mitrany's concept of functionalism dating from the 1940s.

Functionalism rejects federalism as an integration theory. It claims that, firstly, federalism is too political to concentrate on technical, apolitical partnerships.[151] Secondly, it is excessively concerned with the integration of nation states, and has not therefore divorced itself from nation state thinking. This is obsolete, since the nation state itself is no longer the fixed authority that it once embodied: "In national government the definition of authority and the scope of public action are now in a continuous flux, and are determined less by constitutional norms than by practical requirements."[152] In addition to international law, various rules, conventions and "*ad hoc* functional arrangements" also play a major role in the organisation of "common activities" in the states' international relationships with each other.[153] It is precisely these functional arrangements on which functionalists focus their analysis.

Above all, neo-functionalism therefore explains European integration in sectoral terms. This means that the unification process initially takes place in the economic, social and political sectors, in which common (transnational) problems occur, which can also be solved in union (transnationally). This means that integration takes place on a problem-oriented basis, not an idealistic or political basis. Integration leads to the emergence of supranational institutions (such as the High Authority of the ECSC or the European Parliament), whose treaty-based form and structure are determined according to their tasks and functions – the "form follows function" principle therefore prevails to a certain extent.[154]

---

149 Große Hüttmann and Fischer (2005), p. 57.
150 Große Hüttmann and Fischer (2005), pp. 56 – 57.
151 See Wolf (2005), p. 65.
152 Mitrany (1943), p. 13.
153 Mitrany (1943), p. 20.
154 Weidenfeld (2013³), p. 57; Grimmel and Jakobeit (2009), p. 99.

This form of integration has been implemented in practice through the "Monnet method". Jean Monnet, after whom the method is named, stood for European integration in small steps: "I have always felt that the political union of Europe must be built step by step like its economic integration."[155] Monnet, one of the founding fathers of a united Europe, was a French businessman, technocrat and the actual force behind the idea of the Schuman Plan of 1950. As chairman of the French Commissariat géńeral du Plan (Planning Office), he formulated plans for modernising the French economy. He was convinced that the resources of one individual country could not suffice to raise the standard of living in post-war European countries: "It was necessary to transcend the national framework."[156] European co-operation in the economic sector therefore had to be established to create a common market.

European integration was therefore only implemented in those sectors in which the states were willing to collaborate. Above all, this was to be governed through practical issues, not political issues. The ECSC was therefore first founded in 1952. In due course, integration of the coal and steel industry was followed by considerations to also integrate other sectors of the economy, politics and society, such as labour law and socio-political issues.[157]

This incorporation of an increasing number of areas into the community was referred to by the political scientist Ernst Haas as spill-over. Leon N. Lindberg defined the term spill-over in greater detail: "Spill-over refers to a situation in which a given action, related to a specific goal, creates a situation in which the original goal can be assured only by taking further actions, which in turn create a further condition, a need for more action and so forth."[158] A more recent example is the extension of the EU's authority to central areas of home affairs and justice policy, a spill-over resulting from economic integration (single market) and global challenges such as international criminality and terrorism.[159]

In recent years, it has been shown how spill-over drives integration forwards. For example, the ESM and Fiscal Pact became necessary as a result of the European sovereign debt crisis. However, this would probably not have occurred without the Monetary Union. The European banking crisis led to the extension of the ECB's tasks in terms of banking supervision (Single Supervisory Mechanism, SSM) and the introduction of the Single Resolution Mechanism (SRM) for banks in "difficulties". The SSM and SRM are two pillars of the so-called Banking Union, dubbed "the most ambitious integration project since the creation of the

---

155 Monnet (1962), p. 208.
156 Monnet (1962), p. 205.
157 Haas (1958), pp. 269–270.
158 Lindberg (1963), p. 10.
159 Wessels (2008), p. 427.

single currency 14 years ago"[160] by commentators in 2014. With this, the EU undertakes new functions, and a new form had to follow as per the constraints – form follows function.

The theory of neo-functionalism was further differentiated and, in addition to spill-over, a possible reverse development, spill-back, was also taken into consideration.[161] The background to this was the blockade policy of French President Charles de Gaulle, when France prevented decision-making in the Council with its "empty chair policy".[162] Spill-backs are also possible today, at least in theory, because the crisis has led to some voices demanding the return of competencies from Brussels to the member states. Former British Prime Minister David Cameron held a referendum regarding the UK remaining in the EU (held on 23 June 2016, leave won by 52% to 48%).[163] However, the member state's political will to change the Treaty on the European Union is finite.[164] Apart from this, the legal hurdles are relatively high, or at least higher than the majority of constitutional changes at national level.

The main criticism levelled at neo-functionalism was that a certain degree of teleology and automatism is inherent in it. The unification of Europe is almost as unstoppable as a law of nature.[165] Despite all automatism, neo-functionalism also designates the actors of the European integration process, the technocratic and political elites. "In our scheme of integration elites are the leaders of all relevant political groups who habitually participate in the making of public decisions, whether as policy-makers in government, as lobbyists or as spokesmen of political parties. They include the officials of trade associations, the spokesmen of organised labour, higher civil servants and active politicians."[166]

Two interesting aspects can be derived from this for successful lobbying: firstly, an active role in structuring European politics and European integration is assigned to lobbyists. Secondly, the list of political actors refers to possible decision-makers. Reference is made here to parties, the administration, associations and trade unions, all of which may play a role in the decision-making process. Whilst the essential political direction is specified by the European Council consisting of the heads of state and government, it is the EU Commission which has the right of initiative for EU legislation. The parties in the European Parliament form coalitions to assert content in certain legislative proposals, and lobbyists, i.e. from associations and trade unions, attempt to play a part in structuring laws. All actors can be possible contacts and perhaps even "coalition partners" for one's own concern.

---

160 Barker (2014).
161 See the detailed overview in Weidenfeld (2013³), p. 58 ff.; or Wolf (2005), p. 79.
162 With regard to the "empty chair policy", see Loth (2014), pp. 134–142.
163 N.U. (2015b).
164 N.U. (2015e).
165 See Wolf (2005), pp. 76–77.
166 Haas (1958), p. 17.

4.4.3 Liberal intergovernmentalism

Another integration theory is that of intergovernmentalism. In contrast to neo-functionalism, this theory is state-centred: the primary drivers of European integration are not transnational challenges and problems or supranational institutions (such as the High Authority of the ECSC), but the European nation states and their governments. Intergovernmentalism is the central opponent of all theories which prophesy the disappearance of the nation state in Europe:[167] "The nation state is still there (...)."[168]

Stanley Hoffmann, the main advocate of intergovernmentalism in the 1960s, emphasised the leadership of political actors[169] and rejected neo-functionalism as being too technical. He claimed that more than the existing processes and process conditions would be required for integration which could surmount the nation state: "A procedure is not a purpose, a process is not a policy."[170] According to Hoffmann, European integration takes place primarily in the area which he refers to as "low politics". This includes the integration of economic areas such as coal and steel in the ECSC, but also the common single market. He states, however, that such integration successes do not make the leap to more sensitive areas of politics, such as foreign and security policy, which affect the sovereignty of the member states, so-called "high politics".[171] Despite this sensitivity, an increasing integration process is now also emerging in the areas of high politics. With the Maastricht Treaty, for example, the Common Foreign and Security Policy (CFSP) was established as a pillar of the Union on the basis of European Political Cooperation (EPC), and was reformed and strengthened with the Treaty of Lisbon. Together with the areas of home affairs and judicial policy, the CFSP is advancing into the area of high politics. The High Representative of the Union for Foreign Affairs and Security Policy and the European External Action Service (EEAS) are a strong indication of the fact that the areas of high politics can also become part of European integration.[172]

Andrew Moravcsik's liberal intergovernmentalism is a further development of Hoffmann's theories. Whilst Hoffmann believes that the nation states' external image is more that of "self-contained blocks", and that European integration and decision-making processes are determined by the member states' foreign policy, Moravcsik also regards the member states' home affairs policies as relevant to their European political decisions. Firstly, for instance, preferences are formed within a member state under consideration of the political and social power structures prevailing there. Therefore, "a country's behaviour is the result of competition between different societal actors who are competing to influence governmental decisions".[173]

---

167 Grimmel and Jakobeit (2009), p. 134.
168 Hoffmann (1966), p. 863.
169 Weidenfeld (2013[3]), p. 62.
170 Hoffmann (1966), p. 881.
171 Hoffmann (1966), pp. 882, 901; Bieling (2005), pp. 102–103.
172 See Weidenfeld, (2013[3]), p. 63.
173 Steinhilber (2005), p. 177.

Accordingly, the actions of the member states at EU level are also determined by internal, national interests. They therefore act out of national interest, and not on the basis of European strategic or geostrategic considerations. A sobering résumé of liberal intergovernmentalism is therefore: "Ultimately, Moravcsik views European politics as nothing other than the continuation of national state policy interests by other means."[174]

Once preferences have been formed within a member state, bargaining between the states commences. "Governments first define a set of interests, then bargain among themselves in an effort to realize those interests."[175] Moravcsik assumes that the member states' preferences are defined during this bargaining.[176] The supranational institutions of the EU, such as the European Commission, for instance, are necessary to implement and validate the bargaining results, and ultimately to make progress in European integration.[177] However, no power of initiative is attributed to them in the integration process.

According to Moravcsik, the driving force is assigned to the intergovernmental elements, e.g. the Council of the EU, in which the member states' relevant ministers meet, or the European Council, in which the heads of state and government assemble, and which sets the major EU policy initiatives. The EU integration steps are always the results of voluntary negotiations and rational decisions by the governments on the basis of the member states' converging interests and preferences, and not supranational initiatives or "automatic" spill-over.[178]

Moravcsik's reference to preference formation in the member states is particularly important to successful lobbying. It acts as a reminder not only to think in terms of Brussels as a centre in the EU decision-making processes but also to give consideration to the decision-making processes in the member states.

However, lobbyists must also remember that, contrary to Moravcsik's assumption, member state preferences can indeed change during bargaining (e.g. as a result of changes of government or other external changes and day-to-day political stimuli). Nor is preference formation in the member states isolated; it can most certainly be influenced directly or indirectly by other member states. The freedom of movement in Europe and the multi-lingual capability of many EU citizens is also increasingly leading to a European public. Preference formation in the states must no longer be regarded in isolation. Moravcsik simplifies here.[179] He also

---

174 Weidenfeld (2013³), pp. 65–66.
175 Moravcsik (1993), p. 481.
176 See Moravcsik (1993), pp. 497–498, which does not deal with a possible change in national preferences due to internal influences.
177 Moravcsik (1993), p. 507, talks about supranational institutions strengthening the national governments.
178 Steinhilber (2005), pp. 183–184; Moravscik (2002), pp. 604 ff., 609, highlights the importance of the nation states in the political system of the EU in comparison with the importance of the supranational institutions.
179 Steinhilber (2005), p. 181.

overlooks important supranational elements of the EU, such as the majority principle in the European Council or the Commission's right of initiative in legislative proposals as part of the ordinary legislative procedure.

4.4.4 Supranationalism

In the 1990s, the American political scientists Wayne Sandholtz and Alec Stone Sweet developed the integration theory of supranationalism on the basis of neofunctionalism;[180] this analyses "why the European integration process is proceeding irregularly and at varying paces in different sectors. Whilst political decision-making still follows the intergovernmental pattern in some policy areas, it is more appropriately termed supranational governance in other areas."[181]

Supranationalism places particular focus on transnational exchange, which becomes the motor for the emergence of supranational organisations and institutions. Transnational exchange is backed by a transnational society with transnational actors from the economy, the societal sector and politics which want to solve transnational problems, and which need and demand supranational institutions to do so.[182]

The central analysis objects of supranationalism are:

- The development of a transnational society: non-governmental actors which are involved directly or indirectly in the decision-making processes.
- The role of supranational institutions with the authority to drive forwards their own integrative agenda, i.e. which are able to produce, implement and interpret regulations.
- European legislative activity.[183]

The role ascribed to non-governmental actors in the integration process is of crucial importance to lobbying. In addition to European regulations and European institutions, the shift from intergovernmental to supranational governance is also determined by a "transnational society": "(...) those non-governing neutral actors who engage in intra-EC exchange – social, economic, political – and thereby influence directly or indirectly, policy-making processes and outcomes at the European level."[184] This means that the political decision-making processes in Europe are not determined solely by the member states and their governments, but are also extensively influenced by companies and associations, etc.

Supranational institutions in the EU include the European Commission, which has the right of legislative initiative in the ordinary legislative procedure, the European Parliament, with parliamentary members from all 28 member states, or

---

180 Sandholtz and Stone Sweet (1998), p. 5: "Our theory has important affinities with neofunctionalism."
181 Nölke (2005), p. 145; Sandholtz and Stone Sweet (1998), p. 1: "Why does policymaking sometimes migrate from the nation-state level to the European Community?".
182 Sandholtz and Sweet Stone (1998), pp. 11–15.
183 Sandholtz and Sweet Stone (1998), p. 6.
184 Sandholtz and Sweet Stone (1998), p. 9.

also the European Court of Justice, whose authority in structuring the primary law is generally recognised by the member states' law courts.

4.4.5 Multi-level governance

During its first few decades, EC/EU research concentrated primarily on the political integration of the European states. Analyses were conducted into how and in which areas of policy the EC/EU member states gave up their sovereignty in part and how decision-making powers were transferred from the national to the European level and the newly established supranational institutions.[185]

With the increasing supranational competence of the EC/EU and the related shift in political decisions to Brussels, research focus moved from issues concerning European integration and the emergence of European institutions to the question of how political decisions are made in Europe.[186] In other words: government – governance[187] – is the focus of analysis here. This paradigm shift – also called governance turn – was kicked off by theoretical, conceptual considerations[188] as well as real-life factors.

Conceptually, it was recognised that neither intergovernmental nor supranational approaches are able to comprehensively describe the EU.[189] Real-life, political Europe had further developed. For example, European integration had been driven forwards due to the Single European Act and the structure of the common single market in the 1980s or the establishment of the EU through the Maastricht Treaty and its subsequent treaties.[190]

The multi-level governance (MLG) approach, which was particularly developed by Gary Marks and Liesbet Hooghe in the 1990s, deserves emphasising here.[191] In Germany, reference is usually made to "government in the multi-level system". Whilst intergovernmentalism assumes that EU decisions are determined primarily by the member states, the MLG approach questions the central importance of the member states. The majority decisions in the Council alone are leading to a reduction in the influence of an individual member state.[192] The influence of supranational institutions such as the European Parliament, the European Commission and the European Court of Justice has also increased since the Single European Act of 1986.[193] The Commission additionally has the sole right of initiative for EU legislation.[194]

---

185 Kohler-Koch and Rittberger (2009), p. 3.
186 Jachtenfuchs and Kohler-Koch, (2003²), p. 16: this not only involves the transfer of authority but also informal changes in the co-operation between member states and the EU institutions.
187 With regard to the terms government and governance (in German): Jachtenfuchs (2003), p. 495.
188 This refers to continued development from realistic to constructivistic theories.
189 Scharpf (2010), pp. 67 ff.
190 Kohler-Koch and Rittberger (2009), pp. 3–4.
191 Marks (1993); Marks, Hooghe and Blank (1996); Hooghe and Marks (2001).
192 Marks, Hooghe and Blank (1996), p. 350.
193 Marks. Hooghe and Blank (1996), p. 343.
194 By means of a majority decision, however, the Commission can request the European Parliament to submit proposals for issues which the Parliament believes necessitate Union legislation (Article 225 TFEU).

MLG generally places state autonomy for specific areas into question, because it is no longer the nation states (or EU member states) alone which make the decisions in a globalised, complex world. Many issues, particularly environmental policy challenges, are transnational and can no longer be resolved by one state alone. International co-operation between states in resolving these issues is not necessarily of value in itself, as was the case in the federalism approach, for example, but is merely a means to an end.[195]

Decision-making hierarchies break down: intergovernmentalism takes the view that opinion-forming occurs in the member states, and that these then externally represent the opinion which has been formed and negotiate with other states. The hierarchy therefore passes from local and internal to the supranational entity, such as the EU, via the member states. However, research into MLG shows: "From the 1980s, a system of multi-level governance arose, in which national governmental control became diluted by the activities of supranational and subnational actors."[196] Governing is not only undertaken by governments, which are ideally positioned at the top of the decision-making hierarchy, but also by other actors which have a non-hierarchical relationship with one another.[197] "States are an integral and powerful part of the EU, but they no longer provide the sole interface between supranational and subnational arenas, and they share, rather than monopolize, control over many activities that take place in their respective territories."[198] In other words: in the EU, all decision-making levels, supranational, national and sub-national, communicate with and amongst each other.[199] This means, for instance, that the German Länder (states) communicate directly with the EU institutions without choosing to proceed via the national government. The representations of the respective Länder in Brussels are proof of this.

The dwindling importance of the nation states in the EU means that lobbying must not rely solely on national actors and networks but should instead choose a pan-European approach which also includes various actors at the different decision-making levels (local, national, supranational). As there is no clear hierarchy of decision-making levels in the political system of the EU, there is no *one* solitary decision-making level or *one* solitary decision-maker which may be a possible, sole contact for lobbying (see also Chapter 5 for detail).

In the member states, governments can rely on the support of their government majorities in parliament in their work, which simplifies governing. The case in the EU is different. The Commission and the Parliament do not work together in the manner familiar from the member states. For example, the Commission cannot rely on a parliamentary majority for "governing"; it has to seek a compromise

---

195 Jachtenfuchs (2003), p. 499.
196 Marks, Hooghe and Blank (1996), p. 373; Hooghe and Marks (2001), p. 4.
197 Jachtenfuchs (2003), p. 495.
198 Marks, Hooghe and Blank (1996), p. 347.
199 Marks, Hooghe and Blank (1996), p. 346.

with the European Parliament's political groups. *Cum grano salis*, this can be compared to the situation that the American President has no party majority in Congress or that a German government has a majority in the Bundestag, but not in the state assembly, the Bundesrat. Nor can the member state governments which are represented in the Council trust *a priori* in the support of "their" national members of parliament. The parliamentarians "represent those living in particular territories, but not necessarily the governments of those territories".[200] "The particularly characteristic feature of government in the EU is the organisation of opinion-forming in networks. The nodes are the numerous committees in the EU system."[201] An extensive, EU-wide network encompassing institutions, parties and member states is therefore important for successful lobbying.

When the importance of the nation state decreases, that of other stakeholders increases. Not only supranational and sub-national institutions, but also societal stakeholders, play a role, e.g. citizens' initiatives, companies, associations, trade unions and NGOs. They all have access to the institutions of the EU without having to channel their concerns via their nation states.[202] In its decision-making processes, the European Union therefore not only seeks consensus amongst the member states, but also with private groups and organisations, NGOs and companies. Both the Commission and the Council are "geared towards finding ground with stakeholders and accommodating nationally aggregated interests through compromise" (see also Section 4.5.3). Added to this is the fact that decisions are not necessarily made politically, but objectively, because: "The forging of ideology-based majorities is seen as counter-productive to decision-making efficiency."[203] This fosters an objective portrayal of arguments and the consideration of interests. The involvement of non-state and civil society actors in political opinion-forming contributes towards opinion plurality and thus democratisation in the multi-level system of the European Union.[204]

It is therefore set down with corresponding clarity in the Treaty on the European Union that the citizens of the EU are expressly granted the right "to participate in the democratic life of the Union" (Article 10 (3) TEU). By means of citizens' initiatives, the European Commission can even be invited to submit proposals on matters where citizens consider that a legal act is required (Article 11 (4) TEU). In addition, the EU institutions, e.g. the Commission, Parliament and Council, are obliged "by appropriate means, [to] give citizens and representative associations the opportunity to make known and publicly exchange their views in all areas of Union action" (Article 11 (1) TEU). The institutions are also required to "maintain an open, transparent and regular dialogue with representative associations and civil society" (Article 11 (2) TEU).

---

200 Hooghe and Marks (2001), p. 9.
201 Jachtenfuchs and Kohler-Koch (2003[2]), p. 25.
202 Grimmel and Jakobeit (2009), p. 315.
203 Kohler-Koch and Rittberger (2009), p. 9.
204 Weidenfeld (2013[3]), p. 55.

However, the extent to which the increasing politicisation of the EU will extend to the decision-making process remains to be seen. For the first time, the parties nominated top, pan-European candidates for the European elections in May 2014 – e.g. the Jean-Claude Juncker (EPP), Martin Schulz (S&D), Ska Keller and José Bové (Greens/EFA). For the first time in the history of the EU, Jean-Claude Juncker, whose EPP party emerged from the elections as the strongest parliamentary group, was elected as President of the European Commission by the European Parliament – and additionally proposed by the European Council – as specified by the Treaty of Lisbon of 2009 (Article 7 (7) TEU).

It can already be seen that increasing politicisation and ultimately also democratisation (of the EU institutions) do not simplify decision-making in the complex, multi-level system of Europe.[205] Not only is the politicisation of EU decisions emerging, but also the Europeanisation of member state policies and institutions.[206] Europeanisation refers to "Processes of (a) construction (b) diffusion and (c) institutionalisation of formal and informal rules, procedures, policy paradigms, styles, ways of doing and shared beliefs and norms, which are first defined and consolidated in the making of EU decisions and then incorporated in the logic of domestic discourse, identities, political structures and public policies".[207]

This expresses what takes place at national level when the European institutions develop their effect:[208] with around 500 supranational political decisions per year and via legislative acts such as regulations and directives, the EU firstly has a direct, top-down influence on the member states' policies through vertical stimuli (so-called positive integration). This is particularly the case in communitised areas of policy such as the environment and consumer protection.[209] The UK, for example, was forced to accept the "principle of precautionary action and the setting of legal pollution standards" in the environmental policy. From then on, negotiation between industry and environmental inspectors was no longer possible, and was superseded by more formal procedures.[210] However, the EU also limits the member states' scope of action by ruling out member state regulatory options (so-called negative integration),[211] such as e.g. regulations in the area of the single market, which (would) impede the free market and competition.[212] As part of the coalition negotiations conducted to form the German government in 2013, German politicians informed the European Commission about whether, or not, the

---

205 Criticism is levelled here by Kohler-Koch and Rittberger (2009), p. 13, who do not foresee politicisation beyond the national level, as European elections do not really involve governmental offices. However, this assessment dates from 2006.
206 Overview in: Auel (2005); Pollack (2010⁶), p. 37. Héritier (2001), p. 1.
207 Radaelli (2003), p. 30.
208 Auel (2005), p. 294.
209 Auel (2005), p. 293.
210 Example from Héritier (2001), p. 1.
211 Auel (2005), pp. 306–308; Scharpf (2010), p. 69.
212 Auel (2005), p. 303.

discounts on electricity charges for German industrial enterprises were "EU-compliant", and the German Transport Minister met with the EU Commissioner for Transport to co-ordinate a planned passenger car toll.[213] The EU therefore influenced member state policy before it was formulated and structured in the first place. The European Union thus exerted an influence on the formulation of member state policy during its development process.

Secondly, the EU indirectly influences member state policy through horizontal stimuli, since the member states orient their policies to those of other member states (so-called horizontal integration). This means that, at least in some areas, member states attempt to co-ordinate their policies, e.g. foreign and security policy, although this is not always a complete success, as for example in 2003 during the war against Iraq or against Libya in 2011. One other example is tax policy, where the EU fosters co-ordination through minimum standards, as in the case of value added tax.[214]

However, the effects of stimuli from the EU may vary in the member states: whilst EU-compliant regulations already apply in one country, for example, another member state may possibly first have to implement adjustments. The influence of the EU in the different member states is therefore also perceived differently.[215]

Case law is also undergoing Europeanisation. The ECJ is the only entity which is able to interpret the European Treaties. Secondly, national courts are also relinquishing their rights and recognising the ECJ as the last-instance decision-maker. In 2000, for example, the German Federal Constitutional Court relinquished its right to make last-instance rulings in issues of individual freedoms.[216] "As a consequence, European law is routinely enforced in ordinary cases and controversies by the judicial systems of member states."[217]

The Europeanisation of national policy shows that the EU is firmly anchored in the day-to-day politics of the member states at European, national, regional and local level (simply consider communities' pan-European invitations to tender for construction projects) and also political party level.[218] For European lobbying, this therefore results in issues at all EU decision-making levels, including national and regional levels.

Conclusion

All integration theories have strengths and weaknesses. In its own way, each theory attempts to explain the historically evolved complexity of the EU. There are examples from political reality which confirm all of these theoretical approaches.

---

213 N.U. (2013).
214 Auel (2005), pp. 306–309.
215 Héritier (2001), p. 9.
216 Scharpf (2010), p. 72.
217 Scharpf (2010), p. 72.
218 With regard to the Europeanisation of political parties, see Külahci (2012).

Nevertheless, each of these approaches, by itself, appears to fall too short. Even the unbiased analytical concept of multi-level governance is subject to criticism, because there is ultimately no answer to the question of "Who has the power over whom in the EU?"[219]

The European Union remains a political system *sui generis*: neither a federal state nor a confederation of sovereign states. It has intergovernmental and supranational elements. The member states are sovereign, and yet they have relinquished sovereignty to the EU; a crux which has been in existence since the beginning of European integration. As early as 1958, Ernst Haas described the ECSC as a political order *sui generis* – "neither federal nor inter-governmental".[220] In 1993, in the so-called "Maastricht ruling",[221] the German Federal Constitutional Court had attempted to categorise the EU as a "union of states".

In view of this complexity, familiarity with the theoretical access options is all the more important in order to make the "system of the EU" comprehensible and to classify it. The following is important for lobbying: "Traditional statehood is radically changed through this integrated union; regulations are no longer enacted autonomously exclusively through the actions of a sovereign state, but instead find themselves in occasionally complex bargaining processes which take place between representatives of states, Union institutions and stakeholders."[222]

4.5 Political stakeholders in the European Union

The examination of the historic development (Sections 4.2 and 4.3) and the analysis on the basis of political science theories (Section 4.4) have shown how complex the multi-level system of the EU is today. This system is the stage for the actors of the EU political process, as it were. They set the standards and determine policy and European legislation, and interpret and implement it. It is therefore crucially important for lobbying to have an overview of these actors, because these are ultimately all stakeholders in the political process which pursue their own agendas and their own interests. They engage in compromises with one another in many cases, and form coalitions, partly against one another, and in part, they appear to be striving to move in different directions. The stakeholders involved in the political process of the multi-level system of the EU are found on several levels: the first is the supranational level of the European institutions, the second the national level of the member states, comprising both the nation states and – at the subnational level – their regions (e.g. the German Länder).

---

219 Neyer and Wiener (2011), p. 8.
220 Haas (1958), pp. 33–34.
221 Federal Constitutional Court 89, 155 on 21.10.1993.
222 Herz and Jetzelsperger (2008[2]), p. 118.

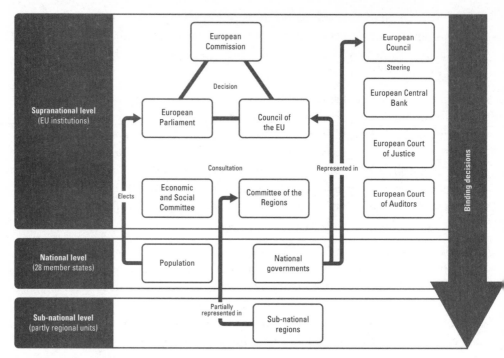

Figure 4.6: The multi-level system of the EU

Another level outside of the organisational, legislative framework of the EU is that of civil society stakeholders.

These three levels do not run parallel – instead, stakeholders at all levels are engaged in constant exchange with one another; some of them are also simultaneously active on several levels. One example of this is the EU member states which, as members of the Council of the EU (see Section 4.5.1.3), are a collective actor at European level. At the same time, however, they are also present as 28 individual member states with national interests – as individual actors which attempt to assert their own interests (see Section 4.5.2).

4.5.1 European (supranational) level: overview of the institutions of the European Union

Against this backdrop and in view of the EU Treaty, the political system of the EU reveals, by necessity, significant differences in comparison with national political systems. Whilst the classic institutions of democratically constituted communities, such as an elected legislature (European Parliament), an executive (European Commission) and a judiciary (European Court of Justice), formally exist as per the constantly pursued democratic principle, some of these institutions' options, functions and competencies deviate significantly from those of their counterparts in the individual states. A fundamental understanding of these institutions is vital to be able to comprehend legislative procedures, decision-making processes and thus also the characteristic procedures of lobbying in Brussels. The fundamentals and the most important institutions of the EU will be described in overview form, and their tasks and functions explained, in the following.

4.5.1.1 European Parliament

The European Parliament is the representative body of the people in the political system of the EU. Since 1979, the Members of the European Parliament have been elected directly by the citizens. Whether the EU legislature, in the form of the European Parliament, corresponds to a normal (national) parliament in terms of its tasks and formulation rights, however, is a matter of dispute.[223] It must be stated that the European Parliament is not a parliament of the European people, but the parliament of the European peoples.[224] In this regard, the European Parliament assumes an important position in mediating political content between the individual member states and the EU.[225]

Originally, the European Parliament was little more than a democratic fig leaf; over time, however, more and more possibilities for exerting an influence, and thus power, were transferred to it, most recently through the Treaty of Lisbon. The Parliament has since become a self-confident actor in the political structure of the EU, particularly in the areas of legislation and budgetary issues.[226] One striking example of the Parliament's increased power is its refusal to exonerate the Commission due to a case of corruption in 1999, which led to the dismissal of the entire Commission under President of the Commission Jacques Santer.

The legal bases of the European Parliament are found in Articles 10, 14, 16, 48 to 50 TEU and Articles 223 to 234, 289, 294 to 297 TFEU. The European Parliament's main tasks, together with the Council, include legislative and budgetary policy-making. In both the ordinary legislative procedure and the budgetary procedure, the Parliament is an equal-ranking legislator alongside the Council. The European Parliament's election function includes the election of the President of the Commission and consent to the appointment of the Commission (further details on this below). The Parliament also supervises the activity of the Council and Commission; it additionally has the power to dismiss the latter. The European Parliament also has rights of consultation in the continued development of the EU system. The representation of, and interaction with, the citizens of the EU are some of its other functions.[227] The Parliament still has no direct right of initiative; its options for influencing the CFSP are also severely limited. In practice, the Parliament makes intensive use of its competencies, and also makes forays into areas which are not directly assigned to it.

---

223 See Wessels (2008), p. 119.
224 See Strohmeier (2007), p. 30.
225 See Bieber, Epiney and Haag (2009[8]), p. 118.
226 See Wessels (2008), p. 119.
227 See Wessels (2008), p. 119.

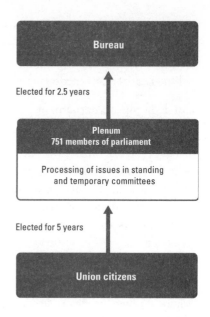

EPP 218 seats	
S&D 190 seats	
ECR 73 seats	
ALDE 70 seats	
GUE/NGL 52 seats	
Greens/EFA 50 seats	
EFDD 45 seats	
ENF 36 seats	
NA 16 seats	

Figure 4.7: The European Parliament (status: 23.6.2015)

The European Parliament's internal organisation is not dissimilar to national parliaments. For example, the members of parliament join forces in parliamentary groups which extensively correspond to the familiar left/right scheme of national, elected assemblies (see Figure 4.7). For example, the conservative members of parliament are members of the EPP group; the social democratic parliamentarians belong to the S&D group. It is chaired by a Bureau headed by the Parliamentary President. European Parliament resolutions are usually adopted with a majority of the votes cast; exceptions exist e.g. in the case of certain legislative procedures, in which the majority of the members (absolute majority) is the determining factor.[228] One significant difference in comparison with national parliaments is the lack of any government-opposition scheme, for which reason *ad hoc* majorities[229] are sought depending on the issue.[230]

The voting behaviour in the plenary is not clear: in addition to voting behaviour according to parliamentary group membership, cross-party voting behaviour characterised by the MEPs' nationality also occurs.[231] However, one very essential difference – which is extremely significant for lobbying within the European Parliament – in comparison with the member state parliaments is that the executive level does not arise from the legislative level: whilst the European Parliament can

---

228 See Wessels (2008), pp. 140 ff.
229 See Weidenfeld (2013³), p. 124.
230 Due, amongst other aspects, to the absence of the government-opposition scheme, the conclusion of a coalition agreement similar to those found in nation state parliaments is rather unlikely at European level in the foreseeable future. Efforts to achieve closer co-ordination are only occasionally made to form a majority, as recently stated by the chairman of the EPP group, Manfred Weber, in a newspaper in September 2014 –see Gutschker (2014).
231 See Wessels (2008), p. 141.

reject or approve the candidate put forwards by the European Council for the office of President of the Commission (Article 17 TEU),[232] and the competence and integrity of the potential Commissioners are subjected to (entirely critical[233]) scrutiny in the respective specialist committees of the European Parliament following their nomination, the Parliament can only consequently accept or reject the Commission as a whole, not individual members. Accordingly, the composition of the Commission does not correspond to the composition of the European Parliament, as is usually the case with national parliaments. Conventional disciplinary mechanisms at member state level – as a general rule, the government line is supported by the parliamentarians of the government parliamentary groups – are therefore eliminated; accordingly, a lobbyist must always keep an eye on the attitude of both the European Parliament and the Commission as regards his concern. This has significant effects on issues of "European coalition building". A further consequence of the fact that the executive level does not arise from the legislative level is closely related to this: there is no parliamentary opposition as such in the European Parliament. Majority and minority positions do not therefore arise through structure, so to speak, but are dependent on the individual case.

The members of parliament's content-related work is carried out in the committees. There are currently 20 standing committees, whose subject matter essentially reflects the policy issues of the Commission and its Directorates General. The specialised policy draft resolutions for the plenary are formulated in the committees. The rapporteurs and co-ordinators, which are designated for each initiative, are responsible for this within the committees. The prepared reports and the details of these are discussed in the committees and finally voted on before being submitted to the plenary as draft resolutions. In this context, it is interesting that parliamentary work is extensively dependent on individual members of parliament, particularly the rapporteurs. These primarily draw up their reports for the committees single-handedly, as there is no research service to the extent found in many national parliaments, such as the German Bundestag.[234]

The European Parliament is appointed and compiled through the national election of its members of parliament. The European elections take place every five years in June, and comply with the respective member state regulations and electoral systems as well as EU standards. As per the TEU and TFEU, a total of 751 seats are available; the mandates are subdivided using a national allocation key according to the principle of declining proportionality, in which there is no seat dis-

---

232 Jean-Claude Juncker was elected as the new President of the Commission by the European Parliament on 15.7.2014. For the first time, the President of the Commission was elected by the European Parliament at the suggestion of the European Council (Article 17 (7) TEU). This article provides for the nomination of a candidate for the office of President of the Commission by the European Council under consideration of the results of the European Parliament elections.

233 See the particulars of the Bulgarian candidate-Commissioner Schelewa in January 2010; see N. U. (2010a).

234 See Joos (2011), pp. 121–122 – also with regard to the so-called shadow rapporteur.

tribution per member state. However, there are at least six seats per member state, with a maximum of 96 seats.[235]

The European Parliament's headquarters are located in Brussels, but one quarter of the sessions are regularly held in Strasbourg, France. Despite the high staffing levels and costs necessary for the requisite translation services, the members of parliament are able to discuss issues in their national language in committee and plenary meetings; however, just a small number of working languages such as English, German or French are predominant in informal meetings.

Due to the constant increase in the options open to it for exerting an influence and for decision-making, the European Parliament has become increasingly important since its establishment, and is now a powerful actor in the political system of the EU. Its recent increases in authority due to the innovations introduced by the Treaty of Lisbon (particularly the co-decision procedure's designation as the "ordinary legislative procedure" in the EU – see Chapter 5) indicate that this trend will continue.

4.5.1.2 European Council

The European Council is the EU's supreme body. This institution is also difficult to categorise in a conventional manner (under constitutional law). For a long time, it stood outside of the EU, and was only elevated to the rank of an EU institution by the Treaty of Lisbon. The Council has its legal bases in Articles 13, 15, 17, 18, 22, 26 TEU and Articles 68, 121, 148, 222, 235 – 236 TFEU. Although it has no direct legislative authority, it is regarded as the EU's most influential entity. The Council provides stimuli for the EU and defines the Union's general political concepts and objectives. It also determines the Union's strategic interests. The European Council encompasses the member states' heads of state and government and the President of the Commission, who are supported by the Foreign Ministers and a Commissioner. The EU states' top-ranking representatives therefore come together in the Council, where they discuss and define the political guidelines for the EU.[236] The European Council convenes at least twice a year (EU summits); it is chaired for two and a half years by the President-in-Office elected by the heads of state and government.[237] The results of the Council meetings are incorporated into so-called policy conclusions. The Council also has decision-making, appointment, voting and dismissal rights. In addition to setting guidelines, the European Council's most important tasks include its function as an electoral and decision-making body, as an international actor (especially the respec-

---

235 See Weidenfeld (2013[3]), p. 117.
236 See Wessels (2008), pp. 155 – 156.
237 Effectively, two meetings regularly take place during each Presidency; the Presidency lasts for six calendar months. The importance of the office of President for the respective official cannot be underestimated; in addition to leadership and steering tasks, he also undertakes informal coordination in matters of dispute, and, to a certain extent, is also the "face" of the EU during the Presidency period.

tive President-in-Office of the Council) and as the "constitutional architect" of the Union.[238] Decisions in the European Council are made by consensus, with "negotiated packages" characteristically being formed.[239]

The importance of the European Council can be gauged, for example, by the great public interest in Council meetings. Although the Council itself does not act in a legislative capacity, its character as a leading political entity in European integration is clearly shown in this.

4.5.1.3 Council of the European Union (Council of Ministers)

The Council is the central institution which bindingly defines and co-ordinates EU policy, and thus makes decisions regarding the political and systemic structure of the EU (see Figure 4.8). With regard to this government or governing function, it is the "primary political steering institution of the EU".[240] In terms of its legislative competencies, it is superior to the European Parliament, as it is responsible for all EU legislative acts. The Council has its legal basis in Articles 13, 16 TEU and Articles 235–243 TFEU. Due to its changing composition of individual, relevant ministers from the member states (further details on this in the following) it is also referred to in the Treaty texts and the vernacular as the Council of Ministers. By being staffed with politicians from the member states, the Council also fulfils an important feedback function as an intergovernmental institution: it mediates between the EU and the nation state executive levels, thus enabling overlapping nation state and European opinion-forming.[241] In this manner, the member states or their governments insert their political interests into the Union level.

This institution is also difficult to compare with related ministerial committees such as the NATO Council, for instance. The Council is the main legislative authority for secondary Union law; in the areas of CFSP and PJC, it has sole decision-making authority.[242] It possesses an indirect right of initiative vis-à-vis the Commission and, following the Parliament's approval, appoints the members of the Commission. Together with the Parliament, it also prepares the draft budget for the Commission. It additionally concludes treaties with non-EU states and international organisations.[243] It undertakes CFSP structuring based on the strategies and objectives defined in the European Council. In addition to adopting general legislative acts, the Council can also pass implementing provisions itself.[244]

---

238 See Wessels (2008), pp. 171 ff.
239 See Wessels (2008), pp. 169 ff.
240 Oppermann, Classen and Nettesheim (2009[4]), p. 104.
241 Bieber, Epiney and Haag (2009[8]), p. 127.
242 See Bieber, Epiney and Haag (2009[8]), p. 125.
243 Partly with the approval of the European Parliament, see Ranacher and Staudigl (2007), pp. 43–44.
244 Bieber, Epiney and Haag (2009[8]), p. 125.

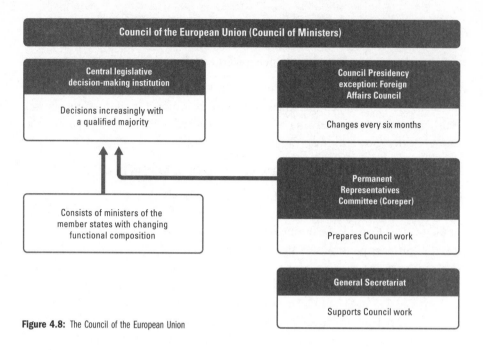

Figure 4.8: The Council of the European Union

The Council's composition differs according to the issues being dealt with. The Council therefore exists in a total of ten different formations: [245]

- General Affairs Council.
- Foreign Affairs Council.
- Economic and Financial Affairs Council (ECOFIN Council).
- Justice and Home Affairs Council.
- Employment, Social Policy, Health and Consumers Council.
- Competitiveness Council.
- Transport, Telecommunications and Energy Council.
- Agriculture and Fisheries Council.
- Environment Council.
- Education, Youth and Culture Council.

The various formations are co-ordinated by the General Affairs Council. The Council meetings themselves are prepared by the Permanent Representatives Committee (Coreper); the detailed work is undertaken by working groups consisting of national civil servants from the member states. [246] The Council's activities are based on its rules of procedure. The Council is a permanent institution; however, its members are not determined *a priori*, but are each delegated to the

---

245 Strictly speaking, "Council" is the name given solely to the common legal form for the meetings of the ten different committees; see Weidenfeld (2013³), p. 130.
246 The designation Coreper is the shortened form of the French title Comité des représentants permanents.

Council according to their executive function in the member states.[247] Council chairmanship switches between the member states every six months.[248] The "team presidency", in which previously defined groups of three states each co-ordinate their chairmanships over a period of 18 months, was introduced with the Treaty of Lisbon.[249] There are three different decision-making procedures in the Council. The vast majority of decisions are made with a qualified majority[250] necessitating 55 % of the member states, which simultaneously represent 65 % of the EU's population. Called the double majority, this voting procedure, which has been in force since 1st November 2014, superseded the triple majority rule commonly practised until then.[251] The clause according to which at least four member states are required to prevent a decision in the Council (blocking minority) was additionally agreed in the Treaty of Lisbon. This is intended to effectively prevent the possibility of a blocking minority by the three biggest countries, Germany, France and Italy.[252]

One further decision-making option in the Council is the principle of unanimity, although this is only applied for certain areas of policy. Decisions with a simple majority are theoretically possible but very rare in practice. The Council is organised, and its meetings managed, by the Permanent Representatives of the member states or by the General Secretariat, headed by the Secretary General. Although all documents are translated into each EU language, the unofficial working languages are once again primarily English, German and French. The meetings take place in Brussels and Luxembourg.

4.5.1.4 European Commission

As the executive level of the EU, the Commission has extensive competencies and powers. Similarly to the EU as an entity under constitutional law, the Commission is an institution *sui generis* which is difficult to subsume using constitutional law definitions. The Commission is legally anchored in Articles 13, 17–18 TEU and 244–250 TFEU, as well as in the Protocol on the Application of the Principles of Subsidiarity and Proportionality. In the past, the Commission's composition and tasks have constantly been the target of reform approaches, latterly as part of the Treaty of Lisbon.

---

247 Bieber, Epiney and Haag (2009[8]), p. 128.
248 One exception is the "Foreign Affairs" Council, which is chaired by the High Representative for the Common Foreign and Security Policy, see Seeger (2008), p. 81.
249 See Seeger (2008), p. 81.
250 See Biebner, Epiney and Haag (2009[8]), p. 130.
251 In this, 74 % of the total votes must be achieved, amounting to the majority of the member states and representing at least 62 % of the EU's total population. An interim solution was implemented, according to which the triple majority can only be required for votes up to 31.3.2017, see Weidenfeld (2013[3]), p. 135.
252 See Weidenfeld (2013[3]), p. 135.

First and foremost, the Commission is fundamentally the "guardian of the Treaties"[253] and, as such, monitors adherence to Union legislation and its subsequent provisions. It is obliged to intervene in the event of violations against them. At the same time, the Commission is the EU's executive institution. It ensures that the legislative acts are adequately implemented in the member states. Particularly during the first few decades of European integration, it was also a "motor of integration", and was extensively co-responsible for determining the pace and direction of the EU's development.[254] It additionally monitors the co-ordination of economic policy in the EU. The Commission has the sole right of initiative in the EU legislative procedure, i.e. only it has the right to table proposals for legislative acts at Union level. Ultimately, however, only the Council of the EU and the European Parliament are able to enact the Commission's draft legislation. In turn, the Commission itself can then enact the necessary implementing provisions in the form of regulations or directives.[255] In certain policy areas such as the area of competition, for instance, the directives directly affect national economic policy.[256] The Commission additionally administers the EU's financial resources and the EU structural funds. Together with the Council, it also represents the EU externally.[257] Due to its strong position within the EU and its external visibility, the (power) political importance of the Commission can hardly be overestimated. It is therefore frequently ranked on an equal footing with the EU and Brussels.

At present, each member state still provides a Commissioner. The President of the Commission is elected by the Parliament; the College is appointed by the Council. The entire Commission requires the approval of the Parliament.[258] Its term of office is five years, and is linked to the Parliament's legislative period.[259] The Commission is responsible to the Parliament, and can be dismissed by it through a no-confidence vote.[260] The Commission's composition should be oriented towards the Parliament's political composition. The principle of collegiate responsibility applies in decision-making and adopting resolutions within the Commission, whereby the President of the Commission has the political leadership and stands out as *primus inter pares*. Decisions are made according to the majority principle, whereby attempts are effectively made to reach a consensus during decision making.[261] The Commission usually meets once a week.

---

253 See Wessels (2008), p. 237.
254 Sabathil, Joos and Keßler (2008), p. 6; now, however, the European Council is occasionally dominant, with the result that the Commission is sometimes referred to as the Council's "junior partner", see Oppermann, Classen and Nettesheim (2009[4]), p. 107.
255 See the section on legislation in the EU.
256 See Oppermann, Classen and Nettesheim (2009[4]), p. 107.
257 The High Representative for the Common Foreign and Security Policy is one of the Vice Presidents of the Commission, but is appointed in a separate procedure.
258 This means that the Parliament can approve the Commission as a College or refuse to approve it as a whole.
259 See Wessels (2008), pp. 240–241.
260 See Wessels (2008), p. 226.
261 See Wessels (2008), pp. 245 ff.

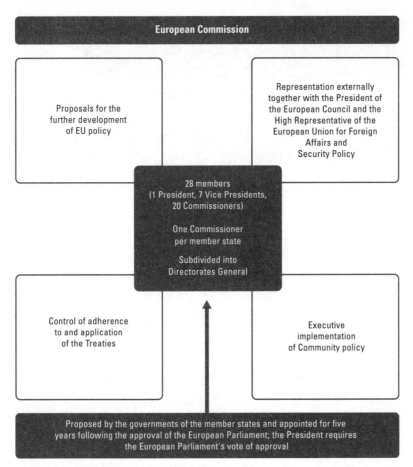

Figure 4.9: The European Commission (status: 26.5.2015)

The President of the Commission has the right to individually structure and sub-divide the responsibilities within the Commission. The Juncker Commission, in which subdivision into clusters was undertaken for the first time, is an example of this structural freedom. Each of the seven Vice Presidents of the Commission heads a specific task area; the Commissioners whose functions fall into the respective cluster in turn belong to these task areas.[262] Through this bundling, President of the Commission Juncker is fostering more effective co-operation in important issues such as the establishment of the energy union or strengthening the economic and monetary union.[263]

The actual administrative apparatus consists of the Directorates General and the services (e.g. General Secretariat, Legal Service). The Directorates General have a functional, hierarchical structure and process specific policy areas; they are exten-

---

262 See European Commission (2015f).
263 See Jean-Claude Juncker's restructuring of the Commission; see Cáceres and Gammelin (2014).

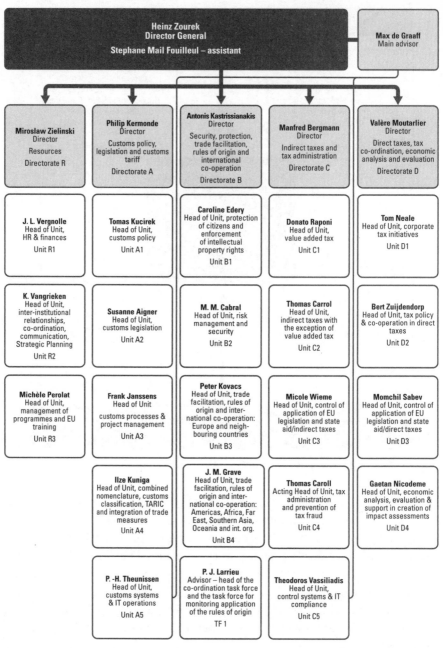

Figure 4.10: Internal organisation of a Directorate General using the example of the Directorate General for Taxation and the Customs Union (status: 26.5.2015)

sively comparable to national ministerial bureaucracies (see Figure 4.10 using the example of the DG for Taxation and the Customs Union).[264] The cabinets, which are directly subordinate to the respective Commissioner, are a powerful special

---

264 See Wessels (2008), p. 247.

feature. They consist of a small number of the respective Commissioner's political confidantes and have the power to issue instructions to the services and Directorates General.[265] Under the chairmanship of the General Secretariat, the cabinets prepare the draft resolutions for the Commission's weekly meeting. The heads of cabinet also confer each week prior to the Commission meeting, and determine which decisions can be made in unanimity (so-called A issues) and which submissions require further discussion in the College of Commissioners (so-called B issues). A Commission decision is usually based on a draft from the responsible Directorate General which has been co-ordinated beforehand with other functionally involved Directorates General. The draft is accordingly co-ordinated between the Directorate General and the cabinet.[266] The extensive influence which the heads of cabinet and the Directors General have on European politics becomes clear against this backdrop.

At present, the Commission has over 30,000 employees,[267] around 2,500 of whom work in the translation service alone.[268] All official announcements are published in all EU languages. The primary working languages within the Commission are English and French. The Commission's headquarters are located in the Berlaymont building in Brussels.

4.5.1.5 Court of Justice of the European Union

The European Court of Justice is one of the EU's oldest institutions, and embodies the Union's judicial level. Its rulings and decisions occasionally have far-reaching consequences which can have a considerable impact on the general public.[269] The Court of Justice's legal bases are found in Articles 13, 19 TEU and 251–281 TFEU. As the supreme institution, it includes the Court of Justice itself, a Court of First Instance and several specialised courts. The European Court of Justice is responsible for all of the Union's legislative acts as well as for the EU's public service. Infringement proceedings, actions for annulment, failure to act and for damages as well as preliminary ruling proceedings are argued before the Court. These may involve disputes between individual member states, between member states and the EU, between the institutions and other bodies, and between individuals and the EU. The Court's powers also extend to the "common space of freedom, security and justice".[270] There is no possibility for appealing against the European Court of Justice's decisions and rulings. The CFSP does not fall extensively into the Court's area of responsibility.

---

265 See Wessels (2008), p. 249.
266 See Wessels (2008), p. 249; the Legal Service also checks each draft for conformity with EU legislation. The General Secretariat, which supports the decision-making process within the Commission and maintains links with other EU institutions during this process, is another especially important element in the legislative procedure.
267 See Bieber, Epiney and Haag (2015[11]), p. 152.
268 See European Commission (2015b).
269 One famous, historic case is e.g. the "Cassis de Dijon decision" from 1979.
270 With the exception of evaluating the validity and proportionality of nation state actions.

The so-called Advocates-General are a special feature.[271] They are not associated with one of the parties to the dispute but, at the end of the proceedings, submit ruling proposals which they formulate by drawing on European legislation, particularly the European Court of Justice's previous case law, of course. The Court's judges are appointed from the member states; their functional suitability must be ascertained in advance. The number of judges and Advocates-General is oriented towards the statutes of the Court of Justice. The European Court of Justice is located in Luxembourg.

4.5.1.6 European Central Bank

The European Central Bank (ECB) is the most important European Economic and Monetary Union (EMU) institution. It is an EU institution with its own statutes and rules of procedure. Together with the national central banks, it forms the European System of Central Banks (ESCB). As a supranational institution, the ESCB is responsible for the EU's monetary policy.[272] The Eurosystem, consisting of the ECB and the respective, national central banks, exists for the euro area, i.e. those EU states which have introduced the euro as the sole currency (the "Eurogroup"). The monetary policy is therefore a completely communitarised policy area which was transferred in full to a European institution with supranational character during the course of the euro's introduction as the sole currency in the euro countries. In the euro area, the ECB is therefore *de facto* the only central bank and thus the "guardian" of the single currency, the euro. Together with the single currency, the ECB is therefore *the* symbol of European unification bar none.

Its legal bases are found in Article 13 TEU and Articles 15, 66, 123, 126–134, 138–141, 219, 263, 265, 271, 282–284, 289, 292, 294, 299 TFEU. The main task of the ECB (or the ESCB) is to guarantee the stability of the euro through price stability. In this, it decides independently, and not bound by directives, on the instruments required to achieve this, such as key interest rates or foreign reserve assets.[273] This therefore rules out the exertion of any political influence by the EU or the euro countries. Insofar as the objective of price stability is not affected, the ECB uses its monetary policy instruments to support the EU's general economic policy objectives. Against this background, the ECB's monetary policy thus far can be deemed restrictive.

In addition to its above listed tasks, the special task of supervising the eurozone's most important banks was also transferred to the ECB through an EU regulation dated 15th October 2013;[274] this officially came into effect in November 2014. The ECB therefore directly supervises around 120 banks in the EU, 21 of which are

---

271 See Bieber, Epiney and Haag (2009[8]), pp. 140–141.
272 See Bieber, Epiney and Haag (2009[8]), p. 145.
273 See Bieber, Epiney and Haag (2009[8]), p. 145.
274 European Council (2013).

German.[275] This significant step of voluntarily relinquishing nation state law to an EU institution marks a further milestone in progressing EU integration.

The ECB is headed by the Governing Council of the ECB, administered by the Executive Board, which consists of the President, the Vice President and four further members.[276] The Executive Board is appointed by the heads of state and government of the member states, and holds office for eight years. The ECB's headquarters are in Frankfurt am Main.

4.5.1.7 Court of Auditors

The European Court of Auditors, which has been in existence since 1975, is an EU institution, and controls the legality and regularity of budgetary use by the EU and its downstream bodies. To do so, it submits an annual statement of accounts. This is the Parliament's most important budgetary control instrument, and is simultaneously the basis of budgetary discharge for the Commission by the Parliament. The European Court of Auditors additionally attests to the reliability of budgetary management, whereby this assessment has thus far been negative.[277] The opinion of the European Court of Auditors must be heard in the case of certain legislative acts, such as the Financial Regulation.[278] The European Court of Auditors' staff of around 900 employees[279] can undertake audits at the EU institutions at any time. Such audits can also be performed in the member states and in countries which receive subsidies and other funds from the EU. However, violations against the regulations cannot be addressed by the European Court of Auditors itself, but can only be reported to the institutions concerned, which can in turn institute abuse proceedings. In this context, the Court of Auditors also works closely together with the European Anti-Fraud Office (Office Européen de Lutte Anti-Fraude – OLAF).

The Court of Auditors' legal bases are set forth in Article 13 TEU and Articles 263, 285 – 287, 319, 322, 325 TFEU. The Court of Auditors is headed for three years by a President appointed from the members of the Court of Auditors. The latter are appointed for six years by the Council, whereby each member state puts forward one candidate. The Court of Auditors' headquarters are located in Luxembourg.

In addition to the institutions introduced above, there are numerous other subordinate EU bodies such as the European Investment Bank, for instance, satellite departments of the institutions such as the European Aviation Safety Agency, Commission advisory and auxiliary bodies such as the Monetary Committee with advi-

---

275 These 120 or so banks constitute approximately 85 % of the balance sheet total of all banks in the euro area (status February 2014); see Federal Ministry of Finance (2014).
276 See Bieber, Epiney and Haag (2009[8]), p. 146.
277 See Federal Ministry of Finance (2009).
278 Bieber, Epiney and Haag (2009[8]), p. 143.
279 See Bieber, Epiney and Haag (2015[11]), p. 159.

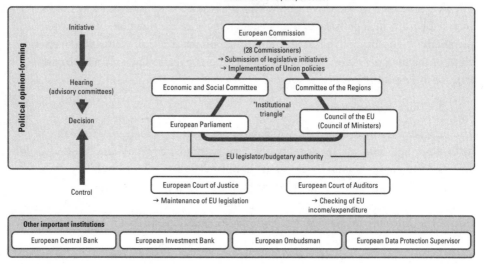

Figure 4.11: Political opinion-forming as part of the European Union's institutional structure

sory status or bodies related to the EU, such as the European Police Office (Europol). Figure 4.11 again shows an overview of political opinion-forming as part of the EU's institutional structure.

4.5.1.8 Other institutions

European Economic and Social Committee

The European Economic and Social Committee (ESC) is an EU body. It consists of representatives of economic and social interest groups. Its tasks are firstly to apprise the Commission, Parliament and Council of the opinion of the respective business, employee and consumer groups affected by legislative acts, and secondly to provide stakeholders with access to the EU institutions. At the same time, the ESC is an integration level for European opinion-forming and interest mediation.[280] In legislative initiatives, the ESC submits statements to the Commission, Parliament and Council. The ESC has its legal bases in Article 13 TEU and Articles 25, 43, 46, 50, 59, 91, 95, 100, 113–115, 148–149, 153, 156–157, 159, 164–166, 168–169, 172–173, 175, 177–178, 182, 188, 192, 194, 300, 301 ff. TFEU, as well as in Article 9 of the Subsidiarity Protocol, the Protocol on the Seats of Institutions and Other EU Bodies and in Article 7 of the Protocol on Transitional Provisions. The ESC has its own rules of procedure and a General Secretariat at its headquarters in Brussels. The ESC's maximum of 350 members are each proposed by the member states and appointed by the Council for five years. The

---

280 Bieber, Epiney and Haag (2009[8]), p. 144.

members are never bound by instructions. They elect a President, who heads the ESC for a period of two years.

Committee of the Regions

Like the ESC, the Committee of the Regions (CoR) is also an EU body. As the Committee of the Regions, it integrates a federalistic element into the EU beneath the member states. It consists of representatives of regional and local authorities, who hold an electoral mandate or who must be politically responsible at the head of an elected committee; their term of office is five years. The committee advises the Commission, the Parliament and the Council. It is obligatory for the above institutions to consult the committee in the areas of transport, regional and environmental policy.[281] The CoR is the institutional expression of the subsidiarity principle. The maximum of 350 seats are distributed degressively proportional to the population size of the member states as per a corresponding Council decision.[282] The CoR's legal bases are found in Article 13 TEU and Articles 91, 100, 148–149, 153, 164–168, 172, 175, 177 –178, 192, 194, 263, 300, 305 ff. TFEU, as well as in Articles 8 and 9 of the Subsidiarity Protocol, the sole article of the Protocol on the Seats of Institutions and Other EU Bodies and in Article 8 of the Protocol on Transitional Provisions. The CoR elects a President for two years from its ranks. The internal organisation is determined through the rules of procedure. The CoR's headquarters are located in Brussels.

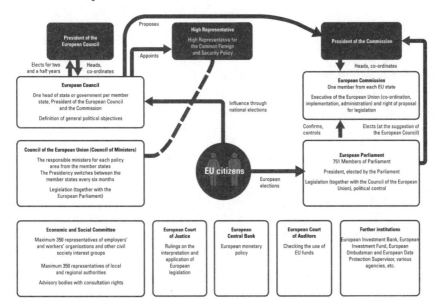

Figure 4.12: The European Union after the Treaty of Lisbon

---

281 See Bieber, Epiney and Haag (2009[8]), p. 145.
282 See Weidenfeld (2013[3]), p. 152.

4.5.2 Member state (national) level

The member states are an integral and significant element of the complex structure of the EU, which cannot be reduced to the fact that, by consistently relinquishing their sovereign rights to the EU, they have become "Europeanised" and are measured against the high level of integration. These member states are, and also remain, actively represented as separate actors in the European structure – not only as part of the European Council's high-profile meetings. Without its member states, there would be no EU. This is made clear by the EU's legal character as a "union of states",[283] but also with regard to its institutional structure (which is ultimately supported through the member states' budget contributions):

- The elections to the European Parliament: as described, these are conducted according to member state law with candidates nominated in the member states (see Section 4.5.1.1).
- The composition of the Commission: each EU member state provides a Commissioner. The member states also propose the President of the Commission via the European Council in interaction with the Parliament (see Section 4.5.1.4).
- There are also options for structural involvement in both institutions, the European Council and the Council of the EU (Council of Ministers), which are anchored in the primary law; these will be explained in greater detail further on.[284]

The member states' diplomatic representations also play a special role in the complex, multi-level system of the EU; this will be portrayed in Section 4.5.2.1 in the following based on the example of the Permanent Representation of the Federal Republic of Germany to the EU. The representations of individual regions of the EU, for example those of some German Länder, are another interesting aspect which is rarely taken note of by the general public (see Section 4.5.2.2).

4.5.2.1 Member state ("permanent") representations

The Permanent Representation of the Federal Republic of Germany to the EU is Germany's embassy to the EU.[285] It plays a key role in mediating German interests in the EU, but also, in reverse, in mediating European issues in Germany. It is, so to speak, the hinge between Germany and the EU, with which it is accredited. Like any other foreign representation or representation to an international organisation such as UNO, it therefore represents German interests amongst the EU institutions, i.e. in the Council of the EU, vis-à-vis the European Commission and the European Parliament. It has around 200 employees, and is headed by the

---

283 In contrast, for example, the federal state system of Germany or Austria, or the centralistic structure of France.
284 See Bieber, Epiney and Haag (2015[11]), p. 137.
285 Permanent Representation of the Federal Republic of Germany (2015d).

Permanent Representative of the Federal Republic of Germany to the EU, currently Ambassador Reinhard Silberberg.[286] Further high-rankng positions include those of the Deputy Permanent Representative and the Representative to the Political and Security Committee. All three positions are held by diplomats of ambassador rank.[287]

In organisational terms, the Permanent Representation is subdivided into three departments (policy department, finance department and economic department), therefore essentially covering all aspects of the EU and European policy.[288] To fulfil its function as Germany's representation and therefore also represent German interests and positions, the Permanent Representation is involved in policy-making as well as decision-making processes, and is thus an indirect part of the European legislative procedure.

Particular emphasis is placed on issues concerning Commission activities and initiatives. For this purpose, own interests and positions are formulated in exchange with the German Government and the Federal Ministries. Whether there are other member states which represent the same, or a similar, standpoint, is also clarified in each individual case and in dialogue with other representations. Finally, analyses and assessments are performed to determine whether corresponding negotiating positions exist, or whether and how these have to be modified to have a realistic chance of asserting the interests or increasing their likelihood of success.[289] To be able to fulfil these tasks, constant functional co-ordination is carried out with the responsible EU institutions.[290]

The Permanent Representation or the Permanent Representative is also formally represented in the EU institutions, more accurately in the European Council and the Council of the EU. For example, the Permanent Representative is a member of the Permanent Representatives Committee (Coreper), which politically prepares the Council meetings and acts as the interface between the working and ministerial levels.[291] The Permanent Representation's working level employees are also involved in the Council working groups, which in turn prepare the Coreper's work and discuss controversial issues in advance.[292] In these ways, Germany's interests are articulated at the political level of the EU, and majorities for Germany's position can be found.

---

286 Status: 20.05.2015, see Permanent Representation of the Federal Republic of Germany (2015b).
287 Permanent Representation of the Federal Republic of Germany (2015c).
288 Permanent Representation of the Federal Republic of Germany (2015e).
289 Permanent Representation of the Federal Republic of Germany (2015f).
290 Permanent Representation of the Federal Republic of Germany (2015).
291 Strictly speaking, the Permanent Representative is a member of Coreper II, in which politically more controversial issues are primarily discussed, see Weidenfeld (2013³) p. 133; with regard to the structure and function of the Council, see Section 4.5.1.3; with regard to the status of the member state representatives, see Oppermann, Classen and Nettesheim (2014⁶), p. 46.
292 Permanent Representation of the Federal Republic of Germany (2015a).

The two committees of the Conference of Representatives of the Member States (Intergovernmental Conference) and the Representatives of the Member States meeting within the Council also require mentioning at this point. The first of these two committees negotiates the amendments to the EU Treaties as per Article 48 TEU (ordinary treaty amendment procedure), whereas specific, individual issues provided for in the Treaties are dealt with in the latter (e. g. appointment of the members of the ECJ), whereby the Council members expressly work as representatives of their member states, not as an institution of the EU.

4.5.2.2 Regional representations

Besides the member states, the sub-national level is also extensively represented in Brussels.[293] Numerous authorities such as regions and communities, which are grouped beneath the nation state (member state) level in legal terms, maintain representative offices or liaison offices there. One example of such a (in this case, actually international) body is the Joint Representation of the European Region of Tyrol-South Tyrol-Trentino.[294] There are now over 200 such establishments in total, two thirds of which are regional representations.[295] The regional representation is living proof of the multi-level system of the EU. Due above all to the subsidiarity principle, the regional actors have their place in this "Europe of the regions", as already demonstrated in the Committee of the Regions (CoR) (Section 4.5.1.8). In a narrower sense, however, the purpose of the entity is naturally determined first and foremost by its position in the political system or the constitutional system of its member state, whereby no strict distinction between the pure representation of regional or local units and the representation of their interests can be made.[296] Accordingly, their radius of action usually also extends far beyond a "shop window" or monitoring function towards professional lobbying work.

The German Länder have assumed a "pioneering role" in this and stand out through their "active lobbying".[297] As partly sovereign constituent states, they are constitutive elements of the federal state structure of the Federal Republic of Germany. Through the Bundesrat, the Länder are important players in the European legislative and political opinion-forming process, and are therefore also a prime example of sub-national state actors within the EU. They have always been anxious to represent their specific state interests vis-à-vis the European institutions, which can occasionally also lead to problems for the Federal Republic of Germany's European policies.[298]

"The Länder shall participate through the Bundesrat in the legislation and administration of the Federation and in matters concerning the European Union" (Arti-

---

293 See Weidenfeld (2013³), p. 156.
294 European Region of Tyrol-South Tyrol-Trentino (2015).
295 See Studinger (2013), p. 12.
296 See Greenwood (2011³), p. 178.
297 Weidenfeld (2013³), p. 156.
298 See Bomberg and Peterson (1998), p. 222.

cle 50 German Constitution). In the German Constitution's so-called "Europe article" (Article 23), the Länder are granted explicit rights of participation in matters concerning the EU via the Bundesrat.[299] Paragraph 2, sentence 1 of this article therefore states: "The Bundestag and, through the Bundesrat, the Länder shall participate in matters concerning the European Union." And paragraph 4 continues: "The Bundesrat shall participate in the decision-making process of the Federation insofar as it would have been competent to do so in a comparable domestic matter, or insofar as the subject falls within the domestic competence of the Länder." If the "interests of the Länder are affected" despite the Federation's responsibility, "the Federal Government shall take the position of the Bundesrat into account" (paragraph 4). At EU level, the "responsibility of the Federation for the nation as a whole" must be maintained (paragraphs 5 and 6); even if the Länder have exclusive legislative authority concerning matters of school education, culture or broadcasting, the rights must always be exercised with the participation of, and in coordination with, the Federal Government (paragraph 6).

As can be seen from the wording of the standard, however, the options of the Länder for participation are limited.[300] They are involved via the Bundesrat, and are reliant on the Federation to "exercise the rights". Ultimately, the Länder are lacking in direct, institutionalised influence over the EU legislative processes.

Wherever options for influencing EU decisions arise, however, the Länder are eager to exert an influence in various ways, and not to remain satisfied with the decision-making competence given via the Bundesrat in terms of the implementation of European legislative acts. They therefore not only implement directives from Brussels, but also – like other sub-national entities – undertake active policy-making in the EU in different ways.[301] For example, the Länder governments have "Ministers for Europe", who deal with the European policy aspects of the Länder. Often, the individual ministries have separate offices which deal with European matters. The Länder Parliaments have also established European Affairs Committees. The 16 Länder Representations in Brussels, which the Länder use as platforms for their European interests, are also a visible sign of their commitment to European politics. The Bavarian Representation, which has around 30 employees, is likely to be the most familiar of these thanks to its representative building.[302]

All of these measures have enabled the Länder to ensure and, in some areas, extend their influence on European policy decisions. This independent effort is also related to the fact that it has thus far been difficult to assert individual Länder interests as part of the Committee of the Regions; the Committee has no real decision-making competence in any case (see the explanations on the Committee

299 See Bomberg and Peterson (1998), p. 223.
300 See also Mayer (2012), p. 221; with regard to the rights of participation, see Mayer (2012), pp. 254–279.
301 See Greenwood (2011³), pp. 184–185.
302 Weidenfeld (2013³), p. 156.

of the Regions in Section 4.5.1.8).[303] The Treaty of Lisbon, which granted the national parliaments, and therefore also the Bundesrat, more extensive, direct rights of participation vis-à-vis the EU, led to progress for the sub-national entities.[304] The new option of being able to file a subsidiarity complaint to the EU institutions prior to the enactment of specific legislative acts is particularly important.[305] If necessary, this can be followed by an action against infringements of the principle of subsidiarity before the European Court of Justice. The EU continues to have numerous obligations to directly notify the national parliaments.[306]

Nor are the individual Länder left in isolation in Brussels as regards the necessary information flow and, if necessary, the exertion of an influence on decision-making at European level. Instead, the Länder maintain the joint body of the "Länder Observer to the European Union", called the Länder Observer.[307] This body has the task of supporting the Bundesrat in the exercise of its rights with regard to EU matters and of informing the Länder about processes which affect them. In particular, the Länder Observer takes part in Council of the EU meetings. The Länder can use its reports to check the extent to which Bundesrat decisions are taken into consideration and implemented by the German Government in the negotiations. The Länder Observer also works closely together with the Permanent Representation of the Federal Republic of Germany to the EU.

Not least because of their self-perception as members of a federation – due to and motivated by both their political and constitutional position – the Länder have recognised the need to participate in political Europe. In all, it can be stated that the Länder are involved in many EU structures, and are therefore in a good position to make their European interests heard.

4.5.3 Civil society (non-state) level

The third group of political stakeholders in the EU is civil society. It stands firstly alongside the actors at European, sovereign level, i.e. the institutions, which are an emanation of European primary law, and secondly alongside the member state actors. The latter are represented in the intergovernmental bodies of the EU, the Council and the European Council. The Permanent Representations of the member states are sometimes the most visible member state actors on the EU stage. In addition to the member states as a whole, however, regions of individual member states are also becoming political actors in the EU (see Section 4.5.2). They are both represented in the Committee of the Regions and present through their own representations in Brussels. Member state bodies such as German Länder Parliaments also have representations in Brussels.

303　Weidenfeld (2013³), p. 153.
304　Degenhart (2009²⁵), p. 52.
305　Degenhart (2009²⁵), p. 52.
306　See Melin (2011), p. 655.
307　The Länder Observer to the EU (2015).

Whilst they are not "state-backed", a special role is nevertheless played by civil society stakeholders in the EU. This role has entirely historic roots. The involvement of civil society in the opinion-forming process has always been part of the democratically constituted European polity. It began, for instance, in the 1950s with the participation of representatives of European stakeholders from the economic and social sectors in the European Economic and Social Committee (EESC) and does not end with the European citizens' initiative of the Treaty of Lisbon, which came into effect on 1st December 2009.[308] In particular, the role of civil society in the political opinion-forming process of the EU was anchored in the primary law by the Treaty of Lisbon. "Every citizen shall have the right to participate in the democratic life of the Union" (Article 10 (3) TEU). By appropriate means, citizens and representative associations have the opportunity to make known and publicly exchange their views in all areas of Union action (Article 11 (1) TEU). To a certain extent, civil society is requested to critically monitor European politics. In addition, the EU institutions have a duty of provision, and are obliged to maintain an "open, transparent and regular dialogue" with civil society and representative associations (Article 11 (2) TEU). The Commission must carry out "broad consultations with parties concerned" (Article 11 (3) TEU). Ultimately, civil society actors also have the option of voluntarily and actively shaping European policy. As part of the European citizens' initiative, citizens can invite the Commission "to submit any appropriate proposal on matters where citizens consider that a legal act of the Union is required" (Article 11 (4) TEU).[309]

The right of democratic participation is also intensively exercised by civil society stakeholders. The European Commission estimates the number of lobbyists employed by associations, organisations, citizens' initiatives and companies, etc. registered in the European Transparency Register to be at least 32,500.[310] This number alone is sufficient reason to take a closer look at this group of actors. The civil society stakeholders also contribute towards the establishment of political openness and increased political effectiveness, with the result that they ultimately underpin their democratic legitimation.[311] This participation is more precisely regulated, for example, in the joint Transparency Register of the European Commission and the European Parliament (see Section 5.3)

---

308 See Seeger and Chardon (2008), pp. 342, 348; Bergmann (2012[4]), s.v. civil society.
309 It should incidentally be mentioned that the wording of the provisions in Article 11 TEU are identical to the regulations of Article 46 in the failed Constitutional Treaty. This is a further example of how similar the Constitutional Treaty and the Treaty of Lisbon are.
310 European Commission (2014c) "In the meanwhile, an estimated 75% of all economically-related organisations and around 60% of the NGOs active in Brussels have sought registration. At present, around 6,500 organisations are registered in total. According to cautious estimates, each organisation employs an average of five individuals, i.e. at least 32,500 lobbyists are now subject to the Transparency Register's code of conduct".
311 Bergmann (2012[4]), s.v. civil society; Seeger and Chardon (2008), p. 344.

The question of what precisely civil society is cannot be answered exhaustively.[312] However, there are certain fixed, key points which can be used to define the term civil society. Civil society is situated between the private sphere and the state, and is a sphere of public action and public debate.[313] It is able to keep the state "in check". It is "strong enough to act as a counterbalance to the state, but without hindering it in its role as keeper of the peace and mediating instance for important stakeholders, and is occasionally capable of preventing it from dominating and atomising the rest of society".[314] Unlike the political parties, the actors of civil society, the stakeholders, do not strive to attain political offices and power. Instead, they attempt to convince state institutions and political parties of their own concerns.[315] Greenpeace Europe, for example, attempts "[to] challenge EU decision-makers to implement progressive solutions".[316] The influence of organised civil society is greatest in the case of detailed political issues. Conversely, the influence of civil society in issues of European integration or the continued development of the political system of the EU appears to be rather minor.[317]

In regard to EU Europe, it is stated that there are still structural, cultural and organisational differences in civil society. A European civil society is still under construction and does not function according to the familiar, national patterns.[318] It is more fragmented; language barriers additionally hamper the development of a common civil society public. Historically, the relationship between the state and civil society has developed differently in the 28 member states. The civil society stakeholders are partly more politically oriented and partly more welfare state oriented. Nevertheless, more and more European, organised, civil society stakeholders which are contributing to the political process of the EU are developing transnationally. The trend towards a European public is already emerging as a consequence of the financial and economic crisis, particularly the period from 2008 to 2010, whose effects are still being felt today.[319] The development of a European civil society is also being specifically fostered with financial resources by the EU. This support is enabling the groups to increase their capability to produce and process policy information. On the other hand, the intention is also to reinforce political pluralism in the EU in this manner.[320]

The organisational core, the instruments of civil society, as it were, is formed by groups which regulate their concerns autonomously. The spectrum ranges from citizens' initiatives and citizens' rights groups, social partners, professional groups, associations, NGOs and interest groups to cultural and educational insti-

---

312 See e.g. Brutta and Verheyen (2002).
313 Nohlen/Schultze (2010⁴), s.v. civil society.
314 Gellner (1994), p. 14.
315 Nohlen and Schultze (2010⁴), s.v. civil society.
316 Greenpeace EU Unit (2015).
317 Seeger and Chardon (2008), p. 345.
318 Seeger and Chardon (2008), p. 342.
319 German Federal Agency for Civic Education (2014).
320 Eising (2012²), pp. 842 ff.

tutions as well as religious communities.[321] The European Commission regards trade unions, employers associations, non-governmental organisations, professional associations, non-profit organisations, and grass-roots groups and organisations via which the citizens take part in local and community life, e.g. churches or religious communities, as belonging to civil society.[322]

The following will now deal with the most important civil society stakeholders at EU level, the associations, the organisations and a civil society group which is important but often overlooked – the media.

4.5.3.1 Associations

Associations are regarded as something akin to "exemplary stakeholders" in organised civil society. They are commonly associated with lobbying[323] – after all, some national associations have already been around for over a hundred years. Associations and trade unions were the first special interest groups in modern industrial societies which were taken note of throughout society and with increased political intensity.[324] Of course, this is also the case at European level: over 100 associations were already established at the inception of political Europe. The European umbrella organisation for industrial and employers' confederations, BUSINESSEUROPE, was founded back in 1958 as UNICE (Union of Industrial and Employers' Confederations of Europe). Public service companies joined forces in 1961 in the CEEP (European Centre of Employers and Enterprises providing Public Services). Both associations have social partner status. The Association of European Chambers of Commerce and Industry (EUROCHAMBRES) was also founded in 1958.[325]

European associations are usually coalitions of national bodies. Of course, the national associations which join forces at European level are primarily those which are particularly affected by EU decisions, for example in the sectors of agriculture, commerce and services; these are joined by employers', industrial and consumer associations.[326] The European associations often act as interfaces between the national associations and Brussels. Via their representative offices, they monitor the EU's political activities and inform the national associations; at the same time, they provide these with access to decision-makers.[327] To a certain extent, their activities are anchored in the primary law, since the associations are expressly mentioned in the Treaties: Article 11 TEU refers to "representative associations" which should have the opportunity to make known and publicly exchange their

---

321 Nohlen and Schultze (2010⁴), s.v. civil society.
322 Seeger and Chardon (2008), p. 343, footnote 1.
323 Lösche (2007), pp. 9–10.
324 With regard to the historic development of associations, particularly in Germany, see Kleinfeld (2007).
325 Eising (2012²), p. 847.
326 Bergmann (2012⁴), s.v. European associations.
327 Michalowitz (2007), p. 78–79.

views in all areas of Union action. The same article states that the institutions must maintain dialogue with the "representative associations" (and civil society). Not least because of this, Brussels is home to a number of umbrella associations which are regarded as especially representative, as they usually represent an entire European industry and bundle the opinions of a high number of associations within the individual member states.

In line with the delimitation and definitions in Chapter 2 and Section 6.4 of this book, the associations are counted as collective interest groups, i.e., they do not represent the interests of individual companies, as do corporate representative offices, for instance, but instead represent an entire industry.[328] The situation of the trade unions is similar; they are also organised by industry (in Germany, e.g. the German metalworkers trade union IG Metall) or as umbrella associations (in Germany, e.g. the DGB). In view of this, the associations have particular tasks and functions within civil society:

- Aggregation of interests.
- Articulation of interests.
- Political participation.
- General function (associations are mediators between society, the economy and politics, and thus contribute towards the legitimation of the political system).[329]

The often heterogeneous composition of associations (e.g. large and small companies or even different industries) results in a usually complicated, bureaucratic and protracted opinion-forming process before interest aggregation is actually achieved. This means not only that valuable time may be lost for professional lobbying, but that the interests of a considerable number of the associations' members may possibly not be taken into consideration (see Section 6.4.1.1). Compromise solutions (the lowest common denominator) are then represented.[330]

The original concept behind the foundation and involvement of associations at European level was to establish the dynamic interaction of economic and social community policies. This concept is an essential characteristic of the democratic state form and way of life. Despite their lack of "punch" ("lowest common denominator"), umbrella associations increase the likelihood of individual, minor actors exerting an influence, becoming integrated and, ultimately, also asserting themselves in the EU.[331]

---

328 Joos (2011), p. 136.
329 Lösche (2007), pp. 14 ff.
330 Michalowitz (2007), pp. 78–79.
331 Matyja (2007), p. 149.

4.5.3.2 Organisations and public interest groups

In addition to the organisational structure of traditional associations, NGOs, churches, media, communities, companies and think tanks, etc. have also increasingly emerged in recent years. Like associations, these organisations and public interest groups also represent their interests in Brussels, and have also developed into genuine political stakeholders.[332] This differentiation between interest groups is due to the extension of the EU's areas of responsibility, which now far exceed mere market integration than ever before[333] (with regard to strengthening the EU externally and internally through the Treaty of Lisbon, see Section 4.3). As late as the 1970s, for example, welfare and socio-political groups were practically non-existent at European level. As the EU became increasingly involved in areas such as consumer protection, the environment, human rights, social and welfare policy, lobbying from these areas also increased. The European Commission itself fosters the emergence of such groups, and attempts to steer their development at the same time, for example with the Platform of European Social Non-Governmental Organisations established in 1995.[334] In this manner, the EU institutions always have access to advisors and dialogue partners for policies in the socio-political sectors, which in turn increase the legitimation of EU initiatives.

The organisations and public interest groups (in contrast to economic interest groups: associations, trade unions) often represent more ideal objectives, attempt to improve the status of underprivileged population groups,[335] are committed to environmental protection (Greenpeace, WWF) or human rights (Amnesty International), and are involved in the health and social sector (Red Cross) or consumer protection (Association of European Consumers).[336] As in the case of associations, certain heterogeneity problems or orientation process difficulties may arise amongst the members of the organisations and public interest groups under certain circumstances.

The organisations' actual influence on EU policies is regarded as relatively limited. There are a number of reasons for this: firstly, regarded historically, the public interest groups' issues were included in the EU's sphere of tasks at a relatively late stage. This means that the organisations and public interest groups have not been present for very long in Brussels; in comparison with the economic groups, this means that they are partly lacking in experience and the organisational structure which, in some cases, has grown over a period of decades.[337] Secondly, the EU remains oriented more extensively towards economic policy. Not all of the European Commission's Directorates General, for instance, deal primarily with the con-

---

332 Lösche (2007), pp. 9–10.
333 Eising (2012²), p. 837.
334 Eising (2012²), pp. 851–852.
335 Eising (2012²), p. 844.
336 Geiger (2006), p. 24.
337 Eising (2012²), p. 851.

cerns of stakeholders from the organisations. Accordingly, their potential contacts are fewer in number. Conversely, a higher number of potential contacts for organisations and public interest groups can be found in the European Parliament which, by nature, has set itself the goal of representing the concerns of citizens in the EU – and therefore also, and particularly, the concerns bundled within the framework of organisations and interest groups.[338]

Nevertheless, public interest groups are not without influence on the procedure and outcome of political decision-making processes. Their options are particularly to be found in the areas of agenda-setting and sensitisation to socio-political and social issues.[339] Increasing professionalisation is also recognisable here: the organisations concentrate on participation in the European political process and less on media work and the mobilisation of public protests,[340] although many of them are now in a position "to turn science into politics through their mass mobilisation when required".[341] Added to this is the fact that, when representing their interests, NGOs occasionally have a credibility lead amongst politicians and the public. They are often regarded *per se* as the counterbalance to economic interests which represent public interests (with regard to the importance of the public interest perspective in lobbying, see above all onepager and perspective change in Chapters 6, 9 and 10).

Think tanks constitute another group of institutions to be counted as organisations and public interest groups. These are research centres which are closely related to a party or a political direction, for example; their work can be purely issue-based, and they are active at the regional, national and supranational level. Others may be closely related to NGOs if, for example, they collect funds for charity purposes. What is common to them all is that they provide advice on policies with (scientific) information, with concepts and strategies, and that their aim is to influence policy-making.[342] This involves the applicability of theoretical knowledge in political practice. However, the effect of the research results on policies can be inhibited if politicians and the administration are aware of the think tank's scientific, ideological thrust.[343] The main representatives at European level are the European Policy Centre (EPC), the Centre for European Policy Studies (CEPS) and the Friends of Europe. Their number and their influence in Brussels are not yet comparable to their corresponding counterparts in Washington.[344]

---

338 Eising (2012²), p. 853.
339 See Eising (2012²), p. 853.
340 Eising (2012²), p. 851.
341 Geiger (2006), p. 24.
342 Badie, Berg-Schlosser and Morlino (2011), s.v. think tank.
343 Joos (2011), p. 160.
344 Geiger (2006), p. 25.

4.5.3.3 Media

Finally, reference should be made to another important group of civil society actors, which are not necessarily identifiable as political stakeholders at first glance: the media. However, they play a particularly important role for civil society in the public arena; due to their influence on the political agenda, they are occasionally referred to as the fourth power in the state, alongside the legislative, executive and judicial levels.[345] This is based on the public task which the media perform in democracies. This includes informing and enlightening the public (i. e. all stakeholders) regarding political issues and processes, but also the issue of statements and criticism, as a result of which they participate in forming so-called public opinion. At the same time, the media function as a link between civil society and political actors. They enable the latter not only to discover what society is thinking or which interests civil society is pursuing, but also to measure their own decisions against this.[346] On the whole, the media therefore help to establish a public sphere in which civil society can form and act. Civil society and the general public develop together. The media enable the representatives of civil society to step out of the private sphere and become (politically) publicly effective.[347] Due to the national fragmentation of EU Europe, a European public only exists in part thus far, or with regard to individual issues such as the Kosovo conflict or the financial crisis.[348] In practice, European politics overcomes this fragmentation by consuming and evaluating the national media in parallel. Politicians, civil servants and employees read the various national newspapers and websites. Each day, press offices evaluate the European media landscape and thus offer a good synoptic overview.

In addition to the classic media, which serve as intermediaries between politics and readers, viewers or listeners, the Internet and social media now enable the political actors, such as the EU institutions, to contact and inform information seekers directly via websites or Facebook profiles. The European Parliament, for instance, uses the European Facebook community to report on political issues and decisions, through which it is most certainly attempting to politicise public opinion. At the same time, civil society actors, such as organisations and, of course, also citizens' initiatives and individual citizens, are enabled to contact politicians directly, and to *react*, but also to become politically *active* themselves, simply and without major obstacles. Politicised civil society can therefore follow the EU's decisions and political activities in real time, so to speak. The social media are slowly turning into a serious platform which enables political communication in both directions.

However, media are not only mediators or platforms for exchanging information. They can also become civil society stakeholders themselves. Due to the feedback loop to politicians, they can most certainly follow the political agenda pro-actively

---

345 von Graevenitz (1999).
346 Bentele, Brosius and Jarren (2013²), s. v. public task.
347 Jäckel (2011⁵), pp. 264–271.
348 Eurotopics (2008).

and exert an influence on it. They co-determine public opinion, and politicians take note of this. Through their choice of news, their type of reporting, through comments and criticism, the media can therefore exert political influence, at least indirectly. In the social media, groups can form and unleash an (artificial) barrage of outrage. Another example is political talk-shows on the television, which have now become part of the political culture.[349] Ideally, this influence is indirect, through the media serving as a neutral platform for the expression of opinions and interests of other stakeholders. However, a certain "colouring" can occur in reporting through the political orientation of media (e.g. newspapers or Internet blogs). A medium itself thus becomes a stakeholder. In lobbying, public affairs agencies occasionally make use of such circumstances and place their campaigns in media which lean towards them or their clients. In summary, it can be stated that, of all civil society stakeholders, the media are more concerned with current, political activities and currently relevant issues, whereas the structurally organised associations and organisations deal primarily with sustainable, more long-term issues.

4.6 Summary

Chapter 4 has outlined the complex (institutional) framework conditions for lobbying amongst the EU institutions against the backdrop of constantly progressing integration.

This was based on three key questions:

- Which consequences arise from the historical course of European orientation? How far has European integration already progressed?
- What are the fundamental changes arising from the Treaty of Lisbon?
- Who are the political stakeholders (from the point of view of lobbyists) in the EU? How is the political system of the EU characterised? How does it differ from the member states as a result of this?
- (1) Over the course of its history, the EU has developed into a multifaceted, highly complex, multi-level system in which political stakeholders can be encountered at sub-national (regional), national (member state) and supranational (EU European) level.
- (2) Large parts of the Treaty of Lisbon (in force since 1st December 2009) correspond to the failed Constitutional Treaty. It was based on the concept of "reverse engineering": instead of writing the Treaty of Lisbon down on a blank sheet of paper, as it were, the Constitutional Treaty was used as the basis, and those passages which had to be amended to achieve unanimous approval of the new text were determined.

---

349 In this sense, for example, member of the Bundestag Friedrich Merz stated the following with regard to Sabine Christiansen's political talk-show: "This programme now determines the political agenda in Germany more than the Bundestag", in: Jäckel (2011[5]), p. 270.

(3) The Treaty of Lisbon significantly strengthened the EU externally. The European Union is a global player and a trade policy heavyweight. In the field of foreign and security policy, the EU is gathering competencies and creating the option of its own foreign policy strategy which is at least partly divorced from the member states. Ultimately, this is an important step towards increased "statehood" for the EU and – at least in the long term – to a reduction of the member states' foreign policy importance.

(4) In addition to refining its external profile, the EU was also strengthened internally. One focus is the transition from the principle of unanimity to the majority principle in the Council in over 40 further cases. The majority decision is thus becoming the usual case (Article 16 (3) TEU) and now covers practically all areas of policy which are crucial to citizens and companies. The result is a considerable loss of influence for the individual member state: whereas a single member state was able to block a decision in the Council whilst the principle of unanimity was valid, a blocking minority is required to achieve this under the majority principle.

(5) The Treaty of Lisbon placed the Parliament on an equal footing with the Council in practically all important areas of policy, thus making it a fully-fledged partner in the legislative procedure. As the "ordinary legislative procedure", the co-decision procedure, in which both the European Parliament and the Council must give their approval to adopt a legislative measure, has now become the usual case.

(6) The European Parliament differs from the member state parliaments. For example, the European Parliament has neither government nor opposition parliamentary groups. The executive level of the EU – with reference to the Commission and (in sub-areas) also the Council – does not arise from the legislative level. In addition to voting behaviour according to parliamentary group membership, cross-party voting behaviour characterised by the MEPs' nationality also frequently occurs. All of this affects issues of "European coalition building" in lobbying, i.e. the formation of alliances amongst the actors at the legislative and executive level: such coalitions usually refer only to individual projects and issues, with the result that new coalitions have to be formed for each concern.

(7) The so-called political science integration theories can be used to reveal recurring patterns and trends in European integration. They additionally analyse the degree to which European integration has already taken place:
   – the federalism theory regards the EU as a union of states. Due to the developments in recent years, however, this categorisation is no longer sufficient, with the result that reference is now made to "supranational federalism" or also a "fusioned federal state" in the context of the EU;
   – above all, the theory of neo-functionalism explains European integration in sectoral terms. This means that the unification process initially takes place in the economic, social and political sectors, in which common (transna-

tional) problems occur, which can also be solved in union (transnational-ly). This means that integration takes place on a problem-oriented basis, not an idealistic or political basis;

– liberal intergovernmentalism is the central opponent of all theories which prophesy the disappearance of the nation state in Europe. It is claimed that the driving force is assigned to the intergovernmental elements, e. g. the Council of the EU, in which the member states' relevant ministers meet, or the European Council, in which the heads of state and government assemble, and which sets the major EU policy initiatives;

– the supranationalism approach includes the development of a transnational society and non-governmental actors, which participate directly or indirectly in the decision-making processes, in its analyses. This means that the political decision-making processes in Europe are not determined solely by the member states and their governments, but are also extensively influenced by companies and associations, etc.;

– the multi-level governance approach (government in the multi-level system) also focuses on the issue of government. This approach questions the central importance of the member states.

(8) The stakeholders involved in the political process of the multi-level system of the EU are found on several levels: the first is the supranational level of the European institutions. The second is the national level of the member states, on which both the nation states and – at the sub-national level – their regions (e. g. the German Länder) are to be found. The dwindling importance of the nation states in the EU means that lobbying must not rely solely on national actors and networks but should instead choose a pan-European approach which also includes various actors at the different decision-making levels.

(9) A further group of political stakeholders in the EU is formed by civil society. It stands firstly alongside the actors at European, sovereign level, i.e. the institutions, which are an emanation of European primary law, and secondly alongside the member state actors. These include the associations, organisations and media.

The complexity of the responsibilities, the decision-making and policy levels in the EU, all of which are interrelated, and in whose context decisions can ultimately no longer be assigned to one (individual) decision-maker, are therefore the background against which the political processes of the EU take place. The various EU institutions are fixed points and possible contacts in the process. However, they are by no means the only political stakeholders in the EU that want to pursue their agenda and insert their own interests. Due particularly to the involvement of stakeholders at member state and civil society level, the number of individual actors – and thus contacts for lobbying – becomes virtually unmanageable in the individual case.

Chapter 5   Legislative procedure and other legal regulations as the framework of lobbying in the European Union

5.1 Introduction and question

Following the provision of an insight into the structure of the political system of the EU and the individual institutions in Chapter 4, Chapter 5 will now deal with the concrete legal bases and the possibilities for specific lobbying at European level. Focus is placed on the following questions:

- What is the role of the individual institutions in EU legislation after Lisbon? What are the characteristics of the "ordinary legislative procedure" (previously: co-decision procedure), which is now the usual case in European legislation? What is the form of the legal framework for the Commission's legislative activity as part of implementing legislation, and what is meant by the term "comitology procedure" (see Section 5.2)?
- What starting points exist for lobbying activities amongst the most important EU institutions, particularly the Council of Ministers, the Commission and the European Parliament, and which rules must the lobbyist observe here, i.e. to what extent is access to the decision-makers at the legislative and executive level subject to legal regulation (see Section 5.3)?

It should be mentioned in advance that some of the following explanations are rather technical and – in the best legal sense – "dry". However, a knowledge of the legal and procedural backgrounds to European legislation, in particular, is the basis and fundamental prerequisite of effective lobbying in Brussels: "He who would build high towers must take time over the foundations."[1]

5.2 Bases of legislation in the EU after Lisbon

As a rule, formal laws are enacted in a uniform procedure at member state level. In Germany, for example, this procedure is defined according to Articles 76ff. of the German constitution. The Bundestag and Bundesrat are always involved in this procedure, the only significant variations being the extent of Bundesrat involvement and whether or not its approval is required. This is not the case in the EU legislative procedure, for which there is still no procedure applicable to all areas of legislation even following the changes introduced through the Treaty of Lisbon.[2]

---

1 A quotation attributed to the Austrian composer Josef Anton Bruckner.
2 With regard to the "old" procedures according to the EC Treaty, see: Bieber, Epiney and Haag (2009), pp. 195ff.

5.2.1 General

As a supranational institution, the EU's activity is based on the powers which have been transferred to it by the 28 member states.[3] Together with general regulations concerning the institutional structure of the EU and corresponding procedural regulations for legislation at European level, these powers are set down in the European Treaties. Since the Treaty of Lisbon, these are the Treaty on the European Union (TEU) and the Treaty on the Functioning of the European Union (TFEU). They and the accompanying Annexes and protocols are also referred to as "primary Union law" and, as the "foundation of the Union" (Article 1 (3) first sentence TEU), can also be regarded as equivalent to national constitutional law, as for example determined in Germany through the German constitution.[4]

These Treaty documents are characterised by the complex interaction of the EU's three principal political actors: the European Commission, the Council of the European Union (shortened to "Council" in the following in compliance with the Treaty documents) and the European Parliament. Based on the Treaties, the EU institutions are able to exercise their powers and, within this framework, jointly enact legislation: secondary legislation.

This secondary legislation can be classified in two ways: firstly according to the type of legislative act (regulations, directives, resolutions, recommendations and opinions[5] or legislative acts with and without legislative character, see Section 5.2.2), and secondly according to the procedure specified for enactment.

As the EU, unlike a nation state, does not have extensive legislative powers, the Treaties at European level do not provide for any uniform procedure applicable to all areas of legislation – even following the ratification of the Treaty of Lisbon. Which procedure is applied is instead set down in the corresponding basis for legislative competence.[6]

A distinction must essentially be made between legislative acts which are enacted as per a legislative procedure and non-legislative acts (see Section 5.2.2).

A variety of procedures, in each of which at least two institutions are always involved, is in turn possible for legislative acts. The ordinary legislative procedure, on which Section 5.2.3 will concentrate in the light of its high practical relevance, has become established as the usual case since the Treaty of Lisbon came into effect.

---

3 See Article 4 (1) TEU and the principle of conferral set down in Article 5 (1) first sentence, (2) TEU and principle of subsidiarity (Article 5 (3) TEU).
4 See Streinz (2012), p. 2.
5 The forms of action of recommendation and opinion are not binding, but are nevertheless regarded as legislative acts in Union law, see Article 288 (1) and (5) TFEU; Schroeder in Streinz (2012a[2]), Article 288 TFEU point 143. However, ordinary and special legislative procedures are not applicable to them.
6 See Streinz (2012), p. 197.

In addition, the enactment of non-legislative acts by the Commission, which is intended to be the exception in concept, is very powerful in practice. Due to its high relevance to lobbying, the implementing legislation, and particularly the comitology procedure, which was reformed in 2011 and is of great importance in practical terms, should be dealt with in greater detail here (see Section 5.2.3.3).

5.2.2 Classification of legislative acts after the Treaty of Lisbon

To exercise their powers, the EU institutions can enact various legislative acts; these are essentially listed in Article 288 TFEU and differ in terms of their respective addressees and binding effect: they can take the form of regulations, directives, resolutions, recommendations and opinions (Article 288 (1) TFEU). Regulations, directives and resolutions are also referred to as "basic legislative acts".

Since the Treaty of Lisbon, however, the legislative acts are not distinguished in terms of the type of legislative act, but according to the procedure applied in their enactment. For example, a distinction is made between legislative acts which are enacted as per a legislative procedure and non-legislative acts. The responsible institutions can essentially enact all types of legislative act in the respective procedure.[7]

- As per Article 289 (3) TFEU, legislative acts are enacted in accordance with a legislative procedure. They constitute the secondary legislation and correspond to basic legislative acts, i.e. they can be issued in the form of regulations, directives or resolutions. The TFEU provides for various legislative procedures, which are specified through the respective legal basis. The usual case for the enactment of legislative acts is now the so-called "ordinary legislative procedure" according to Article 289 (1) in combination with Article 294 TFEU, in which the European Parliament and the Council are involved with equal status (further details on this in Section 5.2.3). So far, it has been applied in the enactment of 54% of legislative acts since the Treaty of Lisbon came into effect. There are also "special legislative procedures", which necessitate express authorisation in the Treaties according to Article 289 (2) TFEU. These are lacking in equal-status involvement; either the Council or the Parliament has the decision-making power; the other respective institution merely issues its approval or assumes an advisory capacity. This particularly includes the consultation procedure, which has been applied in approximately 45% of cases since 2009, and the consent procedure (approximately 1% since 2009), in which the European Parliament has a veto right.[8] What is common to almost all procedures is the fact

---

7 See – also to obtain an extensive overview of the Union institutions' forms of action – the classification of the legislative acts, to which the structure of the Official Journal has been oriented since the Treaty of Lisbon: Annex to the note of the Council of the European Union (2009).

8 For a more exhaustive portrayal of these special legislative procedures, reference is made to the relevant textbooks and manuals on European law; see e.g. Oppermann, Classen and Nettesheim (2014[6]), pp. 180–181.

that the enactment of a legislative act usually necessitates the involvement of at least two EU institutions (at least in terms of the initiative and decision); in fact, all three institutions are usually involved.

- The non-legislative acts can be subdivided into two groups: delegated legislative acts according to Article 290 TFEU and implementing acts in accordance with Article 291 (2) to (4) TFEU (further details in this regard in Section 5.2.3.3). Both empower the European Commission, as the executive institution, to become active in areas which are essentially the prerogative of the legislature (European Parliament and Council), and to enact legislative acts itself to a limited extent determined in advance. The legislation enacted in this manner is therefore also referred to as tertiary legislation. A precise distinction between these two non-legislative acts is sometimes difficult, and is dealt with time and again by the European Court of Justice.[9] However, a distinction can be seen in the fact that the Commission acts in a quasi legislative capacity in the case of delegated legislation, whilst it acts in an executive capacity in the case of implementing acts, and is required to ensure the administrative implementation of the legislative acts.[10] As part of delegated legislation, the Commission has been given the power of further legislation through a legislative act "to supplement or amend certain non-essential elements of the legislative act" (Article 290 (1)(2) TFEU) (this is comparable with the power to issue statutory ordinances under German law); conversely, in the case of implementing acts, the Commission – and, in exceptional cases, the Council – are issued with powers to enact implementing acts, in order to guarantee "uniform conditions for implementing legally binding Union acts", see Article 291 (2) TFEU.

5.2.3 Legislative procedures in the European Union

5.2.3.1 General

Various special considerations, which should be briefly outlined in advance, can be determined in the EU legislative procedures:

- Firstly, the procedure for the enactment and the amendment of primary legislation provisions differ (i.e. in terms of the European Treaties and the accompanying protocols) fundamentally from the secondary law procedures in the areas of legislation of the TEU and TFEU. For the first time in the history of the EU, the Treaty of Lisbon introduced a five-stage procedural sequence for amending and adapting the Treaties; the accompanying regulations can be found in Articles 48 to 50 TEU and in Article 352 TFEU.[11] As this procedure is of very little relevance to lobbying in Brussels, however, it will not be dealt with in greater detail in the following.

---

9 See e.g. European Court of Justice (2014); exhaustively, also Edenharter (2014), pp. 649–650.
10 According to Craig (2011), pp. 672 ff.; Parker and Alemanno (2014), p. 17.
11 See Lieb and Maurer (2009), p. 43.

- Secondly, there are significant differences in terms of the procedure to be adhered to between the areas of the CFSP and co-operation in criminal matters, as regulated in Titles V and VI of the TEU on one hand, and areas regulated in the TFEU on the other hand. As the areas of the TFEU will primarily be of relevance for lobbying, particularly for commercial enterprises and associations, however, this area will not be dealt with at length in the following either.
- Thirdly, as part of the TFEU, there are a variety of different legislative procedures which can only be classified in summary. At least one common feature can be determined for almost all of these procedures: the enactment of a legislative act usually requires the interaction of at least two EU institutions (at least in terms of the initiative and decision). In actual fact, three institutions are usually involved (the Commission initiates, the Parliament and Council are involved in decision-making).

Following the Treaty of Lisbon, what was previously the co-decision procedure (now the "ordinary legislative procedure") has become the usual case in all important areas of the TFEU (see Figure 5.1). Only this procedure will therefore be dealt with in detail in the following (see Section 5.2.3.2).

Involvement of the European Parliament	Council decision-making modes										
	Unanimity		Qualified majority		Simple majority		Special majorities		Rights of the Council chairman		Total	
		%		%		%		%		%		%
Autonomous rights of decision	1	0.33	3	0.99	0	0.00	0	0.00	0	0.00	4	1.32
Co-decision	0	0.00	85	28.29	0	0.00	0	0.00	0	0.00	85	28.29
Approval	15	4.93	7	2.30	1	0.33	2	0.66	2	0.66	25	7.89
Consultation	28	9.21	23	7.57	4	1.32	0	0.00	0	0.00	55	16.78
Notification	7	2.3	10	3.29	0	0.00	0	0.00	0	0.00	22	7,24
No involvement	41	13.49	52	17.11	6	1.97	11	3.62	11	3.62	112	34.87
Total	92	30.26	180	59.54	11	3.62	13	4.28	13	4.28	303	

Figure 5.1: Council's and Parliament's powers to act after the Treaty of Lisbon

5.2.3.2 Ordinary legislative procedure

With the Treaty of Lisbon, the ordinary legislative procedure, and thus the mandatory involvement of the European Parliament in legislation (previously: co-decision procedure), were further enhanced. It is now codified in Article 289 (1) in combination with Article 294 TFEU as the standard procedure for the enactment of legislative acts, and set out in greater detail in a joint declaration by the Parliament, Council and Commission.[12] It is always applied when a Treaty regulation refers to it; see Article 294 (1) TFEU. The Treaty of Lisbon significantly ex-

---

12 European Parliament/Council/Commission (2007a).

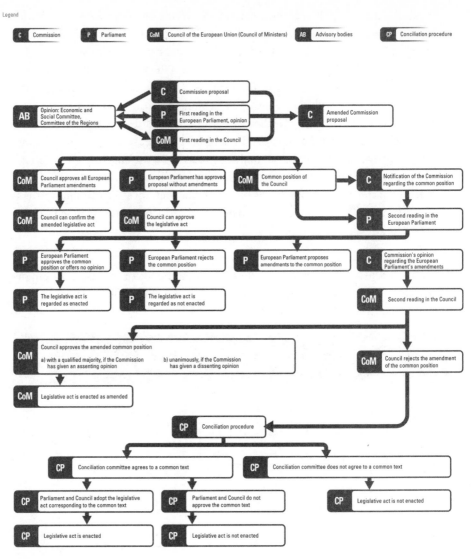

Figure 5.2: The ordinary legislative procedure

tended its scope; it is now applied in 85 areas, also particularly in the area of agriculture, fisheries, freedom, security and legislation, as well as the common trade policy and implementing legislation.[13] In 2014, it formed the basis of approximately 54% of all enacted legislative acts. The ordinary legislative procedure is characterised by the equal-status interaction of the European Parliament and Council in decision-making. The right of initiative still remains exclusively with the Commission, which is open to proposals from external sources. The end prod-

---

13 See Oppermann, Classen and Nettesheim (2014[6]), p. 173; for a complete list, see Gellermann in Streinz (2012a[2]), Article 294 points 6 and 7.

uct of the ordinary legislative procedure is not a formal law, as the name may imply; instead, it takes its name from the form of the procedure. In accordance with Article 289 (1) first sentence TFEU, it can be used for the enactment of regulations, directives or resolutions.

The ordinary legislative procedure consists of at least three to a maximum of six phases, which will be briefly outlined in the following.

5.2.3.2.1 Introduction of the legislative procedure: right of initiative of the Commission

The ordinary legislative procedure is formally initiated by a proposal on the part of the Commission. With a very few exceptions,[14] it has the sole right of proposal and therefore "a formal monopoly for deciding on the time, form and content-related structure of a legislative measure" in accordance with Article 17 (2) TEU.[15] In some cases, the Commission can also be stimulated to implement an initiative from the outside, e.g. through formal requests by the Council (Article 241 TFEU), the European Parliament (Article 192 TFEU) or the new European Citizens' Initiative introduced with the Treaty of Lisbon (Article 11 (4) TEU, Article 24 (1) TFEU). The European Citizens' Initiative, in particular, is viewed as a ground-breaking instrument for increasing citizens' participation at European level. Although only two of the 51 citizens' initiatives requested thus far have been submitted successfully, and the Commission and Parliament see themselves confronted by a high number of practical uncertainties and complexities for the initiators,[16] the list of follow-on measures already implemented by the Commission for the two successful citizens' initiatives[17] show that, in the long term, there is indeed significant potential for exerting an influence at this early stage of legislation.

The preparation of legislative proposals by the Commission is inextricably linked to the right of initiative. This is intended to prepare for agreement amongst all member states in the Council, something which is occasionally difficult to achieve, with the result that this preparatory work is of great importance. Even during this proposal development stage, the Commission is very open to external expertise and opinions. Fixed elements of the preparatory phase include discussions with and opinions by experts as well as public consultations, during which each interested party can assume a position with regard to a current legislative

---

14 Exceptions apply to the areas of judicial (Article 76 in combination with Article 82 ff. TFEU) and police co-operation (Article 76 in combination with Article 87 ff. TFEU) and to administrative co-operation measures (Article 76 in combination with Article 74 TFEU), as one quarter of the member states can also take the initiative in this case (Article 76 b) TFEU).

15 Bieber, Epiney and Haag (2015), p. 210.

16 See European Commission (2015e); for a more detailed list of the procedural prerequisites, an exhaustive analysis of the practical implementation problems as well as improvement suggestions, see the Directorate General for Internal Policies study commissioned by the Committee on Petitions and the Committee on Constitutional Affairs: Directorate for Citizens' Rights and Constitutional Affairs of the European Parliament (2015a).

17 See European Commission (2015d).

proposal via the Internet.[18] Following a reform in 2014, the assessment of the consequences of the specific legislative measures, the so-called impact assessment, is now to be further extended as a formalised procedure and become a fixed part of the preliminary legislative work.[19] The even broader and more structured involvement of external expertise and external opinions can, in all likelihood, be anticipated in the future, particularly in this area of the preparation of legislative acts.

If provided for in the Treaties, consultation of the European Economic and Social Committee and the Committee of the Regions is planned in this phase.

5.2.3.2.2 Further procedure in the Council and Parliament: readings, opinions and conciliation procedures

In accordance with Article 294 (2) TFEU, the proposal developed by the Commission is transferred simultaneously to the Parliament and Council. These always examine the legislative proposal in two readings, unless agreement between the institutions is reached after just one reading.[20] If necessary, a conciliation committee must be formed to guarantee the equal-status consideration of the Parliament's and Council's positions and a proposal supported by both parties. The procedural steps are characterised by close co-ordination and continuous exchange regarding the procedural stages and motives.[21] In the interest of reaching a compromise more easily, the Commission is usually also involved in various ways: firstly, the Rules of Procedure of the Council and Parliament provide for open dialogue with the Commission as regards the motives of the legislative initiative, and informal "trialogues" are formed between the Commission, Parliament and Council throughout the entire legislative procedure on the basis of a joint declaration.[22] Secondly, the Commission not infrequently revises the legislative proposal it has initiated based on the opinions which are submitted.[23] As long as no Council resolution has been adopted in this regard, the Commission can still withdraw and amend its proposal at any time; see Article 293 (2) TFEU. In practice, 72% of legislative acts are enacted in the first reading, 23% in the second reading and only 5% in the third reading after convening a conciliation committee.[24]

---

18 See the Commission's Green Papers, http://ec.europa.eu/green-papers/index_en.htm (last accessed on 28.5.2015).
19 See Alemanno and Meuwese (2013), pp. 3 ff.; Parker and Alemanno (2014), pp. 22 ff.
20 Bieber, Epinay and Haag (2015), p. 213.
21 See Oppermann, Classen and Nettesheim (2014[6]), 176.
22 See principle 7 of the joint declaration regarding the practical modalities of the new co-decision procedure (2007), OJ C145/5: "As part of the co-decision procedure, the institutions often co-operate in the form of "trialogues". This trialogue system has proved effective and flexible, since it has significantly improved the possibilities of reaching an agreement during the stages of the first and second readings and has contributed towards preparation of the conciliation committee's work."
23 See Oppermann, Classen and Nettesheim (2014[6]), p. 176; Gellermann in Streinz (2012a[2]), Article 294 point 17.
24 Parker and Alemanno (2014), p. 16.

5.2.3.2.3 First reading in the European Parliament

In the first reading, the European Parliament develops a position regarding the legislative proposal submitted by the Commission, Article 294 (3) TFEU. In this, it can express its approval or rejection, or submit an amendment proposal, with a simple majority of the members who are present. The Parliament's decision is prepared by a rapporteur, whose report is dealt with firstly in the responsible committee and finally in the plenary.[25] The time requirement for this procedural step is not specified in the legislation; in practice, the development and adoption of the position take an average of eight months.[26] The Parliament's position is conveyed to the Council.

5.2.3.2.4 First reading in the Council

In turn, the Council can approve or reject the European Parliament's position with a qualified majority of the member states.[27] If the Council's position deviates from that of the Commission and an amendment is proposed, a unanimous decision is required in accordance with Article 293 (1) TFEU. The Council can also determine its position before the Parliament's position is defined (so-called general approach); this position is formally decided on at a later point in time.

If the Council approves all of the Parliament's amendment proposals or approves the Parliament's approving position and itself approves the Commission's proposal, the legislative act must be enacted in the version of this position; Article 294 (4) TFEU. The legislative procedure is ended with the enactment of the legislative act in this version.[28]

If the Council does not approve the Commission's proposal of the Parliament's position, it sets down its amendment proposals in a separate position (so-called common position) at first reading. Accompanied by an extensive rationale, this is transferred to the European Parliament; Article 294 (5)-(6) TFEU.

The Council's position is prepared in work groups prior to the formal decision. To do this, the Council first drafts a so-called political agreement, which is then developed in the work groups, legally checked and transformed into the form required for a formal decision to be made. The member state administrations are involved in this work. The Council ultimately has to decide on the position which has been developed in this process. No legal deadline is planned for this; in practice, it takes an average of 18 months, with controversial issues sometimes requiring several years.[29]

---

25 For details on decision preparation, see Article 49 ff., particularly Article 57 ff., of the Rules of Procedure of the European Parliament.
26 See Oppermann, Classen and Nettesheim (2014[6]), p. 176.
27 Article 294 (4)–(5) TFEU in combination with Articles 16 (4) TEU and 238 (2) TFEU.
28 See Bieber, Epinay and Haag (2015), p. 213.
29 Oppermann, Classen and Nettesheim (2014[6]), p. 176.

5.2.3.2.5 Second reading in the Parliament and Council, opinion of the Commission

If the Council's common position deviates from the Commission's or Parliament's proposal, all three actors are again involved.

- **Second reading in the European Parliament**
  Firstly, the European Parliament has to deal with the Council's deviating position within three months of its having been conveyed;[30] Article 294 (7) TFEU. In this second reading, the European Parliament can in turn approve or tacitly accept the Council's position, or reject or amend it. This time, the rejection or amendment of the Council's proposal as part of the second reading requires an (absolute) majority of the parliamentary members; Article 294 (7)(b) and (c) TFEU. As in the procedure of the first reading, the resolution is first prepared in committees before the plenary decides[31] – this consultation focuses exclusively on the Council's common position.
  If the Parliament expressly or tacitly approves the Council's common position, the legislative act must be enacted in the version of this common position, and the legislative procedure is ended; Article 294 (7)(a) TFEU. The proposal is also regarded as tacitly approved in the event that no opinion regarding the position is issued, e.g. because an absolute majority against the proposal is not reached.[32]
  If the Parliament rejects the common position with an absolute majority, the procedure ends without enactment of the legislative act; Article 294 (7)(b) TFEU.
  If the Parliament proposes modifications to the Council's common position, the legislative procedure is continued in a second reading by the Council and a Commission opinion; Article 294 (7)(c) TFEU. The modifications must be forwarded to the Council and Commission.
- **Commission's opinion**
  The Commission is intended to submit an opinion regarding the amendments proposed by the Parliament; Article 294 (7)(c) 2nd clause TFEU. In this, it is intended to express its opinion regarding the Parliament's proposals, but not submit new amendments or withdraw the proposal.[33] Above all, the content of the opinion is relevant with regard to the quorum required for the Council's subsequent decision because, whilst the Council has the option of ignoring a (partially or wholly) negative Commission vote and approving the amendments proposed by the Parliament, this must be done unanimously; Article 294 (9) TFEU.

---

30 In accordance with Article 294 (14) TFEU, the deadline can be extended by a maximum of one month.

31 For more detailed specifications, see Article 64 ff. of the Rules of Procedure of the European Parliament.

32 See Gellermann in Streinz (2012a[2]), Article 294 TFEU point 24; Oppermann, Classen and Nettesheim (2014[6]), p. 178.

33 See Gellermann in Streinz (2012a[2]), Article 294 TFEU point 26 with further references.

Conversely, a qualified majority is sufficient in the event of an opinion which approves all points.

- **Second reading in the Council**
Following their conveyance, the Council in turn has three months'[34] time in which to reach a decision regarding the Parliament's amendment proposals. It can approve the amendments in whole or reject them (also only in part). If the Council unanimously approves all of the Parliament's amendments, the procedure ends and the legislative act is regarded as adopted in the form amended by the Parliament; Article 294 (8)(a) TFEU. If the Commission issues a positive opinion as regards all of the Parliament's amendment proposals, a qualified majority is sufficient for approval by the Council.

If the Council rejects individual or all amendments at the second reading, the President-in-Office of the Council convenes a conciliation committee within six weeks[35] in agreement with the President of the Parliament; Article 294 (8)(b) TFEU.

The phase of the legislative procedure following the adoption of the Parliament's amendment proposals at second reading is characterised by the search for a political compromise which is acceptable to all of the actors. To achieve this, informal meetings and votes also frequently take place between Council, Parliament and Commission representatives.[36] Particularly the involvement of the Commission is important in practice, in order to counteract its issuing a negative opinion and the related requirement of unanimity in the Council, which is difficult to achieve. At the same time, this opens up interesting procedural options for lobbyists who want to prevent an initiative.

5.2.3.2.6 Procedure in the conciliation committee

If the Parliament and the Council fail to reach a common solution at second reading, a conciliation committee is planned. This is intended to develop a compromise proposal within six weeks[37] of being convened; this is based on the positions of both the Council and the Parliament from the second reading; Article 294 (10) TFEU. It consists of 28[38] members, representing both the European Parliament and the Council in equal numbers (or their representatives in the Coreper); the Commission is involved in an advisory capacity in the conciliation committee's work for the purpose of reaching a compromise, see Article 294 (11) TFEU.

Informal co-ordination ("trialogues") between representatives of the three institutions also plays an important role in this stage of the legislative procedure – possible compromises are often sounded out before the conciliation committee

---

34 This deadline can also be extended by one month in accordance with Article 294 (14) TFEU.
35 Extension option: two weeks.
36 Oppermann, Classen and Nettesheim (2014[6]), p. 178.
37 This deadline can be extended by two weeks in accordance with Article 294 (14) TFEU.
38 Oppermann, Classen and Nettesheim (2014[6]), p. 179.

meets.[39] The negotiations themselves are not infrequently conducted in smaller, trilateral work groups. During the formulation of a common draft, the conciliation committee is given wide discretion as regards content.[40] Any draft usually has to be accepted by a simple majority of the Parliament representatives and a qualified majority of the Council representatives; Article 294 (10) TFEU. If the conciliation committee is unable to agree to a common draft, the procedure ends and the legislative proposal is regarded as not enacted; Article 294 (12) TFEU. If the conciliation committee formulates and approves a common draft, a third reading takes place in the Council and Parliament; Article 294 (13) TFEU.

5.2.3.2.7 Third reading in the Council and Parliament

Within six weeks following the submission of the common draft,[41] the Council and Parliament must decide on its final acceptance or rejection; Article 294 (13) and (14) TFEU; amendment proposals are no longer possible. In this case, the Parliament decides with a majority of the votes submitted, and the Council with a qualified majority. Whilst the decision taken in the Council is always identical to that taken in the conciliation committee in practice, due to the politically identical composition of the Council delegation and the Council, the decision reached in the Parliament can most certainly deviate from it: as there is (effectively) no whip line comparable with that of national parliaments at European level, the committee delegation's position does not necessarily have to correspond to the final majority relationships in the Parliament.[42] Failure of the legislative proposal at this stage of the procedure is therefore still possible, e. g. due to failure to take a vote within the deadline, see Article 294 (13) sentence 2 TFEU.

5.2.3.2.8 Publication, announcement and entry into force

In the ordinary legislative procedure, legislative acts can therefore be enacted after the first, second or third reading with consensus support of the Commission's proposal and any amendments by the Parliament and Council. In accordance with Article 297 (1)(1) TFEU, these acts must be signed by the President of the European Parliament and the President-in-Office of the Council. Publication in the Official Journal of the EU is required for the legislative act's validity;[43] the legislation comes into force at the point in time set down within it, or otherwise on the twentieth day following publication; Article 297 (1)(3) TFEU.

---

39 Oppermann, Classen and Nettesheim (2014[6]), p. 179.
40 ECJ, Case C – 344/04, *IATA*, ECR 2006, I-403, recital 58 – 59.
41 Can be extended by two weeks; Article 294 (14) TFEU.
42 So far, such a constellation has arisen in two cases: firstly with regard to the directive on takeover bids 1995/0341 in 2001, and secondly with regard to port services 2001/0147 COD in 2003; Oppermann, Classen and Nettesheim (2014[6]), p. 180.
43 Oppermann, Classen and Nettesheim (2014[6]), p. 183 with further references to ECJ case law.

5.2.3.3 Legislation by the Commission according to Articles 290 and 291 TFEU, particularly comitology

Although focus has shifted to the ordinary legislative procedure through the Parliament and Council since the Treaty of Lisbon, the practical relevance of legislation by the Commission, which is intended to be the exception in concept, is not to be overlooked: approximately 69 % of all European legislative acts were and are enacted by the Commission.[44]

European law distinguishes between basic or primary legal provisions, which are enacted by the legislative institutions, the Council and Parliament, appointed to do so by the Treaties (secondary legislation), and secondary legal provisions or implementing regulations, for whose enactment the respective legislative power is assigned, under strict prerequisites, to different institutions (particularly the Commission) (so-called tertiary legislation). The type of non-legislative act was newly introduced and, in particular, the Commission's powers to enact secondary legal provisions were contractually re-regulated, with the Treaty of Lisbon. A distinction is now made between delegated legislative acts according to Article 290 TFEU and implementing acts in accordance with Article 291 TFEU.[45] In both cases, specific empowerment of the Commission to take action is required, and the legislative acts enacted in this manner by the Commission must be disclosed separately.[46] Whilst legislative powers are transferred to the Commission through the specific legislative act in the area of delegated legislation, legislative powers in the executive area are transferred to it in the case of implementing legislation according to Article 291 TFEU.[47]

5.2.3.3.1 Delegated legislation (Article 290 TFEU)

The delegation of legislative powers to the Commission is intended to relieve the legislative institutions, the Council and Parliament, particularly by keeping detailed technical issues out of the political legislative process, making adaptations of the legislative act to current developments simpler and faster.[48] Article 290 (1) TFEU now expressly opens up the option of issuing the Commission with the power to undertake generally applicable additions or modifications to certain non-essential elements of the legislative act as part of the enactment of a primary legislative act. These additions and modifications can be undertaken in any form

---

44 Blom-Hansen (2011), p. 3.
45 Precise delimitation is often the subject of dispute, not least due to the different extents of these powers and the control mechanisms to be applied between the institutions, and is also dealt with by the ECJ in various proceedings, see e.g. European Court of Justice (2014); exhaustively, also Edenharter (2014), pp. 649–650.
46 For clarification and delimitation from the primary legislative act, the title of delegated legislative acts must be preceded by the word "delegated" in accordance with Article 290 (3) TFEU; implementing acts must be preceded by the word "implementing" in accordance with Article 291 (4) TFEU.
47 Craig (2011), p. 672; Parker and Alemanno (2014), p. 17.
48 Streinz (2012), p. 202.

of a basic legislative act and without the necessary involvement of other institutions or committees with representatives of the member states.[49] However, the Commission is bound to the specified objective, content and time of the delegating legislative act as well as further transfer conditions; Article 290 (1)(2)(2) TFEU. In a similar way to a constitutional materiality proviso, the enactment and amendment of fundamental aspects of the legislative act are reserved for the actual legislative procedure. The exercise and control of delegation, for example in the form of revocation, are transferred to the Council and Parliament, see Article 290 (2) TFEU.

5.2.3.3.2 Implementing legislation by the Commission according to Article 291 (2) TFEU

Implementing acts by the Commission in accordance with Article 291 (2) TFEU are used for administrative implementation of the legislative acts, and are very important in practice. They are an exception to the principle that the implementation of binding Union legislative acts is always the responsibility of the member states through the selection of suitable national implementing provisions (see Article 291 (1) TFEU; principle of subsidiarity). In exceptional cases, the Commission, as an executive institution, can therefore formulate legally binding regulations to control the implementation of a legislative act, which has already been decided on in full in legislative terms, in all member states.[50] This is the case if uniform conditions are required for the implementation of the Union's legislative act and corresponding powers of implementation are transferred to the Commission (or, in exceptional cases, the Council) as part of the enactment of the respective legislative act; Article 291 (2) TFEU.

In contrast to the case of delegated legislation, however, general rules and principles, according to which the member states can control the Commission's exercise of its implementation powers, apply to the enactment of implementing acts by the Commission; Article 291 (3) TFEU. These were implemented by the Council and Parliament with Regulation 182/2011, which came into force on 1st March 2011, and supersede the comitology decision applicable until then.[51] The comitology procedure and the intermesh of the European and national levels are still applied: issue-related committees are involved; under the chairmanship of a non-voting Commission representative, these are comprised of experts and civil servants from the member states. The comitology procedure's scope was extended with the regulation; in particular, the area of the common trade policy is now also includ-

---

49 However, this does not exclude the involvement of external expertise; see Bieber, Epiney and Haag (2015), p. 216; Gellermann in Streinz (2012a[2]), Article 291 TFEU point 12.

50 See Oppermann, Classen and Nettesheim (2014[6]), p. 171; Fabricius (2014), pp. 453–454; Alemanno and Meuwese (2013) also plead for the introduction of the impact assessment in the area of implementing legislation.

51 Article 12 (1) of Regulation 182/2011 of the European Parliament and the Council of 16.2.2011 on laying down the rules and general principles concerning mechanisms for control by member states of the Commission's exercise of implementing powers, OJ 2011 L 55/13.

ed.[52] According to Article 11 of Regulation 182/2011, the Parliament and Council now have a right of notification through the Commission in terms of adherence to the powers of implementation transferred through the basic act.[53]

Instead of the previous five, only two procedures are now applied: the examination procedure and the advisory procedure. In cases of urgency, deviation from this is possible in a simplified procedure. Which procedure is applicable is not specified by the Commission but by the respective basic act; the type and effects of the required legislative act must be taken into consideration in this case (Article 2 (1) Regulation 182/2011). The examination procedure is usually applied (Article 2 (3) Regulation 182/2011). The procedures differ as regards the different importance of the committees' opinion: this is greater in the examination procedure.[54]

- The *advisory procedure* is primarily applied in non-controversial areas, and is rarely used in practice.[55] In this, the committees submit an opinion with a simple majority; whilst these are not binding for the Commission, it should take them into consideration as far as possible in its final decision on the draft implementing act (Article 4 (2) Regulation 182/ 2011).
- The *examination procedure* is usually applied in the case of implementing acts "of general scope", with reference to programmes with significant effects and in the area of common agriculture, fisheries and trade policy, the environment, security, taxation or the protection of the health or safety of humans, animals and plants; Article 2 (2) Regulation 182/2011. The most important, and also most controversial, implementing measures are subject to this procedure.[56] The committee, and therefore indirectly the member states, is afforded an important opportunity for exerting an influence here: the committee can vote on the Commission's proposal with a qualified majority, i.e. can accept or reject it, or not submit an opinion and thus accordingly determine the Commission's scope for action; Article 5 Regulation 182/2011. If the committee approves the Commission's proposal, the Commission can enact the implementing act according to the draft. If the committee rejects the Commission's proposal, the Commission can only enact the implementing act immediately in limited, exceptional cases. However, the Commission can amend the draft and submit it again or submit the rejected draft to the appeal committee. If the comitology committee does not issue an opinion, or not with the required quorum, it is left to the Commission's discretion whether or not it enacts the implementing act. How-

---

52 Daiber (2012), p. 248; Streinz (2012), p. 206.
53 This is derived from the transfer competence as part of the basic act enacted in the ordinary legislative procedure in accordance with Article 291 (3) TFEU; exhaustively and critically in this regard: Fabricius (2014), pp. 454–455; Craig (2011), pp. 683–684.
54 Daiber (2012), pp. 240, 243.
55 See Parker and Alemanno (2014), p. 20, footnote 56.
56 Parker and Alemanno (2014), p. 20; in justified, exceptional cases, the advisory procedure can be applied instead of the examination procedure (Article 2 (3) sentence 2 of Regulation 182/2011), or the examination procedure can also be applied in further areas; Article 2 (2) ("in particular"): see Daiber (2012), pp. 243–244.

ever, it is prevented from enacting if half of the member states contradict, this is provided for in this manner in the basic act, or a legislative act in the area of taxation or the protection of health or safety is involved. The Commission can also amend the proposal or initiate an appeal procedure in this case.

The appeal procedure is similar to the original comitology procedure; in the appeal committee, higher-ranking representatives of the member states make decisions with a qualified majority under the chairmanship of a non-voting Commission representative. They can amend the proposal, accept it, reject it, or not adopt any position; Article 6 (2) Regulation 182/2011: if the appeal committee issues its approval, the implementing act is enacted; if the committee rejects it, it is not enacted. If the appeal committee fails to issue a statement, the Commission is again at liberty to decide.

- In exceptional cases, particularly due to reasons of urgency, implementing acts can be immediately validated even without prior committee involvement (simplified procedure according to Article 8 of Regulation 182/2011).[57]

The Commission's implementing legislation and the comitology procedure are very important in practice. According to the Commission, 302 comitology committees were convened in 2013, in addition to which 970 written procedures were implemented. On this basis, 1,916 committee opinions were forwarded to the Commission, which thereupon enacted 1,716 implementing acts.[58] This is extremely relevant to corporate interests: particularly in the case of detailed regulations, the scope for interpretation permitted by a basic act can be exploited in a company's favour or narrowed to its disadvantage.

5.3 Access to the institutions of the European Union

Following the description of the procedures of particular relevance to the practice of lobbying in Section 5.2, the following explanations will deal with the question of which rules lobbyists have to observe in communication with the individual EU institutions during the course of these procedures. To what extent is access to decision-makers at the legislative and executive levels therefore subject to legal regulation? Not only will the current legal status be described in the following; suggestions for alternative regulation options will also be provided.

5.3.1 General

Since the Treaty of Lisbon and the related, revised version of Article 11 of the EU Treaty (TEU) at the latest, professional lobbyists have become a "fixed element of

57 See Craig (2011), p. 684.
58 For an exhaustive analysis of implementing legislation by policy area: see European Commission (2014a).

EU governance".[59] According to Article 11 (1), "the institutions shall, by appropriate means, give citizens and representative associations the opportunity to make known and publicly exchange their views in all areas of Union action"; according to Paragraph 2, "[t]he institutions shall maintain an open, transparent and regular dialogue with representative associations and civil society".

All EU institutions are therefore firstly under a legal obligation to clearly communicate their initiatives and views in all areas, and to engage in dialogue with the citizens of Europe (thus ultimately also the companies) and their representative associations. Article 11 (3) EU actually contains express provisions in this regard, according to which the European Commission "shall carry out broad consultations with parties concerned in order to ensure that the Union's actions are coherent and transparent".

The accusation that this theoretically very welcome innovation can only be implemented in part in practice, particularly with reference to individual citizens, can hardly be levelled at the parties responsible at European level. For example, the Commission has for some time been conducting public consultations, on diverse EU initiatives,[60] in which individual citizens are welcome to participate in addition to companies, associations and lobbyists. Their comments are published and taken into consideration during the procedure. Nevertheless, there are only a very few cases in which individual persons take up the offer of such dialogue. There are numerous causes for this: firstly, wide areas of the population are still extensively unaware of the EU's legislative and administrative importance. Public reporting and the resulting public outcry regarding the "bureaucratic monster which is the EU" usually occur when the crucial decisions and procedures have long since been reached and completed – at European level. Examples of this include EU legislation on conventional incandescent light bulbs[61] or the recently implemented power restriction for vacuum cleaners[62] due to reasons of environmental protection and energy conservation. In the majority of consultations, a high level of specialist knowledge and personal commitment is additionally required in order to get to grips, as an individual person, with the Green and White Papers, draft directives and regulations, etc. which are published by the EU.

Companies and associations make significantly more frequent use of the opportunity to take part in consultations, although the comparatively low number of consultation contributions regularly seen in practice is also astonishing in this case, given that there are 28 member states and hundreds of thousands of European companies – this number usually lies in the low to medium double digit range.

---

59 See Rödlach-Rupprechter (2014), p. 143.
60 See the list available on the Internet at http://ec.europa.eu/yourvoice/consultations/index_en.htm (last accessed on 22.5.2015).
61 See ecodesign directive 2005/32/EC.
62 See Regulation (EU) No. 666/2013.

The frequency of more extensive – individual – involvement of companies and associations in the actual EU legislative procedures, i.e. ultimately active lobbying, is even lower. This is extensively due to the complexity of the decision-making processes at European level, which is exhaustively described at various points in this book. "In contrast to the national political system, it is often more difficult for those affected to understand the decision-making processes which take place at European level. (…) The difficulties involved in assigning responsibilities are undoubtedly greater at European level. This is not due to a lack of democracy, but to the complexity of democracy at European level, at least at present. In party political terms, the institutional structure consisting of the European Parliament, the member states, the Council and the European Commission is more heterogeneous than in the member states."[63] This is compounded by further, specific difficulties in participating in the decision-making process, such as cultural or language barriers between lobbyists and representatives of the institutions, which are far more relevant at EU level than at member state or national level.

Essentially, however, access to the EU institutions should be readily available to each representative of interests. Whereas the representatives of the EU member states, in particular, usually have constant, "formalised" access to the EU institutions, e.g. via work groups, the representatives of other interests, for example companies, associations, organisations, public affairs agencies or law firms, often have to independently ensure structural access to the institutions.

For some time, this structural access to the institutions has been subjected to increasingly higher formal requirements, which will be dealt with in the following. It can already be stated in advance that the regulation of access to the EU institutions not only has positive aspects: whilst well balanced regulations concerning the "how any why" of access can essentially increase the transparency and professionalism of lobbying, any regulation of access necessarily restricts access as such – the subsequent regulations impact on the "formal, procedural" level and thus restrict access to the relevant contact persons, insofar as these have been identified beforehand. Whether the identified contact person can then be convinced of one's own concern on "the basis of its substance and content" is quite another matter.

5.3.2 Legal bases of regulation

A distinction must first be made between various (legal) provisions which directly or indirectly affect lobbyists in their activities. The criminal law regulations which are possible, at least in theory, in the member states during the course of communication with executive and legislative decision-makers, and through which the illegal exertion of influence is sanctioned, e.g. the offences of bribery or the granting of favours,[64] will not be examined at any greater length in the following. It

---

63 See Linder (2014), p. 48.
64 See Krajewski (2014), pp. 270–271.

goes without saying that a professional lobbyist must behave absolutely lawfully at all times, with the assistance of legal advice if necessary.[65] This starts with the issue of whether – and, if yes, within which scope – a political decision-maker or a civil servant may be invited to dine or to an evening reception.

At EU level, however, there is a range of regulations pertaining specifically to communication and exchange with EU institutions, including, for instance, the Staff Regulations and the Conditions of Employment of the EU, the European Parliament's Code of Conduct, the Transparency Register of the European Commission and European Parliament or the (once again) highly topical transparency initiative under President of the Commission Juncker. All of these will be dealt with exhaustively in the following sections.

Firstly, however, a distinction has to be made between three fundamentally different approaches to regulating lobbying: firstly, self-regulation through professional lobbyist associations, secondly, voluntary institutional registers, and thirdly, binding legal rules.[66]

Whilst professional self-regulation does not essentially require an independent legal basis, the relative powers (legislative competence) must be called into question in the case of voluntary institutional registers (e.g. the current EU Transparency Register, which is based on an interinstitutional agreement between the European Parliament and European Commission) and binding legal rules. The legal situation in this regard is not entirely clear at EU level. Neither the TEU nor the TFEU contains an express legal basis for regulating the relationships between EU institutions and lobbyists. Whilst Article 11 TEU and Article 15 (1) TFEU, which are often cited in this regard, include the principle of transparency which is central in this context, they do not contain any express powers to enact binding EU secondary legislation.[67] In the debate conducted so far with regard to relevant EU competencies, reference has therefore usually been made to Article 352 TFEU, also by the European Commission and the European Parliament[68].[69] Article 352 TFEU is a type of "general clause", which can be invoked when EU Treaty objectives are to be achieved but no express powers exist for this purpose in the Treaty. Under this prerequisite "(…) the Council, acting unanimously on a proposal from the Commission and after obtaining the consent of the European Parliament, shall adopt the appropriate measures".[70] "In view of the Council's reservations about participating in the Parliament's and the Commission's voluntary Transparency Register", Linder refers to this as an "approach promising little success".[71]

---

65 See Joos (2011), p. 120.
66 See Krajeweski (2014), p. 270.
67 See Krajewski (2014), p. 271.
68 See Linder (2014), p. 56.
69 See Krajewski (2014), p. 279.
70 Article 352 (1) sentence 1 TFEU.
71 See Linder (2014), p. 56.

Article 298 TFEU is another possible legal basis for authorisation. According to this, "[i]n carrying out their missions, the institutions, bodies, offices and agencies of the Union shall have the support of an open, efficient and independent European administration", whereby "[i]n compliance with the Staff Regulations and the Conditions of Employment adopted on the basis of Article 336, the European Parliament and the Council, acting by means of regulations in accordance with the ordinary legislative procedure, shall establish provisions to that end". Article 336 is apparently aimed primarily at the European administration, leading to the question of whether rules for the actions of other persons who may influence the administration can also be enacted on this basis. Krajewski affirms this in consideration of the genesis, the systematic position and the sense and purpose of Article 298 TFEU, as the independence of the administration can be ensured in this manner.[72] Conversely, Article 298 TFEU cannot offer an adequate legal basis insofar as regulations concern the Parliament – the legislature – rather than the administration. The literature[73] therefore picks up on the implied powers doctrine again (general principle of EU law), according to which other competencies lead to the implicit existence of a corresponding legal basis in the event that an express legal basis is absent. As a result, the EU accordingly has the power to regulate lobbying at European level in accordance with Article 298 (2) TFEU in combination with the implied powers doctrine.

5.3.3 Legal framework of access to the individual institutions

5.3.3.1 Regulation of access to the European Council

A distinction must be made between the member state and the European level in analysing the rules concerning access to members of the Council or the civil servants.

As regards the member state level, no specific regulations apply under European law to access to the respective, delegated members of the Council and their representatives. However, the member state level, where partially extensive regulations concerning access for lobbyists have been implemented, must be noted. To guarantee correct behaviour here, a lobbyist should obtain information from an expert source in advance. However, a portrayal of the 28 different regulation scenarios is expressly forgone at this point, since it would exceed the scope of this book.

At European level, the general provisions of the Staff Regulations[74] and the Conditions of Employment of the EU[75] (whose content is extensively the same) in

---

72 See Krajewski (2014), pp. 272 ff.
73 See Krajewski (2014), pp. 272 ff. with further references.
74 Regulation 259/68, OJ L 56/1 (1968); with regard to the new version of 2004 Regulation 723/2004, see OJ L 124/I (2004), available on the Internet at: http://ec.europa.eu/civil_service/docs/toc100_en.pdf (last accessed on 3.6.2015).
75 The provisions of the Staff Regulations and the Conditions of Employment of the EU are available on the Internet at: http://ec.europa.eu/civil_service/docs/toc100_en.pdf (last accessed on 3.6.2015).

turn apply to European civil servants and other employees in the service of the Council. There are no specific access regulations with regard to either the Council of the Permanent Representatives Committee (Coreper), as the Council's most important preparatory institution: the code of conduct of the Council and the European Parliament[76] deals exclusively with (internal) organisational issues; nor do the Council's Rules of Procedure contain any standards of relevance to regulation.

5.3.3.2 Regulation of access to Commission members and civil servants

In addition to the general laws, lobbyists must so far adhere, in particular, to the provisions of the Staff Regulations of the EU[77] and the Conditions of Employment of other servants, which are applicable to non-civil servants each time they contact Commission employees and civil servants (the provisions contained in the latter are extensively the same as those in the Staff Regulations with regard to the area of interest here). In 2011, the Commission and Parliament then specified a common register, a code of conduct and a complaints mechanism in an interinstitutional agreement.[78] The Council supports this initiative,[79] but does not maintain a register itself.

The code of conduct is intended to regulate the behaviour of organisations and individual persons towards the EU institutions. It is urgently recommended that professional lobbyists adhere to the code: in addition to the constant requirement of adherence to the counterpart's rules of communication, the poor impression which violations of the code can cause must also be remembered. In the worst case, a lobbyist who fails to adhere to the code by no means least risks the practical loss of his access to the Commission employees. Without being able to deal in legal depth with the high number of individual regulations at this point, at least three regulations require emphasising as being particularly relevant in practice, namely Articles 11, 11a and 12 of the Staff Regulations. These regulations deal with questions of the objectivity, impartiality and duty of loyalty of Commission civil servants and employees:

- For example, Article 11 makes it clear that a civil servant must neither seek nor take instructions which are not attributable to the authority within which he is employed, and that his acceptance of rewards, gifts or payments of any kind is prohibited without the approval of this authority. This ultimately involves a ban on what is already clearly sanctioned by the general penal laws – presumably in all EU member states. It should again be emphasised that such modes of behaviour have nothing to do with lobbying but simply constitute illegal conduct.

---

76 The code of conduct is available on the Internet at: European Commission (2014b); the complete code is outlined in Chapter 2.
77 Regulation 259/68, OJ L 56/I (1968); with regard to the new version of 2004 Regulation 723/2004, see OJ L 124/I (2004).
78 See van Schendelen (2013), p. 311.
79 See European Commission (2015g).

- Article 11a of the Staff Regulations obligates the civil servant, inter alia, to inform the authority within which he is employed about emerging conflicts of interest.
- The general clause in Article 12 of the Staff Regulations, according to which the civil servant must refrain from any behaviour which might reflect adversely upon his position, ultimately includes all actions which may lead to doubt as to the civil servant's objectivity, impartiality or independence from external influences, or to his loyalty to the EU. A lobbyist should always be aware of these regulations, and should refrain from anything which may cause the civil servant to even come close to violating one of the specified rules.

5.3.3.3 Transparency Initiative/Transparency Register

5.3.3.3.1 Boundary conditions and content of the Transparency Register

The EU Transparency Register is based on an interinstitutional agreement concluded between the European Parliament and the European Commission on 23rd June 2011, and is maintained by these institutions.[80] The Commission established a register for lobbyists back in 2008. After the EU Parliament joined the initiative, the register was ultimately extended to form a Transparency Register in 2011. Three years later, the Parliament decided to amend the interinstitutional agreement concerning the register. The new, "second generation" of the register, which was drawn up jointly by the Parliament and Commission, has been applied since January 2015.

In legal terms, interinstitutional agreements are based on Article 295 TFEU. The objective of the Transparency Register is the registration and control of lobbyists' access to executive and legislative decision-makers at EU level.[81] The register is also intended to increase the transparency of the EU decision-making process for citizens. It is additionally aimed at stimulating more active participation in political activities amongst EU citizens. The Transparency Register is intended to answer the following, individual questions:

- Which interests are being pursued?
- Who is pursuing these interests?
- What financial resources are available?[82]

The relationship between the lobbyists and the EU decision-makers is regulated in a code of conduct created for this purpose (see also Section 2.3.5.2 in particular).

The data in the register are the sole responsibility of the respective organisations, and also originate from these organisations. This includes personal information on:

---

80 The interinstitutional agreement was revised after two years. The amended version was then accepted in April 2014. The current agreement is available at: http://eur-lex.europa.eu/legal-content/de/TXT/?uri=uriserv:OJ.L_.2014.277.01.0011.01.ENG (last accessed on 29.5.2015).
81 See Krajewski (2014), pp. 270–271.
82 See European Commission (2015c).

- The organisation acting as a lobbyist or the individual legal entity acting as a lobbyist.
- The lobbyist's represented interests and activities.
- The party on whose behalf the lobbyist is acting;.
- The financial and staffing resources implemented during the course of lobbying.[83]

The Transparency Register defines the various forms of lobbying activities as follows:[84]

- Contacting members, civil servants or other employees of the EU institutions.
- Preparation, dissemination and transfer of written material, information material plus discussion and position papers.
- Organisation of events, meetings or competition measures as well as social events or conferences to which members, civil servants or other employees of the EU institutions have been invited.
- Voluntary contributions and participation in formal consultations regarding planned legislative acts and other legislative acts as well as other consultations.

The main feature common to these activities is the objective of exerting a direct or indirect influence on the decision-making processes at EU level.

At present, approximately 6,500 legal entities are listed in the register. These include self-employed consultants, in-house lobbyists, representatives of various associations, NGOs, religious groups, higher education establishments and agencies.

In return for entry in the Transparency Register, the European Parliament grants registered members – following successful accreditation – special access to its facilities. The Parliament also demands that all speakers representing organisations who are entitled to take part in its committees' public hearings seek registration.[85] Registered lobbyists are also included in E-mail distribution lists in order to keep abreast of current legislative initiatives.[86]

5.3.3.3.2 Critical appraisal

The Transparency Register is one of numerous EU instruments through which the political decision-making process is to be made more open and the opportunities for EU citizens to participate increased.[87] The EU Commission's *transparency*

---

83 See Transparency Register, http://ec.europa.eu/transparencyregister/public/staticPage/
displayStaticPage.do?locale=en&reference=DATA_PROTECTION (last accessed on 3.6.2015).

84 The definition is available at: http://www.europarl.europa.eu/EPRS/EPRS-Briefing-542170-European-
Transparency-Register-FINAL.pdf (last accessed on 5.6.2015).

85 See Transparency Register, http://ec.europa.eu/transparencyregister/public/staticPage/
displayStaticPage.do?locale=en&reference=WHOS_IS_EXPECTED_TO_REGISTER (last accessed on
3.6.2015).

86 European Commission, press release database, http://europa.eu/rapid/press-release_IP-15-3740_en.
htm (last accessed on 3.6.2015).

87 See Transparency Register, http://ec.europa.eu/transparencyregister/public/staticPage/
displayStaticPage.do?locale=en&reference=WHY_TRANSPARENCY_REGISTER (last accessed on
29.5.2015).

portal and the European Parliament's *transparency and ethics* websites are further platforms.[88] Whilst the objective of all of these measures is to be unreservedly welcomed, various Transparency Register weaknesses require closer analysis.

- *Voluntariness of the register:* Even the European Parliament admits that, in its current – non-binding – form, the register is only able to portray a "certain section" of the political lobbying process. It is not able to cover the process completely or give consideration to the various forms of lobbying. The Parliament has therefore set itself the goal of introducing a mandatory register.[89]
- *Verification of the data in the register:* Not only is registration as such voluntary, but the correctness of the specified data is not checked by a third party either. So that the register is able to fulfil its function as a transparency-boosting measure and not create "pseudo-transparency", the level of which is defined by the party to be monitored itself, an independent entity must check and verify the data specified by the registered organisations and individual persons. Trustworthy and professional portrayal of lobbying activities is only possible in this way.[90]
- *Registration of only some of the actors in the area of lobbying:* One further deficit, which is also criticised time and again by lobbyists themselves, is the fact that by no means all of the lobbyists in Brussels fall under the regulations of the European Transparency Initiative.[91] Whilst law firms, for example, are explicitly listed in the Transparency Register, the activities of lawyers are not included in the register's scope when these involve for example "advisory work and contacts with public bodies in order to better inform clients about a general legal situation or about their specific legal position, or to advise them whether or not a particular legal or administrative step is appropriate or admissible under the law as it stands".[92] The activities of social partners as participants in social dialogue are also excluded. Another group of lobbyists which is not subject to the regulations consists of the representatives of local, regional and municipal authorities, such as the representations of the German Länder or Länder parliaments. Nor are the representatives of parties or churches and religious communities ever affected. It is merely "expected" of these groups that they register themselves, despite their similarities to corporate lobbying[93] and their participation in the same procedures in individual cases: if, for example, an oil company makes contact with Members of the European Parliament during the redrafting of an environmental directive, it must seek registration according to the sense of the register; however, the environmental organisation which be-

---

88 For more information, see transparency portal at: http://ec.europa.eu/transparency/index_en.htm; for transparency and ethics see: http://www.europarl.europa.eu/atyourservice/en/20150201PVL00050/Ethics-and-Transparency (last accessed on 3.6.2015).
89 See European Parliament news (5.4.2015).
90 See European Parliament news (5.4.2015).
91 See van Schendelen (2013), pp. 311 ff.
92 See European Parliament (2015b).
93 See van Schendelen (2013), p. 311.

comes involved in the same procedure is not required to do so. Transparency should be independent of the respective perception of the correctness of the represented interest or its ability to achieve a consensus.

To eliminate some of the current registration model's inadequacies, the new Commission under Juncker launched a "Transparency Initiative" in 2014. Even before taking up office, President of the Commission Juncker announced increased transparency in contact with lobbyists in his political guidelines. Since December 2014, the Commission has therefore been publishing all contact between Commissioners, cabinet staff and the Directorate General with lobbyists on its website as part of this initiative. Juncker's objective is therefore the establishment of a mandatory register on a legal basis for all three EU institutions.[94] However, it is unclear how the Commission intends to create greater transparency regarding the experts which advise it without violating data protection regulations.

So far, however, the Juncker Commission has failed to implement its announcements (status July 2016). There is neither a mandatory register nor a new legal basis which includes the Commission, Council and Parliament.

It is problematic that the above points of criticism – with the exception of the first, concerning voluntariness – cannot, in all likelihood, be satisfactorily addressed even on introduction of a new regulation, in the sense of a binding Transparency Register. It is not, therefore, to be anticipated that lawyers' confidentiality obligations will be relaxed: the extensive inviolability of the client-lawyer relationship for state agencies is too valuable a constitutional commodity to be sacrificed for transparency in lobbying. Verification of the data in the register by public sector bodies is also difficult to imagine: to achieve this, companies and associations would have to disclose a significant part of their internal documentation and corporate information, which is unlikely to be politically enforceable, and is certainly legally dubious – companies, too, have basic rights vis-à-vis state bodies.

5.3.3.3.3 *Alternatives to the Transparency Register: binding quality criteria for lobbying*

Adherence to legal, financial and tax regulations – legal and financial compliance – by lobbying actors is of elementary importance, irrespective of the misgivings outlined in the preceding section with regard to current and planned registration regulations. In view of this, a deviating regulation approach which is applicable to all lobbying actors is proposed. Instead of a Transparency Register, the European legislator should define binding quality criteria for all lobbyists (compliance standards).

---

94 See EurActiv.de, at http://www.euractiv.de/sections/eu-innenpolitik/eu-kommission-beschliesst-transparenz-initiative-310338 (last accessed on 3.6.2015).

The following four-pillar principle could be used as a benchmark for compliance standards:

1st pillar: legal compliance

2nd pillar: financial compliance

3rd pillar: data protection

4th pillar: quality management (ISO certification)

1st pillar: legal compliance

Legal compliance should involve adherence to standards which are far more stringent than those specified so far. For example, not only national or EU-wide standards and laws should be taken into consideration in compliance checks, but also international ones such as the US Foreign Corrupt Practices Act. These standards must also be taught in regular training courses for those involved in lobbying, which would also have to be verified by the respective companies or lobbyists.

2nd pillar: financial compliance

As part of financial compliance, all lobbying companies should be subject to mandatory auditing, irrespective of their size and legal form. To guarantee gap-free compliance; business processes, financial accounting and capital flow must be audited in full, not merely at random. The effectiveness of the internal control system and proof of the data in accounting and the annual accounts must also be assessed.

3rd pillar: data protection

An external and independent data protection officer should not only regularly perform the specified audits, but should also be available to the employees as a contact person for data protection issues. The employees should also undergo training on this topic at regular intervals and be kept constantly abreast of the latest developments in this area, e.g. by means of newsletters.

On the whole, the specified measures could lead to equality in treatment, and avoid possible regulation gaps, amongst the lobbying instruments – corporate representative offices, associations, organisations, law firms, public affairs agencies and governmental relations agencies.

4th pillar: quality management (ISO certification)

A quality management (QM) system, which can be guaranteed via QM standard EN ISO 9001, should be ensured for administrative tasks in compliance-relevant areas of lobbying. This particularly includes the areas of finance, accounting, personnel, law and IT. For ISO certification, these areas must be broken down into individual procedures and procedural descriptions, the individual processes checked as regards actuality, appropriateness, plausibility and necessity, and finally reassembled according to ISO-conformant structural principles and procedures. The QM system should additionally be subject to a continuous improvement process.

The EN ISO 9001 standard defines the minimum requirements which the lobbyist's management system would have to fulfil in order to correspond to a specific standard and thus meet, and ultimately guarantee, the client's expectations or official requirements.

In accordance with EU regulations, voluntary management systems are certified by a body accredited for this task, whereby only one national accreditation body exists in each EU member state (in Germany, in accordance with Article 4 (1) Regulation (EC) 765/2008, this is the German Accreditation Body (DAkkS GmbH)), which accredits the certification bodies (Technical Inspection Association (TÜV). This should ensure reliable execution of the specifications defined through the standards.

5.3.3.4 Regulation of access to Members of the European Parliament

Not only the so-called "cash for amendments" scandal in 2011[95] drew attention to this problem, causing the European Parliament to adopt a code of conduct for members of parliament the very same year, since which it has continued to be refined. Amongst other aspects, this code contains the obligation to disclose financial interests, ethical guiding principles and basic principles of conduct.

Article 9 (4) of the Rules of Procedure of the European Parliament (in the following: RoPEP)[96] is particularly relevant with regard to the regulation of lobbyists' access to the Parliament. The importance of direct access to the parliamentary building, as regulated there, to the immediacy of the flow of information is obvious: only if physical access is possible can a lobbyist seek out members of parliament or their employees in their offices or take part in meetings and hearings in the parliamentary building. Accordingly, Article 9 (4) RoPEP describes lobbyists as "persons (...) who desire frequent access to the parliamentary buildings in order to supply the members with information in their own interest or in the interest of third parties within the framework of their parliamentary mandate". To this end, the so-called Quaestors[97] issue badges with a limited period of validity (a maximum of one year) on behalf of the Parliament, and enter the badge holder in a public parliamentary register; however, the prerequisite for entry and the issue

---

95 Starting in the summer of 2010, two reporters from Britain's *Sunday Times* passed themselves off as lobbyists, and attempted, with a (fictitious) offer of 100,000 euros each, to persuade 60 Members of the European Parliament to help pass a specific draft law. Three members of parliament took up this fictitious offer (see Section 2.3.5).
96 The Rules of Procedure of the European Parliament are available at: European Parliament (2015b).
97 Quaestors are six elected members of the Bureau of the European Parliament who are responsible for administrative and finance policy issues which directly affect the Members of the European Parliament, see Article 25 of the Rules of Procedure of the European Parliament.

of the badge is that a lobbyist subjects himself to the code of conduct regulated in Article 3 of Annex IX of the Rules of Procedure.

All in all, the regulations only contain those provisions which a professional, serious lobbyist must in any case observe out of self-interest – such as adherence to general laws. Disclosing the respective, represented interest and not attempting to obtain information by devious means, for example, are matters of course. Any other behaviour would place a lobbyist's good reputation at risk. Whoever attempts to mislead a Member of Parliament with regard to his true intentions is ultimately depriving himself of the foundations of his work.

Further regulations concerning lobbying are planned in the future during the course of the Commission's and Parliament's continuing transparency policy.

5.3.3.5 Regulation of access to the Committee of the Regions (CoR) and the Economic and Social Committee (ESC)

Neither access to the CoR nor the ESC is subject to separate regulations; only the Rules of Procedure of the CoR[98] and ESC,[99] which are very general in issues of access by third parties, have to be observed.

In the final analysis, the absence of detailed regulations can be seen as further proof of the fact that the CoR and ESC are (extensively) of little relevance to lobbying at the European level.

5.3.4 Consequences for the practice of lobbying

Section 5.2 provided an overview of the individual legislative procedures at European level, and Section 5.3 gave an introduction to the legal framework of communication with the individual EU institutions and their members, as well as showing current trends. What conclusions can now be drawn for lobbying at European level from the specifics of the EU's political system and legislative procedures? Firstly, it is vital to ensure that consideration is given to the special features of Europe whilst establishing a lobbying strategy. Approaches which appear practicable at national level are often only second-best solutions or entirely ineffective at European level. Unlike at member state level, there is not, or only very rarely, the one individual, powerful contact person whose conviction is crucial to the success or failure of a concern. Instead, a considerably higher number of decision-makers with different backgrounds and positions have to be addressed at European level, leading to a vast increase in the complexity of, and the effort required in, lobbying in practice (see Section 5.3.4.1). Secondly, the simple "dilution" of the corporate interest as a result of the concern's being shifted from the national to

---

98 The Rules of Procedure of the Committee of the Regions are available at: http://eur-lex.europa.eu/legal-content/EN/ALL/?uri=CELEX:32010Q0109(01) (last accessed on 3.6.2015).

99 The Rules of Procedure of the Economic and Social Committee are available at: http://eur-lex.europa.eu/LexUriServ/LexUriServ.do?uri=CELEX:32010Q1209(01):EN:NOT (last accessed on 3.6.2015).

the European level must be considered: what may have been a strong position in the home member state quickly becomes a marginal problem of little relevance in Brussels (see Section 5.3.4.2).

5.3.4.1 Decisions without decision-makers?[100]

5.3.4.1.1 European Union "complexity trap": is there the one decision-maker?

As has become clear in the preceding Sections 5.2.2 and 5.2.3, the reforms to the Treaty of Lisbon have significantly increased the complexity of the political decision-making processes, and thus also lobbying, in the EU:

1. The Parliament's role was strengthened, thus widening the group of political decision-makers. Whilst the European Parliament is not able to initiate laws, it can block them in all cases requiring mandatory approval.

2. In the Council, decisions in almost all important political fields are no longer subject to the principle of unanimity, but to the majority principle (principle of the double majority of states and population shares).

Conversely, whilst the principle of unanimity still prevailed in many important policy areas, an individual Council member, as a representative of a member state, was often able to block any procedure by refusing to give consent during decisions made in the Council. Nobody was able to bypass the party who was able to exercise a "veto" in this manner for the due decision. This decision-maker was comparatively easy to identify for corporate lobbying.[101] Contact with the Council member could often be established via the veto state's responsible ministry – particularly if the member state intending to implement the veto was the state in which the company itself was based or had its headquarters.[102]

5.3.4.1.2 Ordinary legislative procedure (Article 294 TFEU): the number of decision-makers is increasing

As has already been explained, the majority principle applies in the Council during the ordinary legislative procedure. The votes of at least 55 % of the Council members (i.e. at least 15 member states), which must in turn represent at least 65 % of the EU population, are required for a so-called qualified majority. Consequently, at least four Council members, who must then also represent a total of more than 35 % of the EU population, are required for a blocking minority.[103] The consequence is that one individual member state alone no longer has the option of implementing a "veto". The situation for lobbyists has therefore become more complicated.

---

100 The following chapter contains parts of the author's contribution as published in Joos (2015), pp. 405–418.
101 This not only applies to private companies, but also to associations and organisations (to the entire chapter).
102 See Joos (2011), p. 110.
103 Article 16 (4) TFEU.

So far, lobbyists have relied extensively on the possibility of preventing decisions which, in their view, were not compatible with the represented corporate interests. This will continue to play a role in the future, particularly as companies frequently only become aware of the fact that their interests are in danger when the formal processes are already far advanced. In the Council, a regulation or directive can only be prevented through a blocking minority or amended through a qualified majority. The group of relevant decision-makers has thus become much larger. Cross-member-state networks are now always required, as the classic focus on one member state is no longer sufficient even to prevent a decision.

Frequently, a legislative initiative in the Commission does not start at the upper Commissioner and Director General level but beneath it, at the so-called "working level". Even within the Council, decisions are carefully prepared in both the national governments and in the Council Secretariat. A number of persons are also involved in decision-making within the Parliament. If a draft law is introduced in the European Parliament, the parliamentary committee to which the submission is to be objectively assigned, and the further committees which are to act in an advisory capacity, are additionally defined. In the responsible committee, a rapporteur is in overall charge of supervising the legislative proposal. He can be assisted by so-called "shadow rapporteurs" provided by the parliamentary groups.[104] Added to these are all other members of the advisory committees in which the legislative proposal is dealt with. Ultimately, the final decision is the responsibility of all 751 Members of the European Parliament, consisting of various political parties from a current 28 member states when a majority in the plenary is involved.

Nor should the informal influence of party employees or committee secretariat staff be overlooked. In view of the high number of individual agents, it is difficult to identify and contact the relevant decision-makers in this network of many parallel and successively running processes and to inform them of one's own interests. In combination with the formal and informal procedures, this high level of complexity, even of informal networks, poses a challenge to many lobbyists, including those of major companies, making professional process support by a neutral and objective intermediary unavoidable.

5.3.4.1.3 Informal trialogue as an additional – informal – decision-making level

In addition to the formal procedures and decision-making processes, it is important to obtain information on the informal processes in all EU institutions, and not to overlook these in favour of the formal procedures set down in the Treaties, but to support them through professional monitoring. One striking example of a procedure which is not actually provided for at all in the EU Treaties, particularly the TFEU, is the "informal trialogue" already explained in Section 5.2.3.2.1. This

---

104 See Rules of Procedure of the European Parliament Article 49 (2) and Article 205 (4).

involves meetings and agreements within a limited group, in which representatives of the Commission, the Parliament (usually the rapporteurs) and the Council (usually the Council Presidency) participate.

This trialogue is often applied even prior to parliamentary consultations, i.e. prior to the first reading of a legislative proposal in the Parliament as part of the ordinary legislative procedure, in order to speed up co-ordination between the Commission, Parliament and Council. This is often where crucial compromises in the legislative procedure are achieved.[105] As a consequence of this, compromises in the ordinary legislative procedure are actually reached prior to the first reading and without bringing the case before the conciliation committee in the vast majority of cases.[106]

The informal trialogue can therefore most certainly be regarded as a further (albeit informal) decision-making level. With its focus on content-related work, the activity of classic lobbying is no longer able to cope, particularly with these opaque, informal decision-making processes.

The differences between the member states' political cultures and mentalities also play a role, especially in these less structured, informal processes. Supporting these processes therefore also necessitates profound intercultural expertise as well as knowledge of the persons involved and their political and cultural background.

5.3.4.1.4 Complexity and multi-dimensionality of the procedures and process competence in lobbying

Lobbyists therefore face fundamental "technical" questions that have to be answered continually in parallel with all content-related argumentation, irrespective of whether the interests of a member state, a company, an association or an NGO are being represented. As already explained exhaustively in Chapter 3, practice shows how important process competence is to be able to participate in the European Union's political system and to support decision-making processes. Even the search for the correct contact person often proves to be a challenge for lobbyists. The EU has no executive such as that found in the member states. European lobbying must be undertaken both amongst the European institutions (Parliament, Commission, Council, etc.) and at member state level (Council members). In the EU, legislative functions are exercised by the Council of the EU and the European Parliament. However, the European Parliament is not comparable with national parliaments in view of the fact that there are no governing parties or opposition parties; instead, there are diverse consensus-building processes across national and party boundaries that make it difficult to predict majorities. Not only the relevant, responsible European institutions, but also the member state level (e.g. the

---

105 Weidenfeld (2013³), p. 166; with regard to the informal trialogue in the co-decision procedure prior to the Treaty of Lisbon: Wessels (2008), pp. 229, 345, 361.
106 Jensen/Martisen (2014), p. 5; European Parliamentary Research Service (25.6.2014), p. 2.

individual Council members or the nationally organised parties of the Members of the European Parliament), have to be involved during the legislative procedure. To be successful, one must be able to support the processes promptly at all of these interfaces. Against this background, a lobbyist will constantly have to act under high time pressure and conditions of great uncertainty. European lobbying therefore necessitates not only professional skills but also a good feel for difficulties in a procedure, empathy towards the decision-makers, political sensitivity for the underlying processes and constant information transparency at all interfaces.

Professional lobbying must take account of the paradigm shift due to the significant increase in the importance of procedural issues: its focus must be shifted more towards process-oriented work.

5.3.4.2 Majority decisions amongst 28 member states as a strategic risk for companies: necessity of "European coalition building"?

It has become clear just how extensively the European level has gained in importance for a company's legal environment due to the Treaty of Lisbon and the resulting increase in pure majority decisions: even if a company's national government vehemently supports the corporate concern, it can easily be overruled in Brussels. The consequences for strategic orientation are clear: to be successful in the "Europe of 28 states", the company must position itself more extensively than ever before in accordance with the circumstance that, in addition to its own "home member state", 27 further nationalities are substantially involved in decision-making (at least in terms of the voting majorities required for a decision in the Council or Parliament)[107] – otherwise, what was previously a strong position in the "home member state" may well become a minority position in Brussels, even in the case of companies from populous and economically strong member states.

In Europe, a company must therefore look beyond the "national picture" – not only in the sense that the previously described formal and informal special features of the EU's political system have to be taken into consideration, but also in the sense of looking at the situation from different national positions. In individual cases, this involves significant research, analysis and persuasion effort, as can be outlined using an example: let us assume that a British company is pursuing a specific concern regarding the modification of a proposed regulation which is passing through the European legislative procedure at European level. In this specific case, this concern is only of relevance to British companies since, in its current form, the proposed regulation would lead to significant additional costs solely for British companies due to legal form provisions under British company law. Conversely, no comparable consequences would be anticipated for companies from other

---

107 This could be casually referred to as lobbying according to the motto of "home member state plus 27".

member states. As Members of the European Parliament (MEPs) from other member states would be very unlikely to take up the British cause on their own initiative in such a case, a lobbyist has to find arguments which may possibly not immediately spring to mind in the specific case: what national interests might MEPs from France have to fight for despite the lack of direct relevance to French companies? Might the proposed regulation perhaps have indirect consequences for jobs in France? Does the British company have links to French companies, or does the British company have French subsidiaries, which may sensitise French MEPs to the cause? Might French companies possibly be affected in a similar manner by votes in the near future, i. e. are "specific French problems", which may not be particularly relevant to Britain, looming on the horizon, thus enabling cross-case coalitions to be forged?

At the same time, this expresses a fundamental rule for lobbying in democratic systems: lobbying specifically does not involve being the strongest and loudest "player" on the field. As in a game of chess, the game is not usually won with one single piece but with the best overall position. The common motives for a strategic alliance can be summarised as follows:[108]

- Increased "clout" of the concern by bundling the forces of various actors or opening up otherwise closed channels of communication.
- Focus on individual, key issues which have so far been disregarded, due either to resource reasons or to a lack of consensus, by both associations and individual companies.
- Definition of a clear objective and time constraints.

In other words: the important aspect is to find allies in the sense of one's own concern, in order to jointly achieve an objective. In each individual case, this necessitates a precise analysis of the interests, strengths and weaknesses of the respective actors in order to enable them to be used as optimally as possible for one's own concern in the respective situation. As has been mentioned, the particular difficulty at European level in comparison with the national level (at which regional in-

---

108 See Tydecks in: Rieksmeier (2007), p. 114. However, the author lists one coalition building motive which, in my opinion, should never play a role, namely a "protection function for individual companies that do not wish to expose themselves in a specific topic area in order not to influence their product and brand image". Where such an (opaque) tactic can lead is shown by the case of the pharmaceutical company Roche, for which the Brussels-based PA agency Weber Shandwick received the "Worst Lobby Award 2006" (see "Tagesschau" online from 6.11.2006, http://www.tagesschau.de/wirtschaft/meldung90960.html, last accessed on 4.5.2010): the officially stated objective of a "Cancer United" campaign launched at the beginning of October 2006 was to establish national "anti-cancer plans" in all EU states. Weber Shandwick acted as the campaign's "secretariat". According to information provided by former employees and research conducted by Britain's *Guardian* newspaper, however, the campaign was financed solely by Roche; at the same time, Roche has several anti-cancer drugs in its product portfolio. The "Cancer United" campaign was based on a study paid for by Roche, according to which increased investment in anti-cancer drugs results in a lower cancer mortality rate.

terests also play a role, but usually the crucial one) involves the consideration and utilisation of these actors' national origins.[109]

Such coalitions usually refer only to individual projects and issues, with the result that coalition building has to be undertaken anew for each concern. Creativity and case-based orientation can only be encouraged in this regard. Unexpected options for co-operation occasionally arise: the German Bundesverband Güterkraftverkehr und Logistik (Federal Association of Road Transport and Logistics, BGL), for instance, co-operated with the responsible trade unions in regard to the truck toll.[110] *Geiger* puts this in a nutshell with reference to coalitions amongst individual stakeholders: "[R]egardless of Brent Spar, it may well be that, on a certain EU matter, Greenpeace is the best potential ally of Shell. Never exclude the possibility."[111] The issue of the lack of government formation from legislative level ranks, which was previously addressed in Section 4.5.1.1, is expressed here: under certain circumstances, party or parliamentary group membership has little bearing on the direction taken by an MEP's decision, with the result that here, too, allies for one's own concern have to be sought across party and nationality boundaries.

All in all, the framework conditions for lobbying in Brussels therefore differ fundamentally from the regulations and external circumstances with which a company may well be familiar in its home member state. The company must adapt to these changed framework conditions and consistently address them, so as to utilise them for its own purposes. If it does not merely wish to limit itself to reacting, but to instead have its position taken into consideration in regulation processes and political decisions at European level, it requires strong (process) partners to actively support its interests – partners that not only offer an excellent network and viable contacts in Brussels and the member states' capital cities, but which also possess the corresponding technical know-how in lobbying. These partners are able to communicate wishes and concerns in a targeted and effective manner – particularly beyond national borders.

5.4 Summary

Chapter 5 deals with the specific options of targeted lobbying at European level. To recap, the starting point is formed by two sets of issues:

- What is the role of the individual institutions in EU legislation after Lisbon? What are the characteristics of the "ordinary legislative procedure" (previously: co-decision procedure), which is now the usual case in European legislation?

---

109   In the USA, where majorities amongst Members of Congress and Senators are not always formed across the two major parties' parliamentary groups, but opinion-forming and decision-making are instead often – similarly to the process in the EP – organised via social interest groups, coalition building is a fixed element of the political culture, see Tydecks in: Rieksmeier (2007), p. 112.
110   See Bender/Reulecke (2003), p. 178.
111   Geiger (2006), p. 111.

What is the form of the legal framework for the Commission's legislative activity as part of implementing legislation and what is meant by the term "comitology procedure"?

- What starting points exist for lobbying activities amongst the most important EU institutions, particularly the Council of Ministers, the European Commission and the European Parliament, and which rules must the lobbyist observe here, i.e. to what extent is access to the decision-makers at the legislative and executive level subject to legal regulation?

- The most important results can be summarised as follows:

  (1) Legislation in the EU is highly complex. Whilst formal laws are usually enacted within the framework of a uniform legislative process at member state level, there is still no uniform procedure applicable to all areas of legislation in the EU – even following the changes brought about by the Treaty of Lisbon.[112] A distinction must be made according to both the type of legislative act and the area being dealt with.

  (2) At least one common feature can be determined for almost all of these procedures: the enactment of a legislative act usually requires the interaction of at least two EU institutions (at least in terms of the initiative and decision). In actual fact, three institutions are usually involved (the Commission initiates, the Parliament and Council are involved in decision-making).

  (3) Since the (renamed) TFEU amended through the Treaty of Lisbon came into effect, what was previously the co-decision procedure has now become the usual case in the form of the "ordinary legislative procedure"; the importance of the European Parliament, which is compulsorily involved in decision-making, has accordingly increased. The procedure runs through a maximum of eight phases: (i) Commission's initiative; (ii) first reading in the European Parliament; (iii) first reading in the Council; (iv) second reading in the European Parliament; (v) Commission's opinion; (vi) second reading in the Council; (vii) procedure in the conciliation committee and (viii) third reading in the Council and European Parliament.

  (4) In addition to the formal legislative procedure, the procedure for the enactment of implementing legislation also plays a significant role, particularly the comitology procedure. A distinction must be made between five different procedures in this case: advisory, administrative and regulatory procedures with and without control as well as procedures in the case of protective measures. Common to all procedures is the involvement of issue-related committees consisting of member state experts or civil servants in decision-making regarding the implementing measure. The relevance of these procedures, which are virtually unknown in the public arena, to the representation of corporate interests can be considerable in the specific

---

112 With regard to the "old" procedures according to the EC Treaty: Bieber, Epiney and Haag (2009), pp. 195 ff.

case: particularly in the case of detailed regulations, the scope for interpretation permitted by a basic act can be exploited in a company's favour or narrowed to its disadvantage.

(5) The EU institutions are basically open to external interests and their representatives. Both the Commission employees and the Members of the European Parliament are generally open to dialogue with lobbyists. However, both parties must observe certain legal and ethical boundary conditions in this: for example, the Staff Regulations and the Conditions of Employment of the Commission as well as the Rules of Procedure of the European Parliament set down precise codes of conduct for the institutions' civil servants, salaried employees and political representatives. Separate codes of conduct enacted by the institutions apply to lobbyists; failure to observe these can, for example, be sanctioned by denying access. The lobbying industry has also imposed voluntary self-obligations on itself; however, these are little more than the documentation of general business ethics rules.

(6) In all likelihood, the regulation of access to the EU institutions will continue to increase. A – thus far voluntary – Transparency Register already introduced by the Commission and the Parliament has proved inadequate in the opinion of many people. As part of the outlined Transparency Initiative, the institutions are already working on comprehensive, mandatory registers. Details are not yet foreseeable; the effect of future regulations on the practical activities of lobbyists in Brussels remains to be seen.

Chapter 6 Governmental relations: process management in practice

6.1 Introduction and question

The *how* of lobbying amongst the individual EU institutions has been explained in the preceding chapters. Little differentiation was made here between structural (*who* is active) or process-oriented (*with which tools* is he active) lobbying instruments. These are the questions with which the following explanations will deal.

In the vast majority of cases, the process-oriented instruments, a lobbyist's "toolbox" so to speak, do not differ depending on whether he is employed as a salaried corporate representative or as an external service provider for a client. The following is written primarily from the perspective of corporate lobbying. With some qualifications, however, these explanations also apply to the lobbying work undertaken by associations, organisations and even EU member states and EU regions. However, there are major differences between the outlined lobbying actors in terms of both their professional self-image and their creative power in the specific, individual case. Following an introductory overview of current trends in lobbying (Section 6.2), the explanations will provide answers to the following questions:

- Why does a company require lobbying from a commercial management perspective, particularly from the perspective of stakeholder theory (see Section 6.3)?
- Who are conceivable lobbying actors (structural instruments)? What are their distinguishing characteristics, their costs, strengths and weaknesses (see Section 6.4.1)?
- Which process-oriented instruments are available to a lobbyist, and how should they be used (see Section 6.4.2)?
- In view of the outlined structural and process-oriented instruments, how should a company go about representing its interests in practice? What form might an optimal instrument mix have, and how or by whom should the various instruments be co-ordinated, in both structural and project-specific terms (see Section 6.5)?

6.2 General

In recent years, the field of lobbying has undergone extensive transformation, in both a quantitative and a qualitative regard.[1] For a number of years, for example, an increase in the number of parties involved in lobbying has been observed in

---

1 See Michalowitz (2007), p. 89 with further references plus Coen (2009), pp. 147–168.

Brussels as well as the member states' capital cities.[2] It is unmistakeable that this is related to the constant and continuing political importance of the EU.[3] According to estimates, for instance, only a good 100 interest groups were represented in Brussels in 1959, with 400 in 1970, twice this number in 1980, around 1,200 in 1997, and as many as 2,600 in 2005.[4] Whilst the lack of any registration requirements prevents us from putting a precise figure to the number of lobbyists, the total number of associations, companies, action groups, communication agencies, policy advisors and law firms active in Brussels is likely to be at least 6,500. There are no precise figures; the numbers fluctuate extensively depending on definition and source.[5] Unofficial estimates claim that there may be as many as 100,000 lobbyists active in Washington D.C., which has always been a kind of "lobbying Mecca".[6] According to recent estimates, at least 32,500 lobbyists are claimed to be working in Brussels, which appears to be closing the gap on the US capital in all aspects of lobbying.[7]

The two predominant trends within the industry can also be traced very clearly based on the example of Brussels: firstly, the sharp rise in individual actors in comparison with collective actors (especially associations), and secondly, the increasing professionalisation of lobbying.[8] Whilst associations were the major players on the field into the 1980s, considerable differentiation and heterogenisation has taken place since then; a certain degree of fragmentation can even be observed in the association landscape. As a result of this, two categories of lobbying organisation can now essentially be determined:[9]

- *Collective lobbying:* this includes associations or also informal groupings which represent the interests of an entire industry or a market segment rather than individual companies.

---

2   In February 2015, the German Bundestag's lobby list alone included 2,227 associations; see the respective, latest version at http://www.bundestag.de/dokumente/lobbyliste/-/196912; this does not include individual companies, lawyers, freelancers, etc. (last accessed on 9.2.2015).

3   See Weidenfeld (2013³), p. 154.

4   See Greenwood (2011³), pp. 12–13.

5   See Greenwood (2011³), pp. 12–13.

6   According to press reports, 12,281 lobbyists were registered at the Senate in 2013; this is significantly fewer than official figures suggest, see Fang (2014); Sebaldt (2007), p. 101, states a figure of 33,000 lobbyists; in January 2006, the *Washington Post* dated 29.1.2006 counted 33,000-40,000 lobbyists, Mayberry (2006); the decline in the number of officially registered lobbyists and the simultaneous citation of an estimated 100,000 parties operating in the field of lobbying is explained by the fact that many lobbying activities are not officially registered as such.

7   An estimated 75% of all economically related organisations and around 60% of the NGOs operating in Brussels have now sought registration. At present, around 6,500 organisations are registered in total. According to cautious estimates, each organisation employs an average of five individuals, i.e. at least 32,500 lobbyists are now subject to the Transparency Register's code of conduct, see European Commission (2014c); the figures indicated in this regard also fluctuate: see Traynos (2014); Ducourtieux (2015), p. 2; Speth (2009), p. 8, indicated 15,000 in 2009; the Commission and European Parliament Transparency Register's 2013 annual report counts 5,952 entries up to 31.10.2013, see European Commission and European Parliament (2013).

8   See van Schendelen (2013) pp. 64, 161 ff.; Lahusen (2005).

9   See Michalowitz (2007), pp. 73–74.

- *Non-collective lobbying:* here, a distinction has to be made between the classic corporate representative office (in-house lobbying) and lobbying by external service providers: in the first case, a company employs its own staff or maintains departments for the area of lobbying; in the second case, the company delegates lobbying in whole or in part to external service providers such as agencies and/or law firms.

The latter forms of organisation are exhibiting strong growth: increasingly, individual companies are no longer leaving their lobbying solely to their respective (industry) associations, but are instead undertaking it themselves through their own local representative offices and/or public affairs agencies, law firms or governmental relations agencies.[10] Non-collective approaches enable more individual lobbying tailored to one's specific needs, which associations are often unable to achieve in the same manner (see Section 6.4.1.1). At the same time, this also places the political importance of associations into relation.

The extension and increased diversity of lobbying are due primarily to the extension and deepening of European integration, which has successively extended the EU's competencies to numerous policy areas.[11] However, it is also due to more general trends in society as a whole; on the one hand, the increasing pluralisation, heterogenisation and individualisation of society are giving rise to a high number of new interests and, on the other hand, are leading to the duplication of previously similar interests. The existing structures and institutions are losing their cohesive force and their representation monopoly, as they are no longer able to extensively take up and represent specific and individual interests.[12] In general, this trend can be described as a shift away from traditional corporatistic links between politics and the economy – and particularly those of associations and state.[13] The general increase in the complexity and interdependence of societal action areas is therefore leading to a sharp rise in diverse interests, which is why the number of organised interests is also increasing. Against this backdrop, competition surrounding political importance is also stepping up.[14] This is resulting in the necessity of tailored, individually structured lobbying at all times, in turn leading to differentiation and specialisation in lobbying approaches.

Interest in political representation in Brussels (and in the capital cities of the European member states) will continue to grow, and the number of companies and individual persons working there will increase further in the future: the extension and deepening of European integration alone are leading to a constant increase in the need for lobbying.[15] The growing number of lobbyists is essentially leading to increasing competition amongst service providers in the area of lobbying, and

---

10 See Michalowitz (2007), p. 58.
11 See Lahusen (2004), p. 782.
12 Lahusen (2004), p. 781.
13 See von Winter (2004), p. 764.
14 See Kleinfeld, Willems and Zimmer (2007), pp. 16 ff.
15 See van Schendelen (2013⁴), p. 53.

therefore also stiffer competition for attention by the decision-makers at the legislative and executive level. At the same time, the "market entry barriers" for new lobbyists are high: due to their lack of experience, reputation and cross-institution, -political group and -member state networks, lobbyists who have not yet become established at EU level find it very difficult, in comparison with long-established lobbyists, to position themselves and their concerns at the critical points throughout institutions, political groups and member states.

6.3 Essential element of successful lobbying: stakeholder management

6.3.1 Concept of stakeholder management in the area of political lobbying

Ultimately, lobbying is communication with the company's environment (or the organisation or unit whose interests are being represented). However, clarity regarding the recipients and their interests must be established so that communication does not occur randomly ("scatter effects"), but is instead effective and targeted. Each company is not only a participant in economic markets; it also interacts with society and politics. Companies are additionally elementary parts of the social order. The possible actions and scopes available to a company are not therefore exclusively customer-, market- or industry-dependent. They are also determined by the so-called context environment, which additionally encompasses the legislative and executive levels (see Section 1.2).[16]

Legal and regulatory decisions directly or indirectly determine the company's economic framework conditions.[17] If the company wishes to preserve its existing scopes for action or access new ones, it must include the key decision-makers at the legislative and executive level in its corporate decisions as secondary stakeholders. Examples of this include labour law standards, official regulations or environmental policy specifications. Active involvement in structuring this environment is therefore vital in a globalised world in which companies are confronted with more new economic, social and cultural movements and trends than ever before and are required to react to them. It could even be stated that companies not only have to face up to "corporate social responsibility", but must additionally become aware of their "corporate political responsibility".[18]

Irrespective of whether companies or associations, citizens' initiatives, trade unions, churches or societies are concerned – all of them necessarily act in the conflicting area of economic, social and political objectives which are partly con-

---

16 See Köppl (2008), p. 189; also fundamentally with regard to the embedding of economic actors in the social structure, see Granovetter (1985), pp. 481–510.
17 See Köppl (2008), p. 200.
18 Bohnen (2015), p. 89.

trasting and partly similar. By implementing these objectives, they then clash with social groupings which think differently.

Interest groups which are able to influence the achievement of one's own organisational objectives are called "stakeholders" or "stakeholder groups".[19] A distinction has to be made between primary and secondary stakeholders:

- *Primary stakeholders* are essential to the continued existence of the organisation/the company. They are able to assert a legitimate claim on the basis of a contractual relationship, an exchange relationship or their involvement in value creation. These include, for example, customers, suppliers, investors or the local community.
- *Secondary stakeholders* have no legitimate claim, but are able to influence the organisation or its primary stakeholders, or are in turn influenced by these, for example, environmental protection groups and political decision-makers.[20]

Political decision-makers therefore form part of the external stakeholder group. Anyone who constantly ignores the interests of these stakeholders, and thus the dependencies of one's own organisation within society, will be unable to achieve success in the long term. The skill is instead to consciously recognise and analyse one's own dependency. Only someone who is able to assess and exploit the interests and potential of peers and competitors will be able to successfully pursue his own objectives.

This analysis and integration of the environment is termed stakeholder management.[21] One central segment of the organisational environment is the political or legal system, particularly the legislative and executive level. Legal and regulatory decisions directly and indirectly impact a company's economic framework conditions. If the company wishes to preserve or extend its existing room to manoeuvre, it must give consideration to the corresponding legislative and executive decision-makers in its corporate decisions. For a company, this stakeholder orientation consequently equates to active management of its environment and external relations, and the disclosure of its interests.[22]

Whilst relationships with the primary stakeholders are managed, e.g. through public relations or investor relations, the company also requires a way to communicate with its secondary stakeholders, its "political acceptance markets". This is where lobbying comes into play. Like investor relations, it has a strategic management function, since it analyses and interprets a company's political environment – the "framework conditions" – and helps to optimally structure it according to

---

19 See van Schendelen (2013[4]), p. 171.
20 See Köppl (2008), p. 189.
21 See fundamentally with regard to the topic of stakeholder management: Freeman (2004); Freeman (2010[3]).
22 See Freeman and McVea (2001), p. 8.

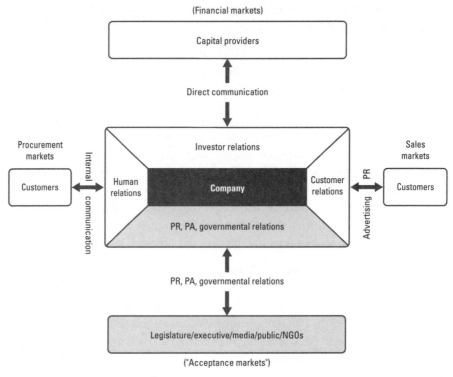

Figure 6.1: Political acceptance markets[23]

the company's objectives.[24] The practical functions of stakeholder management (particularly in terms of long- or longer-term corporate success[25]) include monitoring the political arena, analysing political and social trends and representing corporate interests in the political environment.[26] The concept of "framework conditions" must always refer to the individual company in this process: political and legal framework conditions are generally amongst the most important factors in the corporate environment – just consider the stable political and legal conditions in a state, which are generally regarded as crucial to economic prosperity. Conversely, only the political framework conditions in a more limited sense are relevant to a company's stakeholder management, i.e. market- and industry-specific conditions (direct, specific political circumstances) which specifically affect a company.

Regarded in this manner, the dynamics and relevance of the political and legal framework conditions can vary extensively from industry to industry. Whilst practically all products and services are regulated in one way or another in modern state and legal systems such as the EU and its member states, the more problematic a product or a service is – whether due to reasons of safety such as in the

---

23 Source: Gläser (2010²), p. 24.
24 See Freeman and McVea (2001), p. 9; Köppl (2008), p. 201.
25 See Freeman and McVea (2001), p. 11.
26 See Köppl (2008), p. 189.

aviation industry or environmental reasons such as in the chemicals industry – the more its suppliers are dependent on, and vulnerable to, changes in the framework conditions. Stakeholder management through lobbying is therefore of elementary importance in extensively regulated industries: examples include the energy sector with technology-, environmentally- and safety-related trends and influences, the telecommunications industry with extensive pressure due to the charge regulations in place in the majority of European markets, or the pharmaceuticals industry with the crucial importance of intellectual property rights and drug price regulation.

In such industries, a precise knowledge of relevant political processes – the "how, when and why" of the decision-making processes crucial to structuring the political framework conditions of relevance to companies – and correct identification of the most important decision-makers are of outstanding significance to competitiveness, and can give a company a considerable edge over its competitors. Firstly, these form the basis for the company's strategic decisions: for example, advanced knowledge of an impending change to the framework conditions enables the adjustment of one's own portfolio before that of the competition; involvement in specifically structuring the changes may even be possible through effective process support. A corresponding information flow in terms of one's own content-related concerns and issues[27] also usually results in valuable information regarding the anticipated balance of power of all relevant actors in the company's environment. This basis enables decisions to be made, for instance, as regards how actors with similar interests can bundle their resources more efficiently to achieve a better effect (coalition building). Stakeholder management is consequently a significant module of the corporate strategy and therefore also an important basis for further lobbying measures at the same time.

6.3.2 Stakeholder management in practice

There are various approaches for categorising a company's secondary stakeholders (stakeholder groups). A relevant, secondary stakeholder generally has influence in terms of the company's political framework conditions on the one hand, and is also able to assert its influence on the other hand.[28] One option for distinguishing secondary stakeholder groups, according to their importance to a company, which is easy to apply in practice and compares the positive and negative potential of stakeholders, is also oriented towards these categories. Expressed precisely, this involves assignment to the "support" or "do not support" positions for a concern/interest.

This distinction, together with the related strategic action recommendations for the company, is clearly shown on the basis of the matrix in Figure 6.2.

---

27 "Issues" or "issue management" refers to a company systematically dealing with relevant issues within its environment, i. e. the context environment, see Ingenhoff and Röttger (2008).
28 See van Schendelen (2013[4]), p. 172.

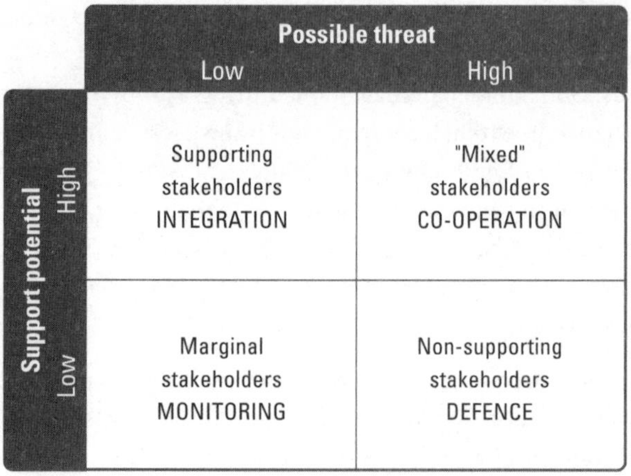

		Possible threat	
		Low	High
Support potential	**High**	Supporting stakeholders INTEGRATION	"Mixed" stakeholders CO-OPERATION
	Low	Marginal stakeholders MONITORING	Non-supporting stakeholders DEFENCE

Based on Wittke/Conzelmann/Schlicht in: Rieksmeier (2007), p. 53 (Table 1)

Figure 6.2: Classification model for stakeholders

Accordingly, fundamental action orientations can be assigned to each type of stakeholder. First and foremost, these are extensively generalised action recommendations if the real reference variables are missing. Whilst it is usually sufficient to monitor marginal stakeholders, e.g. through regular media analysis, it is advisable to include "supporting" stakeholders, i.e. potential sponsors of the concern, with which a common benefit can be generated – through the provision of information, for instance – into one's own strategies.

Wherever possible, interest coalitions should be built, or joint activities implemented to co-operate closely, with "mixed" stakeholder groups. Vis-à-vis "non-supporting" stakeholders, it is important to clearly express opposing standpoints, e.g. in the media, but above all, directly to decision-makers if possible, and to outline the alternative position.

As described above, the achievement of corporate goals is extensively co-determined by the societal environment. Stakeholder management tasks and options must be oriented towards this. The choice of lobbying tools and measures should therefore give consideration to the stakeholders' interests and the company's dependency on them at all times. Of course, stakeholder management can only ever be the preliminary stage for achieving corporate policy objectives. It does, however, provide an indispensable basis for subsequent campaigns and actions.

Reliable stakeholder management essentially encompasses three steps:

1. Identification of the relevant stakeholders.

2. Stakeholder mapping: documentation of the hierarchical structure, and categorisation, of the stakeholders in a stakeholder map.

3. Information management: creation of a stakeholder database.

The necessary reciprocal relationship between these steps over time must also be noted; i.e. when a stakeholder database is finally available, it must, of course, be aligned with the stakeholder map, and further identification of stakeholders must be carried out if necessary. Stakeholder management is therefore an important, continuous task.

6.3.2.1 Step 1: identification of relevant stakeholders

All significant stakeholders and their interests, which are or may be directly or indirectly related to the topic areas of relevance to a specific lobbying project, must first be recorded in an initial step. This first step may appear trivial, but it is vitally important in terms of the overall process of lobbying.[29] Above all, the broadest-based analysis possible at the start of the project is important in order firstly to overcome one's own selective perception (bias), and secondly, to avoid what is presumed to be sound knowledge about persons and their actual political options. As has already been explained (see Section 3.6.1), the formally responsible persons are not always the only, or even the crucial, decision-makers. Secondly, the relevant stakeholders only become apparent at second glance, and often only once the project's concern has undergone a thorough content-related analysis, particularly in the case of complex factual contexts – such as tax regulations, which affect various industries in completely different ways, for instance. In the case of interests represented at EU level, these aspects are compounded by the mixture of diverse institutional and member state interests inherent in the system; the influence of this on the identification of relevant stakeholders in the individual case is not to be underestimated (see Figure 6.3).

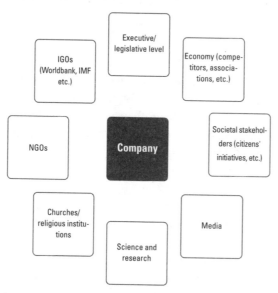

Figure 6.3: Selection of stakeholders with political potential which could influence an organisation (e.g. a company)

---

29 See van Schendelen (2013⁴), p. 172.

The representation of typical stakeholder groups (stakeholders) from the perspective of a company in Figure 6.3 is by no means exhaustive. Apart from "classic" decision-makers, such as persons from the fields of politics and administration who are relevant to decisions, attention must also be paid to other societal stakeholders (e. g. citizens' initiatives, grass-roots movements, etc.) in addition to commerce. The media themselves are not only neutral mediators of information, but also often pursue their own interests in the political arena. Examples include politically prominent series of articles in printed media such as Germany's BILD newspaper, which even drew criticism from the German Federation of Journalists with a series dubbed the "anti-Greece campaign" at the beginning of 2015.[30]

In this context, attention must also be paid to social networks such as Facebook and Twitter, as well as certain bloggers, some of which may occasionally have an extensive public reach and may also receive wide coverage in the classic media.

If relevant to the respective issue, actors from the fields of science and research may also form part of the group of stakeholders. These stakeholders are a significant stakeholder group, particularly in the case of issues with technology relevance.

Finally – even in our extensively secularised society – churches and religious institutions may occasionally be an important stakeholder group. NGOs (non-governmental organisations) such as Greenpeace, Foodwatch and NABU, and IGOs (intergovernmental organisations) – non-profit organisations under state sponsorship which are based on international treaties, such as the WTO (World Trade Organization)[31] – may also be highly important, particularly for lobbying at EU level, since they are able to regularly and effectively influence political decisions.

One further option for distinguishing between stakeholder groups is based on an analysis of the decision-making processes relevant to the assertion of an interest, the role of the stakeholders of relevance within this, their respective form of organisation and their implicit interests or objectives. Specifically, a distinction must be made between two approaches, which must always be used in combination to identify all relevant stakeholders:

- The formal, legal approach.
- The political approach.

The *formal, legal approach* identifies all stakeholders depending on their formal task in a decision-making process, usually in the sense of legal responsibility. State actors, which are categorised according to their purely formal decision-making power, are therefore primarily identified. One example in this case would be the

---

30 See N. U. (2015c).
31 See Gabler Wirtschaftslexikon Online, http://wirtschaftslexikon.gabler.de/Definition/igos.html (last accessed on 11.4.2015).

question of whether an issue falls into the area of authority of the EU or a specific institution of the EU, a member state or its executive or legislative level, or even a downstream unit such as a regional authority. It goes without saying that this approach is indispensable for a lobbying project. The more complex a process is, i.e. the more institutions are involved, the greater the challenge of identifying all relevant persons and groups and of maintaining an overview (which must always be kept up to date) of the official decision-makers. The information required for this can usually be obtained from publicly accessible sources (legal regulations, organisation charts, media reports, etc.).

In contrast to the formal, legal approach, the *political approach* is not based on formal competencies and responsibilities but on real power structures, i.e., an attempt is made in this case to give consideration to the informal power structures as well as the importance of public opinion. It is therefore oriented, so to speak, towards political, empirical values, which the legal approach is unable to do. The problem with the legal, formal approach is that it disregards the further actors, the informal power structures and the power of public opinion. The political approach aims to uncover these actual power relationships – it steers the lobbyist's attention towards associations, NGOs, commissions, advisors, media and public opinion, etc. Whilst some of these actors have no direct agenda-setting power, their importance in individual cases may possibly be greater than that of the formally responsible decision-makers.

The political approach to stakeholder identification is far more difficult in comparison with the formal, legal approach, since it is impossible to implement "from the outside", i.e. without personal experience with the respective persons or knowledge of informal decision-making processes and policy shaping options. Whether a Head of Unit in the European Commission has "the Director General's ear" in specific issues, and the latter is in turn to be regarded as a reliable advisor by the responsible Commissioner, can only be verified through experience from the direct environment of the respective persons. This also applies to the frequent practice of "launching" media reports: without a personal contact in the respective editorial office, it will be virtually impossible to find out who is "behind" a certain article, and even more difficult for the lobbyists' concerns to directly find their way into a specific medium.

Ultimately, not only the actually relevant ("active") stakeholders, but also the potentially relevant stakeholders, must be taken into consideration in both approaches – the formal, legal as well as the political approach. This refers not only to those stakeholder groups which only make an appearance at a later stage of the decision-making process, but also those which are not even identifiable at the beginning. For example, a pure technology issue, such as the authorisation of certain production methods, may turn into a tax issue due to the discovery of fiscal consequences, or an energy issue can quickly become an environmental issue. The identification of stakeholders is therefore a continuous process, which must not be restricted to a list drawn up at the start of a project.

At the very inception of a project, consideration should additionally be given to which resources could, if necessary, be mobilised on the part of relevant stakeholders in order to pursue their own interests.[32]

6.3.2.2 Step 2: stakeholder mapping – categorisation and hierarchical structure

As soon as the relevant stakeholders have been identified, the relationship between one's own organisation or company with these stakeholders is identified and evaluated. This may involve existing or merely latent relationships. Such a "stakeholder group matrix" is initially focussed on the direction of the relevant stakeholder's objectives: are their interests contrary to one's own, or are there matching objectives? In addition, of course, the stakeholders' political weight is also significant. Which potential, which tools the competitors and lobbyists have access to in the pursuit of their own objectives, how likely their use is and what effect could be achieved with them must be analysed in this case.

A precise knowledge of the "playing field" is important for this. The institutional structure, which essentially determines the framework conditions, is first and foremost of crucial importance in this case. In the EU, this includes the European institutions themselves (if germane) and the actors in the member states, such as parties, ministries and parliaments. The decision-making routes, the formal and informal communication channels surrounding the political system, are the basis for the determination and assessment of interests. Ultimately, therefore, the stakeholder analysis must reflect the actual power structure, which cannot usually be derived completely from a formal assessment of the institutions and their rules of procedure.

The identification of one's own organisation's relationships and access routes to the stakeholders (stakeholder map) is primarily intended to create clarity. Hierarchical sorting is a possible structural form, for example: the most important stakeholder, i.e. the one with the greatest relevance to one's own concern, should be listed first in this. This configuration does not necessarily have to reflect the legal circumstances, i.e. the ranking of institutions in accordance with a constitution or bureaucratic sequence, for instance; instead, it can and must also give consideration to informal decision-making structures (see above: political approach).

Sorting within a stakeholder group should therefore also take place according to relevance wherever possible. This arrangement will usually correspond to the hierarchical structure of the institution itself, as the ranking in an administrative organisation (e.g. a Directorate General within the European Commission) certain-

---

32 See van Schendelen (2013[4]), p. 172.

Form of address	Title	First name	Last name	Position	Political group	Member state	Remark
European Parliament							
Mr		Klaus	Heißler	Rapporteur, LIBE committee	PPE	Germany	(...)
Mr		Roberto	Rana-Ranez	Shadow rapporteur, LIBE committee	ALDE	Spain	(...)
Ms		Toula	Portokalos		S&D	Greece	(...)
Mr		Friedrich	Walch		EPP	Austria	(...)
(...)	(...)	(...)	(...)	(...)	(...)	(...)	(...)
European Commission							
Mr		Mindowg	Niakoschius	Commissioner for Economic and Financial Affairs, Taxation and Customs		Lithuania	(...)
Mr		Jean-Pierre	Corgnet	Cabinet member, advisor		France	(...)
Mr		Rudolph	Rabe	Director General	EPP	Austria	(...)
(...)	(...)	(...)	(...)	(...)	(...)	(...)	(...)
Council of the European Union							
Ms	Dr.	Sophia	Berger	Attaché/Permanent Representation of Austria, taxation issues		Austria	(...)
Mr		Mark	Dunleaw	First Secretary/Permanent Representation of Ireland, financial affairs		Ireland	(...)
Mr	Dr.	Reiner	Schneider	Embassy Counsellor/Permanent Representation of Germany, financial affairs		Germany	(...)
Mr		Eimuntas	Tschiurlenis	Attaché/Permanent Representation of Lithuania, financial affairs		Lithuania	(...)
(...)	(...)	(...)	(...)	(...)	(...)	(...)	(...)
European Central Bank							
Mr		Rocco	Savoldi	Financial stability expert, ESRB Secretariat		Italy	(...)

Figure 6.4: Stakeholder map

ly corresponds to the possible effectiveness of the listed persons. Figure 6.4 shows a fictitious example of such a stakeholder map.

6.3.2.3 Step 3: information management – establishment and administration of a stakeholder database

To organise the project and the communication with the relevant stakeholders which takes place during the course of this, it is crucial to systematically record contacts and the related information, and to keep these up to date and manage them.

Information and data management in lobbying projects is gaining in importance to the same extent that political processes and decision-making paths are becoming increasingly complex and important actors are becoming increasingly intermeshed at the same time. The objective of documenting the stakeholders' task areas and positions (and thus possible contact persons), comprehending all changes and thus being able to determine one's scope for negotiations cannot be achieved in any other way. This ultimately involves a certain degree of planning security, in order to avoid having to constantly "fly by sight" and thus prevent the risk of "unknown unknowns" at actor level.

The establishment of a database containing all significant stakeholders is therefore recommended. From a practical point of view, a software-based solution is advisable, whereby special database or contact management software is not absolutely necessary. Conventional applications such as Microsoft Outlook are usually sufficient, or also programmes such as Excel, Access or comparable programs for project-specific, hierarchical databases.

Such a database should first and foremost document fundamental information, such as the names of the respective stakeholders or the responsible contact persons and their contact data. Documenting the contact process is also essential: it should be possible to quickly locate meeting and telephone call agreements and notes, as well as correspondence. Links to the respective stakeholders' public statements and announcements are also appropriate to always maintain an overview of the position they are currently representing. Monitoring and stakeholder mapping therefore intermesh here.

The information exchange which has taken place between the lobbyist and stakeholder is an item of information which is not to be underestimated in a stakeholder map: a lobbyist should always know precisely what information he has passed on to whom at what point in time, or from whom he has received information, and when. Losing track can occasionally have catastrophic results – something that can quickly occur in complex projects with dozens of actors.

Throughout all of this, it is crucial to keep the database up to date at all times. This applies above all to the information on contact partners, from contact data to changes in position within an institution or even departure from their previous sphere of activity altogether. In the political, ministerial field, this occurs relatively often, particularly after elections, and especially during changes of government. Some members of parliament will therefore assume new positions in their political group, switch to a different policy area, perhaps even (in the member state area) be appointed as a state secretary or minister, whereas others may leave parliament. The structures within the institutions also change frequently: departments are re-distributed or chopped and changed; civil servants are promoted, re-posted or assigned new functions. As a variation of a well-known saying, it can be stated that, in the political arena, few things are as persistent as institutional and personnel changes. A lobbyist's lack of knowledge regarding a person's career change can, for instance, ultimately lead to him contacting an incorrect person.

On the whole, it can be stated that systematic stakeholder management through the identification, classification and documentation of relevant actors enables a reliable basis for subsequent lobbying measures. The instruments necessary for the "game of chess that is lobbying" are only in place if one has sufficient knowledge concerning the intentions and possibilities of all conceivable actors. This reveals various scenarios and enables a better assessment of these. This in turn equates to at least a certain degree of planning security for the lobbying process, and can significantly increase its likelihood of success.

6.4 Lobbying instruments

The various lobbying instruments will now be introduced over the next few sections. A distinction will be made between structural and process-oriented instruments. A structural (organisational) distinction must be made between the various organisational forms of the lobbying instruments (see Section 6.4.1), and a procedural (activity-related) distinction between the different ways in which the lobbyist communicates with his addressees (see Section 6.4.2).

6.4.1 Structural instruments

How should a company that wants to have itself effectively represented at European level go about representing its interests against the backdrop of the trends outlined at the beginning of this chapter and the requirements of effective stakeholder management – via an association, its own corporate representative office, an external service provider or a combination of these?

As will be shown, each of these structural instruments performs functions which are both important (see also Figure 6.6) and usually indispensable in practice. However, particularly the association and the corporate representative office each reveal specific deficits, which can hinder the optimal effectiveness of lobbying due to the changed framework conditions (Treaty of Lisbon) – insofar as its "instrument mix" is limited to these. The result (see Section 6.5) will clearly show that the individual structural instruments, in particular, cannot be used as alternatives to one another: instead, effective stakeholder management necessitates a complementary understanding of the different instruments.

6.4.1.1 Collective forms of organisation: lobbying through associations

6.4.1.1.1 General heterogeneity problem

Lobbyists are mediators of interests to the legislative and executive level. Since they involve the organisational bundling of interests, associations are traditionally of particular importance to the political process,[33] as the European institutions' decision-making is vastly simplified if the numerous demands from commerce and society are presented in differentiated form and already processed to form several alternatives – and not just from the perspective of one individual company. Ideally, the discussion concerning the various positions takes place within the associations, as a result of which the actual political opinion-forming and decision-making process can be shortened and structured in manageable form. In this regard, associations can be viewed as (political, economic) opinion-forming instruments.

---

33 See Weidenfeld (2013³), p. 157.

6.4.1.1.1.1 Compulsion to reach a compromise at association level

However, the effect of the traditional, corporatistic arrangements has declined in recent years; this trend will continue in the light of Europeanisation and globalisation.[34] From a macroeconomic perspective, the associations' interest aggregation is to be welcomed, also because association activity undertakes "functions which relieve the state and are self-regulatory".[35] If association decision-making and implementation are regarded from a commercial management perspective, however, three severe disadvantages quickly become apparent:

1. There is little likelihood of companies being able to assert their own interests vis-à-vis deviating positions of members of the same association other than in the form of an often unsatisfactory compromise – a problem which is constantly increasing in intensity due to the growing heterogeneity of the interests of member companies in the associations and as a result of increasing economic globalisation.

2. Lobbying deficits vis-à-vis politicians and the administration additionally arise for companies which cannot assert themselves, or are only able to do so with a weak compromise, in the internal battle of individual interests within the associations.

3. One further disadvantage from the point of view of companies is the association's limited freedom to act, which can be attributed to the constant search for compromise solutions. Whether this limited freedom to act leads to reduced assertiveness, and therefore ultimately to the reduced importance of the association as a whole, is evaluated differently depending on perspective.

According to the experiences of lobbyists, the majority of European civil servants and Members of the European Parliament do not (yet) see any serious weakening of the position of associations in Brussels as a result of the increasing heterogeneity of their members' interests. Interestingly, a high number of companies from the EU member states are of the completely opposite opinion. This different assessment is probably due to the fact that administrative or political decision-makers have a natural interest in being supplied with extensively bundled and objective information wherever possible, in order firstly to structure the process of information intake as efficiently as possible and, secondly, to avoid becoming the plaything of individual interests. Whilst the bundling of information is still most readily expected of associations by the institutions, this is precisely the reason why companies are anticipating the weakening of the associations: companies are fundamentally not interested in the mediation of compromises, but instead want to sensitise the decision-makers to their individual interests,[36] even counter to the interests of their market competitors if necessary.

---

34 See Speth (2006), pp. 43 ff.
35 Haacke (2006), p. 168.
36 See Speth (2006), pp. 45 – 46.

However, the Commission is also increasingly striving to obtain differentiated and practical information, which the larger associations, in particular, are barely able to supply. This is made clear in a statement by a Vice Director General of the Commission: "We usually need to go deeper than the association's view (…) [T]hey are seen as bureaucrats, not the people on the ground who know what they are talking about (…) [T]hese are the people from firms. We need the practical view (…) We are always trying to avoid lowest common denominators."[37]

The fact that an association is not characteristically bound to its members' instructions poses a further problem. On the one hand, this independence may possibly initially lend it greater credibility in its dealings with representatives of the legislative and executive level than is the case with corporate representatives with an imperative mandate. On the other hand, the associations' independence may mean that an individual member company's own interest, which is the subject of internal dispute within the association, cannot be mediated by this association in the specific case: in the most unfavourable case, the interest is not articulated at all if an agreement which is not acceptable for the company is reached.

The associations themselves are entirely aware of the problem of the internal association decision-making structure. Various efforts are therefore already being made to implement reforms, e. g. in the case of BUSINESSEUROPE (formerly UNICE), the umbrella organisation for national, European industrial confederations. These reforms usually involve a shift away from the concept of unanimity and, in addition to national associations, towards also enabling companies to become members, or at least giving them a voice through advisory bodies. BUSINESSEUROPE, for example, has created an Advisory and Support Group consisting of representatives of major European corporations.[38] The intended objective of this body is to give the individual companies an increased say in decision-making at association level and to enable access to their more practically-related information. However, this group also has over 60 members,[39] leading to doubts as regards the efficiency of its decision-making and its assertion of anything more than compromise decisions.

The trend that an increasing number of associations are only accepting companies as members, but not other associations, can also be observed. The association landscape is additionally becoming ever more compartmentalised: numerous associations are specialising exclusively in specific, clearly outlined corporate interests from a single, comparatively small industrial sector, as is the case with the Alliance for Beverage Cartons and the Environment (ACE).[40] Whilst this enables

---

37 Quoted from Greenwood (2002), p. 104.
38 See Greenwood (2002), p. 11; BUSINESSEUROPE organisation, https://www.businesseurope.eu/about-us/asgroup-our-partner-companies (last accessed on 29.7.2016).
39 70 members (status: May 2016), see https://www.businesseurope.eu/about-us/asgroup-our-partner-companies (last accessed on 29.7.2016).
40 See Greenwood (2002), p. 8.

the negative effects of the heterogeneity problem to be lessened, the reduced representation basis goes hand-in-hand with a clearly noticeable decline in agenda-setting options amongst the EU institutions. This is referred to as the conflict between the "membership logic" – i.e. as few members as possible in order to maintain homogeneity – and the "influence logic" – i.e. as many members as possible in order to gain in influence (further details on this in the following).[41] For more than two-thirds of European associations, the problem of reaching a lowest common denominator compromise is now acute: despite the increase in specialised, small associations, the large associations, which only accept national associations as members, continue to make up the majority (58%) of all European associations. Added to these are the 26% of associations which admit both companies as well as other associations as members.[42]

6.4.1.1.1.2 Consequence: conflict between membership logic and influence logic

The associations' work is aimed at lobbying, in the defined sense, amongst the EU decision-makers. The crucial criterion of successful association work is the realisation of members' interests. This firstly requires good, routine contact with members of parliament and civil servants; on the other hand, contact with the management levels of the Commissioner's offices (including the Commissioners themselves) and the management and working level of the Directorates General, as well as ministers, state secretaries and the working levels of the ministries at national level, is crucial to enable involvement in the political, administrative system from two sides, so to speak. In particular, an association finds it easier to make contact with the higher political levels when its macroeconomic importance is sufficiently high.

An association therefore faces the constant dilemma of being as large and extensive as possible on the one hand, in order to attain macroeconomic agenda-setting power, but of minimising the heterogeneity of interests within the association on the other hand, in order to enable it to pursue precise positions which can be sensibly asserted for its members. This is leading, for example, to the fact that, just like the European industrial associations, national associations such as the central association of German industry (BDI) or the most important British industrial association, the Confederation of British Industry (CBI), are maintaining their own representative offices in Brussels in addition to their representation via the European association, BUSINESSEUROPE, to be able to represent their interests independently even if there is a lack of consensus within BUSINESSEUROPE. For the association structure, this means that "the logic of effectively exerting an influence frequently necessitates the formation of inclusive, centralistic association structures";[44] however, the integration of members is "easier for specialised and de-

---

41 See Greenwood (2002), pp. 46–47.
42 See Greenwood (2002), p. 10.
44 Traxler and Schmitter (2002), p. 45.

The European umbrella association CEFIC (European Chemical Industry Council)	
Founded	▪ 1959 ▪ Around 170 employees
Member structure	▪ Directly and indirectly represents approximately 29,000 small, medium and large companies with a total of 1.2 million employees and a worldwide market share of around 17 % ▪ National specialist associations from 22 member states ▪ 8 associated specialist associations ▪ 59 major companies ▪ 597 "business members" of smaller companies ▪ 31 associated companies without their own production plants in Europe ▪ 54 partner companies with interests in the European chemical industry
Publications/ position papers	▪ Issue of "six statements" in 2014
EU political programmes	▪ Six programmes (product stewardship; industrial policy; energy, HSE and logistics; build trust; research and innovation; EU legislation and integration)

Figure 6.5: Example of a European umbrella organisation: CEFIC[43]

centralised associations, since their internalised interests are more homogeneous and the members' opportunities for participation are greater".[45]

The exclusive functionalisation of the associations to the representation of their members' interests results in two mutually influencing factors for an association: the above mentioned membership logic and the influence logic. The former describes the "definition of objectives and priorities, i.e. the internal process of reaching a compromise and consensus, (...) but also control over the members, the safeguarding of 'internal capability to meet obligations'".[46] The influence logic is to be regarded as the representation of members' interests vis-à-vis the decision-makers. The mutual dependency of these two factors arises from the fact that, in order to engage in effective lobbying, which includes the association's negotiating with representatives of the executive and legislative level, the association representatives must be able to rely on the behaviour of their members in the assured sense. This necessitates options for internal sanctions which obligate the association members. Conversely, the internal capability to meet obligations will

---

43 Data according to CEFIC (2015), http://www.cefic.org/ (last accessed on 2.2.2015).
45 Traxler and Schmitter (2002), p. 45.
46 Abromeit (1993), p. 37.

disappear if no lobbying success is achieved by the association. At the same time, however, this means that the strength of the association's negotiating position declines, and ultimately also the importance of the association, making the realisation of interests all the more difficult.[47]

It can therefore be stated that association-based interest mediation often fails to take account of an individual company's interests, or does so inadequately in the event of a compromise solution, due to the interdependence between membership logic and influence logic as well as the pursuit of individual interests instead of the specific pursuit of a formulated group objective by members – arising from the increasing heterogeneity of individual positions, particularly in the case of inclusive, centralistic associations.

6.4.1.1.2 Association-based lobbying "from the inside" and "from the outside"

Association-based lobbying can basically be implemented in two ways: firstly as lobbying "from the inside", and secondly as lobbying "from the outside".

Lobbying from the inside is undertaken from the European institutions. For example, there is hardly a single European Member of Parliament who does not belong to one association or another, or who is at least associated with one in some manner. Leading representatives of interest groups have also risen to important political functions, such as Monika Wulf-Mathies, who was Chairperson of the German Trade Union Federation (DGB) before becoming the EU Commissioner for Regional Policy in 1994. Prior to taking up office, Briton Jonathan Hill, who was appointed as the Commissioner for Financial Stability, Financial Services and Capital Market Union in 2014, attracted controversy, as he held a leading position at Quiller Consultants, a strategic communication consulting company, whose clients include, among others, major British bank HSBC, from 1998 to 2010.[48] In addition, Hill also held political positions; in the 1980s, for example, he was employed as a "special advisor" to Kenneth Clarke, a British minister at that time.[49] However, appropriate lobbying by an association in the European Parliament or at national level is not even guaranteed if certain members of parliament or other officials are committed to an association. Firstly, because their interests do not necessarily match in a specific, individual case; politicians also basically pursue their own objectives, whereby an association's interest may occasionally be inopportune. Added to this is the fact that no Member of Parliament has an imperative mandate. Nor is it ensured that individual members of parliament can assert an association's concern within their own political group, particularly as members of parliament also act as the lobbyists of other associations there, and the day-to-day political situation may be unfavourable for an association's interest. In addition, broad acceptance for the parliamentary mediation of interests is

---

47 See Abromeit (1993), pp. 37–38.
48 See Schmitz (2014); Mason (2014).
49 See Mason (2014).

only achieved in society if a balance of interests between the opposing groups occurs in parliament and compromises are found.

The second type of association-based lobbying is lobbying from the outside. This refers to the actual work of pressure groups in the classic sense, i. e. the establishment and maintenance of contact with representatives from the legislative and executive level as well as the transformation and articulation of association interests. In this case, the larger an association is, the more credible it usually appears. In this context, the above described balance between an association's representative nature and the precision of its opinion should be recalled. However, the size of an association does not equate to its options for structural involvement in the individual case, particularly since, as has already been mentioned, the development of a joint strategy which adequately gives consideration to the interests of all members often involves difficulties, especially at EU level.

6.4.1.1.3 Cultural differences between the EU level and member states as a problem for associations

This is compounded by the fact that many associations have difficulty in adapting flexibly to the multi-level and institutional system of the EU, which is significantly more complex in comparison with the member states' political systems. In contrast to the member states, the criticism of a certain lack of democracy is still being raised at EU level (with regard to the development and the structure of the EU see Chapter 4), which frequently necessitates a different structure for effective lobbying. Whilst the Parliament has again strengthened its position with the extension of the co-decision procedure to the ordinary legislative procedure through the Treaty of Lisbon, those institutions not directly legitimated by the electorate – the Council of the EU and the Commission – still hold crucial, key positions in the legislative process. The European political system is additionally undergoing constant transformation, and European integration remains a slowly but inexorably advancing process in which the decision-making structure may change.[50] Lobbying has to meet this flexibly and adapt itself in order to be effective – a requirement which associations are only able to meet in part due to their often long and complicated institutional decision-making procedures. This also explains the fact that there are several times more non-association lobbyists in Brussels than in Germany's capital city, Berlin, for instance.[51] The relationship between, and the weighting of, association-based and in-house corporate lobbying are also influenced by the political culture of the respective states. In this case, Brussels bears greater similarity to London than Berlin. The associations' difficulty in establishing themselves as a voice for interests between the state and societal groups in

---

50 The institutional structure of the EU has therefore been set down until further notice due to the Treaty of Lisbon's entry into force; however, it remains to be seen how the political processes will run in this structure.

51 A high number of different policy advisory think tanks are therefore also to be found on the Brussels stage, for instance, see Weilemann (2007), pp. 212–219.

Brussels, as in Berlin, is closely related to the fragmented multi-level and institutional system of the EU, "[which] disables the ability for the EU to provide the necessary patronage required for associational strength".[52]

6.4.1.1.4 European and national associations

Against the above outlined background, it is debatable whether the – quasi equal-status – European association or the national association which is active at European level packs a bigger punch vis-à-vis the EU institutions.

6.4.1.1.4.1 European associations

The European associations, in which several national associations of one industry, and occasionally also companies which dominate national markets, join forces, concentrate on lobbying amongst the EU institutions.

Although they are somewhat dated, the words of former EU Commissioner Martin Bangemann still remain true. It remains the case that pressure groups at EU level have still not positioned themselves so "that they (...) exercise the same pressure on political decisions as in the member states". As an explanation, Bangemann states that "European politics does not have the same ranking in the European capitals as national politics. The astonishment, and sometimes also the rude awakening, is therefore all the greater when Brussels has once again eliminated privileges, cut subsidies or increased competition."[53] Another indication of the EU's misunderstood importance can possibly be seen in the fact that many associations do not approach the institutions on their own initiative, as is the case at national level, but that it is instead the Commission itself which acts "as the driving force behind network formation and the organisation of interests" and "systematically organises [association-based] involvement via diverse and differentiated forms of co-operation and co-optation".[54] However, the establishment and expansion of an EU-wide association system went hand-in-hand with EU integration progress.[55] The difficulties "involved in the integration of members (...) are clear. It is becoming more complex and difficult solely due to the numbers of clients across Europe as a whole. Added to this is the fact that the costs and benefits of European integration are highly unlikely to be distributed evenly across the national and sub-national units of one and the same European stakeholder group, with the result that the problems of association-based interest unification are also exacerbated in this qualitative regard."[56] This view is now no longer tenable, as the European associations have since become established in the Brussels arena.[57] The European associations play an important role in lobbying, particular-

---

52 See Greenwood (2002), pp. 50–51.
53 Bangemann (1992), p. 161.
54 Tömmel (1994), p. 278.
55 See Weidenfeld (2013), p. 154.
56 Traxler and Schmitter (1994), p. 46.
57 See Lindloff, Kundolf and Bandelow (2014), p. 216.

ly in pan-EU regulation, e.g. the European Automobile Manufacturers' Association (ACEA) in the case of exhaust emissions.[58] Externally, however, the associations are still barely familiar, because there is no perception of organised pan-European interests due to the lack of a pan-European general public.

One further difficulty of lobbying through the European associations arises from the often levelled criticism of a lack of democracy at EU level. For example, there are hardly any withholding options vis-à-vis the political system, for example, through withholding votes, investment reluctance, boycotts or influencing the media. Like their insertion of personnel into the institutions, the European associations' degree of organisation and mobilisation usually remains low. Due to the usually extensively heterogeneous interest situation within the associations, the members are barely capable of engaging in conflicts. The common political socialisation of association and political elites is particularly difficult, as the sheer size of the EU significantly hampers the establishment of personal contact in comparison with the national level.

The legitimacy of associations is generally measured by their ability to pick up their members' interests and transform them into viable policy objectives. The above clearly shows that this usually involves major difficulties for a European association, and that these difficulties often hinder the adequate representation of a company's individual interests. As a result of this, numerous companies are pursuing a two- or multi-track strategy of association-based lobbying by using their respective national association in addition to the European association in Brussels, and/or by working closely together with the national decision-makers.

In summary, it can therefore be stated that a European association is only fundamentally suitable for asserting individual corporate interests at EU level in exceptional cases, i.e. if the interests within the association are extensively homogeneous. However, the specialist association is usually very good at undertaking one of the defined sub-tasks of lobbying (see Chapter 2), namely the collection of information and also the forwarding of information to decision-makers. Particularly in order to avoid a dearth of internal information vis-à-vis competing companies which meet their information requirements with the assistance of a European association, it is usually advantageous for a company to join its European specialist association or a national association which is active at EU level, and to cover its basic lobbying needs through this association.

6.4.1.1.4.2 National associations

In addition to their own lobbying activities, the national associations are also often members of corresponding European confederations, such asGermany's BDI, France's MEDEF or the UK's CBI, all of which are also members of the Eu-

---

58 See Foy, Bryant and Fontanella-Khan (2014).

ropean umbrella association BUSINESSEUROPE, with the result that overlaps may occur here. The options available to national associations for political involvement at EU level can basically be broken down into the following two forms: firstly, indirect lobbying through involvement in a European association, and secondly, direct lobbying through the activities of the national association representatives at the EU institutions.

For the national association, the first alternative particularly raises the problem of asserting its own interests within the European association due to the high number of the members' individual, and also nationally diverging, interests. The formal difficulties involved in decision-making in European associations have already been mentioned. Only a compromise, which gives consideration to each member, will therefore be possible in the majority of cases. However, this places tight constraints on the effective representation of individual, and also member state-specific, corporate interests. In a past interview, the former Chairman of the Confederation of British Industry (CBI) actually referred to his European umbrella association BUSINESSEUROPE as an "emasculated part of the Brussels establishment that will be increasingly held back to the lowest common denominator within an enlarged Europe".[59] Due to the difficulties involved in adequate decision-making, and to prevent the success of national association work from becoming dependent on the European association, numerous national associations are now choosing to seek representation amongst the EU institutions through their own representatives, with some associations actually maintaining their own national association office in Brussels, in addition to actively structuring European association policy.[60] This enables any of the European association's lobbying deficits to be compensated.

Another problem has its origin at member state level; the Europeanisation of lobbying merely acts as a catalyst here: associations are also significantly declining in importance and assertiveness in their domestic markets. According to a survey conducted in 2003, for instance, only 2.38 % of German companies saw their respective associations as having extensive political importance.[61] Examples in which serious misunderstandings have arisen between the representatives of national industry associations and the political, administrative level additionally raise questions concerning the associations' effectiveness. One past example of this is discussion within the industry surrounding the deposit regulation for beverage cans. Within a national umbrella association, breweries, water bottlers and beverage corporations failed to agree on a common position against the introduction of a deposit on cans. They were therefore "practically voiceless" on this issue

59 See "How Business can influence Europe", in: *Financial Times* dated 17.11.2003, http://search.ft.com/ftArticle?queryText=UNICE+CBI&aje=true&id=031117000975&ct=0 (last accessed on 1.2.2015).
60 Greenwood (2011³), p. 92.
61 See Dehaes and Gräf (2003).

vis-à-vis politicians.[62] An even more extreme example is the dissolution of the German Cigarette Industry Association (VdC) in 2007 due to disputes between the member companies concerning industry policy. Two different industry associations were subsequently established, the German Cigarette Association (DZV) and the German Tobacco Industry Interest Group[63] These examples show the associations' relative decline in importance.[64] The structures within the associations also frequently fail to meet the companies' needs. Whilst the umbrella associations are demanding an "association landscape reform",[65] the partial decline in the effectiveness of national association work appears to underscore this demand.

6.4.1.2 Non-collective forms of organisation

The non-collective instruments are increasingly growing in importance alongside the collective forms of organised lobbying. In this, a distinction has to be made between a company's liaison office or representative office in Brussels (so-called in-house lobbying) and lobbying using external service providers: in the first case, a company employs its own staff or maintains departments for the area of lobbying (see Section 6.4.1.2.1); in the second case, the company delegates lobbying to external service providers such as agencies and/or law firms (see Section 6.4.1.2.2). Finally, co-operation with Brussels-based think tanks – which is of little practical importance thus far – and posting internal employees to the European institutions also deserve a mention.

6.4.1.2.1 In-house lobbying: own corporate representative office

In particular, numerous, large companies have their own corporate representative office in Brussels. This is often used in addition to the respective associations' work in order to represent individual corporate interests. Accordingly, in-house lobbyists are non-collective actors which personally and exclusively represent a company's individual interests in the European political system.[66]

The importance of corporate representative offices – also frequently referred to as liaison offices – has continued to increase in recent years; a figure of around 300 offices in Brussels alone can now be assumed.[67] By no means least, this may well be a consequence of the associations' above outlined weakness in effectively representing the interests of their member companies. At least in partial contrast e.g. to Germany (during the "Bonn republic" period in any case) or France, the associations *de facto* have no supremacy at EU level. All lobbying instruments are initially subject to the same external conditions in terms of their agenda-setting options; in particular, they are equally reliant on the co-operativeness of parliamen-

---

62 See Goffert (2002).
63 See Graw (2008).
64 See Brönstrup (2014).
65 See Priddat (2009), p. 194.
66 See Michalowitz (2007), p. 88.
67 See Greenwood (2013), p. 92; Coen (2009), pp. 147–168; Weidenfeld (2013³), p. 155.

tarians and civil servants in their work. In contrast to associations, however, corporate representative offices are able to react much more flexibly to changes in the factual or political situation; the dependency on the associations' opinion-forming bodies, as described at the beginning, is non-existent. The major advantage of such an office, and the structural lobbying instruments portrayed in the following, in comparison with the associations therefore lies in their strict compliance with the company's instructions – dilution of the company's concerns through the opinion-forming instruments of an association structure is *per definitionem* out of the question. Corporate representatives can also be employed in fields with which the company does not want the responsible association to deal – if the issue in question should not be conveyed to a broader (specialist) public due to reasons of competition, for instance.

Despite these differences, however, a corporate lobbyist – like an association representative – performs an interface function: in-house lobbyists receive "their salary as employees of the company, but they mediate between two parties with different interests"[68] – in a certain manner, they are a "third level" between the company and politicians. This results in important key points for both the framework conditions and content of their activities (see Section 6.4.1.2.1.1) and for the requirement profile of a corporate lobbyist (see Section 6.4.1.2.1.2).

6.4.1.2.1.1 Role and activities of an in-house lobbyist

The role of an in-house lobbyist is oriented both inwards and outwards: within the company, he mediates the relevance and sensitivity of European issues, and ensures that European topics are given the necessary attention by the company's decision-makers. Prior to this, he must undertake – frequently highly specialised – monitoring, and therefore also acts as a "European trend researcher in the political sector" for his employer. This may lead to the occurrence of important strategic stimuli, which are picked up by the company and transformed into corresponding lobbying strategies. Externally, the corporate representative opens up access to the political decision-makers in Brussels, and often also – via the detour of the national representations in Brussels – to the legislative and executive level in the respective member state. To a certain extent, the corporate representative is the company's "face" in the political sphere. He acts as an ambassador, and contributes extensively towards building the company's image on the political stage, whether through his presence at political events or participation in panel discussions as a speaker, etc. Ultimately, corporate representative offices can also be used to flank the activities of the responsible associations – either as a fall-back option in the event that the association's efforts amount to nought or to lend colour to the association's lobbying vis-à-vis the legislative and executive level, in order to highlight the specific interests of their own company over and above the,

---

68 Michalowitz (2007), p. 90.

possibly watered-down, collective position. These offices are also suitable for participating in association work – as "lobbying vis-à-vis lobbyists" so to speak. The issues raised by an association in Brussels can at least be influenced and shaped in this manner.

The fact that major corporations have realised the importance of having their own corporate representative offices can be recognised solely by the staffing levels of some of the offices in Brussels: at Daimler AG, for instance, a department consisting of at least ten full-time staff deals with the pursuit of corporate interests.[69]

6.4.1.2.1.2 Personal requirements for a lobbyist

Two factors are of particular importance to the potential effectiveness of a lobbyist: firstly, the representative nature of the company represented by the lobbyist, and secondly, his individual prerequisites.

The first part of the statement is easy to explain. The representative of a major association or a company which is very important to the macro economy is almost certainly more likely to be heard in Brussels than the representative of a small company – effects of scale come into play here (see also Section 6.4.1.1.4).

Conversely, the issue of the subjective prerequisites or personal framework conditions of effective lobbying requires a more detailed assessment. The representative's personal contact with members of parliament and civil servants is critical here. However, this is frequently difficult to achieve, particularly in view of the high numbers of competitors, since conventionalised channels of communication predominate within the EU institutions. When establishing a dedicated corporate office, it is vital to give consideration to this when selecting the office manager or the individual consultants, in order to minimise the disadvantages vis-à-vis already established competitors as well as start-up difficulties. Employing a former civil servant or Member of Parliament may prove helpful in this case, particularly as these usually have a broad-based network of personal contacts and therefore a good likelihood of obtaining access to the institutions. On selection of a former civil servant, however, it must be remembered that his employment is only essentially advantageous in terms of his former Directorate General. In view of the passage of time and personnel fluctuation, it is self-evident that he can often only exploit existing affinities for the company for a certain period of time: as a result of his departure from the institution, former colleagues' interest in collegial interaction declines over time.

6.4.1.2.1.3 Central problem: trust cannot be bequeathed

Without any doubt, one of the potential strengths of the instrument of the corporate lobbyist is his – *qua* employment relationship – strong sense of loyalty to-

---

69 Michalowitz (2007), p. 90 with further references.

wards the client. Of course, this bond is missing in the case of an association; with an external service provider (further details in the following), it is usually substituted by the contractual duty of allegiance and the economic incentive of the mandate.

However, the mirror image of the lobbyist's loyalty towards his company is the company's bond to an individual person (either a "lone warrior" employed as a corporate representative or the head of the liaison office, who is usually employed to deal with top contacts) and his personal network. This is one of the central disadvantages of the corporate representative in comparison with other lobbying instruments: the trust afforded this person by decision-makers at the legislative and executive level, which is simultaneously a fundamental condition of effective personal networks, cannot be bequeathed. As soon as the corporate representative leaves his position – for whatever reasons – the company also unavoidably loses a large part of its access options. As a rule, not even major corporations will be able to afford to have a large number of high-ranking – i. e. with access to relevant decision-makers – lobbyists on their payroll.[70] The result is extensive dependency (usually) on one individual person, which may pose a risk, particularly within the framework of the usually long drawn-out legislative process at European level. The company's good name alone by no means guarantees that an audience will be found amongst the crucial decision-makers, something which even major corporations have discovered time and again in Brussels.

6.4.1.2.2 External service providers

Co-operation with an external lobbying service provider offers a further option for representing one's interests locally. Even if the company maintains its own representative office in Brussels, such an external service provider can generate significant added value, since the company's internal expertise is supplemented with external competencies. Classically, a distinction has to be made between public affairs agencies and law firms, whose work is particularly content-oriented, and governmental relations agencies, whose work is above all process-oriented. This distinction is crucial, because each of these three external service providers caters to different needs, and therefore also reveals different core competencies. Two special forms of external service providers in EU Europe, which are also primarily content-oriented, will be briefly dealt with at the end of this section: think tanks and posting internal employees to the EU institutions.

6.4.1.2.2.1 Public affairs agencies

Public affairs agencies (PA agencies, sometimes also organised as a department within larger public relations agencies) regularly focus on the content-related as-

---

70 Frequently, even large companies only staff their liaison office in Brussels with just one to two full-time consultants; these may possibly be joined by secretaries and assistants.

pects of lobbying, and less on the procedural area.[71] They perform monitoring services, conduct content-related analyses on specific areas of policy and society (e.g. analyses on the current status of energy policy discussion, on a company's image amongst politicians), perform profile and position analyses e.g. with regard to parliamentarians or Commissioners, advise on the establishment of communication concepts in a company's political environment (in the area of campaign planning, for instance), co-ordinate public relations work in politically sensitive areas in close co-ordination with the company's PR department (creation of press releases, etc.), provide logistical support in contact management and – an important area of business for the agencies – organise events such as panel discussions, political round tables and parliamentary evenings, etc.

As can already be seen from this list, PA agencies primarily have an advisory and supporting function for their clients; often, the actual lobbying work is not left up to them.[72] As a rule, the agencies also have content-related (policy) focuses; using different agencies for different concerns is therefore recommended.

The biggest advantage offered by a PA agency is the flexibility of its use: PA agencies' work is usually project-related, which enables the client to implement them at short notice to support its internal resources. As a general rule, however, the agencies are not suitable as a standalone solution for a company's lobbying.

6.4.1.2.2.2 Law firms

In the case of legally complex issues – which is more often the rule than the exception at European level – both associations and companies rarely rely exclusively on their own legal competence, and make use of external, legal expertise. This has given rise to a highly specialised market, particularly in Brussels, but also in the member states themselves to some extent. However, the service provided by the lawyers concerned is not aimed solely at pure legal advice; instead, these lawyers also offer their political expertise and sensitivity at the interface between legislation, the economy and politics.

The size of the market is difficult to estimate, particularly in the case of law firms, since they, like all other lobbyists, are not obliged to seek registration in the Commission's and Parliament's Transparency Register. According to a search result, 99 law firms were registered there at the beginning of 2015.[73] The US-based law firm DLA Piper appears to be the largest of these: it currently has around 90 professionals in Brussels.[74] Other international law firms such as White & Case, Linklaters and Baker & McKenzie are also active on the market.[75]

---

71 See Sebaldt (2007), p. 112.
72 See Michalowitz (2007), p. 94.
73 See Transparency Register, European Commission (2015c).
74 See law firm website at https://www.dlapiper.com/en/us/people/?region=global&keyword=Brussels&skip=75&sort=relevancy&reload=false&scroll=13294 (last accessed on 2.2.2015).
75 See Transparency Register, European Commission (2015c).

Typical services include advance analysis of the company's legal, political and regulatory environment in Brussels, the monitoring of relevant issues in the area of European legislative policy, the correct assessment and support of crucial legislative procedures, supporting a company in European hearing procedures with expert opinions and position papers or legal preparation for applications or queries to the European institutions. Correct legal work is necessary as part of such indirect measures; this is where the law firms' core competencies lie.[76] Roughly summed up, their work is also primarily content-oriented.

On the whole, the increasing presence of law firms in the field of lobbying is a consequence of the extensive juridification of political and administrative procedures. Whilst Brussels-based law firms are often initially employed merely to deal with legal affairs, their implementation as a structural lobbying instrument arises as a by-product of this activity to a certain extent. As a lobbyist, the law firm represents the interests of one or more clients in the preliminary stages of Brussels' legislation. If this is only undertaken in the specific, individual case, the law firm alone has the advantage of being located in the capital city of Europe, which may possibly compensate for the company's lack of representation in Brussels. The environment from which the law firm's employees come, and their personalities, are once again crucial in this case, in order to achieve the correct diplomatic access to the decision-makers. Usually, this is precisely where the law firms' weakness lies: their core competence is often not in the procedural but rather in the content-related area, namely that of legal consulting. Good legal support is undoubtedly important, particularly when dealing with projects which involve complex legal issues. However, it is no substitute for what above all constitutes effective lobbying: helping to assert the company's concern *in the political process*. In short, "the political activity of lawyers regularly ends at the point at which actual lobbying begins".[77]

Added to this is the legal terminology, a problem which is not to be underestimated in day-to-day political dealings. A good lawyer has learnt to formulate texts as precisely, detailed and unambiguously as possible, which usually results in documents which are complex and extensive in both content and linguistic terms. This frequently occurs at the expense of general comprehensibility and compatibility with the language of politics. "Special transfer work,"[78] i.e. transformation of the legal documents into a text version appropriate to their use and addressees, before a document is forwarded to the respective decision-maker at the legislative and executive level therefore appears all the more important. Detailed formulation proposals, spanning several pages, on specific legislative initiatives should be avoided under all circumstances: on becoming known, this firstly gives the im-

---

76 See Burholt and Reulecke (2007), p. 107; Bender and Reulecke (2003), pp. 154–155.
77 Bender and Reulecke (2003), p. 155; see also Burholt and Reulecke (2007), p. 109: "Lawyers from commercial law firms should not act as political contact mediators."
78 Bender and Reulecke (2003), p. 157.

pression that the tasks of state institutions are extensively being outsourced to private individuals without control; secondly, there is a high risk that the addressees at the legislative and executive level (also not entirely without justification) will feel patronised, and may thus be more inclined to reject the proposal.

6.4.1.2.2.3 Governmental relations agencies

In contrast to law firms and PA agencies, governmental relations agencies' work is not focussed on the area of content-related consulting but on process structuring and support, i. e. on managing actual "active lobbying", with direct contact to the decision-makers at the legislative and executive level. These external service providers, in particular, therefore offer extremely extensive process competence (which can in turn be broken down into process structure and process support competence, see Chapter 10). They can help to reduce the complexity of the multi-level system of the European Union, with its high number of actors, decision-makers and both formal and informal procedures, and to make them manageable. The framework of lobbying processes, particularly in the area of governmental relations (consider legislative procedures and political debates in the EU, for instance), should be long-term and structural, not only project-related, in order to continuously and perspectively support the client's interests in the political arena (see further on, "Project-related or structural (long-term) approach?").

In this form, lobbying is to be regarded as an active undertaking which is dedicated with foresight to targeted communication with executive and legislative decision-makers.

One further, crucial, characteristic of the work of a successful governmental relations agency is perspective change competence (change of perspective from the individual to a public interest perspective). If a discussion paper is written from the perspective of the addressee, this means that, whilst the economic objectives of the company or association are taken into consideration, the advantages of the communicated objective for politicians and also for the general public are primarily emphasised. This process-oriented methodology of making a client's accordingly modified objectives or interests more readily realisable is explained in greater detail in Section 6.4.2.1.7 (onepager) and in Chapter 10 (under perspective change competence) (see also the practical case studies in Chapter 9). Without anticipating results, process support can only lead to the success of a specific lobbying project following a successful change of perspective. An unsuccessful change of perspective offers the client the option of selecting other action options at an early stage and also avoiding the unnecessary use of resources.

Service providers with very different staffing levels can be found on the Brussels market: these include both individual persons – often former officials and elected representatives from the EU institutions – as well as larger agencies with ten or more local employees. These service providers' possible uses are also accordingly varied: whilst a well interconnected "one-man agency" may be suitable for establishing contact and the mediation of content into the political process in individual cases, it very quickly encounters its performance limits in more complex projects. A larger infrastructure and a multitude of lobbyists, who occasionally work simultaneously on various sections of the project, are required in this area.

Such an agency can help the client[79] to make optimal use of its own content competence, i.e. to be able to communicate it to the right decision-maker at the correct point in time. In short, the client is primarily the content provider in this constellation, whereas the service provider is essentially responsible for the process. Of course, there is often no reason why the service provider should not also be given content-related tasks: particularly in long-term, structural working relationships, the agency's responsible employees often acquire extensive-specialist knowledge, which can be put to use to the benefit of the client.

The process-oriented focus of the governmental relations agencies offers central advantages in comparison with other lobbying instruments:

- **No heterogeneity problems**
  As explained in the section on lobbying through associations, their tendency to serve the industry as a whole often leads to the inadequate representation of an individual company's interests – which may occasionally differ extensively from those of the other association members. Against the background of this heterogeneity problem, it is therefore sensible, from the companies' perspective, to extend the basis of lobbying, thus enabling more effective lobbying which is tailored to the companies' own needs; this is something which cannot be accomplished by the associations in the same manner. This extension can be undertaken by the involvement of an external (process) partner. The involvement of such a partner offers advantages in terms of the option of more flexible actions and the possibility of reacting faster. Since it is external, a service provider can also act as an intermediary between (EU) politicians and the client.
- **Tailored service**
  As has already been indicated, there are significant structural differences, which have corresponding qualitative consequences, between the various external service providers. In addition, the personal environment of the acting lobbyists is of crucial importance, in precisely the same manner as that of the employees of a corporate representative office. If an external service provider has networks in Brussels and also in some European capital cities – ideally throughout the EU – there are optimal opportunities for mutual information exchange, which may have a very positive effect on the willingness of EU officials and parliamentarians to engage in dialogue. As a result of this, the external service provider also has the option of not only introducing concerns directly in Brussels but of also

---

79 Whereby this may also involve companies, associations and organisations as well as EU member states and regions; there is no reason why the latter two should not be involved, at least in theory.

coming into contact with the responsible EU institutions via the national levels, thus meeting the requirements of multi-level lobbying. On the whole, the client is therefore able to select a corresponding agency which meets its requirements precisely; the client is not bound to a specified infrastructure (as e. g. in the case of its respective association), and can involve the service provider it its pan-European or global political communication strategy – an important aspect for multinational corporations – or actually develop such a strategy together with the service provider in the first place.

- **Reduced risk of loss of trust**
  As has been described, the dependency of a company, association or organisation on an employed representative in Brussels can lead to difficulties as soon as the representative leaves the company. In short, trust cannot be bequeathed; in practice, transferring the representative's personal network to his successor in the company is usually out of the question. This is a different case with an external service provider: whilst there is, naturally, also a risk of losing personal networks when service provider employees leave, these networks are spread across several shoulders, so to speak; the absence of one lobbyist can usually be compensated by other employees. In addition, the top contacts are usually found at the agency's senior management level, which is subject to low fluctuation. Added to this is the crucial aspect that the executive and legislative level decision-makers' trust is usually related to the governmental relations agency itself, with the result that the loss of personnel can be more readily compensated than in the case of individual representatives. Conversely, if the company's own (and usually its only) representative is replaced, this is equivalent to a "cold start".

Project-related or structural (long-term) approach?

In terms of the time horizon, a distinction can primarily be made between two types of client relationship: firstly, the short-term, merely project-related assignment, and secondly, the long-term, structural support of all of the company's concerns in the area of lobbying.

The project-related use of an external service provider offers the advantage that its individual skills or special contacts can be called upon by selecting them according to the requirements of the individual project, and can therefore be put to optimal use. This can prove entirely expedient in the individual case. On completion of a project, or if only unsatisfactory services are provided, the external service provider can also usually be given notice immediately, as a result of which it can be used more flexibly than a corporate representative office staffed by employees, for instance.

The disadvantages of a purely project-related approach are not to be overlooked: particularly in the case of complex industries and projects, a certain familiarisation time is often required before external third parties have internalised and understood a client's concern to such an extent that they are able to convey it convincingly, credibly and professionally to legislative and executive level decision-makers. Long-term commitment particularly appears to be the key to success here. Added to this is the fact that clients' specific concerns can only be effectively introduced into the European and member state institutions if long-term, trusting working relationships exist. The project-related approach is therefore appropriate for short-term and quickly accomplished assignments focussing on content-related issues. Conversely, structural co-operation between the client and agency (governmental relations agency) is necessary to enable a successful solution in the case of complex and long-term EU issues and procedures requiring, inter alia, intensive process support.

The following three problems arise when external service providers are used on a project-related basis:

1. If the external service provider is engaged by a client in whose industry it has no, or only a very few, viable networks in the European institutions, significant frictional losses occur, or it will not be possible to successfully accomplish a project in the majority of cases.

2. If the service provider is frequently active within an industry, however, it – and ultimately its client – will therefore be confronted with the problem of shifting loyalties: if a lobbyist works for competitor A today, competitor B tomorrow and competitor C the day after, this can only be done credibly and professionally if all of these clients have similar interests. It is obvious that this will very rarely be the case. In the case of law firms, this problem is dealt with using so-called Chinese walls or – in extreme cases – with the rejection of the mandate. It is unclear whether lobbying agencies have such an awareness of the problem – if they do not support their clients structurally, and only ever work according to the principle of "only one interest", i.e. industry exclusivity; however, the door to conflicts of interest and the loss of credibility amongst legislative and executive level decision-makers is wide open.

3. The aspects of conflicts of interest deserve particular emphasis here: during the working relationship, the agencies naturally acquire extremely confidential information concerning the client, its products and its strategy (often far beyond the issue of political communication). Against this background, a client must in any case give careful consideration to what information at all is issued to the service provider and where the element of confidentiality prevents its issue (with the side effect that the service provider, which is "partially flying blind" so to speak, may possibly be unable to represent its clients credibly). If the service provider is provided with all of the required information, however, confidentiality may be ensured through subsequent duties of professional discretion when the working relationship comes to an end, but a not insignificant residual

risk nevertheless remains. Whilst this risk basically occurs in every type of client relationship – it is multiplied the more short-term and interchangeable such a relationship is.

In general, if interests are merely represented as part of a "case-of-emergency service", the client or its concern will not be given the necessary attention in the decision-making process. It has already been explained that the information channels between the economy and the European institutions are not one-way streets – communication processes are based on mutuality, i.e. an MEP or a Commission civil servant will refuse to deal with a company's concerns after a certain time if he, in his function as a decision-maker, does not also benefit from information which he can use as part of his work. However, this can only function independently of day-to-day activities, i.e. particularly during calmer periods. In short, targeted and effective communication with legislative and executive level decision-makers must be initiated at a very early point in time – even before a project has reached the acute stage – and must not leave success to chance later on.

6.4.1.2.2.4 Think tanks

Research institutes or informal groupings of scientists, (former) politicians or businessmen dedicated to research, scientific political consulting and the publication of their research results are referred to as think tanks.[80] Whilst the research conducted by these institutes is essentially scientifically neutral and objective in the majority of cases, they often reveal a certain commitment to ideological premises, which lead to an inductive and interest-led approach from the outset when dealing with the object of the research. Ultimately, think tanks are "a medium for transforming theoretical knowledge into practical relevance".[81] In the EU, however, think tanks have not yet assumed the important position which they occupy in lobbying in the USA, for instance.

Such institutions are frequently supported by well known companies or certain societal groups; scientific independence is therefore not usually ensured. These institutions are generally offensive advertisers of their own ideas, and vehemently represent specific interpretations of the research results. Think tanks therefore often underpin the interests of specific groups, as is clearly shown by the example of Deutsche Bank Research.[82] Irrespective of this, think tanks can most certainly engage in "gentle" involvement at European level, whereby this primarily concerns the macro level.[83] From the point of view of a company, association or organisation, such institutions are only suitable for targeted lobbying to a very limited extent, and are located – according to the categorisation undertaken at the start of

---

[80] For details see Weilemann (2007), pp. 212ff.
[81] Wessels and Schäfer (2007), p. 200.
[82] See e.g. Deutsche Bank Research: this think tank views itself as a monitor of Deutsche Bank's operational environment, https://www.dbresearch.de/ (last accessed on 10.2.2015).
[83] See Wessels and Schneider (2007), p. 210, one example of this is the German-French think tank *Bruegel*, see Bonse (2009), p. 7.

Figure 6.6: Possible structural lobbying instruments at European level

this book (Chapter 2) – more in the area of public relations, possibly that of public affairs, i.e. they are primarily involved in content-oriented lobbying. At best, the scientific underpinning of a client's specific concerns may achieve a certain degree of publicity. Irrespective of this, such results are unlikely to make a big impact in the political arena, particularly if the think tank's scientific, ideological orientation is known.

6.4.1.2.2.5 Posting internal employees to the institutions

Finally, there is also the option of placing an employee from one's own company, association or organisation at the disposal of the European Commission or the European Parliament as an expert. As the employee is not usually paid by the EU institutions for the period of time in question, which may also span several years, posting such a lobbyist will only be a feasible (affordable) option for very large companies, associations and organisations, however. Added to this is the fact that such an employee is only responsible for a specific, limited area within the Commission or the Parliament, with the result that he is usually unable to maintain any multidisciplinary contact with other areas, Directorates General, etc., and can therefore only be of benefit in his specific field of employment. In addition, a seconded employee has no personal decision-making powers.

6.4.1.3 Costs of the various instruments

In addition to the previously analysed, purely qualitative criteria (such as possible operational fields, assertiveness and guaranteed confidentiality), quantitative, and sometimes commercial management, criteria also play an important role in the formulation of an individual lobbying strategy and the selection of specific instruments, of course. To analyse these, the costs of (1) an association membership (particularly content-oriented lobbying); (2) a separate corporate representative office and (3) an external service provider (distinguishing between a primarily content-oriented public affairs agency and a law firm plus a primarily process-oriented governmental relations agency) will be compared in the following, particularly from the point of view of a company, although this is equally valid for other affected parties to a lesser extent.

6.4.1.3.1 Costs of an association

The costs incurred by a company for the activities of the responsible associations in Brussels can only be estimated, since only approximate information is usually provided by both companies and associations. Associations merely state the total costs of their lobbying activities in Brussels; in the 2013/14 financial year, for example, the Federal Association of German Industry (BDI) spent approximately 3.1 million euros, the Confederation of German Employers' Associations (BDA) spent between 1 and 1.25 million euros in 2013, and the Association of German Chambers of Commerce and Industry (DIHK) ran up costs of 2.2 million euros, for direct lobbying work in Brussels.[84] However, these costs cannot be apportioned directly to the member companies: the associations' activities at EU level are already included in the companies' contributions for their membership in national associations, and are not invoiced separately. The company must therefore include the association's national and European activities in a cost-benefit calculation in order to arrive at an evaluation.

The case of associations which operate exclusively at European level is different, of course, whereby the umbrella associations must be disregarded here (they are financed through the member associations' contributions, and therefore only indirectly through the contributions paid by companies). Due to a lack of corresponding publications by associations, however, only examples from empirical studies can be listed at this point: a study encompassing 135 British associations,[85] for instance, revealed annual amounts ranging from 0 to 800,000 euros. The average annual contribution for medium to large EU associations is accordingly approximately 150,000 euros.[86] The spectrum of these costs is dependent on the respective industry, the size (turnover) of the company and the association's range of activities, etc. Against this backdrop, a cost-benefit assessment is only possible on an individual case basis, which would exceed the scope of this book.

However, it is in any case doubtful whether a company which is active at the European level should at all question its membership in the responsible (industry) associations: to some extent, this forms part of its basic lobbying requirements; in addition to negative publicity, leaving the association would cause important sources of information to dry up; the company would also be excluded from the association's agenda-setting options in the case of formal lobbying processes such as hearings and consultations. Against this background, a company will usually have no choice between membership and non-membership.

---

84 All data in accordance with the Transparency Register, European Commission (2015c).
85 See Greenwood (2002), p. 14.
86 See Greenwood (2002), p. 14; the contributions are now almost certainly around 20–30% higher.

6.4.1.3.2 Costs of a corporate representative office in Brussels

Of course, the costs of a company's own liaison office in Brussels cannot be generalised either, since they are dependent on the type and scope of the tasks undertaken as well as the selected structural and process-oriented instruments. Companies do not publish any tenable data in this regard – the only accessible source is the cost factors published in the Transparency Register.[87] However, only the total costs of direct lobbying – usually material costs such as office and travel expenses plus personnel costs – are recorded there. According to a study conducted by the NGO Friends of the Earth Europe,[88] the five biggest budgets for this for 2008 lay between 550,000 and 1.5 million euros. Figure 6.7 shows a selection of figures from major companies.

The considerable differences between some of the companies listed in the Register are interesting, when the costs of direct lobbying in the EU and the USA are compared: BP, for example, states expenditure of 8.07 million US dollars for 2013 in the US lobbying register, as against a mere 1.25 – 1.50 million euros in the EU for the same period, i.e. less than one fifth.[89] Provided that these data are correct, this enables interesting conclusions to be drawn as regards the development potential available for lobbying in Brussels.

Company	EU lobbying expenditure (in euros) (year)
Siemens	4.4 million (2012/2013)
Statoil ASA	2.6 million* (2014)
BASF	2.30 million (2014)
Telefonica	2 million (2014)
BP	1.25 - 1.5 million (2013)
Deutsche Telekom	1.23 million (2013)
Volkswagen	1 - 1.25 million (2013)
ENI	0.6 million (2014)
BNP Paribas	0.6 million (2013)

*Total cost Liason Office Brussels

Figure 6.7: Data from selected companies on expenditure for lobbying in the European Commission Register[90]

In terms of personnel costs, there is no uniform salary structure in the field of lobbying – as in the majority of service industries. A salaried lobbyist's individual remuneration is dependent on his personal background, i.e. by no means least on

---

87 See Transparency Register, European Commission (2015c).
88 See Friends of the Earth Europe (2010).
89 Senate Office of Public Records (2015).
90 All data (rounded in part) in accordance with the Transparency Register, European Commission (2015c).

his connections and access to various points of the executive and legislative level: the more (good) contacts a lobbyist maintains, the more cost intensive he will be for the company. As no tenable data regarding the personnel costs of their representative offices are available from companies either,[91] a few basic cost factors for the head of a corporate representative office in Brussels will be listed as examples.[92]

In addition to former Members of Parliament or top officials from the Commission, leading personalities from other EU institutions or national institutions operating in Brussels are possible as technically suitable corporate representatives, since they offer a widespread and interinstitutional network of relationships as well as very detailed knowledge concerning the intrainstitutional administrative and organisational procedures due to their usually long-term activities. As this group's remuneration is comparatively high, however, it can be assumed that their salary demands for corporate activities will be correspondingly high. Figure 6.8 provides an overview of the current civil servant pay grades within the EU institutions.

Pay grades 1.7.2011	Length of service stages				
	01.	02.	03.	04.	05.
16.	16,919.04	17,630.00	18,370.84		
15.	14,953.61	15,581.98	16,236.76	16,688.49	16,919.04
14.	13,216.49	13,771.87	14,350.58	14,794.83	14,953.61
13.	11,681.17	12,172.03	12,683.51	13,036.39	13,216.49
12.	10,324.20	10,758.04	11,210.11	11,521.99	11,681.17
11.	9,124.87	9,508.31	9,907.86	10,183.52	10,324.20
10.	8,064.64	8,403.76	8,756.90	9,000.53	9,124.87
09.	7,127.99	7,427.52	7,739.63	7,954.96	8,064.86
08.	6,299.95	6,564.69	6,840.54	7,030.86	7,127.99
07.	5,568.11	5,802.09	6,045.90	6,214.10	6,299.95
06.	4,921.28	5,128.07	5,343.56	5,492.23	5,568.11
05.	4,349.59	4,532.36	4,722.82	4,854.21	4,921.28
04.	3,844.31	4,005.85	4,174.18	4,290.31	4,190.20
03.	3,397.73	3,540.50	3,689.28	3,791.92	3,844.31
02.	3,003.02	3,129.21	3,260.71	3,351.42	3,397.73
01.	2,654.17	2,765.70	2,881.92	2,962.10	3,003.02

Figure 6.8: EU officials' pay in euros per month[93]

---

91 See e.g. Olényi, (2010); net monthly salaries of over 6,000 euros are mentioned here (using the example of salaried association lobbyists) – a value which is only usually likely to be achieved by the upper quartile of lobbyists.
92 The extensive spread of these managers' salaries must expressly be taken into consideration in this.
93 Source: European Parliament/Council of the EU (2014).

Nor must it be overlooked that the civil servants are granted considerable benefits such as significant tax breaks, as well as guarantees such as lifetime employment and above-average old-age pensions, by their employer in addition to the above specified emoluments. Many correspondingly experienced civil servants with a good network of relationships will also, of course, be at an age in which they have started a family or have entered into other social commitments. Attractive compensation for the benefits granted by the state are required for them to then give up their secure and very well paid positions in the public sector for corporate work.[94]

Former (long-term) employees of Members of the European Parliament may also be suitable for employment as corporate representatives. They, too, are usually highly familiar with the European political and administrative system and the customs of the political scene in Brussels, and are also equipped with widespread contacts within the institutions. Nevertheless, each individual case must be evaluated by itself: the company must be able to assess in advance whether the (hierarchical) level of a former parliamentary employee's contacts is sufficient to represent the company's interests. As a rule, this will be affirmative in the case of consultant positions and employees of the head of the representative office. However, access to a larger number of decision-makers at higher levels will be rare in this case, although the usually lower salary costs must also be regarded against this background: total salary costs in excess of 80,000 euros per annum (including employer's contributions) are entirely common for such an employee (former employee of a Member of the European Parliament). Personnel costs for further employees in the back-office area of a corporate representative office must also be taken into consideration.

Of course, other expenses such as rent and equipment costs are incurred in addition to the personnel costs of a corporate representative office. These can fluctuate extensively according to the specific case: depending on the location of the property, e. g. at the heart of the governmental area in Brussels or on the outskirts of the city, for instance, the annual rent can vary significantly. False economies should not be applied here, in order to ensure that, firstly, the institutions are only a stone's throw away, and secondly, that the property has a certain representative status.

On the whole, it is clear that, as a structural lobbying instrument, a separate corporate representative office causes high fixed costs. Even when equipped to minimum levels (one to two lobbyists, one team assistant) a basic amount of 0.5 – 1

---

94 Of course, it is not absolutely necessary to give up one's position as a civil servant completely. A leave of absence for several years is also conceivable. In this case, the civil servant incurs no direct financial disadvantages, particularly since he usually continues to progress through the length of service stages and can rejoin public service at the pay grade reached up to then once the leave of absence is over. After a break of several years, however, it is to be anticipated that he will no longer be employed in a significant department or key function, as more experienced or "loyal" civil servants will then be available for these posts. This effective career setback will also necessitate financial compensation by the company.

million euros per year can readily be assumed – with virtually no upward limitations. Even this minimum amount is a sum which will frequently only pay dividends for a company as of a certain turnover level. A corporate representative office, which, as the "face" of the company, also provides content competence in the company's lobbying (content-related interface management) in addition to undertaking image management as a local representative office, is only necessary on reaching a certain size.

6.4.1.3.3 Costs of an external service provider

In terms of the costs of external service providers, a distinction must first be made between the different types of service provider, i.e. primarily content-oriented public affairs agencies and law firms or primarily process-oriented governmental relations agencies.[95]

6.4.1.3.3.1 Public affairs agencies

The costs for the work of a public affairs agency break down into regularly agreed services with fixed prices and activities with variable prices. As regards the first category, the execution of monitoring services can be listed as an example: depending on the scope of the service which is performed, 5,000 – 10,000 euros and more can be incurred per month. The organisation of events also frequently carries a fixed price tag; due to the many possible variants, no statement regarding the costs incurred is possible.

Variably remunerated services regularly include the production of complex analyses and reports as well as the development of complete communication strategies for the client. As in the case of lawyers, generalised statements on the usual fees are extremely difficult; the average fees determined by the Bundesverband Deutscher Unternehmensberater only provide an indication (see Figure 6.9). According to this, the average per diem rates at management level (owner, managing director, partner) for management consultancies with a turnover of over 25 million euros was around 2,200 euros in 2014 (range 1,300 – 3,750 euros). An average of 1,325 euros (range 925 – 2,225 euros) is invoiced for senior consultants. In consulting companies with an annual turnover of less than 250,000 euros, the per diem rates are 1,250 euros (range 800 – 1,925 euros) for management level and 900 euros (range 675 – 1,375 euros) for senior consultants.[96]

It must be remembered that these per diem rates already include all material and personnel costs incurred by the external service provider. Only expenses such as travel and accommodation costs, and costs for conferences and events, etc. are in-

---

95 Costs which can be incurred on commissioning think tanks or posting internal employees to the EU institutions will not be dealt with in greater detail in the following. There are no benchmarks whatsoever for the former; it comes as little surprise that the latter incurs costs for the continued payment of salaries plus any expatriate supplements.
96 See Bundesverband Deutscher Unternehmensberater BDU (2014).

curred in addition to these amounts, as in the case of a corporate representative office or a law firm.

As the external, content-oriented service provider is usually engaged for a specific project or as required by the company, the average costs incurred for it must be calculated depending on the client's needs. No retainer costs are usually incurred; as a rule, the underlying contracts can be terminated at short notice. Consequently, the company only pays for the service which it actually requires. This can range from a few hours per week or even per month up to what is essentially full-time employment, for example in the case of difficult or extensive projects; the costs differ accordingly.

Turnover	Position					
	Partner	Sr. manager	Manager	Sr. consultant	Consultant	Analyst
Over €25 million	2,200	1,825	1,575	1,325	1,175	1,075
Over €5 million	1,900	1,650	1,500	1,275	1,125	975
Over €2.5 million	1,700	1,525	1,300	1,250	1,150	875
Over €1 million	1,700	1,525	1,250	1,175	1,175	850
Over €500,000	1,650	1,325	1,200	1,150	1,075	700
Over €250,000	1,600	1,375	1,150	1,025	900	725
Below €250,000	1,250	1,100	950	900	825	500

Figure 6.9: Fee study 2013 concerning daily rates, mean values for the 2012 financial year[97]

6.4.1.3.3.2 Law firms

As a general rule, law firms invoice according to one of three remuneration models (or a combination of these): fees according to the relevant schedule of charges, hourly or per diem rates, or contingency fees in exceptional cases. Nevertheless, the relevant schedules of charges are only likely to become relevant in the rarest of cases, since the above outlined range of services provided by lawyers in the field of lobbying hardly involves consulting as part of legal disputes. The schedules of charges are usually only mandatory for such cases. In view of the fact that law firms are not usually involved in "direct" lobbying, but are instead concerned more with preparatory (content consulting) work, contingency fees are more of an exception.

Hourly or per diem rates are therefore the usual case. Guideline values can only be indicated to a very limited extent here, since the level of remuneration is dependent on the size of the law firm, the specific task definition and the lawyers involved (the hourly rates usually also vary significantly within a law firm, e.g. between salaried associates and the law firm's partners). Industry services such as

---

97 Bundesverband Deutscher Unternehmensberater BDU e.V.: "Honorarstudie 2013", quoted from http://www.juniorconsultant.net/karriereplanung/honorare-tagessaetze-und-gehaelter/ (last accessed on 11.5.2015).

JUVE offer indications (at least for the German market);[98] according to these, the fixed, average hourly rates in German law firms lie between 230 and 270 euros for associates, and between 280 and 380 euros for partners.[99] It must nevertheless be assumed that, in view of the high level of specialisation of Brussels law firms and national law firms working in the European sector, significantly higher hourly rates will be agreed; charges in excess of 250 euros for associates and over 500 euros for partners appear realistic here. High six-figure sums can therefore be quickly run up for complex legal expert reports, supporting a hearing process or even the production of entire (commented) draft laws.

6.4.1.3.3.3 *Governmental relations agencies*

As has been explained, governmental relations agencies are focussed on process-oriented services, i.e. they do not primarily deliver content, but instead above all provide access to decision-makers, convey information and formulate (procedural) communication strategies. Their work is therefore more structural than merely project-related. As in the case of public affairs agencies, the option of purely variable, i.e. hourly or per diem rate-based, remuneration is available here. In this regard, reference must be made to the explanations in the preceding section.

However, it must be remembered that – in contrast to content-related activity, e.g. the production of a written analysis – neither the effort involved nor the value of the service are frequently reflected in the units of time spent in the individual case or the remuneration paid for this. In extreme cases, a corporate concern can be conveyed in a matter of minutes, for example through a successful telephone call via a high-ranking governmental relations agency contact. If this were invoiced on an hourly basis, the actual worth of the service which is performed would not be measured correctly: the governmental relations agency may well have performed an extremely valuable service for its client, and would receive 100 euros – if an hourly rate of 400 euros is taken as the basis, for example.

Apart from this fee discrepancy, such a calculation would also disregard the governmental relations agency's effort: it has usually taken years to develop this corresponding contact; nor is its activity limited merely to the one-way conveyance of the company's own needs to political decision-makers. Instead, it must be taken into consideration that an EU-wide network also has to be maintained outside of client assignments, which involves significant costs. Network maintenance measures (which are, of course, legal and transparent) range from the (often time consuming and cost intensive) collection and forwarding of information of importance to the decision-maker, also outside of specific customer projects, up to and including attending political events. These measures are crucial factors for successful lobbying.

---

98 See JUVE (2015).
99 Whereby this, as has already been mentioned, involves figures across all fields of "standard", i.e. non-lobbying, legal consultancy.

Against this background, some agencies have switched to combined remuneration models. The agreement of a fixed full cost flat rate (which usually has to be paid on a monthly basis) is necessary in addition to variable remuneration components. Project-related hourly and contingency fees are also possible. Above all, the full cost flat rate, in addition to which the work actually undertaken must also be paid (in part, the allotted number of hours already contained in the full cost flat rate is also agreed), is common, particularly in the case of agencies which work regularly or over a longer period of time for a company, i.e. they are implemented structurally. Lower hourly rates are then to be paid regularly in compensation for the payment of a full cost flat rate, as the service provider's material and back-office costs otherwise contained therein are already remunerated through the flat rate, at least in part.

The level of the full cost flat rate is agreed between the contract partners in each individual case, for which reason no generally applicable statements are possible here. Besides the complexity of the assigned tasks, the allotted number of hours included and other factors, the issue of the service provider's possible industry exclusivity ("only one interest") is of great importance in terms of the specific level of the flat rate. If the service provider works exclusively for just one company within a specific industry, it will regularly seek additional remuneration for this – since it is missing out (subject to corresponding demand) on turnover from further contracts with the client's competitors (opportunity costs). Corresponding exclusivity may be attractive for the company due to two reasons: firstly, the risk of information leaks between the service provider's individual customer relationships can be ruled out in this manner. Whilst a professional agency can and will

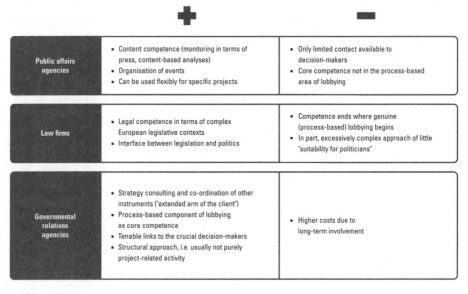

Figure 6.10: Comparison of external service models

guarantee this through Chinese walls, ultimate security can only be ensured by excluding competition. Secondly, the company also ensures the exclusivity of the service provider's contacts through the "only one interest" clause. In an area in which success is extensively dependent on the quality of inroads to decision-makers at the legislative and executive level, this factor should not be underestimated.

6.4.2 Process-oriented instruments

The process-oriented instruments which can be used to specifically undertake lobbying can basically be subdivided into two categories (see Figure 6.11). Firstly, these are the *mono* process-oriented instruments, which are only used by the lobbyist vis-à-vis an individual Member of Parliament, civil servant or other addressee. Secondly, there are the *poly* process-oriented instruments, which can be employed vis-à-vis several addressees, including addressees from various institutions.

Each of the above described structural instruments is fundamentally able to apply all of the following process-oriented instruments for lobbying. However, individual differences arise in terms of the realisation of effective lobbying, e. g. due to the size of an association or the macroeconomic importance of a company with its own representative office. This can lead to preferences as to which process-

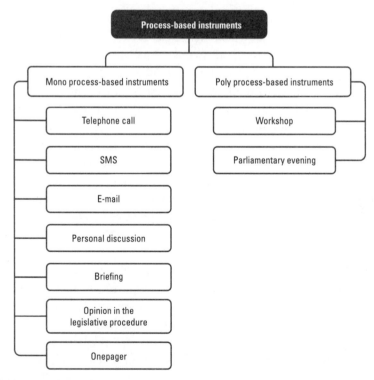

Figure 6.11: Process-oriented lobbying instruments

oriented instrument should be used in each case to achieve the objective in day-to-day business. The mono process-oriented instruments for exchanging information will be analysed first.

6.4.2.1 Mono process-oriented instruments

It must be stated in advance that the mono process-oriented instruments can be transformed very easily into poly process-oriented instruments with the aid of technology. For example, a telephone call can also be aimed at a (small) group of addressees by means of a telephone conference. SMS can be sent to more than just one person, and E-mails can be very easily addressed to a larger group of persons using the cc (carbon copy) and bcc (blind carbon copy) functions or via E-mail distribution lists. One-on-one meetings can also be easily extended to group meetings, etc. In principle, however, the following instruments are always aimed at one recipient. Apart from the caller, the majority of telephone calls only have one other participant. SMS and E-mails are also usually addressed to just one person or a very small group of addressees, with the result that these instruments are categorised as mono process-oriented here. Nevertheless, one should be constantly aware of the fact that they can be very quickly extended to poly process-oriented instruments with all of their advantages and disadvantages.

6.4.2.1.1 Telephone call

The telephone call is probably the most frequently used mono process-oriented lobbying instrument. Regular telephone contact between the lobbyist and elected representatives or civil servants leads to the mutual giving and receiving of information. By transferring objective information which falls into the decision-maker's sphere of interests, the lobbyist can establish a reputation as a reliable provider of information with the person concerned over a certain period of time. The lobbyist, too, can also obtain valuable information, for example on the status of a legislative procedure, which enables him to act specifically and quickly or which may be of benefit elsewhere. Particularly when a partnership-based relationship of trust already exists between the lobbyist and his addressee, the direct transfer of, or the request for, information for specific lobbying is more likely be successful than such an attempt by a different, unknown lobbyist.

6.4.2.1.2 SMS

It may come as a surprise that SMS is listed here as a communication tool, but the advantages are clear. Content can be transported quickly, without complications and personally using SMS. It is therefore also very popular amongst political decision-makers due to its handy format. One well known example is the Federal Chancellor, Angela Merkel, who sends hundreds of short messages each week.[100] The SMS is important for fast, direct contact which simultaneously guar-

---

100 See Quadbeck (2013).

antees a certain degree of confidentiality. Of course, the content has to be short and to the point; in practice, this instrument is thus more suitable for supplementing or confirming information which is already available. By nature, the short messages are not therefore suitable for conveying more extensive, complex issues. The prerequisite for SMS contact is in any case the existence of a personal basis which permits this form of less formal communication. After all, the contact's mobile phone number is required; higher-ranking persons will, of course, only issue this selectively.

6.4.2.1.3 E-mail

Next to the telephone call, the E-mail is the most frequently used mono process-oriented lobbying instrument; its main advantage is the speed with which information can be transferred.[101] It has therefore extensively replaced letters as a common mono process-oriented instrument. However, the E-mail is only suitable for requesting information. As an instrument, E-mail does not enable the establishment of any personal connection between the actors, and is therefore unsuitable for establishing trust between the parties concerned, which is essential to effective lobbying. In contrast to personal discussions, the Member of Parliament or civil servant cannot draw conclusions from his dialogue partner's manner or behavioural signals, or assess the trustworthiness of the information which is obtained. In many cases, the instrument of E-mail does not therefore enable active lobbying, nor is the receipt of anything more than objective, rather superficial information to be anticipated via E-mail.

One aspect of E-mail communication which requires particular emphasis is the level (lack) of security offered by this form of communication; of course, this is also essentially of great importance to all other, electronic and non-electronic, methods of transfer. Not only since it was revealed that electronic data traffic monitoring is undertaken by the secret services (such as the NSA scandal) has it been apparent that E-mails can also be read relatively easily by unauthorised third parties. If the message is not encrypted, it is basically transferred in plain text form, and can therefore be read or even modified in the data transfer systems.[102] In principle, an E-mail is therefore similar to a postcard, which can also be read without authorisation at any time through its entire transportation process. Data can be read on all IT systems via which they are transferred, or can even be altered unnoticed if they are not cryptographically secured. A certain level of protection is only offered by complex end-to-end encryption, but this is only rarely likely to be available in practice. The possibility that information may fall into the wrong hands should always be considered when communicating confidential content, most especially when using E-mail.

---

101 See Sebaldt (2007), p. 113: "Lobbying from a distance".
102 See Federal Office for Information Security (2005).

6.4.2.1.4 *Personal discussion*

Visiting the lobbying addressees, for example parliamentarians or Commission officials, in the respective institutions may also be appropriate. This can lead to an informal discussion between members of parliament or civil servants and the lobbyist, during which information is exchanged to mutual advantage. From the point of view of politicians and Commission officials, a personal discussion is essentially the preferred basis for information exchange.[103] As a general rule, however, this instrument is only suitable if there is genuinely a justified cause for a visit, particularly since this ultimately takes up considerably more of the decision-maker's time than e. g. a telephone call with the same content. Under no circumstances should the lobbyist waste his dialogue partner's time, in the truest sense of the word, with trivialities.

A visit in the European Parliament is particularly favourable, since it is easy to become familiar with further persons via an acquaintance in this location, in which all parliamentarians congregate, and therefore establish personal relationships with them. Conversely, the civil servants of the individual Directorates General within the Commission usually have their offices in various buildings; the likelihood of meeting others via civil servants of one's acquaintance is therefore more limited here (usually limited to the respective Directorate General).

One further advantage for effective lobbying in person, in comparison with a telephone call, lies in the fact that the lobbyist can bring his personality to bear and possibly enhance his power of persuasion through his personal appearance and his personality. The lobbyist can also draw helpful conclusions from his dialogue partner's behaviour, such as his gestures and facial expressions, and can accordingly adapt his own behaviour easily. It should additionally be noted that skilfully addressing decision-makers in person can frequently also lead to success, whereas telephone calls may be warded off by the addressee's receptionist.

Conversely, the disadvantage of (excessively) frequent visits is that they may be perceived as obtrusive.

6.4.2.1.5 *Briefing*

The briefing is a similar instrument. A briefing is the provision of information to the decision-maker for a specific issue during the early preparatory phase of decisions, i.e. even before a draft law, White Paper or Green Paper on the respective concern is available. Such information is usually readily accepted: it must be realised that parliamentarians, in particular, only have a relatively small administrative organisation and consequently – due to a lack of information processed for them – prepare for a pan-European legislative process with only a limited knowledge of the issue which is being dealt with in some cases. The briefing provides the

---

103 See Burson Marsteller (2013), p. 18.

decision-maker with access to objective information from an authoritative source, namely the companies' practical experience; he would otherwise be unlikely to include this information in his considerations, and thus extends the scope of his knowledge regarding the issue.

The briefing requires that the decision-maker is already aware of the lobbyist's corresponding reputation, so that he is interested in the lobbyist's information on the specific issue and gives him his attention. The effectiveness of the briefing is to be regarded as extensively dependent on the selected structural lobbying instrument. Like the lobbyist of a company or an external service provider, who have gained a reputation as competent partners to the decision-maker in question, the representative of a large and important association can also achieve success here. Conversely, the efforts of other service providers or representatives of less important associations, which do not have a corresponding reputation either due to their size or as a result of their previous co-operation with the respective civil servant or Member of Parliament, may be doomed to failure.

6.4.2.1.6 Opinion in the legislative procedure

The opinion is an addition to the briefing. This instrument can be used when a draft, which a company would like to support (or have supported) in the lobbying process, is already available from the institutions in a legislative procedure. Some opinions are submitted unsolicited, some following a request. The Commission, in particular, makes every effort to listen to the biggest associations which are affected, and also companies, regarding an issue, and therefore occasionally requests opinions itself.[104]

Nevertheless, this will occasionally be of little use to a company which wants to specifically represent its own interests. It is therefore often appropriate to submit a separate, unsolicited, opinion to the decision-makers. This firstly necessitates that the company is adequately informed, as quickly as possible, about the official submissions through its structural lobbying instruments. The explanations pertaining to the briefing also apply accordingly if the opinion is to be successful: as a general rule, effective lobbying necessitates either such macroeconomic weight on the part of the company or the lobbyist, or the acquisition of a corresponding reputation, so that attention is given to the presented position.

Clear and understandable formulation is vital in the case of such written input. At European level, attention should always be paid to the addressee's linguistic options: texts should always be written in English, and additionally in the contact person's mother tongue if necessary. In particular, unsolicited submissions should be kept as short as possible.

---

104 One example of many is the "public consultation on patents and standards: a modern framework for standardisation involving intellectual property rights", http://ec.europa.eu/enterprise/newsroom/cf/itemdetail.cfm?item_id=7833 (last accessed on 16.2.2015).

6.4.2.1.7 Onepager

In contrast to all of the above described instruments, which usually indicate the author or the source of the information and arguments, a onepager is an informal communication tool in which information and arguments concerning an issue are summarised "on a white sheet of paper". This has nothing to do with avoiding the public or with secrecy, but is instead intended solely to facilitate use in the continued communication process from the perspective of the decision-maker to whom the onepager is addressed. He can submit it to his own dialogue partners for discussion, without disclosing the source of the text at the same time, which may be strategically unfavourable. Secondly, it is a matter of fact that the quality and power of persuasion of an argument is never evaluated "in a vacuum", but always depending on the environment from which the argument originates. For example, the argument that the prescription of generic drugs is extremely cost-saving in comparison with the original preparations, and that this should therefore be specifically encouraged by law, will not sound especially credible if it is put forth by a generic drug manufacturer or a health insurance company: whilst the former may well be assumed to be pursuing its own interests in the form of its generation of profits, the latter would be faced with the accusation of economy measures at the expense of the health of its insured members. Objectively, however, the argument of greater economy is convincing in many (but not all) cases. If it is therefore put forth by an actor not suspected of pursuing his own interests – such as a recognised health politician – the debate is much more likely to focus on the facts.

In a onepager, the lobbyist is additionally able to demonstrate that its concern does not only apply to its client's individual interest, but that more extensive, factual arguments also speak in favour of this position. A onepager always argues from the perspective of the addressee, and thus from a sphere which may well differ completely from the client's field of interests. Whilst a legislative amendment desired by the client may, above all, possibly have economic advantages for the client itself, it may – when regarded from a different perspective – also offer advantages to the general public, such as the improved provision of a service to the population, improvements in data protection, the preservation of jobs or positive financial effects.

This change of perspective is crucial if only one decision-maker position regarded as being in the common interest can be communicated in the long term, and can be successfully represented in a decision-making process. If difficulties are in turn revealed during the perspective change, this is also an indication of the position's implementation feasibility. The perspective change therefore also acts as a feasibility check.

This perspective change is not always easy to accomplish, as it demands extensive imagination, empathy and understanding for decision theory, cultural, linguistic, interinstitutional, cross-member state and party political aspects, etc. Added to this is the human disposition of believing, due to personal involvement, that one's own positions are without alternative and thus interpreting them as the only possible perspective. This again reveals the problem of the two different spheres based on virtually opposing premises, namely that of politics on the one hand and that of the economy or a company on the other hand. Overcoming this dichotomy from one side is difficult. It necessitates the competence and performance of a professional lobbyist who, as an intermediary, is able to connect both spheres with their respective perceptions and bring about the perspective change (see Chapter 10).

The ideal structure of a onepager is very difficult to describe in general terms. Three basic rules should always be taken into consideration:

- Firstly, the author of the document should obtain precise information on the background, the prior knowledge and the perspectives of possible addressees. Not only does this define the information requirement that is to be met by the document: a specialist politician or a civil servant who has been dealing with this issue for a long while does not have to be presented with the genesis of a legislative initiative together with an assessment of its consequences at great length; he would be bored, and would justifiably feel undervalued. Ideally, a document should start precisely at the point at which the addressee requires information – the volume of text requiring the attention of a top politician or civil servant is too extensive, and his time too precious, to have to deal with what he already knows. Like a lawyer, who will attempt to pick out from a procedural document the arguments in favour of his client from the perspective of the judge, and to weaken the opposing side's arguments, a lobbyist will attempt to make clear the points which are significant from the point of view of his opposite number and to argue them accordingly.
- Secondly, the author should be aware of the limited amount of time available to the addressee. Even an outstandingly written, coherent document with understandable arguments will prove ineffective in the "market of opinions" if it exceeds a certain maximum length or a certain level of complexity. This is not to imply that the addressee would be unable to understand the content: he simply does not have the time. It must be taken into consideration that a top politician or civil servant often has to deal with several hundred pages of text per day, from the press reviews and personal correspondence to a variety of discussion papers and opinions. In the light of this, a line of argument requiring more than one to two pages of text to describe it will be very unlikely to be taken note of effectively.
- Thirdly – one of the most important aspects – the document's content must be convincing. This not only refers to its coherence *per se*; instead, the arguments must also always deal with the counter-arguments, or must at least not disregard these. Honesty and professionalism also pay dividends here: since an issue is usually dealt with by various interest groups, it is highly probable that several

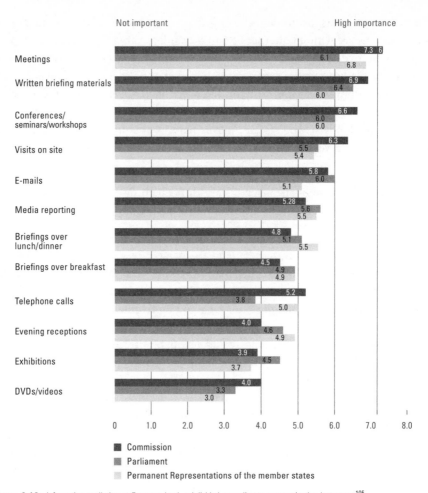

Figure 6.12: Information mediation at European level, subdivided according to communication instrument[105]

discussion papers will also be submitted to an addressee. The discovery of inconsistencies or objective inaccuracies would not then lag far behind; the lobbyist's image and credibility would be significantly damaged.

To meet these requirements, a lobbyist should subject important documents to a quality test, i.e. he should present them to former officials or elected representatives whom he trusts and for whom this issue does not represent a conflict of interests. They are usually able to, firstly, determine very clearly whether a document is aimed at the correct recipient and corresponds to his standpoint, and secondly, (with the unadulterated perspective of an unaffected third party) assess the political saliency of the text and its arguments in detail. Above all, this can be used to authentically check whether, and the extent to which, the necessary change of perspective towards the common good has succeeded.

---

105 Burson Marsteller (2013), p. 18.

The practical importance of written briefing materials (e. g. onepagers) in day-to-day lobbying is extremely high, as shown by a survey conducted in 2013 by the public affairs agency Burson-Marsteller in the Commission, the Parliament and the Permanent Representations of the member states (see Figure 6.12): they are the second most important information instrument after personal meetings.

6.4.2.2 Poly process-oriented instruments

6.4.2.2.1 Workshop

One poly process-oriented instrument is the political workshop. Although it has been declining in importance since the 1990s, it is still used primarily by corporate representative offices and other content-oriented lobbying organisations. In essence, it is a cross-institutional information and discussion event on a specific issue which is usually conducted by or on behalf of a company, association or organisation, and in which the competent representatives of the Commission and the Parliament as well as the company take part. The purpose of such a workshop is to provide the decision-makers with expert and practical knowledge from the company. It is often helpful to have a neutral person with an outstanding reputation and a similar technical background to conduct the workshop. This places the corporate interest in the background vis-à-vis the politicians and civil servants, with the result that they are more likely to indicate their willingness to take part. The particular advantage of this lobbying instrument is the bundling of communication. The relevant civil servants, politicians and experts are seated around one table, and are able to discuss the individual aspects of the issue with one another immediately and without loss of time due to the mutual forwarding of position papers. Objective information and discussion also enhance the corporate representatives' professional authority amongst the representatives of the EU institutions, which is advantageous to their reputation for the future. In this sense, the workshop can also be used as an instrument for polishing the company's image in Brussels at the same time.

6.4.2.2.2 Parliamentary evening

The parliamentary evening is a further option. This is perhaps the most familiar of the poly process-oriented instruments, and is very often used. This therefore occasionally leads to a surfeit, with the result that the invited guests often have the choice between several events on one and the same evening. The parliamentary evening is institution-specific and is above all aimed primarily at the Members of the Parliament and their employees. Commission officials who may be of interest to the company may also be invited if necessary.

The purpose of such an evening is to enable the company's representatives to engage in general dialogue with the parliamentarians and make them familiar to one another. It is therefore used more for public relations work than for specific lobbying in the actual sense; however, image management and the maintenance of contacts are of the utmost importance to a company's reputation and thus to the potential success of lobbying. As a parliamentary evening does not usually involve a specific issue, selection of the participating members of parliament according to their committee membership is not vitally necessary either. Instead, the evening should be used to raise the company's profile in general.

A parliamentary evening is undoubtedly a particularly challenging form of political event, whose success is dependent on highly professional preparation. The parliamentarians and civil servants are faced by a wide and demanding selection of evening events, particularly during the session weeks. In addition, these persons are usually used to the highest of standards – on the one hand in functional terms, and on the other hand in terms of the attention paid to them by a host. The organisers of a parliamentary evening should be aware of these high standards if they wish to successfully enhance their standing and their reputation by means of such an event. The long-term and careful planning of such an evening begins with setting a date, which should be done a minimum of six months in advance. Such an event must always be conducted in a week during which the European Parliament is in session (in Brussels or Strasbourg), as the members of parliament may otherwise be in their home member states, for instance. In addition, the date should be checked in terms of possible, important meeting dates to prevent events from overlapping. At this point, it is also advisable to ask a number of selected members of parliament whether the scheduled date would essentially be favourable. Whether other such events are possibly being scheduled on the possible dates should also be clarified if possible. A great deal of care should also be given to the choice of event location. This may be an hotel with suitable facilities located in the vicinity of the European Parliament, for instance. Once the date has been set, prior notification should be sent as quickly as possible to the group of addressees, together with the polite request to keep the announced date free if possible. It is additionally sensible to undertake lobbying on one's own behalf in this case: an attempt should be made to obtain an early commitment from high-ranking members of parliament,such as the chairpersons of the political groups in the European Parliament, since experience has shown that this increases the attractiveness of the event to the other members of parliament. The actual invitations to the parliamentary evening should be sent approximately three months prior to the event, followed by a reminder closer to the event.

All of this shows how important and extensive good preparation of a parliamentary evening is. The very highest of standards must also be ensured in its performance. It is crucial to remember that a parliamentary evening also requires professional expertise in order to achieve the desired effect within the framework of lobbying.

6.5 Implementation in practice: overall model for structuring effective and efficient lobbying

Against the backdrop of the instruments described in the above, the following section will now deal with implementation in practice – how should a company go about representing its interests? Which combination of the different (structural) instruments offers the optimal mix so that the process-oriented instruments are successful? In other words, what form can a lobbying strategy which is effective and makes efficient use of resources have – in both structural and project-related terms?

To achieve this, the strengths and weaknesses of the individual instruments will first be described on the basis of a quality benchmark, formulated in seven points, for effective lobbying (see Section 6.5.1). Optimal co-ordination of the different activities in the company will be dealt with in a second step (see Section 6.5.2): where should responsibilities be located in the company; how can seamless and resilient structures be established? The third step will then deal with taking stock and the company's subsequent structural foundation in the area of lobbying (see Section 6.5.3): what is the company-specific requirement profile? Which contacts and working relationships are available? Which deficits exist, what image does the company have amongst politicians and the administration? Finally, step four will clearly describe the project-specific establishment of a lobbying strategy (see Section 6.5.4).

6.5.1 Setting quality benchmarks: key elements of effective lobbying for a company

There is undoubtedly no patent recipe for good lobbying – the requirements of each individual industry, each individual company and each individual project are too different. Nevertheless, some key elements can be stated, the quality benchmarks of lobbying, so to speak: lobbying cannot amount to nothing more than developing concepts which "sound great" and then introducing these into the area of the legislative and executive level via more or less random contacts. Good lobbying instead necessitates a cumulatively outstanding supply of information, a feel for timing (see the explanations in Section 3.5 concerning the concept of time slots in lobbying), trustworthy contacts, enthusiasm and assertiveness – if one of these aspects is missing, the company will fail to achieve its objectives, or will only do so by chance.

The following therefore establishes a quality benchmark encompassing seven points. Each of these points will then be briefly explained from the perspective of the structural lobbying instruments: can the respective instrument meet the requirements or are there significant deficits?

Quality benchmarks for lobbying amongst the EU institutions
1. Availability of sources for continuous, extensive **information procurement** and the **identification** of **decision-making processes** based on functioning interconnectedness in the institutions
2. Ability to draw the **correct conclusions** from the information obtained in this manner and to take action at the **right time** (timing)
3. **Tenable, trusting links** to the **responsible** civil servants and elected representatives, not limited solely to randomly distributed actors, but covering a variety of EU committees and institutions (European Parliament, Directorates General of the Commission, etc.)
4. Being in a position to address these contacts **in good time**, i.e. usually quickly
5. Ability to trigger the civil servant's or elected representative's **genuine interest** in the respective concern
6. Possibility of following up or querying the responsible civil servant or elected representative, i.e. for the **longer-term support** of a decision-making process
7. Possibility of contacting the civil servant or elected representative **even when under tremendous time pressure**

Figure 6.13: Quality benchmarks for effective lobbying

These encompass the following individual points:

- *Availability of sources for continuous, extensive information procurement and the identification of decision-making processes based on functioning interconnectedness in the institutions:* the use of an association for covering the "basic requirements" of lobbying is recommended here, particularly due to the breadth of the association-based information approach. An association has very good formal access to the EU institutions – at least if it has the corresponding size and reputation – and thus guarantees a continuous flow of information regarding all public or internal processes at European level. Association membership also ensures, or at least extensively facilitates, involvement in formal participation processes at European level (hearings, etc.). An association appears less suitable for mediating the specific interests and issues of individual member companies. Nor is it always easy for an association to gain access to informal flows of information. The association is often hindered by the heterogeneity problem, which has already been described exhaustively: due purely to factual reasons, it is impossible for an association representative to undertake monitoring for each individual member company (or to identify the corresponding issues at all) and then request detailed information wherever possible. Associations also frequently have a formalised lobbying approach: the provision of information to and from associations generally functions – the corporatistic approach from the member states raises its head here – more readily via official channels than through confidential background discussions. Other instruments therefore appear more suitable, particularly for these points: company-specific monitoring activities limited to generally accessible sources can also be undertaken, for example, by a public affairs agency (a corporate representative office, usually with lower staffing levels, would simply not have the time required to accomplish this in more complex areas), whilst the contacts required for detailed consolidation in the individual case will usually only be available from a corporate representative or an external service provider (governmental relations agency). A law firm should only be implemented in legally complex areas – particularly for the legal evaluation of news and information.

In short, the association is used to supply basic information; public affairs agencies and law firms are used for specific monitoring for individual companies; corporate representative offices and governmental relations agencies are predestined for consolidation and subsequent research in individual cases.

- *Ability to draw the correct conclusions from the information obtained in this manner and to take action at the right time (timing):* the focus here lies on transferring the content-related arguments into processes, i.e. filtering essential information for the company and drawing strategic conclusions for its political position. The information which is obtained can be used, for example, to determine when, how, where and with whom communication is to be undertaken (timing). An association can only guarantee a certain service in this regard, too; due to the heterogeneity problem, however, it encounters its limitations as soon as conflicting interests arise internally. Added to this is that, frequently, an association first has to process new information to meet the needs of the target group due to the diversity of its member companies. However, this deceleration of the (frequently institutionalised) flow of information, e.g. via newsletters, regular briefings, etc. equates to a serious disadvantage in terms of the desired minimisation of the factor of time. Public affairs agencies and law firms implemented by the company can compensate for this to a certain degree, but they too are usually lacking in the procedural know-how to be able to assess the practical, political consequences.

  Accordingly corporate representative offices and governmental relations agencies are also required here; with their procedural expertise (process support competence), the latter, in particular, touch on a (strategic) core competence for correct timing.

- *Trusting contact with the responsible civil servants and elected representatives, not limited solely to randomly distributed actors, but covering a variety of EU committees and institutions (European Parliament, Directorates General of the Commission, etc.):* associations also offer a valuable, basic supply in this case – via the institutionalised channels of communication, they usually have reliable access to a high number of relevant decision-makers. However, it is hardly possible to open up this access exclusively for a single company: by virtue of his office, an association representative is obligated to all association members; in the event of conflicting interests, he cannot dedicate himself to one individual actor without risking his credibility as a representative of an interest group. PA agencies and law firms are usually unsuitable, since their core competence lies more in the content-oriented than in the procedural area. Between corporate representative offices and governmental relations agencies, there are a number of arguments in favour of external service providers: they usually have more tenable networks and, if in doubt, can (in connection with their cross-industry activity for various clients) also contact actors which are only indirectly of relevance to the company's concerns and cannot therefore be covered by the corporate representative during his daily work due to reasons of capacity.

Ultimately, the combination of the networks of corporate representatives and external service providers offers the greatest likelihood of success here.

- *Being in a position to be able to address these contacts in good time, i.e. usually quickly:* in practice, this – purely procedural – core requirement of effective lobbying can virtually only be met by corporate representative offices and governmental relations agencies. The crucial advantages offered by the external service provider may be both the variety of access options available to it and its greater likelihood of introducing subjective corporate interests into the debate, not as such, but instead using objectively credible arguments: as a "lobbyist in both directions", it is therefore frequently more likely to be listened to than a representative sailing under the corporate flag.

- *Ability to trigger the civil servant's or elected representative's genuine interest in the respective concern:* methodical skills are required here rather than characteristics to be specifically assigned to a structural instrument. It has already been explained that the core element of good lobbying involves conveying to one's opposite number why the fulfilment of a concern also lies in the interest to be safeguarded by this party. A Member of Parliament is always interested in the economic success of the companies located in his constituency; a Directorate General will always be interested in the fiscal effects of an initiative; a Member of Parliament or a civil servant can make a concern "his" issue and therefore raise his profile within his own institution. In this regard, each of the lobbying instruments must constantly scrutinise and adjust its own arguments in order not to lose sight of the addressee.

- *Possibility of following up and querying, i.e. for the longer-term support of a decision-making process; possibility of contacting the civil servant or elected representative even when under tremendous time pressure:* tenable networks are required to be able to continuously support a concern without fatiguing or even enervating the responsible officials and elected representatives. The decision-maker must be aware of the lobbyist's professionalism and reliability based on his own experience; he must be able to recognise the advantage of the cooperation to his own work and his own institution. In addition to the previously mentioned ability to change perspectives, this requires that he has already frequently come into contact with the lobbyist regarding content, or will do so, in matters unrelated to the specific concern: for example, a corporate representative who comes into contact with a responsible official for the first time in an export regulation issue will run into difficulties.

The working relationships of a governmental relations agency, which are not limited to just one client, in turn offer a clear advantage here.

This result shows the clear distribution of the individual instruments' strengths and weaknesses: above all, corporate representative offices, associations, public affairs agencies and law firms have content-related strengths. For successful lobbying, these must be supplemented with the process competence offered by governmental relations agencies. Whilst the association ensures an (industry-oriented) basic supply in the area of lobbying, external service providers or a separate corporate representative office are required for company-specific concerns. Further content-related work, such as political analyses, trend research or legal assessments, can best be covered by corporate representative offices, public affairs agencies and law firms. Conversely, the governmental relations agency's strength lies in the procedural area: it structures and supports its clients' lobbying, and performs the actual core activity of introducing the interests into the legislative and executive level.

6.5.2 Co-ordination of the instruments by the company

The variety of available instruments, which – as has just been explained – are sensible in their respective competence areas, must be optimally coordinated to reduce redundancies and frictional losses.[106] The communication and decision-making structures both within the company and between the implemented structural instruments are therefore also crucial to the effectiveness of one of the various structural lobbying approaches. Just as for strategic decisions in corporate departments such as product development, purchasing or sales, a company therefore requires a separate, structurally organised "lobbying" department and, accordingly, also a specific contact person for matters pertaining to this. This internal decision-maker, who distinguishes between the tasks to be performed and co-ordinates between the individual providers, will be referred to as the co-ordinator in the following.

The point in the corporate hierarchy at which the co-ordinator should be located is also dependent on the strategic orientation of the lobbying approach in addition to the type of corporate organisation structure. The co-ordinator should always be located as close to the company's management level as possible in the corporate hierarchy, and also in disciplinary terms, particularly when the lobbying instruments are implemented to obtain information as the basis for far-reaching corporate planning decisions: if lobbying touches on corporate strategy aspects, a comprehensive overview of the overall corporate situation and the option of being able to effectively trigger corresponding strategic shifts are crucial for effective and efficient co-ordination of the instruments.

---

106 With regard to the co-ordination and realignment of the instruments from an organisational science perspective, see Chapter 10.

Due to direct contact between the senior corporate management and the structural lobbying instruments, the co-ordinator therefore minimises the information flow's time lag. The risk of information loss or misallocation is also minimised as far as possible. Optimally, a member of the corporate management assumes the position of co-ordinator. Alternatively – this will be particularly essential in the case of major companies due to the corporate management's wealth of tasks – the co-ordinator should be directly subordinate to the corporate management in disciplinary terms. In addition to a personal advisor, this can be a separately established staff position or the head of the public relations/corporate communication department. In some major companies, the implementation of this knowledge has already led to the establishment of departments for "governmental relations", "governmental affairs" or "policy and agenda-setting"; these report directly – in organisational, content and disciplinary terms – to the corporate management, ideally the chief executive in the case of a publicly limited company.

A governmental relations agency appears to be predestined as the co-ordinator's "extended arm" (in addition to his own employees). Each content-related analysis and strategic decision in the field of lobbying inevitably requires a detailed assessment of what is politically possible (i.e. particularly in process terms). To be able to guarantee this continuously (the implementation feasibility of each concern

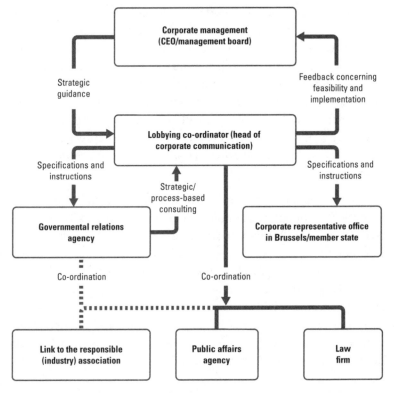

Figure 6.14: Co-ordination of the lobbying instrument mix by the company

should be informally checked before further efforts are undertaken), however, the co-ordinator is reliant on external service providers. Via its broad, ideally EU-wide, contact basis, a governmental relations agency can therefore provide important insights into the Brussels and EU political system (including that of the EU member states) even prior to the start of actual interest mediation. Specific – project-related – planning for the implementation of the various instruments can only be undertaken on such a decision-making basis.

6.5.3 Documentation of the starting point and objective: definition of a general corporate requirement profile in the field of lobbying

The co-ordinator's fundamental, and therefore most important, task is the development of a lobbying strategy specific to the company. A distinction must be made between five stages of development in this procedure (see Figure 6.15).

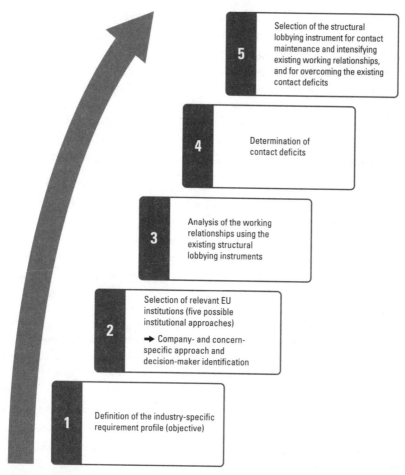

5 Selection of the structural lobbying instrument for contact maintenance and intensifying existing working relationships, and for overcoming the existing contact deficits

4 Determination of contact deficits

3 Analysis of the working relationships using the existing structural lobbying instruments

2 Selection of relevant EU institutions (five possible institutional approaches)

➡ Company- and concern-specific approach and decision-maker identification

1 Definition of the industry-specific requirement profile (objective)

Figure 6.15: Structural establishment of company-specific lobbying

In the first step, the company's industry- and company-specific requirement profile must be defined. At this stage, the definition will always be oriented primarily towards the company's respective industry and its product or service portfolio – naturally, this is where the fundamental direction is set whilst defining the company's interests. The lobbyist's commercial management know-how is required in defining a fundamental strategy, since diverse analytical methods are conceivable. One tool which is relatively simple but frequently used in the development of lobbying strategies is the SWOT analysis;[107] it can be used, for example, to determine risks to the company from the area of industry-specific regulation. Whether and the extent to which other policy areas from neighbouring sectors have to be included in the lobbying process must also be analysed precisely: it is not sufficient, for example, for an automotive company to restrict its activities to the sectors of technology, industry and commerce; instead, the areas of environment, energy and social policy may be important fields of activity under certain circumstances.

The problem analysis then results in corresponding proposals and solution approaches for the lobbying process or the company's fundamental position in the political arena. With a view to sustainable success, the company's superordinate (economic) objectives must always be taken into consideration to guarantee the congruent orientation of the entire corporate strategy. Conversely, it would be accordingly sensible to integrate the political interests into the corporate strategy insofar as is necessary. The long-term coherence of the company's focus and lobbying is guaranteed as a result of this. Of course, the ultimate decision regarding both the content of the solution approaches and their implementation is made by the company itself.

In a second stage, the institutional approaches which appear to be relevant to the company must then be selected from the five which are theoretically available at EU level, i.e. the Council of the EU, the Commission, the Parliament and (theoretically) the Economic and Social Committee and the Committee of the Regions. This results in the spectrum of relevant, company-specific, institutional approaches and therefore the decision-makers acting for the institutions.

The working relationships, i.e. links to relevant decision-makers, that already exist through the company's structural lobbying instruments must then be analysed. In this third stage, the prerequisites which are in place at the company in question attain their particular importance over and above the industry-specific requirements taken into consideration in the first stage.

---

107 A SWOT analysis (Strengths, Weaknesses, Opportunities and Threats) is a simple tool which is used above all in strategic management. It is used to analyse both internal corporate strengths and weaknesses and existing, external opportunities and threats pertaining to the company. The information acquired in this way should be used to support the company's future strategic orientation, e.g. with reference to its structure, portfolio decisions or – as is relevant in this case – questions concerning its positioning in the political arena.

This analysis is followed directly by the determination of contact deficits in a fourth step. These result from a comparison of the industry- and company-specific, relevant institutions and their respective decision-makers, as determined in the first and second stages, with the existing working relationship network analysed in the third stage.

The structural lobbying instruments which reveal the greatest suitability both for maintaining and intensifying already existing contacts in the working relationship network and for overcoming the determined contact deficits under the aspects of effectiveness and efficiency must be selected and implemented in a final, fifth, step. The analysis of the strengths and weaknesses of the respective instruments performed in the preceding sections should be used for strategic planning here.

6.5.4 Implementing and successfully undertaking lobbying projects: fundamental steps

Specific measures can only be implemented once a company has established internal decision-making structures in the area of lobbying, has achieved clarity regarding its interest situation and its own position in Brussels, and has analysed the options for using structural instruments. This applies both to activities which are to be categorised more as general image management in the political, public

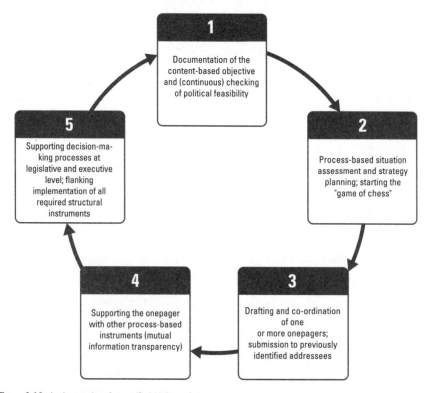

Figure 6.16: Implementation of a specific lobbying project

realm, such as receptions, presentations, conferences or parliamentary evenings, etc., and to specific initiatives for targeted interest mediation. Without the afore-mentioned stock taking, these are inefficient and ineffective, usually require ex-tensive resources and can – in the most unfavourable case – also break "political china". Practice shows that, unfortunately, such an approach is not infrequent – whether this is due to a lack of professionalism on the part of the contractors or a lack of co-ordination on the part of the clients.

How should a specific lobbying project therefore be approached? Of course, there are no patent recipes for this. However, five fundamental steps can be determined; these can be used as a guideline for planning and implementing structured lobby-ing (see Figure 6.16).

6.5.4.1 Documentation of the content-related objective and continuous checking of political feasibility

The project's content-related objective must be documented in the first step. This step must not be confused with the apodictic definition of a benchmark, since there is not just one individual player in the political arena in Brussels. As a gener-al rule, at least two interests, between which the legislative and executive level has to mediate, encounter one another – a completely normal, democratic process. At the same time, however, this necessitates a certain flexibility on the part of the company: one hundred percent realisation of its ideals is hardly realistic; compro-mise solutions are significantly more probable. A certain corridor, within which results which are desirable for the company may lie, should therefore be defined when setting objectives.

What sounds simple is often a task which overburdens actors without experience in Brussels in practice. Outside-in analyses are insufficient, i.e. assessments rely-ing solely on press statements or other manifestations of the views of political decision-makers. Firstly, public statements and actual convictions often lie miles apart. There is nothing illegitimate about this; it is simply a normal, strategic reac-tion by political decision-makers, who do not wish to show their hand without further ado in the political debate. Secondly, public opinion only represents a small part of the aspects essential to decision-making: the actors' personal connec-tions and interests, (often not immediately apparent) party political consider-ations and – a feature specific to Brussels – special, national considerations in the Europe of 28 member states make "simple" answers impossible.

A look behind the scenes appears unavoidable. However, companies are familiar with the necessity of such analyses from an entirely different area, namely that of market research. Before a new product is launched onto the market (often even before the actual development work has begun), companies attempt to decrypt the black box of "consumers" by means of customer surveys, focus groups and "test balloons", etc.: which products are received well, which have no chance of market success? "Political field research" in the area of lobbying, for which – as a result of its primarily procedural focus – a governmental relations agency should be used, functions in a very similar manner. In the sense of a corporate opinion-forming instrument, it is able to informally sound out or continuously check which objectives are achievable to what extent, and where adjustments should be made.

6.5.4.2 Procedural situation assessment and strategy planning

As soon as a feasibility analysis (which has to be updated constantly) has been performed, the "fellow players" on the European stage must be analysed precisely: how are the interests distributed, which other actors are active with which tools? Particularly at European level, this can therefore proceed in completely opposite directions even within one and the same industry, as the dispute surrounding binding CO_2 limit values for motor vehicles showed. Whilst the German automotive industry, whose product portfolio is focussed on larger vehicles, tended to strive towards more generous limit values, French and Italian manufacturers demanded tighter requirements, with vigorous support from their governments – which is highly understandable in commercial terms, since the lion's share of their vehicle fleets consists of sub-compact and compact class vehicles, which are naturally more economical. Determining this even in complex cases necessitates a joint effort by company (content-related side) and the governmental relations agency (procedural side).

A precise analysis of the relevant environment at the legislative and executive level is even more important. One initial step for doing this is to check the legal background of the ongoing procedure: who are the decision-makers concerned, when do which decisions have to be made, where are there possibilities for the legitimate introduction of interests (see Chapter 3)? The options for the latter range from formal participation opportunities such as consultations and hearings to directly addressing elected representatives and officials. A second step is to document one's own contacts which can be used for the specific project, and to assess what can be achieved via these contacts. The governmental relations agency also proves to be predestined for this task – e.g. in co-operation with the association and corporate representative office on the ground in Brussels.

6.5.4.3 Drafting and submitting one or more onepagers

In a third step, the company's content-related ideas must be transformed into a form which is comprehensible for the respective addressee. Such a document is more than simply a written description of one's own position. The change in perspective is central in this process (see also Section 6.4.2.1.7 and Chapter 10). It should not be forgotten that decision-makers at the legislative and executive level often have to make their decisions under time pressure. A concern which is comprehensibly described to them in a limited amount of space is often more likely to be positively received than an interest set down amidst a vast body of text which would require several hours of concentrated work to penetrate. In an individual case, a onepager is additionally the lobbyist's only option for communicating his concern: if he does not have direct contact with the respective decision-maker, but merely persons from his environment (e. g. a parliamentary group or person from the relevant MEP's country), he must lay out his objective so convincingly in this written document that further persuasion may possibly no longer be necessary. The onepager can also be used as a basis for arguments for third parties: particularly in the multi-level system of the EU, a lobbying strategy must not restrict itself only to the European level, but must also include the member state levels. Positions and arguments can also be introduced into the European process via the member states, whether this is achieved formally such as via the Council or informally via the political groups represented in the Parliament. The same also applies to the EU institutions: wherever possible, advocates from both the Commission and the Parliament should be won for one's own position, since practically all important legislative and decision-making procedures now require the involvement of both institutions (see Chapter 5).

6.5.4.4 Flanking the onepager with other structural and process-oriented instruments (mutual information transparency)

A onepager must only be the first step of a strategy – albeit a very significant one. All of the other instruments introduced beforehand must be implemented if this promises success. For example, corporate representatives can take part in formal hearings of the European Parliament; as a flanking measure, work (insofar as this appears sensible) can be undertaken on publicity campaigns via public affairs and public relations agencies. A law firm is required in an advisory capacity, particularly in the case of legally complex procedures and issues.

An association can be an institutional information source (e. g. during the course of hearings and consultations), and can also undertake formalised lobbying; the latter is especially possible when company-specific interests can be embedded in industry-specific or cross-industry interests.[108] Particularly in the case of publicly relevant issues, the political weight assigned to association opinions during hearings and legislative procedures can assume great significance. In qualification, the association's reduced assertiveness at the European level in comparison with their traditional position in the member states must also be pointed out here (see Section 6.4.1.1.4). Albeit more relevant to smaller companies, these additionally have the option of picking up on the association's preliminary work in their own lobbying. Legal analyses, discussion papers and public relations work, etc. are areas in which good work by an association can relieve the burden on a company.[109]

---

108 See Bender and Reulecke (2003), p. 175.
109 Bender and Reulecke (2003), pp. 175–176.

At the same time, this may lead to risks to the credibility of one's own position: to avoid contradictory statements on the part of the association and company, the company should always play as extensive a part as possible in its own association despite independent lobbying. Unfortunately, only a small number of the member companies genuinely play an active role in the work undertaken by many associations. This offers interesting opportunities, particularly for larger companies which undertake their own lobbying:[110] to a certain extent, the association can therefore be granted access to the company's own resources, for instance through the provision of discussion papers or information, etc. On the one hand, such active involvement enables the early detection of contradictory positions in the association, and allows them to be tacked as part of the association's opinion-forming processes. On the other hand, the company can introduce its own positions and – provided that at least some of its own arguments are asserted at association level – obtain strong backing for its own activities in Brussels.

Throughout all of this, the maintenance of mutual information transparency is absolutely essential. For example, a lobbyist must not only ensure that he obtains information from the officials and elected representatives in good time, but should also endeavour to share his information with the crucial decision-makers – only in co-ordination with the client, of course, to prevent the forwarding of confidential information. This is particularly important if the lobbyist is obligated to the principle of only one interest, since information could also be passed on to competitors. A very significant part of lobbying involves the exchange of information; as a general rule, one-way information streets do not function for very long.

6.5.4.5 Supporting decision-making processes at legislative and executive level

Often, a decision-making process or a legislative procedure takes several months or even years, placing high requirements on the presence and flexibility of both the company and its lobbyists. One's own position has to be constantly analysed and readjusted in the light of procedural developments. It is not sufficient to "inject" one's arguments into the process once and then await the (hopefully positive) result. Instead, continuous support of the decision-making processes in Brussels and the member states is required, in order to be able to recognise developments and trends at an early stage and use or repel them. The lobbying cycle is completed: the initially developed strategy may possibly have to be revised, changed situations and proceedings have to be taken into consideration, own lines of argument and onepagers have to be redrafted, etc.

In addition – an aspect which is overlooked even by major corporations in part – a company must also remain a "talking point in Brussels" above and beyond specific concerns and day-to-day problems. Only this ensures that contacts do not fade away, information sources do not dry up, and the company remains present as a trustworthy and reliable partner.

---

110 Bender and Reulecke (2003), pp. 177–178.

6.5.5 Conclusion

It has become clear that lobbying has to be planned meticulously and for the long term, in order to be able to achieve the desired success at the end of the day. First and foremost, the co-ordinator within the company itself is crucial: he must offer the far-sightedness necessary to be able to position his company correctly in the political arena. The involvement of an external process partner in the form of a governmental relations agency can provide him with vital support in both fundamentally positioning the company in the field of lobbying, and in structuring and undertaking specific projects, and is particularly able to cover the procedural share of the tasks. Nevertheless, a governmental relations agency does not render the other instruments – association, corporate representative office, public affairs agency and law firm – superfluous. Quite the opposite – optimal lobbying is a mix of the above instruments, whereby each of these should be implemented according to their individual strengths and weaknesses.

6.6 Summary

Chapter six analyses the instruments and methodology conceivable for targeted lobbying at European level. To recap, the starting point is formed by four questions:

- Who are conceivable lobbying actors (structural instruments)? What are their distinguishing characteristics, their costs, strengths and weaknesses?
- Which process-oriented instruments are available for lobbying, and how should they be used?
- In view of the outlined structural and process-oriented instruments, how should a company go about representing its interests in practice?
- What personal requirements ultimately have to be made on a lobbyist, irrespective of his client (association, company or external service provider)?

The most important results can be summarised as follows:

(1) Companies are not exclusively market participants, but instead interact with society and thus with the stakeholders (stakeholder groups) in a company's environment; these are able to exert a direct or indirect influence, e.g. through legal, particularly regulatory, measures. A precise knowledge of relevant social, political processes and the most important decision-makers is competition-relevant, and can give a company a considerable edge over its competitors. Actively structuring the environment is therefore crucial in the sense of corporate political responsibility. This means that a company must actively manage its environment and disclose its interests. Lobbying is a company's communication with its (political/executive) environment, particularly with society and politicians. This is accomplished through stakeholder man-

agement, which is used to continuously monitor and analyse the stakeholders' interests and potential. Stakeholder management is consequently a significant element of the corporate strategy and therefore also an important basis for further lobbying measures at the same time. In practice, stakeholder management encompasses three steps: the identification of relevant stakeholders, stakeholder mapping and information management.

(2) A distinction must be made between lobbying through collective and non-collective actors in structural terms: the former include associations and project-related groupings of several actors; the latter encompass corporate representative offices and external service providers (public affairs agencies, law firms and governmental relations agencies).

(3) According to estimates, approximately 32,500 lobbyists are working for companies and associations in Brussels alone, with this number set to grow. A significant increase in the number of non-collective actors has been seen recently.

(4) The general growth in demand on the one hand and the increase in the importance of non-collective actors on the other hand are attributable primarily to the progressive extension of the EU's powers, the increasing heterogenisation of corporate interests (resulting in a decline in the associations' cohesive force) and an upsurge in awareness concerning the importance of the decisions being made at European level.

(5) Association work in Brussels is undertaken by both European and national associations. The strengths of both lie in formal lobbying, e.g. as part of public hearings, and as a source of information and monitoring instrument for issues of relevance to industry.

(6) However the representation of corporate interests by associations reveals three weaknesses:

- Compulsion to reach a compromise within the association: the external representation of an interest is preceded by opinion-forming within the association, which often necessitates unsatisfactory compromises ("lowest common denominator") – especially at European level as a result of the further increase in the heterogeneity of interests. The consequence is increasing fragmentation of the association landscape, leading to a reduction in assertiveness (conflict between membership and influence logic).

- Lack of external "punch" on the part of the association: this internal compulsion to find compromise positions prevents the formation of a clear external profile or clear positions even in the case of controversial, detailed issues. Decision paths which are made complicated due to the institutions are not in harmony with a highly dynamic European decision-making environment. The result is a certain sluggishness in the political process.

- The member companies' instructions are not binding: in controversial issues (above and beyond the "lowest common denominator"), there is a risk of a member company's interests not being articulated.

(7) Larger companies have their own liaison offices (corporate representative offices) at EU level; according to estimates, there are currently around 300 such offices in Brussels. Above all, the corporate representative is the company's "face" in the political sphere of Brussels, but also mediates the relevance of European issues within the company, in order to ensure the necessary attention in the case of strategic decisions.

(8) In comparison with the association, a corporate representative offers the advantage of being bound by instructions; any dilution of the company's concerns due to the need to compromise is out of the question. The corporate representative is focussed on processes rather than content. The instrument's central weakness is that the company's contacts are (usually) bundled in one single actor: the trust afforded him by the legislative and executive level is lost on his departing from the company ("trust cannot be bequeathed").

(9) In addition to a corporate liaison office, external service providers are also possible lobbying instruments:

 – Law firms offer a service focussing on content at the interface between legislation and politics, e. g. advance legal analyses, legal policy monitoring and legal consulting support of EU legislative procedures. However, the law firms' political activity usually ends at the point at which actual lobbying begins: on the introduction of relevant interests into the political process.

 – The core competence of public affairs agencies also lies in the content-related rather than the procedural area: their service portfolio includes monitoring, content analyses, planning and execution of campaigns and events in the political sector.

 – Conversely, governmental relations agencies are primarily process partners, i. e. they are used for active lobbying with direct contact to the political decision-makers. Their process support competence offers several advantages in comparison with other structural instruments: firstly, there are no heterogeneity problems; the service is tailored to the client. Secondly, inroads to the decision-makers are not usually linked to individual persons (with the risk of personnel fluctuation); the risk of losing contacts is significantly reduced. Thirdly, the agencies work in various industries over long periods of time, resulting in a wide network and long-term, trusting working relationships with political decision-makers. The agencies therefore usually offer extensive expertise in terms of "European coalition building".

(10) Generalised statements concerning the costs of the various instruments for the company are very difficult. The national association's activities at EU level are not usually invoiced separately (or optionally) to the member companies, but are included in the costs of national membership. Costs of at least 0.5 – 1 million euros per year can be assumed for a separate corporate

representative office in Brussels. Costs for public affairs agencies and law firms are incurred on a project-related basis, and can therefore only be planned and calculated in the individual case. However, purely content-oriented lobbying alone is no longer sufficient for successful lobbying in the multi-level system of the EU since the Treaty of Lisbon came into effect. It must be supplemented by the process-oriented lobbying instruments of a governmental relations agency (see Chapter 10). Within the framework of long-term co-operation, some of these also levy full cost flat rates; hourly remuneration components usually also have to be calculated.

(11) The onepager, a discussion paper drawn up without any indication of authorship, which is forwarded to decision-makers to support one's own position, also requires mentioning in terms of the process-oriented instruments which are used as part of lobbying projects. Onepagers are firstly an important basis for the mediation of complex concerns which cannot be articulated by oral means alone; secondly they are often the only option for being able to present an issue in concentrated and pointed form to the addressed decision-maker. Objective arguments can persuade a decision-maker, irrespective of the underlying author. Above all, however, onepagers describe the concern from a public perspective.

(12) The decision on how – and particularly the structural instruments with which – a company intends to organise the representation of its interests in Brussels should be oriented towards a quality benchmark encompassing seven points: (i) availability of sources for continuous, extensive information procurement and the identification of decision-making processes based on functioning interconnectedness in the institutions; (ii) ability to draw the correct conclusions from the information obtained in this manner and to take action at the right time (timing); (iii) trusting contact with the responsible civil servants and elected representatives, not limited solely to randomly distributed actors, but covering a variety of EU committees and institutions (European Parliament, Directorates General of the Commission, etc.); (iv) being in a position to be able to address these contacts in good time, i. e. usually quickly; (v) ability to trigger the civil servant's or elected representative's genuine interest in the respective concern; (vi) possibility of following up or querying the responsible civil servant or elected representative, i. e. for the longer-term support of a decision-making process and (vii) possibility of contacting the civil servant or elected representative even when under tremendous time pressure.

(13) This result shows the clear distribution of the individual (content- and process-oriented) instruments' strengths and weaknesses: Whilst the association ensures an (industry-oriented) basic supply in the area of content-oriented lobbying, a separate corporate representative office or external service providers are required for company-specific concerns. Additional content-related work (e. g. political analyses or legal assessments) can there-

fore best be covered by public affairs agencies and law firms. Conversely, the governmental relations agency's strength lies in the procedural area: it structures and supports its clients' lobbying and performs the actual core activity of introducing the interests into the legislative and executive level. It is the necessary supplement to content-oriented lobbying.

(14) Co-ordination of the various structural instruments is absolutely crucial to their effectiveness. To achieve this, a separate "lobbying" department and, accordingly, also a separate contact person for all matters pertaining to this ("co-ordinator"), are recommended in the company. To ensure involvement in the corporate strategy, the co-ordinator should be positioned at management level (chairman of the management board/senior management).

(15) A governmental relations agency should be commissioned as the co-ordinator's "extended arm" in addition to his own employees or the company's own corporate representative office: each content-related analysis and strategic decision in the field of lobbying necessitates a detailed assessment of what is politically possible (i.e. particularly in process terms). Via its broad contact basis, the agency can provide important insights into the Brussels political system at an early stage in this case.

(16) The co-ordinator's fundamental task is the development of a specific corporate lobbying strategy. A five-stage procedure appears appropriate: (i) definition of the industry- and company-specific requirement profile; (ii) analysis of the EU institutions to be addressed and the decision-makers acting for these; (iii) determination of the existing working relationships with these decision-makers; (iv) determination of contact deficits and (v) selection of structural instruments for maintaining existing contacts or for overcoming the determined contact deficits.

(17) Specific lobbying projects are also planned and undertaken in five steps: (i) documentation of the content-related objective and continuous checking of political feasibility; (ii) procedural situation assessment and strategy planning; (iii) drafting one or more onepagers and submitting them to previously identified addressees; (iv) flanking the onepager with other structural and process-oriented instruments (mutual information transparency) and (v) supporting decision-making processes at legislative and executive level.

(18) The subjective requirements on a good lobbyist in Brussels can only be generalised to a limited extent. Good training, good contacts, social, linguistic and inter cultural skills, absolute integrity and professionalism are critical. Lobbying in Brussels is significantly more dynamic and offensive than in the member states due to the extensive competition between actors and the basic openness of the institutions; the competition is accordingly much fiercer. A lobbyist must establish a certain status, must be credible and must "make himself interesting" to both parties – the addressee and the client – (mutual information transparency), in order not to founder in view of the strong competition in the "market of opinions, positions and arguments".

Chapter 7 Training: ways to becoming a governmental relations manager

7.1 Introduction and question

The preceding chapters have outlined the particular challenges of modern lobbying in detail:

- The importance of process competence in the European structures of political decision-making and legislation, and the equally varied and complicated EU legislative procedure.
- The complexity of the EU political system.
- The specific methodology of governmental relations.
- Finally, the provision of support to companies and organisations in the observance of their (corporate/commercial) duty of care in averting risks caused by European legislative acts and measures, or acts and measures necessitated by European legislation.

In view of the complex task definitions and challenges, a detailed check is required to assess whether the (predominantly practical) current training adequately prepares a professional lobbyist for his work. Frequently, lobbyist training still proves to be fragmented and not sufficiently interdisciplinary. It is often lacking in the provision of the necessary process competence and the skills to manage processes efficiently in order to break down and reduce the increasing complexity. However, both (process competence and management) are crucial for a profound understanding of (and working in) complex systems such as the EU and for dealing with them.

This chapter will therefore deal with the following questions:

- What are the particular challenges faced by a lobbyist, especially a governmental relations manager who is focussed on process management?
- Are learning by doing or a lobbyist's own (previous) experience in the area of politics and/or administration (revolving door, i.e. actors' switching between politics and stakeholder groups) sufficient to overcome these challenges?
- Does the current (university) training offer adequate preparation to meet these challenges?
- How must training be structured in the future in order to prepare future lobbyists better for their daily work? In other words: what training does a governmental relations manager require?

7.2 Framework conditions and general requirements on a lobbyist

7.2.1 Breaking down and controlling increasing complexity

The globalised world of the 21st century is characterised by increasing complexity in all areas of life – society, science, economy, politics, private life. This world is far too multi-faceted and complex to be controlled, mastered and governed. Regarded globally, neither the United Nations, the G7 nor the G20 are able to guarantee peace and order. It is a "world without driver".[1] However, this no longer manageable complexity is also becoming tangible in smaller areas, for example, in technical progress and the resulting digital revolution which places increased pressure to adapt on each individual. The markets' transformation from sellers' markets to consumer markets is presenting companies with difficult and complex challenges in meeting various, often diverging and changing customer demands. The pressure to adapt is compelling companies to implement complex production sequences, whose complexity they are in turn attempting to reduce through modularisation.[2] In macroeconomic terms, complexity manifests, or has manifested, itself in diverging economic trends or in the financial and economic crisis; this started in 2008 with the bankruptcy of the US American investment bank Lehman-Brothers, and initially appeared to be an American phenomenon. However, it rapidly spread to Europe, where it continued to develop into a sovereign debt and economic crisis, which took years to fight and is still being combated, and whose effects not even experts were, or still are, able to foresee.[3] At the same time, a complex and dynamic, multi-level political system of 28 member states, today's European Union, was established in Europe with the ratifications in the individual member states and the entry into force of the Treaty of Lisbon on 1st December 2009. Such complicated constellations not only equate to increasing complexity for all actors and stakeholder groups, particularly companies, but also pose a major risk to the implementation and achievability of their objectives.[4] It therefore comes as little surprise that newspapers are already talking about the "curse of complexity",[5] in order to draw attention to this central trend.

Above all, complexity is fundamentally a characteristic of ecological, biological and social (and therefore also political) systems. The complexity of a system increases along with the number of its elements (e.g. political actors), with their diversity, various relationships and often diverging interests. And complex, dynamic systems such as the EU produce effects which cannot be explained using simple causal relationships (if A does such and such, then B, etc.). Multi-causality is the

---

1   N.U. (2015 f).
2   As an example of this: Waltl and Wildemann (2014).
3   N.U. (2015); Jost and Stocker (2015).
4   See e.g. the political instability caused by the Ukraine crisis or the terrorist threat posed by IS, Braunberger (2015).
5   N.U. (2015); Walter (2006).

rule.[6] In modern social systems, (political) society is subdivided into a variety of stakeholder groups, all of which pursue their own objectives and interests, and which regard and explain the world from their perspective. However, these groups also have relationships with one another. These relationships are not constant, but can instead change, from mutual antipathy to co-operation.[7] Trade unions, for example, can oppose companies during collective bargaining but also co-operate with them when business interests and jobs are at risk, as evidenced, for instance, when the German metalworkers' trade union IG Metall supported the German Automotive Industry Association (VDA) when a reduction in CO_2 emission limits for passenger cars was on the table.

In such complex and partly diverging social systems, it is becoming increasingly difficult for politicians to provide clear answers to problems, because any political intervention and implemented policy can also have unintended consequences and unexpected effects. The objectives of the various policy areas can always conflict, e.g. social policy versus financial policy, environmental policy versus economic policy and agricultural policy. This means that each problem has to be dealt with in greater detail not only in content-related but also procedural terms with regard to the desired and undesired effects and processes which may be set in motion by the implementation of a policy. There are no longer any simple explanations in a complex world. The consequence will therefore be more detailed work and intensive concentration on the above mentioned problems and processes instead of searching for general, all-encompassing explanations and interpretations of the world.[8]

Just as private individuals are under pressure to adapt, for example, due to technological progress, and in the same way that companies have to adjust to new consumer behaviour, the service of lobbying is also subject to enormous pressure to adapt as a result of complex political systems such as that of the EU, and the complex way in which policies develop. In addition to content-related work, it must now deal above all with breaking down this complexity and with options for controlling it.

In sociology, this increase in complexity is identified as a significant challenge which first has to be recognised by the societal elites, then filtered and broken down in a second step, and finally controlled and managed (see Section 8.1).

The increase in complexity is being reflected in an increase in knowledge. Today, as an integral component of a modern society, knowledge is no longer merely part of the solution, in which a rational and functioning result can be achieved through the application of knowledge; instead, it has also become a problem itself due to its abundance. Knowledge is becoming global. Increasing knowledge is not only

---

6   See La Porte (1975), p. 5.
7   See La Porte (1975), pp. 3–4.; Nassehi (2011), p. 15.
8   See Ruggie (1975), pp. 148 ff.; N.U. (2015); Walter (2006).

constantly being accumulated; it is also available at any time and in any location. The online encyclopaedia, Wikipedia, has superseded the classic, standard encyclopaedias such as Germany's Brockhaus or the UK's Encyclopedia Britannica, and has now become the ultimate synonym for the ubiquitousness, the omnipresence of knowledge in a modern knowledge-based society.[9] This extensive, quantitative increase in knowledge not only provides political decision-makers with support in solution-finding, but also, above all, poses them with a problem. In (political) decisions, an often vast amount of knowledge has to be acquired and filtered, taken into consideration and controlled. This means that, in each decision, decision-makers have to intelligently manage this wealth of knowledge, and require decision-making aids and external support to do so. In the field of political lobbying, the intermediary lobbyist has to provide both parties – politicians and stakeholder groups – with the necessary instruments (e. g. the onepager, see Chapter 6) so that knowledge can become part of the solution and does not remain part of the problem.

Knowledge is traditionally organised into disciplinary "columns" or "silos", e. g. legal knowledge, medical knowledge, political knowledge, commercial knowledge or macroeconomic knowledge. With their specialisation in one core area of knowledge, the various faculties of a university are an expression of this. However, knowledge is also organised into different departments within companies. For example, the sales department is distinct from the research department, just as personnel administration is always separate from (product) marketing, although all of these fields of knowledge can only contribute to the commercial success of a company in unison.

Ultimately, training is also undertaken according to such breakdowns. For instance, students are trained to become political scientists, managers or lawyers.[10] This partitioning is rather unfortunate for training lobbyists, since different problem-solving concepts, which make use of knowledge from all relevant specialist fields, are required to solve complex problems. "Multi-professionalism", the co-operation of diverse professions in one project, is required instead of specialised training and unilateral professionalisation. Multi-professionalism enables the perspective differentiation and the perspective change which are so important to the solution of complex problems. Viewed from different, multi-professional (interdisciplinary) angles, a problem can be segmented and broken down into sub-problems, which are then easier to process and solve.

For lobbying amongst the EU institutions, this means that a European regulation concerning a ban on advertising for alcoholic beverages, for instance, must be regarded from various angles in order to successfully support potential clients in the introduction of their legitimate interests. The European political perspective also

---

9 With regard to the explosion in knowledge, see: Burke (2014).
10 Nassehi (2014), slide 4.

regards such a regulation as an initiative for consolidating European integration by means of a uniform regulation within the 28 member states. By no means least, the European political perspective also gives consideration to questions concerning the health of the populace, and is concerned about the effects of excessive alcohol consumption on the health systems and on society as a whole. Such a legislative proposal can also give rise to possible rival positions between individual member states – advertising alcohol on the television is banned in France, for example, whereas it is permitted in other EU member states – which is not insignificant for a pan-European lobbying approach. However, the legislative procedure can also be regarded from a legal perspective, resulting in questions concerning the approaches: which institutions and their committees are responsible? Which periods of time and deadlines are there? Is such a legislative proposal actually permissible according to the EU Treaties? The commercial perspective may perhaps raise questions concerning the effects of such legislation for the affected companies: what effects would such an advertising ban have on the unit sales or even the continued existence of producers of alcoholic beverages? Above all, these commercial questions also help the lobbyists to understand their clients' concerns better. Only these various perspectives help lobbyists to be able to understand all of the effects of complex problems, and to ultimately solve them, because it is only possible to co-ordinate the various, relevant solution approaches with an in-depth understanding of complex problems and processes.

If a perspective change for a problem is possible, it is the task of the multi-professional elites to identify the various positions and translate them so that they can be understood by all parties involved in the solution. Elites must therefore be able to regard society from different perspectives, and to act as interpreters for specialists as well as the general public.[11] This means that problems and their solutions must always be formulated so that they are understood by the respective target group. In lobbying, this corresponds to the onepager methodology (see Sections 6.4.2.1.7 and 10.4.2), with its perspective change from the individual interest to the common interest perspective. This approach serves to reduce complexity in lobbying by helping to make the concerns of the affected stakeholder groups more understandable, and by ensuring that they are heard in the political process of the EU and become politically usable. It is additionally important for the elites and experts on all sides to be networked, so that they can communicate with each other. This is crucial to successful complexity reduction and problem solving, because "network strategies form the key competence of successful knowledge-based economies"[12] (see Section 3.7).

This fundamental understanding and these fundamental techniques are imperative for training the "next generation" of lobbyists. The training of lobbyists must

11 Nassehi (2014), slide 6.
12 Nassehi (2014), slide 7.

also reflect the forward-looking demand for multi-professionalism. What is needed is not the political scientist, the manager or the lawyer alone, but a cross-section of these and other specialisms with the related skills in order to be able to identify and solve complex problems.

7.2.2 Deciphering the complex multi-level system of the European Union

The EU's development in recent years is a prime example of increasing complexity. The increase from six to the current 28 member states with independent nationalities and cultures, different legal systems and various political systems[13] is the most tangible, outward expression of this growth in complexity. The "European Union complexity trap" has already been described exhaustively in Chapters 4 and 5. This section will therefore merely provide a synopsis and brief description of what is relevant to the training of lobbyists.

The EU's most recent (and, in the opinion of many people, its most central) development step is marked by the Treaty of Lisbon, which came into effect on 1st December 2009. It strengthened the European Union externally and internally. Externally, this is manifested, for example, in the EU's separate legal personality and the newly established External Action Service, headed by the High Representative of the European Union for Foreign Affairs and Security Policy. However, the changes which resulted within the Union are more important for lobbying. They have led to an increase in the complexity of the European political system. The changes within the EU after the Treaty of Lisbon must be analysed against this backdrop.

The Treaty had become necessary to integrate the various new member states into the EU's political system following the EU's so-called eastward enlargement, in order to ensure that the Union remained internally capable of action and making decisions.[14] However, the rising number of members has also led to an increase in complexity, because the growth in members additionally led to a rise in the number of political actors of diverse nationalities and thus the number of contact persons for lobbying in Brussels: the Council has more members, as do the Parliament and the Commission, in which each EU member state is currently represented with one Commissioner. In the public perception, these offices are not concentrated on individual persons such as presidents, Federal chancellors, ministers or opposition leaders. The political system of the EU is oriented more towards negotiations and finding compromises between the institutions and intrainstitutional groups than is the case in the member states.[15]

In addition to the central, federal institutions in Brussels (particularly the Parliament and Commission), the member state decision-making levels also play a role

---

13 With regard to the various political systems in Europe, see: Ismayr (2004²) and (2009⁴).
14 Herz and Jetzelsperger (2008²), pp. 87–88; Weidenfeld (2008), p. 13.
15 Linder (2014), p. 48.

in the EU; these are in turn represented in the Council of the EU and in the European Council. Added to these are regional decision-making levels, which are represented in the Committee of the Regions. However, member states and regions can also play a role in transposing European legislation into national law, such as when EU directives are implemented in German law by the Bundestag and Bundesrat in Germany, as for example in the implementation of European legislation on the rehabilitation and liquidation of banks (Directive 2014/59/EU), in which the Länder assembly also had to issue its approval.[16] This has given rise to a complex multi-level system, which can now only be deciphered down to its very last "ramification" by experts. It is without precedent in this form, and is therefore usually dubbed "*sui generis*".[17]

Above all, the reform measures in the area of political decision-making procedures have become relevant for the daily, practical work of lobbyists. Essentially, these primarily strengthened the role of the Parliament, with its 751 members, by elevating the so-called co-decision procedure to the standard procedure (Article 294 TFEU). In practice, the already complex, formal procedure (see Section 5.3.4.1.2) is supplemented by informal processes and procedures, the importance of which must not be underestimated. These also have to be understood and deciphered in lobbying. Probably the most important example of this is the so-called "informal trialogue" (see Section 5.3.4.1.3), which is not provided for in the EU Treaties. This consists of a limited group in which representatives of the Commission, the Parliament (usually the rapporteurs) and the Council (usually the Council Presidency) participate. It convenes even prior to the first reading of a legislative proposal in the European Parliament, in order to speed up co-ordination between the Commission, Parliament and Council. As the crucial compromises are often achieved there, the informal trialogue can therefore most certainly be regarded as a further (albeit informal) decision-making level.[18]

The Treaty of Lisbon's measures, which subject even more areas of policy in the Council of the EU to the majority principle rather than the principle of unanimity than before, are of equal significance. The majority decision has thus become the usual case (Article 16 (3) TEU), and now covers practically all areas of policy which are crucial to citizens and companies – unanimity is now only required in the Council in exceptional cases. As part of the increased co-operation (Article 20 TEU in combination with Articles 326 to 334 TFEU), decisions which are actually subject to unanimity in the Council can, under certain circumstances, be made via a majority decision. The result is a considerable loss of influence for the individual member state.[19] It is no longer able to block, and therefore prevent, a legislative

---

16 Bundesrat (2014).
17 Schmid and Schünemann (2013²), p. 65.
18 Weidenfeld (2013), p. 166; with regard to the informal trialogue in the co-decision procedure prior to the Treaty of Lisbon: Wessels (2008), pp. 229, 345, 361.
19 See also Joos (2014), p. 34.

proposal by refusing to give its consent in the Council. With the emergence of this dynamic multi-level system and the strengthening of the EU, the individual member states have, so to speak, shifted down one level (or to use sports terminology, they have been "relegated") in terms of their options for involvement in a decision. A member state is now only part of a group of 28. Whilst it was previously possible to concentrate lobbying work on one member state – usually the "home country" of the lobbying company and/or its client – lobbyists now additionally have to deal intensively with the complex, formal and informal political processes and decision-making procedures plus the balances of political power in the EU, and to decipher them after the Treaty of Lisbon.

7.3 Requirements on a lobbyist

The two major tasks of lobbying have already been identified in the above described challenges involved in the decryption and handling of the complex, political processes of the European Union's dynamic, multi-level system. However, further requirements arise from practical lobbying work; these are formulated by the stakeholder groups and politicians, and are what constitute good lobbying from their perspective. To address both parties – stakeholder groups and politicians – equally, however, the lobbyist must be familiar with, and understand, their requirements. Only if this is the case can he successfully establish effective communication between both parties, and mediate and "translate" if required. In this process, it is necessary for the lobbyist to assume the role of an intermediary and trusted mediator.

7.3.1 Knowledge of the world of politics and the world of stakeholder groups

7.3.1.1 Lobbying as an intermediary system

The importance of lobbying in political systems in general and in the political system of the EU in particular was dealt with at the beginning of this book. Lobbying is accordingly an intermediary system: the lobbyist must act as an intermediary between the stakeholder groups and politicians.[20] Only this enables effective and long-term process support, and successful lobbying.

A lobbyist can best meet this intermediary requirement as an external service provider who stands as an independent party between the stakeholder groups and politicians. The external intermediary is able to act outside of hierarchies.

This therefore quickly enables him to obtain relevant information and speedily bring about decisions on the part of the respective stakeholder group, since he has

---

20 Michalowitz (2007b), p. 180.

external access to all hierarchy levels of the company, association or organisation which he represents, from the working level to the management board. Unlike an in-house lobbyist, he does not have to follow fixed chains of command or strictly adhere to rigid hierarchies, i.e. he is independent of internal systems of superiority and subordination or responsibility (e.g. of individual corporate units, specialist departments in associations, etc.).[21] Whilst stakeholder groups make efforts to rectify this in-house lobbyist deficit by positioning the lobbyists as close to the upper hierarchy levels of the respective organisation as possible,[22] the speed of reaction which an external service provider is able to accomplish is nevertheless not usually achieved. Added to this is the fact that, unlike an in-house representative, an external service provider is not integrated in hierarchical or disciplinary terms; this allows him to independently and objectively assess his client's lobbying strategy, and enables improvements or possibly entire strategy changes in good time, something that would not be possible at all, or only at a later point in time, in a system in which he were bound by instructions. Unnecessary costs for the stakeholder group can be avoided in this manner. This problem is very familiar from the area of (non-political) corporate strategy consulting, and is one of the most essential justifications for the existence of international consulting companies such as McKinsey or Boston Consulting.

In addition, an in-house representative will always be regarded by politicians as a representative of his employer, and not as a trusted mediator, unlike an external intermediary, who supports various types of client.

As has been shown, an intermediary is not integrated into the hierarchies either of the stakeholder groups or of the political system. Provided that he has a broad and strong network, he also has access to all hierarchy levels within the legislature and executive, from the employee of a simple Member of the European Parliament to the chairman of a parliamentary group, or from specialist civil servants to the heads of the Directorates General within the European Commission. He can therefore also act freely on this side in the best interests of the respective lobbying project.

The intermediary lobbyist has the option – but also the duty – of acting as the communications interface between stakeholder groups and politicians. Whilst they are all part of society and are reliant on one another, the representatives of stakeholder groups usually have different social backgrounds, or have taken on different characteristics due to their group's professionalisation pressure, and accordingly often pursue objectives which differ from those of political representatives. Religious stakeholder groups such as churches, for instance, are more likely to pursue socio-political, ideological and religious objectives than an NGO which is specialised in environmental issues and orients its efforts and objectives to-

---

21 Joos (2015), p. 417.
22 See Joos (1998), p. 111.

wards these, whereas companies in turn seek to identify possible risks to their commercial success in political decisions, and to eliminate these.

Politics is frequently oriented towards entirely different categories. In addition to content-related, ideological and principle considerations, the central concepts of power, authority and legitimation also play a role here. And politicians often have different expectations of stakeholder groups than the latter have of themselves. They focus on other areas: for example, politicians expect economic representatives to demonstrate public responsibility and safeguard jobs, and not to concentrate so extensively on the generation of profits and the positioning of companies to achieve globalisation.[23] Lobbyists must be able to clarify and explain the different priorities set by the respective, other party.

The intermediary lobbyist forms part of the above mentioned (see Section 7.2.1) translator elites who act as interpreters in the complex area of influence and power between stakeholder groups and politicians. They therefore represent an important "link between public and private actors"[24] by ensuring that legitimate interests are also recognised and adequately taken into consideration by politicians. They therefore help politicians to act closer to civil society, and also help the EU institutions to "maintain an open, transparent and regular dialogue with representative associations and civil society" (Article 11 TEU).

The lobbyist must be able to accept this challenge and, above all, meet it, i.e. he must demonstrate the ability to become aware of the requirements made on him and to meet them professionally. To accomplish this, he must be equipped with a broad cross-section of different skills, encompassing knowledge from the world of both stakeholder groups (e.g. commercial know-how of private companies and trade associations) and politics (e.g. legal and political science knowledge).

In their work as intermediaries, lobbyists must above all be one thing: trusted mediators. Even if they are given an assignment by stakeholder groups, they are required not only to act in the sense of their clients, since trusting communication with politicians will not otherwise succeed. The lobbyist must therefore not only work towards asserting his clients' interests, but must also give consideration to the politicians' interests. This means that he has to meet the politicians' interest in specialist information and specific knowledge, and must provide open and extensive information on an issue so that politicians do not arrive at single-sided conclusions. He must be aware of the fact that politicians and legislators are obligated to objectivity and the common good.[25] Withholding information or, even worse, consciously supplying incorrect information would run counter to the lobbyist's assignment as a trusted mediator between stakeholder groups. Trust would be destroyed and communication between politicians and stakeholder groups therefore

---

23 copes (2014).
24 Michalowitz (2007b), p. 171.
25 See Linder (2014), p. 51.

rendered impossible. This was the case, for example, when the German Farmers' Association attempted to trivialise BSE as a British epidemic and played down the risks for Germany. The consequence of this was 2001's so-called agricultural turnaround in Germany, which saw the Ministry of Agriculture's realignment towards consumer protection by the new Minister, Renate Künast, who then dismissed two heads of department with close ties to the Farmers' Association. Trust between the association and politicians was impaired.[26]

It is also advantageous, against this backdrop, if the lobbyist is an external service provider. Solely out of his own business interests, he will ultimately ensure that a trusting and open relationship with politicians is always maintained. This is the basis of his business – structural and long-term process support over a long period of time would otherwise be inconceivable. He would no longer be able to approach his political contacts with the concerns of new clients if he had not already been able to establish a good, trustworthy reputation with them in preceding encounters and meetings. Only a particularly good reputation as a "trusted advisor" enables a lobbyist to raise his profile and stand out from competitors.[27] At the same time, he must always act openly and as a circumspect service provider; he should concentrate on supporting political decision-making processes and on formulating content and arguments, i.e. he should leave responsibility for the content to his clients, the stakeholder groups.

The position of an intermediary between stakeholder groups and politicians results in specific requirements on the lobbyist; these are constantly reformulated by both parties. A variety of soft skills, which become the lobbyist's permanent tools, are necessary so that these requirements can be met.

7.3.1.2 Requirements on the part of stakeholder groups

7.3.1.2.1 Information

It is primarily important for stakeholder groups (e.g. companies, associations, organisations) to be kept abreast of political activities in Brussels and the member states by their lobbyists. In other words: from their point of view, lobbyists must be the representatives of politicians within the stakeholder groups,[28] and this naturally involves the requirement for information procurement.[29] However, this is not yet sufficient on its own. The requirement also encompasses long-term, structural monitoring combined with an understanding explanation of the political processes, an evaluation of the positions of European decision-makers and the mediation of the results to the client. Extensive descriptive and analytical skills, which should ideally be learnt during the training, must be brought to bear here

---

26 Niemann (2003), pp. 195 – 196; Kempf and Merz (2008), p. 229.
27 Oltmanns (2014), p. 19.
28 See Michalowitz (2007b), p. 180.
29 Interviews with small and medium-sized companies in Bavaria, in: Institute for Marketing, Meyer (2014), slides 37 – 38.

as soft skills in order to be able to identify relevant political topics and issues – "hear the grass grow!"[30] – and mediate them. Obtaining information through monitoring also includes the ability to identify relevant contact persons (key players and/or stakeholders) and political networks. This enables access to be obtained to both the opinion leaders and to the formal and informal, elite groups of decision-makers.[31]

However, this work is not to be misunderstood as passive monitoring. Quite the opposite – the necessary process competence is also demanded of a lobbyist in this area, because he can only derive a strategy for effective and efficient lobbying from the analysed processes if he understands them. This also involves informing the client if lobbying is no longer possible because the right point in time has been missed,[32] for example the policy cycle (see Section 3.4.2) is already too far advanced, a deadline for a hearing has not been adhered to or the EU legislative processes have already progressed too far. A lobbying campaign, which is occasionally costly, particularly if it also includes a media campaign as part of public affairs, can therefore be ended in good time or not launched in the first place. Monitoring and the information flow must be organised so that they are oriented towards the political (decision-making) processes. The relevance of governmental relations, with its process-oriented approach, is again clearly demonstrated here.

7.3.1.2.2 Commercial management thinking and implementation of the clients' (political) objectives

Commercial management thinking is therefore a requirement which is made time and again by the stakeholder groups. A professional lobbyist must always bear the economy of his actions in mind.[33] Naturally, this plays a particularly major role in the case of economic stakeholder groups. As an example, reference should be made to a survey conducted by the Institute for Marketing at the Ludwig-Maximilians-University in Munich amongst small and medium-sized companies. It shows that corporate representatives expect their lobbying measures to deliver a clear benefit in the sense of commercial management understanding. Lobbyists should therefore have a "clear idea of performance and consideration", according to the demand.[34] It should additionally be mentioned that, whilst such commercial management thinking is particularly pronounced in the case of companies, it is also required by other stakeholder groups, the reason being that all clients have to weigh up the costs and benefits of their lobbying work in their budgets. A professional lobbyist must always take this into consideration. The lobbyist is required to demonstrate pragmatic efficiency here as a soft skill. This means that he

---

30 van Schendelen (2014), p. 278.
31 Michalowitz (2007a), p. 77.
32 Horst Seefeld, interviewed in Heitz (2011), p. 128; see also N.U. (2014a).
33 van Schendelen (2012), p. 129.
34 Interviews with small and medium-sized companies in Bavaria, in: Institute for Marketing, Meyer (2014), slides 37–38.

must be able to optimise the resources of time, knowledge and process support in terms of optimal lobbying[35] and work in a solution-oriented manner.[36] Basic commercial management knowledge is therefore crucial in training the next generation of lobbyists; the current training, usually as part of political science seminars (see below), alone is not sufficient for this.

Companies' lobbying objectives can usually be derived in commercial management terms, an aspect which lobbyists must not overlook in their work in addition to the cost/benefit effect. The monitoring of political processes should by all means enable subsequent commercial evaluation. A ban on advertising (e.g. in the case of alcohol and tobacco) or export restrictions (e.g. in the case of production machines) can result in significant (existential) problems for the affected companies and their employees. The planning of important investment decisions on the part of the Commission or a member state government (including in a non-EU country) can also be economically relevant to the clients.[37] However, stakeholder groups such as associations and organisations may also be focussed on other concerns, e.g. social objectives in the case of trade unions and churches or climate protection objectives in the case of environmental associations.

The extent to which a lobbyist has to identify with his clients' objectives is viewed differently. On the one hand, such (strong, internal) identification is, for example, demanded of civil servant lobbyists in the Permanent Representations of the member states to the EU; the case of in-house lobbyists, who are salaried employees and bound by instructions, is similar. Undoubtedly, external lobbyists must also be able to identify, understand and convincingly represent their stakeholder group's objectives in the same manner in which a lawyer represents his client. On the other hand, it is doubtful whether a more extensive "internal obligation" to the stakeholder group is required in order to lend the lobbyist the authenticity to represent it accordingly:[38] as a "classic" lobbyist, a lawyer does not necessarily identify with his client, but instead attempts to represent him as well as possible by optimally exploiting all legal options. Nor must the lobbyist lose sight of his role as an intermediary, i.e. he must not make the mistake of losing sight of the common interest or political perspective of a concern through more or less blindly following the path taken by his client.

7.3.1.2.3 Professional representation of clients' interests

From the point of view of stakeholder groups, the professional representation of their interests is, of course, an important, if not the most central, requirement on a lobbyist. The scope of what is meant by this is extensive: for some, it means the direct assertion of one's own interests. Greenpeace, for example, lists the tasks of

35 van Schendelen (2012), p. 279.
36 Köppl (2003), p. 186.
37 See Nass (2013).
38 van Schendelen (2012), p. 343.

its representative office in Brussels as follows: "Based in Brussels, we monitor and analyse the work of the EU institutions, expose deficient EU policies and laws, and challenge EU decision-makers to implement progressive solutions."[39] Whereby "progressive solutions" refers to the concerns of the stakeholder group. Small and medium-sized companies expect the positive representation of corporate interests.[40] For others, "it is concerned less with the assertion of demands than with the processing of expert assessments",[41] i. e. the provision of information to political decision-makers concerning the possible consequences of a policy. In this regard, stakeholder groups regularly expect lobbyists to offer occasionally long-term knowledge of the institutional procedures and informal decision-making.[42] They should also come equipped with their own viable network and relevant contacts,[43] because "the know-how and access to the responsible parties [are] not available in the majority of companies, and are supplemented through the external know-how of lobbyists".[44]

7.3.1.2.4 Technical know-how and good contacts

In this case, technical "know-how" particularly includes the manner in which the legitimate concerns of stakeholder groups can be introduced. The process instruments available to lobbyists for their practical work were described in detail in Chapter 6. On application of these, an understanding of the informal and formal decision-making processes in the EU is vital, in order to communicate with the correct contact person(s) at the appropriate point in time, for instance. In addition to technical knowledge, access to relevant key players is required (see also Sections 3.6 and 3.7). Ideally, one's own network contains a key figure, who makes the portrayed, legitimate interests his own and effectively introduces these interests into the EU's political process on his own initiative, quasi as a pioneer (endogenic approach).

Establishing such a network poses a challenge even to stakeholder groups with extensive financial and human resources, because access to the political system is often difficult for "outsiders". As a rule, they only have a realistic chance of establishing a tenable network if they are introduced into corresponding circles via already established links to high-ranking personalities (in the form of "trust transfers"). Whilst random acquaintances or friendships with a politician or civil servant may prove helpful in individual cases, they cannot replace a network which has grown over a period of many years of work. Because contact is usually established and maintained during the course of a professional activity; in addition,

---

39 Greenpeace EU Unit (2015).
40 Interviews with small and medium-sized companies in Bavaria, in: Institute for Marketing, Meyer (2014), slides 37 – 38.
41 Wolfgang Anzengruber, CEO of Austria's VERBUND AG, in: Mitterstieler, Offner and Zechner (2011).
42 Michalowitz (2007b), p. 181.
43 Nass (2013).
44 Mitterstieler, Offner and Zechner (2011).

personal exchange at receptions, presentation evenings and recurring lunches or joint leisure activities also plays an important role.[45]

However, a network of contact persona alone is not sufficient. Which national, political, and also social backgrounds the contact has must be taken into consideration in each case. Chapter 2 dealt with the differences in socialisation between politicians and businessmen or managers. The perspective change, which has also been addressed several times, assumes particular importance here. The lobbyist must place himself in his opposite number's respective situation, i.e. firstly that of his clients and secondly that of the contact persons at the executive and legislative level. In the case of the latter, it must be considered whether the introduced concerns are compatible with the common interest and whether the stakeholder groups' arguments are understandable to the contact persons from a common interest perspective. If they are not, the lobbying concern cannot be transposed; all of the technical know-how becomes invalid, and the address file with all of its contacts amounts to nought.

7.3.1.2.5 Soft skills as essential tools: social skills, intercultural and linguistic skills, integrity

Technical know-how, a good network of contacts and knowledge surrounding a necessary perspective change alone are not sufficient for effective and efficient lobbying. The stakeholder groups' requirements can be used to derive a range of soft skills which are crucial factors for the success or failure of a lobbying project: social skills, intercultural and linguistic skills, plus integrity. These are not only soft skills, but indeed the essential tools which are required for the profession, to say nothing of the vocation, of lobbying.

It is not therefore surprising that stakeholder groups demand diplomatic finesse when introducing their interests, namely "precisely the same tact that one would expect of an ambassador".[46] In addition to technical knowledge, this requirement results in a variety of skills which are expected of the professional lobbyist, and which have to be taught and extended during the training. They can be summed up under the generic term "social skills". The lobbyist must be sociable and enjoy meeting new people. This also includes not having any reservations vis-à-vis (high-ranking) civil servants and political decision-makers.[47] Good manners, courteous behaviour and politeness are equally as important as charisma, dialogue skills and a certain degree of sales talent[48] when a concern has to be presented and/or compromises have to be negotiated.[49] He also requires outstanding communication skills in order to be able to present complex issues in brief, succinct

---

45 Joos (2011), p. 202.
46 Wolfgang Ischinger, general representative for governmental relations at Allianz SE in: Nass (2013).
47 Vondenhoff and Busch-Janser (2008), p. 160; Köppl (2003), p. 186.
48 Buholzer (1998), p. 36; Vondenhoof and Busch-Janser (2008), p. 161.
49 Lahusen and Jauß (2001), p. 119.

and generally understandable form.[50] If the lobbyist is impartial and easy-going in his role and work, he is also able to represent the stakeholder groups' concerns authentically and credibly.

Above all, intercultural skills are indispensable for lobbying vis-à-vis the EU institutions in addition to social skills. As lobbying and network building not only take place across parties and institutions, but also across 28 different European nations – if EU officials, politicians or parliamentarians of various nationalities or authorities in EU member states are contacted – the lobbyist must be able to deal with the respective contact persons' various national, socio-cultural and politico-cultural differences.[51] The EU metropolis of Brussels requires extraordinarily skilled handling plus sufficient knowledge of human nature and flexibility to be able to deal adequately with the extensively different mentalities of the EU officials. Sensitivities in this environment must not be underestimated. Even a minor faux-pas, the clumsy handling of a civil servant's national pride, can lead to the permanent loss of contacts here.[52]

Whilst there are now common European standards, for example in the "Brussels microcosm" in general or the "European code of conduct" in particular (see Section 2.3.5.2.1), the Brussels actors are naturally socialised in their national context. For example, the German attitude towards a very formalistic approach is found in Brussels alongside the Southern European tradition, which is perceived as more "laid-back". The lobbyist must meet this circumstance head-on with sufficient skill to adapt to local customs, depending on the situation,[53] with the result that detailed knowledge of the various European cultures is crucial to success, as in the case of an international enterprise.[54] Three interdependent dimensions are ascribed to these intercultural skills: a cognitive dimension (knowledge), an affective dimension (sensitivity) and a communicative and behaviour-related dimension.[55] Above all, transfer skills are important, the ability to also apply these key skills, which are important in one's own culture, to other cultures.[56]

Lobbyist training must find an answer to this enormous challenge. In addition to the obligatory acquisition of English and French language skills, and ideally other European languages, European history, the history of the EU and the special cultural considerations of Europe, particularly in the political culture, must also be dealt with. This theoretical knowledge must be supplemented with practical experience, and tested and examined under all circumstances. An ideal framework for

---

50 Lahusen and Jauß (2001), p. 118.
51 Michalowitz (2007a), p. 78.
52 Joos (2011), p. 203.
53 Joos (2011), p. 203.
54 See the importance of intercultural skills within international companies: Moosmüller (2009), pp. 62–63; or practical manuals for companies: Baumer (2002); Herbrand (2002); Del Fabro (2000).
55 Herbrand (2002) pp. 33–34.
56 Bolten (2012), pp. 128 ff., views terming intercultural skills as a separate ability to act critically, but emphasises the importance of transferring key competencies such empathy, role distance or flexibility in situations and cultures whose rules are not known or only partially known.

this would be semesters abroad or internships in other EU countries, for instance, particularly in member state executive and legislature institutions (government, parliament) or at the EU institutions (e.g. the Commission or Parliament).

The work in Brussels demands extensive linguistic skills of a lobbyist. The administration's general language is French. However, English is spoken as the working language in practically all of the Directorates General within the Commission. Apart from their mother tongue, a few of the older civil servants only speak one of the two aforementioned languages – at different levels. The high importance of personal agility is particularly demonstrated here. For example, a few incomplete sentences spoken in the civil servant's mother tongue (e.g. in Swedish or Spanish) can arouse his liking for a lobbyist, whereas a less flexible actor may possibly find less of an audience. In general, it can be stated that a lobbyist in Brussels should speak at least three languages: in addition to his native language, fluent business English (C2 according to the common European reference framework) and a third language which may be helpful when working together with representatives of the respective nationality. However, a "feel" for different interpretations of terms is also very helpful in the area of legislative lobbying when legal texts are involved.[57]

7.3.1.2.6 Integrity and compliance

A lobbyist's integrity is also of great importance to his acceptance and therefore his potential success. As was exhaustively explained in the analysis in Chapter 2, a lobbyist encounters various prejudices and negative associations in his daily work; it is therefore all the more important that he undertakes this activity with absolute professionalism and integrity: understandably, it is highly unlikely that politicians or civil servants will want to conduct discussions with lobbyists who are alleged to engage in dishonest behaviour. A lobbyist must ensure that he, himself, regards his work as something natural, necessary and legitimate, and not as something clandestine and concealed. Of course, this does not mean that he should forward confidential information to third parties – as in any other business, precise consideration must be given to which data and facts are intended for third parties and which are not.[58] The lobbyist's discretion in establishing trust vis-à-vis the stakeholder groups is absolutely crucial.[59] Unnecessary secretiveness vis-à-vis politicians or even deception concerning one's own intentions and the client are dishonest, and harm both one's own image and that of the profession, i.e. in the long term, they make it more difficult to obtain access to the decision-makers at the legislative and executive level. In addition, it is naturally expected that a lobbyist always adheres to all legal regulations (compliance) (see Section 5.3.3.3 and Section 2.3.5.2).

---

57 Joos (2011), p. 204.
58 Joos (2011), p. 204.
59 Vondenhoff and Busch-Janser (2008), p. 160.

Fundamental requirements of stakeholder groups on lobbying
1. Information 2. Commercial management thinking and implementation of the clients' (political) objectives 3. Professional representation of clients' interests 4. Integrity and compliance

Figure 7.1: Fundamental requirements of stakeholder groups on lobbying

7.3.1.3 Requirements on the part of politicians

7.3.1.3.1 Information

In Chapter 2, it was shown that lobbying is an integral element of the political system in general and the political system of the EU in particular. It is a process of communication between the planners or decision-makers and those affected by a policy. Firstly, it is the assignment of the EU institutions to seek contact with the general public. Article 11 of the TEU explicitly demands that the EU institutions "maintain an open, transparent and regular dialogue with representative associations and civil society". Secondly, politicians are often reliant on the stakeholder groups' relevant information – mediated by the lobbyists – for their decisions. Because lobbying is not only a service for the benefit of the stakeholder groups, but also for the benefit of the political decision-makers[60] (with regard to the exchange of information and expertise, see also the explanations concerning exchange theory in Section 2.3.4.3). Accordingly, politicians also make requirements on good lobbying in addition to the stakeholder groups. The provision of specialist information, expert assessments and arguments is probably the most central requirement. The content and scope of the issues which are decided on at the executive and legislative level are often too complex to be resolved by politicians alone. Cooperation with the stakeholder groups is required here,[61] since they are able to supply the necessary expertise. This includes for example the specialist knowledge of companies, associations and organisations on the very specific issues to which they are committed. These may be questions concerning the economic effects of a draft law, on which affected companies assume a position, or also societal and ethical issues, to which associations and NGOs, for instance, contribute their specialist knowledge. Due to the diversity and complexity of the issues to which political decision-makers are exposed, this can almost be described as the politicians' need for expertise. "For me, a good lobbyist is like a good university professor; he knows everything and can quickly bring the issue to the point",[62] says one Austrian Member of the European Parliament, for example. The reason for this is that the political decision-makers can usually no longer rely solely on their own

60 Römmele and Lorenz (2014).
61 Griesser (2014), p. 63; Römmele and Lorenz (2014).
62 Interview with Paul Rübig, MEP in Heitz (2011), p. 127: "For me, a good lobbyist is like a good university professor; he knows everything and can quickly bring the issue to the point."

knowledge and that of their employees. The EU institutions do not have sufficient manpower to formulate draft laws competently. Political actors and decision-makers are therefore structurally overburdened.[63] They need external input for their decisions: "Information has become a crucial resource."[64]

It is important in this case that the contents, expertise and arguments mediated by the lobbyists are valuable and beneficial to politicians. Political decision-makers have a full appointment calendar and too little time to deal with all of the content in detail. Long dossiers are therefore not usually helpful in conveying a stakeholder group's position. They run the risk of drowning in the sea of petitions and submitted opinions. Top civil servants and politicians simply do not have the time to plough through several hundreds of pages of text each day. In other words: information and arguments must be prepared so that they are brief – ideally outlined on one page (onepager) – and easily understandable, and so that they reduce the complexity of the respective issue, and do not reproduce it in full or even extend it. The information must contribute to the solution, and not make the issue even more complicated. "A win-win situation, from which both decision-makers and lobbyists profit, ideally arises."[65] Lobbyists therefore have to place themselves in the position of their contacts at the executive and legislative level, and accomplish a perspective change from the individual interest of the stakeholder group to the common interest perspective of the political decision-makers; only in this manner do their information and arguments have the chance of being heeded in the political process (with regard to the onepager and perspective change, see Sections 6.4.2.1.7 and 10.4.2.1).

Due to the hoped for gain in knowledge required for their work, politicians do not shy away from personal contact with the stakeholder groups. Research shows that politicians actually appreciate this personal contact, since it offers the opportunity for dialogue, exchanging ideas and also further consultation; personal contact also enables a better assessment of one's opposite number.[66] The politicians have high expectations of such encounters, and demand professionalism from lobbyists. In consideration of these expectations, the following important factors arise for the work and the personality of a lobbyist: transparency, credibility, professionalism, a spotless public image and not merely the representation of individual interests, but additionally consideration of the common interest.[67]

7.3.1.3.2 Information transparency and professional information mediation

Politicians therefore most certainly do appreciate information from lobbyists, because they are ultimately concerned with avoiding the undesired consequences

---

63 Griesser (2014), p. 63.
64 Redelfs (2006), p. 334.
65 Griesser (2014), p. 63.
66 Interviews with members of the Bavarian Landtag, Institute for Marketing, Meyer (2014), slide 47; the European political actors seek contact with lobbyists, see: Linder (2014), p. 47.
67 Interviews with members of the Bavarian Landtag, Institute for Marketing, Meyer (2014), slide 48.

and effects of legislation. As political decision-makers are obligated to promote the common good, however, they demand that the information is transparent, substantiated and reliable.[68] It is expected that lobbyists "put forth honest arguments and are politically neutral".[69] Lobbyists must not withhold or conceal information, but must instead provide full information and also disclose their clients.[70] Of course, the information can be processed to meet the needs of the addressee depending on the contact person: information and arguments referring to the member state may be helpful for representatives of an EU member state, whereas pan-European arguments are important for EU contacts. However, the essential core information must be contained equally for all parties. Information transparency includes the fact that all parties involved in the political process obtain the relevant information. For example, information should not be distributed single-sidedly, but should instead be disseminated to the representatives of all parliamentary groups or be made accessible to all Commission representatives dealing with the issue.[71] This also applies to the Council, with the result that all parties involved in a legislative process (according to Article 294 TFEU) are ultimately in possession of the same level of information. Otherwise, important decision-makers, from whom the information has been knowingly or unknowingly withheld, could feel affronted. If complete information transparency is guaranteed, the political decision-makers' independence and sovereignty are also ensured. If they have access to all relevant information, they can make their decision objectively in the same manner as a judge.[72] Authenticity should again be mentioned in this context as a necessary soft skill for the lobbyist: a lobbyist can only represent his concern honestly and authentically if he also behaves authentically during information mediation. He should therefore remain impartial in his role and his work.

7.3.1.3.3 *Understanding of political processes and culture*

European EU politicians demand a certain degree of empathy, political understanding and knowledge of the political processes and political culture from the stakeholder groups and lobbyists.[73] Certain social skills essentially require mentioning here, such as the rules of social etiquette and politeness already mentioned above (see also Section 7.3.1.2). This also refers to entirely practical, day-to-day aspects, such as the fact that lobbyists keep appointments, arrive punctually and keep things brief, because a political decision-maker's appointment calender is tightly packed. In this context, the working hours within the Brussels institutions also require consideration. For example, office hours in the Commission start between 08.30 and 09.00, and rarely end before 19.00 for the managerial staff. A

---

68 See interview with Paul Rübig, MEP in Heitz (2011), p. 127.
69 Timmerherm (2004), p. 112.
70 With regard to transparency and the disclosure of clients: Leif and Speth (2006a).
71 See Timmerherm (2004), p. 112.
72 See Timmerherm (2004), p. 112.
73 Discussions with European politicians in Heitz (2011), p. 129.

Commission official who takes part in a variety of meetings and internal voting procedures during the day is often very difficult to reach – especially when a little peace and quiet (i. e. sufficient interest, patience and willingness to communicate) are required to be able to put forward a more complex concern. The lobbyists have to go along with the politicians in this regard. This results in the personal requirement on the lobbyist to be flexible and willing to orient his daily agenda – and, moreover, the entire rhythm of his life – towards his target group and give it priority over his private life if necessary.[74]

The fact that lobbyists inform and clarify their clients from the stakeholder groups about the complex, political processes has already been mentioned as a requirement of the stakeholder groups themselves; however, this is also a central requirement from the ranks of politicians, as revealed by a survey conducted by the center of political economy and society berlin (copes) in co-operation with the Quadriga University of Berlin and the magazine "politik & kommunikation" in the EU member state of Germany. 100 political decision-makers from the German Bundestag and ministerial management level, i. e. the legislative and executive level, were polled in 2014: 55 % of respondents gave German top managers a negative testimony as regards their knowledge surrounding decision-making processes in the German Bundestag. 60 % are actually of the opinion that top managers are unfamiliar with the decision-making processes within the parties and parliamentary groups. This is not only concerned with whether political decision-makers do not feel adequately appreciated due to this lack of knowledge on the part of businessmen, but also with whether successful and effective communication can be conducted between both parties. The consequences of this negative assessment for lobbying must be taken very seriously: for instance, the "lack of knowledge concerning political processes" is cited as the "third most frequent reason for the failure of top managers' concerns".[75] Lobbyists have to compensate for this lack of knowledge by keeping their stakeholder groups (in the stated example, companies and managers) abreast and informing them about the formal, and also informal, political processes. Preparation can, of course, be provided by prior legal or political science knowledge from corresponding training and study programmes, or simply a great deal of practical experience.

7.3.1.3.4 Integrity and compliance*

A lobbyist must reveal absolute integrity (see Section 7.3.1.2.6) and must not be open to the accusation of only pursuing single-sided individual interests. In addition, the political decision-makers always want to retain the upper hand in the lobbying communication process. They have therefore established mandatory regulations for communication with lobbyists (see Section 5.3). For lobbying

---

74 Joos (2011), p. 202.
75 copes (2014).
* For a better understanding, parts of this book will be repeated here.

amongst the EU institutions, this is above all the code of conduct, which was established as part of the European Transparency Initiative (ETI) and is again mentioned in this context. Accordingly, lobbyists who seek registration in the voluntary EU Transparency Register have to comply with the following rules when dealing with representatives of the EU.

In addition to the European legislative standards, member state regulations may also be relevant depending on where lobbying takes place or which nationality the persons involved have. For example, § 334 of the German Penal Code (bribery) or § 108e StGB (bribery of members of parliament) would also be relevant to German nationals.[76] However, this is only mentioned for the sake of completeness, because these criminal offences naturally have nothing whatsoever to do with professional lobbying.

In practice, the legal standards are supplemented by voluntary commitments by lobbyists. Both the European Public Affairs Consultancies Association (EPACA) and the Society of European Affairs Professionals (SEAP) recommend that their members are listed in the voluntary Transparency Register and abide by the code of conduct. They have additionally developed their own codes.[77] Companies' in-house lobbying departments must additionally give consideration to the – often much more rigorous – internal compliance regulations. In addition, some lobbying agencies voluntarily undergo various transparency, quality management and compliance audits (financial compliance, legal compliance).[78]

The professionalism of a lobbying company can generally be recognised by how strictly it adheres to codes of conduct and which voluntary commitment and control mechanisms it has imposed on itself. An unprofessional lobbying company interprets the rules more loosely (according to the maxim "What is not expressly prohibited is permissible!"), whereas a professional lobbying company interprets the rules strictly. Only the latter approach enables a relationship of trust to be established between politicians, stakeholders and lobbyists in the long term.[79] In addition, lobbyists – or, to be more accurate, lobbying agencies – also have a competitive interest in strictly interpreting and rigidly adhering to the codes of conduct. Prudent conduct can also make a difference in terms of the desired result, and can therefore increase the effectiveness of lobbying.[80] Adherence to all regulations is crucially important to a lobbyist's compliance and reputation. If even the slightest doubt is cast on his integrity due to (even unconscious!) misconduct, his reputation and credibility are tarnished, if not actually ruined. This can actually make it impossible to remain in this profession.

---

76 Classen (2014), pp. 108–109.
77 EPACA (2015); SEAP (2015).
78 For example, EUTOP International GmbH (2015).
79 van Schendelen (2014), p. 313.
80 van Schendelen (2014), p. 313.

The prudent and lawful behaviour of a lobbyist, compliance, demands both that he adheres to the regulations pertaining to him personally, and also gives consideration to the rules applicable to his contact persons (e.g. the code of conduct for Members of the Commission, the Rules of Procedure of the European Parliament, the Staff Regulations of Officials of the European Economic Community or the Code of Good Administrative Behaviour for Staff of the European Commission in Their Relations with the Public). Whilst these regulations are aimed primarily at EU officials by regulating their contact with the "external world", they also indirectly influence the behaviour of lobbyists. Because a professional lobbyist will be familiar with these regulations for his addressees, and will tailor his own behaviour to them in order not to embarrass his contact person by compelling him to draw attention to these regulations. For example, a lobbyist should know that a Member of the European Commission is not permitted to accept gifts with a value of over 150 euros (Article 1.11 code of conduct for Members of the Commission). This also applies to EU parliamentarians, who may only accept gifts if they are "given in accordance with courtesy usage" and do not exceed a value of 150 euros (Annex 1, Article 5 Rules of Procedure of the European Parliament). The regulations pertaining to EU officials particularly include the Staff Regulations of Officials of the European Economic Community,[81] which for example specify that civil servants must not accept any instructions from persons or organisations outside of their institution; they must carry out the duties assigned to them "objectively, impartially and in keeping with [their] duty of loyalty to the Union" (Article 11). Nor must civil servants "accept ... any honour, decoration, favour, gift or payment of any kind whatever" (Article 11). Information that has not been published must not be disclosed by civil servants (Article 17). Article 12 of the Staff Regulations additionally states: "An official shall refrain from any action or behaviour which might reflect adversely upon his position." However, there are also further regulations. For example, the Commission has also issued a Code of Good Administrative Behaviour for Staff of the European Commission in their Relations with the Public in addition to the Staff Regulations. This provides for example for the protection of personal data and secret information, a principle of non-discrimination, and the proportionality and consistency of the administration. As a result, all stakeholders concerned should therefore be treated equally in contact between the European administration and lobbyists.

However, what is the reality of the lobbyists' behaviour at the EU institutions? Whilst there are significant differences in terms of the quality of lobbying in some cases, representatives of European institutions such as the Parliament or the Commission point out time and again that, to some extent, lobbyists want to make primarily objective information and practical experience useful to the institutions in

---

81 Staff Regulations of Officials of the European Economic Community: Council of the European Economic Community, Council of the European Atomic Energy Community (2015).

Fundamental requirements of politicians on lobbying
1. Informationen
2. Transparency and professional information mediation
3. Understanding of political processes and culture
4. Integrity and compliance

Figure 7.2: Fundamental requirements of politicians on lobbying

a partnership-based relationship.[82] There is always the possibility that lobbyists may manipulate decision-making freedom within the institutions, but the risk of this is relatively low due to the high number of competing interests and the related information which members of parliament and civil servants receive. It can therefore generally be assumed that lobbyists focus on their advice and their practical experience vis-à-vis the EU institutions, and that they do not attempt to apply pressure unfairly.

7.3.1.4 Résumé

The analysis of the requirements on the part of stakeholder groups and politicians shows that lobbying is an important link in communication between both parties. It is interesting that many of the requirements are virtually identical, irrespective of whether they are made by the stakeholder groups or the politicians. Both require good lobbying to provide information exchange with expertise and specialist knowledge from the respective other party's sector. They demand that lobbyists proceed with the greatest possible information transparency and professionalism. Both parties also demand that a lobbyist engages with them, i.e. that he is familiar with their internal, formal and informal processes and the respective internal culture, attunes himself to these and orients his work towards them. Ultimately, it is very important to both parties that all lobbying procedures are always undertaken with integrity and in adherence to all compliance regulations. The lobbyist therefore automatically takes on the role of a translator. As an intermediary, he must reduce the complexity of one party's processes and content for the other party, and process information in such a way that it is understood. He can only successfully provide structural support for political processes in the long term in this manner.

In addition to the requirements, skills and characteristics mentioned in Sections 7.3.1.2 and 7.3.1.3, a lobbyist should above all come equipped with enthusiasm and passion for political, social and economic issues, and particularly for the representation of these (and their interests).[83] The political scientist Rinus van Schendelen refers to these as "general attitudes" which are also required in addi-

---

82 Schulz (2007), pp. 22–23.
83 See Lahusen and Jauß (2001), p. 118: "This includes a basic understanding of how politics functions."

tion to the specific skills.[84] These include pronounced curiosity regarding developments at the centre of the EU, the procedures, issues, personnel decisions and stakeholders, but also regarding issues concerning developments at the "periphery", in the member states, because "with some time lag all these developments may affect the EU playing-field in the near future".[85] This "general attitude" also includes the acquisition of a good general education. It helps to obtain a better overview of issues affecting society as a whole.[86] A good memory for names is more than advantageous when "networking".[87] Due to the variety of topics which a lobbyist has to process, a positive attitude towards "generalisation" is also necessary.[88] He should find it easy to quickly become familiarised with new topics with the care of a researcher, whilst determining valid and reliable facts.[89]

In qualification, it must be acknowledged that all of these skills are only rarely encountered in one single individual; they can therefore usually only be covered by entire teams, as in the case of in-house or association lobbying, or by external service providers such as agencies.[90] The skills and characteristics of each individual lobbyist can additionally be fostered and reinforced with specific training. Conceptual solutions can help to compensate personal imbalances in a team's skills.[91]

7.3.2 Development of skills for the structural and long-term support of political processes

The given framework conditions and the requirements on the part of the stakeholder groups and the politicians lead to the emergence of two key skills which a lobbyist must acquire to be able to successfully provide structural support for political processes in the long term. The first key skill is process competence, in combination with an understanding and the management of complex political systems such as the EU. The second is the ability to reduce complexity (particularly for a lobbyist's contacts within the stakeholder groups and amongst politicians, in order to create the required bases for decision-making).[92]

7.3.2.1 Process competence and an understanding of complex political systems

The EU's development trends, and particularly the reforms brought about by the Treaty of Lisbon, are compelling the adaptation of lobbyists' representation of interests – whether these be the concerns of stakeholder groups or even individual

---

84 van Schendelen (2014), p. 280.
85 van Schendelen (2014), p. 280.
86 Vondenhoff and Busch-Janser (2008), p. 160.
87 Vondenhoff and Busch-Janser (2008), p. 160.
88 Vondenhoff and Busch-Janser (2008), p. 161.
89 van Schendelen (2012), p. 341.
90 Heitz (2011), p. 128.
91 See Buholzer (1998), p. 36.
92 Above all, Section 7.3.2 makes reference to Joos (2014), pp. 40–43.

member states. So far, lobbying has focussed above all on the content to be conveyed, since it was assumed that the essential objective of lobbying is to work towards a specific result with content and objective arguments as part of a decision-making process.[93] Content-related work is therefore at the core of the activity of classic lobbying companies (corporate representative offices, associations, public affairs agencies, law firms): participation in public consultations, drawing up exhaustive argumentation papers and expert opinions, execution of media campaigns. Consequently, extensive attention has thus far been given to training lobbyists in content competence; focus has not been placed on process competence (see Section 7.4.2).[94]

This is remarkable, since the significant development trends in EU politics are concerned far more with procedural questions ("processes"). The new framework conditions, caused by the increase in the EU's powers after the Treaty of Lisbon's entry into force (1st December 2009), are described in Chapters 4 and 5. The fundamental changes to the political system of the EU, the various legislative procedures (Chapter 5) and the institutions and stakeholders involved in these (see Section 4.5) are dealt with in these chapters.

Ever more areas of policy are falling under the complex decision-making procedures of the European Union's dynamic, multi-level system, in which supranational (European), national and regional levels are involved. The actors at the relevant levels do not act in isolation from each other in this. Instead, co-operation and a willingness to compromise are required if an actor wishes to achieve his objectives, each of which is determined through constitutional and political competencies, potential influences and interests.

Primarily procedural questions are raised for the lobbyist – irrespective of whether he is employed by a member state, an NGO or a company. Even the search for the correct contact persons for a concern regularly poses a challenge. There is no uniform executive level – no "government" as understood within the member states – in the EU. European lobbying must instead start at European level (Commission, Council or Coreper, etc.) and at member state level (Council members).[95] The situation concerning European legislative procedures is similar: effective lobbying demands the involvement not only of all three of the responsible EU institutions (Commission, Council and Parliament), but, of course, also the member state level, e.g. the individual Council members or the parties represented in the European Parliament.

---

[93] Definitions in Joos (2011), p. 44; Lösche (2007), p. 20; van Schendelen (2002), pp. 203–204; McGrath (2005), p. 17.
[94] With regard to the concepts of content and process competence, see also Godwin, Ainsworth and Godwin (2013), pp. 216–219.
[95] Griesser (2014), p. 61.

To remain present at all of these interfaces – particularly as high time pressure is usually also a factor – and therefore become successfully involved in decision-making processes in the EU, a lobbyist must possess comprehensive process competence. He must therefore be familiar with the crucial formal and informal decision-making processes, and also have corresponding access options (networks) at all decision-making levels. In view of an EU which now has 28 member states, from Portugal to Finland and from Ireland to Cyprus, this can only be accomplished by a very small number of actors. Often, it is no longer possible to determine the number of decision-makers involved in the decision-making process. Added to this is the fact that political decision-makers often take further criteria into consideration in their decisions in addition to content-related aspects (see Section 3.8).

For instance, an EU Commissioner's decision-making can be influenced by whether the concern is presented by a Directorate General with which he has so far enjoyed good or more negative relations – and also whether it is proposed by persons whom he trusts or does not trust. Whether discussion contributions come from a colleague to whom the Commissioner feels obligated due to previous occurrences may also play a role. And of course – albeit virtually irrelevant at European level – whether an issue originates from the Commissioner's home country will almost certainly be of importance.[96]

It therefore remains to be stated that "the more complex the structure of a procedure – and European procedural law is a prime example of complexity – the greater the relevance of the decision-making structures and processes to a specific decision. Content and arguments remain relevant; however, their individual importance to the result of a decision-making process is in decline".[97]

For the sake of completeness, it must be noted here that the external lobbyist, who is engaged as an intermediary, must also be familiar with his clients' structures and working procedures in addition to the political system and the accompanying processes; because major companies and organisations are often no less complex than the political systems. Just think of a global player with a high number of organisational units and levels, as well as barely manageable parts and variant diversity within its product portfolio.[98] The lobbyist must also know his contact persons and be familiar with the departments' responsibilities in this case, so that he can request information of relevance to the lobbying project and bring about decisions on the part of his client in good time.

Consequently, it must therefore be demanded that, in addition to the establishment of content-related competencies, the acquisition of process competence must also be increasingly fostered in the training of future lobbyists: in addition

---

96 Joos (2015), p. 416.
97 Joos (2014), p. 42.
98 See Bullinger, Spath, Warnecke and Westkämpfer (2009³), pp. 746–747.

to an understanding of complex political systems, and the support and management of complex political (decision-making) processes, this also includes an understanding of the structures and working procedures in major companies, associations and organisations. With process competence, one regains the scope for action which has been lost due to the complexity of the many different and parallel processes, and due to the high number of actors and decision-makers (there is no longer *the one* decision-maker[99]).

7.3.2.2 Reduction of complexity for politicians and stakeholder groups

In addition to an understanding of complex political systems such as the multi-level system of the European Union, and the accompanying political decision-making processes, the lobbyist also faces the task of explaining these complex systems and the related (decision-making) processes to his clients, and then supporting and managing these as required by the clients. To do this, he must be able to minimise this complexity in order to be able to reveal possible (new) scope for action. This therefore involves understanding, reducing and managing complexity.

Both the stakeholder groups and politicians require lobbyists to explain the respective other party's concern briefly, precisely and understandably. This also includes the procedures and the knowledge of internal working methods and functions. The occasionally complex, *formal* political framework conditions and decision-making processes are often unfamiliar, and not necessarily understandable, to the stakeholder groups. As outsiders, the *informal* political processes are usually even more difficult for representatives of the stakeholder groups to understand. In turn, politicians are unfamiliar with the procedures within the various stakeholder groups. The concerns which are brought forth may therefore be too technically specific for the political representatives, even if they appear easily understandable to the stakeholder groups' representatives. However, executive and legislative level contact persons cannot be expected to be generally familiar with the commercial management procedures of a pharmaceuticals manufacturer, the special technical considerations of a solar park or the social challenges faced by a charitable organisation. Politicians constantly complain about being literally swamped with too much information and complex details by lobbyists – a wealth of information which cannot be introduced into the political system or properly processed there. As a rule, time is too short for politicians, their employees and civil servants to be able to get to grips with long dossiers containing complicated details. In other words, both parties – stakeholder groups and politicians – demand the reduction of complexity.

In his work, the lobbyist must therefore not only be able to communicate the concerns of one party (stakeholder groups) to the other party (politicians) – the cognitive skills and soft skills required for this have already been explained in Sec-

---

99 See Joos (2015).

tions 7.3.1.2 and 7.3.1.3; instead, he must also reduce the complexity of the content and the contexts at the same time. The onepager methodology, which significantly helps to reduce complexity, should again be specifically emphasised in this regard. The synopsis of stakeholder groups' concerns on one page helps to portray the complicated content in a form which is easily and generally understandable, and enables the reader to concentrate on the essential aspects despite the wealth of information. Through the explanatory formulation of the political backgrounds, the clear designation of a/the existing problem and the simultaneous submission of possible, proposed solutions, complex issues are processed so that they can be easily absorbed by the political system. This maximum reduction of complexity ensures that the information becomes understandable, and therefore also usable, at each point and for each contact person in the political process.

However, this is only one aspect because, on the other hand, this co-ordination of the information to the political contacts during the onepager process also equates to a reduction of the "European Union complexity trap" for the stakeholder groups. The reason for this is that processing the information necessitates a precise understanding of the political system as well as the formal and informal political processes of the EU. These therefore become less complicated and more understandable for the stakeholder groups. Ultimately, it is this reduction in complexity which enables successful process management, and thus the structural and long-term support of political processes in the first place. The lobbyists' process competence is only really brought to bear through this reduction.

In summary, it remains to be stated that lobbying work is subject to a paradigm shift. It must shift its focus more extensively from content-related work to procedural work, from content to process competence and to the reduction of complexity. Effective lobbying will therefore present many lobbyists with an increasing challenge, because content-related positions and arguments formulated with a great deal of content competence and commitment will not be taken into consideration by the decision-maker if they are introduced for example by the wrong person, at the wrong point in time and at the wrong point in the procedures. The first step is extensive process competence and clever, on-site process management by a neutral and objective intermediary. The reduction of complexity is the second step required for the effective support of political processes and successful lobbying. A way out of the "EU complexity trap" will only be found with extensive process competence and the ability to reduce complexity.[100]

7.3.2.3 Revolving door as an answer?

It appears obvious that the answer, in personnel terms, to the many requirements on a lobbyist is for persons from "politics" (elected representatives, members of the executive level, civil servants, employees of parliamentarians or parliamentary

---

100 Joos (2015); Joos (2014), pp. 40–43.

groups and parties, etc.) to switch to the stakeholder groups. One demand states: "We need much more exchange between politics and commerce, and between commerce and politics".[101] The switch from politics to companies, associations or organisation and vice versa is, indeed, by no means unusual for a career in Brussels,[102] since former politicians and their employees, as well as civil servants, offer precisely that knowledge of the formal and, above all, the informal political processes which is often not available within the stakeholder groups. As a rule, these persons have also been able to establish an extended and tenable network, which they bring with them to their new employers. Conversely, of course, it also occurs that representatives of stakeholder groups switch to politics, such as lucrative positions at the European Commission, and integrate their specialist skills in this manner.

Such a switch from politics to commerce and vice versa is referred to as a "revolving door" effect;[103] the French use the expression "pantouflage" for this. Familiar examples can be found at both national and international level. Following his term of office, for example, former German Bundeskanzler Gerhard Schröder was appointed to the supervisory board of Nord Stream, a subsidiary of Gazprom.[104] From the ranks of the European Commission, for instance, Martin Bangemann, who was the Commissioner for Industrial Policy and Communication at that time, switched to the Spanish company Telefonicà in 1999.[105] The former Commissioner for Enterprise and Industry, Günther Verheugen, became an advisor at the Royal Bank of Scotland, and founded the European Experience Company together with the former head of his cabinet.[106] In addition to these cases, which were widely discussed in the media, "changing sides" takes place very frequently at the lower levels of the political and administrative hierarchy.

Such switches initially raise questions concerning the legal arrangement. Can and should a former politician's free choice of profession be restricted, and an activity outside of politics, for instance in commerce or directly in lobbying, be refused to him? In addition to the legal aspects, this also raises the question of the different socialisation of politicians and decision-makers in companies, associations and organisations, as has already been indicated in the above. Can such differences in cultures – politics and commerce – be negated, and do former politicians slot easily into their new field of employment? Due to the high level of media attention and public criticism, it ultimately remains to be considered whether possible negative reporting does not indeed call the advantages of such a switch – knowledge of the respective other formal and informal procedures and processes or the networks in the other camp – into question.

---

101 For an example of this, see Christ (2013), p. 86.
102 Tansey (2014), p. 257.
103 Leif, (2010), p. 7; Welt (2010), pp. 51–55.
104 E.g. Schwabe and Volkery (2005); Lobbypedia, "Gerhard Schröder".
105 Rubner (2009), p. 122.
106 Corporate Europe Observatory, "Günther Verheugen".

7.3.2.3.1 Switch from politics to commerce

The European Union does not fundamentally reject personnel switching between administration and lobbying, since the EU institutions also ultimately benefit from good relationships with external establishments (information exchange). However, the EU wishes to make such switches as transparent as possible. Diverse regulations have therefore been enacted for the various actors in Brussels: EU officials are subject to the Staff Regulations of Officials of the European Economic Community, Commissioners are subject to a separate code of conduct, as are Members of the European Parliament. Others, such as the members of the Permanent Representations of the 28 member states, however, are not subject to any regulation at EU level.[107]

The Staff Regulations of Officials of the European Economic Community, which are applicable to EU officials, specify the rules for switching to a company, association or organisation for this group of persons. For example, Article 16 of the Staff Regulations states that, after leaving office, civil servants are obliged "to behave with integrity and discretion as regards the acceptance of certain appointments or benefits". This fundamental regulation is underpinned by a duty of information. If a civil servant intends to engage in an occupational activity, whether gainful (e.g. in a company) or not (e.g. at an NGO), within two years of leaving the service, he must inform his institution (e.g. the Commission). If the new activity is related "to the work carried out by the official during the last three years of service" and could lead to a "conflict with the legitimate interests of the institution", the civil servant can be permitted to take up the new activity only subject to appropriate conditions, or he may be forbidden from undertaking it at all. Article 339 TFEU additionally specifies that the EU officials "shall be required, even after their duties have ceased, not to disclose information of the kind covered by the obligation of professional secrecy". Regulations not only exist for civil servants who are leaving service, but also for new recruits. According to Article 11 of the Staff Regulations, applicants must also state possible conflicts of interest. However, it must be remembered that these regulations do not apply to employees without civil servant status, except those who have come into contact with sensitive information. In addition, temporary contracts of employment, which an increasing number of institutions are using, can run for up to six years.[108]

Like the civil servants, the EU Commissioners must "behave with integrity and discretion" on taking up a new occupation after their term of office (Article 245 TFEU). In the event of any breach of these obligations, the ECJ may relieve them of their office at the request of the Council or they may be "deprived of [their] right to a pension or other benefits in its stead". The code of conduct for Members of the Commission (Article 1.2) additionally specifies that Commissioners who

---

107 Tansey (2014), p. 258.
108 Tansey (2014), p. 260.

wish to take up an occupational activity must inform the Commission of this up to 18 months after their term of office has ended. If necessary, the Ethics Committee checks whether the new occupation is compatible with Article 245 TFEU. During a period of 18 months after leaving the Commission, former Commissioners, too, "shall not lobby nor advocate with members of the Commission and their staff for his/her business, client or employer on matters for which they have been responsible within their portfolio as Member of the Commission during their mandate". As a point of criticism, it must be noted here that contacts and networks, which are often established over a period of years, are still helpful even after 18 months – which is probably why Article 245 TFEU contains the general requirement of integrity and discretion.[109] Others consider 18 months to be too short – after all, former Commissioners still receive a transitional allowance for a period of no less than 36 months after leaving office.[110]

The code of conduct for Members of the European Parliament (Article 6) states: "Former Members of the European Parliament who engage in professional lobbying or representational activities directly linked to the European Union decision-making process may not, throughout the period in which they engage in those activities, benefit from the facilities granted to former Members under the rules laid down by the Bureau to that effect." In other words, they could be denied access to the European Parliament, which is otherwise open to each former member. However, not even those former members of parliament who engage in lobbying activity have to explicitly return their parliamentary badge, and thus continue to obtain access.[111]

Despite criticism from certain quarters, these clear regulations are not in place to fundamentally prevent the switch from politics to lobbying, but are instead intended to regulate it in transparent form in order to eliminate or minimise conflicts of interest in advance. On adherence to the regulations, there is therefore nothing to prevent the revolving door, at least in legal terms; it may actually help to build a bridge between the different cultures of politicians on the one hand and the stakeholder groups on the other hand.

7.3.2.3.2 Problems of the different socialisation of politicians and decision-makers from commerce

Observers and commentators are not convinced about the value of the practical experience and political knowledge of lobbyists who were previously employed for long periods in politics or administration. However, some believe that precisely such personnel switches are responsible for the success of effective and efficient lobbying, since former politicians, EU officials and employees are familiar with the political culture and its formal and informal (decision-making) processes; they

---

109 Classen (2014), p. 272.
110 Tansey (2014), p. 259.
111 Tansey (2014), p. 259.

offer insider knowledge and know how to communicate in the respective environment. In addition, they usually also have a viable network.[112]

Others view the situation more critically. They claim that the two cultures are too different for personnel exchange to be able to help effectively to improve understanding on both sides; because a good politician is not necessarily also a good lobbyist. Due to the different socialisation of politicians and business leaders, the shift away from politics is not always easy, and many people find it difficult to find their feet in the new environment. In general, politicians do not always appear to come to terms with the culture in companies. The time horizon of politics is measured in legislative periods, whereas the quarterly reports often set the pace in (major) companies. One example of the difficulties of switching from politics to a company is the case of Hessen's former premier, Roland Koch, who was forced to give up his position of CEO at the construction corporation Bilfinger after just three years.[113]

Whereas high-ranking, executive-level politicians or parliamentarians, in particular, have been able to enjoy relatively extensive independence in their work, and were integrated more indirectly into organisational structures and hierarchies, they are usually part of strict hierarchies and structures in a company, association or organisation. Whilst a minister is bound by cabinet discipline and a parliamentarian by parliamentary group discipline, both are primarily responsible solely to their own conscience. In a company, however, loyalty is to the owners and investors or – if present – also one's direct superior. The hierarchies are therefore significantly more tangible. In addition, switching from the role of the "courted" to that of the "courtier" must also be accepted. Whereas politicians seek and appreciate public attention, lobbyists usually work with great discretion and personal reticence.[114]

The commercial benefit of such switches for companies is constantly being questioned due to these problems,[115] because the arrival of a political expert "from the outside" can also have a disrupting effect on the previous structures and employees within an organisation. Whilst the new arrival usually also facilitates contact with politicians and the EU institutions, such a new concentration of power, e.g. in the area of a corporate representative office, can be "an affront" to the corporate management and other important departments and managers within the company.[116] Problems can also arise outside of the organisational area. These can also become noticeable in the case of other stakeholder groups, particularly associations, if similar hierarchies and structures predominate there. However, these

---

112 Heitz (2011), p. 129; Althaus (2006), p. 323; Vondenhoff and Busch-Janser (2008), p. 163.
113 Vogt (2014); conversely, Baden-Württemberg's former premier, Lothar Späth, who was CEO of Jenoptik, is an example of a successful switch.
114 Vondenhoff and Busch-Janser (2008), p. 165.
115 Vondenhoff and Busch-Janser (2008), pp. 164–165; Lahusen (2004), p. 785.
116 Coen (2009), p. 159.

problems are less prevalent when politicians and civil servants switch to an external service provider such as a governmental relations agency, since the hierarchies there are usually flat, and the former political and administrative representatives have sufficient scope to bring their expertise to bear.

7.3.2.3.3 Revolving door as a dead end? Image problems for politicians and stakeholder groups

The switch from politics to commerce and vice versa is often viewed very critically by the general public. As has already been explained, anti-lobby groups and the media usually take offence at such a move, which is entirely above board in legal terms. Such negative reporting can have a damaging effect on a stakeholder group or a company.

On its website, for instance, the anti-lobby group ALTER-EU demands that the revolving door be "blocked", and wants to see even tighter rules and increased transparency implemented for such personnel transfers.[117] Such switches are also viewed critically by the Corporate Europe Observatory (CEO), which has established a "Revolving Door Watch" online. The switches undertaken by former EU officials, Members of the European Parliament, Commissioners and other employees of EU institutions or EU-near establishments such as the Permanent Representations of the member states are reported and assessed there.[118] Besides specialised websites, however, mainstream media are also interested in personnel switches from politics to commerce. In Germany, for example, media criticism was attracted by the Head of the Federal Chancellery, Roland Pofalla's, move to Deutsche Bahn AG; that of the Minister of State in the Federal Chancellery, Eckart von Klaeden, to Daimler AG and the switch by the Parliamentary State Secretary in the Federal Ministry of Transport and Digital Infrastructure, Katharina Reiche, to the Verband kommunaler Unternehmen e. V. (VKU (German Association of Municipal Companies)).[119]

However, the revolving door in the opposite direction, from commerce to politics, also attracts criticism. On his appointment to the position of Commissioner for Financial Stability, Financial Services and Capital Market Union in the autumn of 2014, Briton Jonathan Hill, who had already made several professional moves between commerce and politics in his home country, was criticised for having being employed at Quiller Consultants, where he represented the interests of the London Stock Exchange and the major bank HSBC, amongst others. Spaniard Miguel Arias Cañete suffered a similar fate, attracting criticism from both the general public and the European Parliament for his links to the oil industry. He was compelled to sell off his stakes in two oil companies before he was able to become EU

---

117 ALTER-EU (2015).
118 Corporate Europe Observatory, "RevolvingDoorWatch".
119 Bollmann (2015).

Commissioner for Energy and Environmental Protection.[120] It is entirely usual for top positions to be held by representatives from the economy. Mario Draghi, the President of the ECB, was previously employed as a Vice President at the investment bank Goldman Sachs.

Although there are no legal grounds to prevent switches from politics to commerce and vice versa, and the corresponding regulations have been adhered to, negative reporting can indeed harm the image of former politicians' new employers. On switching from commerce to politics, the latter is also criticised for its closeness to the former. This then occasionally leads to accusations such as "cronyism" and "string-pulling", and ultimately, the revolving door can also cause major damage to the standing of politics.[121] A company, an association or an organisation must therefore always weigh up in each case whether the specialist knowledge gained on recruiting a former politician compensates for possible "negative press".

Such accusations and the related reporting are a further reason why a lobbyist should act as an intermediary between politics on one side and companies, associations and organisations on the other side. As he stands outside of both systems as a professional, trusted mediator, he is not subject to accusations of cronyism or particular closeness to one side or another. He remains equidistant, i. e. he maintains an equal distance from both cultures. Added to this is the fact that switches usually take place from politics to commerce, and that actual knowledge exchange takes place particularly in this one direction. The fundamental problem of overcoming hierarchies, which is necessary for efficient and effective lobbying, still remains in this case, because the "switchers" are also integrated into the respective hierarchies of a company, association or organisation. In turn, the network and trust are again held by just one person, and cannot be easily passed on to possible successors. The revolving door can therefore quickly prove to be a one-way street.

7.4 Status quo of "vocational education and further training for lobbyists"

7.4.1 Existing methods of education and further training

The need for professional lobbying amongst EU institutions continues to grow as the political importance of the EU increases. The EU's influence has been increasing continuously since the 1980s: starting with the strengthening of the single market through the Single European Act (1987), and continuing to increase with the establishment of the Union through the Maastricht Treaty (1993), up to and

---

120 N.U. (2014); Lobby Control, "After hearing: Hill and Cañete remain unacceptable as EU Commissioners!".
121 Leif (2010), pp. 7–8.

including the intensification of European integration with the Treaty of Lisbon (2009). The number of lobbyists in Brussels is also increasing along with this political influence. In 1997, around 14,000 lobbyists[122] were assumed. Today, unofficial estimates vary between 15,000 and 20,000.[123] It is assumed that this number could increase still further in the coming years.[124] Even now, the European Commission states that there are approximately 6,500 organisations registered in the Transparency Register, which it administers together with the European Parliament. This means that at least approximately 32,500 lobbyists, who would be bound by the Transparency Register's code of conduct, are active in Brussels.[125] Added to these are all of the persons not registered in the Transparency Register, e.g. a high number of lawyers involved in this field, but also the representatives of state establishments such as the representations of the German Federal Länder and Länder parliaments.

The lobbyists' training and résumés are as varied as their number in the "lobbying capital" of Brussels is high. Depending on whether lobbying is performed by corporate representative offices, associations, public affairs agencies, law firms or governmental relations agencies, the lobbyists have undergone different training and offer different professional backgrounds, whether this be legal, political science or other social sciences training and/or work in the field of politics. In part, lobbying in the broader sense is also carried out by think tanks or public relations agencies, some of whose employees may have undergone different training, such as in the field of marketing. Despite the emerging trend towards professionalisation for the vocation of lobbying, the path to becoming a lobbyist is not yet institutionalised, but is instead very varied and unclear. The route via the revolving door has already been outlined (see Section 7.3.2.3). If lobbyists enter the sector via "non-political" professions, they often come from the fields of PR or journalism. Others, who gain a direct foothold in lobbying, have usually studied law, political science, communication science or another social science or humanistic subject such as history.[126]

However, there are also study programmes aimed specifically at future generations of lobbyists. In the UK, for example, future lobbyists generally study the (classic) subjects of Philosophy, Politics and Economics (PPE) in Oxford or Human, Social and Political Sciences (HSPS) in Cambridge.[127] The current train-

---

122 Joos (1998), p. 119.

123 Honsig-Erlenburg (2014); Lobby Control, "Lobbying in the EU", estimates the number to be 20,000; for a precise analysis of the estimates, see: Heitz (2011), pp. 131–134.

124 Heitz (2011), p. 134.

125 European Commission (2014c): "An estimated 75% of all economically related organisations and around 60% of the NGOs operating in Brussels have now sought registration. At present, around 6,500 organisations are registered in total. According to cautious estimates, each organisation employs an average of five individuals, i.e. at least 32,500 lobbyists are now subject to the Transparency Register's code of conduct".

126 See: Lahusen and Jauß (2001), p. 116; Althaus (2006), pp. 326–327.

127 Zetter (2012), p. 64; until 2013, the study programme in Cambridge was called Social and Political Sciences (SPS).

ing is therefore usually fundamental, i.e. undergone during the first study programme (up to the Bachelor qualification or Diploma), and therefore reveals specialisation in a specific specialist or working area. However, interdisciplinary training would be advantageous for lobbying, with its requirements on legal, political and intercultural understanding (to name just a few of the requirements). The content of the individual, classic study programmes is therefore often only of indirect relevance to the work of a lobbyist. Politics, for example, is completely different in scientific and practical terms. Added to this is the fact that methodical knowledge and skills, plus an in-depth and differentiated understanding of political processes, which is particularly important in the "EU complexity trap", are not necessarily part of the curricula. This knowledge is often only acquired during professional practice, as it has not been dealt with during the training.

Initial attempts are being made to enable future lobbyists with subject-specific training to undergo adequate advanced training through offers in the graduate field, of course. For instance, corresponding Master programmes are available for students who have already completed an initial study programme, e.g. the programmes for European studies and international relations; these Master programmes include for example the Master in European Political and Administrative Studies at the College of Europe in Bruges,[128] the Master in Public Affairs at the SciencesPo in Paris[129] and the Master of Public Administration (MPA) and the Executive Master of Public Administration (EMPA) at the Institute of Public Affairs at the London School of Economics (LSE).[130] The Master of Science (MSc) in Public Affairs and Lobbying at London Brunel University,[131] the Master of Science (MSc) in Corporate Communication at Robert Gordon University in Aberdeen[132] or the one-year Master in European Public Affairs (MA EPA) at the University of Maastricht are aimed more specifically at lobbying, at least according to their designations.[133]

The Executive Master of Public Management at the Hertie School of Governance in Berlin[134] or the MBA in Public Affairs and Leadership at Quadriga University, also in Berlin, are aimed more towards further training for active lobbyists.[135] In Belgium, the American University in Brussels offers the one-week European Public Affairs and Advocacy Institute for US American students, but also explicitly for practising lobbyists, according to its American role model.[136]

In addition to universities, there are also non-academic providers or professional associations which are specialised in course programmes and workshops for lob-

---

128 College of Europe (2015b).
129 SciencesPo (2015).
130 LSE (2015).
131 Brunel University, London (2015).
132 Robert Gordon University, Aberdeen (2015).
133 Spoormans and Vanboonacker (2005); Maastricht University (2015).
134 Hertie School of Governance (2015).
135 Quadriga University, Berlin (2015).
136 American University (2015).

byists, such as the European Training Academy from Budapest, which has an office and provides tuition in Brussels,[137] the Chartered Institute for Public Relations[138] or the Public Relations Consultants Association,[139] both located in the UK. In turn, the Confederation of German Employers' Associations (BDA) trains its junior staff itself in part, and has established a junior managing director programme, a two-year traineeship, for this purpose.[140]

At first glance, this appears to meet the need for adequate training for lobbyists: "So universities have certainly woken up to the fact that public affairs and lobbying are now established careers, and students will opt to study the subject at both undergraduate and postgraduate level."[141] In Europe, however, the academic discipline of lobbying or public affairs is still being established, and is defined by its search for a "clear identity". This identity search, as well as concept definition and delimitation of the subject from other disciplines, display a "healthy and vibrant disciplinary evolution".[142] This is indeed an essential step, because such scientification and the establishment of a formal, theoretical basis are also an expression of the professionalisation of lobbying as a vocation.[143] It can be seen that education and further training are moving in the right direction. The various study programmes and training courses almost certainly offer a helpful collection of knowledge modules which support activity in the field of lobbying; however, it remains to be seen whether they deal with the necessary, special requirements such as process competence and complexity reduction, or offer preparation for the tasks of intermediary process supporter and translator between stakeholder groups and politicians.

7.4.2 Objectives and content of the current education and further training

More precise assessment of the current education and further training options reveals the extensive fragmentation and lack of uniformity of the range, in terms of both form and content. A formal distinction therefore has to be made between Bachelor study programmes, Master study programmes and non-academic offers. Some of these take one to two years, others just two weeks, as may be the case with advanced training courses. The content also differs widely, from classic, more political science-based study programmes to pure practical courses. Added to this is the fact that lobbyists are usually recruited from fields of study such as law or political science, history and other humanities. Nor are the academic options necessarily interdisciplinary; they are usually located in one single faculty. At present, the training is therefore often lacking in the necessary depth and breadth which a

---

137 European Training Academy (2015).
138 Chartered Institute of Public Relations (2015).
139 PRCA (2014).
140 BDA.Die Arbeitgeber (2015).
141 Zetter (2011[2]), p. 64.
142 McGrath, Moss and Harris (2010), pp. 346–347.
143 Althaus (2006), p. 328.

lobbyist must offer for his work as an independent, intermediary, structural process supporter, i.e. as a governmental relations manager. It is particularly this interdisciplinary nature which helps to prepare him for this role of translator between the world of politics and the world of stakeholder groups.

The training objectives of the study programmes are also often very global; as a rule, for instance, "lobbyist" is only stated as a primary vocational goal in the practically oriented training courses. In the case of the other offers, the option of subsequently working in the field of lobbying is only one amongst many. The Master in Public Policy at the University of Erfurt, for instance, prepares its graduates "for careers in international public service and non-governmental organisations".[144] According to the programme description, those who obtained their Bachelor in Politics, Philosophy and Economics at Oxford became "eminent philosophers, political scientists and economists, as well as heads of state, distinguished public servants, politicians, industrialists, financiers, journalists, and a host of other professionals".[145] Study programmes such as the Master in European Political and Administrative Studies (MEPA) at the College of Europe in Bruges, whose curriculum is primarily centred on the European Union, are also oriented more towards students who subsequently intend to work in European and national institutions. Nevertheless, the "private sector" is also listed here, which may well ultimately refer to nothing other than lobbying.[146]

As part of this development, a requirement for the political analysis of major, global trends such as climate change, terrorism or financial market reform, which is intended to help provide advice to decision-makers in executive level and stakeholder group organisations, is recognised on the part of the trainees, for instance. This new generation of public affairs experts is "capable of analysing and interpreting – and even anticipating – major environmental trends and developments, and capable of counselling organizational leaders about how best to respond to the challenges that such trends present".[147] By increasingly looking at the broader political context, however, there is a risk that the "feel" for day-to-day political business, with its formal and informal decision-making processes in EU Europe, such as the informal trialogue, will be lost in this lobbyist training.

One further deficit – particularly in the academic training – is the lack of focus on the "practical" methods of lobbying for structural and long-term process support, such as dealing intensively with the process-oriented lobbying instruments (see Chapter 6), particularly the perspective change from the individual interest to the common interest perspective (onepager methodology). The ability to precisely analyse the individual decision-making processes, decision-making bases and decision-making horizons of the political decision-makers is equally as important.

---

144 University of Erfurt (2015).
145 PPE (2015).
146 College of Europe (2015a).
147 McGrath, Moss and Harris (2010), p. 347.

Despite all recognisable shifts towards professionalisation, lobbyists' training is not yet tailored to the actual needs which meet the requirements of a lobbyist in the role of an objective intermediary, or the requirements of the stakeholder groups and politicians. The courses are usually too global in nature, and are aimed at students with different vocational goals, one of which may also be lobbying in the sense of the structural and long-term process support of governmental relations. If the further training is aimed at practising lobbyists, the necessary, theoretical breadth and depth are often lacking – particularly in the case of courses which only last for a few weeks – in order to grasp all of the facets of the profession of lobbying, and particularly governmental relations.

A *prima facie* analysis of the formal and content-related criteria alone shows that not all of these courses can be equivalent, and that students and subsequent employers cannot rely on a uniform level of education and further training. However, such a uniform and binding level (throughout Europe) would be an important prerequisite for permanently raising the quality of lobbying and improving its reputation as an area of employment. The lobbyists' training could be subject to binding standards similar to those (at least within the individual EU member states) applicable to the training undergone by lawyers, teachers or doctors. The great importance of lobbying in the political process would justify this, and the professional ethos amongst lobbyists themselves – as for example in the case of lawyers and doctors – would be further extended and reinforced, which is in turn likely to impact very positively on lobbying compliance and transparency in general. Specific training for the governmental relations manager, who monitors the political (decision-making) processes in Brussels and in the EU member states as an objective intermediary between politicians and stakeholder groups, is therefore urgently required.

7.5 New approaches in education and further training

In conclusion to the preceding analysis, courage should be taken in implementing new approaches to lobbyist training. The current training of lobbyists is usually not targeted, and does not prepare the lobbyists optimally for their professional tasks. The majority of the training courses are too broad-based for this, and are aimed at students with extremely diverse vocational goals. However, the courses aimed specifically at lobbying also differ extensively in terms of their scope and depth. What is lacking is a uniform level of training.

Suggestions for the goal-oriented, academic training of a new generation of lobbyists will now be outlined in the following. Such training should enable the graduates to understand, analyse and decipher complex political systems, in order to support the many parallel and successive processes and procedures, and to reduce their complexity with the necessary process competence. In short, the graduates must be enabled to manage complexity. This applies primarily to the complexity of the multi-level system of the European Union, but also to the not insignificant (formal and informal) complexity of the majority of the member states' political systems, such as the federalism of the Federal Republic of Germany.[148] It follows from this that such training should be oriented first and foremost towards governmental relations, as this is the only sub-sector of lobbying whose primary tasks are process management and the reduction of complexity. The objective of the training is therefore the governmental relations manager.

The governmental relations manager comes into play wherever he is required to represent stakeholder groups vis-à-vis the executive and legislative level, and to act as an intermediary between the spheres of politics and the economy. Through the structural and long-term support of political processes, he is able to recognise potential risks to his clients and prepare strategic decisions.

In addition to the classic workplace of an external governmental relations agency, governmental relations managers are also required in companies, associations and organisations: there, they organise in-house lobbying and establish structures which enable smooth co-operation with external service providers. This also applies to public bodies, from the member state representations at the EU to member state ministries. Scientists actually recommend that even these public bodies establish their own work groups for their lobbying within the EU.[149] These may then also engage external agencies, with whom co-operation has to be coordinated.

To be able to meet the requirements made on lobbying by the stakeholder groups and politicians, to learn the "crucial tools of the trade" in terms of breaking down complexity by means of process competence, future governmental relations manager training must ideally be offered as a postgraduate study programme – a Master in Governmental Relations – similar to the numerous MBA programmes which are already available. In the preceding, initial study programme (e.g. Bachelor programme), future lobbyists should undergo in-depth, specialist training in an area of relevance to governmental relations (e.g. political science, business administration, law, etc.). Through this study programme, the candidates acquire the academic depth required for the Master in Governmental Relations, as well as theoretical and content-related knowledge which are fundamental to the further training. The specific requirements made on the lobbyist will only then be dealt with in interdisciplinary form during the subsequent Master study programme, to which students from the various specialist areas will be admitted. Such a Master study programme can ultimately be used to establish a uniform level of training and uniform standards in lobbying. Initial pioneers, who have recognised and are implementing these approaches, are already proceeding in this direction. For ex-

---

148 See Linder (2014), p. 48.
149 van Schendelen (2013), p. 2.

> ### The six modules of a possible Master in Governmental Relations
>
> 1. European law module
> 2. Political science module
> 3. Process management and complexity reduction module
> 4. Intercultural skills module
> 5. Language module
> 6. Practical module

Figure 7.3: The six modules of a possible Master in Governmental Relations

ample, the Ludwig-Maximilians-University in Munich has been offering an undergraduate seminar, "Convincing Political Stakeholders", specifically on governmental relations within the EU for the past several years as part of a Master study programme at the Munich School of Management; this seminar is organised and conducted by the author as a visiting lecturer.[150]

Two years should be planned for a Master in Governmental Relations due to the wealth of material. This length of time would then also enable the integration of a practical semester, in which the students can put the theoretical knowledge which they have learnt into practice in the day-to-day business of lobbying.

The high number of tasks and requirements made by stakeholder groups and politicians would suggest that a possible curriculum for a Master in Governmental Relations should have an interdisciplinary structure.[151] Only in this way can the students develop an understanding of all of the areas in which governmental relations are involved. Thanks to these insights into various specialist areas, they are also optimally prepared for their future tasks as intermediaries and translators. They are therefore familiarised with various specialist fields, concepts and approaches at an early stage, take these skills on board, and are also able to apply them practically and build bridges between them if necessary. Six central modules emerge as part of an interdisciplinary structure of the Master in Governmental Relations; these can be supplemented by others if necessary: European law, political science, complexity reduction and process management, intercultural competence, languages and a practical module. These serve as suggestions and discussion contributions to the debate concerning the future training of lobbyists.

7.5.1 European law module

Knowledge of European law is crucial to governmental relations manager training. In this module, the students are familiarised with the legal bases and the organisation of the EU (polity), with its institutions (see Chapter 4) as well as the for-

---

150 LMU. Institute for Marketing, "Announcement of Master Seminar Convincing Political Stakeholders", http://www.marketing.bwl.uni-muenchen.de/1_aktuelles/schwarzes_brett/ ausschreibung_eutop_seminar1/index.html (last accessed on 10.2.2015).

151 With regard to interdisciplinary nature, see van Schendelen (2014), p. 282.

mal procedures and decision-making processes. Knowledge of the relevant compliance regulations and rules of procedure (e.g. of the Parliament) is also necessary for practical lobbying.

First and foremost, this module must highlight the differences between primary and secondary European legislation (see Chapter 5). The primary law – particularly the Treaty on the European Union (TEU) and the Treaty on the Functioning of the European Union (TFEU) – result in the basic, legal structure and the organisational structure of the EU as a whole. However, the European law module will also show the legal bases of the multi-level system of the European Union, the interaction of the various decision-making levels as part of the formal processes. The changes brought about by the Treaty of Lisbon are of particular importance here, since this strengthened the EU outwardly (e.g. due to its separate legal personality) and inwardly (e.g. the *de facto* "communitarisation" of many areas of policy).

The secondary legislation involves the legislation laid down by the EU (see typology of legislative acts, Chapter 5). As the primary law, which can only be amended with unanimity in the Council, is not usually the objective of lobbying, focus will be placed on dealing with the secondary legislation. These are the legislative acts which can significantly influence the stakeholder groups' daily work, and which may possibly even determine their success or failure. These may include legislative acts concerning environmental regulations, working time regulations, bans on advertising or import quotas. Such legislative acts are usually the target of lobbying campaigns.

The various legislative acts, such as the ordinary legislative procedure according to Article 294 TFEU or the procedure for the enactment of implementing legislation according to Articles 290 and 291 TFEU, are essential in this context. Knowledge of these formal procedures provides future governmental relations managers with an overview of the (formal) decision-making processes in the EU.

In this context, the various rules of procedure of the EU institutions are also relevant for the daily practice of governmental relations, since these regulate the lobbyists' access to their contact persons in politics. Knowledge of these regulations is vital for lobbyists to deal with legislative and executive level decision-makers with integrity (compliance).

7.5.2 Political science module

Whereas the European law module offers a formal overview of the structure and organisation of the EU and its decision-making processes, the political science module provides information in parallel on how these formal specifications are brought to life in daily political practice. The political processes and the political culture of the EU are analysed more precisely. The future training would therefore meet one of the central requirements made by politicians.

As theoretical bases, this firstly includes an explanation of European integration (see Chapter 4) and its history plus – secondly – an understanding of political processes (policy cycle), which result in the potential time slots for successfully implementing lobbying projects (see Chapter 3).

With its analytical procedures, political science can contribute to practical governmental relations, above all, in terms of researching informal political procedures and processes. For instance, one central, informal procedure, which is not provided for in the Treaties (TEU, TFEU), but with which governmental relations managers must be familiar under all circumstances, is the informal trialogue, which usually takes place prior to the first reading in the European Parliament as part of an ordinary legislative procedure (see Chapter 5). Political science can additionally provide important information for governmental relations via the importance of networks in decision-making and obtaining majorities in the Council and Parliament. One further, central element of this module is individual decision-making amongst political decision-makers, in which political arguments, such as the involvement of the politician's home constituency or party political orientation, also frequently play a role in addition to objective arguments.[152]

7.5.3 Process management and complexity reduction module

The first two modules primarily make the complexity of the multi-level system of the European Union, and its often parallel formal and informal decision-making procedures, clear to the students. In the third module, commercial management and organisational science findings are used to teach how this complexity can be deciphered, reduced and managed with process competence. This module therefore makes a crucial contribution to the professionalisation of the vocation of "lobbying". Even today, lobbying is increasingly being regarded as a "modern manager vocation".[153] This is why reference is also made to "public affairs management"[154] or "public affairs officer".[155] A new generation of lobbyists, "which is going about its business in a more sober but highly effective manner",[156] is emerging. However, only a Master in Governmental Relations will enable this claim to be bindingly implemented at a uniform level with uniform standards.

Specifically, the application of the lobbying process instruments (see Chapter 6) will be taught in the "process management and complexity reduction" module within the framework of practical examples and lobbying cases. Focus is placed on the following questions: how is a stakeholder analysis performed? How is a usable key player list created? How can a tenable network be established? How is a per-

---

152 A more precise analysis of individual decision-making with the aid of the Gaussian normal distribution and the law of large numbers can be found in Section 3.8.
153 Vondenhoff and Busch-Janser (2008), p. 159.
154 van Schendelen (2014), p. 60.
155 Köppl (2003), p. 181.
156 Gross-Halbuer, Neumann and Niewsmann (2014).

spective change accomplished with the onepager methodology, and when is a onepager used? The module therefore prepares students for the important task of the governmental relations manager as an intermediary who mediates between the world of the stakeholder groups and the world of politicians, and who acts as an interpreter. The instruments learned here can be used to meet the requirements made by both the stakeholder groups and politicians (see Section 7.3). Process management helps to retain an overview amidst the high number of procedures and decision-making processes which often run in parallel, and to reduce their complexity in supporting political processes.

Process management also includes an understanding of commercial management organisation and costs. How can the lobbying instruments be used effectively and efficiently? The stakeholder groups' understanding of performance and consideration should also be mentioned in this regard: what can a client expect from his lobbyist? Commercial management training additionally increases the students' understanding of the procedures, issues and problems of commercial clients, which facilitates co-operation with this client group.

7.5.4 Intercultural skills module

With 28 member states with different peoples and cultures, intercultural skills are crucial for day-to-day governmental relations work. This module therefore involves European studies and the application of soft skills in the intercultural field. Here, European studies refers to knowledge of European history, European (economic) geography, social life and the various European (political) cultures. This represents the basic, theoretical knowledge in this module. The acquisition of soft skills, such as good manners and diplomatic finesse, and the intercultural implementation of these, form the second element of this module. This knowledge is not only taught in theory, but is also taken on board in practical terms on the basis of interactive elements such as case studies or role plays.

This is important, because networks and political majorities are not only formed across parties and institutions in the EU, but also across various European nations. If EU and member state civil servants, Commissioners and members of government as well as parliamentarians of diverse nationalities and/or institutions are addressed in several member states, it must be possible to show an understanding of, and to deal at length with, the diverse national, socio-cultural and politico-cultural differences of the respective contact persons.[157] Important key competencies of one's own culture (such as empathy, politeness or communication skills) must be "translated" in order to also enable them to be applied to other cultures. Ultimately, therefore, this module also involves the role of the governmental relations manager as a translator and a "reducer" of (intercultural) complexity.

---

157 Michalowitz (2007), p. 78.

7.5.5 Language module

However, governmental relations managers are also required to be translators in the literal sense of the word. In-depth language training is required for the optimal implementation of intercultural skills, with the result that great importance must be attached to the study of European foreign languages. In particular, advanced courses should also be offered for English and French, the two most common languages in Brussels, and in one or other of the EU's total of 24 official languages, so that the students can extend their existing knowledge of these languages with important, specialist political and legal terms. It must be possible to understand legal texts, expert opinions, documents and other written correspondence correctly. In legal texts such as regulations or directives, for instance, it is often linguistic nuances which may define, extend or restrict the scope or the prerequisites of a regulation.

7.5.6 Practical module

Even the very best academic training is of no worth if it fails the acid test in practice.[158] Purely academic training offers a good foundation for lobbying, and enables theoretical, intellectual access to the formal procedures in the executive, legislative and judicial institutions, but it is only able to provide a limited insight into constitutional reality as well as formal and, above all, informal political practice. It does not provide any direct insight into day-to-day political processes such as meetings or committee sessions, for instance; at best, it is able to describe and analyse these from an external perspective, e. g. using the minutes of meetings (if accessible). Consequently, the academic training must be supplemented by a practical training component – the knowledge of a governmental relations manager "cannot simply be imparted through courses".[159]

A mandatory internship in an EU institution or establishment should be a significant element of the training. In particular, internships should be undertaken at an institution which is also regarded as a relevant contact for lobbying, i. e. at the European Parliament, the Commission, the Council or also the Permanent Representations of the member states or the representative offices of regions and regional parliaments. Such internships are important, and offer the opportunity to start establishing one's own networks.[160] This method is particularly valuable for learning the rules "which are not written down anywhere, and which one can only get to know and learn to apply if it has been possible to take them on board in the organisation".[161]

---

158 See Chahoud (2010), p. 21.
159 See Heitz (2011), p. 129; with regard to the importance of practical elements in academic training in the field of European public affairs, see also Spoormans and Vanboonacker (2005); for Germany: Althaus (2006), pp. 321 – 323.
160 Zetter (2011[2]), p. 65.
161 Althaus (2006), p. 323.

As this involves a Master course, there will also be candidates who have already obtained experience of working full time at one of the relevant institutions after their Bachelor study programme. They may be permitted to forgo the mandatory internship in order to shorten their study programme.

Such a curriculum could be implemented to meet the essential requirements made on lobbying by the stakeholder groups and politicians, and to prepare the future governmental relations managers for their tasks as intermediary process supporters, translators and "complexity reducers". The candidate's general attitude cannot be taught; it can merely be fostered. A genuine, fundamental interest in the politics of the EU and its member states must be present.

In summary, it can be stated that a governmental relations manager must continuously train his multiple intelligences in order to be successful. This means he must first deal with training and developing his rational, mental intelligence (IQ) through the completion of academic training, a Master in Governmental Relations. However, a lobbyist must also promote the development of his social and emotional intelligence. Of the soft skills, dealing with people from various European cultures on a daily basis above all demands empathy. Knowledge of the compliance regulations trains integrity and moral intelligence, a further factor for success. A certain degree of physical intelligence also contributes to success. This includes physical fitness. This is necessary to withstand the extensive stress to which the profession occasionally leads. It is self-evident that a governmental relations manager must also pay attention to his physical condition and health. To establish contacts and build networks, he must be able to adapt to the often not inconsiderable levels of stress in his clients' daily work and politics (see Sections 7.3.1.2 and 7.3.1.3).[162]

The above list of criteria, to which a potential lobbyist is subject, and against which he must measure himself, is long. If these criteria are met, there is no longer anything standing in the way of a successful, new generation of lobbyists – governmental relations managers.

7.6 Summary

The vocational profile of a lobbyist is not clearly defined. In particular, the general public has no clear concept of the work undertaken by a lobbyist. Germany's Federal Employment Agency regards the "political advisor" as a professional group with "different methods of access".[163] Indeed, academics and lobbyists themselves state: "Most persons in EU public affairs are self-made people";[164] lobbying is "not

---

162 With regard to the multiple intelligences, see e.g. Wetzel (2007), p. 14.
163 Federal Employment Agency (2015); see also Althaus (2006), p. 317.
164 van Schendelen (2014), p. 281.

an independent profession per se",[165] and "lobbyists have no specific vocational profile".[166] Some even state incisively: "No formal qualifications whatsoever are required to be a lobbyist."[167] But do the complex challenges which lobbyists face in the dynamic, multi-level system of the European Union not necessitate a well trained specialist who can meet the requirements of the stakeholder groups (e.g. companies, associations, organisations and possibly also the EU member states and EU regions) and European politicians? Instead of self-made generalists, do we not need professional, highly specialised governmental relations managers, who are able to credibly act as intermediaries between stakeholder groups and politicians?

Against this backdrop, Chapter 7 dealt with the following key questions:

- What are the particular challenges faced by a lobbyist, especially a process-oriented governmental relations manager?
- Is learning by doing, or a lobbyist's own (previous) experience in the area of politics and/or administration (revolving door, i.e. actors' switching between politics and stakeholder groups) sufficient to overcome these challenges?
- Does the current (university) training offer adequate preparation to meet these challenges?
- How must training be structured in the future in order to prepare future lobbyists better for their daily work? In other words: what training does a governmental relations manager require?

(1) The most essential tasks of lobbyists include deciphering and reducing complexity, and therefore making political issues and developments manageable and planable for their clients. Due to complex political systems such as that of the EU and the complex way in which policies develop, the service of "lobbying" is under enormous pressure to adapt. In addition to content-related work, it must now deal above all with breaking down this complexity and with options for controlling it. The "European Union complexity trap" has already been described exhaustively in Chapters 4 and 5.

(2) The requirements on good lobbying are therefore varied. In summary, it can be stated that the stakeholder groups expect information procurement, commercial thinking, professional lobbying, integrity and compliance. Similarly, politicians demand information and expertise, information transparency and professional information mediation, an understanding of the political culture, integrity and compliance. Language, social and intercultural skills are additionally required as soft skills on the political stage of the EU. There are already various approaches to academic training for lobbyists. Professionalisation is emerging, but this is still in its infancy.[168]

---

165 Kleinfeld, Zimmer and Willems (2007), interview with Cornelia Yzer, pp. 278–279 and interview with Wolf-Dieter Zumpfort, p. 275.
166 Heitz (2011), p. 128.
167 Althaus (2006), p. 320.
168 van Schendelen (2014), p. 281.

(3) The current education and further training on offer reveals the extensive fragmentation and lack of uniformity of the range, in terms of both form and content. The training objectives of the study programmes are often very global; as a rule, for instance, "lobbyist" is only stated as a primary vocational goal in the practically oriented training courses. In the case of the other offerings, the option of working in the field of lobbying after graduation is only one amongst many.

(4) Students and future employers cannot rely on a uniform level of vocational education and further training. However, such a uniform and binding level (throughout the EU) would be an important prerequisite for permanently raising the quality of lobbying and improving its reputation as an area of employment.

(5) One further deficit – particularly in the academic training – is the lack of focus on the "practical" methods of lobbying for structural and long-term process support, such as dealing intensively with the process-oriented lobbying instruments (see Chapter 6), particularly the perspective change from the individual interest to the common interest perspective (onepager methodology, Chapter 10). The ability to precisely analyse the individual decision-making processes, decision-making bases and decision-making horizons of the political decision-makers is equally as important (see Chapter 3).

(6) To solve these problems, the introduction of a special Master study programme – a Master in Governmental Relations – is proposed; this would have an interdisciplinary structure and encompass specialist areas such as European law, political science, business administration, intercultural skills and languages in various modules. Both hard skills such as process competence and analytical thinking, and soft skills such as social competence and integrity should be taught and fostered. It is important to supplement the academic training with practical, i.e. practically oriented, components.

(7) Special training for governmental relations managers, particularly a Master in Governmental Relations, would be a significant step forwards in the professionalisation and definition of lobbying as a vocation, whilst simultaneously meeting the requirements of politicians and stakeholder groups. Such training would also contribute to increased quality and professionalism and, as a result of this, to an improved image of lobbying in general. Firstly, an authentic vocational profile could emerge; secondly, academic involvement in the topic of lobbying would promote further research, thereby further increasing the acceptance of lobbying. Lobbying in general, and governmental relations management in particular, would therefore have the opportunity to be recognised for what they are, namely a necessary element of the democratic political system of the EU and its member states.

Chapter 8   Discourse: future challenges

8.1 Professionalism means translation competence

By Armin Nassehi

Demanding professionalism from actors of different varieties is a platitude. And the statement that success and professionalism go hand-in-hand with one another could almost be a tautology, because how else should professionalism be demonstrated other than through being successful – if one does not wish to make use of a completely impractical and therefore ideological concept of professionalism that falls apart in the course of time, instead of being able to specify the conditions for success under respective, societal constellations?

Conversely, as can be seen from the complex mix of societal structures, it is becoming increasingly less possible to explain success as the simple application of the right measure in the respective situations, problems or challenges. Professionalism is not therefore simply the application of expert knowledge to an issue, but must instead anticipate that the issue contains an inherent complexity, which cannot be controlled simply by applying knowledge or skills. This not only transforms professionalisation strategies into a difficult undertaking which requires a long-term structure, but virtually compels one to raise questions concerning the conditions, and therefore the professionalisation strategies, which make professionalism possible.

In order to develop corresponding criteria, a look will first be taken at so-called classic professions – these include vocations with client contact, particularly the priesthood, doctors and lawyers, i.e. ultimately graduates of classic faculties, which have been of particular importance to modernisation processes (Section 8.1.1). From here, the train of thought will then lead to the question of what has characterised classic elites in modern society, and which competencies new elites must develop (Section 8.1.2). This will be followed by a more precise definition of professionalism as translation competence (Section 8.1.3). The section will be rounded off with a brief remark concerning the concept of lobbying (Section 8.1.4).

8.1.1 Classic professions

According to a widely accepted definition, professions are vocations which deal with the fundamental concepts of human life and co-existence. The classic professions include the priest, who deals with the relationship between man and his creator, the lawyer, whose work is based on the individual's relationship with his fellow human beings, and the textbook professional, the doctor, who focuses on man's relationship with his body. In extensively trivialised form, Rudolf Stichweh's[1] historic reconstruction of the social importance of classic professions could be summed up as follows: because the stated, fundamental conflicts were regarded as so central that a doctor could actually tell a king what he had to do with regard to his health, professionals were one of the bridging concepts which introduced the transition from a hierarchically to a functionally differentiated society. In contrast to traditional authorities, whose influence was based on an incontestable, hereditary status, the authority of professional vocations is fed by functional, acquired rights. On the one hand, this can be described as the birth of reason from the spirit of paternalism,[2] inasmuch as rationality and reason also asserted themselves as the driving forces behind actions throughout society as professional authorities became established.

On the other hand, this is not only a step towards the establishment of reason and rationality, but also towards their pluralisation. A traditional, all-sorting generator of order is instead superseded by various, area-specific rationalities, which are unable to co-ordinate society as a whole either individually or together. Whilst this plurality is initially inherent in the professional figures themselves, it also increasingly turns against them.

However, let us first deal with the historic constellation: since the 19th century at the latest, one of the instances of mediation between the promise of symmetry and asymmetrical orders in modern society can be seen in the establishment of experts, or, to be more accurate, classic professionals. This refers to figures such as the doctor, the priest or the lawyer, and also, to a certain extent, professors, teachers and possibly politicians; all of these are figures whose "reasonableness" was demonstrated above all in their entitlement to be able to assert generalities, speak in advocative terms and make uncontested decisions. Not for no reason are medical experts, in particular, seen as the prototype of those classic professionals who have the opportunity to deal with the fundamental, existential problems and conflicts of man with great effectiveness, significant prestige, the right to single-sided dialogue positions and, by no means least, with little risk of contradiction. With an unclear, but historically thoroughly satiated typology, it can be stated that the priest is responsible for fundamental conflicts of personnel identity, i.e. for the fragility and fragmented nature of one's own life. The lawyer mediates in inner-worldly conflicts and, through the judicial system, is equipped with an impartiality which takes the side of overall legal order, whereas the doctor is concerned with the fundamental problem of physical and mental integrity. Amongst other aspects, the extensive normative power of these professionals has brought forth nothing less than modern, self-responsible man, who submits to "reason", and whose freedom it has proved possible to restrict through an insight into the necessity of an appropriate, moral lifestyle. Not for no reason did these professional po-

---

1 See Stichweh (1997; 2005).
2 See Nassehi (2010).

sitions garner themselves with high moral standards, with a habitus of inapproachability and with a form of communication more akin to the style of proclamations.

This constellation has changed extensively. Strangely, the danger posed to expertise and professionalism appears to be inversely proportional to the performance and efficiency of their activities – and not, as could be expected, merely due to criticism concerning the habitus of these old professions. Indeed, this is most evident in the field of medicine.[3] On the one hand, it is progress in medicine and the life sciences themselves which has led to decisions which are shifting away from the tightly delimited routines of professional knowledge. On the other hand, however, it is also attributable to a changed society, in which perpetuation of the "symmetrical asymmetry" of classic industrial society's modernity is succeeding less and less.

It is worthwhile taking a look at the sociological theory of professions itself in order to shed light on this transformation. The classic theory of professions established for example by Talcott Parsons in the 1930s clearly bears witness to the trust which was placed in the symmetrical-asymmetrical power of professionals in the classic, modern age. For Parsons, the role of professional, classically that of the doctor, is not only one which is in any case equipped with an undisputed difference in knowledge, but one which expresses the asymmetry of society as a whole, in which universalistically oriented interests stand above purely individualistic interests. Parsons distinguishes a businessman from a professional as follows, for instance: "Business men are, for instance, expected to push their financial interests by such aggressive measures as advertising. They are not expected to sell to customers regardless of the probability of their being paid, as doctors are expected to treat patients. In each immediate instance in one sense the doctor could, if he did these things according to the business pattern, gain financial advantages which conformity with his own professional pattern denies him. It is not obvious that he is 'sacrificing' his interest for the benefit of others."[4] The doctor's universalistic authority in this case does not result from an overall societal hierarchy, but from a belief in the universalistic importance of rational, scientific knowledge. Parsons states: "There is a very important sense in which the professional practitioner in our society exercises authority. We speak of the doctor as issuing 'orders' even though we know that the only 'penalty' for not obeying them is possible injury to the patient's health. [...] This professional authority has a peculiar sociological structure. It is not based on a generally superior status, as in the authority a southern white man tends to assume over any Negro, nor is it a manifestation of superior 'wisdom' in general or of higher moral character. It is rather based on the superior 'technical competence' of the professional man. He often exercises his author-

---

3 See Saake (2003).
4 Parsons (1939), p. 464.

ity over people who are, or are reputed to be his superiors in social status, in intellectual attainments or in moral character. This is possible because the area of professional authority is limited to a particular technically defined sphere."[5]

This is not cited here to make any kind of a statement regarding the professional role of a doctor, but to demonstrate how strange a position which ascribes a competence, which is effectively assigned a universalistic importance, to the medical expert in this unbroken manner, appears to us today. What is interesting about Parsons' position is not the role which he assigns to the professions. His belief that scientific rationality is more rational than tradition, for instance, can also be disregarded as a phenotypic character of nearly 70-year-old texts. Parsons' belief that the professional universalist's employment of his competence across societal stratification in a virtually egalitarian manner requires an explanation is also understandable. Conversely, it is what Parsons does not regard as requiring further explanation which is of interest. Parsons assumes apparently stable asymmetries, namely the asymmetry between a more universalistic and a more individualistic perspective. For him, the extent to which clients actually comply with the professionals' instructions, and why this is so, requires no further clarification. In the case of the classic profession, this means that all parties – both the expert and the layman – hold fast to the specific asymmetry between the expert and the layman. In this sense, modernity therefore enabled the voluntarism of the individual due to the circumstance that the asymmetry between universalistic/rational/scientific norms was kept so stable that it was even able to maintain its stability across other asymmetries, such as the stratification, cultural or also sexual differences. Communicating on equal terms was not an option.[6]

From a current perspective, this theory of professions appears downright curious, but it most certainly has a documentary character. The profession-critical counter-movement found most prominently in the writings of Elliot Freidson no longer occurs in the contemporary sociology of professions.[7] The present day sociology of professions is above all interested in the performance, the showman-like, character of professional action, i.e. it is interested in practical questions concerning how professionals succeed in portraying themselves in specific situations so that the layman "functions" as a layman.[8]

What has apparently not changed, however, is this: to date, it is ultimately firmly maintained that professionals are above all concerned with two aspects: firstly with the self-administration of special knowledge, and secondly, with the processing of asymmetries between professionals and clients. Albeit subject to criticism, this image has been preserved – and it may still be valid, at least for the medical

---

5 Parsons (1939), p. 460.
6 See Nassehi (2007), p. 386 ff.
7 See Freidson (1975).
8 See Hitzler (1994); Pfadenhauer (2003).

profession, but also for teaching vocations, perhaps also for variations of the priesthood and judges. If one considers, for instance, the radical criticism to which medical professionalism has been exposed in recent decades, it must be empirically stated, in contrast, that the specific handling of asymmetries had to be preserved here, even under current conditions, so that treatment of the sick remains possible.[9]

And a second aspect is of particular importance to the context subject to discussion here. In the classic theory of professions, the activity of businessmen is virtually excluded from the cosmos of professionalism, with the clear reasoning that these persons are first and foremost concerned with individual interests, with economic gain, and not, therefore, with universalistic values above and beyond specific interests. Apart from the idealisation of the classic professions, this reflects the undervaluation of the knowledge and skills which are required in professions other than the classic professions.

The question would therefore be as follows: when one considers lobbying, strategies for integrating or convincing political stakeholders, can one rely on something such as professionalism? This question is at least an indication of the fact that professionalism has to be considered in a completely different light today – and the issue being dealt with here may possibly be a paradigmatic case for the question of how professionalism concepts have to be extended.

8.1.2 A new form of professionalism?

Professionalism must not simply be confused with professional expertise. As in the case of classic professionalism concepts, this also involves not simply applying professional expertise to a specific object, or a specific issue or task. It will in any case have to be assumed that professional types of actor offer this professional expertise. What is also crucial here, however, is that the particular, professional competence involves performing transfer services. What, in the case of the classic professionals, was the opportunity for example to transform medical knowledge into the actions of a physician, and to thus offer clients/patients the option of co-operation under asymmetrical conditions, is now something more akin to symmetry management. Above all, what is symmetrical here is the fact that it involves encountering partners, other stakeholders on an equal footing, and making them offers, persuading them, conveying a different perspective. This therefore also involves client contact, no longer the classic, asymmetrical constellation between professionals and clients, but ultimately something approaching "inter-professional" contact – because one's counterpart, with his inherent complexity, is much more an active part in this complex situation and far less a passive recipient of services than the classic client.

---

9 See Nassehi (2010); Saake (2008); Atzeni (2016).

Even these preliminary remarks clearly show that professionalism in the stricter sense cannot merely involve pillar-like partial competencies, but is more of a transfer competence which is closely related to the structure of modern society. As explained in Section 1.1.3, conflicts in modern, functionally differentiated societies are increasingly emerging as translation conflicts between different societal logics – conflicts which have to translate their respective perspectives (one could also say: languages and conditions for success) into each other in order to be able to arrive at decisions.

The representation and assertion of interests are not then simply a trial of strength between communicating tubes. It does not involve asserting something against others by force, at least not in the sense that an effect is simply achieved by applying sufficient force and power. This would not only be a simplistic perspective, because it does not anticipate the inherent complexity of the counterpart; instead, it only anticipates resistance. Such a perspective would also make the option of further co-operation impossible, quite apart from the fact that balances of power can easily be reversed and therefore offer few sustainable solutions. What is instead involved today is determining how actors arrive at common solutions from different perspectives – and if not that, then different solutions which are acceptable to both. One has to learn to anticipate the other perspective – not in order to adopt it, and by no means in order to reach consensuses, but in order to realistically assess the options which may be structurally available for solutions. To express it clearly, the conditions for success between political and economic forms of action are so different that consensus on the issue between the conflicting persons does not even have to be the solution. This is not at all concerned with the persons as such; instead, it is concerned with action options, it is concerned with different logics, it is concerned with the structural logics which are available, and it is concerned with making solutions plausible to different sub-audiences. We are familiar with such forms from collective bargaining, in which the actors involved are often more in agreement than is structurally possible. We are familiar with it from coalition negotiations in politics, in which it is also, but not only, important that persons understand one another, but in which, above all, the different interests and plausibilities are the determining factors behind co-operation options. We are familiar with it from corporate fusions, in which existing structures with different traditions, self-images and expectations have to be merged. We are also familiar with it from the area of interdisciplinary scientific approaches; this does not involve the different disciplines' merging their respective, partial results to form a whole, but instead in their mutually challenging one another to change their questions and solution perspectives with regard to the same object.

Re-thinking professionalism therefore means dealing with different perspectives – and not, to emphasise this once again, accepting different perspectives. As an approach to such a new challenge for professionalism, it is worthwhile taking a brief look at how elites or elite positions have changed over the course of the modernisation process.

The elite discourse is a modern discourse. Who has to lead, who can lead, and even how this leadership is to be undertaken, were as yet beyond question in the old world. And if the question was asked, the answer was clear: the leaders, of course, who had inherited both their authority and their legitimation. Only the rise of the nation state in politics, the rise of companies in the economy, the (at least to some extent) democratisation of the educational sector, the juridification of transactions as a generator of equality and, by no means least, the scientification of knowledge led to the fact that decision-making leadership, representation and legitimation became contingent. One now had to "choose", and this is precisely why the elites are also called elites: the "chosen ones". The discourse concerning the question of the appropriate selection of elites, of managers and decision-makers, thus becomes a crucial question for the self-reproduction of societies.

Thoughts initially turn to politics. The modern, democratic politician is a visible type, whose elite position is characterised particularly through celebrity and familiarity. The modern political system would be entirely inconceivable without the construction of such a type. Another type is almost certainly the economic elite type, which is not characterised primarily through celebrity, but whose conditions for success instead unfold more in the background. Further types would be scientific elites, artistic avant-gardes, etc. Even at first glance, it can clearly be seen that an indication of the functional differentiation of modern society is reflected in the differentiation of societal elites. And the differentiation of societal functional systems for politics, the economy, science, law, art, etc. is almost certainly the crucial background to the differentiation of achievement and functional elites, whose selection criteria each arise independently for the specific function.[10] And undoubtedly, correspondingly differentiated profession cultures, each of which have their own rules and customs, traditions and conflicts in terms of selection and succession regulations, can be determined. All of this has not remained unobserved, and has for example been described for the specific, German case of Ralf Dahrendorf[11] as a pillar formation of partial elites. However empirically correct and plausible this argument may be in terms of social theory, it occasionally has an all too sublimating function in the debate surrounding elites. This at least eliminates the problem of the term elite's immediately evoking thoughts of the domination of an elitist group and clique, and reduces the issue of elites to career opportunities and paths, and to the question concerning the efficiency of functionally-differentiating elite circulation. It could then be said that, to some extent, functional differentiation is the solution to the problem of societal elites. This means that elites forfeit

---

10 See Münkler (2000), p. 80.
11 See Dahrendorf (1965).

their dominating position over society as a whole in favour of opinion leadership in functional sub-systems. The power of the functional and achievement elites is therefore obtained exclusively from the respective structures of the functional systems.

An incorrect image is now sometimes obtained of the functionally differentiated society. Discussion surrounding differentiating logics, which have shifted apart from one another during the course of the societal modernisation process, is at least misleading. At first glance, it appears that this differentiation process is leading to the complete independence of partially systemic functional areas. Indeed, economic aspects can only prove themselves in an economic setting, the law can only prove itself in a legal setting, and scientific truth can only prove itself according to internal, scientific criteria, etc. Salvation cannot be had for money, power cannot assert any truth, and health cannot be decreed by legal ruling. However, it is also entirely accurate to state that the functional areas extensively interact with one another, and take on the "other side's" world in translated form. For example, intervention into medical activity is entirely possible by means of a court ruling, political power most certainly can disrupt scientific work, and whilst salvation can no longer be bought today, some kind of financial payment may well improve one's conditions for participating in religious communication. And – this is the issue here – economic interests certainly can be translated into political demands.

Such constellations indicate that modern societies are not centrally integrated, but that the different functions instead mutually encounter one another in real time. Solutions therefore have to be found at precisely the interfaces between the different functions and perspectives – simply because a modern society is not already integrated in terms of its functions, and therefore has to deal productively with the differences.

This can be used to derive the theory that both the discourse surrounding elites and the societal constitution of elite positions, of culmination points for far-reaching decisions, can be regarded as a reaction to the integration problem of a functionally differentiated society. Elites, it can now be concluded, ultimately protest against the structure of modern society and against their respective, monolithically professionalised functional elites, by attempting to undermine functional differentiation. This applies both to the "old" elites of the marriage of nation state autonomy assumptions and to the "new" elites of the present.

The classic, modern elites of the functional systems appear to have more or less become paper tigers – constructed political personalities, ingenious artists, dispassionately calculating business managers, supreme judges obligated to the blindness of the legal system, good professors. This caricature shows how little satiated the reduction of the elite problem to these functional elites is. If elites are actually those actors who are not only the affected parties, but in whom decisions of some scope culminate, then elites are almost certainly no longer only those who have achieved a certain status, as visible functional elites, in stable organisational contexts of the functional systems under the contemporary conditions of a functionally differentiated society. Even today, the crucial positions appear to be those which are able to act on the differences between the functional systems; in system theory terms, those which are able to act at the structural coupling points. Under the present conditions, such couplings are being stabilised increasingly less through national state closure or their simulation. Ultimately, the "old" elites were visible elites, whose visibility also ensured representation of the societal community of the national framework.

Conversely, the "new" elites are instead those which invisibly master juggling with the difference between the distinctions which form the functional system. Loyalties which have arisen from traditional bonds therefore no longer generate elites, nor do the old-boy networks of classic national and industrial societal modernity; this is instead accomplished through the art of playing with the inherent logic of the functional systems and exploiting the mutual irritability of political power, economic power and legal decision-making power. The key competence for these elites is no longer the domestication of their own auxiliary troops or the potential threat of applying their monopoly on the use of force, but is instead a more epistemologically founded competency. To state this again in terms of system theory, it is the capability of specifically applying second-order observation to the coupling of functional systems. The fundamental issue of these "new" elites would be a kind of role acceptance, or, to be more accurate, translation work: how can political perspectives be translated into economic perspectives, and vice versa; how is scientific knowledge portrayed from the political perspective, how can moral conflicts be translated into non-moral, legal terminology, etc.? This is now precisely where the concept of translation comes into play as a central mechanism of how a new form of professionalism is to be conceived. What is applicable to literature and to cultures in translation research also applies to functional contexts. In the same way as a post-colonial migrant – or his literary representation as an author and translator – perches like a parasite on the differences between cultures, the new elites also cling fast to the distinctions between functional contexts like parasites. They appear to be ensuring, in an entirely new manner, what was also expected of the "old" elites: integration in the sense of the mutual limitation of functional systems, a function which ultimately contradicts the structure of modernity. In this sense, the "new" elites are also protesting against the structure of modern society – and are simultaneously confirming it by showing that integration and functional co-ordination do not precede the functionally differentiated structure of society but are, at best, a localised, fragile sequence of specific contexts which is becoming increasingly fragile, particularly in the transnational decoupling of functional contexts. All of the prerequisites for a professionalisation concept for lobbying processes have thus been designated, and now merely have to be merged.

8.1.3 Professionalism as translation competence

Corporate lobbying and the persuasion of political stakeholders and decision-makers are practices which are located directly at the interfaces at which the main task and the crucial competence of new elites, which can effectively be called "differentiation elites",[12] and which must above all offer a specific form of translation competence, are required. The professionalism of the type required here is no longer the classic professionalism with asymmetrical client contact, but rather a professionalism which is able to undertake mutual translation services. Whereas classic professionalism is characterised by single-sided asymmetry, something akin to double asymmetry is present here, namely two mutual translation perspectives, because the interests of one side must be translated by the other side into the other side's own interest position, and must in turn be communicated so that they are compatible from the other perspective. To some extent, this type of professionalism must deal with different levels of reality and meaning simultaneously, and develop criteria for the conditions under which, when and, above all, in which form this double asymmetry is addressed, remains an anathema or must actually be maintained.

Perhaps it is now becoming clear why it was worthwhile to start with the characterisation of classic professionalism. It is also concerned above all with conveying specialist knowledge to a counterpart or an audience which has to solve other problems than the professional himself. The form of asymmetry would particularly be reduced, in cultural terms, due to the fact that the professional is not ultimately assumed to have own interests, but has instead elevated the interests in an overall societal interest. This is precisely what is meant by the common interest orientation of the classic professionals. Against this background, the economic or political interest of a corporate representative or a party politician appeared to be almost an individualistic figure, and thus ultimately driven "only" by interest. In civil society, and in classical political philosophy since Hegel, interests have occurred as private interests. This ultimately means that these are simply interests which have no relation to a general public or to the centre of society. In a society in which the general public can simply no longer be thought of as the central state or moral form, the meaning of interests is also consequently transformed.

Interests are therefore ultimately the medium in which the action objectives arise from the respective perspective of different functions, problem-solving concepts and conditions for success. Economics is not then conceivable above and beyond interests – just as politics is always encoded as an interest, even if representatives of corresponding institutions do not co-ordinate any specific interests at all. We are used to constantly scrutinising a politician's words for political interests, just as a corporate or association representative is perceived as a representative of interests, completely irrespective of what he says.

---

12 See Nassehi (2004; 2006).

The following is a brief marginal note: the crisis experienced by the classic professionals, whose power and exclusivity has most certainly declined in comparison with classic modernity, is also revealed by the fact that they are now also assumed to have something akin to an interest; this is likely to mean that the common interest orientation of such specific knowledge is subject to increasing doubt, as can be observed to an ever increasing extent in the case of the doctor, the lawyer, the priest, and also the teacher or professor.

It should have become clear that interests can no longer simply be handled as private interests today, i.e. as a particular instance. Of course, interests are always own interests, but the trick is precisely how to achieve a balance of interests with the objective of positioning one's own interest accordingly. In this regard, professionalism today can only refer to the ability to formulate interests such that they cannot simply be put forward and asserted with more or less power in a functionally differentiated society. Within the respective functional logics, of course, interests are opposing forces. Companies are in competition for the same market, and act as competitors. And political actors have to assert themselves against political competitors and fight for limited electoral votes. Equally, scientists battle to find the right solution, for the scant resource of reputation, and are in competition for quotable sentences. However, these similar opposing forces can be overcome with specialist knowledge; they necessitate strategies which apply the respective, own logic of the respective, own field.

Conversely, the professionalism involved here finds a counterpart which has to come to terms with other logics. In a public administration, in European authorities or in a party politician, a corporate representative of an industry association, for instance, finds a counterpart whose conditions for success follow logics other than one's own. Competencies which are able to represent the own interests not simply before other interests, but instead before differing interests, are required at these points. This is where professionalism comes into play as a translation competence which has to master precisely this difference, and must therefore be a professionalism which acts directly on the differentiated societal structure of modernity.

8.1.4 Brief Appendix: lobbying re-thought

This also results in a differentiated picture of what lobbying might be. To express this in shortened form: the art of lobbying does not lie in asserting oneself against other interests, but instead involves acquiring the ability to identify differing interests and to find a language for translation in order to ensure that the conditions for success can be met. Sustainable solutions in such settings are only conceivable if each side can translate the form of interests into that of the respective other side, and thereby include these interests in its own condition for success. Talk of a win-win situation is a clichéd platitude, but it hits the nail on the head here: in classic competition amongst businessmen, amongst politicians, amongst scientists, i. e. amongst similar stakeholders, there are always winners and losers. In this case, competition is actually a crucial mechanism which brings forth creativity and innovations, because it tightens the selection criteria and ensures paths which would not be taken without competition. This is not intended to cast doubt on the fact that there are ordering mechanisms other than competition, but in fiercely contested areas surrounding scant resources, competition arises even in locations in which this would not be assumed.

The representation of interests vis-à-vis players in other fields, playing according to other logics and rules, such as the representation of an industry association's interests vis-à-vis the European Parliament, follows different rules. This does not involve competition in the stricter sense, but is instead concerned with making interests compatible with each other. It should now have become clear that this type of professionalism is more similar to the classic type than was thought. It anticipates a benefit for the opposite number, since the establishment of motives for making the different perspectives compatible and achieving a coupling, at least temporarily, is not otherwise possible. This concept should incidentally also enable successful rehabilitation of the topos of interest, because interests are more than just private interests in a functionally differentiated society. They may possibly be necessary to arrive at solutions in a structurally disintegrated society – temporarily, provisionally and, particularly because of this, reliant on mutual trust.

8.2 Convincing political stakeholders: specifics and challenges for SMEs using the example of Bavaria
By Anton Meyer, Michael Dürr and Lena-Marie Rehnen

Classic examples of political lobbying usually involve DAX-30 companies, which often have their own representative office in Brussels. The lobby registers of the parliaments in Brussels and Berlin are therefore tantamount to a "Who is who" of multinational corporations, financial institutions, global players and industrial lobbyists – i.e. major, global corporations.[13] However, structured representation is not only necessary in the case of major companies; small and medium-sized enterprises (SMEs) also require the political representation of their interests. Due to multinational corporations' institutionalisation, their strong market position and their superior financial resources in the assertion of their political interests, SMEs can quickly suffer competitive disadvantages without effective and efficient political lobbying. Using the example of SMEs in Bavaria, Business Administration M.Sc. students at the Institute for Marketing at Ludwig-Maximilians-University in Munich investigated the specifics and challenges of political lobbying for SMEs.

---

13 See European Parliament/European Commission (2012).

The Bavarian SMEs will firstly be introduced, and the current organisation of their political lobbying described in the following. The results of an empirical study concerning current problems and possible changes required in the political lobbying of Bavarian SMEs will then be presented.

8.2.1 What are SMEs in Bavaria?

Small and medium-sized enterprises are defined differently in the literature. At European level, for instance, various size classes are used for classification; at national level, classification is undertaken with reference to various subsidy programmes, and separate definitions are used at German Länder level. In this case, reference will be made to the definition in the report on medium-sized Bavarian companies.[14] It is published every five years by the Bavarian Ministry of Economic Affairs and Media, Energy and Technology. The last version, dating from 2010, which covers the period of time between 2005 and 2009, contains the very specific delimitation which is used in the following: SMEs are companies with fewer than 500 employees and annual turnover of less than 50 million euros.

The qualitative definition of medium-sized enterprises, as used by the Institut für Mittelstandsforschung (institute for research into medium-sized enterprises) in Bonn, also encompasses the majority of all family-owned companies.[15] In these cases, the ownership and leadership rights are united in the person of the entrepreneur. The terms SME and family-owned company are therefore often used synonymously.

In the example of Bavaria, the official statistics state that there are approximately 574,000 Bavarian SMEs. These represent 99.7 % of all companies operating in Bavaria. They form the backbone of the Bavarian economy. Bavarian SMEs primarily consist of companies with an annual turnover of up to 1 million euros. 72 % of these are micro-enterprises, which only generate 5 % of the total turnover of all SMEs.

Measured against their number of employees and generated turnover, the SMEs are very important. For instance, the aforementioned 574,000 Bavarian SMEs generated a total turnover of 347 billion euros in 2008, the year in which reliable data were last acquired. These 574,000 enterprises break down into the following categories: 50 % of all enterprises generate turnover of less than 100,000 euros. 90 % of the enterprises generate turnover of less than 1 million euros. And only 0.3 % of all companies in Bavaria generate turnover in excess of 50 million euros. These approximately 1,800 companies with over 50 million euros in turnover are the so-called major companies, which are excluded from our investigation (see Figure 8.1).

---

14 See Bavarian Ministry of Economic Affairs, Infrastructure, Transport and Technology (2010), p. 10.
15 See Institut für Mittelstandsforschung (2015).

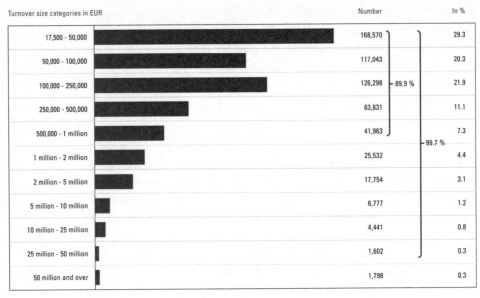

Turnover size categories in EUR | Number | In %

17,500 - 50,000	168,570	29.3
50,000 - 100,000	117,043	20.3
100,000 - 250,000	126,298	21.9
250,000 - 500,000	63,831	11.1
500,000 - 1 million	41,963	7.3
1 million - 2 million	25,532	4.4
2 million - 5 million	17,754	3.1
5 million - 10 million	6,777	1.2
10 million - 25 million	4,441	0.8
25 million - 50 million	1,602	0.3
50 million and over	1,798	0.3

89.9 %

99.7 %

575,609 companies in total

Source: Bavarian Office for Statistics and Data Processing: sales tax statistics; IfM Bonn calculations

Figure 8.1: Companies in Bavaria in 2008 by turnover size category – number and percentage[16]

Turnover size categories in EUR | Number | In %

17,500 - 50,000	5.3	0.6
50,000 -100,000	8.4	1.0
100,000 - 250,000	20.1	2.3
250,000 - 500,000	22.5	2.6
500,000 - 1 million	29.5	3.3
1 million - 2 million	35.7	4.0
2 million - 5 million	54.9	6.2
5 million - 10 million	47.2	5.4
10 million - 25 million	68.3	7.7
25 million - 50 million	55.3	6.3
50 million and over	534.2	60.6

9.7 %

39.4 %

575,609 companies in total

Source: Bavarian Office for Statistics and Data Processing: sales tax statistics; IfM Bonn calculations

Figure 8.2: Company turnover in 2008 in Bavaria by turnover size category – in millions of euros and as a percentage[17]

---

16 Bavarian Ministry of Economic Affairs, Infrastructure, Transport and Technology (2010), p. 12.
17 Bavarian Ministry of Economic Affairs, Infrastructure, Transport and Technology (2010), p. 13

Measured against turnover size categories, the following picture emerges: together, enterprises with turnover of up to 1 million euros per year generate 10% of the total turnover of all companies in Bavaria (see Figure 8.2). The classic SMEs, i.e. those with a turnover of up to 50 million euros per annum, generate 39.4% of the total turnover of all companies in Bavaria.[18]

72% of the Bavarian SMEs are sole proprietorships and 14% GmbHs (private limited companies). Measured against turnover, the GmbH legal form makes up 37% and the GmbH & Co. KGs (private limited companies with limited partnerships) make up 20%.[19] The majority of the SMEs belong to the manufacturing industry, the service industry and the trade sector.[20]

8.2.2 How is political lobbying organised amongst Bavarian SMEs?

Theoretically, the SMEs' need for political lobbying can be determined on the basis of the resource-based and the resource dependence view.[21] In the ideal case, SMEs have access to rare and valuable resources which cannot be imitated, substituted or transferred, and with which they achieve their competitive advantage. On the other hand, this resource-based view reveals an external dependency due to links to the environment.[22] Political regulations specify the SMEs' action framework; these can extensively limit their ability to act, and can endanger both their competitive advantages and their competitiveness.

SMEs are usually organised in associations which support them in their political lobbying. As amalgamations of industry and service interests as well as professional bodies, as classic representatives of the interests of SMEs in politics, these are of particular importance to medium-sized enterprises. For instance, around 70% of the 574,000 SMEs in Bavaria are organised in specialist associations. The Vereinigung der bayerischen Wirtschaft e.V. (vbw – Bavarian Industry Association) includes a total of 137 specialist associations which cover various industries.[23] Added to these, of course, are also the corresponding, national central and umbrella associations. The respective associations usually maintain good contact with the member companies. They prepare content-related concerns and are regarded as important opinion leaders in the industry.

Organisation and lobbying through associations are not only national and European topics. Braun and Dietsche[24] analysed the network of shrimp traders between Bangladesh and Germany, and established that there is barely any contact between companies and the government: "As sole companies, as individual im-

---

18 See Bavarian Ministry of Economic Affairs, Infrastructure, Transport and Technology (2010), p. 13.
19 See Bavarian Ministry of Economic Affairs, Infrastructure, Transport and Technology (2010), p. 15.
20 See Deloitte & Touche GmbH Wirtschaftsprüfungsgesellschaft/LMU (2011), p. 36.
21 See Ulrich and Barney (1984), p. 471.
22 See Ulrich and Barney (1984), p. 471.
23 See Vbw (2015).
24 See Braun and Dietsche (2009), pp. 249 ff.

porters, they have no chance whatsoever to talk to any government departments. This has to take place via associations."[25]

The chambers of commerce and industry, and guilds, also play an important role with regard to political lobbying. Due to mandatory memberships and contributions, the chambers of commerce and industry have access to all Bavarian companies, and additionally offer a nationwide and international network as well as extensive financial resources.

Figure 8.3 shows the multi-layered association structures for SMEs. It reveals the integrative, institutional consolidation of the political representation of Bavarian SMEs' interests by the associations. The individual points represent the SMEs' heterogeneous, individual interests. For instance, the members' financial interests are bundled in specialist associations, those of the specialist associations in umbrella associations, and then those of the umbrella associations in central associations. These central associations are also usually the points of contact for politicians. The multi-layered structure clearly shows the complexity of political lobbying. The individual associations act at different levels, and often reveal diverging interests.

The small, industry-specific, specialist associations suffer from a lack of resources, a lack of "punch" and, due to their scant resources, also from a lack of differentiated competencies in various fields and at various levels of political lobbying. This

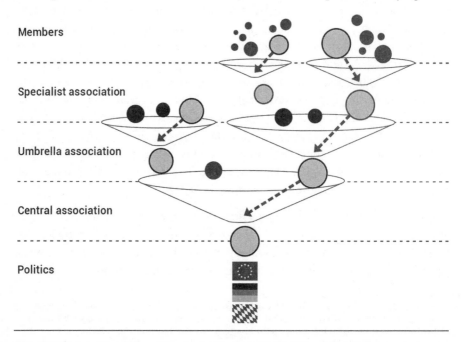

Figure 8.3: Structure of the multi-layered, integrative, institutional consolidation of the association structures

25 Braun and Dietsche (2009), p. 262.

is the difference in comparison with umbrella associations, the majority of which are well structured, broad-based and equipped with extensive competencies. Due to their available resources and specific departments, they offer a broad range of activities.[26]

In a case study concerning the German, family-owned company Knauf and its subsidiaries in Russia, where the company is regarded as an SME, Holtbrügge and Puck[27] show that the company uses various options to exert an influence on Russian legislation. Firstly, for instance, requests are submitted via official associations to the State Duma, in order to exert political influence, such as in the case of legislative amendments. Knauf also maintains close relationships with the Russian chamber of commerce and industry (TPP), although these are used more for public relations work in Russian media than for lobbying activities. However, Knauf does not rely solely on the associations' work, and, in addition to this indirect contact to the Russian legislature, also has direct access to the Russian State Duma through personal contact with several members of parliament. This example clearly shows that political lobbying solely via associations is often insufficient.[28] Figure 8.4 shows Knauf's extensive stakeholder network in Russia.

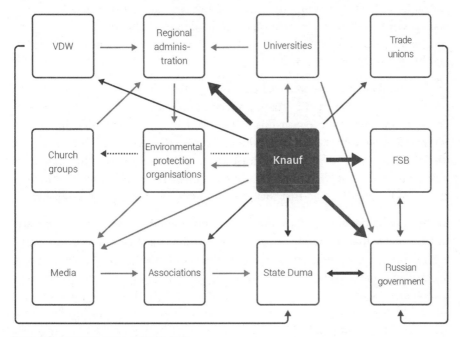

Figure 8.4: Stakeholder network of Knauf in Russia

---

26 See Institute for Marketing (2014).
27 See Holtbrügge and Puck (2009), pp. 226–227.
28 See Holtbrügge and Puck (2009), p. 228.

8.2.3 What are the current problems involved in political lobbying?

In January 2014, 12 students from the Ludwig-Maximilians-University in Munich conducted a qualitative study regarding political lobbying in Bavaria together with EUTOP International GmbH as part of a project course during their Business Administration M.Sc. study programme at the Institute for Marketing. The students conducted structured interviews not only with ten representatives of Bavarian SMEs, but also with nine politicians from various parties and 11 representatives of associations and agencies.[29] The objective of the investigation was the development of a market analysis for political lobbying amongst medium-sized companies under consideration of general market characteristics and market trends as well as existing competition structures. According to the results of this non-representative study, many SMEs believe that there is a significant need for improvement in political lobbying for SMEs by their association. The results indicate that, at least in individual associations, there is a great deal of interest heterogeneity and delayed evidence of problems. The content-related diversity and multi-layered nature of collective lobbying can equate to sub-optimal effectiveness. There is a lack of financial resources for individual representation and, in part, a lack of understanding of political processes and institutionalised contact management. Individual associations may be dominated by powerful members, and "small members" are often dissatisfied. A lack of competencies at national and EU level are also remarked on.

In the chamber of commerce and industry's report on medium-sized Bavarian companies,[30] economic policy framework conditions are regarded as a risk to economic development in the near future, not just for major companies (more than 500 employees), but also amongst the surveyed SMEs (see Figure 8.5). On the whole, it can therefore be stated, at least for the near future, that efficient and effective political lobbying in Bavaria is of great importance from the point of view of the Bavarian SMEs, and that this most certainly has room for improvement.

As far as we can see, there is extensive agreement amongst politicians in Bavaria and Germany that the competitiveness of medium-sized companies and SMEs must continue to be supported and strengthened. Under certain circumstances, the challenge involved in this is in organising structured exchange between SMEs and politicians, and in getting the representatives of both sides to listen to one another. The medium-sized companies often have difficulties in putting their own expectations of good political lobbying into words. These expectations are for example transparency, a strong network, specialist competence and professionalism. The SMEs' lack of resources for representing their individual, political interests is clearly revealed in this context.[31] In this, SMEs are most certainly at a disadvan-

---

29 See Institute for Marketing (2014).
30 See chamber of commerce and industry for Munich and Upper Bavaria (2012), p. 8.
31 See Institute for Marketing (2014).

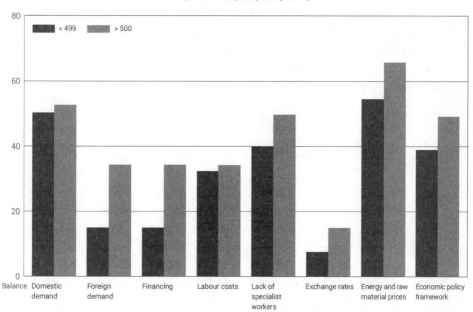

Which risks do you foresee for your company's economic development over the coming twelve months
(Data in %; multiple responses possible)

Figure 8.5: Chamber of commerce and industry report on medium-sized companies (2012), p. 8

tage in comparison with bigger companies which regularly have access to a high budget for lobbying work.[32]

These disadvantages could at least be compensated in part by co-operating with SMEs with similar interests. At the same time, the disadvantages of the high interest heterogeneity of institutional lobbyists which occurs in some cases could also be avoided. Individual SMEs would therefore develop greater political "punch". The negative association influence caused by predominating interest heterogeneity can be compensated through tailored coaching and pooling. Only in this manner will the SMEs, too, be able to break through major industry's dominance.

8.2.4 Conclusion

As an important element of the Bavarian economy, SMEs are primarily represented politically via their association membership at present. The strong role of the associations in political lobbying is characterised by trust and credibility. Political lobbying by specialist associations can go hand-in-hand with structural and procedural "shortcomings". The effectiveness of political lobbying is weakened by polling heterogeneous, individual interests and due to the comparatively scant resources which are available. In order to prevent the SMEs' competitiveness from

---

32 See Anger (2009).

suffering as a result of this, there is a need to improve the individual, political representation of SMEs' interests. Associations composed of SMEs with similar interests are a solution approach in which the implementation of structural instruments and procedural control are important. Only through interconnectedness and the accompanying pooling of resources will SMEs be able to stand up to multinational corporations and overcome the challenges posed by rapidly changing markets in the future.

Chapter 9 Case studies on lobbying projects with structural process support

In the following chapter, the importance of process competence for the success of lobbying projects vis-à-vis the EU decision-makers will be made tangible in practical terms on the basis of two fictitious case studies.[1] The entire project is structurally supported procedurally by an external service provider for governmental relations (as an intermediary) in this case.

The procedure of a lobbying project and its process support by an external governmental relations agency will be portrayed on the basis of the case studies "Advertising bans for spirits, beer and wine" (Section 9.1) and "Regulation for (...) reducing the CO_2 emissions of new passenger cars" (Section 9.2), thereby providing a deeper insight into the practice of governmental relations at the interface between politics, the economy and society within the EU. Without structural support (process support competence)[2] by an external, neutral process partner, effective lobbying, whose temporal scope is foreseeable, and which is successful on the whole in terms of the content-related objectives achieved, is hardly possible any longer, particularly under the current framework conditions set out by the Treaty of Lisbon. Process competence is now a vital requirement of successful long-term lobbying in Europe: however "good" an argument is, it will not be heard if it is not introduced in the correct form and at the right point in time to the appropriate decision-makers according to the specified rules. The content-related component is then extensively overshadowed by the deficient procedural component – with correspondingly disadvantageous effects for the concern.

The basic problem of communication in the context of lobbying concerns the parallel existence of different political and economic levels of communication: companies and associations, as "senders", and the executive and legislative levels, as "recipients", regard an issue from different perspectives; they have different social backgrounds, see different problems and therefore often do not speak the same language. Whilst companies and associations, for instance, tend to communicate their own individual interests, in unfiltered form, as demands to politicians and view their own economic advantages as the crucial element, decision-makers at the executive and legislative level have other points of reference: they are ultimately obligated to the interests of the institution (executive) or the electorate (legislature) which they represent or – without any pathos – the common interest. In light of this, it is not difficult to foresee that a concern is more likely to be asserted if its "sender" is able to assume the "recipient's" perspective. A lobbyist must therefore give consideration to his opposite number's position, or that of the com-

---

1 The case studies are based on authentic lobbying cases. All names have been changed. The circumstances, figures and statistics are also fictitious, but are extensively based on reality.
2 With regard to the individual competencies, see Chapter 10 for a summary.

mon interest, when communicating a concern – only this prevents the accusation of mere self-interest from being levelled at him (perspective change competence).

The fictitious lobbying projects outlined in the following are each structurally supported by an intermediary, complementary to the company's/companies' own content-oriented lobbying structures. In its individual steps, the intermediary's approach is oriented towards Chapter 6 (Section 6.5.4) as a guideline for planning and implementing structured lobbying.

After outlining the initial situation and the circumstances, a chronological sequence will be maintained and subdivided into five steps:

- Step 1: documentation of the (content-related) objective and continuous checking of political feasibility.
- Step 2: procedural situation assessment and strategy planning.
- Step 3: drafting one or more onepagers and submitting them to previously identified addressees at the legislative and executive level.
- Step 4: flanking the onepager with other structural and process-oriented instruments (mutual information transparency).
- Step 5: supporting decision-making processes at legislative and executive level.

In addition to these individual stages, the results of the lobbying processes of both case studies will also be subjected to "success controlling", i.e. whether, and the extent to which, the company/companies was/were able to achieve its/their objectives due to the assignment of an external governmental relations agency will be assessed.

9.1 Case 1: "advertising bans for spirits, beer and wine?"

9.1.1 Circumstances/initial situation

The consumption of alcohol poses a major problem to public health in the EU. Adolescents are particularly at risk due to excessive alcohol consumption: in the 15 to 29 age group, 10 % of female deaths are attributable to alcohol abuse; this figure actually rises to 25 % amongst males. Press reports concerning excessive alcohol consumption ("binge drinking") amongst adolescents appear time and again. In total, approximately 7.4 % of health disorders and premature deaths are attributable to alcohol; in addition, around 10,000 alcohol-related road traffic accidents occur each year.

Against this background, the European Commission defined various fields of action in October 2006 as part of its EU strategy to reduce alcohol-related harm; within these areas, high-priority measures were to be implemented to counter the effects of harmful alcohol consumption. In the Commission's opinion, this also included the commercial communication undertaken by manufacturers of alcoholic beverages (advertising). Thus far, the industry had been required, through voluntary commitments, to advertise its alcohol products responsibly. In the Commission's view, however, the results of these voluntary commitments did not lead to the desired success. It was now considering imposing an extensive ban on advertising alcoholic beverages (spirits, wine and beer), comparable with the ban on tobacco advertising implemented in 2005, by means of a regulation harmonised throughout the EU. The Commission's initiative was supported by the World Health Organization (WHO), which demanded a ban on, or the extensive curtailing of, direct or indirect advertising for alcoholic beverages in all media as well as the limitation of sponsoring by alcohol manufacturers in its *Global strategy to reduce the harmful use of alcohol* from 2010 and the *Alcohol Action Plan 2012– 2020* adopted in 2011. It also insisted on the regulation of new forms of commercial communication for alcoholic beverages, e.g. in social networks, and on the regulation of the content and scope of other commercial communication for alcoholic beverages.

In political Europe, it was expected that the Commission would shortly table a draft regulation in the form of a directive, in order to assert an EU-wide advertising ban for alcoholic beverages. Subsequent to this, after running through the ordinary legislative procedure and the entry into force of such a directive, the member states would then be given a legal framework within which they would be required to implement this advertising ban. In such a procedure, the individual member states are always allowed some leeway in structuring their regulations.

Europe's second-largest beer brewing company is the "Bayernbräu" brewery, whose headquarters are located in Germany. The company generates the majority of its turnover in Germany, followed by the UK, Spain and Italy, where it also operates its own bottling plants, as in Germany. The European beer market is led by Belgium's "Prime Brew Co." (which is also the world's biggest beer manufacturer); the industry's number three ("DutchBrew") has its headquarters in the Netherlands. Germany produces the most beer (98 million hectolitres/year), followed in second and third place by the UK (45 million hectolitres/year) and Poland (36 million hectolitres/year).

A total of approximately two million jobs are directly or indirectly related to the beer brewing industry in the EU. In addition, the spirits and wine industry directly and indirectly employs a total of approximately 0.8 million people throughout the EU. In a discussion at an event in Brussels, the head of Bayernbräu's political communication department heard by chance about a planned directive for imposing an advertising ban on alcoholic beverages throughout the EU. Alarmed by this, he asked an acquainted contact within the European Commission's responsible Directorate General (DG) "Health and Consumer Protection" (SANCO) about the status and further details of the planning. Following brief research, this person was not only able to confirm the initiative, but actually provided a schedule for the planned directive.

Date	Event
March 2013	Commission publishes proposals regarding advertising ban/restrictions.
June 2013	European Parliament committees begin an exchange of views on the draft directive on advertising bans.
September 2013	European Parliament working document is published, produced by lead rapporteur in Environment, Public Health and Food Safety Committee (ENVI).
January 2014	Opinions on rapporteur report and revised draft due from all other European Parliament advisory committees.
February 2014	**Final vote in ENVI committee**, taking into account opinions of other advisory committees, is submitted to the European Parliament for a plenary vote.
February 2014	**First reading** to take place. This aims to consolidate the views of the European Parliament, the Council of the European Union and the European Commission. If there is agreement the text of the legislation will also be determined.
April 2014	If necessary a **second reading** is to take place to allow for further negotiation before finalisation of the form of the legislation.
2015	Directive is expected to come into force.

Figure 9.1: Preliminary schedule of the "advertising ban for alcoholic beverages' directive

A specific draft text for a directive, in which the advertising ban was explicitly set out and detailed, was already available, too. Time was of the essence. It was clear to the head of Bayernbräu's communication that a lobbying concept had to be drawn up immediately, in order to achieve amendments to the draft text. The objective was to completely eliminate the planned advertising ban for alcoholic beverages from the directive's formulation.

In his considerations, however, the head of communication discovered that, whilst his company has good links to officials and elected representatives at the executive and legislative levels in Germany, it had barely any channels to the crucial EU institutions. The high degree of complexity also became apparent to him in appraising the political decision-making procedures for the adoption of the directive: since the Treaty of Lisbon came into force at the end of 2009, the Council of the EU has been making its decisions according to the majority principle in the majority of essential policy areas. The requirement of unanimity in the Council has become the exception; the majority decision is the usual case.[3] Decisions in the Council now require a qualified majority of votes (double majority, i. e. at least 55 % of the member states, which represent 65 % of the EU's population, have to cast their votes); a blocking minority must consist of at least four member states, which represent 35 % of the EU's population. An individual member state alone is therefore no longer able to block a Council decision with its dissenting vote.

---

3   See Joos (2014), pp. 34–35.

The head of communication was compelled to realise that these new regulations go hand-in-hand with a significant loss of importance for the individual member states – i.e. that his own, national network would not be sufficient. To achieve his objective of preventing the advertising ban on alcoholic beverages, a "European approach" with cross-institution, -parliamentary group and -member state networks was required. As Bayernbräu did not have such networks at its disposal, the head of communication ultimately arranged for an external governmental relations agency to be engaged to represent the company's interests. This decision was preceded by a discussion within the company regarding whether it would be sufficient to have the procedure supported by the company's own corporate representative office in Brussels and the "German Brewers' Association (Deutscher Brauer-Bund – DBB)",[4] of which Bayernbräu was in any case a member. However, the company's own corporate representative office did not have the networks deemed necessary by the corporate management; within the association, significant differences of opinion between the member companies and associations from the various member states became apparent from the very beginning, with the result that effective (unanimous) lobbying appeared very unlikely.

9.1.2 Step 1: documentation of the (content-related) objective and continuous checking of political feasibility

To plan the co-operation between Bayernbräu and the governmental relations agency, and to define a basis for a strategy, both parties met for a kick-off meeting. In this, focus was placed above all on Bayernbräu's objectives and concerns, on the basis of which the agency intended to develop a strategy.

During this meeting, it quickly became apparent that the governmental relations agency could not only offer procedural support, but that it could also undertake content-related work: each of the brewery's individual concerns and project elements was checked as regards its "political feasibility".[5] During this procedure, it emerged that Bayernbräu's most rigorous demand – the complete waiver of an advertising ban and other regulation – could not be conveyed politically, as the issue of "alcohol consumption amongst adolescents" was subject to controversial discussion amongst Europe's general public, and the procedure was already relatively far advanced. The agency urgently advised the company not to stick rigidly to its own standpoint, since this would eliminate any chance of reaching a compromise – this was determined in advance during informal discussions in the European Parliament and the European Commission. Instead, the agency recommended the formulation of several "realistically achievable core objectives (must-haves)",[6] which could genuinely be achieved. The key objectives that were eventu-

---

4 The corporate representative office, association, public affairs agency and law firm are the four "classic" lobbying instruments.
5 See Joos (2011), p. 215.
6 See Joos (2011), p. 215.

ally emphasised were to retain the voluntary commitment of manufacturers of alcoholic beverages and for them to advertise their products responsibly.

9.1.3 Step 2: procedural situation assessment and strategy planning

Once Bayernbräu's core objectives had been determined during the kick-off meeting, the governmental relations agency developed a strategy for implementing them in close consultation with the brewery.

A team, whose members were exclusively responsible for Bayernbräu, was first formed within the agency: a senior consultant was dedicated to process management, and undertook contact management and conducting discussions with the members of parliament and civil servants. He also acted as a permanent contact vis-à-vis Bayernbräu's head of communication, and ensured complete information transparency. To guarantee regular co-ordination, a telephone conference was scheduled every two weeks, or also more frequently as required.

Two further team members were responsible above all for content-related questions, and provided their senior consultant with support wherever necessary. They were responsible for monitoring and research, as well as for drafting and continuously updating the discussion papers, and for all other written correspondence. An important part of their work was concerned with identifying the actors involved and with attentively following their arguments; in this manner, the national and European associations, the Commission's responsible Directorate General (SANCO), the World Health Organization and other opponents of advertising measures for alcoholic beverages were to be subjected to detailed monitoring in this project. This enabled the agency to register the involved actors' arguments and all public statements (including contradictions and discrepancies in the arguments), and to formulate tenable counter-arguments.

The governmental relations agency used one of its contacts in the Directorate General SANCO to determine the time framework for its strategy, and discovered that the Commission had not yet conclusively adopted the final text of the directive. This therefore enabled amendment proposals to be submitted and, accordingly, an influence to be exerted on the formulation of the directive's text. However, the agency warned that the possible time frame for this was only very limited. Earlier involvement in the procedure – in the sense of preventive lobbying – would have been better, but the time pressure would have been even greater if the Commission had already submitted the proposal to the Council and Parliament.

A timeline was initially drawn up to provide both the agency and Bayernbräu's head of communication with a constant overview. All important dates were listed in this, such as the directive's introduction into the European Parliament, the committee meetings, any public hearing or the consultations in the Council and the Parliament. As the dates could be shifted at any time, the timeline was regularly updated during the project. The point in time at which the political contact persons were addressed had to be oriented towards this timeline. For instance, it proved sensible to get in touch with the responsible contact persons, e.g. the rapporteur within the European Parliament's responsible committee, directly prior to the corresponding committee meeting in which the planned directive was on the agenda.

Figure 9.2 shows the timeline (under consideration of the above mentioned preliminary schedule for the planned directive) of the complete legislative procedure up to implementation in the member states (in this specific case, the procedure ended – by no means least as a result of the agency's involvement – with the first reading in the Parliament; the procedure is shown in full due to didactic reasons).

In a second step, the team now drew up a key player analysis as the basis of its plans to address the political decision-makers.

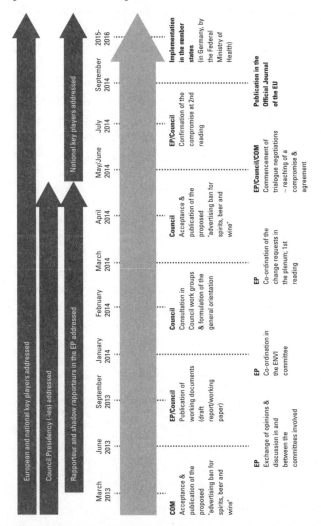

Figure 9.2: Timeline/complete legislative procedure ("advertising ban for alcoholic beverages" directive)

In addition to the European Commission, which had the right of initiative, the Council of the EU and the European Parliament were also involved in the ordinary legislative procedure for adopting the directive concerning the "advertising ban for alcoholic beverages". This means that the representatives of these institutions primarily had to be integrated into the lobbying strategy.

From the European Commission, the Director General of the responsible Directorate General SANCO, the responsible head of unit for "Public Health" and the Policy Officer in charge[7] were included in the key player list.

The Members of the European Parliament who were concerned with the topic of "health" were listed, including the members of the responsible "Environment, Public Health and Food Safety (ENVI)" committee[8] plus its chairman, but also those committee members from countries in which Bayernbräu generated the majority of its turnover and has its own bottling plants; besides Germany, this involved the UK, Spain and Italy. The agency assumed that these Members of the European Parliament (MEPs) would take particular interest in the concerns to be discussed, since the bottling plants also provided jobs. Particular consideration was also given to the rapporteurs and shadow rapporteurs[9] responsible for the issue of the "health of the population/influences of alcohol on health". Thanks to their function in the procedure, these were able to exert a specific influence on the formulation of the legislative text, with the result that addressing them appeared particularly sensible in this case. The members of the advising "Internal Market and Consumer Protection (IMCO)" and "Civil Liberties, Justice and Home Affairs (LIBE)" committees were also registered.

At member state level, the State Secretaries and heads of department of the responsible ministries – the Ministries of Health[10] and Finance[11] as well as the Ministries of Justice and Consumer Protection[12] were included in the list. The German contact persons in the Council of the EU were therefore also registered. In addition, the Council representatives of those European member states whose domestic companies would have been particularly affected by an advertising ban for alcoholic beverages – namely the responsible ministers of the member states of Belgium and the Netherlands, in which the headquarters of Europe's largest brew-

---

7 An organisational chart for the Directorate General (since 2015 "Health and Food Safety") is available at http://ec.europa.eu/dgs/health_consumer/chart.pdf (last accessed on 26.1.2015).

8 Available at http://www.europarl.europa.eu/committees/en/envi/members.html (last accessed on 26.1.2015).

9 "This person [the rapporteur] is primarily responsible for dealing with the Commission's proposal, and prepares a committee decision proposal and the European Parliament's decision. (…) As the rapporteur for a Commission initiative therefore always comes from a specific parliamentary group, (…) each of the other parliamentary groups itself designates a representative from its ranks. This representative is referred to as the respective parliamentary group's 'shadow rapporteur'. (…) Both the rapporteur and the shadow rapporteurs play a central role in the functioning of the parliamentary system." From: Centre for European Policy cep (2015a).

10 Organisational chart available at Federal Ministry of Health (2015).

11 Organisational chart available at Federal Ministry of Finance (2015).

12 Organisational chart available at Federal Ministry of Justice and Consumer Protection (2015).

eries are located – were also taken into consideration. The representatives of those countries with the highest overall beer production were also taken into account: besides Germany, this included the UK and Poland. It could be assumed that these member states' national economies would have been significantly affected by an advertising ban for alcoholic beverages, thus placing jobs at risk.

The Bayernbräu head of communication's network was also included in the key player list. This encompassed the managing director of an association related to the industry, trade union representatives and a business journalist, for instance.

In addition to creating and updating the timeline and the key player list, the agency also continued its content-related work, and continuously compared the opposing side's arguments against those of its client. This guaranteed that the discussion was always conducted according to the latest information and that the opposing side's arguments were taken into consideration in the client's own communication.

As part of the further strategy, Bayernbräu's head of communication and the agency employees discussed whether flanking measures in the area of "public affairs" appeared sensible, such as advertising campaigns or major discussion events. The agency urgently advised against this, since topics such as "the consumption of alcohol by adolescents" or even so-called "binge drinking" were always perceived by the general public, and discussed in the media, in very critical terms.[13] As a specific example of this, it referred to the public debates conducted in Germany; e.g. in 2004, these led to extensive legal restrictions on the advertising and sale of so-called "alcopops" (alcoholic soft drinks).[14] The head of communication thereupon decided solely to address the key players without any accompanying media campaigns.

9.1.4 Step 3: drafting a onepager and submitting it to previously identified addressees at the legislative and executive level

As the legislative process had already begun, the agency was required to work quickly and in a targeted manner. To be able to put the concern forward effectively and succinctly, it suggested the use of a onepager (see Chapter 6 for details).

To do this, the agency employees drew up a one-page document, in close coordination with the head of communication, containing all relevant information and the essential line of argument.[15] The problem involved in drawing up the onepager was not, as is otherwise frequently the case, in arousing a European awareness of the problem both at the company itself and in the legislative and executive

---

13 See, for instance: Lachmann (2014).
14 Amongst other aspects, an "alcopop tax" was introduced on 2.8.2004: Federal Ministry of Finance (2014a).
15 See Joos (2011), p. 217.

level contact persons – this was already in existence. For instance, the consumption of alcohol, particularly by adolescents, is regarded as a European problem which endangers the health of Europe's population as a whole. Instead, the difficulty was to convincingly demonstrate that the planned advertising ban for alcoholic beverages would not lead to an improvement in health or to the protection of adolescents, and that it was not therefore appropriate. Arguments which supported this theory were developed in close consultation with the client; for instance:

- Advertising for alcoholic beverages does not necessarily lead to the consumption of these beverages. This has been proved by scientific studies e.g. in Canada and Norway.
- (Alcohol) advertising only influences adolescents to a very minor degree. The behaviour of family and friends, who serve as examples, is far more important.
- The excessive consumption of alcohol is not a group-specific problem of adolescents, but occurs – irrespective of age – throughout the entire population. Conversely, a significant percentage of adolescents do not consume any alcohol whatsoever.

The agency was aware that the responsible political decision-makers were compelled to implement measures in order to protect adolescents from the dangers of alcohol ("decision-maker's perspective"). As discussed during the kick-off meeting, maintaining and extending the industry's voluntary commitments in terms of the limitation of advertising and the execution of prevention and clarification measures were therefore suggested as a compromise within the onepager. It was also indicated that support would be provided to politicians in the execution of independent educational programmes, in which adolescents were to be enabled to learn how to consume alcohol in a responsible manner. Proposals for tightening the age limits for purchasing alcoholic beverages and controlling these limits more strictly were also tabled.

On completion of the onepager, which actors were to be personally addressed when, and in which sequence, was decided in close co-operation between the agency and Bayernbräu on the basis of the key player list. To do this, the agency's senior consultant undertook appointment co-ordination and organisation, and accompanied the head of communication to the meetings with the political decision-makers. The agency undertook all of the organisation in the run-up to these meetings, i.e. it dealt with appointment arrangement and also ensured that the curricula vitae of all parties involved were sent in addition to dispatching the onepager in advance. The curricula vitae enabled each of the participants to prepare for the meetings in detail.

Since not only German-speaking actors were to be contacted, the onepager was additionally translated into all of the addressees' languages.

9.1.5 Steps 4 and 5: implementation of the onepager and supporting decision-making processes at legislative and executive level

9.1.5.1 Lobbying vis-à-vis the European Commission

Although the European Commission had already introduced the draft text of the directive into the legislative procedure, dialogue was sought with the Director of the responsible Directorate General SANCO and with the Head of Unit for Public Health, who were also registered as key players in the key player list. During these discussions, it again became clear that earlier involvement of the agency in the sense of "preventive lobbying" would have been sensible: whilst the Director and his Head of Unit were open to the arguments contained in the onepager, their willingness to subsequently amend the text appeared to be very limited. However, the agency was able to reassure the head of communication that the desired formulation change would in any case only have pertained to the draft directive. It was debatable whether the Council and Parliament would ultimately have approved this draft at all. As the approval of both institutions therefore had to be ensured under all circumstances, the text amendment could also be postponed until a later stage in the co-decision procedure. However, the meeting was most certainly not to no avail, as the Commission representatives were able to confirm the existing schedule and the timeline which had been established.

9.1.5.2 Lobbying vis-à-vis the Council

The Council and the European Parliament still had the option of introducing amendments to the draft text of the directive. In the following step, the agency therefore concentrated on organising meetings with Council representatives.

The agency particularly focussed on those Council representatives who were significantly affected by the issue of the "ban on advertising for alcohol". As determined in the key player list, this involved Belgium, the Netherlands, the UK and Poland in addition to Germany. Major manufacturers of alcoholic beverages, and therefore jobs which were extensively at risk due to the planned directive, were located in these countries.

As the agency did not have links to all of these governments, a "detour approach" was taken (indirectly contacting an addressee via third parties): the respective, responsible ministers and decision-makers in the governments were to be addressed via the agency's "national contacts"[16] and won over for the line of argument. During the course of this, the agency contacted personally known Members of the European Parliament and further actors at national level, including the State Secretary from the German Ministry of Health, for instance, and familiarised them with the onepager. The respective governments and thus the most important decision-makers in the Council were therefore sensitised to the directive's topic and the related problems for the company, in order to enable them to act at European level to push through a correspondingly amended version of the directive.

---

16 See Joos (2011), p. 218.

In addition, other important actors in the most extensively affected states were encouraged to take action in Brussels: for instance, one MEP, who was very well known to the agency, was not only able to persuade the Belgian Minister of Health of the onepager's arguments, but also drew the attention of the managing director of Belgium's "Prime Brew Co.", the largest manufacturer of beer in the EU, to the topic. In turn, the managing director approached the Belgian executive to encourage its members to act on the issue in Brussels.

In the Netherlands, the headquarters of the EU's third-largest beer manufacturer, "DutchBrew", the agency mobilised further advocates. In addition to sensitising the Dutch government and the managing director of "DutchBrew", a Member of the European Parliament who was known to the agency drew the attention of the Dutch beer and spirits industry associations to the looming advertising ban. These reacted with alarm, and they began to lobby the European Commission and the European Parliament with regard to this issue.

9.1.5.3 Lobbying vis-à-vis the European Parliament

Once the members of the Council had been made aware of the client's concern, the agency then turned to the Members of the European Parliament, in order to draw their attention to the client's interest.

As had been determined beforehand through research, the "Environment, Public Health and Food Safety (ENVI)" committee was in overall charge in the European Parliament; the "Internal Market and Consumer Protection (IMCO)" and "Civil Liberties, Justice and Home Affairs (LIBE)" committees were involved in an advisory capacity. In an initial step, the agency drew the attention of the responsible rapporteur in the ENVI to the client's concern. To do this, Bayernbräu's head of communication conducted a personal discussion with the rapporteur – through the agency's mediation – in order to explain the arguments contained in the onepager, which had been sent prior to the meeting appointment. The head of communication was accompanied by the agency's senior consultant, who acted as a neutral mediator during the discussion. This appointment was of particular importance, as the rapporteur was to draw up the ballot proposal ("report") for the plenary. The rapporteur was additionally contacted by other MEPs, which were known to the agency and had already proved helpful in addressing the Council, with regard to the draft directive and possible amendments to its text. Similar to the approach employed in lobbying vis-à-vis the Council, the instrument of indirectly contacting the addressees was again used.

The representatives and shadow rapporteurs were also included. Initially, the majority of members of parliament were not convinced that a ban on advertising alcohol was not appropriate. However, a majority was subsequently obtained in the responsible committee (ENVI) for the desired amendments, particularly through the arguments contained in the onepager. This committee's final report gave consideration to all of the items of significance to Bayernbräu.

Subsequent to the creation of this final report in the responsible committee, the European Commission, Council and European Parliament commenced negotiations as part of the informal trialogue (see Section 5.3.4.1.1.2), in order to reach an agreement prior to the first reading in the Parliament. The objective was to adopt the directive without protracted discussions. Against this backdrop, the agency's strategy of approaching all of the parties involved in the procedure at an early stage proved very helpful and efficient: clearly formulated arguments, oriented towards the common interest, but also content-related misgivings, had been submitted to all dialogue partners, with the result that the Council and Parliament representatives ultimately succeeded in persuading the Commission to amend the formulations in the directive in favour of Bayernbräu – an agreement was reached at first reading.

9.1.6 Result: achievement of objectives

The majority of the members of parliament voted for an amended directive; whilst this did not contain the advertising ban for alcoholic beverages, the industry's voluntary commitments were tightened.

The project-related strategy planning, with all organisational details such as the creation of a key player list and a timeline, and the drafting of the onepager, had paid off. By addressing all three of the EU institutions – the Commission, Council and Parliament – corresponding majorities were found irrespective of parliamentary groups and nationalities.[17] With its process competence and thanks to its cross-party and -member state network, the governmental relations agency helped the client's concern to succeed. In addition to the agency's actual work as a structural process partner, the client's content competence was also optimally implemented.

9.2 Case 2: "regulation for defining the modalities for achieving the objective of reducing the CO_2 emissions of new passenger cars by 2020"

9.2.1 Circumstances/initial situation

As the progress made up to 2013 with regard to the reduction of CO_2 emissions, particularly in the automotive industry, was not yet sufficient for the European Commission, the Commission deemed it necessary to revise the regulation on the reduction of CO_2 emissions by new passenger cars (Regulation (EC) 443/ 2009) which came into effect in 2009 following protracted negotiations. The previous regulation provided for a reduction in the average CO_2 output of an automotive manufacturer's passenger car fleet to 95 g CO_2/km by 2020.

At the beginning of November 2014 the attention of a German automotive manufacturer with factories in three further EU member states was drawn to the imminent amendment of the regulation by the automotive industry's European um-

---

17 See Joos (2011), p. 221.

brella association. In detail, the manufacturer of (primarily) premium mid-size and luxury class vehicles discovered that the Commission's proposed regulation was to be submitted to the European Parliament and the Council in just four weeks. Within the European Commission, the Directorate General (DG) Environment was responsible for the dossier.

Further research on the proposed regulation revealed that, whilst the Commission was planning to retain the emission target of 95 g CO_2/km by 2020, it intended to modify the calculation of this average value. Above all, the reduction in the multiple crediting of particularly efficient vehicles (so-called "super credits") from a factor of 2.5 to 1 for the years 2020 to 2023, which is intended to reward manufacturers for launching especially efficient vehicles onto the market at an early stage, gave the parties responsible within the German manufacturer's management board considerable cause for concern. Added to this was the maximum creditable number of 20,000 passenger cars planned by the Commission in the above stated period of time. As a consequence of this, low-emission passenger cars would have less of an impact when calculating the average value. Achieving the CO_2 target value would therefore be more difficult for the manufacturers of higher-emission passenger cars, whereas manufacturers of lower-emission passenger cars would be able to attain the target values more easily.

The senior management feared that the new regulations would lead to competitive disadvantages for the German automotive industry, particularly in comparison with the quickly growing markets in Asia and the USA, where far more generous crediting systems are implemented. In turn, this would have negative effects on production and employment in Germany. The German manufacturer's objective was accordingly to bring about a corresponding amendment of the draft text, in order to give greater consideration to company-specific interests.

After consulting the company's in-house legal department with regard to the proposed new regulations' conformity with European legislation and the significant aspects of the ordinary legislative procedure in the EU, the management board finally engaged a governmental relations agency located in Brussels.

What was particularly interesting about the assignment of an external service provider as a process supporter was the fact that, due to its membership of both the national and the European industry association, the manufacturer could at least have covered its basic lobbying requirements via the associations, as classic lobbying instruments. On closer scrutiny, however, it became clear that associations were not an adequate instrument for individual lobbying, because the European association's members also included French and Italian automotive manufacturers in addition to German manufacturers; with their sub-compact and mid-size class vehicles, the former offer different product ranges, serve different market segments, and therefore also make different requirements on the regulatory environment. Generally, this pluralistic interest situation in associations leads to the

fact that only the lowest common denominator of all concerns is often represented outwardly. In addition, opinion-forming within associations is often slow; appropriate reactions to immediate challenges are not always forthcoming.[18] Despite the unanimity of all its members regarding content, the national association's lack of "punch" in the form of viable contacts has proved problematic in the
context of the Europeanisation of lobbying.[19]

As outlined in the following, the problems of the association's minimal consensus
and lack of "leverage" were ultimately resolved by employing an external process
supporter.

9.2.2 Step 1: documentation of the (content-related) objective and continuous checking of political feasibility

The company's management formulated its content-related lobbying objectives
based on the Commission's amendment proposals outlined in the preceding section. As a consolidated opinion was emerging amongst the national association
members, and this was also backed by the German Industrial Union of Metal
Workers, the manufacturer initially co-ordinated closely with the national association. In parallel, the external service provider was to undertake the process-
oriented part of the lobbying at national and European level. However, it emerged
at a relatively early stage that the commissioned service provider had more tenable links to the relevant decision-makers at EU level. As a result of this, the agency
was able to ensure communication which was more sustainable and tailored exactly to the legislative process than the national association, whereupon procedural co-ordination with the industry association was scaled back. In the light of the
plurality of interests prevailing in the European association, co-operation with
this body was forgone from the word go, in order to avoid any co-ordination
problems and frictional losses.

It emerged even during the content-related objective determination phase that the
consultation spectrum provided by the engaged governmental relations agency
would not be restricted merely to procedural steps, but that it would also include
a content-related component. The reason being that consultation was required,
above all, in terms of the political feasibility of the content-related changes desired
by the client. As the client's most rigorous demand of persuading the European
Commission to withdraw its proposed regulation could not be conveyed politically in this case, the agency played an important role in terms of the identification
of realistic requirements. The examination and consideration of feasible issues by
the agency were based on a broad range of information stemming from a variety
of informal discussions with decision-makers within the Commission, Council
and Parliament. The client's objectives were subsequently formulated as follows:

---

18 See Joos (2011), pp. 138 ff.
19 See Joos (2011), pp. 147–148.

the achievement of a change to the text of the proposed regulation, with the result that the maximum possible "super credits" could be retained even after 2020, without calling the EU-wide specification of an average value of 95 g CO_2/km for the passenger car fleets into question.

9.2.3 Step 2: procedural situation assessment and strategy planning

Based on the content analysis undertaken in step 1 (Section 9.2.2), the external service provider then developed a specific project strategy. Within the agency, project implementation was undertaken by a three-person team which had already gained experience with European legislation in the area of environmental policy. To guarantee efficient project control, the advisor team's internal organisation was clearly structured. A senior consultant was responsible for the procedural component. He was consequently responsible for contact management and for communication with members of parliament and civil servants. Throughout the entire project, he was additionally available to the client as a central contact person, in order to ensure trust-based information exchange. The other team members covered organisational support. This included both monitoring and research tasks as well as the formulation and updating of position papers (onepagers). At the start of the project, the following questions had to be answered to define the specific approach points for articulating the client's interests: which procedure is being applied? Where are we in the legislative process? Who are the actors involved?

The agency's contacting the responsible Commission staff from the Directorate General Environment revealed that, whilst the public consultation of stakeholders had already been completed and the Directorate General Environment had already formulated a draft text, this had not yet been officially adopted by the Commission. The regulation text was still undergoing inter-service consultation, i.e. it was still being functionally co-ordinated between the individual Directorates General. Content-oriented assessment by the responsible members of the Commissioner's cabinet – i.e. political co-ordination – was also still forthcoming. Before the College of Commissioners officially accepted the text, the heads of cabinet would first have to approve the regulation's text in an intermediate step. This meant that, in theory, it was still possible to influence the formulation of the proposed regulation before it was officially submitted to the Council and Parliament; however, the time slot available for this offered very little scope in practical terms. From the point of view of preventive lobbying, even earlier involvement in the procedure would have been advantageous. Involvement during the formulation of the Commission's political discussion paper – the so-called Green Paper – would have been optimal.[20] A proactive approach could then have been taken to exert an influence on the Directorate General Environment's draft text at an early stage.

---

20 See Joos (2011), p. 47.

In the next step, the agency checked the procedural framework of the regulation text's imminent revision. As this involved the ordinary legislative procedure, the regulation also had to be accepted by the Council and the European Parliament, in addition to the Commission (right of initiative), before coming into force. Consequently, two additional actors had to be included in the lobbying strategy. As the regulation's amendment touched on environmental policy issues, the Committee of the Regions would also submit an opinion in addition to the European Economic and Social Committee's obligatory opinion.

Based on this information, the agency began to draw up key player lists, i.e. it began to identify the responsible persons in the institutions concerned. Within the Commission, the Director General, the Head of Unit dealing with the issue and the responsible Policy Officer within the Directorate General Environment were first identified. The cabinet member responsible within the Environment Commissioner's cabinet was also identified as a relevant contact. In the Parliament, the rapporteur and the parliamentary groups' shadow rapporteurs were identified.[21] The largest parliamentary group's committee co-ordinators were also taken into consideration as contacts. Finally, the committee chairman and his deputies were identified.

Within the Council, the responsible actors at ambassador, head of unit and attaché level in the Permanent Representations (PR) of the relevant member states were initially identified. Particular attention was also paid to the responsible actors of the biannually rotating Council Presidencies, which co-ordinated the Council's work during the legislative consultations. At national level, the responsible civil servants (State Secretary, Head of Department, Head of Unit) in the German Ministry of the Environment, who were represented in the Council's committees, were selected.

In addition to the key player analysis, one member of the agency's team implemented a monitoring process, as a result of which the content-related component of the issue was continuously covered and institutional questions pertaining to the legislative process were clarified. These steps formed the foundation for conveying the client's content-related concepts to the previously determined addressees at the legislative and executive level in the form of a onepager.

9.2.4 Step 3: drafting one or more onepagers and submitting them to previously identified addressees

As initially mentioned, it was above all the lack of progress made by the automotive industry in climate protection which played a crucial role in the revision of the existing regulation for the Commission. This resulted in two lobbying challenges from the client's perspective. Firstly, the topic of climate protection was a

---

21 These were only identified following transfer to the responsible committee and nomination by the parliamentary groups.

sensitive issue which was unsuitable for broad-based media campaigns and which, under certain circumstances, may have led to counter-campaigns by environmental protection or non-governmental organisations (NGOs). Secondly, the legislator's primarily climate policy-based motivation resulted in the fact that a lack of attention vis-à-vis the German automotive manufacturer's positions was to be anticipated on the part of the European decision-makers. "Open doors" and willing dialogue partners could not therefore be assumed. In order to thus avoid being confronted with a weakened starting position due to the client's position being regarded merely as the particular interests of an individual member state in Brussels, this risk had to be counteracted with specific information work.

Since the legislative process had already started and, in this case, the Commission's proposed regulation would be officially accepted in a matter of weeks, specific and immediate action was required. The client's most significant lines of argument were summarised in the form of a onepager (see Chapter 6). On a total of one page, the tripartite structure of the onepager contained passages on the background and status quo of the regulatory situation, an analysis of the negative effects of the new legislative initiative on the affected stakeholders and, finally, specific proposals for resolving the previously defined problems. In addition to the factual arguments, the European dimension of the issue had to be particularly highlighted in order to sustainably introduce the concern vis-à-vis the different actors at EU level. The formulation of a onepager entitled "Germany", which primarily emphasised the importance of the German automotive sector to the single European market, and the formulation of a onepager entitled "EU", aimed at support for implementing the EU climate protection objectives, was the appropriate method for achieving this aim. Once the onepagers had been co-ordinated several times between the client and the agency, the compatibility of the company's interests with public interest was rendered visible (common interest perspective) and communicated in the language of the decision-makers to the previously identified contact persons (see step 2 in Section 9.2.3).

9.2.5 Step 4: flanking the onepager with other structural and process-oriented instruments (mutual information transparency)

In addition to the support provided by the onepager in the decision-making process, more extensive measures, from the areas of public affairs and public relations, for instance, must always be weighed up depending on the situation. The repertoire of possible measures can encompass background discussions with experts, the organisation of parliamentary evenings or also the triggering of public debate via social media channels or by contacting media representatives. The objective of all of these instruments is to draw the attention of relevant actors to the issue via the circuitous route of publicity (indirect lobbying).[22]

---

22 See Joos (2011), pp. 180 ff.

In view of the high sensitivity of the issue of climate protection in public debate, effective media measures had to be implemented cautiously in order not to provoke any negative backlash. Due to the fact that the client also received backing for its position from the metalworkers' trade union in addition to the national automotive association, a symposium conducted by these two actors, with effective media coverage, proved to be a helpful instrument in obtaining content-related interpretation sovereignty at national level. Because of the unusual consonance between the association and the trade union, this alliance additionally offered the potential for making an impact at European level. However, the lobbying continued to focus primarily on the instrument of governmental relations, as will be clearly shown in the following section.

9.2.6 Step 5: supporting decision-making processes at legislative and executive level

9.2.6.1 Lobbying vis-à-vis the European Commission

On completion and transfer of the onepager entitled "EU" to the Commission, the agency subsequently scheduled personal meetings with the key players previously identified within the Directorate General Environment, i.e. with the Director General, the responsible Head of Unit and the administrative civil servant (Policy Officer). The agency's established network played an important role in appointment arrangement and acceptance. The responsible Commission official and the agency representative were already familiar with one another from a previous project. The meetings were therefore able to take place against the backdrop of an existing factual and relationship level.

Nevertheless, it was initially unclear how the Commission officials would react to the client's outlined concern. The possibilities for content-related intervention were also limited due to the procedural progress of the Commission's draft. Whilst the Commission representatives showed that they understood the client's position at working level, their willingness to subsequently amend the text of the Directorate General's legislative draft was still limited.

Once this became apparent, the agency sought, in the sense of the two-dimensional approach to lobbying vis-à-vis the Commission, dialogue with the Chef de Cabinet – who prepares the weekly meeting of all Commissioners together with his counterparts – and with the member of the Environment Commissioner's cabinet responsible for the dossier. Making political contact via the Commissioner's personal staff also held little promise of success, since the Environment Commissioner had already indicated to his employees that he intended to stick to his political line. It was therefore unlikely that the functional path via the Directorate General and the political route via the cabinet would lead to the desired objective. At this point, an amendment to the text would in any case only have affected the Commission's proposed regulation. However, subsequently contacting the Commission could indeed prove helpful, as it plays an important role both as part of the "informal trialogue" during the first reading and also in the event that a conciliation committee is convened.

After consulting the client, the agency therefore initially concentrated on the Council and the Parliament, where a text amendment was finally achieved during the further course of the ordinary legislative procedure.

9.2.6.2 Lobbying vis-à-vis the Council

Following the official acceptance of the proposed regulation by the College of Commissioners, the text was transferred to the Council. The national automotive association's previously established links to the German Ministry of the Environment, specifically to the State Secretary's personal advisor and the head of the Europe and International Affairs sub-department, proved helpful at this point. Thanks to the use of the onepager entitled "Germany", the Federal Ministry's attention was brought to the client's concern, as a concern pertaining to the German automotive industry as a whole, and its support in this matter was assured via the Council at EU level. An initial, interim objective was therefore achieved.

As the Council's work at EU level is primarily determined by the Permanent Representatives Committee (Coreper), the next step involved addressing the ambassadors of the member states in the Permanent Representations in Brussels. An existing link to the Head of Unit in Germany's Permanent Representation proved to be an important starting point in this regard, as she was persuaded of the client's concern thanks to the specific use of the onepager.

In view of the double majority required in the Council since the Treaty of Lisbon came into effect, the agency pointed out to the client that it would not be sufficient to exert an influence on the Council solely via one individual member state. The support of further member states was necessary in order to orchestrate opinion-forming across national boundaries in the Council in the sense of the client's concern.[23] It was appropriate in this case to firstly approach those member states in which the client's production plants were located. The agency additionally conducted research into which other member states were economically dependent on the German automotive industry. Two member states were identified in this manner. However, a trusting relationship with the Permanent Representation only existed in one of these cases. Lobbying in the case of the other four countries therefore had to be undertaken by means of a detour approach: in the case of the second country with a production plant, success was achieved in convincing the responsible, national minister of the relevance of the issue specifically via a Member of the European Parliament. The two actors' long-term co-operation in national party committees, which was previously brought to light through the agency's research work, played a significant role in this.

---

23 Multi-dimensional lobbying in the multi-level system (see Joos (2011), pp. 72, 110).

The lobbying process in the third member state, via an MEP's contact with the national ministry, was similarly successful. The minister was encouraged to take action in the Council via a former employee of the Member of Parliament, who had since relocated to the national ministry, where he was responsible for the issue.

The relevant ministers in the two member states with economic dependency on German automobile production were approached via the agency's contacts. The industrial associations located there also pricked up their ears, and additionally approached the national executive, demanding that it safeguard jobs within the supply industry. Thanks to this "twin track" approach, these member states also took action to provide support in Brussels.

9.2.6.3 Lobbying vis-à-vis the European Parliament

The agency's strategic approach focussed primarily on lobbying vis-à-vis the responsible committee (ENVI). The first point of contact here was the rapporteur, who would draw up the ballot proposal (report) for the plenary. A onepager was transferred to, and a personal meeting subsequently scheduled with, the rapporteur in order to convince him of the client's suggestions. In the meanwhile, the MEPs previously contacted by the agency, focussing on the Council, had already independently approached the rapporteur and outlined the client's concern to him (endogenic approach). In this case, the rapporteur additionally originated from Germany, and was therefore generally receptive to a German company's content-related input.

The second target group alongside the rapporteur was the so-called shadow rapporteurs of the other parliamentary groups. They were also sensitised to the issue, in order to ensure the greatest possible majority for the ballot in the committee and the plenary. To additionally ensure the support of the other committee members for the client's concern, the agency recommended approaching the two biggest parliamentary groups' (EPP and S&D) committee co-ordinators.

Irrespective of party membership, the German members of the ENVI were won over to the client's concern due to the agency's factual arguments and professional approach. However, a critical situation arose when the Italian committee chairman (EPP), supported by his French deputy (S&D), increasingly intervened into the committee consultations and introduced amendment proposals in favour of the Italian and French automotive industry and to the disadvantage of the German automotive industry. Further members of parliament were won over as supporters through the *ad hoc* preparation of additional arguments and repeatedly approaching the office managers of the co-ordinators and the MEPs from countries in which German automotive industry production plants and/or suppliers were located. Ultimately, the submitted amendment requests were rejected by a majority in the committee's final vote, and a committee report which was positive from the client's perspective was accepted.

As the Commission, Council and Parliament had already commenced informal meetings ("informal trialogue") following the committee's vote, in order to reach an early agreement as part of the first reading, the strategy of having approached the key players within each of the institutions in a similar manner proved particularly helpful. The content-related misgivings were therefore sufficiently familiar to the institutions' negotiation teams, and Council and Parliament representatives were able to persuade the Commission to intervene in favour of the client and ultimately reach an agreement at first reading.

9.2.6.4 Lobbying vis-à-vis the Committee of the Regions and the Economic and Social Committee

In order to lend the client's interest greater impact, the Committee of the Regions (CoR) and the Economic and Social Committee (ESC) were additionally included in the lobbying strategy. In the case of the former, the German automotive association undertook important mediation work vis-à-vis the German members of the CoR. The CoR therefore adopted a position which was clearly in favour of the client's concern as regards the Commission's proposal.

In terms of the ESC, the link to the S&D co-ordinator in the ENVI proved useful since, as a member of the national metalworkers' trade union IG Metall management board, she maintained a good relationship with the German trade union members in the ESC. An opinion which favoured the client was also adopted here thanks to the initially described, national consonance between the industrial association and the trade union.

9.2.7 Result: achievement of objectives

In contrast to the Commission's draft, the version of the regulation adopted at first reading by the Parliament and Council contained the represented company's positions as formulated at the start of the project. Lobbying vis-à-vis the Council and Parliament, via which a cross-member and cross-group majority was achieved in both institutions, proved particularly successful here. The flanking, structural support measures during the informal trialogue or via the CoR and ESC also contributed positively to the formation of a corresponding opinion in the EU's multi-level system.

The company benefited from engaging an external service provider for governmental relations by gaining access to its process competence and broad network. The required access to decision-makers would not have been achievable as part of the company's own association memberships or its own liaison offices (corporate representative offices).

Chapter 10   Summary and outlook: necessity of supplementing and updating the instruments for successful lobbying in the European Union in the light of the Treaty of Lisbon

10.1 Lobbying as an economic asset for companies[*]

The paradigm shift from the focus on content-oriented to process-oriented lobbying, which was particularly triggered by the changes resulting from the Treaty of Lisbon, has been emphasised in the preceding chapters. Based on this, the following, final, chapter of this book will introduce a more extensively differentiated, process-oriented approach to lobbying which makes reference to organisational science. In this, the process competence which is crucial within the framework of lobbying is broken down into three fundamental elements:

- Firstly, the provision of the required procedural structures (particularly the EU-wide contact networks and the EU-wide organisational and personnel structures of a structural lobbying instrument).
- Secondly, perspective change competence.
- Thirdly, process support competence.

In this, the example of an independent, external service provider in lobbying (governmental relations agency as an intermediary) will be used as the basis for showing how the client's content competence has to be intermeshed with the intermediary's process competence for a specific lobbying project, in order to enable success to be achieved under the changed framework conditions of lobbying in the EU. Finally, this complementary procedure of client and intermediary must be made tangible on the basis of a "formula for successful lobbying".

Political lobbying serves to achieve corporate objectives which are crucial from a commercial management perspective:

- Repelling corporate, competitive disadvantages.
- Avoidance of errors.
- Achieving and safeguarding competitive advantages.[1]

These corporate objectives are universal, i.e. they apply across industries. The question of how these objectives can be achieved as efficiently as possible is the object of commercial management organisation theory and, as part of the so-called "organisational problem", is determined by the following three variables:

---

[*]   This not only applies to private companies, but also to associations and organisations (for the entire chapter).
1   See working definition of the term lobbying in Section 2.2.2 and in Joos (1998), p. 27.

- "Objectives".
- Constraining "conditions" which cannot be influenced ("framework conditions").
- "Tools" or "instruments".[2]

10.2 Objectives of lobbying (involvement in decision-making processes)

As has been explained in detail in Sections 2.2 and 6.4, lobbying is an intermediary system for mediating economic policy interests in the broadest sense:[3] as such an intermediary system, lobbying links the two external systems of politics and the economy by overcoming the existing communication barriers through its mediation activity. It acts as a type of translation mechanism between the two systems; by transforming the information from both of the external systems, it enables the respective, other system to receive the interests articulated by the partner.[4] This results in the interaction of the determining variables of the organisation problem between politicians and companies (between their objectives, the framework conditions and instruments). For a portrayal of the intermediary character of lobbying in the light of these variables, see Figure 2.3 (in Section 2.2.2.2).

In the sense of commercial management organisation theory, political lobbying is a corporate "tool" or the "instrument" for achieving the respective corporate objectives. However, it does not always passively accept the existing conditions (framework conditions), but is often involved in structuring them: the essential objective of any lobbying is involvement in executive and legislative level decision-making processes through the introduction of the company's arguments and positions.

The initiative for a European directive as a legislative act is usually regarded as a given exogenous factor. Essentially, of course, it is also conceivable for a legislative process for a specific directive to be initiated by a company. In this case, the objective would be endogenous. Another, far more frequent, example of an endogenous objective is the acquisition of subsidies.[5] As endogenous objectives are dependent on numerous factors such as the industry and the size of the company, for instance, it is very difficult to make generally applicable or transferable statements here. Conversely, the problem of involvement in an emerging EU legislative act is identical for all affected companies in the case of an exogenous objective.[6] It can also fundamentally be stated that the company-related action require-

---

2   See Joos (1998), p. 36.
3   The importance of the exchange of information and issues in the political decision-making process is one of the topics dealt with in Chapter 3.
4   Joos (1998), p. 85.
5   Joos (1998), p. 87.
6   Joos (1998), pp. 87–88.

ments are determined from the outside in an exogenous objective, whereas the company itself determines its individual action requirements in the case of an endogenous objective.[7] Due to these reasons, the explanations provided here are limited exclusively to exogenous objectives for lobbying.

The objectives of lobbying are of considerable importance as part of the problem of organising or structuring lobbying, particularly since the specific approaches and potential lobbying instruments have to be oriented towards them. The best possible constellation of approaches and instruments has to be found and implemented in order to achieve a set objective. In turn, the latter is dependent on further factors:

- The orientation of the given framework conditions, which cannot be influenced and under which organisation has to take place (see Section 10.3).
- The establishment of mutual information transparency (through communication/mediation between politicians and companies), i. e. the availability of all information relevant to a decision (see Sections 7.3.1.2 and 6.5.4.4).
- The special role of the factor of time, i. e. in terms of the point in time at which the action is required (see above all Section 3.5).

Essentially, optimal lobbying is therefore characterised by its ability to deal with exogenous objectives, which usually arise at short notice depending on the situation, using the most flexible possible lobbying instruments.[8]

10.3 Framework conditions – reform due to the Treaty of Lisbon

The framework conditions of corporate activities are the political and legal prerequisites and attendant circumstances of the product and geographical markets in which the company is active (with regard to the framework conditions, see above all Chapter 5 for details). The Treaty of Lisbon specifies the EU's political, legal framework conditions (with regard to the "political system of the EU", see Chapter 4 and above all Section 4.3 for details). Coming into effect on 1st December 2009, this Treaty has fundamentally reformed the political system of the EU. The significant points of these framework conditions will again be described in the following.

10.3.1 Treaty of Lisbon: "United States of Europe"!

It is interesting that the heads of state and government still succeeded in pushing through the Reform Treaty of Lisbon even after the referenda concerning the Constitutional Treaty for Europe (TCE) had failed in mid-2005 in France and the Netherlands; because ultimately, the Treaty of Lisbon has taken over the majority

---

7 Joos (1998), p. 89.
8 Joos (1998), p. 88.

of the Constitutional Treaty's substance. Bertie Ahern, the Prime Minister of Ireland at the time of ratification, claims that 90% of the Constitutional Treaty found its way into the Treaty of Lisbon.[9] Expert assessments on this issue vary between 80 and 95%[10] – something of which the majority of citizens, private companies, associations and organisations within the EU are likely to be unaware.

With regard to the differences and important innovations, see Section 4.3 for details. As a result, it is still *de facto* possible to talk of a "United States of Europe", despite the failed constitution – although some of its aspects have been watered down, of course.

The EU is an internally solid union of states, whose stable legal bases are set more firmly in concrete than those of some of the member states: an amendment of the EU Treaty is normally significantly more difficult to achieve than the amendment of national constitutions. For instance, a two-thirds majority of the members in the Bundestag and Bundesrat is required to amend the German Constitution (Article 79 (1 and 2) GG). The regulation concerning how the EU Treaty can be amended (Article 48 TEU) is an innovation of the Treaty of Lisbon. Reforms to the Treaty now require special amendment procedures; in these, a distinction is made between an *ordinary* and a *simplified amendment procedure*, whereby the latter does not necessarily require ratification by the national parliaments. However, a unanimous decision in the European Council, i.e. by the national governments of all EU member states, is necessary in each case.

A state's withdrawal from the Union has been regulated for the first time since Lisbon (Article 50 TEU). In harmony with its constitutional regulations, each member state can now decide to withdraw from the EU (Article 50 (1)). The precise procedure – declaration of the withdrawal decision vis-à-vis the European Council, conclusion of a withdrawal agreement including the regulation of the future legal relationship between the withdrawing state and the EU – is regulated in sub-sections 2 and 3. The period of time until withdrawal is completed is also specified in accordance with Article 50 (3): the guideline value is two years. Withdrawing from the EU is entirely possible in purely legal terms.

However, the actual difficulties are not of a legal nature; instead, they arise following withdrawal. Even if it is theoretically possible for each member state to withdraw, it is *de facto* not possible due to the tight "intermesh" with other member states on the single market (particularly at economic level). For the euro countries, withdrawal from the EU also means exiting the monetary union and reintroducing the state's own national currency. The related risks and costs are barely calculable. This also applies to non-euro countries. Apart from "threats", the first precedent has occurred with the Brexit referendum on 23 June 2016.

---

9 Bertie Ahern in an interview: "90% [of the constitution] are still there. (...) These amendments have not led to any spectacular changes to 2004's Treaty" (*Irish Independent* from 24th June 2007).
10 See Phinnemore (2013), p. 143.

Up to this (theoretical) time of withdrawal, the member states must abide by, and subject themselves to, the EU's ("ground") rules.

10.3.2 Strengthening the European Union

The Treaty of Lisbon's main objective was a fundamental reform of the EU's political system.[11]

10.3.2.1 Outwardly

The objective was to lend the EU – which was previously regarded as a chorus of many voices rather than as a common voice of the member states in foreign policy terms – a coherent and visible external image and enable it to speak with one voice.[12] This problem was tackled using three measures.

- The EU now has a separate legal personality (Article 47 TEU); consequently, it is able to conclude international treaties or join international organisations, and therefore become more tangible as a partner for non-Community countries and international organisations.[13]
- As a foreign policy "face" and contact person for international partners, the Reform Treaty also introduced the office of the High Representative of the Union for Foreign Affairs and Security Policy – ultimately a kind of EU Foreign Minister – (Article 27 (2 and 3)). The High Representative is simultaneously the Chairman of the Council of Foreign Ministers and Vice President of the Commission (Article 18 (4) TEU).
- According to Article 27 (3) TEU, the newly established European External Action Service (EEAS), which is made up of officials of the Commission, the Council Secretariat and the diplomatic services of all member states, is subordinate to the High Representative.

Although the principle of member state unanimity in outwards decision-making has been retained to all extents and purposes (apart from a very few, tightly delimited exceptions: see Article 31 TEU) – i.e. the EU remains unable to act until a unanimous solution has been found – the above mentioned three measures give the EU the option of its own foreign policy strategy which is at least divorced from the member states in part.[14] This is an important step towards increased "statehood" for the EU and – at least in the long term – towards a reduction of foreign policy importance for the member states.[15]

---

11 See Woods and Watson (2012), p. 17; Seeger (2008), p. 63.
12 See Maurer (2008), p. 13; Giegerich and Wallace (2010), pp. 451 ff.
13 See Bieber, Epiney and Haag (2013), § 3 Ri 49 ff.; Murswiek (2008), p. 66.
14 See Mix (2013), p. 2.
15 See Joos (2014), p. 33.

10.3.2.2 Inwardly

Inwardly, only the areas of social security and social policy plus operational police co-operation are still subject to the principle of unanimity, in addition to tax harmonisation and EU budgetary policy. These are joined by individual areas of environmental policy.[16] The background to this is that the individual member states' ability to block decisions is to be reduced, and the EU's ability to act improved, in the light of an environment which is changing rapidly as a result of global crises and challenges.

The inwardly directed reform measures described in the following had a significantly greater impact on the area of political decision-making procedures, and therefore on the practice of lobbying.

10.3.3 Multi-level system, ordinary legislative procedure, informal trialogue

It stands to reason that an individual member state had more influence on individual decisions in a "Europe of 6 states" than is the case in today's "Europe of 28 states". However, the extensive transition from the principle of unanimity to the majority principle in the case of decisions in the Council is significant – and involves considerably more complex effects in practice: since the Treaty of Lisbon, at the latest, decisions are made according to the majority principle in most important policy areas. In other words, an individual member state can no longer block or significantly influence an EU legislative procedure in these policy areas.

10.3.3.1 Multi-level system

Today's European Union of 28 member states is a dynamic, complex, multi-level system in whose political decision-making processes European, national and regional levels are involved. By no means least because of this, European procedures are difficult to understand. It is even more difficult to specifically introduce an individual member state's concerns into the system. The situation has deteriorated even further due to the Treaty of Lisbon and the related structural and institutional changes. At the same time, the importance of the EU is growing continuously.

An increasing number of policy and legislative areas, which were previously the responsibility of nation states, are now decided on at EU level (in Brussels and Strasbourg).

10.3.3.2 Ordinary legislative procedure (Article 294 TFEU): the number of decision-makers is increasing

With the Treaty of Lisbon, the previous co-decision procedure (in which the Parliament is involved in legislative decisions) was elevated to the standard proce-

---

16 See Joos (2014), pp. 35–36.

dure. The Parliament became a fully-fledged partner in the legislative procedure in practically all important areas of policy.[17] At the same time, the EU's democratic legitimation was increased by enhancing the role of the European Parliament in the legislative procedure. Three EU institutions are involved in what is now the ordinary legislative procedure (Article 294 TFEU): the European Commission, the European Parliament and the Council of the EU. The Commission submits a proposal to the Parliament and the Council; the latter two institutions then decide on it. However, the decision-making procedure is complicated. In formal terms, reaching a compromise may take up to three readings in the Parliament and Council, with the involvement of a conciliation committee (in the second reading).

For lobbying, this means:

- The necessity of always being kept abreast of the procedure and the important dates of committee meetings, plenary sessions and Council meetings, etc.
- The difficulty of identifying the crucial decision-makers: the number of decision-makers in legislative and executive decision-making processes is increasing; essentially, decisions with numerous "decision-makers" are emerging (phenomenon of "decisions without the one decision-maker/very few decision-makers").

In the ordinary legislative procedure, the majority principle applies in the Council. The votes of at least 55% of the Council members (i.e. at least 15 member states), which must in turn represent at least 65% of the EU population, are required for a so-called qualified majority. As a result, at least four Council members, which must represent a total of more than 35% of the EU's population, are required for a blocking minority (Article 16 (4) TFEU). The consequence of this is that one member state alone is no longer able to submit a "veto" and thus block a decision or steer it in its desired direction.

The situation for lobbyists has therefore become more complicated.

- So far, lobbyists have relied extensively on the possibility of preventing decisions which, in their view, were not compatible with the represented corporate interests. This will continue to play a role in the future, particularly as companies frequently only become aware of the fact that their interests are in danger when the formal decision-making processes are already far advanced. In the Council, however, a regulation or directive can only be prevented with a blocking minority or amended with a qualified majority.
- The group of relevant decision-makers has therefore become much larger after Lisbon. Cross-member state networks are therefore required, as the classic focus on one member state is no longer sufficient even to prevent a decision.

---

17 See Selck and /Veen (2008), p. 18.

10.3.3.3 Informal trialogue: an additional decision-making level

In addition to the formal procedures and decision-making processes, it is also important to keep abreast of the informal processes in the EU, and to monitor and support both these and the formal processes. One striking example of an informal procedure – i. e. one which is not regulated by law – is the "informal trialogue". It is not provided for in the TFEU, but is nevertheless frequently implemented prior to the first reading in the Parliament as part of the ordinary legislative procedure. The informal trialogue involves meetings between a small group of individuals, in which representatives of the Commission, the Parliament (usually the rapporteur) and the Council (usually the Council Presidency) take part.

This trialogue is a procedural, sovereign tool for structuring and speeding up coordination between the Commission, Parliament and Council. Crucial compromises are often achieved in the trialogue.[18] As a result of this, a compromise in the ordinary legislative procedure can be reached in over 80 % of cases at first reading.[19] The informal trialogue can therefore most certainly be regarded as a further (albeit informal) decision-making level.

10.3.4 Shift in focus from content to process competence

The EU's development trends, and particularly the reforms brought about by the Treaty of Lisbon, are exerting high pressure to adapt on the representation of interests – whether these be the concerns of member states or individual industries and companies. If one assumes that the primary objective of lobbying is to work towards a specific result with content, i. e. factual arguments, as part of a decision-making process,[20] the practical focal point prior to the Treaty of Lisbon lay less on process competence and far more on content competence.[21]

The so-called "classic", structural lobbying instruments (see "structural instruments" in detail in Section 6.4.1) include:

- Corporate representative offices.
- Associations.
- Public affairs agencies.
- Law firms.

These classic instruments usually dedicate the vast majority of their time to the content-related preparation of lobbying, drawing up exhaustive expert reports and discussion papers, conducting media campaigns and taking part in public hearings, etc. This is noticeable, since the significant development trends in EU

---

18 See Weidenfeld (2013), p. 166.
19 See Jensen and Martinsen (2014), p. 5; European Parliamentary Research Service (2014), p. 2.
20 Definitions in Joos (2011), p. 44; Lösche (2007), p. 20; van Schendelen (2002), pp. 203–204; McGrath (2005), p. 17.
21 With regard to the concepts of content and process competence, see also Godwin, Ainsworth and Godwin (2013), pp. 216 ff.

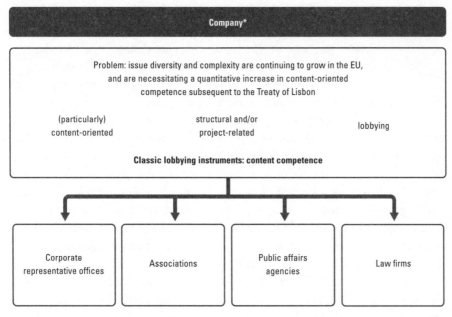

Figure 10.1: Classic lobbying instruments

politics are much more concerned with procedural questions (processes) of European policy.

However, as soon as specific involvement in decision-making processes is concerned, content-related work and focussing on arguments alone are not sufficient. In a complex, multi-level system such as the EU, with decision-makers at regional, national and European level, procedural questions are at least equally as crucial to the success of lobbying amongst the European Union's institutions. Content-related arguments fail to reach their target audience at all unless the relevant, complex decision-making processes are observed beforehand: which of the various legislative procedures is applied? When and what should be communicated to whom, and in which form? Who is responsible for what at which point in time in the procedure? Which periods of grace have to be observed?

10.3.5 Increase in complexity and paradigm shift

10.3.5.1 Increase in the complexity of European decision-making processes

The political, legal framework conditions of corporate activities in EU Europe have changed fundamentally due to the Treaty of Lisbon at the latest. This Reform Treaty has triggered an increase in the complexity of European decision-making processes.

Even the search for the correct contact person often turns out to be a challenge for lobbyists. The EU has no executive such as that found in classic nation states. It is pointless to analyse the issue of whether the EU's legal status bears similarity to that of a state, a confederation, a federation or another entity under international law. It is *sui generis* – a new entity, for which the old categories are too tightly de-limited. European lobbying must be applied both amongst the European institutions (Parliament, Commission, Council, etc.) and at member state level (Council members). In the EU, legislative functions are exercised by the Council of the EU and the European Parliament. However, the European Parliament is not compa-rable with national parliaments in respect to the fact that there are no governing political groups or opposing political groups; instead, there are diverse consensus-building processes across national and party boundaries that make it difficult to predict majorities. Not only the relevant, responsible European institutions (ac-cording to Article 294 TFEU, the Commission, Council and Parliament), but also the member state level (e. g. the individual Council members or the nationally or-ganised parties of the Members of the European Parliament) have to be involved during the legislative procedures. Successful lobbying must be able to monitor the processes promptly at all of these interfaces. Against this background, a lobbyist will constantly have to act under high time pressure and conditions of great un-certainty. European lobbying therefore necessitates not only professional skills but also a good feel for difficulties in a procedure, empathy towards the decision-makers, political sensitivity for the underlying processes and constant information transparency at all interfaces.[22]

When dealing with the EU and its actors at regional, national and European level, a company and its lobbyists fall into a genuine "complexity trap", from which even major company groups are unable to escape: careful process management and a high level of process competence, which the company itself is unable to sus-tainably maintain, are required to cope with this complexity.[23] Many companies are not even aware of this problem. Others recognise the increasing necessity of procedural knowledge and procedural management, but ultimately have no effec-tive tools which they are able to implement to make the structures of European decision-making more transparent.[24] Even if businessmen and managers have re-cognised the importance of the political framework conditions and decisions in the member states, and especially in the European Union, to their commercial success, they are often unable to cope in view of the complex processes in the in-stitutions. They are increasingly viewing themselves as no longer able to iden-tify the formal and informal decision-makers that are genuinely of relevance to them. The political processes are intransparent to them. They do not know where,

---

22 Joos (2015), pp. 408 – 409.
23 Joos (2015), pp. 410 ff.; for further detailed information on process management and competence, see also Joos (2014), pp. 29 – 45.
24 See Joos (2015), pp. 410 ff.

when or how they can communicate their interests in such a way that they are heard.[25]

10.3.5.2 Paradigm shift in lobbying: process competence

Triggered by this increase in the complexity of European decision-making processes in an increasingly heterogeneous environment, we are experiencing a paradigm shift – a sharp rise in the importance of "processes" in politics in comparison with "content-related arguments". Content and arguments are necessary even in complex political procedures. However, only their communication by the right person to the right addressee at the right time, in the right place and in the right manner, subject to a knowledge of the decision-makers' objectives, interests and ways of thinking, as well as the informal and formal decision-making rules, is sufficient for these to be taken note of and asserted. An argument which is not introduced in a specific stage of the decision-making process runs the risk of no longer being taken into consideration.

Lobbyists therefore face fundamental "technical" questions that have to be answered continually in parallel with all content-related arguments, irrespective of whether the interests of a member state, a company, an association or an NGO are being represented. Practice shows how important process competence is to be able to participate in the EU's political dealings and support decision-making processes. The consequence of this for political lobbying in the EU is that process competence becomes as important as content competence, and actually surpasses it in importance as the complexity of a decision-making process increases (for an illustration, see Figure 10.2).

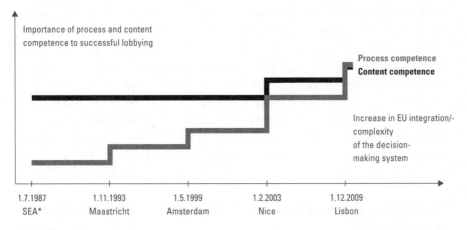

Figure 10.2: Change in the importance of process and content competence for successful lobbying during the development of the EC or EU

---

25 Joos (2015), pp. 410 ff.

Professional lobbying must take account of the paradigm shift due to the significant increase in the importance of procedural questions: its focus must be shifted more towards procedural work. The "complexity trap" that is the EU can only be escaped with extensive process competence. Help can only be provided through external, professional process support by an intermediary who constantly monitors European processes (see Section 10.4.1). Extensive process competence and clever on-site process management by a neutral and objective intermediary are the key to reducing complexity.

10.4 Lobbying instruments: additions and continued development (intermeshing content competence with process competence)

In light of the fundamental changes described in the above, the company's political lobbying tools have to be reconfigured. Here, commercial management organisation theory makes a distinction between structural and procedural organisation:[26]

- *Structural organisation (structure):* increase in thus far primarily content-oriented instruments and extension by process-oriented lobbying instruments (establishment and maintenance of required structures and networks).
- *Procedural organisation (process-oriented methodology):* application of a process-oriented methodology of lobbying ("process" at least with equal status in comparison with "content").

The distinction between structural and procedural organisation is used to express the analytical breakdown between structure and process. Both usually analyse identical objects, but from different perspectives.[27] In the final analysis, both are concerned with the optimised management of (work) procedures and processes. With reference to professional lobbying, this means giving consideration to the paradigm shift due to the significant increase in the importance of procedural questions, and increasingly shifting the focus to procedural work. Adaptation to these new framework conditions makes it necessary for companies to check and further develop their own structural and procedural organisation – this otherwise leads to a risk of extensively forfeiting structural options, which often goes unnoticed by many actors.

10.4.1 External intermediary: key to reducing complexity (structural organisation)

The objective of any corporate management team is to represent the interests of its company as well as possible. A neutral, objective – and therefore necessarily

---

26 According to Kosiol (1962).
27 See Kosiol (1962), p. 32.

external – intermediary is an appropriate key to reducing complexity under the framework condition changes brought about by the Treaty of Lisbon. This intermediary represents extensive process competence and intelligent, pan-EU process management. The establishment and maintenance of the structures described in the following are barely possibly any longer for an individual company or for lobbying undertaken by the company itself.

A detailed "intermediary" requirement profile, which must encompass the competencies and prerequisites described in the following, arises for successful lobbying in EU Europe. It must be remembered in this case that the intermediary concentrates on the structural process support of lobbying (process management), whereas the company remains responsible for content-related management (content competence).

10.4.1.1 Process structure competence (PStC)

The process structure competence of the intermediary, an agency specialised in governmental relations, encompasses two separate sub-areas; as such, these represent independent competencies which are interdependent:

- EU-wide spacial, personnel and organisational capacities (management competence).
- Tenable EU-wide networks (production competence).

10.4.1.1.1 Management competence

Management competence exists in the form of reservation of the required geographical, personnel and organisational capacities throughout the EU.

- *Spacial capacities:* the challenge for successful lobbying in EU Europe involves establishing networks throughout Europe's capital cities, ideally with own offices or also structural co-operation partners. The background to this is that the European Parliament is not comparable to the national parliaments, since there are no governing or opposing political groups. Instead, diverse consensus-forming processes across national and party boundaries are required. It is therefore extremely difficult to predict majorities. In addition to the respective, responsible European institutions (according to Article 294 TFEU, the Commission, Council and Parliament), the individual Council members or the parties of the Members of the European Parliament, which are organised on nation state lines, must be involved at member state level.
- *Personnel capacities:* experienced teams with professional interface management competence vis-à-vis a) "the parties concerned" and b) "decision-makers". In addition to its employees, the intermediary's (the specialised governmental relations agency's) team should also encompass structural advisors, including former, top legislative and executive level officers and public figures from several EU member states.

- *Organisational capacities:* the intermediary also keeps the organisational structures on constant standby, in order to simultaneously be able to act as a task force in the event of a crisis, and as a service unit, and additionally to provide insurance against undesired changes to the legal and political framework conditions. Ultimately, the intermediary should offer organisational capacities which correspond, or bear similarity to, the following four business models: a) facility management; b) highly specialised engineering bureau; c) fire brigade and d) insurance company.

10.4.1.1.2 Production competence

Production competence is based on the tenable, EU-wide, cross-institution, cross-parliamentary group and cross-member state networks of the intermediary's own employees, structural advisors and structural co-operation partners, and on external networks. Professional process support (see Section 10.4.2.2) necessitates the establishment and maintenance of a corresponding, tenable network; this can only be achieved with an enormous effort which exceeds even the capacities of major companies. The resulting requirement can therefore only be met by an external service provider (intermediary) which is specialised in governmental relations, and which is able to structurally support processes. In short, companies, associations and organisations require professional process support by an external intermediary complementary to their own structures (see Section 10.4.2).

10.4.1.2 Procedure complementary to the company's content competence (CC)

The intermediary always works complementary to the company and its "classic" lobbying instruments. Due to the continuing increase in the complexity of the significant decision-making procedures, all competencies must be individually and project-specifically intermeshed ("combination and dosing") in each individual legislative or executive initiative. The independent intermediary's interface management between the company and its instruments on the one hand, and the legislative and executive level on the other hand, is crucial in this.

10.4.1.3 Prerequisites for the acceptance of the intermediary within the company and the legislative and executive level

The governmental relations agency must meet the following additional prerequisites in order to be accepted by both the company and also the legislative and executive level.

10.4.1.3.1 Neutrality and independence

An intermediary can concentrate on its role as a neutral and objective (trusted) mediator between commerce and politicians; it is independent of the "affected party" and the "decision-maker". As an external, it is outside of a company's hierarchies (and also those of politics), i. e. it is independent of internal sections (individual corporate units, specialist departments, etc.). Subject to corresponding process structure competence, such an intermediary can make contact with both politicians and companies at all levels, something which would be impossible for in-house lobbyists to achieve. Thanks to its process management competence, it is therefore also able, for instance, to give a CEO action recommendations.[28]

10.4.1.3.2 Highest standards of compliance

This independent, external intermediary is specialised in process management, and guarantees the very highest standards of compliance (legal compliance, financial compliance, data protection, ISO 9001). The intermediary lobbyist not only has to be independent and external, but must also meet the highest standards of compliance. This is what helps him to stand out from the competition. The professionalism of a lobbyist can generally be recognised by the codes of conduct to which he has subjected himself.

10.4.1.3.3 Industry competition exclusion clause

The intermediary should always work exclusively for just one company per industry. This principle ("only one interest") is fundamental to credibility vis-à-vis political decision-makers.

10.4.2 Process-oriented methodology of the intermediary (procedural organisation)

The specifically process-oriented methodology (approach) of the intermediary, which is necessary to be able to successfully manage the processes of lobbying under the framework conditions of the Treaty of Lisbon, will be described in the following.

10.4.2.1 Perspective change competence (PCC)

10.4.2.1.1 Onepager

A onepager is an informal communication tool in which information and arguments concerning an issue, for example an association's or a company's concerns, are summarised "on a blank sheet of paper". This has nothing to do with avoiding the public or with secrecy, but is instead intended solely to facilitate use in the continued communication process from the perspective of the decision-maker to whom the onepager is addressed (e.g. the rapporteur). He can submit it to his own dialogue partners for discussion, without disclosing the source of the text at the same time, which may be strategically unfavourable (see Section 6.4.2.1.7). As a rule, executive and legislative level decision-makers have a tight schedule, and have very little time to devote to the innumerable requests made on them. This is why the special procedural instrument – the onepager – has been developed.

---

28 Under time pressure and "directly", without having to keep to "diplomatic forms".

In order to bring a concern forwards quickly and effectively, whilst remaining efficient, it is set down on a single sheet of paper, on which all relevant information and the association's or company's significant lines of argument are summarised in a form appropriate to the addressee. During the further procedure, the onepager is co-ordinated several times between the client and the agency; finally – in various versions – it is adapted to the corresponding recipient and transferred to the previously identified decision-makers in the Commission and Parliament. Such a discussion paper must be formulated in a factual and balanced manner in terms of its structure and language, and must be written from the recipient's perspective ("endogenous approach"). The complexity of the arguments must be aimed at the addressee's understanding and prior knowledge as well as his time constraints.

The onepager additionally has a fixed structure and is subdivided into three parts:

1. *Background:* introductory, neutral description of the circumstances, which also particularly explains the procedural backgrounds in addition to the significant content-related aspects. In each case, the content is selected according to the procedural background.

2. *Problem:* a description of why the current situation or the planned, new regulation (legislative initiative, legislative amendment, etc.) leads (or would lead) to problems for the general public, of which the addressee is a part.

3. *Solution:* a short and succinct description of how the problem could be solved.

The task of this extraordinarily important procedural instrument not only involves its use to provide assistance in the creation of information transparency, on the basis of which further strategic decisions can be made, for those affected on the corporate and the political sides. From a commercial management perspective, the onepager also clearly establishes, at the very start of a project, whether or not successful lobbying is possible with a very high level of probability.

10.4.2.1.2 Perspective change from the individual interest (perspective of those affected) to a common interest

In the context of lobbying, the fundamental problem of communication between companies or associations, i.e. commerce, on one side and political decision-makers on the other side involves the fact that commerce, as the sender, and politicians (executive and legislative), as the recipients, communicate on entirely different levels. In particular, commerce tends to communicate its own individual interests to politicians in the form of demands; it has its sights set on its own economic advantages. However, it is significantly easier to assert one's own concerns if the interests of politicians or the general public are also taken into consideration, thereby preventing the accusation of mere self-interest from being levelled.

The discussion paper must be written from the perspective of the addressee, the point of view of the recipient; it must therefore take an endogenous approach.

This means that, whilst the economic objectives of the company or association are taken into consideration, the advantages of the communicated objective to politicians and also the general public have to be emphasised (perspective change). Decision theory, cultural, linguistic, interinstitutional, cross-member state and party political aspects, etc. are taken into consideration on an interdisciplinary basis in this procedure (onepager methodology).

Experience has shown that the desired perspective change is unsuccessful in approximately 5–15 % of cases (see Section 3.8.2), which *de facto* rules out successful lobbying. In such cases, the company is recommended not to take any action. Then, however, the advantage to the company is that it can select other action options at an early stage, and that the unnecessary implementation of resources is additionally avoided. If the perspective change is successful, however – which occurs in 85–95 % of all cases – process support competence is crucial to the achievement of the objective. The perspective change therefore simultaneously serves as a feasibility check to determine whether or not successful lobbying is possible with a very high level of probability.

10.4.2.2 Process support competence (PSuC)

Structural process support is the object of this entire book, and has been exhaustively dealt with in the individual chapters, particularly in practically understandable terms in the case studies in Chapter 9.

Where projects have successfully undergone a perspective change, their continued progress confirms the finding that the more complex a decision-making system is, the more important procedural know-how and long-term, structural process support (process support competence) become to the successful achievement of objectives in comparison with content-related arguments (content competence). The content-related aspect remains a necessary, but no longer a sufficient, condition for success.

Each day, employees and advisors throughout the EU have to structurally support all interfaces in the long term, so that the result of the onepager methodology can lead to the success of the specific lobbying project. Experience shows that major projects have usually failed as a result of minor aspects. Organisational mistakes or misunderstandings can no longer be afforded in a complex decision-making system. The continuous support of the company (process support competence) is an essential factor for success in this, since loyalties and coalitions, in particular, can change at any time during a decision-making procedure in a complex system – quite apart from the problem of practical mistakes. Constantly checking and coordinating all interfaces, and updating the onepager as required by the situation, are therefore critical.

Following the above described, far-reaching changes brought about by the Treaty of Lisbon, each issue or concern must be weighted and rethought according to the current situation, and must be adapted to the respective, prevailing power structure and the majority situations. Above all, procedural questions are raised: what is the opinion of the Council or the Parliament? Is the Commission willing to submit an initiative? The lobbying instruments also have to be weighted anew each time. The balance between content- and process-oriented instruments must be weighed up carefully. The level of complexity has to be checked for each individual case. The more complex the decision-making processes, the more important the extensive process competence becomes (and vice versa). Depending on this, the content – process weighting has to be decided on anew in each case ("dosing" between content and process competence).

10.5 Success formula for complexity management in successful lobbying

Prior to the Treaty of Lisbon, successful lobbying consisted primarily of content competence. Since the Treaty of Lisbon, at the latest, successful lobbying (SL) in the complex decision-making system of the EU results from the combination of the company's content competence and the neutral, objective intermediary's process structure competence. The sum of these two is raised to the power of perspective change competence (onepager methodology) and multiplied by process support competence. In this, the client's content competence (CC) and the intermediary's process structure competence (PStC) represent the structural instruments, whilst perspective change competence (PCC) and process support competence (PSuC) are the process instruments of successful lobbying. To express this differently: usually, the sum of the client's content competence and the intermediary's process structure competence will only lead to a successful lobbying result in the complex decision-making system of the EU if the onepager methodology and process support competence are also applied at the same time. As has already been mentioned at the beginning, the essential elements – i.e. the required competencies and instruments – of successful lobbying under the new framework conditions of the Treaty of Lisbon can be expressed using the following formula for visualisation purposes; this does not involve the mathematically correct representation of laws.

$$SL = (CC + PStC)^{(PCC * PSuC)}$$

Figure 10.3: Formula for success

10.6 Result and outlook

Content-related work is important. In the complex multi-level system of the EU, however, focussing solely on content-related work in lobbying can no longer lead to success. The decision-making processes have become too complex for this. Supporting the entire decision-making process is therefore becoming increasingly important. Added to this is the fact that, as shown in this book, decisions are usually not as predetermined as they may sometimes appear. Within complex political systems such as the EU, a profound and differentiated understanding of processes and their structural, sustainable support have now become elements that are central to the success of lobbying projects. In addition, concerns must always be translated into the other party's perspective, in order to formulate them such that a decision can be made (see Nassehi in Section 1.1). The complexity of a decision-making process is therefore significantly reduced. To express it differently, a professional lobbyist must constantly remain on the ball and know exactly what the procedures are. He must know where, when, by whom and at which point of a process he can become involved with a chance of success.[29]

The more complex the design of a system, the more extensively the successful communication of content is dependent on the conveyor's process competence. The importance of process competence in relation to content competence therefore grows in parallel with the complexity of a decision-making system.

From the point of view of classic, content-oriented lobbying (i.e. for corporate representative offices, associations, public affairs agencies and law firms), this is a sobering conclusion. The situation often proves difficult for many lobbyists, because the content-related positions developed with a great deal of effort and commitment are not taken into consideration by the decision-maker if they are introduced into the procedure by the wrong person, at the wrong time and in the wrong place. Professional process support necessitates the establishment and maintenance of a cross-institutional, cross-parliamentary group and cross-member state network. The enormous effort required for this exceeds even the capacities of major companies. This results in a growing need for professional process support, which has to be undertaken by an external service provider who structurally supports the processes. This party is outside of a company's hierarchy (and also that of politics), i.e. it is independent of internal systems of hierarchical structure or also accountability, and, as an intermediary, can make contact with both politicians and companies at all levels, something which would be impossible for in-house lobbyists to achieve.[30] The importance and necessity of an intermediary within mutual market relationships, and the requirement of an intermediary in lobbying, as derived from this, have already been analysed by Meyer and Me-

---

29 See Joos (2015).
30 Joos (2015).

indl in Section 1.3. Such an intermediary forms part of the new elites of a complex society; above all, these elites must possess perspective change competence now and in the future. This means that they must be able to mediate between various specialist and professionalisation areas, and to "translate" (see Nassehi in Section 8.1). The supporting pillars in this case are compliance and exclusivity ("only one interest"), in order to achieve acceptance by the company as well as the legislative and executive level in the long term.

In addition to content-related arguments, a structural process partner has also become a vital necessity in order to continue to be able to successfully support the lobbying undertaken by private companies, associations and organisations vis-à-vis the legislative and executive level within the EU and selected member states. Ultimately, each management team should check whether the existing structure of its lobbying is still sufficient, under the described framework condition changes, to enable it to completely fulfil its duties of care.[31] A company must constantly ensure that it enjoys functioning communication with its stakeholders (these also include politicians), in order to acquire and retain its "licence to operate" (see Meyer et al. in Section 1.2). The structural intermeshing of content-related and procedural competencies has now become a significant factor in the success of lobbying projects in the EU.

---

[31] In this case, a duty of care vis-à-vis the *primary stakeholders*: these have a contractual relationship with the company (e.g. investors, employees, suppliers, customers, etc.). The difference as opposed to *secondary stakeholders* is that there are no direct contractual relationships with the latter, but that they exert an influence on the well-being of the company (e.g. executive, legislature, associations, NGOs, media).

References and further reading

Abrams, F.W. (1951) "Management's Responsibilities in a Complex World", in: *Harvard Business Review* 29(3), 29–34

Abromeit, H. (1993) *Interessenvermittlung zwischen Konkurrenz und Konkordanz: Studienbuch zur Vergleichenden Lehre politischer Systeme*, Opladen

Ackoff, R.L. (1981) *Creating the corporate future. Plan or be planned for*, New York

Adamek, S. and K. Otto (2008) *Der gekaufte Staat. Wie Konzernvertreter in deutschen Ministerien sich ihre Gesetze selbst schreiben*, Opladen

Aguinis, H. and A. Glavas (2012) "What We Know and Don't Know About Corporate Social Responsibility a Review and Research Agenda", in: *Journal of Management* 38(4), pp. 932–968

Akerlof, G.A. (1970) "The Market for 'Lemons'. Quality Uncertainty and the Market Mechanism", in: *Quarterly Journal of Economics* 84(3), pp. 488–500

Albrecht, J. (2011) "Search Theory. The 2010 Nobel Memorial Prize in Economic Sciences", in: *Scandinavian Journal of Economics* 113/2, pp. 237–259

von Alemann, U. and F. Eckert (2006) "Lobbyismus als Schattenpolitik", in: *Aus Politik und Zeitgeschichte* 15/16/2006, pp. 3–10

von Alemann, U. and R.G. Heinze (1981) "Kooperativer Staat und Korporatismus. Dimensionen der Neo-Korporatismusdiskussion", in: *Neokorporatismus*, ed. von Alemann, Frankfurt/Main, pp. 43–61

Alemanno, A. and A. Meuwese (2013) "Impact Assessment of EU Non-Legislative Rulemaking. The Missing Link of 'New' Comitology", in: *ELJ* (19) 2013, pp. 76–92, http://ssrn.com/abstract=2178128 (last accessed on 28.5.2015)

Allen, F. and A.M. Santomero (1998) "The Theory of Financial Intermediation", in: *Journal of Banking & Finance* 21, pp. 1461–1485

Allison, G.T. (1971) *The Essence of Decision. Explaining the Cuban Missile Crisis*, Boston

ALTER-EU (2015) "Block the Revolving Door", http://alter-eu.org/block-the-revolving-door (last accessed on 29.7.2016)

Althaus, M. (2006) "Lobbying als Beruf. Karrierewege in der Interessenrepräsentation", in: *Die fünfte Gewalt. Lobbyismus in Deutschland*, ed. Thomas Leif/Rudolf Speth, Wiesbaden, pp. 317–332

Althaus, M. (2013) "Unternehmen und Grassroots-Lobbying", in: *Grassroots-Campaigning*, ed. Rudolf Speth, Wiesbaden, pp. 61–89

Althaus, M., Geffken, M. and S. Rawe (ed.) (2005) *Handlexikon Public Affairs*, Münster

Altmeyer, J. (2009) "Der Tag danach", in: *Politik und Kommunikation* v. 1.10.2009 (printed version 8/2009), http://www.politik-kommunikation.de/ressorts/artikel/der-tag-danach/seite/0/1 (last accessed on 29.7.2016)

Amann, M., S. Becker, F. Dohmen and G. Traufetter (2013) "Im War Room der Demokratie", in: *Der Spiegel* 49/2013

American Marketing Association (2013) "Marketing", https://www.ama.org/AboutAMA/Pages/Definition-of-Marketing.aspx (last accessed on 13.4.2015)

American University (2015) "European Public Affairs and Advocacy Institute", http://www.american.edu/spa/ccps/EPAAI.cfm (last accessed on 10.2.2015)

Anderson, E. and R.L. Oliver (1987) "Perspectives on Behavior-Based versus Outcome-Based Salesforce Control Systems", in: *Journal of Marketing* 51/4, pp. 76–88

Anderson, P. and E. Anderson (2002) "The New E-Commerce Intermediaries", in: *MIT Sloan Management Review* 43 (summer), pp. 53–62

Anger, H. (2009) "Was Wirtschaftsverbände für EU-Lobbying zahlen", in: *Handelsblatt Online* from 2.6.2009, http://www.handelsblatt.com/politik/deutschland/interessenvertretung-was-wirtschaftsverbaendefuer-eu-lobbying-zahlen/3189512.html (last accessed on 10.2.2015)

Arnold, L.M. (2008) "Die Entstehung der europäischen Dienstleistungsrichtlinie im Spannungsfeld der organisierten Interessen. Eine Fallstudie zum Einfluss von Gewerkschaften und Unternehmerverbänden im Europäischen Parlament", *Hertie School of Governance, Working Papers 36*

Atzeni, G. (2016) *Professionelles Erwartungsmanagement. Zur soziologischen Bedeutung des Arzt-Narrativs*, Baden-Baden

Auel, K. (2005) "Europäisierung nationaler Politik", in: *Theorien der europäischen Integration*, ed. H.J. Bieling and Lerch, Wiesbaden, pp. 293–318

Backhaus, K. and M. Voeth (20109) *Industriegütermarketing*, Munich

Badie, B., Berg-Schlosser, D. and L. Morlino (2011) *International Encyclopedia of Political Science*, 8 vols. Los Angeles

Baecker, D. (ed.) (2009) *Niklas Luhmann. Einführung in die Systemtheorie*, Heidelberg

Bailey, J. P and Y. Bakos (1997) "An Exploratory Study of the Emerging Role of Electronic Intermediaries", in: *International Journal of Electronic Commerce* 1/3, pp. 7–20

Baligh, H.H. and L. E Richartz (1964) "An Analysis of Vertical Market Structures", in: *Management Science* 10/4, pp. 667–689

Balmer, J.M. Tand E.R. Gray (2003) "Corporate brands. What are they? What of them?", in: *European Journal of Marketing* 37/(7/8), pp. 972–997

Bangemann, M. (1992) *Mut zum Dialog. Wege zu einer europäischen Industriepolitik*, Bonn

Barker, A. (2014) "Marathon talks seal EU bank union", in: *Financial Times* from 21.3.2014

Barnard, C. (1938) *The functions of the executive*, Cambridge

Barone, M., A. Miyazaki and K. Taylor (2000) "The Influence of Cause-related Marketing on Consumer Choice. Does one Good Turn Deserve Another?", in: *Journal of the Academy of Marketing Science* 28/2, pp. 248–262

Basu, A.K.R. Lal, V. Srinivasan and R. Staelin (1985) "Salesforce Compensation Plans. An Agency Theoretic Perspective", in: *Marketing Science* 4/4, pp. 267–291

Baumer, T. (2002) *Handbuch Interkulturelle Kompetenz*, Zürich

Bavarian Ministry of Economic Affairs, Infrastructure, Transport and Technology (2010) "Mittelstandsbericht 2010", http://www.mittelstand-in-bayern.de/fileadmin/user_upload/stmwivt/Publikationen/Mittelstandsbericht.pdf (last accessed on 10.2.2015)

Baye, M.R. and J. Morgan (2001) "Information Gatekeepers on the Internet and the Competitiveness of Homogeneous Product Markets", in: *American Economic Review* 91/3, pp. 454–474

BDA.Die Arbeitgeber (2015) "GFN Programm", http://www.arbeitgeber.de/www/arbeitgeber.nsf/id/KA_GFN_Programm (last accessed on 10.2.2015)

Bebnowski, D. (2013) "Der trügerische Glanz des Neuen. Formierte sich im Protest gegen 'Stuttgart 21' eine soziale Bewegung?", in: *Stuttgart 21. Ein Großprojekt zwischen Protest und Akzeptanz*, ed. F. Brettschneider/W.Schuster, Wiesbaden, pp. 127–148

Bender, G. and L. Reulecke (2003) *Handbuch des deutschen Lobbyisten. Wie modernes Politikmanagement funktioniert*, Frankfurt am Main

Benjamin, W. (1992) "The task of the translator", in: *Theories of Translation. An Anthology of Essays from Dryden to Derrida*, ed. R. Schulte and J. Biguenet, Chicago, pp. 71–82

Bennedsen, M. and S.E. Feldmann (2006) "Lobbying Bureaucrats", in: *Scandinavian Journal of Economics* 108.4, pp. 643–668

Bentele, G. and Brosius, H.B. and O. Jarren (ed.) (2013[2]) *Lexikon Kommunikations- und Medienwissenschaft*, Wiesbaden

Bergmann, J. (ed.) (2012[4]) *Handlexikon der Europäischen Union*, Baden-Baden

Berle, A.A. and G. Means (1932) *The Modern Corporation and Private Property*, New York

Bernauer, T., Jahn, D., Kuhn, P. and S. Walter (2013[2]) *Einführung in die Politikwissenschaft*, Baden-Baden

Bhargava, H.K. and V. Choudhary (2004) "Economics of an Information Intermediary with Aggregation Benefit", in: *Information Systems Research* 15/1, pp. 22–36

Bhattacharya, S. and A.V. Thakor (1993) "Contemporary Banking Theory", in: *Journal of Financial Intermediation* 3/1, pp. 2–50

Bianco, K. (2008) "The Subprime Lending Crisis: Causes and Effects of the Mortgage Meltdown", CCH Mortgage Compliance Guide and Bank Digest, http://business.cch.com/images/banner/subprime.pdf (last accessed on 27.1.2015)

Bieber, R., Epiney, A. and M. Haag (2009[8]) *Die Europäische Union. Europarecht und Politik*, Baden-Baden

Bieber, R., Epiney, A. and M. Haag (2013[10]) *Die Europäische Union. Europarecht und Politik*, Baden-Baden

Bieber, R., Epiney, A. and M. Haag (2015[11]) *Die Europäische Union. Europarecht und Politik*, Baden-Baden

Bieling, H. J. (2005) "Intergouvernmentalismus", in: *Theorien der europäischen Integration*, ed. Hans-Jürgen Bieling/Marika Lerch, Wiesbaden, pp. 91–116

Blau, P. M. (1964) "Justice in Social Exchange", in: *Sociological Inquiry* 34/2, pp. 193–206

Blom-Hansen, J. (2011) *The EU Comitology System in Theory and Practice. Keeping an Eye on the Commission?*, Houndsmills

Blum, S. and K. Schubert (2009) *Politikfeldanalyse*, Wiesbaden

Boatright, J. R. (2006) "What's Wrong – and What's Right – With Stakeholder Management", in: *Journal of Private Enterprise* 21/2, pp. 106–130

Bohnen, J. (2015) "Werdet politisch!", in: *Cicero – Magazin für politische Kultur*, 2/Feb.

Böhret, C., Jann, W. and E. Kronewett (1988) *Innenpolitik und Politische Theorie*, Opladen

Bollmann, R. (2015) "Merkels teure Freunde", in: *Frankfurter Allgemeine Sonntagszeitung* from 8.2.2015, p. 22

Bolten, J. (2012) *Interkulturelle Kompetenz*, Erfurt

Bomberg, E. and J. Peterson (1998) "European Union Decision Making. The Role of Sub-National Authorities", in: Political Studies 46.2, pp. 219–235

Bonse, E. (2009) "Neues Denken aus dem alten Europa", in: *Handelsblatt* from 27.7.2009

Bouwen, P. (2001) "Corporate Lobbying in the European Union. Towards a Theory of Access", *Working Paper SPS No. 2001/5*, European University Institute Badia Fiesolana, San Domenico (FI)

Bouwen, P. (2002) "Corporate Lobbying in the European Union. The Logic of Access", in: *Journal of European Public Policy* 9.2002, pp. 365–390

Braun, B. and C. Dietsche (2009) "Unternehmensnetzwerke und Stakeholderansprüche im Handel mit Entwicklungsländern", in: *Internationales Risikomanagement. Auslandserfolg in grenzüberschreitenden Netzwerken*, ed. Torsten M. Kühlmann/Hans-Dieter Haas, Munich, pp. 247–275

Braun, S., Blechschmidt, P., Brössler, D. and N. Fried (2010) "Merkel, die Getriebene", in: *Süddeutsche Zeitung* from 27.10.2010, http://www.sueddeutsche.de/politik/die-kanzlerin-inder-krise-merkel-die-getriebene-1.946810 (last accessed on 26.2.2015)

Braunberger, G. (2015) "Die Rückkehr des Risikos", in: *Frankfurter Allgemeine Zeitung* from 20.1.2015, p. 18

Brealey, R., Leland, H. E. and D. H. Pyle (1977) "Informational Asymmetries, Financial Structure and Financial Intermediation", in: *The Journal of Finance* 32/2, pp. 371–387

Brettschneider, F. (2011) "Kommunikation und Meinungsbildung bei Großprojekten", in: *Aus Politik und Zeitgeschichte* 44-45/ 2011, pp. 40–47

Brönstrup, C. (2014) "Firmen und Konzerne nehmen Lobbyarbeit selbst in die Hand", in: *Der Tagesspiegel* from 6.10.2014, http://www.tagesspiegel.de/themen/agenda/bdi-bleibt-aussen-vor-firmen-undkonzerne-nehmen-lobbyarbeit-selbst-in-diehand/10799810.html (last accessed on 16.2.2015)

Brückner, M. (2013) *Prozesse politischer Entscheidungsfindung im institutionellen Kontext der Europäischen Union. Eine Einzelfallstudie über den Gesetzgebungsprozess zur Etablierung des Europäischen Innovations- und Technologieinstituts (ETI)*, [Dissertation mach.] Düsseldorf, http://docserv.uni-duesseldorf.de/servlets/DerivateServlet/Derivate-27869/Dissertation_Br%C3%BCckner_2013.pdf (last accessed on 18.3.2015)

Brunel University London (2015) "Public Affairs and Lobbying MSC", http://www.brunel.ac.uk/courses/postgraduate/public-affairs-and-lobbying-msc (last accessed on 10.2.2015)

Brunn, G. (2002) *Die Europäische Einigung von 1945 bis heute*, Stuttgart

Brunn, G. (2009^3) *Die Europäische Einigung von 1945 bis heute*, Stuttgart

Brutta, M. and N. Verheyen (2002) "Akteure der Zivilgesellschaft. Individuelle Ressourcen, soziale Basis, Vergesellschaftung: Berlin, 18.-20. April 2002", in: *Historical Social Research/Historische Sozialforschung* 27.2/3 (100/101), pp. 294–299

Buholzer, R. (1998) *Legislatives Lobbying in der Europäischen Union. Ein Konzept für Interessengruppen*, Bern

Bullinger, H. J., Spath, D., Warnecke, H. J. and E. Westkämpfer (ed.) (2009^3) *Handbuch Unternehmensorganisation. Strategien, Planung, Umsetzung*, Wiesbaden

Bundesagentur für Arbeit (2015) "Politische/r Berater/in", http://berufenet.arbeitsagentur.de/berufe/resultList.do?resultListItemsValues=14963&duration=&suchweg=begriff&searchString=%27+Politischer+Berater*+%27&doNext=forward ToResultShort (last accessed on 11.2.2015)

Bundesamt für Sicherheit in der Informationstechnik (2005) "Gefährdungskatalog GO – Elementare Gefährdungen", https://www.bsi.bund.de/DE/Themen/ITGrundschutz/ITGrundschutzKataloge/Inhalt/_content/g/g05/g05077.html (last accessed on 16.2.2015)

Bundesgesundheitsministerium (2015) organisational chart, http://www.bmg.bund.de/fileadmin/dateien/Downloads/O/Organisationsplan/Organigramm_BMG_Stand_080115.pdf (last accessed on 26.1.2015).

Bundesministerium der Finanzen (2009) http://www.bundesfinanzministerium.de/nn_1308/DE/Wirtschaft__und__Verwaltung/Europa/Betrugsbekaempfung/14286.html (last accessed on 26.1.2015)

Bundesministerium der Finanzen (2014) "EZB übernimmt Bankenaufsicht im Euroraum", http://www.bundesfinanzministerium.de/Content/DE/Pressemitteilungen/Finanzpolitik/2014/11/2014-11-04-PM44-ezb-uebernimmt-bankenaufsicht.html (last accessed on 11.2.2015)

Bundesministerium der Finanzen (2014a) "Verbrauchsteuern", http://www.bundes finanzministerium.de/Web/DE/Themen/Zoll/Verbrauchsteuern/verbrauchsteuern.html (last accessed on 27.1.2014)

Bundesministerium der Finanzen (2015) organisational chart, http://www.bundes finanzministerium.de/Content/EN/Downloads/organigramm-german.pdf?__blob=publicationFile&v=8 (last accessed on 26.1.2015).

Bundesministerium für Justiz und Verbraucherschutz (2015) organisational chart, http://www.bmjv.de/SharedDocs/Downloads/DE/Organisationsplan/Organisationsplan_DE_20150108.pdf;jsessionid=36B2F54568F7273D1E056FC4567E1F5B.1_cid334?__blob=publication File (last accessed on 26.1.2015).

Bundesrat (2014) "Sanierung und Abwicklung von Banken", http://www.bundesrat.de/DE/plenum/plenum-kompakt/14/928/928-pk.html (last accessed on 9.2.2015)

Bundesverband der Deutschen Industrie BDI (2009) "Europäisches Parlament 2004–2009. Zusammensetzung, Ansprechpartner und Empfehlungen für Interessenvertreter", http://www.bdi.eu/download_content/Marketing/Broschuere_EU_Parlament_2009-2014.pdf (last accessed on 19.3.2015)

Bundesverband der Unternehmensberater BDU e.V.(2014) press release "Beraterhonorare steigen 2014 nur moderat", http://www.bdu.de/media/115115/beraterhonorare_2014.pdf (last accessed on 29.7.2016)

Bundeszentrale für politische Bildung (2010) "Nicht-Regierungsorganisationen (NGOs)", http://www.bpb.de/nachschlagen/zahlenundfakten/globalisierung/52808/ngos (last accessed on 14.3.2015)

Bundeszentrale für politische Bildung (2014) "Zivilgesellschaft in Europa", http://www.bpb.de/politik/wahlen/europa-wahl/71376/zivilgesellschaft-in-europa (last accessed on 30.4.2015)

Bündnis 90/Die Grünen (2013) "Einfach mal probieren", http://www.gruene.de/themen/moderne-gesellschaft/einfach-mal-probieren-gute-gruende-fuer-den-veggie-day.html (last accessed on 27.2.2015)

Burani, N. (2008) "Matching, search and intermediation with two-sided heterogeneity", in: *Review of Economic Design* 12/2, pp. 75–117

Burdett, K. and K.T. Judd (1983) "Equilibrium Price Dispersion", in: *Econometrica* 51/4, pp. 955–969

Burholt, C. and L. Reulecke (2007) "Public Affairs – Rechtsberatung zum frühestmöglichen Zeitpunkt", in: *Praxisbuch Politische Interessenvermittlung – Instrumente – Kampagnen – Lobbying*, ed. Jörg Rieksmeier, Wiesbaden, pp. 106–111

Burke, P. (2014) *Die Explosion des Wissens. Von der Encyclopédie bis Wikipedia*, Berlin

Burson Marsteller (2013) "A Guide to Effective Lobbying in Europe. The View of Policy-Makers"

Burt, R.S. (1992) *Structural Holes. The Social Structure of Competition*, Cambridge

Burt, R.S. (1997) "The Contingent Value of Social Capital", in: *Administrative Science Quarterly* 42/2, pp. 339–365

Butters, G.R. (1977) "Equilibrium distributions of sales and advertising prices", in: *The Review of Economic Studies* 44/3, pp. 465–491

von Byeme, K. (1996) *Theorie der Politik im 20. Jahrhundert. Von der Moderne zur Postmoderne*, Frankfurt/Main

Cáceres, J. and C. Gammelin (2014) "Juncker baut EU-Kommission grundlegend um" in: *Süddeutsche Zeitung* from 19.11.2014, http://www.sueddeutsche.de/politik/

designierterpraesident-juncker-baut-eu-kommission-grundlegend-um-1.2113489 (last accessed on 19.5.2015)

Callies, C. (2010) *Die neue Europäische Union nach dem Vertrag von Lissabon. Ein Überblick unter Berücksichtigung ihrer Implikationen für das deutsche Recht*, Tübingen

Calton, J. M. and N. B. Kurland (1996) "A theory of stakeholder enabling. Giving voice to an emerging postmodern praxis of organizational discourse", in: *Postmodern management and organization theory*, ed. D. Boje, R. P. Gephart Jr. and T. J. Thatchenkery, London/New Delhi, pp. 154–177

Campbell, D. T. (1961) "Conformity in Psychology's Theories of Acquired Behavioral Dispositions", in: *Conformity and deviation*, ed. I. A. Bergand B. M. Bass, New York, pp. 101–142

Campbell, T. S. and W. A. Kracaw (1980) "Information Production, Market Signalling, and the Theory of Financial Intermediation", in: *The Journal of Finance* 35/4, pp. 863–882

Carroll, A. B. (1979) "A three-dimensional conceptual model of corporate performance", in: *Academy of Management Review* 4/4, pp. 497–505

Centre for European Policy cep (2015) definition "Informeller Trilog", http://www.cep.eu/suche.html?id=16&L=0&q=informeller+trilog (last accessed on 27.1.2015)

Centre for European Policy cep (2015a) definition "Berichterstatter/Schattenberichterstatter", http://www.cep.eu/publikationen/eu-lexikon/eintrag.html?title=Schattenberichterstatter&sword_list[]=berichterstatter&no_cache=1 (last accessed on 27.1.2015)

Chahoud, A. (2010) "Wer? Der Public Affairs-Berater", in: *Karriereguide Public Affairs*, ed. F. Busch-Janser and M. Pötter, Berlin, pp. 19–22

Chamber of Commerce and Industry for Munich and Upper Bavaria (2012) "IHK-Mittelstandsreport Bayern 2012", http://www.muenchen.ihk.de/de/standortpolitik/Anhaenge/ihk-mittelstandsreportbayern-2012.pdf (last accessed on 20.11.2013)

Chan, Y. S. (1983) "On the Positive Role of Financial Intermediation in Allocation of Venture Capital in a Market with Imperfect Information", in: *The Journal of Finance* 38/5, pp. 1543–1568

Chartered Institute of Public Relations (2015) "Public Affairs Diploma", http://www.cipr.co.uk/courses/public-affairs-diploma (last accessed on 10.2.2015)

Chemmanur, T. J. and P. Fulghieri (1994) "Investment Bank Reputation, Information Production, and Financial Intermediation", in: *The Journal of Finance* 44/1, pp. 57–79

Chircu, A. M. and R. J. Kauffman (1999) "Strategies for Internet Middlemen in the Intermediation/Disintermediation/Reintermediation Cycle", in: *Electronic Markets* 9/1, pp. 109–117

Christ, H. (2013) interview "Zwischen den Welten", in: *Zeitschrift für Politikberatung*, 2/2013

Chun, R. and G. Davies (2006) "The influence of corporate character on customers and employees: exploring similarities and differences", in: *Journal of the Academy of Marketing Science* 34/2, pp. 138–146

Clark, C. (2012) *Sleepwalkers. How Europe went to War in 1914*, London

Clarkson, M. B. E. (1995) "A Stakeholder Framework for Analyzing and Evaluating Corporate Social Performance", in: *Academy of Management Review* 20/1, pp. 92–117

Classen, A. (2014) *Interessenvertretung in der Europäischen Union. Zur Rechtmäßigkeit politischer Einflussnahme*, Wiesbaden

Clemens, G., Reinfeld, A. and G. Wille (2008) *Geschichte der europäischen Union*, Paderborn

Coase, R. H. (1937) "The Nature of the Firm", in: *Economica* 4/16, pp. 386–405

Coen, D. (2007) "Empirical and theoretical studies in EU lobbying", in: *Journal of European Public Policy* 14.3, pp. 333–345

Coen, D. (2009) "Business Lobbying in the European Union", in: *Lobbying the European Union. Institutions, Actors, and Issues*, ed. D. Coen and J. Richardson, Oxford, pp. 145–168

Coen, D. and J. Richardson (2009) "Learning to Lobby the European Union. 20 Years of Change", in: *Lobbying the European Union. Institutions, Actors, and Issues*, ed. D. Coen and J. Richardson, Oxford, pp. 3–19

College of Europe (2015a) "Course Information", https://www.coleurope.eu/website/study/european-political-and-administrative-studies/academic-programme (last accessed on 10.2.2015)

College of Europe (2015b) "MA in European Political and Administrative Studies (MEPA)", https://www.coleurope.eu/website/study/ma-european-political-and-administrative-studies (last accessed on 10.2.2015)

Committee of the Regions (CoR) (2015) http://europa.eu/about-eu/institutions-bodies/cor/index_de.htm (last accessed on 2.2.2015)

copes (2014) fact sheet "Politische Entscheider beurteilen Reputation der Topmanager"

Corporate Europe Observatory, "Günther Verheugen", http://corporateeurope.org/revolvingdoorwatch/cases/g-nter-verheugen (last accessed on 10.2.2015)

Corporate Europe Observatory, "Revolving-DoorWatch", http://corporateeurope.org/revolvingdoorwatch (last accessed on 11.2.2015)

Cosimano, T.F. (1996) "Intermediation", in: Economica 63/249, pp. 131–143

Coudenhove-Kalergi, R. (1923) Pan-Europa, Vienna

Council of the European Energy Community (2015) "Regulation No. 31 (EEC) 11 (EAEC) laying down the Staff Regulations of Officials and the Conditions of Employment of Other Servants of the European Economic Community and the European Atomic Energy Community", http://eurlex.europa.eu/LexUriServ/LexUriServ.do?uri=CON-SLEG:1962R0031:20140101:EN:PDF (last accessed on 29.5.2015)

Council of the European Union (2009) Council Note from 14.12.2009 (17392/09) "Structure of the Official Journal – Adaptation following the entry into force of the Lisbon Treaty", http://register.consilium.europa.eu/doc/srv?l=EN&f=ST%2017392%202009%20INIT (last accessed on 3.5.2015)

Craig, P. (2011) "Delegated Acts, Implementing Acts and the New Comitology Regulation", in: European Law Review 36. pp. 671–687

Craig, P. (2011[2]) "Institutions, Power, and Institutional Balance", in: The Evolution of EU Law, ed. P. Craig and G. De Búrca, Oxford, pp. 41–84

Craig, P. (2014) "Comitology, Rulemaking and the Lisbon Settlement. Tensions and Strains", in: Oxford Legal Studies Research Paper No. 75/2014, http://papers.ssrn.com/sol3/papers.cfm?abstract_id=2512368## (last accessed on 28.5.2015)

Cronin, D. (2013) Corporate Europe. How Big Business Sets Policies on Food, Climate and War, London

Crouch, C. (2008) "Postdemokratie", in: Neue Gesellschaft Frankfurter Hefte 4/2008, pp. 4–7

CSU (2013) "Regierungsprogramm", http://www.csu.de/programm/csu_regierungsprogramm_2013-2018_der_bayernplan/# 14 (last accessed on 27.2.2015)

Culpan, R. and J. Trussel (2005) "Applying the agency and stakeholder theories to the Enron debacle. An ethical perspective", in: Business and Society Review 110/1, pp. 59–76

Cummins, J.D. and N.A. Doherty (2006) "The economics of insurance intermediaries", in: Journal of Risk and Insurance 73/3, pp. 359–396

Cyert, R.M. and J.G. March (1963) A behavioral theory of the firm, New Jersey

Daase, C. and C. Friesendorf (2010) Rethinking Security Governance, London

Dahrendorf, R. (1965) Gesellschaft und Demokratie in Deutschland, Munich

Daiber, B. (2012) "EU-Durchführungsrechtsetzung nach Inkrafttreten der neuen Komitologie-Verordnung", in: Europarecht EuR 2/2012, pp. 240–253

Danquart, P. (2011) "Joschka und Herr Fischer", ARD broadcast from 28.5.2013

Darby, M.R.and E. Karni (1973) "Free competition and the optimal amount of fraud", in: Journal of Law & Economics 16/1, pp. 67–88

Dawson, L.M. (1969) "The human concept. New philosophy for business. Marketing concept outmoded today", in: Business Horizons 12/6, pp. 29–38

Degenhart, C. (2009[25]) Staatsrecht I – Staatsorganisationsrecht, Heidelberg

Dehaes, D. and P.L. Gräf (2003) "Zweite Liga – Lobbying in der Hauptstadt, früher fest in der Hand der Wirtschaftsverbände, zerfasert", in: WirtschaftsWoche 31/2003, p. 26-27

Del Fabro, R. (2000) "Interkulturelle Kompetenz im Unternehmen. Die historische Dimension", in: Historical Social Research 25, 3/4, pp. 75–113

Deloitte & Touche GmbH Wirtschaftsprüfungsgesellschaft/LMU (2011) "Fit für morgen – Effiziente und flexible Unternehmenssteuerung: Studie zum AXIA-Award 2011 in Bayern", http://www2.deloitte.com/

content/dam/Deloitte/de/Documents/
Mittelstand/Axia-Award/axia-award-2011-
studie-bayern.pdf (last accessed on
29.7.2016)

Der Beobachter der Länder bei der Europäischen Union (2015)
http://www.laenderbeobachter.de (last accessed on 19.03.2015)

Derrida, J. and L. Venutti (2001) "What is a 'relevant' translation?", in: *Critical Inquiry* 27/2, pp. 174–200

Devuyst, Y. (2012) "The Constitutional and Lisbon Treaties", in: *The Oxford Handbook of the European Union*, ed. E. Jones, A. Menon and S. Weatherill, Oxford, pp. 163–178

Diamond, D.W. (1984) "Financial Intermediation and Delegated Monitoring", in: *Review of Economic Studies* 51/3, pp. 393–414

Diamond, P. (1987) "Consumer Differences and Prices in a Search Model", in: *The Quarterly Journal of Economics* 102/2, pp. 429–436

Diekmann, F. (2014) "Abspaltung von Kohle, Gas und Atom: Wie sich E.on neu erfindet", in: *Spiegel Online* from 1.12.2014, http://www.spiegel.de/wirtschaft/unternehmen/e-on-wie-sich-der-konzern-neu-erfindet-a-1005954.html (last accessed on 14.3.2015)

Dill, W.R. (1976) "Strategic management in a kibitzer's world", in: *From strategic planning to strategic management*, ed. I.H. Ansoff, R.P. Declerck and R.I. Hayes, Oxford, pp. 125–136

Diller, H., Haas, A. and B. Ivens (2005) *Verkauf und Kundenmanagement. Eine prozessorientierte Konzeption*, Stuttgart

Directorate General Health and Food Safety (SANTE) (2015) organisational chart, http://ec.europa.eu/dgs/health_consumer/chart.pdf (last accessed on 26.1.2015)

Donaldson, T. and L.E. Preston (1995) "The stakeholder theory of the corporation. Concepts, evidence, and implications", in: *Academy of Management Review* 20/1, pp. 65–91

Donnelly, J.H. (1976) "Marketing intermediaries in channels of distribution for services", in: *The Journal of Marketing* 40(1), pp. 55–57

Downs, A. (1968) *Ökonomische Theorie der Demokratie*, Tübingen

Draper, D.W. and J.W. Hoag (1978) "Financial Intermediation and the Theory of Agency",

in: *Journal of Financial and Quantitative Analysis* (13)4, pp. 595–611

Driessen, P.H., Kok, R.A. and B. Hillebrand (2013) "Mechanisms for stakeholder integration. Bringing virtual stakeholder dialogue into organizations", in: *Journal of Business Research* (66/9), pp. 1465–1472

Drucker, P.F. (1946) *Concept of the Corporation*, New York

Drucker, P.F. (1965) *The Future of Industrial Man*, New York

Ducourtieux, C. (2015) "Bruxelles, terre bénie des lobbies", in: *Le Monde* from 28.1.2015Dye, T. (1976) *Policy Analysis. What governments do, why they do it, and what difference it makes*, Tuscaloosa

Eberlein, B. and E. Grande (2014[3]) "Entscheidungsfindung und Konfliktlösung", in: *Lehrbuch der Politikfeldanalyse*, ed. Klaus Schubert/Nils Bandelow, Munich, pp. 151–177

Ebers, M. and W. Gotsch (2006) "Institutionenökonomische Theorien der Organisation", in: *Organisationstheorien*, ed. A. Kieser and M. Ebers, Stuttgart, pp. 247–306

Edenharter, A. (2011) "Die Komitologie nach dem Vertrag von Lissabon. Verschiebung der Einflussmöglichkeiten zugunsten der EU-Kommission?", in: *Die Öffentliche Verwaltung* (16), pp. 645–650

Eichner, V. and H. Voelzkow (1994) (ed.) *Europäische Integration und verbandliche Interessenvermittlung*, Marburg

Eisenhardt, K.M. (1989) "Agency Theory. An Assessment and Review", in: *Academy of Management Review* 14(1), pp. 57–74

Eising, R. (2012[2]) "Interessenvermittlung in der Europäischen Union", in: *Verbände und Interessengruppen in den Ländern der Europäischen Union*, ed. W. Reutter, Wiesbaden, pp. 837–860

Eising, R. and B. Kohler-Koch (1999) "Introduction. Network governance in the European", in: *The Transformation of Governance in the European Union*, ed. R. Eising and B. Kohler-Koch, London, pp. 3–13

Eising, R. and B. Kohler-Koch (2005) "Interessenpolitik im Europäischen Mehrebenensystem", in: *Interessenpolitik in Europa*, ed. R. Eising and B. Kohler-Koch, Baden-Baden, pp. 11–78

Emerson, R.M. (1954) "Deviation and Rejection. An Experimental Replication", in: *American Sociological Review* 19(6), pp. 688–693

Emerson, R.M. (1976) "Social Exchange Theory", in: *Annual Review of Sociology* (2), pp. 335–362

ENVI (2015) "Members of the Environment, Public Health and Food Safety Committee (ENVI) in the European Parliament", http://www.europarl.europa.eu/committees/en/envi/members.html (last accessed on 26.1.2015).

Erdmann, H. (1988) *Neopluralismus und institutionelle Gewaltenteilung*, Opladen

E.ON (ed.) (2014) press release from 30.11.2014, http://www.eon.com/content/eon-com/en/media/news/press-releases/2014/11/30/new-corporate-strategy-eon-to-focus-on-renewables-distribution-networks-and-customer-solutions-and-to-spin-off-the-majority-of-a-new-publicly-listed-company-specializing-in-power-generation-global-energy-trading-and-exploration-and-production.html/ (last accessed on 14.3.2015)

EPACA (2015) "Code of Conduct", http://www.epaca.org/code-of-conduct/text-of-code (last accessed on 29.5.2015)

Eschenburg, T. (1955) *Herrschaft der Verbände?*, Stuttgart

Europaregion Tirol-Südtirol-Trentino (2015) http://www.alpeuregio.org/index.php/de/ (last accessed on 20.5.2015)

European Commission (2001) "Consultations conducted for the preparation of the White Paper on Democratic European Governance", http://ec.europa.eu/governance/whats_new/consultation_report.pdf (last accessed on 29.5.2015)

European Commission (2006) Green Paper "European Transparency Initiative", COM (2006) 194 final, http://europa.eu/documents/comm/green_papers/pdf/com2006_194_en.pdf, (last accessed on 9.4.2015)

European Commission (2013) "Multiannual Financial Framework (2014–2020)", http://ec.europa.eu/budget/mff/index_en.cfm (last accessed on 27.4.2015)

European Commission (2014) White Paper "Towards more effective EU merger control", http://eur-lex.europa.eu/legal-content/EN/TXT/PDF/?uri=CELEX:52014DC0449

European Commission (2014a) "Report from the Commission on the working of committees during 2013 from 16.9.2014", COM (2014) 572 final, http://ec.europa.eu/transparency/regdoc/rep/1/2014/EN/1-2014-572-EN-F1-1.PDF (last accessed on 2.5.2015)

European Commission (2014b) "Transparency Register/Code of Conduct", http://ec.europa.eu/transparencyregister/public/staticPage/displayStatic-Page.do;TRPUBLICID=vGQnVm1YYJHVkJPpgsYGn8JCZQ4b6TG76Tg9GnD6jZlKvJXMpk41!1756804907?locale=en&reference=CODE_OF_CONDUCT (last accessed on 29.5.2015)

European Commission (2014c) "The revised Transparency Register, MEMO/14/302 from 15.4.2014", http://europa.eu/rapid/press-release_MEMO-14-302_en.htm (last accessed on 11.2.2015)

European Commission (2015a) "Billiger im Ausland telefonieren. Die EU will Roaming-Gebühren abschaffen", http://ec.europa.eu/deutschland/pdf/europawahl/faktencheck_-roaminggebuehren_und_billigeres_telefonieren.pdf (last accessed on 8.5.2015)

European Commission (2015b) "The European Commission's in-house translation service", http://ec.europa.eu/dgs/translation/whoweare/index_en.htm (last accessed on 12.2.2015)

European Commission (2015c) "European Transparency Register", http://ec.europa.eu/transparencyregister/public/homePage.do?redir=false&locale=en (last accessed on 29.5.2015)

European Commission (2015d) "European Citizens' Initiative – Official Register", http://ec.europa.eu/dgs/secretariat_general/followup_actions/citizens_initiative_en.htm (last accessed on 28.5.2015)

European Commission (2015e) "Report from the Commission to the European Parliament and the Council: Report on the application of Regulation (EU) No. 211/2011 on the citizens' initiative" from 31.3.2015, COM (2015) 145 final, http://ec.europa.eu/transparency/regdoc/rep/1/2015/EN/1-2015-145-EN-F1-1.PDF (last accessed on 28.5.2015)

European Commission (2015f) "The Commission's Structure", http://ec.europa.eu/about/structure/index_en.htm#td (last accessed on 19.5.2015)

European Commission (2015g) "Transparency Register. Transparency and the EU", http://ec.europa.eu/transparencyregister/public/staticPage/displayStaticPage.do?locale=en&reference=WHY_TRANSPARENCY_REGISTER (last accessed on 30.5.2015)

European Commission and European Parliament (2013): "Transparency Register. Annual Report 2013", http://ec.europa.eu/transparencyregister/public/staticPage/displayStaticPage.do?locale=en&reference=ANNUAL_REPORT (last accessed on 19.6.2015)

European Council (2006) "Presidency Conclusions", http://www.consilium.europa.eu/ueDocs/cms_Data/docs/pressData/en/ec/90111.pdf (last accessed on 27.1.2015)

European Council (2007) "Schlussfolgerungen des Vorsitzenden", http://www.consilium.europa.eu/uedocs/cms_data/docs/pressdata/de/ec/94935.pdf (last accessed on 27.1.2015)

European Council (2009) "Presidency Conclusions", http://www.consilium.europa.eu/uedocs/cms_data/docs/pressdata/en/ec/108622.pdf (last accessed on 27.1.2015)

European Council (2013) "Regulation (EU) No. 1024/2013 from 15.10.2013 conferring specific tasks on the European Central Bank concerning policies relating to the prudential supervision of credit institutions, http://eurlex.europa.eu/LexUriServ/LexUriServ.do?uri=OJ:L:2013:287:0063:0089:EN:PDF (last accessed on 11.2.2015)

European Court of Justice (2014) Judgement from 18th March 2014, Case C 427/12 Commission/Parliament and Council, http://curia.europa.eu/juris/document/document.jsf?text=&docid=149385&pageIndex=0&doclang=EN&mode=req&dir=&occ=first&part=1 (last accessed on 2.5.2015)

European Economic and Social Committee (ESC) (2015) http://europa.eu/about-eu/institutions-bodies/ecosoc/index_en.htm (last accessed on 2.2.2015).

European Parliament (2015) "Fraktionen", http://www.europarl.de/de/europa_und_sie/das_ep/glossar.html (last accessed on 18.3.2015)

European Parliament (2015a) "Directorate General for Internal Policies: Directorate for Citizens' Rights and Constitutional Affairs of the European Parliament (2015) European Citizens' Initiative – First lessons of implementation", http://www.europarl.europa.eu/RegData/etudes/STUD/2014/509982/IPOL_STU%282014%29509982_EN.pdf (last accessed on 28.5.2015)

European Parliament (2015b) "Rules of Procedure of the European Parliament, 8th Parliamentary Term", http://www.europarl.europa.eu/sides/getLastRules.do?language=EN&reference=TOC (last accessed on 30.5.2015)

European Parliament News (5.4.2015) "Sylvie Guillaume: 'There is a strong demand from citizens for an obligatory transparency register'", http://www.europarl.europa.eu/news/en/news-room/20150205STO19401/Guillaume-Strong-demand-from-citizens-for-an-obligatory-transparency-register (last accessed on 3.6.2015)

European Parliament/Council of the EU (2009) "Regulation (EC) No. 443/2009 of the European Parliament and of the Council of 23 April 2009 setting emission performance standards for new passenger cars as part of the Community's integrated approach to reduce CO2 emissions from light-duty vehicles", OJ EU, http://eur-lex.europa.eu/legal-content/EN/TXT/?uri=URISERV:mi0046 (last accessed on 2.2.2015)

European Parliament/Council of the EU (2011) "Regulation (EU) No 182/2011 of the European Parliament and of the Council of 16 February 2011 laying down the rules and general principles concerning mechanisms for control by Member States of the Commission's exercise of implementing powers", OJ 2011 No. L 55/ 13 ff., http://eur-lex.europa.eu/legal-content/EN/TXT/?uri=CELEX:32011R0182 (last accessed on 2.5.2015)

European Parliament/Council of the EU (2014) "Regulation (EU) No 422/2014 of the European Parliament and of the Council of 16 April 2014 adjusting with effect from 1 July 2011 the remuneration and pensions of officials and other servants of the European Union and the correction coefficients applied thereto", OJ EU L129/5, http://eur-lex.europa.eu/legal-content/EN/TXT/?uri=uriserv:OJ.L_.2014.129.01.0005.01.ENG&toc=OJ:L:2014:129:TOC (last accessed on 8.8.2015)

European Parliament/Council of the EU/Commission of European Communities (2007) "Declaration on the occasion of the 50th anniversary of the signature of the Treaties of Rome" (Berlin Declaration), http://europa.eu/50/docs/berlin_declaration_en.pdf (last accessed on 27.1.2015)

European Parliament/Council of the EU/European Commission (2007a) "Joint Declaration of the European Parliament, the Council and the Commission of 13 June 2007 on practical arrangements for the codecision procedure, also Annex XX of the Rules of Procedure of the European Parliament", OJ C145/5, http://www.europarl.europa.eu/sides/getDoc.do?pubRef=-//EP//TEXT+RULES-EP+20150909+ANN-20+DOC+XML+V0//EN&language=EN&navigationBar=YES (last accessed on 29.7.2016)

European Parliament/European Commission (2012) "Annual Report on the operations of the Transparency Register 2012, Presented by the Secretaries General of the European Parliament and the European Commission to European Parliament Vice President Rainer Wieland and European Commission Vice President Maros Šefčovič", http://www.europarl.europa.eu/atyourservice/en/20150201PVL00050/Ethics-and-transparency (last accessed on 29.7.2016)

European Patent Office (2013) "Unitary Patent", https://www.epo.org/law-practice/unitary/unitary-patent.html (last accessed on 27.4.2015)

European Commission (2000) "The Commission and Non-Governmental Organisations. Building a Stronger Partnership." Discussion Paper, http://aei.pitt.edu/6506/1/001499_1.PDF?origin=publication_detail (last accessed on 15.1.2015)

European Commission (2001) "European Governance – A White Paper. (COM(2001) 428 final)", http://eur-lex.europa.eu/legal-content/EN/TXT/PDF/?uri=CELEX:52001DC0428&rid=2 (last accessed on 15.1.2015)

European Commission (2005 – 2015) "Policy Evaluation", http://ec.europa.eu/trade/policy/policy-making/analysis/policy-evaluation/ (last accessed on 20.2.2015)

European Commission (2014a) COMMISSION DECISION of 25.11.2014 on the publication of information on meetings held between Members of the Commission and organizations or self-employed individuals, http://ec.europa.eu/news/2014/docs/c_2014_9051_en.pdf (last accessed on 29.5.2015)

European Commission (2014b) "Human Resources. Key Figures Card" http://ec.europa.eu/civil_service/docs/hr_key_figures_en.pdf (last accessed on 13.3.2015)

European Training Academy (2015) http://www.eu-academy.eu/ (last accessed on 10.2.2015)

EUROSTAT (2014) "Population on 1 January – Persons", http://ec.europa.eu/eurostat/tgm/table.do?tab=table&language=en&pcode=tps00001&tableSelection=1&footnotes=yes&labeling=labels&plugin=1 (last accessed on 13.6.2015).

Eurotopics (2008) "Medias: A need to catch up on Europe", http://archiv.eurotopics.net/en/home/presseschau/archiv/magazin/medien-verteilerseite-neu/europaeische-oeffentlichkeit/interview-herzog/ (last accessed on 5.5.2015)

EUTOP International GmbH (2015) "Governance/ISO 9001", http://www.eutop.com/de/governance-iso-9001/index.html (last accessed on 29.5.2015)

Faber, M., Manstetten, R. and T. Petersen (1996) "Homo politicus und homo oeconomicus. Die Grenzen der politischen Ökonomie im Hinblick auf die Umweltpolitik", *Department of Economics, Discussion Paper Series* 237, Heidelberg

Faber, M., Petersen, T. and J. Schiller (2002) "Homo oeconomicus and homo politicus in Ecological Economics", in: *Ecological Economics* (20), pp. 323 – 333

Fabricius, C. (2014) "Das Kontrollrecht von Rat und Parlament nach der Komitologie-Durchführungsverordnung", in: *Europäische Zeitschrift für Wirtschaftsrecht* (12), pp. 453 – 456

Fang, L. (2014) "Where Have All the Lobbyists Gone?", in: *The Nation* from 19.2.2014, http://www.thenation.com/article/178460/shadow-lobbying-complex (last accessed on 10.2.2015)

Ferguson, N. (2011) *Civilization. The West and the Rest*, London

Figge, F. and S. Schaltegger (2000) *Was ist 'Stakeholder Value'. Vom Schlagwort zur Messung*, Working Paper, Chair of Environmental Management, University of Lüneburg

de Figueiredo, J.M. (2004) "Timing, intensity, and composition of interest group lobbying. An analysis of structural policy windows in the states", Working Paper 10588, National Bureau of Economic Research, Cambridge (Massachusetts), http://web.mit.edu/jdefig/www/papers/state_lobby.pdf (last accessed on 18.3.2015)

Fischer, S. (2011) "Deutschlands Alleingang. Nach Fukushima. Ein europaweiter Atomausstieg bleibt eine politische Illusion", in: *Süddeutsche Zeitung* from 17.5.2011

Fleming, L. and D. M. Waguespack (2007) "Brokerage, Boundary Spanning, and Leadership in Open Innovation Communities", in: *Organization Science* (18)2, pp. 165–180

Foy, H., Bryant, C. and J. Fontanella-Khan (2014) "Carmakers lobby to delay EU efforts to upgrade emission testing", in: *Financial Times* from 21.4.2014, http://www.ft.com/cms/s/0/e05baf80-c57f-11e3-a7d4-00144feabdc0.html#axzz3Ru8fY9SY (last accessed on 16.2.2015)

Fraenkel, E. (1964) *Deutschland und die westlichen Demokratien*, Stuttgart

Freeman, R. E. (1984) *Strategic Management. A Stakeholder Approach*, Boston

Freeman, R. E. (2004) "The Stakeholder Approach Revisited", in: *Zeitschrift für Wirtschafts- und Unternehmensethik* 5(3), pp. 228–241

Freeman, R. E. (2010³) *Strategic Management. A Stakeholder Approach*, Cambridge

Freeman, R. E. and J. McVea (2001) "A Stakeholder Approach to Strategic Management", Working Paper No. 01–02, Darden Graduate School of Business Administration, University of Virginia

Freidson, E. (1975) *Dominanz der Experten. Zur sozialen Struktur medizinischer Versorgung*, Munich (Orig. 1970)

Frevel, B. (2004) *Demokratie*, Wiesbaden

Friedrich, C. J. (1964) "Nationaler und internationaler Föderalismus in Theorie und Praxis", in: *Politische Vierteljahresschrift* 5(2), pp. 154–187

Friedrich, C. J. (1968) *Trends of Federalism in Theory and Practice*, New York

Friends of Earth Europe (2010) http://www.foeeurope.org/corporates/pdf/Lobbying_in_Brussels_April2010.pdf (17.2.2015)

Gammelin, C. and G. Hamman (2005) *Die Strippenzieher. Manager, Minister, Medien –wie Deutschland regiert wird*, Berlin

Gammelin, C. and R. Löw (2014) *Europas Strippenzieher. Wer in Brüssel wirklich regiert*, Berlin

Gehring, H., Delinic, T. and M. Paul (2009) "Vaclav Klaus unterschreibt Lissabonner Vertrag", Konrad Adenauer Stiftung, http://www.kas.de/wf/doc/kas_17971-1522-1-30.pdf?091103171447 (last accessed on 27.1.2015)

Geiger, A. (2006) *EU lobbying handbook. A guide to modern participation in Brussels*, Berlin

Gellner, E. (1994) *Bedingungen der Freiheit. Die Zivilgesellschaft und ihre Rivalen*, Stuttgart

German Bundestag (2007) "Entwurf eines Gesetzes zum Vertrag von Lissabon" from 13.12.2007, publication of the Bundestag 16/8300

Geyskens, I. , Steenkamp, J. B. and N. Kumar (2006) "Make, Buy, or Ally. A Transaction Cost Theory Meta-Analysis", in: *Academy of Management Journal* 49(3), pp. 519–543

Giegerich, B. and W. Wallace (2010) "Foreign and Security Policy", in: *Policy-Making in the European Union*, ed. H. Wallace, M. A. Pollack and A. R. Young (2010⁶), Oxford, pp. 431–456

Gläser, M. (2010²) *Medienmanagement*, Munich

Göbel, H. (2008) "Im Bundestag schwindet die Wirtschaftskompetenz", in: *Frankfurter Allgemeine* from 18.8.2008, http://www.faz.net/s/Rub4D8A76D29ABA43699D9E59C0413A582C/Doc~E018AD61B444D43FB83F29FE719A477D8~ATpl~Ecommon~Scontent.html (last accessed on 29.6.2009)

Godwin, K. R., Ainsworth, S. and E. K. Godwin (2013) *Lobbying and policymaking. The public pursuit of private interests*, Los Angeles

Goffert, D. (2002) "Die Firmen brauchen Lobbying à la carte", in: *Handelsblatt* from 20.11.2002

Gopalan, R. , Nanda, V. and V. Yerramilli (2011) "Does Poor Performance Damage the Reputation of Financial Intermediaries? Evidence from the Loan Syndication Market", in: *The Journal of Finance* (66)6, pp. 2083–2120

von Graevenitz, G. (ed.) (1999) *Vierte Gewalt? Medien und Medienkontrolle*. UVKMedien, Constance

Granovetter, M. S. (1973) "The Strength of Weak Ties", in: *American Journal of Sociology* 78(6), pp. 1360–1380

Granovetter, M. S. (1983) "The Strength of Weak Ties. A Network Theory Revisited", in: *Sociological Theory* (1), pp. 201–233

Granovetter, M. S. (1985) "Economic Action and Social Structure. The Problem of Embeddedness", in: *Amercian Journal of Sociology* 91(3), pp. 481–520

Graw, A. (2008) "Die Raucher-Lobby führt Krieg gegen sich selbst" in: *Die Welt* from 6.5.2008, http://www.welt.de/politik/article1970681/Die-Raucher-Lobby-fuehrt-Krieggegen-sich-selbst.html (last accessed on 16.2.2015)

Greenpeace EU Unit (2015) http://www.greenpeace.org/eu-unit/en/ (last accessed on 30.4.2015)

Greenwood, J. (2002) *The Effectiveness of EU Business Associations*, Basingstoke

Greenwood, J. (2011[3]) *Interest Representation in the European Union*, Basingstoke

Griesser, P. (2014) "Lobbying im Mehrebenensystem der EU. Licht und Schatten", in: *Lobbying in der Europäischen Union. Zwischen Professionalisierung und Regulierung*, ed. D. Dialer/M. Richter, Wiesbaden, pp. 59–69

Grimmel, A. and C. Jakobeit (ed.) (2009) *Politische Theorien der Europäischen Integration. Ein Text- und Lehrbuch*, Wiesbaden

Große Hüttmann, M. and T. Fischer (2005) "Föderalismus", in: *Theorien der europäischen Integration*, ed. Hans-Jürgen Bieling/Marika Lerch, Wiesbaden, pp. 41–64

Gross-Halbuer, A., Neumann, P. and A. Niewsmann (2014) "Bahn frei?", in: *Focus* from 13.1.2014, p. 23

Gründinger, W. (2012) *Lobbyismus im Klimaschutz. Die nationale Ausgestaltung des europäischen Emissionshandelssystems*, Wiesbaden

Gupta, S. and H.W. Kim, (2007) "The Moderating Effect of Transaction Experience on the Decision Calculus in On-Line Repurchase", in: *International Journal of Electronic Commerce* 12(1), pp. 127–158

Gutschker, T. (2014) "Große Koalition in Straßburg" in: *Frankfurter Allgemeine* from 21.09.2014, http://www.faz.net/aktuell/politik/europaeische-union/eu-parlamentgrosse-koalition-in-strassburg-13164431.html (last accessed on 5.3.2015)

Gyrd-Jones, R.I.and N. Kornum (2013) "Managing the co-created brand. Value and cultural complementarity in online and offline multi-stakeholder ecosystems", in: *Journal of Business Research* 66(9), pp. 1484–1493

Haacke, E. (2006) "Wirtschaftsverbände als klassische Lobbyisten – auf neuen Pfaden", in: *Die fünfte Gewalt. Lobbyismus in Deutschland*, ed. T. Leif and R. Speth, Wiesbaden, pp. 164–187

Haas, E.B. (1958) *The Uniting of Europe. Political, Social and Economical Forces, 1950–1957*, London

Hagel III, J. and J.F. Rayport (1997) "The Coming Battle for Customer Information", in: *Harvard Business Review* 75(1), pp. 53–65

Hailey, A. (1975) *The Moneychangers*, New York

Hamilton, A., Madison, J., Jay, J. and B. Zehnpfennig (2007) *Die Federalist Papers*, Munich

Han, G. (2011) "Risky Business. The Effect of Structural Holes on Risk Taking", Paper presented at the American Sociological Association

Händler, E.W. (2012) "Das Wissen der Ökonomie. Theorie und Praxis, Formen und Grenzen", in: *Merkur* (66) pp. 89–101

Haratsch, A., Koenig, C. and M. Pechstein (2010[7]) *Europarecht*, Tübingen

Hardinghaus, B. (2007) "Im Lobbyland", in: *Der Spiegel*. 30/2006

Hartlapp, M., Metz, J. and C. Rauh (2014) *Which Policy for Europe? Power and Conflict inside the European Union*, Oxford

Hartmann, J., Meyer, B. and B. Oldopp (2002) *Geschichte der politischen Ideen*, Wiesbaden

Hauser, H. (2011) "European Union lobbying post Lisbon. An economic analysis", in: *Berkeley Journal of international law* 29(2), pp. 680–709

Hauswald, H. and A. Hack (2013) "Impact of Family Control/Influence on Stakeholders' Perceptions of Benevolence", in: *Family Business Review* 26(4), pp. 356–373

Heide, J. B and G. John (1988) "The Role of Dependence Balancing in Safeguarding Transaction-Specific Assets in Conventional Channels", in: *Journal of Marketing* 52(1), pp. 20–35

Heitz, H. (2011) *Lobbyismus in der EU aus der Praxis für die Theorie* (Dissertation University of Vienna), Vienna

Hennig-Thurau, T., Malthouse, E.C., Friege, C., Gensler, S. , Lobschat, L., Rangaswamy, A. and B. Skiera (2010) "The impact of new media on customer relationships", in: *Journal of Service Research* 13(3), pp. 311–330

Herbrand, F. (2002) *Fit für fremde Kulturen. Interkulturelles Training für Führungskräfte*, Bern

Héritier, A. (2001) "Differential Europe", in: *Differential Europe. The European Union Impact on National Policymaking*, ed. A. Héritier, D. Kerwer, C. Knill, D. Lehmkuhl, M. Teutsch and A.C. Douillet, Lanham, pp. 1–22

Herrnstein, R.J.and C. Murray (1994) *The Bell Curve. Intelligence and Class Structure in American Life*, New York

Hertie School of Governance (2015) "Executive Master of Public Administration (Executive MPA)", http://www.hertie-school.org/empm/ (last accessed on 10.2.2015)

Herz, D. and C. Jetzelsperger (2008[2]) *Die Europäische Union*, Munich

Hesketh, I. (2014) "History is past politics and politics is present history. Who said it?", in: *Notes and Queries* 61(1), pp. 105–108

Hess, T. and B. von Walter (2006) "Toward Content Intermediation. Shedding New Light on the Media Sector", in: *International Journal on Media Management* 8(1), pp. 2–8

Hillebrand, B., Driessen, P.H.and O. Koll (2015) "Stakeholder Marketing. Theoretical Foundations and Required Capabilities", in: *Journal of the Academy of Marketing Science* 43(4), pp. 411–428

Hitzler, R. (1994) "Wissen und Wesen des Experten. Ein Annäherungsversuch – zur Einleitung", in: *Expertenwissen. Die institutionalisierte Kompetenz zur Konstruktion von Wirklichkeit*, ed. R. Hitzler, A. Honer and C. Maeder, Opladen, pp. 13–31

Hofmann, T. and S. Frevel (2007) "Politisches Krisenmanagement aus Unternehmenssicht", in: *Praxisbuch Politische Interessenvermittlung – Instrumente – Kampagnen – Lobbying*, ed. J. Riesmeier, Wiesbaden, pp. 78–88

Hoffmann, S. (1966) "Obstinate or Obsolete? The fate of the nation-state and the case of western Europe", in: *Daedalus* 95(3), pp. 862–915

Holscher, C. (1977) *Sozio-Marketing. Grundprobleme und Lösungsansätze zum Marketing sozialer Organisationen*, Essen

Holtbrügge, D., Berg, N. and J.F. Puck (2007) "To Bribe or to Convince? Political Stakeholders and Political Activities in German Multinational Corporations", in: *International Business Review* (16)1, pp. 47–67

Holtbrügge, D. and J.F. Puck (2009) "Stakeholder-Netzwerke als Instrument des strategischen Risikomanagements. Das Beispiel ausländischer Unternehmungen in Russland", in: *Internationales Risikomanagement. Auslandserfolg in grenzüberschreitenden Netzwerken*, ed. T.M. Kühlman and H.D. Haas, Munich, pp. 213–246

Homans, G.C. (1958) "Social Behavior as Exchange", in: *American Journal of Sociology* 63(6), pp. 597–606

Homburg, C. and H. Krohmer (2009) *Grundlagen des Marketingmanagements. Einführung in Strategie, Instrumente, Umsetzung und Unternehmensführung*, Wiesbaden

Honsig-Erlenburg, M. (2014) "Wie viele Lobbyisten arbeiten in Brüssel?", in: *derStandard.at* from 14.2.2014, http://derstandard.at/1389859863728/Wie-viele-Lobbyisten-arbeiten-in-Bruessel (last accessed on 11.2.2015)

Hooghe, L. and G. Marks (2001) "Multi-Level Governance in the European Union", in: *Multi-Level Governance and European Integration*, ed. L. Hooghe and G.Marks, New York, pp. 1–32

Horster, D. (2005) *Sozialphilosophie*, Leipzig

House of Commons (1947) The Official Report (5th Series), 11 November 1947, Vol. 444, cc. 206–207

Ingenhoff, D. and U. Röttger (2008[2]) "Issue Management", in: *Unternehmenskommunikation. Kommunikationsmanagement aus Sicht der Unternehmensführung*, ed. M. Meckel and B.F. Schmid, Wiesbaden, pp. 325–354

Institute for Marketing at the LMU. Meyer, A. (2014) "Projektkurs. Marktanalyse für eine politische Interessenvertretung. Interne Abschlusspräsentation", Munich

Institut für Mittelstandsforschung (2015) "KMU-Definition des IfM Bonn", http://www.ifm-bonn.org/definitionen/mittelstandsdefinition-kmu-des-ifm-bonn/ (last accessed on 10.2.2015)

Ismayr, W. (ed.) (2004[2]) *Die politischen Systeme Osteuropas*, Opladen

Ismayr, W. (ed.) (2009[4]) *Die politischen Systeme Westeuropas*, Wiesbaden

Jachtenfuchs, M. (2003) "Regieren Jenseits der Staatlichkeit", in: *Die neuen Internationalen Beziehungen*, ed. G. Hellmann, K. Wolf and D. Zürn, Baden-Baden, pp. 495–517

Jachtenfuchs, M. and B. Kohler-Koch (2003[2]) "Regieren und Institutionenbildung", in: *Europäische Integration*, ed. M Jachtenfuchs and B. Kohler-Koch, Opladen, pp. 11–46

Jachtenfuchs, M. and B. Kohler-Koch (2004) "Governance and Institutional Development" in: *European Integration Theory*, ed. A. Wiener and T. Diez, Oxford, pp. 97–115

Jäckel, M. (2011[5]) *Medienwirkungen. Eine Studie zur Einführung*, Wiesbaden

Jann, W. and K. Wegrich (2014[3]) "Phasenmodelle und Politikprozesse: Der Policy Cycle", in: *Lehrbuch der Politikfeldanalyse*, ed. K. Schubert and N. Bandelow, Munich, pp. 97–131

Janning, F. (2009) "Gemeinwohlorientierung durch Neokorporatismus? Verbändeorganisation und Interessenvermittlung in der deutschen Verbraucherschutzpolitik", in: *Interessensvermittlung in Politikfeldern. Befunde der Policy- und Verbändeforschung*, ed. B. Rehder, T.von Winter and U. Willems, Wiesbaden, pp. 132–155

Jansen, D. (2003²) *Einführung in die Netzwerkanalyse. Grundlagen, Methoden, Forschungsbeispiele*, Wiesbaden

Jarren, O. and P. Donges (2011³) *Politische Kommunikation in der Mediengesellschaft. Eine Einführung*, Wiesbaden

Jensen, M.C. (2002) "Value Maximization, Stakeholder Theory, and the Corporate Objective Function", in: *Business Ethics quarterly* (12)2, pp. 235–256

Jensen, M.C. and W.H. Meckling (1976) "Theory of the firm. Managerial behavior, agency costs and ownership structure", in: *Journal of Financial Economics* 3(4), pp. 305–360

Jensen, M.C. and W.H. Meckling (2000) "Theory of the firm. Managerial behavior, agency costs, and ownership structure", in: *A Theory of the firm. Governance, Residual Claims, and Organizational Forms*, ed. M.C. Jensen, Cambridge, pp. 83–135

Jensen, M.D. and D.S. Martinsen (2014) "Out of time? National Parliaments and Early-Decision-Making in the European Union", in: *Government and Opposition*, 45(4), pp. 1–31

Jevons, W.S. (1871) *The theory of political economy*, London

Jones, T.M. (1995) "Instrumental Stakeholder Theory. A Synthesis of Ethics and Economics", in: *Academy of Management Review* 20(2), pp. 404–437

Jones, T.M. and W. Felps (2013) "Shareholder Wealth Maximization and Social Welfare", in: *Business Ethics quarterly* 23(2), pp. 207–238

Jones, T.M., Felps, W. and G.A. Bigley (2007) "Ethical theory and Stakeholderrelated Decisions. The Role of Stakeholder Culture", in: *Academy of Management Review* 32(1), pp. 137–155

Jones, T.M. and A. C Wicks (1999) "Convergent Stakeholder Theory", in: *Academy of Management Review* 24(2), pp. 206–221

Joos, K. (1998) *Interessenvertretung deutscher Unternehmen bei den Institutionen der Europäischen Union. Mit Beispielen aus der Versicherungs-, Energie- und Verkehrssicherheitsbranche*, Berlin

Joos, K. (2011) *Lobbying im neuen Europa. Erfolgreiche Interessenvertretung nach dem Vertrag von Lissabon*, Weinheim

Joos, K. (2014) "Erfolg durch Prozesskompetenz. Paradigmenwechsel in der Interessenvertretung nach dem Vertrag von Lissabon", in: *Lobbying in der Europäischen Union. Zwischen Professionalisierung und Regulierung*, ed. D. Dialer and M. Richter, Wiesbaden, pp. 29–45

Joos, K. (2015) "Entscheidungen ohne Entscheider? Prozesskompetenz ist der entscheidende Erfolgsfaktor für die Reduzierung von Komplexität in der Interessenvertretung bei den Institutionen der Europäischen Union", in: *Always Ahead im Marketing. Offensiv, digital, strategisch*, ed. S. Bartsch and C. Blümelhuber, Wiesbaden, pp. 405–416

Joos, K. and F. Waldenberger (2004) *Successful Lobbying in the New Europe*, Berlin

Jost, S. and F. Stocker (2015) "Draghis riskanter Psycho-Trick mit Euro Billionen", in: *Die Welt* from 26.1.2015, http://www.welt.de/finanzen/article136780324/Draghisriskanter-Psycho-Trick-mit-Euro-Billionen.html (last accessed on 9.2.2015)

Judt, T. (2006) *Geschichte Europas seit 1945*, Munich

Juncker, J.C. (2014) "A New Start for Europe. My Agenda for Jobs, Growth, Fairness and Democratic Change", https://ec.europa.eu/priorities/publications/president-junckers-political-guidelines_en (last accessed on 29.4.2015)

JUVE Verlag für juristische Information GmbH (2015), http://www.juve.de/rechtsmarkt/stundensaetze (last accessed on 10.2.2015)

Kahneman, D. and A. Tversky (1979) "Prospect Theory. An Analysis of Decision under Risk", in: *Econometrica* 47(2), pp. 263–292

Kaiser, R. (2010) "Zeitfenster in der europäischen Politik. Die Rolle der EU-Kommission als politischer Unternehmer", in: *Iablis. Jahrbuch für Europäische Prozesse*, http://www.iablis.de/iablis_t/2010/kaiser10.html (last accessed on 25.2.2015)

Karpen, U., Nünke, A. and N. Breutz (2008) *Gesetzescheck. Die Gesetzgebung der Großen Koalition in der ersten Hälfte der Legislatur-*

periode des 16. Deutschen Bundestages (2005-2007), Bielefeld

Karr, K. (2007) *Democracy and Lobbying in the European Union*, Fankfurt/Main

Kaunert, C. (2009) "Commentary Editorial. The Lisbon Treaty and the Constitutionalization of the EU", in: *Journal of Contemporary European Research* 5(3), pp. 465–471

Kempf, U. and H.G. Merz (ed.) (2008) *Kanzler und Minister 1998-2005. Biographisches Lexikon der deutschen Bundesregierungen*, Wiesbaden

Kennes, J. and A. Schiff (2008) "Quality infomediation in search markets", in: *International Journal of Industrial Organization* 26(5), pp. 1191–1202

Kerscher, K.J. (2013) *Homo Oeconomicus und Menschenbild. Form und Wesen einer betrachtenswerten Spannung*, Marburg

Kevenhörster, P. (2008³) *Politikwissenschaft. Band 1. Entscheidungen und Strukturen der Politik*, Wiesbaden

Keynes, J.M. (1920) *The Economic Consequences of the Peace*, New York

Kim, D.J., Ferrin, D.L. and H.R. Rao (2008) "A Trust-Based Consumer Decision-Making Model in Electronic Commerce. The Role of Trust, Perceived Risk, and Their Antecedents", in: *Decision Support Systems* 44(2), pp. 544–564

Kirchgässner, G. (2013⁴) *Homo Oeconomicus. Das ökonomische Modell individuel-len Verhaltens und seine Anwendung in den Wirtschafts- und Sozialwissenschaften*, TübingenKleinfeld, R. (2007) "Die historische Entwicklung der Interessenverbände in Deutschland", in: *Interessenverbände in Deutschland*, ed. T. von Winterand U. Willems, Wiesbaden, pp. 51–83

Kleinfeld, R., Willems, U. and A. Zimmer (2007) "Interessenvermittlung – zentrale Agenda der Politikwissenschaft", in: *Lobbying. Strukturen. Akteure. Strategien*, ed. R. Kleinfeld, U. Willems and A. Zimmer, Wiesbaden, pp. 7–35

Klink, D. (2008) "Der ehrbare Kaufmann – Das ursprüngliche Leitbild der Betriebswirtschaftslehre und individuelle Grundlage für die CSR-Forschung", in: *Zeitschrift für Betriebswirtschaft* 78(3), pp. 57–79

Knoepfel, P., Larrue, C., Varone, F. and S. Veit (2011) *Politikanalyse*, Opladen

Kohler-Koch, B., Conzelmann, T. and M. Knodt (2004) *Europäische Integration – Europäisches Regieren*, WiesbadenKohler-

Koch, B. and C. Quittkat (2011) *Die Entzauberung partizipativer Demokratie. Zur Rolle der Zivilgesellschaft bei der Demokratisierung von EU-Governance*, Frankfurt/Main

Kohler-Koch, B., and B. Rittberger (2009) "A Futile Quest for Coherence. The Many Frames of EU-Governance", in: *European Multi-Governance. Contrasting Images in National Research*, ed. B. Kohler-Koch and F. Larat, Cheltenham, pp. 3–18

König, J.G. (2007) *Die Lobbyisten. Wer regiert uns wirklich?*, Düsseldorf

Köppl, P. (2003) *Power Lobbying. Das Praxishandbuch der Public Affairs. Wie professionelles Lobbying die Unternehmenserfolge absichert und steigert*, Vienna

Köppl, P. (2008²) "Lobbying und Public Affairs. Beeinflussung und Mitgestaltung des gesellschaftspolitischen Unternehmensumfeldes", in: *Unternehmenskommunikation. Kommunikationsmanagement aus Sicht der Unternehmensführung*, ed. M. Meckel and B.F. Schmid, Wiesbaden, pp. 187–220

Köppl, S. (2006) "Verbände als Organisationen im Neokorporatismus", in: *Klassiker der Verbändeforschung*, ed. M. Sebaldt and A. Straßner, Wiesbaden, pp. 275–288

Köppl, S. (2008) "Von der Verfassungskrise zum Vertrag von Lissabon – die EU auf dem Weg zu mehr Effizienz und Demokratie?", in: *Gesellschaft – Wirtschaft – Politik (GWP)*, (2), pp. 227–238.

Köppl, S. and T. Nerb (2006) "Verbände als Dialogpartner im kooperativen Staat", in: *Klassiker der Verbändeforschung*, ed. M. Sebaldt and A. Straßner, Wiesbaden, pp. 289-304

Kornum, N. and H. Mühlbacher (2013) "Multi-stakeholder Virtual Dialogue. Introduction to the Special Issue", in: *Journal of Business Research* 66(9), pp. 1460–1464

Korschun, D. and S. Du (2013) "How Virtual Corporate Social Responsibility Dialogs Generate Value. A Framework and Propositions", in: *Journal of Business Research* 66(9), pp. 1494–1504

Kosiol, E. (1962) *Organisation der Unternehmung*, Wiesbaden

Kotler, P. and G. Armstrong (1994⁶) *Principles of Marketing*, London

Krahmann, E. (2003) "Conceptualizing Security Governance" in: *Cooperation and Conflict* 38(1), pp. 5–26

Krahmann, E. (2010) "Security Governance and Networks. New Theoretical Perspectives on Transatlantic Security", in: *Cambridge Review of International Affairs* 18(1), pp. 19–34

Krajewski, M. (2014) "Rechtsfragen der Regulierung von Lobbying gegenüber EU-Institutionen", in: *Lobbying in der Europäischen Union. Zwischen Professionalisierung und Regulierung*, ed. D. Dialer and M.Richter, Wiesbaden, pp. 269–282

Kreimeier, N. (2009) "Beamte klagen über Lobbyismus", in: *Financial Times Deutschland* from 12.10.2009

Kretschmer, H. and W. Elbe (2007) "Issues Management", in: *Praxisbuch Politische Interessenvermittlung – Instrumente – Kampagnen – Lobbying*, ed. J. Rieksmeier, Wiesbaden, pp. 89–94

Kriele, M. (2003) *Einführung in die Staatslehre. Die geschichtlichen Legitimitätsgrundlagen des demokratischen Verfassungsstaates*, Stuttgart

Kuhn, N. (2007) "Mit Blick auf den Reichstag", in: *Der Tagesspiegel* from 11.11.2007, http://www.tagesspiegel.de/magazin/ karriere/art292,2417282 (last accessed on 16.3.2015)

Kuhn, T. S. (2012[4]) *The Structure of Scientific Revolutions*, Chicago

Külahci, E. (ed.) (2012) *Europeanisation and Party Politics. How the EU Affects Domestic Actors, Patterns and Systems*, Colchester

Küpper, H. U. (2011) *Unternehmensethik. Hintergründe, Konzepte, Anwendungsbereiche*, Stuttgart

Lachmann, G. (2014) "Jugendliche wollen das Komasaufen nicht lassen", *Die Welt* from 7.4.2014, http://www.welt.de/politik/ deutschland/article126660275/Jugendliche-wollen-das-Komasaufen-nicht-lassen.html (last accessed on 27.1.2015)

Lahusen, C. (2004) "Institutionalisierung und Professionalisierung des europäischen Lobbyismus", in: *Zeitschrift für Parlamentsfragen* (4), pp. 777–794

Lahusen, C. (2005) *Kommerzielle Beratungsfirmen in der Europäischen Union*, in: *Interessenpolitik in Europa*, ed. R. Eising and B. Kohler-Koch, Baden-Baden, pp. 251–280

Lahusen, C. (2007) "Institutionalisierung und Professionalisierung des europäischen Lobbyismus", in: *Zeitschrift für Parlamentsfragen* 35(4), pp. 777–794

Lahusen, C. and C. Jauß (2001) *Lobbying als Beruf. Interessengruppen in der Europäischen Union*, Baden-Baden

Landeszentrale für politische Bildung Baden-Württemberg, "Die Energiewende 2011", http://www.lpb-bw.de/energiewende.html (last accessed on 25.1.2015)

Lang, A. and P. Leifeld (2008) "Die Netzwerkanalyse in der Policy-Forschung. Eine theoretische und methodische Bestandsaufnahme", in: *Die Zukunft der Policy-Forschung. Theorien, Methoden, Anwendungen*, ed. F. Janning and K. Toens, Wiesbaden, pp. 223–241

Langguth, G. (2007) "Lobbyismus und Politikberatung in der EU", in: *Politikberatung und Lobbying in Brüssel*, ed. S. Dagger and M. Kambeck, Wiesbaden, pp. 183–264

Langguth, G. (2009) "Triumph des Pragmatismus", in: *Spiegel Online* from 15.11.2009, http://www.spiegel.de/politik/ deutschland/triumph-des-pragmatismus-wie-merkelihre-macht-absichert-a-661175.html (last accessed on 26.2.2015)

Langhorst, A. K. and K. Ullrich (2008) "Der Ratifikationsprozess des Vertrags von Lissabon", Konrad Adenauer Stiftung from 21.5.2008, http://www.kas.de/wf/doc/ kas_13784-544-1-30.pdf (last accessed on 27.1.2015)

Laplume, A. O., Sonpar, K. and R. A. Litz (2008) "Stakeholder Theory. Reviewing a Theory that Moves Us", in: *Journal of Management* 34(6), pp. 1152–1189

La Porte, T. R. (1975) "Organized Social Complexity. Explication of a Concept", in: *Organized Social Complexity. Challenge to Politics and Policy*, ed. T. R. La Porte, Princeton, pp. 3–39

Laswell, H. (1956) *The Decision Process. Seven Categories of Functional Analysis*, Maryland

Laumen, A. and A. Maurer (2006) "Jenseits des 'Permissive Consensus'", Stiftung Wissenschaft und Politik, http://www.swp-berlin. org/fileadmin/contents/products/ arbeitspapiere/korrKS_EU_Oeffentl_Meinung.pdf (last accessed on 27.1.2015)

Lee, J., Son, J. Y. and K. S. Suh (2010) "Can Market Knowledge from Intermediaries Increase Sellers' Performance in On-Line Marketplaces?", in: *International Journal of Electronic Commerce* 14(4), pp. 69–102

Leif, T. (2010) "Von der Symbiose zur Systemkrise", in: *Aus Politik und Zeitgeschichte* (19), pp. 3–9

Leif, T. and R. Speth (2006) "Zehn zusammenfassende Thesen zur Anatomie des Lobbyismus in Deutschland und sechs praktische

Lösungsvorschläge zu seiner Demokratisierung", in: *Die fünfte Gewalt. Lobbyismus in Deutschland*, ed. T. Leif and R. Speth, Wiesbaden, pp. 351–354

Leif, T. and R. Speth (2006a) "Die fünfte Gewalt", in: *Zeit Online* from 22.2.2006, http://www.zeit.de/online/2006/10/lobbyismus (last accessed on 10.2.2015)

Leland, H. E. and D. H. Pyle (1977) "Informational asymmetries, financial structure, and financial intermediation", in: *Journal of Finance* 32(2), pp. 371–387

Lieb, J. and A. Maurer (2009) Der Vertrag von Lissabon, Diskussionspapier der FG 1, 2009/09 und FG 2, 2009/04, April 2009, SWP Berlin

Lindberg, L. N. (1963) *The Political Dynamics of European Economic Integration*, Stanford

Linder, C. (2014) "Lobbyismus und Interessenvertretung auf europäischer Ebene. Zwischen Professionalisierung und Regulierung", in: *Lobbying in der Europäischen Union. Zwischen Professionalisierung und Regulierung*, ed. D. Dialer and M. Richter, Wiesbaden, pp. 47–58

Lindloff, K., Kundolf, S. and N. C. Bandelow (2014) "Europäisches Parlament und Interessenverbände als Akteure und Adressaten europäischer Verkehrspolitik. Eine interaktionsorientierte Betrachtung", in: *Interessengruppen und Parlamente*, ed. J. von Blumenthal and T. von Winter, Wiesbaden, pp. 211–232

Lindner, C. (2015) Interview: "Unsere Politik ist klar auf Inhalte orientiert", http://www.liberale.de/content/lindner-interview-unsere-politik-ist-klar-auf-inhalteorientiert (last accessed on 27.2.2015)

Lipgens, W. (1985) *Documents on the History of European Integration*, Vol. 1, Berlin

Lipgens, W. and W. Loth (1988) *Documents on the History of European Integration*, Vol. 3, Berlin

Lobby Control, "Lobbyismus in der EU", https://www.lobbycontrol.de/schwerpunkt/lobbyismus-in-der-eu/ (last accessed on 11.2.2015)

Lobby Control, "Nach Anhörung. Hill und Cañete als EU-Kommissare bleiben inakzeptabel!", https://www.lobbycontrol.de/2014/10/nach-anhoerung-hill-und-caneteals-eu-kommissare-bleiben-inakzeptabel/ (last accessed on 11.2.2015)

Lobbypedia, "Gerhard Schröder", https://lobbypedia.de/wiki/Gerhard_Schr%C3%B6der (last accessed on 10.2.2015)

Lösche, P. (2006) "Lobbyismus als spezifische Form der Politikberatung", in: *Handbuch Politikberatung*, ed. S. Falk, A. Römmele, D. Rehfeld and M. Thunert, Wiesbaden, pp. 334–342

Lösche, P. (2007) *Verbände und Lobbyismus in Deutschland*, Stuttgart

Loth, W. (2014) *Europas Einigung. Eine unvollendete Geschichte*, Frankfurt/Main

LSE (2015), "Institute of Public Affairs", http://www.lse.ac.uk/IPA/Home.aspx (last accessed on 10.2.2015)

Luhmann, N. (1984) *Soziale Systeme. Grundriss einer allgemeinen Theorie*, Frankfurt/Main

Luhmann, N. (1988) *Die Wirtschaft der Gesellschaft*, Frankfurt/Main

Luhmann, N. (1997) *Die Gesellschaft der Gesellschaft*, Frankfurt/Main

Luo, X. and N. Donthu (2007) "The role of cyber-intermediaries. A framework based on transaction cost analysis, agency, relationship marketing and social exchange theories", in: *Journal of Business & Industrial Marketing* 22(7), pp. 452–458

Lusch, R. F., Brown, S. W. and G. J. Brunswick (1992) "A generic framework for explaining internal vs. external exchange", in: *Journal of the Academy of Marketing Science* 20(2), pp. 119–134

Lusch, R. F. and S. L. Vargo (2006) "Service-dominant logic. Reactions, reflections and refinements", in: *Marketing theory* 6(3), pp. 281-288

Maastricht University (2015) "European Public Affairs", http://www.maastrichtuniversity.nl/web/Faculties/FASoS/Target-Groups/ProspectiveStudents/MastersProgrammes/EuropeanPublicAffairs.htm (last accessed on 10.2.2015)

Majone, G. (2006) "Agenda Setting", in: *The Oxford Handbook of Public Policy*, ed. M. Moran, M. Rein and R. Goodin, Oxford, pp. 228–250

Malthouse, E. C., Haenlein, M., Skiera, B., Wege, E. and M. Zhang (2013) "Managing customer relationships in the social media era. Introducing the social CRM house", in: *Journal of Interactive Marketing* 27(4), pp. 270–280

Mangiameli, S. (2012) "The institutional design of the European Union after Lisbon", in: *The European Union after Lisbon. Constitutional basis, economic order and external action*, ed. H.-J. Blanke and S. Mangiameli, Berlin, pp. 93–128

Manzeschke, A. (ed.) (2010) *Sei Ökonomisch! Prägende Menschenbilder zwischen Modellbildung und Wirkmächtigkeit*, Berlin

March, J.G. and H.A. Simon (1958) *Organizations*, New York

Marcoux, A.M. (2003) "A fiduciary argument against stakeholder theory", in: *Business Ethics Quarterly* 13(1), pp. 1–24

Margolis, J.D. and J.P Walsh (2003) "Misery loves companies: Rethinking social initiatives by business", in: *Administrative Science Quarterly* 48(2), pp. 268-305

Markovsky, B. (1993) "Profits of Omission", in: *Contemporary Sociology* 22(2), pp. 153–155

Marks, G. (1993) "Structural Policy and Multilevel Governance in the EC", in: *The State of the European Community. The Maastricht Debates and Beyond*, ed. A.Cafruny and G.G. Rosenthal, Boulder, pp. 391–410.

Marks, G., Hooghe, L. and K. Blank (1996) "European Integration from the 1980s. State-Centric v. Multi-level Governance", in: *Journal of Common Market Studies* 34(3), pp. 341–378

Mason, R. (2014) "Lord Hill, the former lobbyist pitching for the Tories in Europe", in: *The Guardian* from 15.7.2014, http://www.theguardian.com/politics/2014/jul/15/lord-hill-tories-europe-lobbyist-cameron (last accessed on 10.2.2015)

Mass, P. (2010) "How Insurance Brokers Create Value. A Functional Approach", in: *Risk Management and Insurance Review* 13(1), pp. 1–20

Mast, C. (2008^3) *Unternehmenskommunikation. Ein Leitfaden*, Stuttgart

Matyja, M. (2007) "Interessenverbände im Entscheidungsprozess der Europäischen Union", in: *Lobbying. Strukturen. Akteure. Strategien*, ed. R. Kleinfeld, U. Willems and A. Zimmer, Wiesbaden, pp. 148–167

Matzler, K., Pechlaner, H. and B. Renzl (2003) "Werte schaffen – Perspektiven einer stakeholderorientierten Unternehmensführung", in: *Werte schaffen – Perspektiven einer stakeholderorientierten Unternehmensführung*, ed. K. Matzler, H. Pechlaner and B. Renzl, Wiesbaden, pp. 3–20

Maurer, A. (2008) "Der Vertrag von Lissabon. Anreize für eine demokratischere und handlungsfähigere Europäische Union", Diskussionspapier der FG 1, 2008/08, April 2008, SWP Berlin

Maxwill, P. (2015) "Wahlwerbung in Hamburg", in: *Spiegel Online* from 12.2.2015 http://www.spiegel.de/politik/deutschland/hamburg-schraege-wahlplakate-von-cduspd-gruenen-linken-fdp-a-1016279.html (last accessed on 26.2.2015)

Mayberry, D. (2006) "Zeroing In: On Numbers and Notions in the News. 37,000? 39,402? 11,500?" in: *Washington Post* from 29.1.2006, http://www.washingtonpost.com/wp-dyn/content/article/2006/01/28/AR2006012800042.html (last accessed on 17.2.2015)

Mayer, M. (2012) *Die Europafunktion der nationalen Parlamente in der Europäischen Union*, Tübingen

Mayntz, R. and F.W. Scharpf (1995) "Der Ansatz des akteurzentrierten Institutionalismus", in: *Gesellschaftliche Selbstregulierung und politische Steuerung*, ed. R. Mayntz and F.W. Scharpf, Frankfurt/Main, pp. 39–72

Mazower, M. (2008) *Hitler's Empire. Nazi Rule in Occupied Europe*, London

McGrath, C. (2005) *Lobbying in Washington, London and Brussels. The Persuasive Communication of Political Issues*, Lexington/Mellen

McGrath, C., Moss, D. And P. Harris (2010) "The Evolving Discipline of Public Affairs", in: *Journal of Public Affairs* (10), pp. 335–352

Meadows, D.H., Meadows, D.L., Randers, J. and W.W. Behrens (1972) *The limits to growth*, Washington

Mecke, I., Piekenbrock, D. and D. Sauerland (2014) *Gabler Wirtschaftslexikon*, http://wirtschaftslexikon.gabler.de/Archiv/4487/markt-v12.html (last accessed on 21.4.2014)

Meeker, B.F. (1971) "Decisions and Exchange", in: *American Sociological Review* 36(3), pp. 485–495

Meffert, H. and M. Bruhn (2003^4) *Dienstleistungsmarketing. Grundlagen – Konzepte – Methoden*, Wiesbaden

Meffert, H. and M. Bruhn (2012^7) *Dienstleistungsmarketing. Grundlagen – Konzepte – Methoden*, Wiesbaden

Meffert, H., Burmann, C. and M. Kirchgeorg (2008) *Marketing*, Heidelberg

Meffert, H., Burmann, C. and M. Kirchgeorg (2012^{11}) *Grundlagen marktorientierter Unternehmensführung, Konzepte, Instrumente, Praxisbeispiele*, Wiesbaden

Melin, P. (2011) "Die Rolle der deutschen Bundesländer im Europäischen Rechtsetzungsverfahren nach Lissabon", in: *Europarecht EuR* 5(2011), pp. 655–682

Merkel, A. (2014) "Rede von Bundeskanzlerin Merkel zum 5. Treffen der Nobelpreisträger am 20.8.2014", http://www.bundes-regierung.de/Content/DE/Rede/2014/08/2014-08-20-lindau.html (last accessed on 10.3.2015)

Merz, M., He, Y. and S. Vargo (2009) "The evolving brand logic. A service-dominant logic perspective", in: *Journal of the Academy of Marketing Science* 37(3), pp. 328–344

Meyer, A. and J.H. Davidson (2001) *Offensives Marketing. Gewinnen mit POISE: Märkte gestalten – Potenziale nutzen*, Freiburg

Meyer, A. and C. Holscher (1993²) "Sozio-Marketing", in: *Marketing-Systeme – Grundlagen des institutionalen Marketing*, ed. P.W. Meyer and A. Meyer, Stuttgart, pp. 221–262

Meyer, A. and A. Niedermeier (2011) "Lebensqualität – ein neuer Leitwert für ein nachhaltiges Wirtschaften von Dienstleistungsunternehmen", in: *Beiträge zum Dienstleistungsmarketing – Forschung –Aktuelle Forschungsfragen und Forschungsergebnisse*, ed. Sabine Fließ, Wiesbaden, pp. 1–23

Meyer, P.W. (1973) *Die machbare Wirtschaft. Grundlagen des Marketing*, Essen

Meyer, P.W. (1996⁴) "Der integrative Marketingansatz und seine Konsequenzen für das Marketing", in: *Integrierte Marketingfunktionen*, ed. Paul Werner Meyer, Stuttgart, pp. 13–30

Meyer, T. (2003) *Was ist Politik?*, Opladen

Meyer, T. (2010³) *Was ist Politik?*, Wiesbaden

Michalowitz, I. (2007) *Lobbying in der EU*, Vienna

Michalowitz, I. (2007b) "Die Rationalität Europäischer Interessenvertretung. Prinzipale, Agenten und Tausch im maritimen Transport", in: *Lobbying. Strukturen. Akteure. Strategien*, ed. R. Kleinfeld, U. Willems and A. Zimmer, Wiesbaden, pp. 169–195

Michalowitz, I. (2014) "Warum die EU-Politik Lobbying braucht? Der Tauschansatz als implizites Forschungsparadigma" in: *Lobbying in der Europäischen Union. Zwischen Professionalisierung und Regulierung*, ed. D. Dialer and M. Richter, Wiesbaden, pp. 17–28

Miller, V. (2007) "EU Reform. A new Treaty or an Old Constitution", Research Paper 07/64, House of Commons Library, http://www.parliament.uk/business/publications/research/briefing-papers/RP07-64/eureform-a-new-treaty-or-an-old-constitution (last accessed on 27.1.2015)

Miller, V. (2009) "The Treaty of Lisbon. Government and Parliamentary views on a referendum", House of Commons Library, http://www.parliament.uk/business/publications/research/briefing-papers/SN05071/thetreaty-of-lisbon-government-and-parliamentary-views-on-a-referendum (last accessed on 28.1.2015).

Misik, R. and M. Reimon (2014) *Supermarkt Europa. Vom Ausverkauf unserer Demokratie*, Vienna

Mitchell, R.K., Agle, B.R. and D.J. Wood (1997) "Toward a Theory of Stakeholder Identification and Salience. Defining the Principle of Who and What Really Counts", in: *Academy of Management Review* 22(4), pp. 853–886

Mitrany, D. (1943) *A Working Peace System. An Argument for the Functional Development of International Organizations*, London

Mittag, J. (2008) *Kleine Geschichte der Europäischen Union. Von der Europaidee bis zur Gegenwart*, Münster

Mitterstieler, E., Offner, A. and W. Zechner (2011) "Warum die Unternehmen Lobbyisten brauchen", in: *Wirtschafts Blatt* from 23.3.2011, http://wirtschaftsblatt.at/home/nachrichten/oesterreich/1182085/index?from=suche.intern.portal (last accessed on 9.1.2015)

Mix, D.E. (2013) *The European Union. Foreign and security policy*, CRS Report for Congress 7-5700

Monnet, J. (1962) "A ferment of Change", in: *Journal of Common Market Studies* 1(3), pp. 203–211

Moosmüller, A. (2009) "Kulturelle Risiken in der internationalen Unternehmenstätigkeit", in: *Internationales Risikomanagement. Auslandserfolg in grenzüberschreitenden Netzwerken*, ed. T.M. Kühlmann and H.-D. Haas, Munich, pp. 61–82Moravscik, A. (1993) "Preferences and Power in the European Community. A Liberal Intergovernmentalist Approach to the EC", in: *Journal of Common Market Studies* 31(4), pp. 473–524

Moravscik, A. (2002) "Reassessing Legitimacy in the European Union", in: *Journal of Common Market Studies* 40(4), pp. 603–624

Morgan, R.M. and S.D. Hunt (1994) "The commitment-trust theory of relationship marketing", in: *The Journal of Marketing* 58(3), pp. 20–38

Mouffe, C. (2007) *Über das Politische. Wider die kosmopolitische Illusion*, Frankfurt/Main

Müller-Armack, A. (1956) "Soziale Marktwirtschaft", in: *A. Müller-Armack. Ausgewählte Werke – Wirtschaftsordnung und Wirtschaftspolitik*, ed. E.Dürr, H.Hoffmann, E. Tuchtfeld and C. Watrin (1976²), Freiburg im Breisgau, pp. 243–249

Münkler, H. (2000) "Werte, Status, Leistung. Über die Probleme der Sozialwissenschaften mit der Definition von Eliten", in: *Kursbuch* 139, pp. 76–88

Münkler, H. (2013) "Politische Ideengeschichte und moderne politische Theorie. Ein einführender Überblick, in: *Studienbuch Politikwissenschaft*, ed. M.G. Schmidt, F. Wolf and S. Wurster, Wiesbaden, pp. 21–50Munzel, A. and C. Ullmer (2009) *Übersicht Stakeholder-Entwicklung*, unpublished Working Paper, Institute for Marketing, Munich

Murswiek, D. (2008) *Der Vertrag von Lissabon und das Grundgesetz (Rechtsgutachten)*, Freiburg

Nass, M. (2013) "Türöffner und Welterklärer", in: *Zeit Online* from 2303.2013, http://www.zeit.de/2013/12/Lobbyismus-Spitzenbeamte-Konzerne (last accessed on 9.1.2015)

Nassehi, A. (2004) "Eliten als Differenzierungsparasiten. Skizze eines Forschungsprogramms", in: *Elitenmacht*, ed. Ronald Hitzler, Wiesbaden, pp. 25–42

Nassehi, A. (2006) "Differenzierungseliten in einer 'Gesellschaft der Gegenwarten'", in: *Deutschlands Eliten im Wandel*, ed. H. Münkler, G. Straßenberger and M. Bohlender, Frankfurt/Main, pp. 255–274

Nassehi, A. (2007) "Organisation, Macht, Medizin. Diskontinuitäten in einer Gesellschaft der Gegenwarten", in: *Moderne Mythen der Medizin. Studien zur organisierten Krankenbehandlung*, ed. I. Saake and W. Vogd, Wiesbaden, pp. 379–398

Nassehi, A. (2010) "Asymmetrie als Problem und als Lösung", in: *Grenzen des Paternalismus*, ed. B. Fateh-Moghadam, S.Sellmaier and W.Vossenkuhl, Stuttgart, pp. 341–345

Nassehi, A. (2011) *Gesellschaft der Gegenwarten. Studien zur Theorie der modernen Gesellschaft II*, Berlin

Nassehi, A. (2012) "Ökonomisierung als Optionssteigerung. Eine differenzierungstheore-

tische Perspektive", in: *Soziale Welt* 63, pp. 403–420

Nassehi, A. (2014) "War die Zukunft früher besser? Gesellschaftliche Trends über eine Gesellschaft, deren Zukunft nie beginnen kann", presentation in Munich from 11.7.2014

Nassehi, A. (2015) *Die letzte Stunde der Wahrheit. Warum rechts und links keine Alternativen mehr sind und Gesellschaft ganz anders beschrieben werden muss*, Hamburg

Nelson, P. (1974) "Advertising as Information", in: *Journal of Political Economy* 82(4), pp. 729–754

Neukirch, R. (2009) "Ich, Merkel", in: *Der Spiegel* 26/2009

Neville, B. and B. Menguc (2006) "Stakeholder multiplicity. Toward an understanding of the interactions between stakeholders", in: *Journal of Business Ethics* 66(4), pp. 377–391

Neyer, J. and A. Wiener (2011) "Introduction. The State of the Art of a Non-State-Oriented Political Theory", in: *Political Theory of the European Union*, ed. J. Neyer and A. Wiener, Oxford, pp. 1–2

Niemann, E. (2003) "Das Interessengeflecht des Agrobusiness", in: *Die Stille Macht. Lobbyismus in Deutschland*, ed. T. Leif and R. Speth, Wiesbaden, pp. 186–221

Nohlen, D. (ed.) (1998) *Lexikon der Politik*, Vol. 7, Munich

Nohlen, D. and R.O. Schultze (ed.) (2010⁴) *Lexikon der Politikwissenschaft. Theorien, Methoden, Begriffe*, Munich

Nölke, A. (2005) "Supranationalismus", in: *Theorien der europäischen Integration*, ed. H.-J. Bieling and M. Lerch, Wiesbaden, pp. 145–169

Nord, W.R. (1969) "Social exchange theory. An integrative approach to social conformity", in: *Psychological Bulletin* 71(3), pp. 174–208

Nowag, J. (2012) "Changing the Competition Regime without altering the Treaty's chapter on competition?", in: *The Treaty of Lisbon and the Future of European Law and Policy*, ed. M. Trybus and L. Rubini, Cheltenham, pp. 398–413

N.U. (2003a) "Beratungsresistenz der Politiker steigt", in: *Frankfurter Allgemeine Zeitung* from 17.02.2003

N.U. (2003b) "Die Lobby-Republik", in: *Manager Magazin* from 1.8.2003, http://www.managermagazin.de/unternehmen/karriere/a-259242.html (last accessed on 15.5.2008)

N.U. (2005) "Die unsichtbare Gefahr", in: *Der Spiegel* 14/2005

N.U. (2007) "Jobverlust durch Klimaschutz?", in: *Zeit Online* from 28.1.2007, http://www.zeit.de/online/2007/05/klimaautos-glos (last accessed on 24.4.2015)

N.U. (2008) "Timeline Northern Rock bank crisis", in: *BBC News* from 5.8.2008, http://news.bbc.co.uk/2/hi/business/7007076.stm (last accessed on 27.1.2015)

N.U. (2009a) "Die Wahlprogramme der großen Parteien", in: *Hamburger Abendblatt* from 5.6.2009, http://www.abendblatt.de/politik/europawahl/article107518203/Die-Wahlprogramme-der-grossen-Parteien.html (last accessed on 26.2.2015)

N.U. (2009b) "Präsenz, Ehrlichkeit und Seriosität. Politikberater Klemens Joos über ein Geschäft das Fingerspitzengefühl erfordert", in: *Profil* 10/2009

N.U. (2009c) "Vor dem Spiel", in: *Wirtschafts-Woche* 40/2009

N.U. (2009d) "Wissen, wer wichtig wird", in: *Financial Times Deutschland* from 10.9.2009

N.U. (2010a) "Bulgarische Kandidatin Schelewa gibt auf" in: *Spiegel Online* from 19.1.2010, http://www.spiegel.de/politik/ausland/0,1518,672706,00.html (last accessed on 12.2.2015)

N.U. (2010b) "Lobbyismus ist eine latente Gefahr für den Rechtsstaat", in: *Börsenzeitung* from 2.3.2010

N.U. (2011a) "Atomkanzlerin erklärt ihren Ausstieg", in: *Süddeutsche Zeitung* from 9.6.2011, http://www.sueddeutsche.de/politik/regierungserklaerung-zur-energiewendemerkel-erklaert-den-atomausstieg-zur-herkulesaufgabe-1.1106773 9 (last accessed on 15.3.2015)

N.U. (2011b) "Two Euro MPs quit amid lobbying allegations", in: *BBC News* from 21.3.2011, http://www.bbc.com/news/world-europe-12806955 (last accessed on 29.4.2015)

N.U. (2011c) "Von der Leyen fordert 'Vereinigte Staaten von Europa'", in: *Die Welt* from 28.8.2011, http://www.welt.de/politik/article13570835/Von-der-Leyen-fordert-Vereinigte-Vereinigte-Staaten-von-Europa.html (last accessed on 12.5.2015)

N.U. (2013) "Union und SPD suchen im Koalitionspoker EU-Rückendeckung", in: *Reuters Deutschland* from 5.11.2013 http://de.reuters.com/article/topNews/idDEBEE9A404720131105 (last accessed on 19.5.2015)

N.U. (2014) "Designierter EU Kommissar muss nachsitzen", in: *Zeit Online* from 1.10.2014, http://www.zeit.de/politik/ausland/2014-10/eu-kommission-canete-navracsics (last accessed on 11.2.2015)

N.U. (2014a) "Kodex-Kommission geht ins Lobbygeschäft", in: *Handelsblatt* from 26.6.2014, p. 19

N.U. (2014b) "Schäuble – Parlament für Euro-Länder vorstellbar", in: *Reuters Deutschland* from 28.1.2014, http://de.reuters.com/article/domesticNews/idDEBEEA0R00O20140128 (last accessed on 12.5.2015)

N.U. (2014c) "Was die wichtigsten Parteien versprechen", in: *Tagesschau.de* from 5.5.2014, http://www.tagesschau.de/europawahl/parteien_und_programme/programmvergleichstart104.html (last accessed on 26.2.2015)

N.U. (2015) "Der Fluch der Komplexität", in: *Frankfurter Allgemeine Zeitung* from 21.1.2015, p. 21

N.U. (2015a) "EU-Kommission bremst ihre Beamten aus", in: *Frankfurter Allgemeine Zeitung* from 23.1.2015

N.U. (2015b) "EU Referendum in Großbritannien", in: *Spiegel Online* from 12.5.2015, http://www.spiegel.de/politik/ausland/davidcameron-will-eu-referendum-in-grossbritannien-vorziehen-a-1033315.html (last accessed on 15.5.2015)

N.U. (2015c) "Kritik vom Journalistenverband: 'Bild' soll Anti-Griechenland-Kampagne stoppen", in: *Spiegel Online* from 26.2.2015, http://www.spiegel.de/kultur/gesellschaft/bild-zeitung-kritik-von-djv-an-anti-griechenland-kampagne-a-1020718.html (last accessed on 11.4.2015)

N.U. (2015d) "Neue E.on-Gesellschaft heißt Uniper", in: *Spiegel Online* from 27.4.2015, http://www.spiegel.de/wirtschaft/unternehmen/e-on-neue-gesellschaft-heisst-uniperklaus-schaefer-vorstand-a-1030939.html (last accessed on 8.5.2015)

N.U. (2015e) "Nur London will den Vertrag ändern", in: *Frankfurter Allgemeine Sonntagszeitung* from 31.5.2015

N.U. (2015f) "Welt ohne Lenker", in: *Süddeutsche Zeitung* from 5.1.2015

Nye, M.J. (2003) "Introduction. The Modern Physical and Mathematical Sciences", in: *The Cambridge History of Science. Volume 5. The Modern Physical and Mathematical Sciences*, ed. M.J. Nye, Cambridge, pp. 1–17

Olényi, S. (2010) "Die Überzeugungstäter", in: *Spiegel Online* from 27.4.2010, http://www.spiegel.de/unispiegel/jobund beruf/0,1518,690457,00.html (last accessed on 8.8.2015)

Olson, M. (1985) *Aufstieg und Niedergang von Nationen*, Tübingen

Oltmanns, T. (2014) "Die Zukunft des Lobbyismus. Professionalisierung als Erfolgsfaktor", in: *Verbändereport* 6, pp. 18–23

Open Europe (2007) "A Guide to the Constitutional Treaty", http://www.mehr-demokratie.de/fileadmin/pdf/2007-09-openeurope-guide.pdf (last accessed on 27.1.2015)

Oppermann, T., Classen, C. D. and M. Nettesheim (2009[4]) *Europarecht. Ein Studienbuch*, Munich

Oppermann, T., Classen, C. D. and M. Nettesheim (2014[6]) *Europarecht. Ein Studienbuch*, MunichPalonen, K. (2003) "Four Times of Politics. Polity, Politicking, and Politicization", in: *Alternatives. Global. Local. Political* 28(2), pp. 171–186

Papier, H.-J. (2007) "Lobbyismus und parlamentarische Demokratie", http://www.frei heit.org/webcom/show_article.php/_c-85/_nr-1312/_p-1/i.html (last accessed on 27.5.2015)

Parasuraman, A., Zeithaml, V. A. and L. L. Berry (1985) "A Conceptual Model of Service Quality and its Implications for Future Research", in: *Journal of Marketing* 25(2), pp. 41–50

Parasuraman, A., Zeithaml, V. A. and L. L. Berry (1988) "SERVQUAL. A Multiple-Item Scale for Measuring Consumer Perceptions of Service Quality", in: *Journal of Retailing* 64(1), pp. 12–37

Parasuraman, A., Zeithaml, V. A. and L. L. Berry (1994) "Alternative Scales for Measuring Service Quality. A Comparative Assessment Based on Psychometric and Diagnostic Criteria", in: *Journal of Retailing* 70(3), pp. 201–230

Parker, R. and A. Alemanno (2014) "Towards Effective Regulatory Cooperation under TTIP. A Comparative Overview of the EU and US Legislative and Regulatory Systems", http://trade.ec.europa.eu/doclib/docs/2014/may/tradoc_152466.pdf (last accessed on 30.4.2015)

Parliament of the United Kingdom, "Whips", http://www.parliament.uk/about/mps-and-lords/principal/whips (last accessed on 17.3.2015)

Parsons, T. (1939) "The Professions and Social Structure", in: *Social Forces* 17(4), pp. 457–467

Pastowski, S. (2004) *Messung der Dienstleistungsqualität in komplexen Marktstrukturen. Perspektiven für ein Qualitätsmanagement von Hochschulen*, Wiesbaden

Payne, A., Ballantyne, D. and M. Christopher (2005) "A stakeholder approach to relationship marketing strategy: The development and use of the six markets model", in: *European Journal of Marketing* 39 (7/8), pp. 855–871

Peng, M. W.and A. S. York (2001) "Behind Intermediary Performance in Export Trade. Transactions, Agents, and Resources", in: *Journal of International Business Studies* 32(2), pp. 327–346

Permanent Representation of the Federal Republic of Germany to the European Union Brussels (2015) "Abstimmung mit den EU-Institutionen und ihren beratenden Organen", http://www.bruessel-eu.diplo.de/Vertretung/bruessel__eu/de/01-Rolle-St_C3_A4V/01-03-EU-Institutionen/03-EUInstitutionen.html (last accessed on 20.5.2015)

Permanent Representation of the Federal Republic of Germany to the European Union Brussels (2015a) "Ausschuss der Ständigen Vertreter (AStV) und die Ratsarbeitsgruppen (RAG)", http://www.bruessel-eu.diplo.de/Vertretung/bruessel__eu/de/01-Rolle- St_C3_A4V/01-01-AStV/AStV__RAG.html (last accessed on 20.05.2015)

Permanent Representation of the Federal Republic of Germany to the European Union Brussels (2015b) "Der Ständige Vertreter", http://www.bruessel-eu.diplo.de/Vertretung/bruessel__eu/de/02-St_C3_A4V/02-01-Botschafter__Stv/St_C3_A4ndigerVertreter.html (last accessed on 20.5.2015)

Permanent Representation of the Federal Republic of Germany to the European Union Brussels (2015c) "Der Ständige Vertreter, Stellvertreter und PSK-Botschafter", http://www.bruessel-eu.diplo.de/Vertretung/bruessel__eu/de/02-St_C3_A4V/02-01-Botschafter__Stv/01-Botschafter__Stv.html (last accessed on 20.5.2015)

Permanent Representation of the Federal Republic of Germany to the European Union Brussels (2015d) "Die Deutsche Botschaft in Brüssel", http://www.bruessel-eu.diplo.de/Vertretung/bruessel__eu/de/Deutsche-Botschaft.html, (last accessed on 11.8.2015)

Permanent Representation of the Federal Republic of Germany to the European Union Brussels (2015e) "Die einzelnen Abteilungen", http://www.bruessel-eu.diplo.de/Vertretung/bruessel__eu/de/02-St_C3_A4V/02-02-Abteilungen/02-Abteilungen.html (last accessed on 8.8.2015)

Permanent Representation of the Federal Republic of Germany to the European Union Brussels (2015f) "Die Rolle der Ständigen Vertretung", http://www.bruesseleu.diplo.de/Vertretung/bruessel__eu/de/01-Rolle-St_C3_A4V/0-rolle-st_C3_A4v.html (last accessed on 23.5.2015)

Peteraf, M. A. (1993) "The Cornerstones of Competitive Advantage. A Resource-Based View", in: *Strategic Management Journal* 14(3), pp. 179–191

Petersen, S. (2000) *Manager des Parlaments. Parlamentarische Geschäftsführer im Deutschen Bundestag – Status, Funktion, Arbeitsweise*, Opladen

Pfadenhauer, M. (2003) *Professionalität. Eine wissenssoziologische Rekonstruktion institutionalisierter Kompetenzdarstellungskompetenz*, Opladen

Pfeffer, J. and G. R. Salancik (1978) *The external control of organizations. A resource dependence perspective*, New York

Phillips, R. A. (1997) "Stakeholder Theory and a Principle of Fairness", in: *Business Ethics Quarterly* 7(1), pp. 51–66

Phillips, R. A. (2003) *Stakeholder theory and organizational ethics*, San Francisco

Phillips, R. A. (2011) *Stakeholder Theory, Impact and Prospects*, Cheltenham

Phillips, R. A. (2014) "Stakeholder, Ethik und Unternehmensleistung", in: *Delivering Tomorrow – Zuhören, gestalten, Wert schaffen. Erfolgsfaktor Stakeholdermanagement*, ed. Deutsche Post AG, Bonn, pp. 25–31

Phinnemore, D. (2013) *The Origins and Negotiation of the Lisbon Treaty*, London

Picot, A. (1991) "Ökonomische Theorien der Organisation. Ein Überblick über neuere Ansätze und deren betriebswirtschaftliches Anwendungspotential", in: *Betriebswirtschaftslehre und ökonomische Theorie,* ed. D. Ordelheide, B. Rudolph and E. Büsselmann, Stuttgart, pp. 143–170

Picot, A., Dietl, H. M. and E. P. Franck (2008[5]) *Organisation. Eine ökonomische Perspektive,* Stuttgart

Picot, A., Reichwald, R. and R. T. Wigand (2003[5]) *Die grenzenlose Unternehmung. Information, Organisation und Management,* Wiesbaden

Piekenbrock, D. and A. Hennig (2013[2]) *Einführung in die Volkswirtschaftslehre und Mikroökonomie,* Berlin

Pillkahn, U. (2012) *Innovationen zwischen Planung und Zufall. Bausteine einer Theorie der bewussten Irritation*, Norderstedt

Pollack, M. A. (2010[6]) "Theorizing EU Policy-Making", in: *Policy-Making in the European Union,* ed. H. Wallace, M. A. Pollack and A. R. Young (2010[6]), Oxford, pp. 15–44

Pollak, J. and P. Slominski (2012[2]) *Das politische System der EU*, Vienna

Pollert, A., Kirchner, B. and J. M. Polzin (2013) *Duden Wirtschaft von A-Z. Grundwissen für Schule und Studium, Beruf und Alltag,* Berlin

Porter, M. E. and M. R. Kramer (2006) "The link between competitive advantage and corporate social responsibility", in: *Harvard Business Review* 84(12), pp. 78–92

Posey, L. L. and S. Tennyson (1998) "The Coexistence of Distribution Systems under Price Search: Theory and some Evidence from Insurance", in: *Journal of Economic Behavior and Organization* 35(1), pp. 95–115

Posey, L. L. and A. Yavaş (1995) "A Search Model of Marketing Systems in Property-Liability Insurance", in: *Journal of Risk and Insurance* 62(4), pp. 666–689

Post, J. E., Preston, L. E.and S. Sachs (2002) *Redefining the corporation. Stakeholder Management and Organizational Wealth,* Stanford

PPE (2015), "Course Information", http://www.ppe.ox.ac.uk/index.php/course-information (last accessed on 10.2.2015)

Prahalad, C. K.and G. Hamel (1990) "The Core Competence of the Corporation", in: *Harvard Business Review* 68(3), pp. 79 ff.

Prahalad, C. K. and V. Ramaswamy (2004) "Co-creation experiences. The next practice in value creation", in: *Journal of Interactive Marketing* 18(3), pp. 5–14

Pratt, J. W., Wise, D. A. and R. Zeckhauser (1979) "Price Differences in Almost Competitive Markets", in: *The Quarterly Journal of Economics* 93(2), pp. 189–211

Pratt, J. W. and R. Zeckhauser (1985) "Principals and Agents. An Overview", in: *Principals and Agents. The Structure of Business,* ed. J. W. Pratt and R. Zeckhauser, Boston, pp. 1–35

PRCA (2014) "Introduction to Public Affairs", http://www.prca.org.uk/pr-training-introduction-to-public-affairs-14-may-2014 (last accessed on 10.2.2015)

Precht, M., Kraft, R. and M. Bachmaier (2005[7]) *Angewandte Statistik*, Vol. 1, Oldenburg

Pressler, F. (2013) *Die erste Weltwirtschaftskrise. Eine kleine Geschichte der Großen Depression*, Munich

Priddat, B.P. (2009) *Politik unter Einfluss. Netzwerke, Öffentlichkeiten, Beratungen, Lobby*, Wiesbaden

Püschner, M. (2009), "Der Fraktionsreferent. Ein Politischer Akteur?", in: *Aus Politik und Zeitgeschichte* 38, pp. 33-40

Quadbeck, E. (2013) "Angela Merkel – Politik per Handy", in: *Rheinische Post* from 25.10.2013, http://www.rp-online.de/politik/angela-merkel-politik-per-handy-aid-1.3770877 (last accessed on 17.2.2015)

Quadriga University Berlin (2015) "MBA Public Affairs & Leadership", http://www.quadriga.eu/studium/mba-public-affairsand-leadership (last accessed on 10.2.2015)

Radaelli, C.M. (2003) "The europeanization of public policy", in: *The politics of Europeanization*, ed. K. Featherstone and C.M. Radaelli, Oxford, pp. 27–56

Ranacher, C. and F. Staudigl (2007) *Einführung in des EU-Recht*, Vienna

Redelfs, M. (2006) "Mehr Transparenz gegen die Macht der Lobbyisten", in: *Die fünfte Gewalt. Lobbyismus in Deutschland*, ed. T. Leif and R. Speth, Wiesbaden, pp. 333–350

Reinhard, W. (2007) *Geschichte des modernen Staates*, Munich

Reutter, W. and P. Rütters (2007) "Mobilisierung und Organisation von Interessen", in: *Interessenverbände in Deutschland*, ed. T. von Winter and U. Willems, Wiesbaden, pp. 119–138

Rhodes, R.A.W. (2007) "Understanding Governance. Ten Years On", in: *Organizational Studies* 28(8), pp. 1243–1264

Rickens, C. (2004) "Wässriges Steuergesetz", in: *Manager Magazin* from 20.10.2004, http://www.manager-magazin.de/unternehmen/artikel/a-323905.html (last accessed on 8.5.2015)

Rickens, C. (2006) "Die ignorante Elite", in: *Manager Magazin* 10/2006, http://www.manager-magazin.de/magazin/artikel/a-438294.html (last accessed on 8.8.2015)

Rieksmeier, J. (ed.) (2007) *Praxisbuch Politische Interessenvermittlung – Instrumente – Kampagnen – Lobbying*, Wiesbaden.

Robert Gordon University Aberdeen (2015) "MSc Corporate Communication and Public Affairs", http://www.rgu.ac.uk/course/masters-corporate-communications-degree (last accessed on 10.2.2015)

Rogge, J.-C. (2010) "Die Rationalität des politischen Unternehmers", in: *Studentische Untersuchungen der Politikwissenschaft und Soziologie* 2(3), pp. 206–219

Römmele, A. and Y. Lorenz (2014) "Sagenumwobene Anzugträger. Herrschen in der EU in Wirklichkeit die Lobbyisten?", in: *Focus Online* from 18.5.2014, http://www.focus.de/politik/experten/hertieschool/bruessel-im-wahlkampf-sagenumwobene-anzugtraeger-herrschen-in-der-eu-in-wirklichkeit-die-lobbyisten_id_3849299.html (last accessed on 10.2.2015)

Rose, F. (1999) *The economics, concept, and design of information intermediaries. A theoretic approach*, Heidelberg

Rosen, K.M. (2013) "Financial Intermediaries as Principals and Agents", in: *Wake Forest Law Review* 48(3), pp. 625–642

Ross, S.A. (1973) "The Economic Theory of Agency. The Principal's Problem", in: *The American Economic Review* 63(2), pp. 134–139

Ross, S.A. (1989) "Institutional Markets, Financial Marketing, and Financial Innovation", in: *The Journal of Finance* 44(3), pp. 541–556

Rousseau, J.-J. (2005; original 1762) *Der Gesellschaftsvertrag oder die Grundsätze der Staatsstruktur*, Frankfurt/Main *(Du Contrat Social ou Principes du Droit Politique*, Amsterdam 1762)

Rowley, T.J. (1997) "Moving beyond dyadic ties. A network theory of stakeholder influences", in: *Academy of Management Review* 22(4), pp. 887–910

Rüb, F. (2006) "Die Zeit der Entscheidung. Kontingenz, Ambiguität und die Politisierung der Politik. Ein Versuch", in: *Hamburg Review of Social Sciences* 1(1), pp. 1–34

Rubinstein, A. and A. Wolinsky (1987) "Middlemen", in: *The Quarterly Journal of Economics* 102(3), pp. 581-594

Rubner, J. (2009) *Brüsseler Spritzen. Korruption, Lobbyismus und die Finanzen der EU*, Munich

Ruggie, J.G. (1975) "Complexity, Planning and Public Order", in: *Organized Social Complexity. Challenge to Politics and Policy*, ed. T.R. La Porte, Princeton, pp. 119–150

Saake, I. (2003) "Die Performanz des Medizinischen", in: *Soziale Welt* 54, pp. 429–459

Saake, I. (2008) "Moderne Todessemantiken. Die Biographisierung des Sterbenden", in: *Moderne Mythen der Medizin. Studien zur organisierten Krankenbehandlung*, ed. I. Saake and W. Vogd, Wiesbaden, pp. 237–264

Sabathil, G., Joos, K. and B. Keßler (ed.) (2008) *The European Commission. An Essential Guide to the Institutions, the Procedures and the Policies*, London

Sachs, S. and E. Rühli (2011) *Stakeholders Matter. A new Paradigm for Strategy in Society*, New York

Sandholtz, W. and A. Stone Sweet (1998) "Integration, Supranational Governance, and the Institutionalization of the European Polity", in: *European Integration and Supranational Governance*, ed. W. Sandholtz and A. Stone Sweet, Oxford, pp. 1–26

Santomero, A.M. (1984) "Modeling the Banking Firm. A Survey", in: *Journal of Money, Credit and Banking* 16(4), pp. 576–602

Scharpf, F.W. (2000) *Interaktionsformen. Akteurzentrierter Institutionalismus in der Politikforschung*, Opladen

Scharpf, F.W. (2004) "Legitimationskonzepte jenseits des Nationalstaats", MPIfG Working Paper 04/06

Scharpf, F.W. (2010) "Multi-Level-Europe. The case for multiple concepts", in: *Handbook on Multi-level Governance*, ed. M. Zürn, S. Wälti and H. Enderlein, Cheltenham, pp. 66–79

van Schendelen, R. (2002) *Machiavelli in Brussels. The art of lobbying the EU*, Amsterdam

van Schendelen, R. (2006) "Brüssel. Die Champions League des Lobbying", in: *Die fünfte Gewalt. Lobbyismus in Deutschland*, ed. T. Leif and R. Speth, Wiesbaden, pp. 132–162

van Schendelen, R. (2007) "Trends im EU-Lobbying und in der EU-Forschung", in: *Lobbying. Strukturen. Akteure. Strategien*, ed. R. Kleinfeld, U. Willems and A. Zimmer, Wiesbaden, pp. 65–92

van Schendelen, R. (2012) *Die Kunst des EU-Lobbyings. Erfolgreiches Public Affairs Management im Labyrinth Brüssels*, Berlin

van Schendelen, R. (2013) "Public Affairs im Europäischen Mehrebensystem, Europäische Bewegung Deutschland (Interview)", in: *EU-in-Brief* 3, pp. 2–5

van Schendelen, R. (2013[4]) *The Art of Lobbying in the EU. More Machiavelli in Brussels*, Amsterdam

van Schendelen, R. (2014) *More Machiavelli in Brussels. The art of lobbying the EU*, Amsterdam

Schmale, W. (2000) *Geschichte Europas*, Vienna

Schmedes, H.-J. (2010) "Das Mosaik der Interessenvermittlung im Mehrebensystem Europas", in: *Aus der Politik und Zeitgeschichte* 19, pp. 22–27

Schmergal, C. (2009) "Zwei Welten", in: *WirtschaftsWoche* 33

Schmid, B. and B. Lyczek (2008[2]) "Die Rolle der Kommunikation in der Wertschöpfung der Unternehmung", in: *Unternehmenskommunikation. Kommunikationsmanagement aus Sicht der Unternehmensführung*, ed. M. Meckel and B.F. Schmid, Wiesbaden, pp. 3–150

Schmid, S. and W. Schünemann (2013[2]) *Die Europäische Union*, Baden-Baden

Schmidt, M.G. (2008) *Demokratietheorien. Eine Einführung*, WiesbadenSchmidtchen, D. (1993) "Neue Politische Ökonomie von Normen und Institutionen", in: *Jahrbuch für neue Politische Ökonomie* 12, pp. 1–10.

Schmitt, C. (1932) *Der Begriff des Politischen*, Berlin

Schmitter, P.C. (1974) "Still the Century of Corporatism?", in: *The Review of Politics* 36(1), pp. 58–131

Schmitter, P.C. (1979) "Still the Century of Corporatism?", in: *Trend towards Corporatist Intermediation*, ed. P.C. Schmitter and G. Lehmbruch, London, pp. 7–52

Schmitz, G.P. (2014) "Designierter EU-Finanzkommissar Hill: Mr. Lobby muss nachsitzen", in: *Spiegel Online* from 1.10.2014, http://www.spiegel.de/wirtschaft/soziales/jonathan-hill-britischer-kandidat-fuer-eukommission-muss-nachsitzen-a-994939.html (last accessed on 10.2.2015)

Schneider, S. (2007) "Die Statthalterin", in: *Die Welt* from 8.12.2007, http://www.welt.de/die-welt/article1441286/Die_Statthalterin.html (last accessed on 15.3.2015)

Schneider, V. (2014[3]) "Akteurskonstellationen und Netzwerke in der Politikentwicklung, in: *Lehrbuch der Politikfeldanalyse*, ed. K. Schubert and N. Bandelow, Munich, pp. 259–287

Scholes, M., Benston, G.J. and C.W. Smith (1976) "A Transactions Cost Approach to the Theory of Financial Intermediation", in: *The Journal of Finance* 31(2), pp. 215–231

Schreyögg, G. (2008⁵) *Organisation. Grundlagen moderner Organisationsgestaltung*, Heidelberg

Schuckel, M. and W. Toporowski (2007) *Theoretische Fundierung und praktische Relevanz der Handelsforschung*, Wiesbaden

Schultz, S. (2015) "Deutschland klagt gegen EU-Kommission", in: *Spiegel Online* from 16.2.2015, http://www.spiegel.de/wirtschaft/soziales/energiewende-deutschlandklagt-vor-eugh-wegen-beihilfe-a-1018807.html (last accessed on 2.0.2015)

Schulz, M. (2007) "Ziel und Quelle. Politikberatung und das EP", in: *Politikberatung und Lobbying in Brüssel*, ed. S. Dagger and M. Kambeck, Wiesbaden, pp. 21–31

Schwabe, A. and C. Volkery (2005) "Neuer Job. Schröder verrubelt seinen Ruf", in: *Spiegel Online* from 12.12.2005, http://www.spiegel.de/politik/deutschland/neuer-job-schroeder-verrubelt-seinen-ruf-a-389956.html (last accessed on 10.2.2015)

Schwaiger, M. (2004) "Components and Parameters of Corporate Reputation – An Empirical Study", in: *Schmalenbach Business Review* 54(1), pp. 46–71

SciencesPo (2015) "Master Affaires Publiques", http://master.sciences-po.fr/fr/content/master-affaires-publiques (last accessed on 10.2.2015)

SEAP (2015) "Society of European Affairs Professionals (SEAP) Code of Conduct", http://www.seap.be/wp-content/uploads/2013/11/Code-of-Conduct.pdf (last accessed on 29.5.2015)

Sebaldt, M. (2007) Strukturen des Lobbying. Deutschland und die USA im Vergleich, in: *Lobbying. Strukturen. Akteure. Strategien*, ed. R. Kleinfeld, U. Willems and A. Zimmer, Wiesbaden, pp. 92–123

Seeger, S. (2008) "Die Institutionen- und Machtarchitektur der Europäischen Union mit dem Vertrag von Lissabon", in: *Lissabon in der Analyse. Der Reformvertrag der Europäischen Union*, ed. Werner Weidenfeld, Baden-Baden, pp. 63–98

Seeger, S. and M. Chardon (2008) "Mehr Gehör für gesellschaftliche Interessen? Gelegenheitsstrukturen für Interessenvertretung in der EU vor und nach dem Vertrag von Lissabon", in: *Zeitschrift für Politikberatung (ZPB)* 1.3(4), pp. 341–358

Selck, T. and T. Veen (2008) *Die politische Ökonomie des EU-Entscheidungsprozesses. Modelle und Anwendungen*, Wiesbaden

Senate Office of Public Records (2015), http://www.senate.gov/pagelayout/legislative/g_three_sections_with_teasers/lobbyingdisc.htm#lobbyingdisc=lda (last accessed on 10.2.2015)

seo-united.de "Content is King", http://www.seo-united.de/glossar/contentis-king/ (last accessed on 13.3.2015).

Shevchenko, A. (2004) "Middlemen", in: *International Economic Review* 45(1), pp. 1–24

Shostack, L. G. (1977) "Breaking free from Product Marketing", in: *Journal of Marketing* 41(2), pp. 73–80

Siegele, J. (2007) *Lobbying. Praktische Grundlagen für wirtschaftliche, politische und kommunale Entscheidungsprozesse*, Vienna

Simms, B. (2012) "Towards a mighty union. How to create a democratic European superpower", in: *International Affairs* 88(1), pp. 49–60

Simms, B. (2013) *Europe. The Struggle for Supremacy. 1453 to the Present*, London

Simon, H. (1985) *Goodwill und Marketingstrategie*, Wiesbaden

Sinn, H.-W. (2013) "Verschärfung der C02-Grenzwerte schadet Wirtschaft und Umwelt", in: *WirtschaftsWoche* from 25.5.2013

Smith, K. G., Carroll, S. J. and S. J. Ashford (1995) "Intra- and Interorganizational Cooperation. Toward a Research Agenda", in: *Academy of Management Journal* 38(1), pp. 7–23

Snower, D. J. (2014) "Adieu, Homo Oeconomicus", in: *Süddeutsche Zeitung* from 11./12.10.2014

Solomon, M. R., Surprenant, C., Czepiel, J. A. and E. G. Gutman (1985) "A Role Theory Perspective on Dyadic Interactions. The Service Encounter", in: *Journal of Marketing* 49(1), pp. 99–111

SPD (2013), "Regierungsprogramm", http://www.spd.de/linkableblob/96686/data/20130415_regierungsprogramm_2013_2017.pdf (last accessed on 27.2.2015)

Spence, A. M. (1974) *Market Signaling. Informational Transfer in Hiring and Related Screening Processes*, Cambridge

Speth, R. (2006) "Wege und Entwicklungen der Interessenpolitik", in: *Die fünfte Gewalt. Lobbyismus in Deutschland*, ed. T. Leif and R. Speth, Wiesbaden, pp. 38–52

Speth, R. (2009) "Machtvolle Einflüsterer", in: *Das Parlament* 15/16

Spoormans, H. and S. Vanboonacker (2005) "Problem-based Learning in European Public Affairs", in: *Journal of Public Affairs* 11(2), pp. 95–103

Spulber, D. F. (1996a) "Market Making by Price-Setting Firms", in: *The Review of Economic Studies* 63(4), pp. 559–580

Spulber, D. F. (1996b) "Market Microstructure and Intermediation", in: *The Journal of Economic Perspectives* 10(3), pp. 135–152

Spulber, D. F. (1998) *The Market Makers. How Leading Firms Create and Win Markets*, New York

Spulber, D. F., Pandian, J. R. and P. L. Robertson (2003) "The Intermediation Theory of the Firm. Integrating Economic and Management Approaches to Strategy", in: *Managerial and Decision Economics* 24(4), pp. 253–266

Steinhilber, J. (2005) "Liberaler Intergouvernmentalismus", in: *Theorien der europäischen Integration*, ed. H.-J. Bieling and M. Lerch, Wiesbaden, pp. 169–196

Steinmann, H. (1973) "Zur Lehre von der 'Gesellschaftlichen Verantwortung der Unternehmensführung' – Zugleich eine Kritik am Davoser Manifest", in: *Wirtschaftsstudium* 10, pp. 467–473

Steuart, J. (1767) *An Inquiry into the Principle of Political Economy. Being an Essay on the Science of Domestic Policy in Free Nations*, London

Steurer, R., Langer, M., Konrad, A. and A. Martinuzzi(2005) "Corporations, stakeholders and sustainable development. A theoretical exploration of business–society relations", in: *Journal of Business Ethics* 61(3), pp. 263–281

Stichweh, R. (1997) "Professions in Modern Society", in: *International Review of Sociology* 7, pp. 95–102

Stichweh, R. (2005) "Wissen und Professionen in einer Organisationsgesellschaft", in: *Organisation und Profession*, ed. T. Klatetzki and V. Tacke, Wiesbaden, pp. 31–45

Stigler, G. J. (1961) "The Economics of Information", in: *The Journal of Political Economy* 69(3), pp. 213–225

Straßner, A. (2006) "Ernst Fraenkel. Verbände als Manifestation des Neopluralismus", in: *Klassiker der Verbändeforschung*, ed. M. Sebaldt and A. Straßner, Wiesbaden, pp. 73–89

Streinz, R. (2012) *Europarecht*, Heidelberg

Streinz, R. (ed.) (2012a[2]) *EUV/AEUV. Vertrag über die Europäische Union und Vertrag über die Arbeitsweise der Europäischen Union*, Munich

Strohmeier, G. (2007) "Die EU zwischen Legitimität und Effektivität", in: *Aus Politik und Zeitgeschichte* 10, pp. 24–30

Studinger, P. (2013) *Wettrennen der Regionen nach Brüssel. Die Entwicklung der Regionalvertretungen*, Wiesbaden

Sveiby, K. E. (1997) *The new organizational wealth. Managing & measuring knowledge-based assets*, San Francisco

Tansey, R. (2014) "The EU's Revolving Door Problem. How Big business Gains Privileged Access", in: *Lobbying in der Europäischen Union. Zwischen Professionalisierung und Regulierung*, ed. D. Dialer and M. Richter, Wiesbaden, pp. 257–268

Thaa, W. (2013) "'Stuttgart 21' – Krise oder Repolitisierung der repräsentativen Demokratie?", in: *Politische Vierteljahresschrift* 1, pp. 1–20

Thibaut, J. W. and H. H. Kelley. (1959) *The Social Psychology of Groups*, New York

Thommen, J.-P. (2003[2]) *Glaubwürdigkeit und Corporate Governance*, Zürich

Thompson, G. and C. Driver (2005) "Stakeholder Champions. How to Internationalize the Corporate Social Responsibility Agenda", in: *Business Ethics. A European Review* 14(1), pp. 56–66

Tietmeyer, A. (2003) Interview "Interessenvertretung als Teil des demokratischen Prozesses", in: *Zeitschrift für Politikberatung* 6(3-4)

Tillack, H.-M. (2015) *Die Lobby-Republik. Wer in Deutschland die Strippen zieht*, Berlin

Timmerherm, H. (2004) "Lobbying ist keine Einbahnstraße", in: *Politikberatung in Deutschland. Praxis und Perspektiven*, ed. S. Dagger, C. Greiner, K. Leinert, N. Meliß and A.Menzel, Wiesbaden, pp. 111–132

Tömmel, I. (1994) "Interessenartikulation und transnationale Politikkooperation im Rahmen der EU", in: *Europäische Integration und verbandliche Interessenvermittlung*, ed. V. Eichner and H. Voelzkow, Marburg, pp. 263–282

Tönnies, F. (1887) *Gemeinschaft und Gesellschaft*, Leipzig

Töpfer, A. (2008[2]) "Krisenkommunikation. Anforderungen an den Dialog mit Stakeholdern in Ausnahmesituationen", in: *Unternehmenskommunikation. Kommunikations-*

management aus Sicht der Unternehmensführung, ed. M. Meckel and B. F. Schmid, Wiesbaden, pp. 355–402

Toporowski, W. (1999) "Der Baligh-Richartz-Effekt. Kontaktkostenreduktion durch die Einschaltung von Handelsbetrieben", in: *Wirtschaftswissenschaftliches Studium 2*, pp. 81–83

Traxler, F. and P. C. Schmitter (1994) "Perspektiven europäischer Integration, verbandlicher Interessenvermittlung und Politikformulierung", in: *Europäische Integration und verbandliche Interessenvermittlung*, ed. V. Eichner and H. Voelzkow, Marburg, pp. 45–70

Traynor, I. (2014) "30,000 lobbyists and counting: is Brussels under corporate sway?" in: *The Guardian* from 8.5.2014, http://www.theguardian.com/world/2014/may/08/lobbyists-european-parliament-brussels-corporate (last accessed on 2.2.2015)Treaty on the Functioning of the European Union (TFEU) (2009) OJ, 2012/C 326/01, http://eur-lex.europa.eu/legal-content/EN/TXT/?uri=CELEX:12012E/TXT (last accessed on 28.5.2015)

Treaty on the European Union (TEU), OJ, 2012/C 326/01, http://eur-lex.europa.eu/legal-content/EN/TXT/?uri=CELEX:12012M/TXT (last accessed on 28.5.2015)

Ulrich, D. and J. Barney (1984) "Perspectives in organizations. Resource dependence, efficiency, and population", in: *Academy of Management Review* 9(3), pp. 471–481

Ulrich, H. (1968) *Die Unternehmung als produktives soziales System*, Bern

Ulrich, P. (1997) *Integrative Wirtschaftsethik. Grundlagen einer lebensdienlichen Ökonomie*, Bern

Ulrich, P. (2014) "Stakeholder-Beziehungen – Warum sie so wichtig sind", in: *Delivering Tomorrow – Zuhören, gestalten, Wert schaffen. Erfolgsfaktor Stakeholdermanagement*, ed. Deutsche Post AG, Bonn, pp. 16–24

University of Erfurt (2015) "Public Policy", http://www.uni-erfurt.de/studium/studienangebot/master/public-policy/ (last accessed on 10.2.2015)

Vallaster, C. and S. von Wallpach (2013) "An online discursive inquiry into the social dynamics of multi-stakeholder brand meaning co-creation", in: *Journal of Business Research* 66(9), pp. 1505–1515

Vandekerckhove, W. and N. A. Dentchev (2005) "A network perspective on stakeholder management. Facilitating entrepreneurs in the discovery of opportunities", in: *Journal of Business Ethics* 60(3), pp. 221–232

Varadarajan, P. R. and A. Menon (1988) "Cause-related Marketing. A Coalignment of Marketing Strategy and Corporate Philanthropy", in: *The Journal of Marketing* 52(3), pp. 58–74

Vargo, S. L. and R. F. Lusch (2004) "Evolving to a new dominant logic for marketing", in: *Journal of Marketing* 68(1), pp. 1–17

Vargo, S. L. and R. L. Lusch (2008) "Service-dominant logic. Continuing the evolution", in: *Journal of the Academy of Marketing Science* 36(1), pp. 1–10

Vbw (2015) "Wir über uns", http://www.vbwbayern.de/vbw/%C3%9Cber-uns/index.jsp (last accessed on 10.2.2015)

Vershofen, W. (1930) *Wirtschaft als Schicksal und Aufgabe*, Darmstadt

Vogt, R. (2014) "Das Roland-Koch-Experiment. Brutalst möglich gescheitert", in: *Zeit Online* from 5.8.2014, http://www.zeit.de/wirtschaft/2014-08/roland-koch-bilfinger-scheitern (last accessed on 11.2.2015)

Vondenhoff, C. and S. Busch-Janser (2008) *Praxishandbuch Lobbying*, Berlin

Vorländer, H. (1999) *Die Verfassung. Idee und Geschichte*, Munich

Vowe, G. (2005) "Rechner, Spieler, Bürger. Ein Blick durch 'Des Vetters Eckfenster' auf die Marktteilnehmer", in: *Markt – Literarisch*, ed. T. Wegmann, Bern, pp. 87–99

van Waarden, F. and K. van Kersbergen (2004) "Governance" as a bridge between disciplines. Cross-disciplinary inspiration regarding shifts in governance and problems of governability, accountability and legitimacy" in: *European Journal of Political Research* 43, pp. 143–171

Wahlers, G. (2009) "Einleitung", in: *Das Gemeinwohl in einer globalisierten Welt*, ed. G. Wahlers, Berlin, pp. 3–4

Waldermann, A. (2009) "Atom-Lobby plante Wahlkampf minutiös", in: *Spiegel Online* from 23.9.2009, http://www.spiegel.de/wirtschaft/soziales/internes-strategiepapier-atomlobby-plante-wahlkampf-minutioes-a-650172.html (last accessed on 29.7.2016) von Walter, B. and T. Hess (2005) *Content-Intermediation – Konzept und Anwendungsgebiete*, Munich

Walter, F. (2007) "Partei der Büroleiter", in: *Spiegel Online* from 29.5.2007, http://www.spiegel.de/politik/deutschland/0,1518,485370,00.html (last accessed on 24.4.2009)

Walter, H. (2006) "Der Fluch der Komplexität", in: *Handelsblatt* from 19.6.2006, p. 19

Waltl, H. and H. Wildemann (2014) *Modularisierung der Produktion in der Automobilindustrie*, Munich

Wareham, J., Zheng, J.G. and D. Straub (2005) "Critical Themes in Electronic Commerce Research. A Meta-Analysis", in: *Journal of Information Technology* 20(1), pp. 1 – 19

Watt, N. (2014) "Eurozone countries should form United States of Europe, says EC vice-president", in: *The Guardian* from 17.2.2014, http://www.theguardian.com/world/2014/feb/17/eurozone-countries-united-states-europe-viviane-reding (last accessed on 20.5.2015)

Weber, M. (1984) "Soziologische Grundbegriffe", Tübingen (Wirtschaft und Gesellschaft, 1922/1925, Erster Teil, Kapitel I. "Soziologische Grundbegriffe")

Weber, M. (1988) "Der Reichspräsident", in: *Gesammelte Politische Schriften*, pub. by Johannes Winkelmann, Stuttgart, pp. 498 – 501Weidenfeld, W. (2008) "Der Vertrag von Lissabon als historischer Schritt der Integration Europas. Aufbruch aus der Krise", in: *Lissabon in der Analyse. Der Reformvertrag der Europäischen Union*, ed. W. Weidenfeld, Baden-Baden, pp. 13 – 27

Weidenfeld, W. (2013[3]) *Die Europäische Union*, Munich

Weidenfeld, W. (2013b) *Die Europäische Union. Akteure – Prozesse – Herausforderungen*, Munich

Weidenfeld, W. and W. Wessels (ed.) (2006[9]) *Europa von A-Z. Taschenbuch der europäischen Integration*, Baden-Baden

Weilemann, P.R. (2007) "Im Brüsseler Think Tank Biotop – zur Kultur politischer Beratung in der Hauptstadt Europas", in: *Politikberatung und Lobbying in Brüssel*, ed. S. Dagger and M. Kambeck, Wiesbaden, pp. 212 – 219

Wellman, B. and S.D. Berkowitz (ed.) (1988) *Social Structures. A Network Approach*, New York

Welt, R. (2010) "Multikulti. Als Quereinsteiger in die Public Affairs-Beratung", in: *Karriereguide Public Affairs*, ed. F.Busch-Janser and M. Pötter, Berlin, pp. 51 – 56

Wernerfelt, B. (1984) "A Resource-based View of the Firm", in: *Strategic Management Journal* 5(2), pp. 171 – 180

Wessels, W. (2008) *Das politische System der Europäischen Union*, Wiesbaden

Wessels, W. and V. Schäfer (2007) "Think Tanks in Brüssel. 'Sanfte' Mitspieler im EU-System? – Möglichkeiten und Grenzen der akademisch geleiteten Politikberatung", in: *Politikberatung und Lobbying in Brüssel*, ed. S. Dagger and M. Kambeck, Wiesbaden, pp. 197 – 211

Wetzel, C. (2007) *Soft Skills und Erfolg in Studium und Beruf. Eine vergleichende Studie von hochbegabten Studenten und Unternehmensberatern*, Münster

Wheeler, D. and R. Davies (2004) "Gaining goodwill. Developing stakeholder approaches to corporate governance", in: *Journal of General Management* 30(2), pp. 51 – 74

White, H.C. (1981) "Where Do Markets Come From?", in: *American Journal of Sociology* 87, pp. 517 – 547

White, H.C. (2002) *Markets from Networks. Socioeconomic Models of Production*, Princeton

Wiegand, R. (2009) "Ministerialrat Dr. Hektik", in: *Süddeutsche Zeitung* from 17.9.2009

von Winter, T. (2004) "Vom Korporatismus zum Lobbyismus. Paradigmenwechsel in Theorie und Analyse der Interessenvermittlung", in: *Zeitschrift für Parlamentsfragen* 4, pp. 761 – 776Wiese, H. (2010[5]) *Mikroökonomik. Eine Einführung*, Berlin

Williamson, O.E. (1975) *Markets and hierarchies. Antitrust analysis and implications*, New York

Williamson, O.E. (1985) *The economic institutions of capitalism. Firms, markets, relational contracting*, New York

Wolf, D. (2005) "Neo-Funktionalismus", in: *Theorien der europäischen Integration*, ed. H.-J. Bieling and M. Lerch, Wiesbaden, pp. 65 – 90

Wood, D.J. (1991) "Corporate social performance revisited", in: *Academy of Management Review* 16(4), pp. 691 – 718

Wooders, J. (1997) "Equilibrium in a Market with Intermediation is Walrasian", in: *Review of Economic Design* 3(1), pp. 75 – 89

Woods, L. and P. Watson (2012[11]) *Steiner & Woods, EU Law*, Oxford

Yavaş, A. (1995) "Can Brokerage Have an Equilibrium Selection Role?", in: *Journal of Urban Economics* 37(1), pp. 17–37

Young, A.R. (2010[6]) "The European Policy Process in Comparative Perspective", in: *Policy-Making in the European Union*, ed. H. Wallace, M.A. Pollack and A.R. Young, Oxford

Zahariadis, N. (2003) *Ambiguity and Choice in Public Policy. Political Decision Making in Modern Democracies*, Washington D.C.

Zaheer, A. and G. Soda (2009) "Network Evolution. The Origins of Structural Holes", in: *Administrative Science Quarterly* 54(1), pp. 1–31

Zakhem, A.J., Palmer, D.E. and M.L. Stoll (2008) *Stakeholder Theory. Essential Readings in Ethical Leadership and Management*, Amherst/New York

Zeithaml, V.A. (1981) "How Consumers Evaluation Processes Differ Between Goods and Services", in: *Marketing of services*, ed. J.H. Donnelly and W.R. George, Chicago, pp. 186–190

Zeithaml, V.A. and M.J. Bitner (2003[2]) *Services Marketing: Integrating Customer Focus across the Firm*, Boston

Zetter, L. (2011[2]) *Lobbying. The Art of Political Persuasion*, Petersfied

Zinkhan, G.M. (1994) "Structural Holes. The Social Structure of Competition", in: Journal of Marketing 58(1), pp. 152–155

About the authors

Dr. Klemens Joos studied business administration at Ludwig-Maximilians-University in Munich, where he obtained his doctorate on the topic of "Representing the Interests of German Companies vis-à-vis the Institutions of the European Union" in 1997. After working as a personal assistant to a Member of the European Parliament, he founded EUTOP International GmbH in 1990. Since then, EUTOP has dealt with structural and long-term support work for lobbying undertaken by private companies, associations and organisations amongst the institutions of the European Union and selected member states. EUTOP International GmbH in Munich has subsidiaries in Brussels, Frankfurt, Berlin, Vienna, Budapest and Prague, further offices in Paris, Rome and London, as well as sales representations in Beijing, Tokyo and New York. It is specialised in process-oriented, structural governmental relations (PSGR®). Klemens Joos heads the EUTOP Group as the managing partner. His doctorate was followed by further publications on the topic of lobbying which are available in German, English and Japanese. Since 2013, Klemens Joos has also been visiting lecturer at the Faculty of Business Administration at Munich's LMU (Munich School of Management) for the subject of "Convincing Political Stakeholders".

Prof. Anton Meyer is professor of business administration and marketing at Ludwig-Maximilians-University in Munich. As one of the pioneers in the German-speaking area, he has been dealing with questions of customer orientation, market- and resource-oriented corporate management, service marketing, sales, brand management, digital marketing, sustainability, quality of life and stakeholder orientation in numerous scientific and practically-oriented publications, projects and presentations for over 30 years. In his publications on offensive marketing and stakeholder management, he is a proponent of integrated marketing, which aims to actively drive markets and customer relationships with an eye to the future, and which promotes the relativisation of single-sided shareholder value orientation in favour of increased stakeholder value orientation in the sense of the social market economy.

He understands marketing as a mindset, management function and activity which run through all of a company's or an organisation's hearts and minds, processes, departments and areas; firstly, these are oriented towards superior customer benefits and secondly, they give consideration to the perspectives and interests of the various stakeholders (employees, financial backers, suppliers, citizens, politicians, "NGOs", etc.), in order to enable long-term profit generation.

Prof. Armin Nassehi, who was raised in Munich, Landshut, Gelsenkirchen and Teheran, studied philosophy, sociology and educational sciences in Münster and at FernUniversität Hagen (distance-learning university) from 1979 to 1985.

Born in Tübingen, Armin Nassehi obtained his doctorate with his work entitled "Die Zeit der Gesellschaft" in 1992. Since 1998, he has been professor of sociology at Ludwig-Maximilians-University in Munich. His areas of research include sociological theory, cultural sociology, political sociology and organisational sociology. Within these areas, he particularly conducts research into the genesis of decisions in complex situations and the clash of different societal perspectives. He has been a member of the senate and the university council at Ludwig-Maximilians-University in Munich since 2009. Armin Nassehi is also a board member of the Munich Center for Ethics, and has been a member of the Hanover-based Research Institute for Philosophy's board since 2012. He is also engaged in diverse areas outside of the university, and is active in journalism and in television productions. He regularly publishes articles in diverse media, for instance, including *SZ, FAZ* or *DIE ZEIT*. In 2010, the ARD-alpha television channel broadcast a series entitled "GmbH – Gesellschaft mit beschränkter Haftung", which dealt with the facets of our society. Since 2012, he has been responsible for the publishing of the reissued "Kursbuch".